SETTLE A [W9-CAV-485]
WITH THE DEFINITIVE
REFERENCE GUIDE
TO OUR WORLD OF WONDERS

SCOOTIN'EST BOOTS: The biggest country line dance took place in Lebanon, TN, where 2,578 people danced to the "Boot Scootin' Boogie" on July 30, 1994. [p. 352]

MOST-MARRIED FELLA: Record-holder Glynn "Scotty" Wolfe made it 28, besting his own record for monogamous marriages on June 27, 1994. [p. 474]

THE 200-G FLEA: The common flea *Pulex irritans* is the champion jumper among fleas, jumping 130 times its own height—subjecting itself to a force of 200 *g*! [p. 87]

LONGEST-DELAYED MESSAGE PICKUP: A message in a bottle thrown from a ship out of Cairns, Queensland, Australia, on June 9, 1910, finally reached land on Moreton Island, Queensland, on June 6, 1983. [p. 252]

PLUS!!!!
THE 3,000-ACRE GARBAGE DUMP [p. 216]
THE 8^1/$_2$-YEAR STRIKE [p. 433–34]
THE 18-DAY SPEECH [p. 440]
THE 94,080-SQUARE-FOOT MAZE [p. 221]

AND
THE WORLD'S LARGEST MASS WEDDING [p. 476], THE LOUDEST ANIMAL [p. 43], THE TALLEST ROLLER COASTER [p. 223], AND THE MOST VIOLENT VOLCANIC ERUPTION [p. 145].

Bantam Books in the Guinness Series

THE GUINNESS BOOK OF RECORDS 1996

THE
GUINNESS
BOOK
OF
RECORDS
1996

Editor
Peter Matthews

Founding Editor
Norris McWhirter

Deputy Editor (U.S. Edition)
Christine Heilman

BANTAM BOOKS
NEW YORK • TORONTO • LONDON • SYDNEY • AUCKLAND

This edition contains the complete text of the original hardcover edition.
NOT ONE WORD HAS BEEN OMITTED.

THE GUINNESS BOOK OF RECORDS 1996
A Bantam Book / Published by arrangement with
Guinness Publishing, Ltd.

Bantam edition / April 1996

"Guinness International" is a registered trademark
of Guinness Publishing Ltd.

CONTENTS

FEATURES

SPORTS & GAMES

INTRODUCTION

WELCOME TO THE 35th edition of *The Guinness Book of Records*. From the largest burrito to the largest terrorist bombing, the most-traveled flight attendant to the most-watched trial, the oldest DNA to the longest search for E.T., the book has been completely revised and updated to include a wide variety of new records.

ONCE AGAIN, WE have included "On the Record" interviews with some of the record-holders to give a greater insight into the effort required to earn a place in our pages, while the sample of "Letters to the Editor" gives an indication of the kinds of notable achievements we were unable to accept.

ALTHOUGH THE PRESENTATION of the book has changed over the years, people have had the same fascination with the Guinness brand of superlatives since the publication of the first edition in Great Britain in 1955.

THE BOOK WAS the brainchild of Sir Hugh Beaver, a Guinness executive. After a day of game shooting in Ireland, Beaver and his shooting party began to wonder which bird was the fastest game bird in Europe. The exten-

THE SIX GOLDEN RULES OF RECORD-BREAKING

1. Choose to beat a record that is in the current edition.

2. Remember that if the record you want to try to beat is not in the book, your chances of its being introduced are slim. You might improve those chances by ensuring that your record activity is a measurable one with plenty of popular appeal.

3. Check with us about two months before you proceed. The record you have in mind could easily have changed since publication.

4. Follow the guidelines on rules and authentication that we can provide for your record attempt.

5. Produce documentation at all stages. We cannot send out witnesses, so we need all the proof you can gather.

6. Please be patient. Regrettably, it can take four to six weeks for us to get back to you, longer if your claim requires further research on our part.

sive library at Castlebridge House, the site of the shoot, could not provide the answer.

BEAVER THOUGHT THERE must be similar debates going on nightly in pubs and inns throughout the British Isles, while the patrons partook of his employer's brew. He decided to produce a book to settle these arguments.

BEAVER CHALLENGED NORRIS and Ross McWhirter, statisticians in London, to compile a book of records. The first copy was bound by the printers in 1955. The book shot to the top of the British best-seller list, and each successive annual edition has done the same.

OVER THE LAST four decades the book has become a worldwide success. The first United States edition was published in 1956. Editions in France (1962) and Germany (1963) followed. The 1996 edition will be published throughout the world, and *The Guinness Book of Records* has now been printed in 37 languages.

THE PURPOSE OF *The Guinness Book of Records* has always been to provide accurate, easy-to-find information on achievements in every field of endeavor. The book has also become a unique outlet for individuals to demonstrate their talents.

GUINNESS WANTS TO help people achieve their record-breaking ambitions. The criteria used to establish a record are as follows: the record must be measurable, must be independently corroborated, must be completely objective, and should preferably be the subject of worldwide interest and participation. Unique skills, unusual happenings and one-of-a-kind occurrences do not qualify for entry into the book.

IF YOU WISH to attempt a published record, please write to the following address requesting the guidelines for that event:

The Guinness Book of Records
U.S. Edition
Guinness Publishing Ltd.
33 London Road
Enfield
EN2 6DJ
England

Fax number: 011-44-181-366-7849

IF YOU WOULD like to attempt a potential new record category, you should submit a written proposal outlining your idea to the same address.

WE ARE A very small editorial team, and we receive hundreds of letters every week. Please submit your request at least two months in advance of your attempt so that we can give your inquiry the attention it deserves.

ACKNOWLEDGMENTS

THE CREATION OF a new edition of *The Guinness Book of Records* is very much a team effort. Space prevents me from mentioning all of the talented and dedicated people who put together the 1996 edition, but the contributions of Gary Krebs, Dawn Gratton, Amanda Ward and Caleb Crain have been especially valuable.

I would also like to thank the individuals and organizations who took time to help us with our research, and the record-breakers, whose enthusiasm and hard work inspire us to make the book better every year.

Christine Heilman
Deputy Editor, U.S. Edition

HUMAN BEING

ORIGINS

Human beings (*Homo sapiens*) are a species in the subfamily Homininae of the family Hominidae of the superfamily Hominoidea of the suborder Simiae (or Anthropoidea) of the order Primates.

Earliest primates Primates appeared in the Paleocene epoch, about 65 million years ago. The earliest members of the suborder Anthropoidea are known from both Africa and South America in the early Oligocene, 30–34 million years ago. Finds from the Fayum, Egypt may represent primates from the Eocene period, 37 million years ago.

Earliest hominoid A jawbone with three molars, discovered in the Otavi Hills, Namibia on June 4, 1991, was dated at 12–13 million years and named *Otavi pithecus namibiensis*.

Earliest hominid An Australopithecine jawbone with two molars, each two inches long, was found near Lake Baringo, Kenya in February 1984 and dated to 4 million years ago by associated fossils and to 5.4–5.6 million years ago through rock correlation by potassium–argon dating.

Parallel tracks of hominid footprints extending over a distance of more than 80 feet were discovered in Laetoli, Tanzania in 1978, by Paul Abell and Dr. Mary Leakey, in volcanic ash dating to 3.6 million years ago. The footprints seemed to belong to three individuals, the tallest of which was estimated to have been 3 ft. 11 in. tall.

***Earliest of the genus* Homo** *Homo habilis*, or "handy man," from Olduvai Gorge, Tanzania was identified and named by Louis Leakey, Philip Tobias and John Napier in 1964 after a suggestion from Prof. Raymond Arthur Dart (1893–1988). The greatest age attributed to fossils of this genus is about 2.4 million years for a piece of cranium found in western Kenya in 1965.

The earliest stone tools are abraded core-choppers dating from *c.* 2.7 million years ago. They were found in Hadar, Ethiopia in 1976 by Hèléne Roche (France). Finger-held (as opposed to fist-held) quartz slicers found by Roche and Dr. John Wall (New Zealand) close to the Hadar site by the Gona River can also be dated to *c.* 2.7 million years ago.

***Earliest* Homo erectus** The oldest example of *Homo erectus* ("upright man"), the direct ancestor of *Homo sapiens*, was discovered by Eugène Dubois (Netherlands) in Trinil, Java in 1891. Javan *H. erectus* was redated to 1.8 million years in 1994.

United States Over 500 artifacts 11,000 to 16,000 years old were found in Washington Co., PA in April 1973 after being brought to the attention of the University of Pittsburgh by Albert Miller, whose family owned the land. The site dates to the Pre-Clovis Paleo-Indian culture and it is believed that the *Homo sapiens* Paleo-Indians were the first inhabitants of the site. The dig, led by Dr. James Adovasio, started in June 1973 and lasted until June 1983.

In 1968, a burial site containing bones of two individuals believed to be an infant and an adolescent was uncovered by construction workers in Wilsall, MT. The bones were dated by the MAS technique to at least 10,600 years ago. The remains are believed to be of members of the Paleo-Indian culture, with the artifacts in the style of the Clovis Age.

GUESS WHAT?

Q. WHERE IS THE OLDEST STRUCTURE BUILT BY HUMANS?

A. LOOK IN "ORIGINS" (BUILDINGS & STRUCTURES)

Oldest human body   The body of a Late Stone Age man, who is thought to have died *c.* 3300 B.C., was found almost perfectly preserved in an Austrian glacier in September 1991.

Oldest mummy   The oldest known mummy is that of a high-ranking young woman who was buried *c.* 2600 B.C. on a plateau near the Great Pyramid of Cheops at Giza, or Al-Gizeh, Egypt. Her remains, which appear to represent an early attempt at mummification, were discovered in a 6-foot-deep excavation on March 17, 1989, but only her skull was intact. She is believed to have lived in the lost kingdom of Ankh Ptah.

The oldest complete mummy is of Wati, a court musician of *c.* 2400 B.C., from the tomb of Nefer in Saqqâra, Egypt, found in 1944.

BIRTH AND FAMILIES

MOTHERHOOD

Most children born to one mother   In a total of 27 confinements, the wife of Feodor Vassilyev, a peasant from Shuya (near Moscow), Russia gave birth to 69 children, comprising 16 pairs of twins, seven sets of triplets and four sets of quadruplets. The case was reported to Moscow by the Monastery of Nikolskiy on February 27, 1782. Only two of the children born in the period *c.* 1725–65 died in infancy.

The world's most prolific mother is currently Leontina Albina (née Espinosa) of San Antonio, Chile, who in 1981 produced her 55th and last child. Her husband, Gerardo Secunda Albina (Alvina), states that they were married in Argentina in 1943 and had five sets of triplets (all boys) before coming to Chile. Only 40 children (24 boys and 16 girls) survive.

OTZI:

TRAVELER FROM THE PAST

Reinhold Messner (left), the record-setting mountaineer, was one of the first people to realize the significance of the find. (*Gamma/P. Hanny*)

In September 1991, two German mountaineers discovered a human body in a melting glacier in the Ötztal Alps, on the Austrian–Italian border. At first, the body was thought to belong to a man who disappeared in the area earlier this century. But the objects recovered from the surrounding ice told a different story: the man in the glacier was a Neolithic traveler who died 5,300 years ago.

Ötzi, as the man was nicknamed, was an amazing archeological find. Ötzi did not have a ceremonial burial with a few specially chosen items; he died alone, in his ordinary clothes, with his everyday possessions. And his body and belongings were preserved incredibly well in the glacier ice; if he had been buried in soil, only his ax blade, his stone tools and possibly his skeleton would have survived.

Ötzi was 35–40 years old when he froze to death on the mountainside. He was about 5 ft. 3 in. tall, and he wore a leather loincloth, fur leggings, leather shoes stuffed with grass, a fur tunic, a grass cloak, and a fur hat with a chin strap.

Judging from the objects Ötzi carried, it seems likely that he was a shepherd or a hunter. Among his belongings were a copper ax; a bow and flint-tipped arrows; a birchbark container for carrying embers, containing charcoal flakes and still-green Norway maple leaves; part of a net made from twisted grass cords; two pieces of birch fungus, which contains a natural antibiotic; and the remains of some of his food: a sloe berry and splinters of gnawed ibex bone.

No one knows the original destination of this traveler from the past, but Ötzi's arrival in a 20th-century European laboratory has given scientists unique insight into life in the Neolithic age.

Oldest human body   The body of a Late Stone Age man, who is thought to have died *c.* 3300 B.C., was found almost perfectly preserved in an Austrian glacier in September 1991.

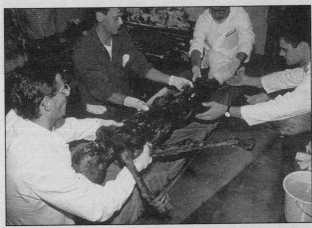

Ötzi apparently died lying on his left side; slight movements of the glacier pushed his body into its present position, with the left arm forced under the chin. (*Gamma/G. Hinterleitner*)

Oldest mother Menopause is the end of a woman's reproductive life and occurs in the majority of women between the ages of 45 and 55 years. However, recent hormone treatment techniques have led to post-menopausal women becoming pregnant. It is therefore now feasible for a woman of *any* age to give birth.

Rossanna Della Corte of Canino, Italy gave birth at age 63 on July 18, 1994.

BABIES

Heaviest single birth Big babies (i.e., those over 10 pounds) are usually born to mothers who are large, overweight or have some medical problem such as diabetes. Anna Bates (née Swan; 1846–88), a 7-ft.-5½-in. Canadian woman, gave birth to a boy weighing 23 lb. 12 oz. (length 30 inches) at her home in Seville, OH on January 19, 1879, but the baby died 11 hours later.

Heaviest twins The world's heaviest twins, weighing a total 27 lb. 12 oz., were born to Mrs. J.P. Haskin of Fort Smith, AR on February 20, 1924.

Heaviest quadruplets The world's heaviest quadruplets, two girls and two boys weighing a total of 22 lb. 15¾ oz., were born to Tina Saunders at St. Peter's Hospital, Chertsey, England on February 7, 1989.

Heaviest quintuplets Two cases have been recorded for heaviest quintuplets, each set weighing a total of 25 pounds. The first set was born on June 7, 1953 to Mrs. Lui Saulian of Zhejiang, China, and the second set to Mrs. Kamalammal of Pondicherry, India on December 30, 1956.

Lightest single birth A premature baby girl named Madeline, weighing 9.9 ounces, was reported to have been born on June 27, 1989 at the Loyola University Medical Center, Maywood, IL.

Lightest twins Anne Faith Sarah (14.8 ounces) and John Alexander (15.5 ounces) were born to Wendy Kay Morrison at Ottawa General Hospital, Ontario, Canada on January 14, 1994.

First test tube baby Lesley Brown, age 31, gave birth by cesarean section to Louise (5 lb. 12 oz.) in Oldham General Hospital, Oldham, England at 11:47 P.M. on July 25, 1978. Louise was conceived by in vitro fertilization on November 10, 1977.

United States Elizabeth Jordan Carr (5 lb. 12 oz.) was delivered by cesarean section to Judy Carr, age 28, in Norfolk General Hospital, Norfolk,

---

OH, BABY!

The heaviest baby born to a healthy mother was a boy weighing 22 lb. 8 oz. who was born to Carmelina Fedele of Aversa, Italy in September 1955.

VA on December 28, 1981. Elizabeth was conceived by in vitro fertilization on April 15, 1981. Dr. Howard Jones of Eastern Virginia Medical School performed the procedure.

First birth from a frozen embryo   Zoe (last name withheld) was delivered by cesarean section weighing 5 lb. 13 oz. on March 28, 1984 in Melbourne, Australia. Scientists from Monash University announced the birth.

United States   A 9-lb.-8-oz. boy was delivered by cesarean section on June 4, 1986 to Monique (last name withheld), age 36, in Cottage Hospital, Santa Barbara, CA. A second child was born on October 23, 1989 by the same procedure, and it is believed that this is the only case of siblings from frozen embryos. Dr. Richard Marrs was in charge of the procedure.

Most-premature baby   James Elgin Gill was born to Brenda and James Gill on May 20, 1987 in Ottawa, Ontario, Canada 128 days premature and weighing 1 lb. 6 oz.

United States   Ernestine Hudgins was born on February 8, 1983 in San Diego, CA about 18 weeks premature and weighing 17 ounces.

Most-premature twins   Joanna and Alexander Bagwell were born 114 days premature on June 2, 1993 in Oxford, England.

United States   Joshua and Evan Ernsteen were born 112 days premature on August 18, 1992 at Evanston Hospital, Evanston, IL. Sarah Constance and Riley Scott Winstead were also born 112 days premature, on May 3, 1994, at Trinity Hospital, Minot, ND.

Most-premature triplets   The lightest and most-premature triplets in the United States were Brandi Nichole, Christian Kipling and Kelli Amanda Karasiewicz, born to Rick and Gwen Karasiewicz on December 9, 1980 in Columbia, SC, 88 days premature and weighing 1 lb. 11 oz., 1 lb. 15 oz. and 1 lb. 10 oz. respectively.

Most-premature quadruplets   Tina Piper of St. Leonards-on-Sea, England had quadruplets on April 10, 1988, after 26 weeks of pregnancy. Oliver, 2 lb. 9 oz. (d. February 1989), Francesca, 2 lb. 2 oz., Charlotte, 2 lb. 4½ oz., and Georgina, 2 lb. 5 oz., were born at The Royal Sussex County Hospital, Brighton, England.

MULTIPLE BIRTHS

Conjoined twins   Conjoined twins were formerly called Siamese twins, after the celebrated Chang and Eng ("Left" and "Right") Bunker, born in Meklong, Thailand on May 11, 1811. They were joined by a cartilaginous band at the chest. In 1843, they married Sarah and Adalaide Yates of Wilkes County, NC, and fathered 10 and 12 children respectively. Chang and Eng died within three hours of each other on January 17, 1874, age 62.

Rarest type   The most extreme form of conjoined twins is dicephales tetra-brachius dipus (two heads, four arms and two legs). The only fully reported example is Masha and Dasha Krivoshlyapovy, born in Russia on January 4, 1950.

Earliest successful separation On December 14, 1952, xiphopagus (joined at the sternum) girls were successfully separated at Mount Sinai Hospital, Cleveland, OH by Dr. Jac S. Geller.

Longest-parted twins With the help of New Zealand's television program *Missing* on April 27, 1989, Iris Johns (born Iris Haughie) and Aro Campbell (born Aro Haughie), who were born on January 13, 1914, were reunited after 75 years' separation.

United States Fraternal twins Lloyd Earl and Floyd Ellsworth Clark were born on February 15, 1917 in Nebraska. They were parted when they were four months old and lived under their adopted names, Dewayne William Gramly (Lloyd) and Paul Edward Forbes (Floyd). Both men knew that they had been born twins, but they were not reunited until June 16, 1986, having been separated for over 69 years.

Longest interval between births Jackie Iverson of Saskatoon, Canada gave birth normally to a boy, Christopher, on November 21, 1993, a girl, Alexandra, on November 29, 1993, and was delivered of another boy and girl, Matthew and Sarah (by cesarean section), on November 30, 1993—all over a period of 10 days.

Longest interval between twins Mrs. Danny Petrungaro (née Berg; b. 1953) of Rome, Italy, who had been on hormone treatment after suffering four miscarriages, gave birth normally to a girl, Diana, on December 22, 1987, but the other twin, Monica, was delivered by cesarean on January 27, 1988, 36 days later.

Fastest triplet birth Bradley, Christopher and Carmon were born naturally to Mrs. James E. Duck of Memphis, TN in two minutes on March 21, 1977.

Quindecaplets Dr. Gennaro Montanino of Rome, Italy removed the fetuses of 10 girls and five boys from the womb of a 35-year-old woman on July 22, 1971. This unique instance of quindecaplets was caused by a fertility drug.

Highest number at a single birth The highest number reported at a single birth were two males and eight females in Bacacay, Brazil on April 22, 1946. Reports of 10 at a single birth were also received from Spain in 1924 and from China on May 12, 1936.

The highest number medically recorded is nine (nonuplets), born to Geraldine Broderick at Royal Hospital for Women, Sydney, Australia on June 13, 1971. None of the five boys (two stillborn) and four girls lived for more than six days. The birth of nine children has also been reported on at least two other occasions: Philadelphia, PA on May 29, 1971; and Bagerhat, Bangladesh *c.* May 11, 1977; in both cases none of the babies survived.

Most sets of multiple births in a family *Quadruplets* Four sets, to Mme. Feodor Vassilyev, Shuya, Russia (b. 1707) (see MOTHERHOOD).

Triplets 15 sets, to Maddalena Granata, Italy (1839–*fl.* 1886).

Twins   16 sets, to Mme. Vassilyev (see above). Barbara Zulu of Barbeton, South Africa had three sets of girls and three mixed sets in seven years (1967–73). Anna Steynvaait of Johannesburg, South Africa produced two sets within 10 months in 1960.

DESCENDANTS

Most children fathered   The last Sharifian emperor of Morocco, Moulay Ismail (1672–1727), known as "The Bloodthirsty," was reputed to have fathered a total of 525 sons and 342 daughters by 1703 and to have achieved a 700th son in 1721.

Most descendants   At his death on October 15, 1992, Samuel S. Must, age 96, of Fryburg, PA had 824 living descendants—11 children, 97 grandchildren, 634 great-grandchildren and 82 great-great-grandchildren.

Seven-generation family   Augusta Bunge (née Pagel; b. October 13, 1879) of Wisconsin received news of the arrival of her great-great-great-great-grandson, Christopher John Bollig, on January 21, 1989.

Great-great-great-grandmother   Harriet Holmes of Newfoundland, Canada became the youngest living great-great-great-grandmother on March 8, 1987 at age 88 years 50 days.

Longest lineage   The lineage of K'ung Ch'iu or Confucius (551–479 B.C.) can be traced further than that of any other family. His great-great-great-great-grandfather K'ung Chia is known from the eighth century B.C. His 85th lineal descendants, Wei-yi (b. 1939) and Wei-ning (b. 1947), live today in Taiwan.

LONGEVITY

Oldest person   The greatest *authenticated* age to which any person has ever lived is 120 yr. 237 days, in the case of Shigechiyo Izumi of Tokunoshima, Japan. He was born on June 29, 1865 and was recorded as a 6-year-old in Japan's first census of 1871. Izumi died of pneumonia on February 21, 1986.

Oldest living person   Jeanne Louise Calment was born in France on February 21, 1875, when Ulysses S. Grant was president of the United States. She met Vincent van Gogh in her father's hardware store when she was 14. Now 120 years old, she lives in a nursing home in Arles, southern France.

Oldest twins   Eli Shadrack and John Meshak Phipps were born on February 14, 1803 in Affington, VA. Eli died in Hennessey, OK on February 23, 1911 at age 108 yr. 9 days.

On June 17, 1984, identical twin sisters Mildred Widman Philippi and Mary Widman Franzini of St. Louis, MO celebrated their 104th birthday. Mildred died on May 4, 1985, 44 days short of the twins' 105th birthday.

THE LIFE OF JEANNE CALMENT

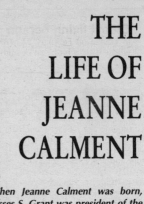

When Jeanne Calment was born, Ulysses S. Grant was president of the United States. Since then, she has lived through many of the major events that have shaped the world today. These events have occurred in all areas of life—social, political, scientific and technological—many of them in Calment's homeland of France.

She has lived through two world wars, the invention of incandescent lighting, cars, airplanes, and many other things that are taken for granted today.

Asked on her 120th birthday what kind of future she expected, she replied, "a very short one."

Momentous events in Calment's lifetime:

Louis Blériot crossed the English Channel on July 25, 1909. This was the first flight over the ocean by a heavier-than-air craft. The cover of *Le Petit Journal* (August 8, 1909) shows him completing his crossing over the white cliffs of Dover.

The Eiffel Tower opened on March 31, 1889 as part of the Centennial Exposition to commemorate the French Revolution. It was originally viewed as a temporary structure and was to be dismantled in 1910. However, because of its usefulness in many scientific fields such as astronomy and meteorology, it was saved from destruction and remained the world's tallest building until 1930.

Louis Pasteur made a wide and varied contribution to science, most notably in the fields of microbiology and chemistry. Pasteur is best known for the development of the pasteurization process, but he also worked with vaccines, especially for rabies and anthrax. *Le Petit Journal*, October 13, 1895, mourns his death.

The **Tour de France,** the world's premier cycling event, was first held in July 1903. The winner was Maurice Garin; he also won the following year, as celebrated in this poster, but was disqualified four months later for having accepted a ride in a car. Millions now watch the race every summer.

World War I saw French troops marching through Strasbourg on November 22, 1918. Strasbourg, in the Alsace region, was annexed by Germany during the Franco-Prussian War (1870–71) but returned to France after the Treaty of Versailles. Germany occupied the city again during World War II.

Jeanne Calment recalls meeting **Vincent van Gogh** in her father's shop in Arles and selling him colored pencils. *Sunflowers* (Les Tournesol), which was painted by van Gogh during his stay in Arles in 1888, was sold at auction on March 30, 1987, for a then world record price of £22,500,000 (excluding buyer's premium) (approx. $39,900,000).

AUTHENTIC LONGEVITY RECORDS

Country	Age	Name	Born	Died
Japan	120 yr. 237 days	Shigechiyo Izumi	Jun. 29, 1865	Feb. 21, 1986
France	120 yr. 40 days	Jeanne Louise Calment	Feb. 21, 1875	fl.* April 1995
United States	116 yr. 88 days	Carrie White (née Joyner)	Nov. 18, 1874	Feb. 14, 1991
United Kingdom	115 yr. 229 days	Charlotte Hughes (née Milburn)	Aug. 1, 1877	Mar. 17, 1993
Canada	113 yr. 124 days	Pierre Joubert	Jul. 15, 1701	Nov. 16, 1814
Australia	112 yr. 330 days	Caroline Maud Mockridge	Dec. 11, 1874	Nov. 6, 1987
Wales	112 yr. 292 days	John Evans	Aug. 19, 1877	Jun. 10, 1990
Spain	112 yr. 228 days	Josefa Salas Mateo	Jul. 14, 1860	Feb. 27, 1973
Norway	112 yr. 61 days	Maren Bolette Torp	Dec. 21, 1876	Feb. 20, 1989
Morocco	112 yr. +	El Hadj Mohammed el Mokri (Grand Vizier)	1844	Sep. 16, 1957
Poland	112 yr. +	Roswlia Mielczarak	1868	Jan. 7, 1981
Netherlands	111 yr. 354 days	Thomas Peters	Apr. 6, 1745	Mar. 26, 1857
Sweden	111 yr. 350 days	Hulda Johansson	Feb. 24, 1882	fl. February 1994
Ireland	111 yr. 327 days	Katherine Plunket	Nov. 22, 1820	Oct. 14, 1932
Scotland	111 yr. 238 days	Kate Begbie	Jan. 9, 1877	Sep. 5, 1988

South Africa	111 yr. 151 days	Johanna Booyson	Jan. 17, 1857	Jun. 16, 1968
Italy	111 yr. 60 days	Chelidonia Merosi	Oct. 11, 1883	fl. February 1995
Czechoslovakia	111 yr. +	Marie Bernatková	Oct. 22, 1857	fl. October 1968
Germany	111 yr.	Maria Corba	Aug. 15, 1878	fl. March 1990
Finland	111 yr. +	Fanny Matilda Nystrom	Sep. 30, 1878	1989
Northern Ireland	110 yr. 234 days	Elizabeth Watkins	Mar. 10, 1863	Oct. 31, 1973
Denmark	110 yr. 60 days	Anne Kathrine Matthiesen	Nov. 26, 1884	fl. February 1995
Yugoslavia	110 yr. +	Demitrius Philipovitch	Mar. 9, 1818	fl. August 1928
Greece	110 yr. +	Lambrini Tsiatoura	1870	Feb. 19, 1981
USSR	110 yr. +	Khasako Dzugayev	Aug. 7, 1860	fl. August 1970

Superior claims but insufficient documentation

Brazil	124 yr. 30 days	Maria do Como	Mar. 6, 1871	fl. April 1995
United States	121 yr. +	Mark Thrash	Dec. 1822	Dec. 17, 1943
Spain	114 yr. 335 days	Benita Medrana	Dec. 29, 1864	Jan. 28, 1979
South Africa	114 yr. +	Susan Johanna Deporter	1840	Aug. 4, 1954

Note: fl. is the abbreviation for the Latin floruit, meaning he or she was living at the relevant date.

Oldest living identical twins Marian Elise Lamb Bechtelheimer and Mary Elizabeth Lamb Sheridan are the oldest living identical twins in the United States. They were born on March 11, 1895, in Santa Barbara, CA.

Oldest triplets Faith, Hope and Charity Cardwell were born on May 18, 1899 in Elm Mott, TX. Faith died on October 2, 1994, at the age of 95 yr. 137 days.

Oldest living triplets The oldest living triplets in the United States are Annis Ruth Nolan, Sarah Rubye Waggoner, and Frances Rebecca Waggoner, born on June 15, 1905.

Mildred Widman Philippi and Mary Widman Franzini of St. Louis, MO celebrated their 104th birthday on June 17, 1984. Mildred died on May 4, 1985. (*Gamma/Stricklin*)

Oldest quadruplets Adolf, Anne-Marie, Emma and Elisabeth Ottman were born in Munich, Germany on May 5, 1912. Adolf died on March 17, 1992, at the age of 79 yr. 316 days.

United States The Morlok quads of Lansing, MI—Edna, Wilma, Sarah and Helen—celebrated their 64th birthday on May 18, 1994.

Most living ascendants Megan Sue Austin of Bar Harbor, ME had a full set of grandparents and great-grandparents and five great-great-grandparents, making a total of 19 direct ascendants, when she was born on May 16, 1982.

THE BODY

HEIGHT

Body growth is determined by growth hormone, which is produced by the pituitary gland in the brain. The true height of human giants or dwarfs is frequently obscured by exaggeration or understatement and by commercial dishonesty. The only admissible evidence on the actual height of giants is that collected since 1870 under impartial medical supervision. Nine feet is the limit towards which the tallest giants tend and 22 inches is the limit towards which the shortest adult dwarfs tend (compare the average length of newborn babies, which is 18–20 inches).

Tallest man The tallest man in medical history of whom there is irrefutable evidence was Robert Pershing Wadlow, born on February 22, 1918, in Alton, IL. Weighing 8½ pounds at birth, he began his abnormal growth at the age of two, following a double hernia operation. At age 10 he was 6 ft. 5 in. tall.

On June 27, 1940, Dr. C.M. Charles of Washington University's School of Medicine in St. Louis, MO, and Dr. Cyril MacBryde measured Robert Wadlow at 8 ft. 11.1 in. (arm span 9 ft. 5¾ in.) in St. Louis. Wadlow died 18 days later on July 15, 1940, weighing 439 pounds, in a hotel in Manistee, MI as a result of a septic blister on his right ankle caused by a poorly fitting brace. He was buried in Oakwood Cemetery, Alton, IL in a coffin measuring 10 ft. 9 in.

Wadlow's greatest recorded weight was 491 pounds on his 21st birthday. His shoes were size 37AA (18½ inches) and his hands measured 12¾ inches from the wrist to the tip of the middle finger.

Tallest woman The tallest woman in medical history was Zeng Jinlian (b. June 26, 1964) of Yujiang village in the Bright Moon Commune, Hunan Province, central China, who measured 8 ft. 1¾ in. when she died on February 13, 1982. This figure represented her height with assumed normal spinal curvature, because she suffered from severe scoliosis (curvature of the spine) and could not stand up straight. She began to grow abnormally from the age of four months and stood 5 ft. 1½ in. before her fourth birth-

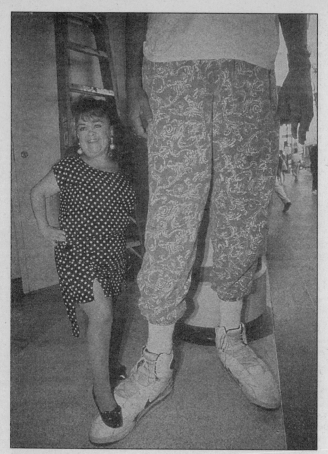

Haji Mohammad Alam Channa is currently one of the world's tallest people. His friend is Poquita Nunez; she measures 42 inches tall. (*Gamma/Giboux/Liaison*)

day. Her hands measured 10 inches and her feet were 14 inches long. Her parents and her brother were of normal size.

Tallest living person   Both Haji Mohammad Alam Channa (b. 1956) of Bachal Channa, Sehwan Sharif, Pakistan, and the world's tallest living woman, Sandy Allen, are approximately 7 ft. 7¼ in. tall.

Tallest living woman Sandy Allen, born June 18, 1955, in Chicago, IL, weighed 6½ pounds at birth, but started growing abnormally soon afterwards. At 10 years of age she stood 6 ft. 3 in., and she measured 7 ft. 1 in. when she was 16. On July 14, 1977, at 7 ft. 7¼ in., Allen underwent a pituitary gland operation that inhibited further growth. She now weighs 462 pounds and takes a size 16 EEE shoe.

Most variable stature Adam Rainer (1899–1950), born in Graz, Austria, measured 3 ft. 10½ in. at age 21. He then suddenly started growing at a rapid rate, and by 1931 he had reached 7 ft. 1¾ in. He became so weak as a result that he was bedridden for the rest of his life. When he died on March 4, 1950, age 51, he measured 7 ft. 8 in. and was the only person in medical history to have been both a dwarf and a giant.

Tallest married couple Anna Hanen Swan (1846–88) of Nova Scotia, Canada was said to be 8 ft. 1 in. tall but she actually measured 7 ft. 5½ in. At the church of St. Martin-in-the-Fields, London, England on June 17, 1871, she married Martin van Buren Bates (1845–1919) of Whitesburg, KY, who was 7 ft. 2½ in. tall, making them the tallest married couple on record.

Most dissimilar couple Fabien Pretou (b. June 15, 1968), 6 ft. 2 in. tall, married Natalie Lucius (b. January 19, 1966), 3 ft. 1 in. tall, in Seyssinet-Pariset, France on April 14, 1990.

Tallest identical twins Michael and James Lanier (b. November 27, 1969) of Troy, MI both measured 7 ft. 1 in. at age 14 years and now stand 7 ft. 4 in. Their sister Jennifer is 5 ft. 2 in. tall.

Heather and Heidi Burge (b. November 11, 1971) of Palos Verdes, CA are both 6 ft. 4¾ in. tall.

Shortest man The shortest mature person of whom there is independent evidence is Gul Mohammad (b. February 15, 1957) of Delhi, India. On July 19, 1990, when he was examined at Ram Manohar Hospital, New Delhi, he was 22½ inches tall and weighed 37½ pounds. The other members of his immediate family are of normal height.

Shortest woman Pauline Musters was born in Ossendrecht, Netherlands, on February 26, 1876, and measured 12 inches at birth. At nine years of age she was 21.65 inches tall and weighed only 3 lb. 5 oz. She died on March 1, 1895 in New York City at age 19. Although she was billed at 19 inches, a postmortem examination showed her to be exactly 24 inches tall (there was some elongation after death). Her mature weight varied from 7½ to 9 pounds.

GUESS WHAT?

Q. How tall was the tallest gorilla?

A. Look in "Primates" (Living World)

Shortest living woman   Madge Bester (b. April 26, 1963) of Johannesburg, South Africa is 25½ inches tall. She suffers from *Osteogenesis imperfecta*, a disease characterized by brittle bones and skeletal deformities, and she is confined to a wheelchair. Her mother, Winnie, is not much taller, measuring 27½ inches.

Madge Bester (far right) of Johannesburg, South Africa is the world's shortest living woman; she is just 25.5 inches tall. (*Gamma/D. Bar*)

Shortest twins   Matjus and Bela Matina (1903–c. 1935) of Budapest, Hungary, who later became United States citizens, were both 30 inches tall.

Shortest living twins   John and Greg Rice (b. December 3, 1951) of West Palm Beach, FL both measure 34 inches.

The shortest identical twin sisters are Dorene Williams of Oakdale and Darlene McGregor of Alameda, CA (b. 1949), who each stand 4 ft. 1 in. tall.

Oldest dwarf   Hungarian-born Susanna Bokoyni ("Princess Susanna") of Newton, NJ died at age 105 on August 24, 1984. She was 3 ft. 4 in. tall.

WEIGHT

Heaviest man   The heaviest person in medical history was Jon Brower Minnoch (b. September 29, 1941) of Bainbridge Island, WA, who had suffered from obesity since childhood. The 6-ft.-1-in. former taxi driver weighed 392 pounds in 1963, 700 pounds in 1966, and 975 pounds in September 1976.

In March 1978, Minnoch was rushed to University Hospital, Seattle, saturated with fluid and suffering from heart and respiratory failure. A dozen firemen used an improvised stretcher to move him from his home to a ferryboat. When he arrived at the hospital he was put in two beds lashed together. It took 13 people just to roll him over. Consultant endocrinologist Dr. Robert Schwartz calculated that Minnoch must have weighed more than 1,400 pounds when he was admitted. A great deal of this was water accumulation due to his congestive heart failure. After nearly 16 months on a 1,200-calorie-a-day diet, he was discharged at 476 pounds. In October 1981, he had to be readmitted, having put on 197 pounds. When he died on September 10, 1983 he weighed more than 798 pounds.

Heaviest living man   The heaviest living man is T.J. Albert Jackson (born Kent Nicholson in 1941), also known as "Fat Albert," of Canton, MS. He has weighed as much as 891 pounds and has a 120-inch chest, a 116-inch waist, 70-inch thighs and a 29½-inch neck.

Heaviest woman   The heaviest woman ever recorded is Rosalie Bradford (U.S.; b. 1944), who registered a peak weight of 1,200 pounds in January 1987. In August of that year she developed congestive heart failure and was rushed to a hospital. She was put on a carefully controlled diet and by February 1994 weighed 283 pounds. Her target weight is 150 pounds.

Heaviest twins   Billy Leon and Benny Loyd McCrary, alias McGuire (b. December 7, 1946), of Hendersonville, NC weighed 743 pounds (Billy) and 723 pounds (Benny) and had 84-inch waists in November 1978. As professional tag-team wrestling performers they were billed at weights up to 770 pounds. Billy died in Niagara Falls, Ontario, Canada on July 13, 1979.

Greatest weight loss   *Dieting*   The greatest recorded slimming feat by a man was that of Jon Brower Minnoch (see HEAVIEST MAN), who had reduced to 476 pounds by July 1979, a weight loss of at least 920 pounds in 16 months.
   Rosalie Bradford (see HEAVIEST WOMAN) went from a weight of 1,200 pounds in January 1987 to 283 pounds in February 1994, a loss of a record 917 pounds.

Sweating   Ron Allen (b. 1947) sweated off 21½ pounds of his weight of 239 pounds in Nashville, TN in 24 hours in August 1984.

Greatest weight gain   The reported record for weight gain is held by Jon Brower Minnoch (see HEAVIEST MAN) at 196 pounds in 7 days in October 1981 after readmittance to University Hospital, Seattle, WA. Arthur Knorr (U.S.; 1916–60) gained 294 pounds in the last six months of his life.

Most dissimilar couple   The greatest weight difference recorded for a married couple is roughly 1,300 pounds in the case of Jon Brower Minnoch (see HEAVIEST MAN) and his 110-pound wife Jeannette in March 1978.

Lightest person   The lightest adult was Lucia Zarate (Mexico, 1863–89). At age 17, she measured 26½ inches, and weighed 4.7 pounds. She "fattened up" to 13 pounds by her 20th birthday. At birth she had weighed 2½ pounds.

HANDS AND FEET

Longest fingernails   Fingernails grow at a rate of about 0.02 inches a week—four times faster than toenails. As of February 25, 1995, the aggregate measurement of Shridhar Chillal's fingernails (b. 1937, Pune, Maharashtra, India) was 226 inches for the five nails on his left hand (thumb 52 inches, index finger 40 inches, middle finger 43 inches, ring finger 46 inches, and pinkie 45 inches). He last cut his nails in 1952.

Shridhar Chillal has the longest fingernails in the world; he last cut them in 1952. (*Gamma/Bartholomew-Liaison*)

Fewest toes   The 2-toed syndrome exhibited by some members of the Wadomo tribe of the Zambezi Valley, Zimbabwe and the Kalanga tribe of the eastern Kalahari Desert, Botswana is hereditary via a single mutated gene. They are not handicapped and can walk great distances without discomfort.

Largest feet   If cases of elephantiasis are excluded, then the biggest feet currently known are those of Matthew McGrory (b. May 17, 1973) of Pennsylvania, who wears size 26 shoes.

Balancing on one foot   The duration record for balancing on one foot is 55 hr. 35 min., by Girish Sharma in Deori, India, October 2–4, 1992. In this contest the disengaged foot may not be rested on the standing foot, nor may any object be used for support or balance.

Motionlessness   António Gomes dos Santos of Zare, Portugal stood motionless for 15 hr. 2 min. 55 sec. on July 30, 1988 at the Amoreiras Shopping Center, Lisbon, Portugal.

CHESTS, WAISTS AND NECKS

Largest chest measurement   In the extreme case of Robert Earl Hughes (U.S.; 1926–58) the chest measurement was 124 inches, and T.J. Albert Jackson, currently the heaviest living man, has a chest measurement of 120 inches.
   The largest muscular chest measurement is that of Isaac Nesser of Greensburg, PA, at 74$^{1}/_{16}$ inches.

Largest waist   The largest waist ever recorded was that of Walter Hudson (1944–91) of New York; it measured 119 inches at his peak weight of 1,197 pounds.

Smallest waist   The smallest waist in someone of normal stature was that of Ethel Granger (1905–82) of Peterborough, England, reduced from a natural 22 inches to 13 inches over the period 1929–39. A measurement of 13 inches was also claimed for the French actress Mlle. Polaire (real name Emile Marie Bouchand; 1881–1939).

Longest neck   The maximum measured extension of the neck by the successive fitting of copper coils, as practiced by the women of the Padaung or Kareni tribe of Myanmar, is 15$^{3}/_{4}$ inches.

DID YOU KNOW?

It has been estimated that the eye muscles move 100,000 times a day or more. Many of these eye movements take place during the dreaming phase of sleep.

HAIR AND SKIN

Longest hair   Human hair grows at a rate of about half an inch per month. If left uncut, it will usually grow to a maximum of 2–3 feet.

The longest documented hair belongs to Mata Jagdamba of Ujjain, India (b. 1917). Her hair measured 13 ft. 10½ in. on February 21, 1994.

United States   The hair of Diane Witt of Worcester, MA measured over 12 ft. 8 in. in March 1993.

Most valuable hair   On February 18, 1988, a bookseller from Cirencester, England paid £5,575 ($10,035) for a lock of hair from the head of British naval hero Lord Nelson (1758–1805) at an auction held in Crewkerne, England.

Hair splitting   Alfred West (Great Britain; 1901–85) succeeded in splitting a human hair 17 times into 18 parts on eight occasions.

Longest beard   The beard of Hans N. Langseth (b. 1846, Norway) measured 17½ feet at the time of his burial in Kensett, IA in 1927. It was presented to the Smithsonian Institution, Washington, D.C., in 1967.

The beard of Janice Devêree, "the bearded lady" (b. Bracken Co., KY, 1842), was measured at 14 inches in 1884.

Longest mustache   The mustache of Kalyan Ramji Sain of Sundargarth, India, grown since 1976, reached a span of 133½ inches (right side 67¾ inches and left side 65¾ inches) in July 1993.

United States   Paul Miller of Alta Loma, CA had grown a mustache measuring nine feet long as of February 3, 1995.

Fastest shaving   The fastest barbers are Denny Rowe and Tom Rodden. Denny Rowe shaved 1,994 men in 60 minutes with a retractor safety razor in Herne Bay, England on June 19, 1988, taking an average of 1.8 seconds per volunteer and drawing blood four times. Tom Rodden of Chatham, England shaved 278 volunteers in 60 minutes with a straight razor on November 10, 1993, averaging 12.9 seconds per face. He drew blood once.

Most tattoos   The ultimate in being tattooed is represented by Tom Leppard of the Isle of Skye, Scotland. He has chosen a leopard-skin design, with all the skin between the spots tattooed saffron yellow. The area of his body covered is approximately 99.2 percent.

The world's most decorated woman is strip artiste "Krystyne Kolorful" (b. December 5, 1952, Alberta, Canada). Her 95 percent bodysuit took 10 years to complete.

Bernard Moeller of Pennsylvania has the most separate designs, with 14,000 individual tattoos up to January 1993.

MUSCLES

Largest muscle   Muscles normally account for 40 percent of male body weight, and 35 percent of female body weight. The bulkiest of the 639 named muscles in the human body is usually the gluteus maximus or buttock muscle, which extends the thigh. A woman's uterus, which normally weighs about one ounce, can increase its weight during pregnancy to more than 2.2 pounds.

Longest muscle The sartorius is a narrow, ribbonlike muscle that runs from the pelvis across the front of the thigh to the top of the tibia below the knee.

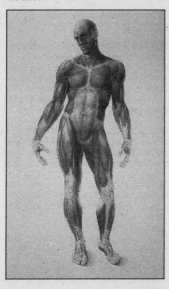

The sartorius, the longest muscle in the human body, runs from the pelvis and across the front of the thigh to the top of the tibia below the knee. (*Science Photo Library/J. Daugherty*)

Smallest muscle The stapedius, which controls the stapes (see SMALLEST BONE), is less than 0.05 inches long.

Strongest muscle The two masseters, one on each side of the mouth, are responsible for the action of biting. In August 1986, Richard Hofmann (b. 1949) of Lake City, FL achieved a bite strength of 975 pounds for approximately two seconds in a research test using a gnathodynamometer at the College of Dentistry, University of Florida. This figure is more than six times the normal biting strength of these muscles.

GUESS WHAT?

Q. WHICH ELEMENT HAS THE HIGHEST TENSILE STRENGTH?

A. LOOK IN "ELEMENTS" (SCIENCE & TECHNOLOGY)

Longest muscle name The *levator labii superioris alaeque nasi* runs inwards and downwards on the face, with one branch running to the upper lip and the other to the nostril.

Largest biceps Denis Sester of Bloomington, MN has a right bicep measuring 30³/₄ inches cold.

TEETH

Tooth enamel is the only part of the human body that remains basically unchanged throughout life. It is also the hardest substance in the body.

Earliest teeth The first deciduous or milk teeth normally appear in infants at 5–8 months, these being the upper and lower jaw first incisors. Molars usually appear at 24 months, but a case published in Denmark in 1970 documented a 6-week-premature baby with eight teeth at birth, four of which were in the molar region.

Most valuable tooth A tooth belonging to scientist Isaac Newton (1643–1727) was sold in London, England in 1816 for £730 ($3,650). A nobleman purchased it and had it set in a ring, which he wore constantly.

Earliest false teeth From discoveries made in Etruscan tombs, partial dentures of bridgework type were being worn in what is now the Tuscany region of Italy as early as 700 B.C. Some were permanently attached to existing teeth and others were removable.

Lifting and pulling with teeth Walter Arfeuille of Ieper-Vlamertinge, Belgium lifted weights totaling 621 pounds a distance of 6³/₄ inches off the ground with his teeth in Paris, France, on March 31, 1990.

Robert Galstyan of Masis, Armenia pulled two railroad cars coupled together, weighing a total of 483,197 pounds, a distance of 23 feet along a railroad track with his teeth at Shcherbinka, Greater Moscow, Russia on July 21, 1992.

OUCH!

Brother Giovanni Battista Orsenigo of Rome, Italy, a dentist, saved all the teeth he extracted from 1868 to 1904. In 1903, the number was found to be 2,000,744 teeth—an average of 185 teeth, or nearly six total extractions, each day.

BONES

Longest bone Excluding a variable number of sesamoids (small rounded bones), there are 206 bones in the adult human body, compared with 300 in children (as they grow, some bones fuse together). The thigh bone or femur is the longest. It usually constitutes 27.5 percent of a person's stature, and may be expected to be 19³/₄ inches long in a 6-foot-tall man. The

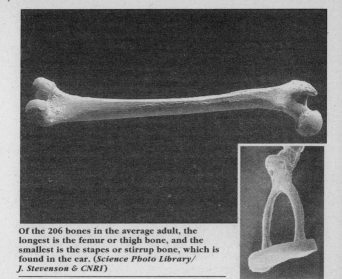

Of the 206 bones in the average adult, the longest is the femur or thigh bone, and the smallest is the stapes or stirrup bone, which is found in the ear. (*Science Photo Library/ J. Stevenson & CNRI*)

longest recorded bone was the 29.9-inch femur of the German giant Constantine, who died in Mons, Belgium, on March 30, 1902, at age 30. The femur of Robert Wadlow, the tallest man ever recorded, measured an estimated 29½ inches.

Smallest bone   The stapes or stirrup bone, one of the three auditory ossicles in the middle ear, measures 0.10–0.13 inches long and weighs 0.03–0.066 grains.

Most expensive skull   The skull of Emanuel Swedenborg (1688–1772), the Swedish natural philosopher and theologian, was bought in London, England by the Royal Swedish Academy of Sciences for £5,500 ($10,505) on March 6, 1978.

VISION

Highest acuity   The human eye is capable of judging relative position with remarkable accuracy, reaching limits of between three and five seconds of arc.

In April 1984, Dr. Dennis M. Levi of the College of Optometry, University of Houston, Houston, TX repeatedly identified the relative position of a thin bright green line within 0.85 seconds of arc. This is equivalent to a displacement of one fourth of an inch at a distance of one mile.

Light sensitivity   Working in Chicago, IL in 1942, Maurice H. Pirenne detected a flash of blue light of 500 nm in total darkness, when as few as five quanta or photons of light were available to be absorbed by the rod photoreceptors of the retina.

BRAINS

Heaviest brain   In December 1992, Dr. T. Mandybur and Karen Carney of the Department of Pathology and Laboratory Medicine at the University of Cincinnati, Cincinnati, OH reported a brain from a 30-year-old man weighing 5 lb. 1.1 oz.

Lightest brain   The lightest "normal" or nonatrophied brain on record was one weighing 1 lb. 8 oz. It belonged to Daniel Lyon (Ireland), who died in 1907 at age 46 in New York. He measured just over five feet tall and weighed 145 pounds.

Mathematical computation   Shakuntala Devi of India multiplied two 13-digit numbers (7,686,369,774,870 × 2,465,099,745,779) randomly selected by the Computer Department of Imperial College, London, England on June 18, 1980, in 28 seconds. Her answer, which was correct, was 18,947,668,177,995,426,462,773,730. Some experts on calculating prodigies refuse to give credence to Devi on the grounds that her achievements are so vastly superior to the calculating feats of any other judged prodigy that the evaluation must have been defective.

Memorization   Bhandanta Vicittabi Vumsa (1911–93) recited 16,000 pages of Buddhist canonical texts in Yangon, Myanmar in May 1974. Gon Yangling, 26, memorized more than 15,000 telephone numbers in Harbin, China, according to the Xinhua News Agency.

Memorizing cards   Dominic O'Brien (Great Britain) memorized on a single sighting a random sequence of 40 separate decks of cards (2,080 cards in all) that had been shuffled together, with only one mistake, at the BBC studios, Elstree, England on November 26, 1993. The fastest time to memorize a single deck of shuffled cards is 42.01 seconds, by Tom Groves at Jesus College, Cambridge, England, on November 3, 1994.

The United States record is held by Frost McKee of Georgetown, TX, who memorized on a single sighting a random sequence of 36 separate decks of cards (1,872 cards in all) that had been shuffled together, with only eight mistakes, at the Ramada Inn, Georgetown, TX on October 17–18, 1992.

Memorizing pi   Hideaki Tomoyori (b. 1932) of Yokohama, Japan recited *pi* from memory to 40,000 places in 17 hr. 21 min., including breaks totaling 4 hr. 15 min., on March 9–10, 1987 at the Tsukuba University Club House.

Longest and shortest dreams   Dreaming sleep is characterized by rapid eye movements known as REM. The longest recorded period of REM is one of 3 hr. 8 min. by David Powell at the Puget Sound Sleep Disorder Center, Seattle, WA on April 29, 1994. At the other extreme, in July 1984, the Sleep Research Center, Haifa, Israel recorded no REM in a 33-year-old male with a shrapnel brain injury.

VOICE AND BREATHING

Lung power   The inflation of a standard 35-ounce meteorological balloon to a diameter of eight feet in a timed contest was achieved by Nicholas Mason (England) in 45 min. 2.5 sec. for the BBC *Record Breakers* television program on September 26, 1994.

DID YOU KNOW?

The normal intelligible outdoor range of a man's voice in still air is 600 feet. The *silbo*, the whistled language of the island of La Gomera in the Canaries, is intelligible across the valleys at five miles under ideal conditions. There is a recorded case of the human voice being detectable at a distance of $10^1/_2$ miles across still water at night.

Fastest talker   Few people are able to speak *articulately* at a sustained speed greater than 300 words per minute.

Steve Woodmore of Orpington, England spoke 595 words in a time of 56.01 seconds, or 637.4 words per minute, on the British TV program *Motor Mouth* on September 22, 1990.

Sean Shannon, a Canadian residing in Oxford, England, recited Hamlet's soliloquy "To be or not to be" (260 words) in a time of 24 seconds (equivalent to 650 words per minute) on British Broadcasting Corporation's *Radio Oxford* on October 26, 1990.

Talking backwards   Steve Briers of Kilgetty, Wales recited the entire lyrics of Queen's album *A Night at the Opera* backwards at British Broadcasting Corporation North-West Radio 4's *Cat's Whiskers* on February 6, 1990 in a time of 9 min. 58.44 sec.

Loudest scream   Simon Robinson of McLaren Vale, South Australia produced a scream of 128 decibels at a distance of 8 ft. 2 in. at The Guinness Challenge in Adelaide, Australia on November 11, 1988.

Loudest shout   Annalisa Wray (b. April 21, 1974) of Comber, Northern Ireland achieved 121.7 decibels when shouting the word "Quiet" at the Citybus Challenge, Belfast, Northern Ireland on April 16, 1994.

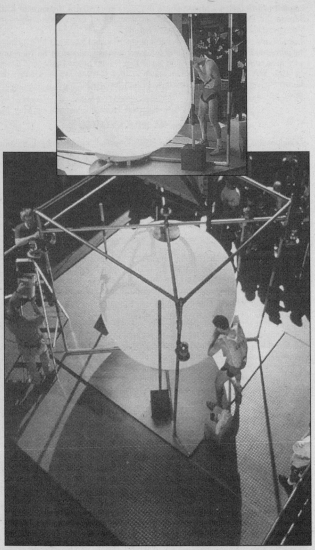

Nicholas Mason demonstrates his claim to have the world's most powerful lungs. (*BBC*)

Loudest whistle   Roy Lomas achieved 122.5 decibels at a distance of 8 ft. 2 in. in the Deadroom at the British Broadcasting Corporation studios in Manchester, England on December 19, 1983.

Fastest sneeze   The fastest speed at which particles expelled by sneezing have ever been measured to travel is 103.6 MPH.

Loudest snoring   Kåre Walkert (b. May 14, 1949) of Kumla, Sweden, who suffers from the breathing disorder apnea, recorded peak levels of 93 dBA while sleeping at the Örebro Regional Hospital, Sweden on May 24, 1993.

Fastest yodeling   The most rapid recorded yodel is 22 tones (15 falsetto) in one second, by Thomas Scholl of Munich, Germany on February 9, 1992.

ACHOO!

The longest sneezing fit ever recorded is that of Donna Griffiths (b. 1969) of Pershore, England. She started sneezing on January 13, 1981 and sneezed an estimated 1 million times in the first 365 days. Griffiths achieved her first sneeze-free day on September 16, 1983—the 978th day.

BLOOD

Most common blood group   On a world basis, Group O is the most common (46 percent), but in some areas, for example Norway, Group A predominates.

United States   The most common subgroup in the United States is O+, which is found in 38.4 percent of the population.

Rarest blood type   The rarest type in the world is a type of Bombay blood (subtype h-h) found so far only in a Czechoslovak nurse in 1961, and in a brother (Rh positive) and sister (Rh negative) surnamed Jalbert in Massachusetts, reported in February 1968.

United States   The rarest generic blood group is AB–, which occurs in only 0.7 percent of persons in the United States.

Largest blood transfusion   A 50-year-old hemophiliac, Warren C. Jyrich, required 2,400 donor units of blood, equivalent to 1,900 pints of blood, when undergoing open heart surgery at the Michael Reese Hospital, Chicago, IL in December 1970.

Largest vein   The largest is the inferior vena cava, which returns the blood from the lower half of the body to the heart.

Largest artery   The largest is the aorta, which is 1.18 inches in diameter where it leaves the heart. By the time it ends at the level of the fourth lumbar vertebra it is about 0.68 inches in diameter.

Highest blood alcohol level   The University of California Medical School, Los Angeles reported in December 1982 the case of a confused but conscious 24-year-old female, who was shown to have a blood alcohol level of 1,510 mg per 100 ml. After two days she discharged herself.

CELLS

Largest cell   The megakaryocyte, a blood cell, measures 200 microns. It is found in the bone marrow, where it produces the platelets that play an important role in blood clotting.

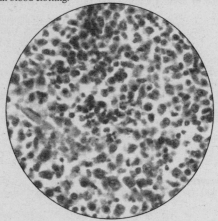

A micrograph of human red bone marrow shows the blood-producing cells. Two examples of the body's largest cell, the megakaryocyte, are visible (large nuclei); these cells produce platelets and measure 200 microns. (*Science Photo Library/ A. & Hanns-Frieder Michler*)

Smallest cells   Brain cells in the cerebellum measure about 0.005 mm.

Longest cells   Motor neurons can be 4¼ feet long. They have cell bodies in the lower spinal cord with axons that carry nerve impulses down to the big toe.

Fastest turnover of body cells   The body cells with the shortest life are in the lining of the alimentary tract (gut), where the cells are shed every three days.

Longest-living cells   Brain cells last for life. They may be three times as old as bone cells, which live 25–30 years.

Most abundant cell   The body contains approximately 30 billion red blood cells. The function of these cells is to carry oxygen around the body.

ILLNESS AND DISEASE

Commonest disease   The commonest noncontagious diseases are periodontal diseases such as gingivitis (inflammation of the gums). Few people completely escape the effects of tooth decay during the course of their lives.

The commonest contagious disease in the world is coryza (acute nasopharyngitis), or the common cold.

Highest mortality   A number of diseases are generally considered to be universally fatal. AIDS (Acquired Immune Deficiency Syndrome) and rabies encephalitis, a virus infection of the central nervous system, are well-known examples. The *disease* rabies, however, should not be confused with being bitten by a rabid animal. With immediate treatment, the virus can be prevented from entering the nervous system, and chances of survival are high.

The pneumonic form of plague (bacterial infection), which caused the Black Death of 1347–51, killed everyone who caught it—some 75 million people worldwide.

U.S. AIDS CASES

TOP 5 FIVE

State	Cases
New York	83,197
California	78,084
Florida	43,978
Texas	30,712
New Jersey	25,089

Metropolitan Area	Cases
New York	71,934
Los Angeles	27,247
San Francisco	20,750
Miami	14,050
Washington, D.C.	12,527

Centers for Disease Control, December 31, 1994

Leading cause of death In industrialized countries, diseases of the heart and blood vessels account for more than 50 percent of deaths. The most common of these are heart attacks, strokes, and gangrene of the lower limbs, usually due to atheroma (degeneration of the arterial walls) obstructing the flow of blood.

Most commonly dispensed drug The drug Premarin, generally prescribed during estrogen replacement therapy as a method for treating the symptoms of female menopause, was dispensed 36,818,000 times in the U.S. in 1994.

T O P
10
T E N

U.S. DISPENSED DRUGS

Drug	Times Dispensed
Premarin	36,818,000
Amoxil	27,159,000
Zantac	25,630,000
Synthroid	22,963,000
Trimox	22,138,000
Lanoxin	21,744,000
Procardia	20,507,000
Vasotec	18,801,000
Proventil	17,471,000
Prozac	15,161,000

National Prescription Audit Plus, IMS America, Ltd., 1994

BODY TEMPERATURE

Standard body temperature is 98.6°F; the coolest parts are the hands and feet; the hottest is the center of the brain.

Highest body temperature Willie Jones, 52, was admitted to Grady Memorial Hospital, Atlanta, GA on July 10, 1980 with heatstroke on a day when the temperature reached 90°F with 44 percent humidity. His temperature was found to be 115.7°F. After 24 days he was discharged "at prior baseline status."

Lowest body temperature People may die of hypothermia with body temperatures of 95°F. The lowest authenticated body temperature is 57.5°F, for Karlee Kosolofski, age two, of Regina, Saskatchewan, Canada on February 23, 1994. She had been accidentally locked out of her house for six hours in a temperature of –8°F. Despite severe frostbite, which required the amputation of her left leg above the knee, she has made a full recovery.

The scream of Simon Robinson (Australia) measured 128 dBa on November 11, 1988 [See page 29]. (*Bob Burton*)

MEDICAL EXTREMES

Cardiac arrest The longest period of cardiac arrest in which the victim survived is four hours in the case of a Norwegian fisherman, Jan Egil Refsdahl (b. 1936), who fell overboard in the icy waters off Bergen on December 7, 1987. He was rushed to nearby Haukeland Hospital after his body temperature fell to 77°F and his heart stopped beating, but he made a full recovery after he was connected to a heart–lung machine normally used for heart surgery.

United States On October 9, 1986, Allen Smith, age two, fell into the Stanislaus River in Oakdale, CA. He was spotted 90 minutes later and rushed to Modesto Memorial Hospital, where two hours later his heart began beating again spontaneously.

Longest coma Elaine Esposito (1934–78) of Tarpon Springs, FL never stirred after an appendectomy on August 6, 1941, when she was age six. She died on November 25, 1978 when she was 43 yr. 357 days old, having been in a coma for 37 yr. 111 days.

Eating Michel Lotito (b. June 15, 1950) of Grenoble, France, known as Monsieur Mangetout ("Mr. Eat-Everything"), has been eating metal and glass since 1959. Gastroenterologists have X-rayed his stomach and described his ability to consume two pounds of metal per day as unique. His diet since 1966 has included 10 bicycles, a supermarket cart (in 4½ days), seven TV sets, six chandeliers, a Cessna light aircraft and a computer. He is said to have provided the only example in history of a coffin (handles and all) ending up inside a man.

Longest without food and water The longest recorded case of survival without food *and* water is 18 days by Andreas Mihavecz, then 18, of Bregenz,

Austria, who was put in a holding cell on April 1, 1979 in a local government building in Höscht, and then totally forgotten by the police. On April 18, 1979, he was discovered close to death. He had been a passenger in a car that crashed.

GULP!

The heaviest object extracted from a human stomach was a 5 lb. 3 oz. ball of hair from a 20-year-old female compulsive swallower at the South Devon and East Cornwall Hospital, England, on March 30, 1895.

Largest gallbladder   On March 15, 1989 at the National Naval Medical Center in Bethesda, MD, Prof. Bimal C. Ghosh removed a gallbladder that weighed 23 pounds from a 69-year-old woman. The patient had been complaining of increasing swelling around the abdomen, but after removal of this enlarged gallbladder, which weighed more than three times as much as the average newborn baby, she felt perfectly well and left the hospital 10 days later.

Largest gallstones   A gallstone weighing 13 lb. 14 oz. was removed from an 80-year-old woman by Dr. Humphrey Arthure at Charing Cross Hospital, London, England on December 29, 1952.

Most gallstones   In August 1987, it was reported that 23,530 gallstones had been removed from an 85-year-old woman by Dr. K. Whittle Martin at Worthing Hospital, Sussex, England, after she complained of severe abdominal pain.

Highest g force endured   Race car driver David Purley (1945–85) survived a deceleration from 108 MPH to zero in a crash at Silverstone, near Towcester, England on July 13, 1977 that involved a force of 179.8 g. He suffered 29 fractures, three dislocations and six heart stoppages.

The highest g value endured voluntarily is 82.6 g for 0.04 seconds by Eli L. Beeding, Jr. on a water-braked rocket sled at Holloman Air Force Base, NM on May 16, 1958. He was subsequently hospitalized for three days.

Heat endurance   The highest dry-air temperature endured by naked men in U.S. Air Force experiments in 1960 was 400°F, and by heavily clothed men 500°F.

Hemodialysis   Brian Wilson of Edinburgh, Scotland has suffered from kidney failure since 1964, and has been on dialysis since May 30, 1964.

Longest hospital stay   Martha Nelson was admitted to the Columbus State Institute for the Feeble-Minded in Ohio in 1875 and died in January 1975 at age 103 yr. 6 mo. in the Orient State Institution, OH after spending more than 99 years in hospitals.

Munchausen's syndrome The most extreme recorded case of the rare and incurable condition known as Munchausen's syndrome (a continual desire to have medical treatment) was William McIloy (b. 1906), who cost Britain's National Health Service an estimated £2.5 million ($4 million) during his 50-year career as a hospital patient. During that time he had 400 major and minor operations, and stayed at 100 different hospitals using 22 aliases. The longest period he was ever out of the hospital was six months. In 1979, he hung up his bedpan for the last time, saying he was sick of hospitals, and retired to an old people's home in Birmingham, England, where he died in 1983.

Most injections Samuel L. Davidson (b. July 30, 1912) of Glasgow, Scotland has had, at a conservative estimate, 77,200 insulin injections since 1923.

Longest in "iron lung" Dorothy Stone (b. June 2, 1928) of Liss, England has been in a negative pressure respirator since 1947. John Prestwich (b. November 24, 1938) of Kings Langley, England has been dependent on a respirator since November 24, 1955.

Pill-taking The highest recorded total of pills swallowed by a patient is 565,939 between June 9, 1967 and June 19, 1988 by C.H.A. Kilner (1926–88) of Bindura, Zimbabwe.

Postmortem birth The longest gestation interval in a postmortem birth was one of 84 days in the case of a girl born on July 5, 1983 to a brain-dead woman in Roanoke, VA who had been kept on a life support machine since April.

HIC!

Charles Osborne (1894–1991) of Anthon, IA hiccupped every 1¹/₂ seconds for 69 yr. 5 mo., until February 1990. He began hiccupping in 1922 when he was slaughtering a hog. He was unable to find a cure, but led a reasonably normal life during which he had two wives and fathered eight children.

Swallowing The worst reported case of compulsive swallowing of objects involved an insane female, Mrs. H., who at the age of 42 complained of a "slight abdominal pain." She proved to have 2,533 objects, including 947 bent pins, in her stomach. These were removed by Dr. Chalk and Dr. Foucar in June 1927 at the Ontario Hospital, Canada.

Largest tumor An ovarian cyst weighing an estimated 328 pounds was drained from a patient during the week prior to removal of the cyst shell by Dr. Arthur Spohn in Texas in 1905. The patient made a full recovery.

The largest tumor ever removed *intact* was a multicystic mass of the ovary weighing 303 pounds. The 3-foot-diameter growth was removed in its entirety in October 1991 from the abdomen of an unnamed 35-year-old woman by Prof. Katherine O'Hanlan of Stanford University Medical Center, California. The patient weighed 210 pounds after the 6-hour operation and has made a full recovery.

Underwater submergence In 1986, 2-year-old Michelle Funk of Salt Lake City, UT made a full recovery after spending 66 minutes under water.

DOCTORS

Most dedicated doctor Since 1943, Dr. M.C. Modi, a pioneer of mass eye surgery in India, has performed as many as 833 cataract operations in one day. He has visited 46,120 villages and 12,118,630 patients, and has performed a total of 610,564 operations to February 1993.

Dr. Robert B. McClure of Toronto, Ontario, Canada performed a career total of 20,423 major operations from 1924 to 1978.

Medical families The eight sons and two daughters of Dr. William and Beryl Waldron of Knocknacarra, Ireland all qualified as doctors at University College, Galway, between 1976 and 1990. The Barcia family of Valencia, Spain has had the same medical practice for seven generations, since 1792.

OPERATIONS

Longest operation An operation of 96 hours was performed on Gertrude Levandowski from February 4 to February 8, 1951 in Chicago, IL to remove an ovarian cyst. During the operation, her weight fell from 616 pounds to 308 pounds.

Most operations endured From July 22, 1954 to the end of 1994, Charles Jensen of Chester, SD had 970 operations to remove the tumors associated with basal cell nevus syndrome.

Oldest patient The greatest recorded age at which anyone has undergone an operation is 111 yr. 105 days in the case of James Henry Brett, Jr. (1849–1961) of Houston, TX. He had a hip operation on November 7, 1960.

Earliest general anesthesia The earliest recorded operation under general anesthesia was for the removal of a cyst from the neck of James Venable by Dr. Crawford Williamson Long (1815–78), using diethyl ether $(C_2H_5)_2O$, in Jefferson, GA on March 30, 1842.

Cardiopulmonary resuscitation Brent Shelton and John Ash completed a 130-hour-long CPR marathon (cardiopulmonary resuscitation—15 compressions alternating with two breaths) from October 28 to November 2, 1991 at Regina, Saskatchewan, Canada.

First heart transplant Louis Washkansky, age 55, was operated on at the Groote Schuur Hospital, Cape Town, South Africa between 1 A.M. and 6 A.M., on December 3, 1967, by a team of 30 headed by Prof. Christiaan

Neethling Barnard. The donor was Denise Ann Darvall, age 25. Washkansky lived for 18 days.

United States   The first heart transplant was performed on a 2½-week-old baby boy at Maimonides Hospital, Brooklyn, NY on December 6, 1967 by a team of 22 headed by Dr. Adrian Kantrowitz. The donor was a newborn infant. The patient lived 6½ hours. The first adult transplant was performed at the Stanford Medical Center in Palo Alto, CA on January 6, 1968 by Dr. Norman E. Shumway on 54-year-old Mike Kasperak. Mr. Kasperak lived 14 days. From December 1967 until December 31, 1993 there have been 16,378 heart transplants. The greatest number performed in one year is 2,293, in 1993.

First double heart transplant   In the United States, the first operation was performed on Darrell Hammarley, age 56, at the Stanford Medical Center in Palo Alto, CA on November 20, 1968. The first heart implanted failed to beat steadily and was replaced by a second transplant two hours later.

Longest surviving heart transplant patient   Dirk van Zyl of Cape Town, South Africa (1926–94) survived for 23 yr. 57 days, having received an unnamed person's heart in 1971.

Youngest heart transplant patient   Paul Holt of Vancouver, British Columbia, Canada underwent surgery at Loma Linda Hospital in California on October 16, 1987 at age 2 hr. 34 min. He was born six weeks premature weighing 6 lb. 6 oz.

First animal-to-human heart transplant   In the United States, the first operation was carried out on January 23, 1964 at the University of Mississippi Medical Center in Jackson, MS by a team of 12 headed by Dr. James D. Hardy. The patient, age 64, received the heart of a chimpanzee, which beat for 90 minutes.

Dr. Christiaan Barnard led the team that performed the first successful heart transplant. (*South African Embassy, London*)

U.S. INPATIENT PROCEDURES

Procedure	Number per year
Arteriography and angiocardiography	1,771,000
Episiotomy	1,611,000
Diagnostic ultrasound	1,458,000
Computerized axial tomography	1,286,000
Fetal EKG	1,241,000
Cardiac catheterization	1,028,000
Cesarean section	921,000
Endoscopy of small intestine	864,000
Respiratory therapy	819,000
Repair of current obstetric laceration	790,000

Centers for Disease Control, 1994

First heart–lung–liver transplant On December 17, 1986 at Papworth Hospital, Cambridge, England, Mrs. Davina Thompson (b. February 28, 1951) of Rawmarsh, England underwent surgery for seven hours by a team of 15 headed by chest surgeon Dr. John Wallwork and Prof. Sir Roy Calne.

First five-organ transplant Tabatha Foster (1984–88) of Madisonville, KY, at 3 yr. 143 days of age received a transplanted liver, pancreas, small intestine, portions of stomach and large intestine in a 15-hour operation at the Children's Hospital, Pittsburgh, PA on October 31, 1987. Before the operation, she had never eaten solid food.

First artificial heart implant On December 1–2, 1982 at the Utah Medical Center, Salt Lake City, UT, Dr. Barney B. Clark, 61, of Des Moines, WA was the first recipient of an artificial heart. The surgeon was Dr. William C. DeVries. The heart was a Jarvik-7 designed by Dr. Robert K. Jarvik. Dr. Clark died on March 23, 1983, 112 days later. William J. Schroeder survived 620 days with an artificial heart in Louisville, KY from November 25, 1984 to August 7, 1986.

First synthetic heart implant Haskell Karp, age 47, of Skokie, IL, received the first synthetic heart implant on April 4, 1969, at St. Luke's Episcopal Hospital, Houston, TX. Dr. Denton A. Cooley led the team of doctors, which included the developer of the heart, Dr. Domingo Liotta. The synthetic heart was replaced by a human transplant on April 7.

First kidney transplant   Dr. Richard H. Lawler (U.S.) performed the first transplant of a kidney in a human at Little Company of Mary Hospital, Chicago, IL, on June 17, 1950. The first successful kidney transplant operation was performed at Peter Bent Brigham Hospital (now Brigham and Women's Hospital) in Boston, MA on December 23, 1954 by a team of surgeons headed by Dr. John P. Merrill. The patient, Richard Herrick, age 23, received a kidney from his identical twin, Ronald.

Longest surviving kidney transplant patients   From 1977, when figures were first gathered, until 1993, there have been a total of 136,986 kidney transplants in the United States. The greatest number performed in one year is 10,894, in 1993.

The longest surviving kidney transplant patient is Johanna Leanora Rempel (née Nightingale; b. 1948) of Red Deer, Alberta, Canada, who was given a kidney from her identical twin sister Lana Blatz on December 28, 1960. The operation was performed at the Peter Bent Brigham Hospital, Boston, MA. Both Johanna and her sister have continued to enjoy excellent health, and both have borne healthy children.

U.S. CAGES OF DEATH

Cause	Deaths per year
Heart disease	739,860
Cancer	530,870
Stroke	149,740
Chronic obstructive pulmonary diseases	101,090
Accidents	88,630
Pneumonia and influenza	81,730
Diabetes	55,110
HIV/AIDS	38,500
Suicide	31,230
Homicide	25,470

Centers for Disease Control, December 31, 1994

First lung transplant   In the United States, the first operation took place on June 11, 1963 at the University of Mississippi Medical Center in Jackson, MS. The surgery, which was headed by Dr. James D. Hardy, lasted three hours and involved the replacement of the patient's left lung. The patient, John Richard Russell, survived 18 days.

LIVING WORLD

ANIMAL KINGDOM

Oldest land animals Animals moved from the sea to the land 414 million years ago, according to discoveries made in 1990 near Ludlow, England. The first known land animals include two kinds of centipede and a tiny spider found among plant debris. However, it is believed that all three species were fairly advanced predators—and must therefore have been preying on animals that lived on land even before they did.

Greatest concentration A swarm of Rocky Mountain locusts (*Melanoplus spretus*) that flew over Nebraska on July 20–30, 1874 covered an area estimated at 198,600 square miles. The swarm must have contained at least 12.5 trillion insects, with an aggregate weight of about 27.5 million tons.

Largest colony The black-tailed prairie dog (*Cynomys ludovicianus*), a rodent of the family Sciuridae found in the western United States and northern Mexico, builds huge colonies. A single "town" discovered in 1901 contained about 400 million individuals and was estimated to cover 24,000 square miles.

Largest flying creature The largest-ever flying animal was the pterosaur (*Quetzalcoatlus northropi*). About 70 million years ago it soared over what is now Texas, Wyoming and New Jersey; Alberta, Canada; and Senegal and Jordan. Partial remains discovered in Big Bend National Park, TX in 1971 indicate that this reptile must have had a wingspan of 36–39 feet and weighed about 190–250 pounds.

Largest animal-made structure The largest structure built by living creatures is the 1,260-mile-long Great Barrier Reef, off Queensland, Australia, covering an area of 80,000 square miles. It consists of millions of dead and living stony corals (order Madreporaria or Scleractinia). Over 350 species of coral are found on this reef, and its accretion is thought to have taken 600 million years.

Loudest animal sound The low-frequency pulses made by blue whales when communicating with each other have been measured up to 188 decibels, making them the loudest sounds emitted by any living source. They have been detected 530 miles away.

Noisiest animal The male howler monkey (*Alouatta*) of Central and South America makes a sound that has been described as a cross between the bark of a dog and the bray of a donkey, and can be heard clearly for distances of up to 3.1 miles.

Most acute hearing Because of their ultrasonic echolocation abilities, bats have the most acute hearing of any terrestrial animal. Most species use frequencies in the 20–80 kHz range, although some can hear frequencies as high as 120–250 kHz. This compares with a limit of almost 20 kHz for humans, and 280 kHz for the common dolphin (*Delphinus delphis*).

THE *CLOUDS* THAT *CRAWLED*

In July 1874, enormous swarms of Rocky Mountain locusts descended on Nebraska and the surrounding frontier settlements, causing inestimable agricultural damage and loss to the pioneers of the region. Many had only recently brought their families to settle there, and had already endured the effects of the persistently hostile climate, with raging storms in one season and intolerable drought in the next.

Newspapers and historical documents contain graphic descriptions of the insects' unmitigated attack on the communities of Nebraska. They flew through the air in dense clouds and fell to the ground in gray, oily clusters. They laid eggs in the ground that would later hatch in droves, prolonging the cyclical suffering of the pioneers for years to come. According to the *Daily State Journal* of November 30, 1874, 10,000 people had been left destitute and $1.5 million in aid was needed to allow them to survive for just one more year. The swarm covered an area estimated at 198,600 square miles as it flew over Nebraska, and it was at its worst on July 20–30, 1874.

A disheveled tree (above) shows the kind of damage that a swarm of locusts can cause. The Nebraska swarm of 1874 destroyed vegetation in this way across thousands of miles. (*Jacana/J. Robert*)

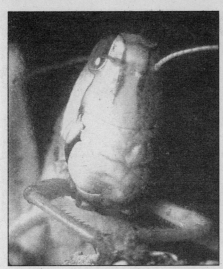

Face to face with one
of the locusts.
(*Jacana/A. Kernels-
Dragesco*)

"They covered the ground almost like a blanket. They jumped to the right and left as you walked through them, opening a pathway and closing in behind you as you passed. I had some young celery plants in the garden that I was especially proud of and I covered them with some large pie-plant leaves in the morning. When I came home at noon the pie-plant leaves were eaten and the celery leaves were eaten; not a scrap of anything green remained. The grasshopper brigades also ate all the leaves on my little trees, leaving them as bare as in winter. Even the weeds were not spared by the destroying hosts.

These swarms passed over us often like vast flying squadrons. When they did not stop you could see them, as I have said before, only by looking towards the sun and shading your eyes when you could see their wings shining in the sunlight. Those were tragic days indeed. It became pathetic to see a man standing in that attitude by his little home watching the shining clouds above and waiting to see if a changing wind would send destruction from the air and leave him and his little household destitute."

Recollections of a Pioneer Lawyer, Othman A. Abbott; from the *Nebraska History Magazine*, Volume XI, July–September 1928.

Greatest concentration of animals A huge swarm of Rocky Mountain locusts (*Melanoplus spretus*) covered an estimated area of 198,600 square miles as they flew over Nebraska in July 1874.

Vampire bats have such acute hearing that they can identify frequencies 6–10 times higher than humans can hear. (*Jacana/ G. Ziesler*)

Largest eye   The Atlantic giant squid has the largest eye of any animal, living or extinct. It has been estimated that one specimen found at Thimble Tickle Bay, Newfoundland, Canada had eyes 15³/₄ inches wide—almost the width of this open book.

Most acute sense of smell   The male emperor moth (*Eudia pavonia*) can detect the sex attractant of the female at a range of 6.8 miles upwind. This scent has been identified as one of the higher alcohols ($C_{16}H_{29}OH$), of which the female carries less than 0.0001 mg. The chemoreceptors on the male moth's antennae are so sensitive that they can detect a single molecule of scent.

Strongest animal   In proportion to their size, the strongest animals are beetles of the family Scarabaeidae, found mainly in the tropics. In one test, a rhinoceros beetle (*Dynastinae*) supported 850 times its own weight on its back (compared with 25 percent of its body weight for an adult elephant). As a comparison, in a trestle lift humans can support 17 times their own body weight.

Strongest bite   Experiments carried out with a Snodgrass gnathodynamometer (shark-bite meter) at the Lerner Marine Laboratory in Bimini, Bahamas revealed that a 6-ft.-6³/₄-in.-long dusky shark (*Carcharhinus obscurus*) could exert a force of 132 pounds between its jaws. This is equivalent to a pressure of 22 tons per square inch at the tips of the teeth. The bites of larger sharks, such as the great white (*Carcharodon carcharias*), must be even stronger but have never been measured.

Most dangerous animal   Malarial parasites of the genus *Plasmodium*, carried by mosquitoes of the genus *Anopheles*, have probably been responsible for half of all human deaths, excluding deaths caused by wars and accidents, since the Stone Age.

Most poisonous animal   The brightly-colored poison-arrow frogs (*Dendrobates* and *Phyllobates*) of South and Central America secrete some of the most deadly biological toxins known to man. The skin secretion of the golden poison-arrow frog (*Phyllobates terribilis*) of Colombia is the most poisonous; this frog is so dangerous that scientists have to wear thick gloves to pick it up in case they have cuts or scratches on their hands.

Most prodigious eater   The larva of the Polyphemus moth (*Antheraea polyphemus*) of North America consumes an amount equal to 86,000 times its own birth weight in the first 56 days of its life. In human terms, this would be equivalent to a 7-pound baby taking in 300 tons of nourishment.

Greatest weight loss   During a 7-month lactation period, a 132-ton female blue whale (*Balaenoptera musculus*) can lose up to 25 percent of her body weight nursing her calf.

Slowest growth   The deep-sea clam (*Tindaria callistiformis*) of the North Atlantic takes 100 years to grow to $\frac{1}{3}$ of an inch in length.

Longest suspended animation   Two specimens of the desert snail (*Eremina desertorum*) were presented to the British Museum (Natural History) in London as dead exhibits in 1846. They were placed on display, but four years later, in March 1850, it was found that one of the snails was still alive. This hardy little creature lived for another two years before it fell into a torpor and then died.

Greatest powers of regeneration   The sponges (Porifera) can regrow from tiny fragments of themselves. If a sponge is pushed through a fine-meshed silk gauze, each piece of separated tissue will live as an individual and grow into a full-sized sponge.

Fastest reproduction   A single cabbage aphid (*Brevicoryne brassicae*) could theoretically (with unlimited food and no predators) give rise in a year to a mass of descendants weighing 906 million tons.

MAMMALS

Largest mammal   The largest mammal, and the largest animal ever recorded, is the blue whale (*Balaenoptera musculus*), which grows from a barely visible ovum to a weight of over 28 tons one year after birth. Newborn calves measure 20–26 feet long and weigh up to 6,614 pounds.

Heaviest   A female blue whale weighing 190 tons and measuring 90 ft. 6 in. was caught in the Southern Ocean on March 20, 1947.

Longest   In 1909, a female blue whale measuring 110 ft. 2½ in. long was landed at Grytviken, South Georgia, Falkland Islands in the South Atlantic.

Largest land mammal   *Indricotherium* (= *Baluchitherium* or *Paraceratherium*), a long-necked, hornless rhinocerotid that roamed across western Asia and Europe about 35 million years ago, was first known from bones discovered in the Bugti Hills of Baluchistan, Pakistan in 1907–08. A restoration in the American Museum of Natural History, New York City measures 17 ft. 9 in. to the top of the shoulder hump and 37 feet in total length. The most likely maximum weight of this gigantic browser was revised in 1993 to 12–22 tons from earlier estimates of 37 tons.

Modern   The average bull of the African bush elephant (*Loxodonta africana africana*) stands 9 ft. 10 in.–12 ft. 2 in. at the shoulder, and weighs 4.4–7.7 tons. The largest specimen ever recorded was a bull shot on November 7, 1974, in Mucusso, Angola. Lying on its side, the elephant measured 13 ft. 8 in. in a projected line from the highest point of the shoulder to the base of the forefoot, indicating that its standing height must have been about 13 feet. Its weight was computed to be 13.5 tons.

Tallest   The tallest elephants are those of the endangered desert race from Damaraland, Namibia, which have proportionately longer legs than other elephants. The tallest recorded example was a bull shot near Sesfontein, Damaraland on April 4, 1978, after it had allegedly killed 11 people and caused widespread crop damage. Lying on its side, this elephant measured 14½ feet in a projected line from the shoulder to the base of the forefoot, indicating a standing height of about 13 ft. 10 in. It weighed an estimated 8.8 tons.

Largest toothed mammal   The lower jaw of a sperm whale (*Physeter macrocephalus*), measuring 16 ft. 5 in. long and exhibited in the British Museum (Natural History) in London, belonged to a bull reputedly measuring nearly 84 feet. However, the longest officially measured specimen was a male measuring 67 ft. 11 in. long, captured in the summer of 1950 off the Kurile Islands in the northwest Pacific Ocean.

Tallest mammal   The giraffe (*Giraffa camelopardalis*), found in the dry savanna and open woodland areas of Africa south of the Sahara, is the tallest mammal and the tallest living animal. The tallest individual ever recorded was a Masai bull (*G. c. tippelskirchi*) named George, received at Chester Zoo, Chester, England on January 8, 1959 from Kenya. His horns *almost* grazed the roof of the 20-foot-high Giraffe House when he was nine years old. George died on July 22, 1969.

Smallest mammal   Savi's white-toothed pygmy shrew (*Suncus etruscus*) has a head–body length of 1.32–2 inches and a tail length of 0.94–1.14 inches, and weighs 0.05–0.09 ounces. It is found along the Mediterranean coast and southwards to Cape Province, South Africa.

Fastest land mammal   Over a short distance (i.e., up to 600 yards) the cheetah (*Acinonyx jubatus*) of the open plains of East Africa, Iran, Turkmenistan and Afghanistan has a probable maximum speed of about 60 MPH on level ground.

Over a short distance, the cheetah is the fastest land mammal in the world. (*Jacana/Y. Arthus-Bertrand; Jacana/F. Polking; Jacana/Varin/ Visage*)

The pronghorn antelope (*Antilocapra americana*) of the western United States, southwestern Canada, and parts of northern Mexico has been observed to travel at 35 MPH for four miles, at 42 MPH for one mile, and at 55 MPH for half a mile.

Fastest marine mammal On October 12, 1958, a bull killer whale (*Orcinus orca*), measuring an estimated 20–25 feet long, was timed at 34.5 MPH in the eastern North Pacific. Similar speeds have also been reported for Dall's porpoise (*Phocoenoides dalli*) in short bursts.

Slowest mammal The three-toed sloth of tropical South America (*Bradypus tridactylus*) has an average ground speed of 6–8 feet per minute (0.07–0.1 MPH), but in the trees it can accelerate to 15 feet per minute (0.17 MPH).

Oldest mammal No other mammal can match the age of 120 years attained by humans, but it is probable that the closest approach is made by the Asiatic elephant (*Elephas maximus*). The greatest age that has been verified with certainty is 78 years in the case of a cow named Modoc, which died in Santa Clara, CA on July 17, 1975. Certain whale species are believed to live even longer, although little is known about this. The fin whale (*Balaenoptera physalis*) is probably the longest-lived, with a maximum attainable lifespan estimated at 90–100 years.

Deepest dive On August 25, 1969, a bull sperm whale (*Physeter macrocephalus*) was killed 100 miles south of Durban, South Africa after it surfaced from a dive lasting 1 hr. 52 min. Inside its stomach were two *Scymnodon*, small sharks found only on the sea floor. At this distance from land the water is over 10,473 feet deep for a radius of 30–40 miles, which suggests that the sperm whale can descend over 9,840 feet when looking for food. The deepest authenticated dive was made in 1991 by a bull sperm

The Largest Litter of bear cubs, named Konrad, Paul, Christian, Johannes and Günther, were born at Haag Wildlife Park, Austria, on January 6, 1993. (*Tierpark Haag*)

whale off the coast of Dominica. Scientists from the Woods Hole Oceanographic Institute recorded a dive of 6,560 feet, lasting a total of 1 hr. 13 min.

Sleepiest mammals Some armadillos (Dasypodidae), opossums (Didelphidae) and sloths (Bradypodidae and Megalonychidae) spend up to 80 percent of their lives sleeping or dozing. The least active of all mammals are probably the three species of three-toed sloths in the genus *Bradypus*.

Highest-living mammal By a small margin, the highest-living mammal is the large-eared pika (*Ochtona macrotis*), which has been recorded at a height of 20,106 feet in high-altitude Asian mountain ranges. The yak (*Bos mutus*), of Tibet and the Sichuanese Alps, China, climbs to an altitude of 20,000 feet when foraging.

Largest herds The largest herds on record were herds of springbok (*Antidorcas marsupialis*) that migrated across the plains of the western parts of southern Africa in the 19th century. One herd estimated to be 15 miles wide and more than 100 miles long was reported from Karree Kloof, Orange River, South Africa in July 1896.

Largest litter The greatest number of young born to a *wild* mammal at a single birth is 31 (30 of which survived) in the case of the tailless tenrec (*Tenrec ecaudatus*), found in Madagascar and the Comoro Islands.

GUESS WHAT?

Q. How long was the longest dream?

A. Look in "Brains" (Human Being)

Longest gestation period The Asiatic elephant (*Elephas maximus*) has an average gestation period of 609 days (over 20 months) and a maximum of 760 days.

Shortest gestation period The shortest gestation period for a mammal is 12–13 days, which is common in several species. These include the Virginia opossum (*Didelphis marsupialis*) of North America, and the water opossum or yapok (*Chironectes minimus*) of central and northern South America. On rare occasions, gestation periods of as little as eight days have been recorded for some of these species.

Youngest breeder The female true lemming (*Lemmus lemmus*) of Scandinavia can become pregnant at the age of 14 days. The gestation period is 16–23 days, and litter size varies from 1 to 13. Lemmings are also prolific animals; one pair was reported to have produced eight litters in 167 days.

Largest tusks The longest tusks (excluding prehistoric examples) are a pair from an African elephant (*Loxodonta africana*) from Zaire preserved in the National Collection of Heads and Horns kept by the New York Zoological Society (Bronx Zoo), New York City. The right tusk measures 11 ft. 5½ in. along the outside curve and the left tusk measures 11 feet. The combined weight of the tusks is 293 pounds.

Heaviest A pair of African elephant (*Loxodonta africana*) tusks in the British Museum (Natural History), London from a bull shot in Kenya in 1897 weighed 240 pounds (length 10 ft. 2½ in.) and 225 pounds (length 10 ft. 5½ in.) respectively, giving a total weight of 465 pounds. Their combined weight today is 440½ pounds.

Longest horns The longest horns of any living animal are those of the water buffalo (*Bubalus arnee = B. bubalis*) of India, Nepal, Bhutan, and Thailand. One bull shot in 1955 had horns measuring 13 ft. 11 in. from tip to tip along the outside curve across the forehead.

Domestic animal The largest spread on record is 10 ft. 6 in. for a Texas longhorn steer. The horns are currently on exhibition at the Heritage Museum, Big Springs, TX.

Largest antlers The record antler spread or rack of any living species is 6 ft. 6½ in. from a moose (*Alces alces*) killed near the Stewart River in the Yukon Territory, Canada in October 1897. The antlers are now on display in the Field Museum, Chicago, IL.

CARNIVORES

Largest carnivore The largest of all carnivores is the polar bear (*Ursus maritimus*). Adult males typically weigh 880–1,300 pounds and have a nose-to-tail length of 95–102 inches.

The male of the Kodiak bear (*Ursus arctos middendorffi*), a subspecies of brown bear found on Kodiak Island and the adjacent Afognak and Shuyak islands in the Gulf of Alaska, AK, is usually shorter in length than the polar bear but more robustly built.

Smallest carnivore The least or dwarf weasel (*Mustela nivalis*) has a head–body length of 4.3–10.2 inches, a tail length of 0.5–3.4 inches, and a weight of 1–7 ounces. This species varies in size more than any other mammal; the smallest individuals are females living in the north of the range (especially Siberia), and in the Alps.

Largest feline The male Siberian tiger (*Panthera tigris altaica*) averages 10 ft. 4 in. long from the nose to the tip of the extended tail, stands 39–42 inches at the shoulder and weighs about 585 pounds.

An Indian tiger (*Panthera tigris tigris*) shot in northern Uttar Pradesh in November 1967 measured 10 ft. 7 in. between pegs (11 ft. 1 in. over the curves) and weighed 857 pounds (compared with 9 ft. 3 in. and 420 pounds for an average adult male).

Captive The largest tiger in captivity, and the heaviest on record, is a Siberian male named Jaipur, owned by animal trainer Joan Byron-Marasek of Clarksburg, NJ. In October 1986, Jaipur was 10 ft. 11 in. long and weighed 932 pounds.

Smallest feline The rusty-spotted cat (*Priongilurus rubiginosus*) of southern India and Sri Lanka has a head–body length of 13.8–18.9 inches and an average weight of 2 lb. 7 oz. (female) and 3 lb. 5 oz.–3 lb. 8 oz. (male). The black-footed cat (*Felis nigripes*) of southern Africa is almost as small.

PRIMATES

Largest primate The male eastern lowland gorilla (*Gorilla g. graueri*) of eastern Zaire has a bipedal standing height of up to 5 ft. 11 in. and weighs up to 386 pounds.

Tallest The greatest height (top of crest to heel) recorded for a gorilla in the wild is 6 ft. 5 in. for a mountain bull shot in the eastern Congo (Zaire) on May 16, 1938.

Heaviest The heaviest gorilla ever kept in captivity was a mountain bull named N'gagi, who died in the San Diego Zoo in California on January 12, 1944 at age 18. He weighed 683 pounds at his heaviest in 1943 and was 5 ft. 7³/₄ in. tall.

Smallest primate The smallest true primate (excluding tree shrews, which are normally classified separately) is the rufous mouse lemur (*Microcebus rufus*) of Madagascar. It has a head–body length of 4–4.9 inches, a tail length of 5–5.9 inches, and a weight of 1.6–3.2 ounces.

Oldest primate The greatest irrefutable age recorded for a nonhuman primate is 59 yr. 5 mo. for a chimpanzee (*Pan troglodytes*) named Gamma, who died at the Yerkes Primate Research Center in Atlanta, GA on February 19, 1992. Gamma was born at the Florida branch of the Yerkes Center in September 1932.

Monkey The world's oldest monkey, a male white-throated capuchin (*Cebus capucinus*) named Bobo, died on July 10, 1988 at age 53.

SEALS AND SEA LIONS

Largest pinniped The largest of the 34 known species of pinniped is the southern elephant seal (*Mirounga leonina*) of the sub-Antarctic islands. Bulls average 16¹/₂ feet long from the tip of the inflated snout to the tips of the tail flippers, have a maximum girth of 12 feet, and weigh 4,400–7,720 pounds. The largest accurately measured specimen was a bull weighing at least 4 tons and measuring 21 ft. 4 in. after flensing (stripping of the blubber or skin). Its original length was estimated to be about 22¹/₂ feet. The seal was killed in the South Atlantic at Possession Bay, South Georgia on February 28, 1913.

Live The largest reported live specimen is a bull from South Georgia, nicknamed Stalin. It was tranquilized by members of the British Antarctic Survey on October 14, 1989, when it weighed 5,869 pounds and measured 16 ft. 8 in. long.

Smallest pinniped The smallest pinniped, by a small margin, is the Galápagos fur seal (*Arctocephalus galapagoensis*). Adult females average 47 inches long and weigh about 60 pounds. Males are usually considerably larger, averaging 59 inches long and weighing around 140 pounds.

Oldest pinniped   The greatest authenticated age for a pinniped has been estimated by scientists at the Limnological Institute, Irkutsk, former USSR to be 56 years for the female Baikal seal (*Phoca sibirica*) and 52 years for the male, based on cementum layers in the canine teeth.

Fastest swimmer   The maximum swimming speed recorded for a pinniped is a short spurt of 25 MPH by a California sea lion (*Zalophus californianus*).

Deepest dive   In May 1989, scientists testing the diving abilities of northern elephant seals (*Mirounga angustirostris*) off the coast of San Miguel Island, CA documented an adult male that reached a maximum depth of 5,017 feet.

BATS

Largest bat   The world's largest bat in terms of wingspan is the Bismarck flying fox (*Pteropus neohibernicus*) of the Bismarck Archipelago and New Guinea. One specimen preserved in the American Museum of Natural History in New York City has a wingspan of 5 ft. 5 in.

United States   Mature specimens of the large mastiff bat (*Eumops perotis*), found in southern Texas, California, Arizona and New Mexico, have a wingspan of 22 inches.

Smallest bat   The smallest bat in the United States is the Western pipistrelle (*Pipistrellus hesperus*), found in the western United States. Mature specimens have a wingspan of 7.9 inches.

Oldest bat   The greatest age reliably reported for a bat is 32 years for a banded female little brown bat (*Myotis lucifugus*) in the United States in 1987.

Largest colony   The largest concentration of bats is in Bracken Cave, San Antonio, TX, where up to 20 million Mexican free-tailed bats (*Tadarida brasiliensis*) assemble.

Deepest descent   The little brown bat (*Myotis lucifugus*) has been recorded at a depth of 3,805 feet in a zinc mine in New York State.

DID YOU KNOW?

The largest rodent is the capybara (*Hydrochoerus hydrochaeris*) of northern South America, which has a head and body length of 3$\frac{1}{4}$–4$\frac{1}{2}$ feet and can weigh up to 145 pounds, although one exceptional cage-fat specimen attained 250 pounds.

RODENTS

Smallest rodent The northern pygmy mouse (*Baiomys taylori*), found in Mexico, Arizona and Texas, and the Baluchistan pygmy jerboa (*Salpingotus michaelis*) of Pakistan both have head–body lengths of as little as 1.42 inches and a tail length of 2.84 inches.

EEEEK!

A population of house mice (*Mus musculus*) numbering 83,000 individuals per acre was found in the dry bed of Buena Vista Lake, Kern County, CA in 1926–27.

Oldest rodent The greatest reliable age reported for a rodent is 27 yr. 3 mo. for a Sumatran crested porcupine (*Hystrix brachyura*) that died in the National Zoological Park, Washington, D.C. on January 12, 1965.

Longest hibernation Arctic ground squirrels (*Spermophilus parryi*), found in northern Canada and Alaska, hibernate for nine months of the year.

DEER

Largest deer An Alaskan moose (*Alces alces gigas*) standing 7 ft. 8 in. between pegs and weighing an estimated 1,800 pounds was shot on the Yukon River in the Yukon Territory, Canada in September 1897.

Smallest deer The smallest true deer (family Cervidae) is the southern pudu (*Pudu puda*), which is 13–15 inches tall at the shoulder and weighs 14–18 pounds. It is found in Chile and Argentina.

Oldest deer A red deer (*Cervus elaphus scoticus*) named Bambi (b. June 8, 1963) died on January 20, 1995, at the advanced age of 31 yr. 8 mo. The deer was owned by the Fraser family of Kiltarlity, Scotland.

United States A red deer age 26 yr. 8 mo. (*Cervus elaphus scoticus*) died in the Milwaukee Zoo, Milwaukee, WI on June 28, 1954.

KANGAROOS

Largest kangaroo The male red kangaroo (*Macropus rufus*) of central, southern and eastern Australia measures up to 5 ft. 11 in. tall when standing in its normal position, and up to 9 ft. 4 in. in total length (including the tail). It can weigh up to 198 pounds.

Fastest kangaroo The fastest speed recorded for a marsupial is 40 MPH for a mature female eastern gray kangaroo (*Macropus giganteus*).

Highest kangaroo jump A captive eastern gray kangaroo once cleared an 8-foot fence when an automobile backfired, and there is also a record of a hunted red kangaroo clearing a stack of timber 10 feet high.

STEADY TEDDY

Oldest pony The oldest pony in the United States is Teddy, who is 53 years old. He is owned by Kathy Pennington of Virginia Beach, VA.

The secrets to a long life? Clean your teeth once a year, trim your hooves every six weeks, and stay out of things you shouldn't get into.

That's how Teddy, a Shetland pony "almost at least 53 years old," keeps going, with a little t.l.c. from owner Katherine Pennington. Pennington, a full-time nurse and part-time farmer, keeps six horses and ponies who are past retirement age (typically between 25 and 30 years old).

When Teddy was examined by a vet eight years ago, Pennington got the news that her pony had reached at least 45 years, the point when a pony's or horse's teeth stop changing. After that point, no clear dating can be done. "So we knew he was 45 back then. His papers are long since lost. For years he's been traded from farm to farm for equipment, or a dog, or whatever. If he was standing around when farmers were trading and someone had a little child (under four) who could ride him, he'd go."

Teddy answered a call from Purina's Equine Senior horse food for the oldest horse in the nation, and he won, far and away. Now that his photograph (hard-won, out of a 2-hour photo session) has appeared on the back of Purina's food bag, Pennington gets letters—including one addressed to Teddy from the governor of Virginia—and calls from all over. "People call to check on his health, as if he were an ill relative. One woman from Texas was sure he was the pony she'd had as a girl. Her family bought him from a traveling circus." If that story could be proved to be true, Teddy would be 71.

Nobody knows Teddy's real story—except Teddy himself. "I really do wonder," muses Pennington, who plans to keep him until he dies. "There's a lot of stuff in his head that I'd love to know."

Same pony, different year: Teddy with 3-year-old Elizabeth Frieden in 1980 (above) and with 17-year-old Frieden in 1994 (below). (*David Hansen; Kathy Pennington*)

Longest kangaroo jump   During a chase in New South Wales, Australia in January 1951, a red kangaroo made a series of bounds that included one of 42 feet. There is also an unconfirmed report of an eastern gray kangaroo jumping nearly 44½ feet on level ground.

HORSES

Earliest domestication   Evidence from Ukraine indicates that horses may have been ridden earlier than 4000 B.C.

Largest horse   The tallest and heaviest documented horse was the shire gelding Sampson, bred by Thomas Cleaver of Toddington Mills, England.
   This horse, which was foaled in 1846, measured 21.2½ hands (7 ft. 2½ in.) in 1850 and was later said to have weighed 3,360 pounds.

Largest mules   Apollo (foaled 1977) and Anak (foaled 1976), owned by Herbert L. Mueller of Columbia, IL, are the largest mules on record. Apollo measures 19.1 hands (6 ft. 5 in.) and weighs 2,200 pounds, with Anak at 18.3 hands (6 ft. 3 in.) and 2,100 pounds. Both are the hybrid offspring of Belgian mares and mammoth jacks.

Smallest horse   The stallion Little Pumpkin (foaled April 15, 1973), owned by J.C. Williams Jr. of Della Terra Mini Horse Farm, Inman, SC, stood 14 inches tall and weighed 20 pounds on November 30, 1975.

Breed   The Falabela of Argentina was developed by Julio Falabela of Recco de Roca, Argentina. The smallest example was a mare that stood 15 inches and weighed 26¼ pounds.

Oldest horse   The greatest age reliably recorded for a horse is 62 years in the case of Old Billy (foaled 1760), bred by Edward Robinson of Woolston, England. Old Billy died on November 27, 1822.

Oldest pony   The greatest age reliably recorded for a pony is 54 years for a stallion (foaled 1919) owned by a farmer in central France.

United States   The oldest pony in the United States is Teddy, who is 53 years old. He is owned by Kathy Pennington of Virginia Beach, VA.

DOGS

The canine population of the United States for 1993 was estimated by the Pet Food Institute to be 53 million. There was at least one dog kept as a pet in 37.7 percent of U.S. households.

Largest dog   The heaviest and longest dog ever recorded is Aicama Zorba of La-Susa (whelped September 26, 1981), an Old English mastiff owned by Chris Eraclides of London, England. In November 1989, Zorba was recorded as weighing 343 pounds, standing 37 inches at the shoulder, and measuring 8 ft. 3 in. from nose to tail.

Tallest   Shamgret Danzas (whelped 1975), owned by Wendy and Keith Comley of Milton Keynes, England, was 41½ inches tall, or 42 inches when his hackles were raised, and weighed up to 238 pounds. He died on October 16, 1984.

Smallest dog   The smallest dog on record was a matchbox-sized Yorkshire terrier owned by Arthur Marples of Blackburn, England. This tiny creature, which died in 1945 at the age of nearly two years, stood 2½ inches tall at the shoulder and measured 3¾ inches from the tip of its nose to the root of its tail. It weighed four ounces.

GUESS WHAT?

Q.   HOW BIG WAS THE LARGEST TEAM OF SLED DOGS?

A.   LOOK IN "SLED DOG RACING" (SPORTS & GAMES)

United States   The smallest dog in the United States is Chelsi Dijon, a 1¾-pound toy poodle belonging to Dollie Childs of Dothan, AL.

Oldest dog   An Australian cattle-dog named Bluey, owned by Les Hall of Rochester, Victoria, Australia, was obtained as a puppy in 1910 and worked among cattle and sheep for nearly 20 years. He was put to sleep on November 14, 1939 at the age of 29 yr. 5 mo.

Longest-serving guide dog   The longest period of active service reported for a guide dog is 14 yr. 8 mo. (August 1972–March 1987) in the case of a Labrador retriever bitch named Cindy-Cleo (whelped January 20, 1971), owned by Aaron Barr of Tel Aviv, Israel. The dog died on April 10, 1987.

Hearing   Donna, a hearing guide dog owned by John Hogan of Pyrmont Point, Australia, has completed 10 years of active service in Australia to 1995, and served for eight years prior to that in New Zealand.

Most guide dogs placed   In the United States, the record for the most guide dogs placed with users is held by the Seeing Eye of Morristown, NJ, with a total of 230 placements in 1991.

Most prolific sire   The greatest sire ever was the champion greyhound Low Pressure, nicknamed Timmy (whelped September 1957), owned by Bruna Amhurst of London, England. From December 1961 until his death on November 27, 1969, he fathered over 3,000 puppies.

Highest jump   The canine "high jump" record for a leap and a scramble over a smooth wooden wall (without ribs or other aids) is 12 ft. 2½ in., achieved by an 18-month-old lurcher dog named Stag at the annual Cotswold Country Fair in Cirencester, England on September 27, 1993. The dog is owned by Mr. and Mrs. P.R. Matthews of Redruth, England.

U.S. DOGS

Breed	Registrations
Labrador Retriever	126,393
Rottweiler	102,596
German Shepherd	78,999
Golden Retriever	64,322
Poodle	61,775
Cocker Spaniel	60,888
Beagle	59,215
Dachshund	46,129
Dalmatian	42,621
Pomeranian	39,947

American Kennel Club; 1994

Longest jump A greyhound named Bang jumped 30 feet while chasing a hare at Brecon Lodge, Gloucestershire, England in 1849. He cleared a 4-ft.-6-in. gate and landed on a hard road, damaging his pastern bone.

Best tracker In 1925, a Doberman pinscher named Sauer, trained by Detective-Sergeant Herbert Kruger, tracked a stock thief 100 miles across the Great Karroo, South Africa by scent alone.

Top show dog The greatest number of Best-in-Show awards won by any dog in all-breed shows is 203, compiled by the Scottish terrier bitch Ch. Braeburn's Close Encounter (whelped October 22, 1978) by March 10, 1985. She is owned by Sonnie Novick of Plantation Acres, FL.

Largest dog show The centennial of the annual Crufts show, held at the National Exhibition Center in Birmingham, England on January 9–12, 1991, had a record 22,993 entries.

Drug sniffing Snag, a U.S. Customs Labrador retriever trained and partnered by Jeff Weitzmann, has made 118 drug seizures worth a canine record $810 million.

   The greatest number of seizures by dogs is 969 (worth $182 million) in 1988 alone by Rocky and Barco, a pair of malinoises patrolling the Rio Grande Valley ("Cocaine Valley") along the Texas border, where the pair were so proficient that Mexican drug smugglers put a $30,000 price on their heads. The dogs hold the rank of honorary Sergeant Major and always wear their stripes when they are on duty.

Zorba, the largest, longest and heaviest dog ever recorded, with his owner, Chris Eraclides of London, England. (*Chris Eraclides*)

CATS

The feline population of the United States for 1993 was estimated by the Pet Food Institute to be 64 million. There was at least one cat in 32.9 percent of the households in the United States.

Largest cat   The heaviest domestic cat was a neutered male tabby named Himmy, owned by Thomas Vyse of Redlynch, Queensland, Australia. When Himmy died of respiratory failure on March 12, 1986 at the age of 10 yr. 4 mo., he weighed 46 lb. 15¼ oz. (neck 15 inches, waist 33 inches, length 38 inches).

Smallest cat   A male blue point Himalayan-Persian cat named Tinker Toy, owned by Katrina and Scott Forbes of Taylorville, IL, is just 2¾ inches tall and 7½ inches long.

Oldest cat   The oldest reliably recorded cat was a female tabby named Ma, owned by Alice St. George Moore of Drewsteignton, England. This cat was put to sleep on November 5, 1957 at age 34.

Largest cat show   The largest cat show in the United States was the Purina Cat Chow/CFA Invitational held at the Cervantes Convention Center, St. Louis, MO, November 19–20, 1988. It attracted a record 814 entries.

Best climber   On September 6, 1950, a 4-month-old kitten belonging to Josephine Aufdenblatten of Geneva, Switzerland followed a group of climbers to the top of the 14,691-foot Matterhorn in the Alps.

Most prolific cat   A tabby named Dusty (b. 1935) of Bonham, TX produced 420 kittens during her life. She gave birth to her last litter (a single kitten) on June 12, 1952.

TOP
10
TEN

U.S. CATS

Breed	Registrations
Persian	47,022
Maine Coon	3,852
Siamese	2,881
Abyssinian	2,447
Exotic	1,507
Scottish Fold	1,250
American Shorthair	1,143
Oriental American Shorthair	1,123
Birman	957
Burmese	884

Cat Fanciers' Association, Inc., 1994

Oldest feline mother In May 1987, Kitty, owned by George Johnstone of Croxton, England, produced two kittens at age 30, making her the oldest feline mother on record. She died in June 1989, just short of her 32nd birthday, having given birth to a known total of 218 kittens.

RABBITS

Largest rabbit In April 1980, a 5-month-old French lop doe weighing 26.45 pounds was exhibited at the Reus Fair in northeast Spain.

Smallest rabbit The Netherland dwarf and the Polish dwarf both have a weight range of 2–2½ pounds when fully grown. In 1975, Jacques Bouloc of Coulommière, France announced a new cross of these two breeds that weighed 14 ounces.

LARGEST PET LITTERS

Animal/Breed	No.	Owner	Date
Cat *Burmese/Siamese*	19[1]	V. Gane, Church Westcote, England	Aug. 7, 1970
Dog *American foxhound*	23	W. N. Ely, Ambler, PA	Jun. 19, 1944
St Bernard	23[2]	R. and A. Rodden, Lebanon, MO	Feb. 6–7, 1975
Great Dane	23[3]	M. Harris, Little Hall, England	June 1987
Ferret *Domestic*	15	J. Cliff, Denstone, England	1981
Gerbil *Mongolian*	14[4]	S. Kirkman, Bulwell, England	May 1983
Guinea pig	12	Laboratory specimen	1972
Hamster *Golden*	26[5]	L. and S. Miller, Baton Rouge, LA	Feb. 28, 1974
Mouse *House*	34[6]	M. Ogilvie, Blackpool, England	Feb. 12, 1982
Rabbit *New Zealand white*	24	J. Filek, Cape Breton, Nova Scotia, Canada	1978

[1] *Four stillborn.*
[2] *Fourteen survived.*
[3] *Sixteen survived.*
[4] *Litter of fifteen recorded in the 1960s by George Meares, geneticist-owner of gerbil-breeding farm in St Petersburg, FL, using special food formula.*
[5] *Eighteen killed by mother.*
[6] *Thirty-three survived.*

Most prolific rabbits The most prolific domestic breeds are the New Zealand white and the Californian. Does produce 5–6 litters a year, each comprising 8–12 kittens, during their breeding life (compare with five litters and 3–7 young for the wild rabbit).

Longest ears "Sweet Majestic Star," a champion black English lop rabbit owned by Therese and Cheryl Seward of Exeter, England, had ears measuring 28½ inches long and 7¼ inches wide. He died on October 6, 1992. The ears of his grandson "Sweet Regal Magic" are the same length.

BIRDS

Oldest bird fossil Two partial bird skeletons were found in Texas in rocks dating from 220 million years ago. Named *Protoavis texensis* in 1991, the pheasant-sized creature has caused much controversy by pushing the age of birds back many millions of years from the previous record, that of the more familiar *Archeopteryx lithographica* from Germany. It is still unclear whether *Protoavis* will be widely accepted as a true bird, making *Archeopteryx* the earliest unambiguous fossil bird.

Largest bird Males of the flightless North African ostrich (*Struthio c. camelus*) have been recorded up to nine feet in height and 345 pounds in weight.

Heaviest flying bird The heaviest flying birds are the Kori bustard or paauw (*Ardeotis kori*) of northeast and southern Africa and the great bustard (*Otis tarda*) of Europe and Asia. Weights of 42 pounds have been reported for the former, and there is an unconfirmed record of 46 lb. 4 oz. for a male great bustard shot in Manchuria that was too heavy to fly. The heaviest reliably recorded great bustard weighed 39 lb. 11 oz.

Tallest flying bird Cranes, tall waders of the family Gruidae, can stand almost 6 ft. 6 in. high.

Heaviest bird of prey An adult male Andean condor (*Vultur gryphus*) has an average weight of 20–27 pounds. An oversized male California condor (*Gymnogyps californianus*) now preserved in the California Academy of Sciences at San Francisco weighed 31 pounds. This species is appreciably smaller than the Andean condor and rarely exceeds 23 pounds.

Largest wingspan The wandering albatross (*Diomedea exulans*) of the southern oceans has the largest wingspan of any living bird. The largest specimen was a very old male with a wingspan of 11 ft. 11 in., caught by members of the Antarctic research ship U.S.G.S. *Eltanin* in the Tasman Sea on September 18, 1965.

Smallest bird Adult male bee hummingbirds (*Mellisuga helenae*) of Cuba and the Isle of Pines are 2.24 inches long, half of which is taken up by the bill and tail (females are slightly larger). Adult males weigh 0.056 ounces (females are slightly heavier).

Smallest bird of prey The black-legged falconet (*Microhierax fringillarius*) of southeast Asia and the white-fronted or Bornean falconet (*Microhierax latifrons*) of northwestern Borneo each have an average length of 5$^1/2$–6 inches (excluding a 2-inch tail) and weigh about 1$^1/4$ ounces.

Most abundant bird The red-billed quelea (*Quelea quelea*), a seed-eating weaver of Africa south of the Sahara, has an estimated adult breeding population of 1.5 billion, and at least 200 million are slaughtered annually without having any impact on this number.

United States The red-winged blackbird (*Agelaius phoeniceus*) has an estimated population of at least 30 million. The blackbird is found throughout the country, except for desert and mountainous regions.

Most talkative bird A number of birds are renowned for their ability to reproduce words, but the African gray parrot (*Psittacus erythacus*) excels in this ability. A female named Prudle, in the care of Iris Frost of Seaford, England, won the "Best Talking Parrot-like Bird" title at the National Cage and Aviary Bird Show in London each December for 12 consecutive years (1965–76) and retired undefeated. Prudle, who had a vocabulary of nearly 800 words, was taken from a nest at Jinja, Uganda in 1958 and died in 1994.

Largest vocabulary Puck, a budgerigar owned by Camille Jordan of Petaluma, CA, had a vocabulary estimated at 1,728 words on January 31, 1993.

Fastest-flying bird The peregrine falcon (*Falco peregrinus*) reaches record speed levels when swooping from great heights during territorial displays, or when catching prey in midair. In one series of German experiments, a velocity of 168 MPH was recorded at a 30° angle of descent, rising to a maximum of 217 MPH at an angle of 45°.

United States America's fastest bird is the white-throated swift (*Aeronautes saxatilis*), which has been estimated to fly at speeds of 200 MPH.

Fastest wing-beat The wing-beat of the horned sungem (*Heliactin cornuta*), a hummingbird living in tropical South America, is 90 beats per second.

Fastest bird on land The ostrich can run at a speed of up to 40 MPH when necessary.

Fastest swimmer The gentoo penguin (*Pygoscelis papua*) has a maximum burst of speed of *c.* 17 MPH.

Slowest-flying bird During courtship flights, the American woodcock (*Scolopax minor*) and the Eurasian woodcock (*S. rusticola*) have been timed at 5 MPH.

Oldest bird The greatest irrefutable age reported for any bird is over 80 years for a sulfur-crested cockatoo (*Cacatua galerita*) named Cocky, who died at London Zoo, England in 1982.

Domestic The longest-lived domesticated bird is the domestic goose (*Anseranser domesticus*), which can live for 25 years. On December 16, 1976, a gander named George, owned by Florence Hull of Thornton, England, died at the age of 49 yr. 8 mo. He was hatched in April 1927.

Longest flight The greatest distance covered by a banded bird is 14,000 miles, by an Arctic tern (*Sterna paradisaea*). The tern was banded as a nestling on July 5, 1955 in the Kandalaksha Sanctuary on the White Sea coast, Russia, and was captured alive by a fisherman eight miles south of

An ostrich can run at up to 40 MPH when necessary. (*Jacana/ J-P Varin.*)

A Ruppell's vulture collided with an aircraft at an altitude of 37,000 feet. (*Jacana/Ferrero/Labat*)

Fremantle, Western Australia on May 16, 1956. The bird had probably flown south via the Atlantic Ocean and then circled Africa before crossing the Indian Ocean.

Highest-flying bird The highest irrefutable altitude recorded for a bird is 37,000 feet for a Ruppell's vulture (*Gyps rueppellii*) that collided with a commercial aircraft over Abidjan, Ivory Coast on November 29, 1973. The impact damaged one of the aircraft's engines, causing it to shut down, but the plane landed safely. Enough feather remains were recovered to allow the Museum of Natural History in Washington, D.C. to make a positive identification of this high-flier, which is rarely seen above 20,000 feet.

United States The highest verified altitude record for a bird in the United States is 21,000 feet for a mallard (*Meleagris gallopavo*) that collided with a commercial jet on July 9, 1963 over Nevada. The jet crashed, killing all aboard.

Most airborne bird After leaving its nesting ground, the sooty tern (*Sterna fuscata*) remains continuously aloft from 3–10 years as a sub-adult before returning to land to breed.

Longest feathers The longest feathers grown by any bird are those of the Phoenix fowl or Yokohama chicken (a strain of red junglefowl *Gallus gallus*), bred in Japan since the 17th century. In 1972, a tail covert measuring 34 ft. 9½ in. was reported for a rooster owned by Masasha Kubota of Kochi, Shikoku, Japan.

WATCHING THE BIRDIE

Phoebe Snetsinger, the world's leading bird-watcher, is renowned for her thorough approach to identifying birds. She has seen 80 percent of the world's recognized species, or 90 percent of the genera, and all the familes but one.

Bird-watching Phoebe Snetsinger of Webster Groves, MO has logged 7,772 of the 9,700 known species since 1965, representing over 80 percent of the known total.

Although Snetsinger has heard evidence of 100 additional species, she only considers "countable" those she sees well enough to identify precisely.

Snetsinger (left) with companions in Szechwan, China, May 1990. (*Phoebe Snetsinger*)

Snetsinger with companion Fern Piersol and a boatman in Papua New Guinea, August 1990. (*Phoebe Snetsinger*)

"From the beginning I've been fascinated by the problems of identification, and it has always been a key ingredient of my birding style to learn in advance the important features of any birds, especially the new ones, that I might see on any trip I plan. It's vitally important to me to be able to know and recognize what I'm seeing. I keep a card-file record system which gives me quick reference to my entire experience with any given species.

"I didn't start watching birds until I was 35, a married woman with small children, when various factors combined to provide the vital trigger. The first 15 years of my birding career consisted of learning how to do it and acquiring the necessary skills and knowledge, all through local birding, first in Minnesota, and then in St. Louis, Missouri, which has been my home for nearly 30 years. My horizons expanded gradually to include most of North America and a few foreign locations as my family grew and we all gained independence.

"From age 50 until my present 63 I've been threatened with periodic recurrences of malignant melanoma and consequent surgery, all of which has led me into a 'now or never' approach to international birding and an ongoing succession of short-term goals. I've had the good fortune to be able to pursue this to a degree I never dreamed possible.

"Within the next year or so I hope to have seen 8,000 of the world's 9,700-plus bird species, and to know something about the rest of them. Then I'll plan to continue birding at a less frantic pace and pursue especially some high-priority species. I prefer to be called a 'birder' or 'bird-watcher' rather than 'lister' or 'twitcher,' because my main interest lies in observing, learning about and identifying birds rather than the strictly numerical approach of 'ticking' or 'twitching' a large number of species."

Deepest dive   In 1990, a depth of 1,584 feet was recorded for an emperor penguin (*Aptenodytes forsteri*) in the Ross Sea, Antarctica. An emperor penguin at Cape Crozier, Antarctica remained submerged for 18 minutes in 1969.

Sharpest vision   It has been calculated that a large bird of prey can detect a target object at a distance three or more times greater than that achieved by humans; thus a peregrine falcon (*Falco peregrinus*) can spot a pigeon at a range of over five miles under ideal conditions.

Greatest field of vision   The woodcock (*Scolopax rusticola*) has eyes set so far back on its head that it has a 360° field of vision, enabling it to see all around and even over the top of its head.

Highest g force   Experiments have revealed that the beak of the red-headed woodpecker (*Melanerpes erythrocephalus*) hits the bark of a tree with an impact velocity of 13 MPH. This means that when the head snaps back the brain is subject to a deceleration of about 10 g.

Longest bill   The bill of the Australian pelican (*Pelicanus conspicillatus*) is 13–18½ inches long.
   The longest bill in relation to overall body length belongs to the sword-billed hummingbird (*Ensifera ensifera*) of the Andes from Venezuela to Bolivia. The bill measures four inches long and is longer than the bird's body.

Shortest bill   The bill of the glossy swiftlet (*Collocalia esculenta*) is almost nonexistent.

Largest egg   On June 28, 1988, a 2-year-old cross between a northern and a southern ostrich (*Struthio c. camelus* and *Struthio c. australis*) laid an egg weighing a record 5.1 pounds at the Kibbutz Ha'on collective farm, Israel.

Smallest egg   The vervain hummingbird (*Mellisuga minima*), of Jamaica and two nearby islets, lays the smallest eggs. Two specimens measuring less than 0.39 inches long weighed 0.0128 ounces and 0.0132 ounces.

United States   Eggs laid by the Costa hummingbird (*Calypte coastae*) measure 0.48 inches long and 0.33 inches in diameter with a weight of 0.017 ounces.

Longest incubation   The longest incubation period is that of the wandering albatross (*Diomedea exulans*), with a range of 75–82 days. There is an isolated case of an egg of the mallee fowl (*Leipoa ocellata*) of Australia taking 90 days to hatch, against its normal incubation of 62 days.

Shortest incubation   The shortest incubation period is 10 days for the shore lark (*Eremophila alpestris*), lesser whitethroat (*Sylvia curruca*) and several other passerine species.

Largest nest   The incubation mounds built by the mallee fowl (*Leipoa ocellata*) of Australia measure up to 15 feet high and 35 feet across, and it has been calculated that the nest site may involve the mounding of 8,829 cubic feet of material weighing 331 tons.

Smallest nest   The smallest nests are built by hummingbirds (Trochilidae). The nest of the vervain hummingbird (*Mellisuga minima*) is about half the size of a walnut, while the deeper one of the bee hummingbird (*M. helenea*) is thimble-sized.

Bird-watching   Phoebe Snetsinger of Webster Groves, MO has logged 7,772 of the 9,700 known species since 1965, representing over 80 percent of the known total.

24 hours   The greatest number of species spotted in a 24-hour period is 342, by Kenyans Terry Stevenson, John Fanshawe and Andy Roberts on day two of the Birdwatch Kenya '86 event held November 29–30.

REPTILES

Oldest reptile fossil   A reptile fossil, nicknamed "Lizzie the Lizard," was found on a site in Scotland by palaeontologist Stan Wood in March 1988. The 8-inch-long reptile is estimated to be 340 million years old, 40 million years older than previously discovered reptiles. "Lizzie" was officially named *Westlothiana lizziae* in 1991.

CROCODILIANS

Largest crocodile   There are four protected estuarine crocodiles at the Bhitarkanika Wildlife Sanctuary, Orissa State, India that measure over 19 ft. 8 in. long. The largest individual is more than 23 feet long.

Smallest crocodile   The dwarf caiman (*Paleosuchus palpebrosus*) of northern South America is the smallest living crocodilian. Females rarely exceed a length of four feet, and males rarely grow to more than 4 ft. 11 in.

Oldest crocodile   The greatest age authenticated for a crocodile is 66 years for a female American alligator (*Alligator mississippiensis*) that arrived at Adelaide Zoo, South Australia on June 5, 1914 as a 2-year-old, and died there on September 26, 1978.

LIZARDS

Largest lizard   Adult male komodo dragons or oras (*Varanus komodoensis*), found on the Indonesian islands of Komodo, Rintja, Padar and Flores, average 7 ft. 5 in. long and weigh about 130 pounds. The largest specimen to be accurately measured was a male presented to an American zoologist in 1928 by the Sultan of Bima. In 1937, this animal was put on display at St. Louis Zoological Gardens, St. Louis, MO for a short period. It then measured 10 ft. 2 in. long and weighed 365 pounds.

Longest lizard   The slender Salvadori or Papuan monitor (*Varanus salvadori*) of Papua New Guinea has been measured at up to 15 ft. 7 in. long, but nearly 70 percent of the total length is taken up by the tail.

GOLIATH

THE GALÁPAGOS TORTOISE

In 1960, two tiny Galápagos tortoises (*Geochelone elephantopus ele-phantopus*) were brought to The Life Fellowship Bird Sanctuary (then the New Age Ranch) in Seffner, FL by a UNESCO researcher. One of them, later named Goliath, weighed just two pounds. In the 35 years since then, Goliath has grown to record-breaking proportions and is now the world's largest tortoise. When he was coaxed onto the platform of a government-certified scale in 1988, he was found to weigh 785 pounds; in October 1994, he weighed 849 pounds. By tortoise standards Goliath is quite young, and he is still growing. At his present rate, he is likely to pass the 900-pound mark in a few years. He eats well, but not *too* well—his weight is in proportion to his size and he is in fact fit and lean.

According to Greg A. Moss, General Curator of Life Fellowship, Goliath shows the same levels of comprehension a dog might display. He is affectionate towards workers at the Sanctuary, and when touched by someone he knows, he rises on all four legs and extends his head to be petted. As autumn approaches, Goliath is the first to use the heated winter house; others in his paddock have to become accustomed each year to being closed up overnight.

Ramon P. Noegel, Director of the Life Fellowship Bird Sanctuary, with six male Galápagos tortoises. He has his hand on Goliath's shell. Goliath measures 53⅝ inches long, 40½ inches wide, and 27 inches high. (*Life Fellowship Bird Sanctuary*)

The Life Fellowship Bird Sanctuary has a herd of 44 *gigantea*, believed to be the largest herd in the Americas. In seven breeding seasons (1987–93), Life Fellowship hatched and kept alive 411 Galápagos tortoises, an unparalleled achievement for any captive herd of these endangered giants outside their habitat in the Galápagos. In 1994 alone the Sanctuary hatched 74 Galápagos tortoises. (*Life Fellowship Bird Sanctuary*)

Largest tortoise

A Galápagos tortoise (*Geochelone elephantopus elephantopus*) named Goliath, who has lived at the Life Fellowship Bird Sanctuary in Seffner, FL since 1960, measures 53⅝ inches long, 40½ inches wide and 27 inches high, and weighs 849 pounds.

Goliath enjoys a healthy snack. (*Life Fellowship Bird Sanctuary*)

Smallest lizard   *Sphaerodactylus parthenopion*, a tiny gecko indigenous to the island of Virgin Gorda, one of the British Virgin Islands, is the world's smallest lizard. It is known from only 15 specimens, including some pregnant females found August 10–16, 1964. The three largest females measured 0.70 inches from snout to vent, with a tail of roughly the same length.

Oldest lizard   The greatest age recorded for a lizard is over 54 years for a male slow worm (*Anguis fragilis*) kept in the Zoological Museum in Copenhagen, Denmark from 1892 until 1946.

Fastest lizard   The highest speed measured for any reptile on land is 21.7 MPH for a spiny-tailed iguana (*Ctenosaura*) from Costa Rica, in a series of experiments by Professor Raymond Huey from the University of Washington and colleagues at the University of California, Berkeley, CA.

TURTLES

Largest turtle   A male leatherback found dead on the beach at Harlech, Wales on September 23, 1988 measured 9 ft. 5½ in. long from nose to tail, and nine feet across the front flippers. The turtle weighed an astonishing 2,120 pounds.

United States   The greatest weight reliably recorded in the United States is 1,908 pounds for a male leatherback captured off Monterey, CA on August 29, 1961, which measured 8 ft. 4 in.

Smallest turtle   The stinkpot or common musk turtle (*Sternotherus odoratus*) has an average shell length of three inches when fully grown, and a weight of only eight ounces. The smallest marine turtle is the Atlantic ridley (*Lepidochelys kempii*), which has a shell length of 19.7–27.6 inches and a maximum weight of 175 pounds.

Fastest turtle   The fastest speed claimed for any reptile in water is 22 MPH by a frightened Pacific leatherback turtle.

GUESS WHAT?

Q.   How fast is the fastest human swimmer?

A.   Look in "Swimming" (Sports & Games)

Deepest dive   In May 1987, it was reported by Dr. Scott Eckert that a leatherback turtle (*Dermochelys coriacea*) fitted with a pressure-sensitive recording device had dived to a depth of 3,973 feet off the Virgin Islands in the West Indies.

Largest tortoise   A Galápagos tortoise (*Geochelone elephantopus*) named Goliath, who has lived at the Life Fellowship Bird Sanctuary in Seffner, FL since 1960, measures 53⅝ inches long, 40½ inches wide, and 27 inches high, and weighs 849 pounds.

Oldest tortoise   The greatest age recorded for a tortoise is over 152 years for a male Marion's tortoise (*Testudo sumeirii*), brought from the Seychelles to Mauritius in 1766 by the Chevalier de Fresne, who presented it to the Port Louis army garrison. This specimen was accidentally killed in 1918.

SNAKES

Longest snake   A reticulated python (*Python reticulatus*) measuring 32 ft. 9½ in. was shot in Celebes, Indonesia in 1912. This species is also found in southeast Asia and the Philippines.

United States   There are three species of snake in the United States with average measurements of 8 ft. 6 in. These include the indigo snake (*Drymarchon corais*), the eastern coachwhip (*Masticophis flagellum*) and the black ratsnake (*Elaphe obsoleta*), all found in the southeastern United States.

Longest venomous snake   The king cobra (*Ophiophagus hannah*), also called the hamadryad, averages 12–15 feet long and is found in southeast Asia and India. An 18-ft.-2-in. specimen, captured alive near Fort Dickson in the state of Negri Sembilan, Malaysia in April 1937, later grew to 18 ft. 9 in. in London Zoo, England. It was destroyed at the outbreak of war in 1939 to avoid the risk of escape.

Shortest snake   The very rare thread snake (*Leptotyphlops bilineata*) is known only from Martinique, Barbados and St. Lucia. The longest known specimen measured 4¼ inches, and had such a thin body that it could have entered the hole left in a standard pencil after the lead has been removed.

Shortest venomous snake   The namaqua dwarf adder (*Bitis schneider*) of Namibia has an average adult length of eight inches.

Heaviest snake   The anaconda (*Eunectes murinus*) of tropical South America and Trinidad is nearly twice as heavy as a reticulated python (*Python reticulatus*) of the same length. A female shot in Brazil *c.* 1960 was never weighed, but as it measured 27 ft. 9 in. long with a girth of 44 inches, it must have weighed about 500 pounds. The average adult length is 18–20 feet.

Heaviest venomous snake   The eastern diamondback rattlesnake (*Crotalus adamanteus*) of the southeastern United States is probably the heaviest venomous snake. One specimen, measuring 7 ft. 9 in. long, weighed 34 pounds.

Oldest snake   The greatest reliable age recorded for a snake is 40 yr. 3 mo. 14 days for a male common boa (*Boa constrictor constrictor*) named Popeye, who died at the Philadelphia Zoo, PA on April 15, 1977.

Most venomous snake   All sea snakes are venomous. The species *Hydrophis belcheri*, which lives around the Ashmore Reef in the Timor Sea, has a myotoxic venom 100 times as toxic as any land snake.

Most venomous land snake   The 5-ft.-7-in. small-scaled or fierce snake (*Oxyuranus microlepidotus*) is found mainly in the Diamantina River and Cooper's Creek drainage basins in Channel County, Queensland, and western New South Wales, Australia. Its venom is several times more toxic than that of the tiger snake (*Notechis scutatus*) of South Australia and Tasmania. One tiger snake yielded 0.00385 ounces of venom after milking, enough to kill 250,000 mice.

United States   The most venomous snake in the United States is the coral snake (*Micrurus fulvius*). In a standard LD99–100 test, which kills 99–100 percent of all mice injected with the venom, it takes 0.55 grain of venom per 2.2 pounds of mouse weight injected intravenously. In this test, the smaller the dosage, the more toxic the venom.

Most snakebites   More people die of snakebites in Sri Lanka than in any comparable area in the world. An average of 800 people are killed annually on the island by snakes, and more than 95 percent of the fatalities are caused by the common krait (*Bungarus caeruleus*), the Sri Lankan cobra (*Naja n. naja*), and Russell's viper (*Vipera russelli pulchella*).

The saw-scaled or carpet viper (*Echis carinatus*) bites and kills more people in the world than any other species. Its geographical range extends from West Africa to India.

Longest fangs   The highly venomous gaboon viper (*Bitis gabonica*) of tropical Africa has the longest fangs of any snake. In one 6-foot-long specimen, they measured almost two inches long.

Fastest snake   The fastest-moving land snake is probably the aggressive black mamba (*Dendroaspis polylepis*) of the eastern part of tropical Africa. This snake can achieve speeds of 10–12 MPH in short bursts over level ground.

Most snakes milked   Over a 10-year period ending in December 1970, Bernard Keyler, a supervisor at the South African Institute for Medical Research in Johannesburg, South Africa, personally milked 780,000 venomous snakes, obtaining 870 gallons of venom. He has never been bitten.

FROGS

Largest frog   The rare African giant frog or goliath frog (*Conraua goliath*) is found in Cameroon and Equatorial Guinea. A specimen captured in

April 1989 on the Sanaga River, Cameroon by Andy Koffman of Seattle, WA had a snout-to-vent length of 14½ inches (34½ inches over all with legs extended) qand weighed 8 lb. 1 oz. on October 30, 1989.

Smallest frog *Sminthillus limbatus* of Cuba measures 0.34–0.5 inches long (snout-to-vent) when fully grown. It is the smallest frog and the smallest amphibian.

Longest jump by a frog   (*Distances in frog-jumping competitions represent the aggregate of three consecutive leaps.*)
The greatest distance covered by a frog in a triple jump is 33 ft. 5½ in. by a South African sharp-nosed frog (*Ptychadena oxyrhynchus*) named Santjie at a frog derby held at Lurula Natal Spa, Paulpietersburg, Natal, South Africa on May 21, 1977.

United States   At the annual Calaveras Jumping Jubilee held at Angels Camp, CA, an American bullfrog (*Rana catesbeiana*) called Rosie the Ribeter, owned by Lee Guidici of Santa Clara, CA, leaped 21 ft. 5¾ in. on May 18, 1986.

FISH

Largest fish   The rare plankton-feeding whale shark (*Rhincodon typus*) is found in the warmer areas of the Atlantic, Pacific, and Indian Oceans. The longest specimen to have been scientifically measured was captured off Baba Island near Karachi, Pakistan on November 11, 1949. It measured 41½ feet long, 23 feet around the thickest part of the body and weighed an estimated 16½–23 tons.

Largest predatory fish   The largest predatory fish is the rare great white shark (*Carcharodon carcharias*). Adult specimens average 14–15 feet long, and generally weigh 1,150–1,700 pounds. There are many claims of huge specimens up to 33 feet long and, although few have been authenticated, there is plenty of circumstantial evidence to suggest that some great whites grow to more than 20 feet long.

Largest freshwater fish   The largest fish that spends its whole life in fresh or brackish water is the rare pla buk or pa beuk (*Pangasianodon gigas*) found only in the Mekong River and its major tributaries in China, Laos, Cambodia and Thailand. The largest specimen, captured in the River Ban Mee Noi, Thailand, was reportedly 9 ft. 10¼ in. long and weighed 533½ pounds.

Smallest fish   The shortest marine fish—and the shortest vertebrate—is the dwarf goby (*Trimmatom nanus*) of the Chagos Archipelago, central Indian Ocean. In one series of 92 specimens collected by the 1978–79 Joint Services Chagos Research Expedition of the British Armed Forces, the adult males averaged 0.34 inches long and the adult females 0.35 inches.

Smallest freshwater fish The shortest and lightest freshwater fish is the dwarf pygmy goby (*Pandaka pygmaea*), a colorless and nearly transparent species found in the streams and lakes of Luzon in the Philippines. Adult males measure only 0.28–0.38 inches long and weigh 0.00014–0.00018 ounces.

Fastest fish The cosmopolitan sailfish (*Istiophorus platypterus*) is considered to be the fastest species of fish over short distances, although the practical difficulties of measuring make data extremely difficult to secure. In a series of speed trials carried out at the Long Key Fishing Camp, FL, one sailfish took out 300 feet of line in three seconds, which is equivalent to a velocity of 68 MPH (compare with 60 MPH for the cheetah).

Deepest-living fish Brotulids of the genus *Bassogigas* are generally regarded as the deepest-living vertebrates. The greatest depth from which a fish has been recovered is 27,230 feet in the Puerto Rico Trench in the Atlantic by Dr. Gilbert L. Voss of the U.S. research vessel *John Elliott*, who caught a 6½-inch-long *Bassogigas profundissimus* in April 1970. It was only the fifth such brotulid ever caught.

Oldest fish In 1948, the death of an 88-year-old female European eel (*Anguilla anguilla*) named Putte was reported by the aquarium at Hälsingborg Museum, Sweden. She was allegedly born in 1860 in the Sargasso Sea, in the North Atlantic, and was caught in a river as a 3-year-old elver.

Oldest goldfish Goldfish (*Carassius auratus*) have been reported to live for over 50 years in China, although there are few authenticated records.

A goldfish named Fred, owned by A.R. Wilson of Worthing, England, died on August 1, 1980 at 41 years of age.

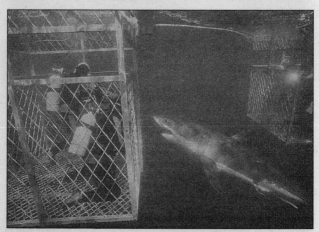

A great white shark, the world's largest predatory fish.
(*Jacana/K. Deacon/Auscape*)

Shortest-lived fish   Certain species of the family Cyprinodontidae (killifish), found in Africa, the Americas, Asia and the warmer parts of Europe, normally live for about eight months.

Most eggs   The ocean sunfish (*Mola mola*) produces up to 300 million eggs at a single spawning, each of them measuring about 0.05 inches in diameter.

Fewest eggs   The mouth-brooding cichlid *Tropheus moorii* of Lake Tanganyika, East Africa, produces seven eggs or fewer during normal reproduction.

Most valuable fish   The Russian sturgeon (*Huso huso*) is the most valuable fish. In 1924, a 2,706-pound female was caught in the Tikhaya Sosna River; it yielded 541 pounds of best-quality caviar, which would be worth $300,000 on today's market.

The 30-inch-long Ginrin Showa koi, which won the supreme championship in nationwide Japanese koi shows in 1976, 1977, 1979 and 1980, was sold two years later for 17 million yen (about $165,000). In March 1986, this ornamental carp was acquired by Derry Evans, owner of the Kent Koi Centre near Sevenoaks, England, for an undisclosed sum, but the 15-year-old fish died five months later.

Most ferocious fish   The razor-toothed piranhas of the genera *Serrasalmus* and *Pygocentrus* are generally considered to be the most ferocious freshwater fish in the world. They live in large South American rivers, and will attack any creature, regardless of size, if it is injured or making a commotion in the water. On September 19, 1981, more than 300 people were reportedly killed and eaten when an overloaded passenger-cargo boat capsized and sank as it was docking at the Brazilian port of Obidos.

Most venomous fish   The most venomous fish are the stonefish (Synanceiidae) that live in the tropical waters of the Indo-Pacific, and in particular *Synanceia horrida*, which also has the largest venom glands. Direct contact with the spines of its fins, which contain a strong neurotoxic poison, can prove fatal.

Most electric fish   The electric eel (*Electrophorus electricus*) is found in the rivers of Brazil, Colombia, Venezuela and Peru. An average-sized specimen can discharge one amp at 400 volts, but measurements up to 650 volts have been recorded.

STARFISH

Largest starfish   The largest of the 1,600 known species of starfish is the very fragile brisingid *Midgardia xandaras*. One specimen, collected by the Texas A & M University research vessel *Alaminos* in the southern part of the Gulf of Mexico in 1968, measured 4½ feet tip to tip, but the diameter of its disc was only 1.02 inches.

Smallest starfish The asterinid sea star *Patiriella parvivipara* was discovered by Wolfgang Zeidler on the west coast of the Eyre peninsula, South Australia in 1975. It has a maximum radius of only 0.18 inches and a diameter of less than 0.35 inches.

Most destructive starfish The crown of thorns (*Acanthaster planci*) of the Indo-Pacific region and the Red Sea has 12–19 arms and can measure up to 24 inches in diameter. It feeds on coral polyps and can destroy 46½–62 square inches of coral in one day. It has been responsible for the destruction of large parts of the Great Barrier Reef off Australia.

Deepest-living starfish The greatest depth from which a starfish has been recovered is 24,881 feet for a specimen of *Porcellanaster ivanovi* collected by the Soviet research ship *Vityaz* in the Mariana Trench *c.* 1962.

CRUSTACEANS

Largest crustacean The takashigani or giant spider crab (*Macrocheira kaempferi*) is the largest, although not the heaviest, of all Crustacea (a category that includes crabs, lobsters, shrimp, prawns, crawfish, etc.). It is found in the deep waters off the southeastern coast of Japan. One specimen had a claw-span of 12 ft. 1½ in. and weighed 41 pounds.

Freshwater A species of crayfish or crawfish (*Astacopis gouldi*) found in the streams of Tasmania, Australia has been measured up to two feet long and weighing as much as nine pounds. In 1934, an unconfirmed weight of 14 pounds (total length 29 inches) was reported for one specimen caught at Bridport, Tasmania, Australia.

Heaviest crustacean The heaviest crustacean, and the largest species of lobster, is the American or North Atlantic lobster (*Homarus americanus*). On February 11, 1977, a specimen weighing 44 lb. 6 oz. and measuring 3 ft. 6 in. from the end of the tail fan to the tip of the largest claw was caught off Nova Scotia, Canada. This lobster was later sold to a New York restaurant owner.

Greatest concentration An enormous swarm of krill (*Euphasia superba*) estimated to weigh 11 million tons was tracked by U.S. scientists off Antarctica in March 1981.

SCORPIONS

Largest scorpion The largest of the 800 or so species of scorpion is a species called *Heterometrus swannerderdami* from southern India. Males

The emperor scorpion, one of the largest scorpions in the world, measures a spine-chilling seven inches long. (*Jacana/P. & C. Vasselet*)

frequently attain a length of more than seven inches from the tips of the pedipalps or "pincers" to the end of the sting. One specimen found during World War II measured 11.5 inches in overall length. The tropical emperor or imperial scorpion (*Pandinus imperator*) of West Africa also grows to seven inches; the largest on record is a male from Sierra Leone that measured 9.01 inches.

Smallest scorpion The *Microbothus pusillus* found on the Red Sea coast measures about half an inch long.

Most venomous scorpion The Palestine yellow scorpion (*Leiurus quinquestriatus*) ranges from the eastern part of North Africa through the Middle East to the shores of the Red Sea. Fortunately, the amount of venom it delivers is very small (0.000009 ounces) and adult lives are seldom endangered; however, it has been responsible for a number of fatalities among children under the age of five.

SPIDERS

Largest spider The largest spider is the goliath bird-eating spider (*Theraphosa leblondi*) of the coastal rain forests of Surinam, Guyana, and French Guiana, but isolated specimens have also been reported from Venezuela and Brazil. A male specimen collected by members of the Pablo San Martin Expedition at Rio Cavro, Venezuela in April 1965 had a leg span of 11.02 inches.

Heaviest spider Female bird-eating spiders are more heavily built than males, and in February 1985 Charles J. Seiderman of New York City captured a female example near Paramaribo, Surinam that weighed a record peak 4.3 ounces before its death from molting problems in January 1986. Other measurements included a maximum leg span of 10½ inches, a total body length of four inches, and 1-inch-long fangs.

Smallest spider   The *Patu marplesi* (family Symphytognathidae) of Western Samoa in the Pacific is the smallest spider. The type specimen (male), found in moss at *c.* 2,000 feet in Madolelei, Western Samoa in January 1965, measured 0.017 inches overall—about the size of a period on this page.

Oldest spider   The longest-lived of all spiders are the tropical bird-eaters (family Theraphosidae). A female specimen collected in Mexico in 1935 lived for an estimated 26–28 years.

United States   The longest-lived species of American spider is the *Rhecosticta californica* of the family Theraphosidae, which has an average life span of 25 years.

Most venomous spider   The most venomous spiders are the Brazilian wandering spiders of the genus *Phoneutria*, and particularly the Brazilian huntsman *P. fera*, which has the most active neurotoxic venom of any living spider. These large and highly aggressive creatures frequently enter human dwellings and hide in clothing or shoes. When disturbed they bite furiously several times, and hundreds of accidents involving these species are reported annually. When deaths occur, they are usually in children under the age of seven. Fortunately, an effective antivenin is available.

Fastest spider   The long-legged sun spiders of the order Solifugae live in the arid semidesert regions of Africa and the Middle East. They feed on geckos and other lizards and can reach speeds of over 10 MPH.

WORMS

Longest earthworm   The species *Microhaetus rappi* (= *M. microhaetus*) is found in South Africa. In *c.* 1937, a giant earthworm measuring 22 feet long when naturally extended and 0.8 inches in diameter was collected in the Transvaal.

Shortest earthworm   *Chaetogaster annandalei* measures less than 0.02 inches long.

Worm-charming   At the first World Worm Charming Championship, held in Willaston, Cheshire, England on July 5, 1980, Tom Shufflebotham charmed a record 511 worms out of the ground (a 9.84-square-foot plot) in the allotted time of 30 minutes. In this contest, garden forks or other implements are vibrated in the soil by competitors to coax up the worms, but water is banned.

INSECTS

It is estimated that there may be as many as 30 million species of insect—more than 90 percent of all plant and animal species put together—but most have yet to be discovered and thousands are known only from a single type specimen.

Oldest insect fossil A shrimplike creature found in 1991 in rocks 420 million years old may be the oldest insect. Found in Western Australia, this euthycarcinoid was a large (five inches long) freshwater predator.

Oldest DNA The oldest fossil DNA was found in a 120–135-million-year old weevil encased in amber from Lebanon.

Oldest insect The longest-lived insects are the splendor beetles (Buprestidae). On May 27, 1983, a *Buprestis aurulenta* appeared from the staircase timber in the the home of Mr. W. Euston of Prittlewell, England, after 47 years as a larva.

Heaviest insect The heaviest insects are the Goliath beetles (family Scarabaeidae) of Equatorial Africa. The largest are *Goliathus regius*, *G. meleagris*, *G. goliathus* (= *G. giganteus*) and *G. druryi*, and in one series of fully grown males (females are smaller) the lengths from the tips of the small frontal horns to the end of the abdomen measured up to 4.33 inches and the weights ranged from 2½–3½ ounces.

CRUNCH!

The largest cockroach is *Megaloblatta longipennis* of Colombia.

A preserved female specimen of *M. longipennis* in the collection of Akira Yokokura of Yamagata, Japan measures 3.81 inches long and 1.77 inches across.

Longest insect *Pharnacia kirbyi* is a stick insect from the rain forests of Borneo. A specimen in the Natural History Museum, London, England has a body length of 12.9 inches and a total length, including the legs, of 20 inches.

Smallest insect The "feather-winged" beetles of the family Ptiliidae (= trichopterygidae) and the "battledore-wing fairy flies" (parasitic wasps) of the family Mymaridae are smaller than some species of protozoa (single-celled animals).

Lightest insect The male bloodsucking banded louse (*Enderleinellus zonatus*) and the parasitic wasp (*Caraphractus cinctus*) may each weigh as little as 5,670,000 to an ounce. Eggs of the latter each weigh 141,750,000 to an ounce.

Loudest insect At 7,400 pulses per minute, the tymbal organs of the male cicada (family Cicadidae) produce a noise (officially described by the U.S. Department of Agriculture as "tsh-ee-EEEE-e-ou") detectable more than a quarter of a mile distant.

The swallowtail butterfly beats its wings only 300 times a minute, less than any other insect. (*Jacana/P. Lorne*)

Fastest-flying insect A maximum speed of 36 MPH for the Australian dragonfly *Austrophlebia costalis* has been recorded for short bursts.

Fastest wing-beat The fastest wing-beat of any insect under natural conditions is 62,760 per minute by a tiny midge of the genus *Forcipomyia*. This insect's 0.00045-second muscular contraction–expansion cycle represents the fastest muscle movement ever measured.

Slowest wing-beat The slowest wing-beat of any insect is 300 per minute by the swallowtail butterfly (*Papilio machaon*). The average for all insects is 460–636 per minute.

Fastest-moving insect The fastest-moving insects are large tropical cockroaches; the record is 3.36 MPH, or 50 body lengths per second, registered by *Periplaneta americana* at the University of California at Berkeley in 1991.

Most legs The centipede *Himantarum gabrielis*, found in southern Europe, has 171–177 pairs of legs.

Largest egg The largest egg laid by an insect belongs to the 6-inch-long Malaysian stick insect *Heteropteryx dilitata* and measures an immense 1/2 inch long; this makes it larger than a peanut. Some insects—notably mantids and cockroaches—lay egg *cases* that are much larger, but these contain as many as 200 individual eggs.

Highest g force The click beetle (*Athous haemorrhoidalis*) averages 400 *g* when "jack-knifing" into the air to escape predators. One example measuring half an inch long and weighing 0.00014 ounces that jumped to a height of 11¾ inches was calculated to have endured a peak brain deceleration of 2,300 *g* by the end of the movement.

Largest termite mound In 1968, W. Page photographed a specimen south of Horgesia, Somalia estimated to be 28½ feet tall.

Largest grasshopper The largest grasshopper is an unidentified species from the border of Malaysia and Thailand measuring 10 inches long and capable of leaping 15 feet.

Largest flea Siphonapterologists recognize 1,830 varieties, of which the largest known is *Hystrichopsylla schefferi*, which was described from a single specimen taken from the nest of a mountain beaver (*Aplodontia rufa*) at Puyallup, WA in 1913. Females are up to 0.3 inches long.

Longest flea jump The champion jumper among fleas is the cat flea (*Ctenocephalides felis*), which has been known to reach a height of 34 inches in a single jump. The common flea (*Pulex irritans*) is capable of similar feats. In one American experiment carried out in 1910, a specimen allowed to leap at will performed a long jump of 13 inches and a high jump of 7¾ inches. In jumping 130 times its own height a flea subjects itself to a force of 200 *g*.

Largest dragonfly *Megaloprepus caeruleata* of Central and South America has been measured up to 4.72 inches long with a wingspan of up to 7.52 inches.

United States The giant green darner (*Anax walsinghami*), found in the West, has a body length of up to 4½ inches.

Smallest dragonfly The smallest dragonfly is *Agriocnemis naia* of Myanmar. A specimen in the British Museum (Natural History), London, England had a wing spread of 0.69 inches and a body length of 0.71 inches.

United States The smallest dragonfly in the United States is the elfin skimmer (*Nannothaemis Bella*), which has a body length of 4/5 of an inch.

Largest butterfly Females of the Queen Alexandra's birdwing butterfly (*Ornithoptera alexandrae*) of Papua New Guinea may have a wingspan exceeding 11 inches and may weigh over 0.9 ounces.

United States The largest *native* butterfly in the United States is the giant swallowtail (*Papilio cresphontes*), found in the eastern states, with a wingspan of up to six inches.

Smallest butterfly The smallest of the 165,000 known species of Lepidoptera is a micro-moth called *Stigmella ridiculosa*, which has a wingspan of 0.079 inches and a similar body length. It is found in the Canary Islands.

United States The smallest butterfly in the United States is the pygmy blue (*Brephidium exilis*), found in the Southeast, with a wingspan of ³/₈–³/₄ inches.

Longest butterfly migration distance A tagged female monarch or milkweed butterfly (*Danaus plexippus*) released by Donald Davis at Presqu'ile Provincial Park near Brighton, Ontario, Canada on September 6, 1986 was recaptured 2,133 miles away, on a mountain near Angangueo, Mexico on January 15, 1987. This distance was obtained by measuring a line from the release site to the recapture site, but the actual distance traveled could be double this figure.

Largest butterfly farm The largest butterfly farm in the United States is Butterfly World, in Coconut Creek, FL, which accommodates 2,000 butterflies in authentic rain forest or North American conditions. About 80 species of butterfly can be seen at any one time, and in the course of a year up to 300 species are shown in the three large screened aviaries for display and 36 separate screen enclosures for breeding.

MOLLUSKS

Largest mollusk The giant squid, *Architeuthis dux*, is the largest invertebrate and the largest mollusk. The heaviest ever recorded was a 2.2-ton specimen that ran aground in Thimble Tickle Bay, Newfoundland, Canada on November 2, 1878. Its body was 20 feet long, and one tentacle measured 35 feet long.

Gastropod The largest known gastropod is the trumpet or baler conch (*Syrinx aruanus*) of Australia. One specimen collected off Western Australia in 1979 and now owned by Don Pisor of San Diego, CA had a shell 30.4 inches long with a maximum girth of 39³/₄ inches. It weighed nearly 40 pounds when alive.

Longest mollusk A 57-foot giant *Architeuthis longimanus* was washed up on Lyall Bay, Cook Strait, New Zealand in October 1887. Its two long, slender tentacles each measured 49 ft. 3 in.

Most venomous mollusk The two related species of blue-ringed octopus, *Hapalochlaena masculosa* and *H. lunulata*, found around the coasts of Australia and parts of southeast Asia, carry a neurotoxic venom so potent that their relatively painless bite can kill in a matter of minutes. It has been estimated that each individual carries sufficient venom to cause the paralysis (or death) of 10 adult people. Fortunately, blue-ringed octopuses are not very aggressive and normally bite only when they are taken out of the water and provoked. These mollusks have a radial spread of 4–8 inches.

The most venomous gastropods are cone shells (genus *Conus*), all of which can deliver a fast-acting neurotoxic venom. Several species are capable of killing people, but the geographer cone (*Conus geographus*) of the Indo-Pacific is considered to be one of the most dangerous.

Oyster opening　The record for opening oysters is 100 in 2 min. 20.07 sec., by Mike Racz in Invercargill, New Zealand on July 16, 1990.

Snail racing　On February 20, 1990, a garden snail named Vern, owned by Sally DeRoo of Canton, MI, completed a 12$\frac{1}{5}$-inch (31-centimeter) course at West Middle School in Plymouth, MI in a record 2 min. 13 sec. at 0.092 inches per second.

This oversized snail is the largest on land; it is found in Africa and has a shell length of 10^3/$_4$ inches. (*Jacana/Mero*)

JELLYFISH

Largest jellyfish　An Arctic giant jellyfish (*Cyanea capillata arctica*) that washed up in Massachusetts Bay had a bell diameter of 7 ft. 6 in. and tentacles stretching 120 feet.

Most venomous jellyfish　The Australian sea wasp (*Chironex fleckeri*) or box jellyfish (*Chironex fleckeri*) is the most venomous cnidarian in the world. Its cardiotoxic venom has caused the deaths of at least 70 people off the coast of Australia alone in the past century, with some victims dying within four minutes if medical aid is not available. One effective defense is women's pantyhose, oversized versions of which were once worn by Queensland lifeguards at surfing tournaments.

SPONGES

Largest sponge   The barrel-shaped loggerhead sponge (*Spheciospongia vesparium*) of the West Indies and the waters off Florida can measure up to 3 ft. 6 in. high and three feet in diameter.

Heaviest sponge   In 1909, a wool sponge (*Hippospongia canaliculatta*) measuring six feet in circumference was collected off the Bahamas. When taken from the water it weighed 80–90 pounds, but after it had been dried and cleaned it weighed 12 pounds. (This sponge is now preserved in the National Museum of Natural History, Washington, D.C.)

Smallest sponge   The widely distributed *Leucosolenia blanca* measures 0.11 inches in height when fully grown.

Deepest-living sponges   Sponges have been recovered from depths of up to 18,500 feet.

DINOSAURS

Heaviest dinosaur   The main contender for the heaviest dinosaur is probably the titanosaurid *Antarctosaurus giganteus* ("Antarctic lizard") from Argentina and India, at 45–88 tons. A new titanosaurid from Argentina, *Argentinocaurus*, was estimated in 1994 to have weighed up to 110 tons based on its vast vertebrae.

Tallest and largest dinosaur   The *Brachiosaurus brancai* ("arm lizard") from the Tendaguru site in Tanzania is dated as Late Jurassic (150–144 million years ago). The site was excavated by German expeditions during the period 1909–11 and the bones prepared and assembled at the Humboldt Museum in Berlin. A complete skeleton was constructed from the remains of several individuals and put on display in 1937. It is also the largest and tallest mounted dinosaur skeleton, measuring 72 ft. 9½ in. in overall length (height at shoulder 19 ft. 8 in.), and has a raised head height of 46 feet. The animal probably weighed 30–40 tons.

Largest dinosaurs   The sauropod dinosaurs, a group of long-necked, long-tailed, four-legged plant-eaters, lumbered around most of the world during the Jurassic and Cretaceous periods, 208–65 million years ago.

Largest carnivorous dinosaur   The largest flesh-eating dinosaur recorded so far is *Tyrannosaurus rex* ("king tyrant lizard"), which 70 million years ago reigned over what are now the states of Montana, Wyoming and Texas and the provinces of Alberta and Saskatchewan, Canada. The largest and heaviest example, as suggested by a discovery in South Dakota in 1991, was 19½ feet tall, had a total length of 36½ feet and weighed an estimated 6–8 tons.

Longest dinosaur   In 1991, a diplodocid from New Mexico named *Seismosaurus halli* was estimated to be 128–170 feet long based on comparisons of individual bones.

Smallest dinosaur   *Compsognathus* ("pretty jaw") of southern Germany and southeast France, and an undescribed plant-eating fabrosaurid from Colorado, both measured 29½ inches from the snout to the tip of the tail and weighed about 15 pounds.

DID YOU KNOW?

The sauropod *Mamenchisaurus* ("mamenchi lizard") of the Late Jurassic of Sichuan, China had the longest neck of any animal that has ever lived. The neck measured 36 feet—half the total length of the dinosaur.

Most brainless dinosaur   *Stegosaurus* ("plated lizard"), which roamed across Colorado, Oklahoma, Utah and Wyoming about 150 million years ago, measured up to 30 feet long but had a walnut-sized brain weighing only 2½ ounces. This represented 0.004 of 1 percent of its computed body weight of 1.9 tons (compare with 0.074 of 1 percent for an elephant and 1.88 percent for a human).

Largest footprints   In 1932, the gigantic footprints of a large bipedal hadrosaurid ("duckbill") measuring 53½ inches long and 32 inches wide were discovered in Salt Lake City, UT, and other reports from Colorado and Utah refer to footprints 37–40 inches wide. Footprints attributed to the largest brachiosaurids also range up to 40 inches wide for the hind feet.

Largest dinosaur eggs   The *Hypselosaurus priscus* ("high ridge lizard"), a 40-foot-long titanosaurid that lived about 80 million years ago, laid the largest eggs. Examples found in the Durance valley near Aix-en-Provence, France in October 1961 would have had, uncrushed, a length of 12 inches and a diameter of 10 inches (capacity 5.8 pints).

DINOSAUR DNA:

THE REAL

JURASSIC PARK

In the movie *Jurassic Park*, scientists created living dinosaurs from preserved dinosaur DNA. During 1994 and 1995, real scientists claimed they had taken the first steps toward making this unbelievable story come true. Could we see living dinosaurs someday?

DNA, short for deoxyribonucleic acid, is a complex molecule that carries genetic information. Every cell in every species of plant or animal contains DNA unique to that species. DNA, which is divided into units called genes, is passed from parents to offspring and forms a blueprint for the physical development of an individual organism.

Before 1990, ancient DNA had been extracted from some fossils, and many scientists hoped this would open up a whole new area of research. However, DNA is a delicate molecule, and it breaks down rapidly after a plant or animal dies. In many cases, the DNA that was extracted from fossils was not originally part of those fossils; it was DNA from bacteria involved in the decay process. Original DNA could only be found when fossils had been preserved in very unusual ways.

Michael Crichton, in his book *Jurassic Park*, suggested that dinosaur DNA might be found inside the digestive systems of blood-sucking insects preserved in amber, the ancient resin of coniferous trees. Insects were often trapped in the sticky resin and preserved instantly, with no chance for decay. Indeed, in 1993, when the movie was released, DNA was extracted from a dinosaur-age insect, a 120-million-year-old weevil. So at least part of Crichton's prediction came true—but what about finding dinosaur DNA?

The first reports of dinosaur DNA came in 1994 from two teams, one led by Scott Woodward of Brigham Young University, Utah, and one led by Jack Horner of Montana State University. In both cases, the dinosaur bones were Late Cretaceous in age, perhaps 80 million years old, and were preserved in lowland sediments, some of them in association with coals.

These reports have not been widely accepted, however, since neither team has yet been able to prove that the DNA they found was entirely free from contamination. The search continues!

Termites trapped in 25-million-year-old amber. (*Gamma/Novovitch/Liaison*)

Oldest DNA Proteins, the building blocks of life, normally disappear rapidly from carcasses. Original proteins are only rarely found in fossils, but in 1993, DNA, the specialized genetic-coding protein, was recovered from a weevil that became trapped in amber 120–135 million years ago in what is now Lebanon.

A model diplodocus (above) roams through a lake. Is this the shape of things to come? (*Jacana/ J.-P. Varin*)

Dinosaur DNA was first found in bones from a dinosaur like Edmontosaurus (above). (*Matthew Hillier © Guinness Publishing*)

PLANT KINGDOM

Oldest plant   "King Clone," the oldest-known clone of the creosote plant (*Larrea tridentata*), found in southwest California, was estimated in February 1980 by Prof. Frank C. Vasek to be 11,700 years old.

Northernmost plant   The yellow poppy (*Papaver radicatum*) and the Arctic willow (*Salix arctica*) survive, the latter in an extremely stunted form, on the northernmost land at Lat. 83° N.

Southernmost plant   Lichens resembling *Rhinodina frigida* were found in Moraine Canyon at Lat. 86° 09′ S, Long. 157° 30′ W in 1971, and in the Horlick Mountain area, Antarctica at Lat. 86° 09′ S, Long. 131° 14′ W in 1965.

The southernmost flowering plant is the Antarctic hair grass (*Deschampsia antarctica*), which was found at Lat. 68° 21′ S on Refuge Island, Antarctica on March 11, 1981.

Highest-living plant   The greatest certain altitude at which any flowering plants have been found is 21,000 feet on Mt. Kamet (25,447 feet) in the Himalayas by N.D. Jayal in 1955. They were *Ermania himalayensis* and *Ranunculus lobatus*.

Deepest-living plant   Plant life was found at a depth of 884 feet by Mark and Diane Littler off San Salvadore Island, Bahamas in October 1984. The maroon-colored algae survived although 99.9995 percent of sunlight was filtered out.

Deepest roots   The greatest reported depth to which roots have penetrated is a calculated 400 feet for a wild fig tree at Echo Caves, near Ohrigstad, Transvaal, South Africa.

Longest roots   A single winter rye plant (*Secale cereale*) has been shown to produce 387 miles of roots in 1.801 cubic feet of earth.

Fastest-growing plant   Some species of the 45 genera of bamboo have been found to grow up to three feet per day (0.00002 MPH).

BLOOMS AND FLOWERS

Earliest flower   A flower believed to be 120 million years old was identified in 1989 by Dr. Leo Hickey and Dr. David Taylor of Yale University from a fossil discovered near Melbourne, Victoria, Australia. The flowering angiosperm, which resembles a modern black pepper plant, had two leaves and one flower and is known as the Koonwarra plant.

United States   The fossil of a flowering plant with palmlike imprints was found in Colorado in 1953 and dated about 65 million years old.

Largest bloom   The mottled orange-brown and white parasite *Rafflesia arnoldii* has the largest of all blooms. The plant attaches itself to cissus vines in the jungles of southeast Asia. Its blooms are as much as three feet across, with petals ³/₄ of a inch thick, and weigh up to 36 pounds.

Inflorescence   The largest inflorescence (as distinct from the largest of all blooms) is that of *Puya raimondii*, a rare Bolivian monocarpic member of the Bromeliaceae family. Its erect panicle (diameter eight feet) emerges to a height of 35 feet, and each of these bears up to 8,000 white blooms.

Largest bouquet   A team of community helpers and students led by Susan Williams of Victoria, British Columbia constructed a giant bouquet of 10,011 roses measuring 41.9 feet long in August 1994.

Smallest flowering and fruiting plant   The floating, flowering aquatic duckweed (*Wolffia angusta*) of Australia, described in 1980, is only 0.024 inches long and 0.013 inches wide. It weighs about .00001 ounces and its fruit, which resembles a minuscule fig, weighs .000025 ounces.

United States   The smallest plant regularly flowering in the United States is *Wolffia globosa*, found in the San Joaquin Valley, central California, and in rivers draining the Sierra Nevada Mountains. The plant weighs about 150 micrograms, and is 0.015–0.027 inches long and 0.011 inches wide.

GUESS WHAT?

Q. How long is the longest paper lei?

A. Look in "Big Deals" (Human Achievement)

Fastest-growing flowering plant   It was reported from Tresco Abbey, Isles of Scilly, Great Britain in July 1978 that a *Hesperoyucca whipplei* of the family Liliaceae grew 12 feet in 14 days, a rate of about 10 inches per day.

Slowest-flowering plant   The rare *Puya raimondii*, the largest of all herbs, was discovered at 13,000 feet in Bolivia in 1870. The panicle of this plant emerges after about 80–150 years of the plant's life and then dies. One specimen planted near sea level at the University of California's Botanical Garden, Berkeley in 1958 grew to 25 feet and bloomed as early as August 1986 after only 28 years.

Tallest orchid   The tallest of all orchids is *Grammatophyllum speciosum*, a native of Malaysia. Specimens have been recorded up to 25 feet high.
   There are five species of vanilla orchid that are vines and can spread to almost any length depending on the environment. These orchids root in the ground and will grow in any direction over their surroundings.

United States   The tallest of all American orchids is the *Eulophia ecristata*, with a recorded height of 5.6 feet.

FLOWERS, FRUITS AND VEGETABLES

World Records

In the interest of fairness and to minimize the risk of mistakes being made, all plants should, where possible, be entered in official international, national or local garden contests. Only produce grown primarily for human consumption will be considered for publication. The assistance of *Garden News* and the World Pumpkin Confederation is gratefully acknowledged.

Type	Size	Grower/Location	Year
Apple	3 lb. 2 oz.	Miklovic family, Caro, MI	1992
Beetroot	40 lb. 8 oz.	I. Neale, Newport, Wales	1994
Cabbage	124 lb.	B. Lavery, Llanharry, Wales	1989
Cantaloupe	62 lb.	G. Draughtridge, Rocky Mount, NC	1991
Carrot¹	15 lb. 7 oz.	I. Scott, Nelson, New Zealand	1978
Celery	46 lb. 1 oz.	B. Lavery, Llanharry, Wales	1990
Chrysanthemum	8 ft. 10 in.	M. Comer, Desford, England	1992
Cucumber²	20 lb. 1 oz.	B. Lavery, Llanharry, Wales	1991
Dahlia	25 ft. 7 in.	R. Blythe, Nannup, Western Australia	1990
Garlic	2 lb. 10 oz.	R. Kirkpatrick, Eureka, CA	1985
Grapefruit	6 lb. 8½ oz.	J. and A. Sosnow, Tucson, AZ	1984
Grapes	20 lb. 11½ oz.	Bozzolo y Perut Ltda, Santiago, Chile	1984
Green bean	48 in.	Bill Rogerson, Robersonville, NC	1994
Leek (pot)	12 lb. 2 oz.	P. Harrigan, Linton, Northumberland, England	1987
Lemon	8 lb. 8 oz.	C. and D. Knutzen, Whittier, CA	1983
Long Gourd	110⅝ in.	Peter Waterman, NY	1994
Marrow	108 lb. 2 oz.	B. Lavery, Llanharry, Wales	1990
Okra	19 ft. 9⅜ in.	David Mikulka, FL	1994
Onion	12 lb. 4 oz.	M. Ednie, Anstruther, Scotland	1994
Parsnip	171¾ in.	B. Lavery, Llanharry, Wales	1990

Petunia	13 ft. 8 in.	B. Lawrence, Windham, NY	1985
Philodendron	1,114 ft.	F. Francis, University of Massachusetts	1984
Pineapple[3]	17 lb. 12 oz.	E. Kamuk, Ais Village, WBNP, Papua New Guinea	1994
Potato[4]	7 lb. 13 oz.	K. Sloane, Patrick, Isle of Man	1994
Pumpkin	990 lb.	H. Bax, Ashton, Ontario, Canada	1994
Radish	37 lb. 15 oz.	Litterini family, Tanunda, South Australia	1992
Rhubarb	5 lb. 14 oz.	E. Stone, East Woodyates, England	1985
Runner bean	39½ in.	J. Taylor, Shifnal, England	1986
Rutabaga	53 lb. 8 oz.	P. Lillie, Uxbridge, Ontario, Canada	1993
Squash	900.5 lb.	J. & C. Lyons, Baltimore, Canada	1994
Strawberry	8.17 oz.	G. Anderson, Folkestone, England	1983
Sunflower[5]	25 ft. 5½ in.	M. Heijms, Oirschot, Netherlands	1986
Tomato	7 lb. 12 oz.	G. Graham, Edmond, OK	1986
Tomato plant[6]	53 ft. 6 in.	G. Graham, Edmond, OK	1985
Watermelon	262 lb.	B. Carson, Arrington, TN	1990
Zucchini	64 lb. 8 oz.	B. Lavery, Llanharry, Wales	1990

[1] *A 6 ft.-10½-in.-long carrot was grown by Bernard Lavery of Llanharry, Wales in 1991.*

[2] *A Vietnamese variety 6 ft. long was reported by L. Szabo of Debrecen, Hungary in September 1976. A.C. Rayment of Chelmsford, England grew one measuring 43½ inches in 1984–86.*

[3] *Pineapples weighing up to 28 lb. 11 oz. were reported from Tarauaca, Brazil in 1978.*

[4] *One weighing 18 lb. 4 oz. was reported dug up by Thomas Siddal in his garden in Chester on Feb. 17, 1795. A yield of 515 lb. was achieved from a 2½-lb.-parent seed by Bowcock planted in April 1977.*

[5] *A sunflower with a head measuring 32¼ inches in diameter was grown by Emily Martin of Maple Ridge, British Columbia, Canada in September 1983. A fully mature sunflower measuring just 2⅓ inches was grown by Michael Lenke of Lake Oswego, OR in 1985 using a patented bonsai technique.*

[6] *It was reported at the Tsukuba Science Expo Center, Japan on Feb. 28, 1988 that a single plant produced 16,897 tomatoes.*

FLOWERS, FRUITS AND VEGETABLES

U.S. National Records

In the interest of fairness and to minimize the risk of mistakes being made, all plants should, where possible, be entered in official international, national or local garden contests. Only produce grown primarily for human consumption will be considered for publication. The assistance of *Garden News* and the World Pumpkin Confederation is gratefully acknowledged.

Bushel Gourd	231.5 lb.	Richard Wright, NJ	1992
Collard[1]	41¼ in. tall	B. Rackley, Rocky Mount, NC	1989
Corn	31 ft. tall	D. Radda, Washington, IA	1946
Dahlia	16 ft. 5 in.	S. & P. Barnes, Chattahoochee, FL	1982
Eggplant	5 lb. 5¼ oz.	J. & J. Charles, Summerville, SC	1984
Kohlrabi	36 lb.	E. Krejci, Mt. Clemens, MI	1979
Lima bean	14 in.	N. McCoy, Hubert, NC	1979
Onion	7½ lb.	N. W. Hope, Tempe, AZ	1984
Peanut	4 in.	E. Adkins, Enfield, NC	1990
Pepper	13½ in.	J. Rutherford, Hatch, NM	1975
Pepper plant	12 ft. 3 in.	F. Melton, Jacksonville, FL	1992
Rutabaga	53.35 lb.	J. & M. Evans, Palmer, AK	1994
Squash	821 lb.	L. Stellpflug, Rush, NY	1990
Sweet potato	40¾ lb.	O. Harrison, Kite, GA	1982
Tomato (cherry)	28 ft. 7 in.	C. H. Wilber, Crane Hill, AL	1985
Zucchini	35.6 lb.	D. Schroer, Homer, AK	1992

[1]*This same collard holds the record for greatest width, measuring 62 inches from leaf tip to leaf tip at its widest point.*

Mel Ednie with his world record onion. (*Guinness Publishing/M. Good*)

Mr. I. Neale with the record-setting beet he grew in 1994. (*Guinness Publishing/M. Good*)

Herman Bax and his world record pumpkin. (*William Rankin*)

Exhibitors and exhibits at the 1994 Baytree Giant Vegetable show, Spalding, England. (*Guinness Publishing/ M. Good*)

Largest orchid flower   In 1886, *Pathiopedilum sanderianum* was discovered in the Malay Archipelago. The petals of this orchid's flower are reported to grow up to three feet long in the wild. A specimen grown in Somerset, England in 1991 had three flowers averaging two feet from the top of the dorsal sepal to the bottom of the ribbon petals, giving a record stretched length of four feet.

United States   The largest flowering orchid in the United States is the yellow ladyslipper (*Cypripedium calceolus*) of the Pubescens variety. Its petals grow up to seven inches long.

Largest cactus   The saguaro (*Cereus giganteus* or *Carnegiea gigantea*) is found in Arizona, southeastern California and Sonora, Mexico. The green fluted column is surmounted by candelabra-like branches rising to a height of 57 ft. 11¾ in. in the case of a specimen discovered in the Maricopa Mountains, near Gila Bend, AZ on January 17, 1988.

An armless cactus 78 feet high was measured in April 1978 by Hube Yates in Cave Creek, AZ. It was toppled in a windstorm in July 1986 at an estimated age of 150 years.

The saguaro cactus of the Arizona desert grows extremely slowly, sprouting less than one inch in its first 10 years of life and growing by less than four inches a year thereafter. (*Jacana/F. Gobier*)

Largest rhododendron Examples of the scarlet *Rhododendron arboreum* reach a height of 65 feet on Mt. Japfu, Nagaland, India. The cross-section of the trunk of a *Rhododendron giganteum*, reputedly 90 feet high, from Yunnan, China, is preserved at Inverewe Gardens, Highland, Scotland.

Largest rose tree A Lady Banks rosé tree at Tombstone, AZ has a trunk 163 inches in circumference, stands nine feet high and covers an area of 8,660 square feet. It is supported by 77 posts and several thousand feet of piping, which allows 150 people to be seated under the arbor. The cutting came from Scotland in 1884.

Largest hanging basket A giant hanging basket measuring 20 feet in diameter and containing about 600 plants was created by Rogers of Exeter Garden Centre, Exeter, England in 1987. Its volume was approximately 4,167 cubic feet and it weighed an estimated 4.4 tons.

FRUITS AND VEGETABLES

Longest daisy chain A 16-person team from Good Easter, England made a daisy chain measuring 6,980 ft. 7 in. in seven hours on May 27, 1985.

Most calorific fruit An analysis of 38 fruits commonly eaten raw (as opposed to dried) shows that the avocado has the highest calorific value, with 741 calories per pound.

GUESS WHAT?

Q. Where is the largest vineyard?

A. Look in "Agriculture" (Business & Law)

Least calorific fruit The cucumber (*Cucumis sativus*) has only 73 calories per pound.

Cucumber slicing Norman Johnson of Blackpool, England set a record of 13.4 seconds for slicing a 12-inch cucumber, $1\frac{1}{2}$ inches in diameter, at 22 slices to the inch (total 264 slices) at West Deutscher Rundfunk in Cologne, Germany on April 3, 1983.

Apple peeling Kathy Wafler of Wolcott, NY produced a single unbroken apple peel measuring 172 ft. 4 in. from a 20-ounce apple in 11 hr. 30 min. at Long Ridge Mall, Rochester, NY on October 16, 1976.

Apple picking George Adrian of Indianapolis, IN picked 15,830 pounds of apples in eight hours on September 23, 1980.

Most jack-o'-lanterns   The record for most jack-o'lanterns in one place at one time is 10,540, on October 29, 1994. The pumpkins were carved for the Harvest Festival in Keene, NH.

Largest jack-o'-lantern   The largest jack-o'-lantern in the world was carved from a 827-pound pumpkin by Michael Green, Regina Johnson and Daniel Salcedo at Nut Tree, CA on October 30, 1992.

Potato peeling   On September 19, 1992, Marj Killian, Terry Anderson, Barbara Pearson, Marilyn Small and Janene Utkin peeled 1064 lb. 6 oz. (net) of potatoes to an institutional cookery standard with standard kitchen knives in 45 minutes at the 64th Annual Idaho Spud Day celebration, held in Shelley, ID.

LEAVES

Largest leaves   The largest leaves of any plant belong to the raffia palm (*Raphia farinifera* = *R. raffia*) of the Mascarene Islands in the Indian Ocean, and the Amazonian bamboo palm (*R. taedigera*) of South America, whose leaf blades may measure up to 65½ feet long, with petioles up to 13 feet.

United States   The largest leaves to be found in outdoor plants in the United States are those of the climbing fern (*Lygodium japonicum*) of the Gulf coast, with leaves of 23 feet.

Largest undivided leaf   *Alocasia macrorrhiza* is found in Sabah, Malaysia. A leaf of this specimen discovered in 1966 was 9 ft. 11 in. long and 6 ft. 3½ in. wide, with a surface area of 34.12 square feet.

Most-leaved clovers   A 14-leafed white clover (*Trifolium repens*) was found by Randy Farland near Sioux Falls, SD on June 16, 1975. A 14-leafed red clover (*T. pratense*) was reported by Paul Haizlip at Bellevue, WA on June 22, 1987.

SEEDS

Largest seed   The single-seeded fruit of the giant fan palm *Lodoicea maldivica* (= *L. callipyge*, *L. seychellarum*) can weigh 44 pounds. Commonly known as the double coconut or coco de mer, it is found wild only in the Seychelles in the Indian Ocean.

Smallest seed   The smallest are those of epiphytic (nonparasitic plants growing on others) orchids, at 28,129.81 million seeds per ounce (compare with grass pollens at up to 6 billion grains per ounce).

Most durable seed   A plausible but inconclusive claim for the longevity of seeds has been made for the Arctic lupine (*Lupinus arcticus*) found in frozen silt at Miller Creek, Yukon, Canada in July 1954 by Harold Schmidt. The seeds were germinated in 1966 and were radiocarbon dated to at least 8000 B.C. and more probably to 13,000 B.C.

GRASSES

Commonest grass Bermuda grass (*Cynodon dactylon*) is native to tropical Africa and the Indo-Malaysian region, but it extends from Lat. 45° N to 45° S. It is possibly the most troublesome weed of the grass family, affecting 40 crops in over 80 countries. The Callie hybrid, selected in 1966, grows as much as six inches per day, and stolons reach 18 feet long.

Tallest grass A thorny bamboo culm (*Bambusa arundiancea*) felled at Pattazhi, Travancore, India in November 1904 was 121½ feet tall.

WEEDS

Largest weed The giant hogweed (*Heracleum mantegazzianum*), originally from the Caucasus, reaches 12 feet tall and has leaves three feet long.

Most damaging weed The purple nutsedge, nutgrass or nutsedge (*Cyperus rotundus*) is a land weed native to India. It attacks 52 crops in 92 countries, including the United States, where it is primarily found in the southern states.

Aquatic The most widespread aquatic weed is the water hyacinth (*Eichhornia crassipes*), which is a native of the Amazon basin but extends from Lat. 40° N to 45° S.

Tallest weed The tallest weed in the United States is the Melaleuca tree (*Melaleuca quinquenervia*), introduced to the Florida and Gulf coasts from Australia in 1900. Growing to an average of 39 feet, the weed has infested 3.7 million of the 4.7 million acres of Florida wetlands. The tree is very dense and is not destroyed by fire, although it is a fire hazard because it contains essential petroleums that spread fire quickly.

Largest weed mat The greatest area covered by a single clonal growth is that of the wild box huckleberry (*Gaylussacia brachycera*), a mat-forming evergreen shrub first reported in 1796. A colony covering about 100 acres was found on July 18, 1920 near the Juniata River, PA. It has been estimated that this colony began 13,000 years ago.

TREES

Oldest tree species The maidenhair tree (*Ginkgo biloba*), which first appeared about 160 million years ago during the Jurassic era, survives today as a living species. It has been grown since *c.* 1100 in Japan.

Oldest tree The *potential* life span of a bristlecone pine (*Pinus longaeva*) is estimated at nearly 5,500 years, and that of a giant sequoia (*Sequoiadendron giganteum*) at perhaps 6,000 years. The oldest recorded tree is the "Eon Tree," a coast redwood (*Sequioa sempervirens*) in Humboldt County, CA. This tree, which fell in December 1977, stood about 250 feet tall and was believed to be at least 6,200 years old.

Living A bristlecone pine named Methuselah, growing at 10,000 feet on the California side of the White Mountains, has been confirmed as 4,700

The maidenhair tree of Zhejiang, China first appeared about 160 million years ago during the Jurassic era. (*Jacana/R. Durand*)

years old. In March 1974, it was reported that this tree had produced 48 live seedlings.

Most massive tree   General Sherman, a giant sequoia (*Sequoiadendron giganteum*) standing in Sequoia National Park, CA, is 275 feet tall. In 1991, it had a girth of 102.6 feet, measured 4½ feet above the ground. General Sherman has been estimated to contain the equivalent of five billion matches. The red-brown bark may be up to 24 inches thick in parts.

Greatest spread   The great banyan (*Ficus benghalensis*) in the Indian Botanical Garden, Calcutta, has 1,775 prop or supporting roots and a circumference of 1,350 feet. It covers some three acres and dates from before 1787.

Greatest girth   A circumference of 190 feet was recorded for the European chestnut (*Castanea sativa*) known as the "Tree of the Hundred Horses" (*Castagno di Cento Cavalli*) on Mount Etna, Sicily, Italy in 1770 and 1780. The tree is now in three parts, widely separated.

United States   The giant sequoia named General Sherman in Sequoia National Park, CA has a girth of 102.6 feet, measured 4½ feet above the ground.

Tallest tree   An Australian eucalyptus (*Eucalyptus regnans*) at Watts River, Victoria, Australia, was reported in 1872 to measure 435 feet tall. It almost certainly measured over 500 feet originally.

Living   The tallest tree currently standing is the "National Geographic Society" coast redwood (*Sequoia sempervirens*) in Humboldt Redwoods State Park, CA. It was measured at 365 feet by Ron Hildebrant of California in October 1991.

Tallest Christmas tree   A 221-foot Douglas fir (*Pseudotsuga menziesii*) was erected at Northgate Shopping Center, Seattle, WA in December 1950.

Fastest tree climb   On July 3, 1988, Guy German of Sitka, AK climbed up a 100-foot tree trunk and back down to the ground in 24.82 seconds at the World Championship Timber Carnival in Albany, OR.

Fastest-growing tree   Discounting bamboo, which is not classified as a tree but as a woody grass, the fastest rate of growth recorded is 35 ft. 3 in. in 13 months by an *Albizzia falcata* planted on June 17, 1974 in Sabah, Malaysia.

Slowest-growing tree   Excluding *bonsai*, the 14th-century Oriental art of cultivating miniature trees, the extreme in slow growth is represented by the *Dioon edule* (Cycadaceae) in Mexico, whose average annual growth rate is 0.03 inches; a specimen 120 years old measured four inches high.

Most isolated tree   It is believed that the nearest companion to a solitary Norwegian spruce on Campbell Island is over 120 nautical miles away in the Auckland Islands.

Tree sitting   The duration record for staying in a tree is more than 24 years, by Bungkas, who went up a palm tree in Bengkes, Indonesia in 1970 and has been there ever since. He lives in a nest made from branches and leaves. Repeated efforts have been made to persuade him to come down, but without success.

Tree planting   Three hundred schoolchildren and adults from Walsall, England planted 1,774 trees in 17 hr. 20 min. (over six days), between November 25 and December 5, 1993.

Largest forest   The largest forested areas in the world are the vast coniferous forests of northern Russia, lying between Lat. 55° N and the Arctic Circle. The total wooded area amounts to 2.7 billion acres (25 percent of the world's forests), of which 38 percent is Siberian larch. The former USSR is 34 percent forested. In comparison, the largest area of forest in the tropics is the Amazon basin, amounting to some 815 million acres.

United States   The largest forest in the United States is the Tongass National Forest (16.7 million acres) in Alaska. The United States is 32.25 percent forested.

Longest avenue of trees   The Nikko Cryptomeria Avenue, measuring a total 22 miles, comprises three parts converging on Imaichi City in the Tochigi Prefecture of Japan. It was planted in the period 1628–48, and over 13,500 of its original 200,000 Japanese cedar (*Cryptomeria japonica*) trees survive, at an average height of $88\frac{1}{2}$ feet.

MICROBES

Largest protozoan   The largest known protozoans in terms of volume are the extinct calcareous foraminifera (*Foraminiferida*) of the genus *Nummulites*. Individuals measuring up to six inches wide have been found in the Middle Eocene rocks of Turkey.

The largest existing protozoan, a species of the *Stannophyllum* (Xenophyophorida), can exceed this in length (9³/₄ inches has been recorded) but not in volume.

Largest bacterium   The *Epulopiscium fishelsoni* inhabits the intestinal tract of the brown surgeonfish (*Acanthurus nigrofuscus*) from the Red Sea and

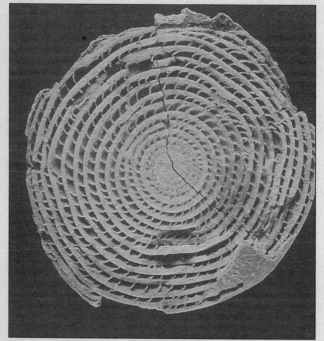

Nummulites laevigatus from the Middle Eocene rocks of Turkey, an example of the largest known protozoans in terms of volume. (*Jacana/N. Le Roy*)

the Great Barrier Reef. Measuring 80 by 600 µm or more and therefore visible to the naked eye, this mega-microorganism, first discovered by Israeli researchers in 1985, is a million times larger than the human food poisoner *Escherichia coli*.

Smallest free-living entity   The smallest of all free-living organisms are pleuro-pneumonialike organisms of the *Mycoplasma*. One of these, *Mycoplasma laidlawii*, first discovered in sewage in 1936, has a diameter during its early existence of only 0.0000001 m. Examples of the strain known as H.39 have a maximum diameter of 3×10^{-7} m and weigh an estimated 1×10^{-16} g.

Smallest protophyte   The marine microflagellate alga *Micromonas pusilla* has a diameter of less than 0.00008 inches.

Fastest bacterium   The rod-shaped bacillus *Bdellovibrio bacteriovorus*, which is two micrometers long, can move 50 times its own length in one second, using a polar flagellum rotating 100 times per second. This equivalent to a human sprinter reaching 200 MPH.

Fastest protozoan   The protozoan *Monas stigmatica* can move a distance equivalent to 40 times its own length in a second. No human can cover even seven times his own length in a second.

Fastest protozoan reproduction   The protozoan *Glaucoma*, which reproduces by binary fission, divides as frequently as every three hours. Thus, in the course of a day, it could become a great-great-great-great-great-grandparent and the progenitor of 256 descendants!

Highest-living bacterium   In April 1967, the National Aeronautics and Space Administration (NASA) reported that bacteria had been discovered at an altitude of 25½ miles.

Toughest bacterium   The bacterium *Micrococcus radiodurans* can withstand atomic radiation of 6.5 million röntgens, or 10,000 times the dose that would be fatal to the average person. In March 1983, John Barras (University of Oregon) reported bacteria from sulfurous seabed vents thriving at 583°F in the East Pacific Rise at Lat. 21° N.

Oldest bacterium   Viable bacteria were reported in 1991 to have been recovered from sediments 3–4 million years old from the Sea of Japan.

Living   In 1991, it was reported that live bacteria were found in the flesh of a mastodon (an ancestor of the elephant) from Ohio that died 12,000 years earlier and which, on the evidence of spear marks found in the ribs, represented the first proof of humans killing a prehistoric animal. The bacteria gave the flesh a bad smell even after such a long time.

FUNGI

Largest fungus A single living clonal growth of the underground fungus *Armillaria ostoyae* was reported in May 1992 as covering some 1,500 acres in the forests of Washington State. Estimates based on its size suggest that the fungus is 500–1,000 years old, but no attempts have been made to estimate its weight. Also known as the honey or shoestring fungus, it fruits above ground as edible gilled mushrooms.

Largest edible fungus A giant puffball (*Calvatia gigantea*) measuring 8 ft. 8 in. in circumference and weighing 48½ pounds was found by Jean-Guy Richard of Montreal, Canada in 1987.

Largest tree fungus The largest recorded tree fungus is the bracket fungus *Rigidoporus ulmarius* growing from dead elm wood on the grounds of the International Mycological Institute at Kew, England. It measured 59 by 56¾ in. with a circumference of 14 ft. 10¾ in.

United States In April 1992, Freda Kaplan of San Ramon, CA found a puffball (*Langermannia gigantea*) measuring 7 ft. 3 in. in circumference on the Wiedemann ranch in San Ramon.

Heaviest fungus A clonal growth of the fungus *Armillaria bulbosa* was reported on April 2, 1992 to be covering about 37 acres of forest in Michigan. It was calculated to weigh over 110 tons, which is comparable with the weight of a blue whale. The organism is thought to have originated from a single fertilized spore at least 1,500 years ago.

Heaviest edible fungus A chicken of the woods mushroom (*Laetiporus sulphureus*) weighing 100 pounds was found in the New Forest, England by Giovanni Paba of Broadstone, Dorset, England on October 15, 1990.

Most poisonous fungus The yellowish-olive death cap (*Amanita phalloides*) is responsible for 90 percent of fatal poisonings caused by fungi. The estimated lethal amount for humans, depending on body weight, is about 1¾ ounces of fresh fungus. From 6 to 15 hours after eating, the victim experiences vomiting and delirium, followed by collapse and death. Among its victims was Cardinal Giulio de' Medici, Pope Clement VII (b. 1478), on September 25, 1534.

Highest fungal spore count A count of 5,686,861 per cubic foot was recorded near Cardiff, Wales on July 21, 1971.

ZOOS, AQUARIA AND PARKS

Oldest zoo   The oldest existing public zoo is the Zoological Society of London, England, founded in 1826. In January 1993, the collection comprised 18,128 specimens, housed in Regent's Park, London, England (36 acres) and at Whipsnade Park, England (541 acres; opened May 23, 1931).

United States   The Philadelphia Zoo received its charter from the state of Pennsylvania in 1859, but did not open to the public until 1874. Lincoln Park Zoo, a 60-acre public park owned by the city of Chicago, received a gift of two swans from Central Park, New York City in 1868 to start its collection. By 1870, a "small barn and paddocks" had been built to house additional animals that had been donated by the public. The current facility covers 35 acres.

According to the American Association of Zoological Parks and Aquariums, the top zoo for attendance is Lincoln Park Zoo, with 4 million visitors each year.

Largest aquarium   In terms of volume of water held, the Living Seas Aquarium, opened in 1986 at the Epcot Center near Orlando, FL, is the largest, with a total capacity of 6.25 million gallons. It contains over 3,000 fish, representing 65 species.

The largest in terms of marine life is the Monterey Bay Aquarium in California. The aquarium was opened on October 20, 1984 at a cost of $55 million. It contains over 6,500 specimens (525 species) of fauna and flora in its 86 tanks. The volume of water held is 1 million gallons. The average annual attendance is 1.7 million visitors; however, in 1985, there were 2.3 million visitors, the highest for any aquarium in the United States.

Largest park   The National Park of North-Eastern Greenland covers 375,289 square miles and stretches from Liverpool Land in the south to the northernmost island, Odaaq Ø, off Pearyland. Established in 1974 and enlarged in 1988, the park is largely covered by ice and is home to a variety of protected flora and fauna, including polar bears, musk-ox and birds of prey.

United States   The largest public park in the United States is Wrangell-St. Elias National Park and Preserve in Alaska. Of a total 13.2 million acres, the National Park section covers 8.33 million acres and the Preserve comprises 4.88 million acres.

Largest game reserve   Etosha National Park, Namibia was established in 1907, and now covers an area of 38,427 square miles.

Most national parks visited   From 1991 to January 16, 1995, Eloise and Charles Shields visited 370 of the national parks in the United States. They have traveled over 68,500 miles in their van.

EARTH & SPACE

THE UNIVERSE

A light-year is the distance traveled by light (at a speed of 186,282.397 miles per second) in one tropical year (365.24219878 mean solar days at January 0, 12 hours Ephemeris time in A.D. 1900). This is equivalent to 5,878,499,814,000 miles.

Largest structure in the universe   In June 1994, the discovery of a cocoon-shaped shell of galaxies about 650 million light-years across was announced by Georges Paturel (France) and his colleagues.

Remotest object   The record red shift is 4.897 for the quasar PC 1247 + 3406. If it is assumed that there is an "observable horizon," where the speed of recession is equal to the speed of light, then this quasar appears to be 13.2 billion light-years away.

Remotest galaxy   The remotest galaxy is the radio source 8C 1435 + 635, which has a red shift of 4.25, equivalent to a distance of 13 billion light-years.

Largest galaxy   The central galaxy of Abell 2029 is 1.07 billion light-years away in the Virgo cluster. The galaxy has a major diameter of 5.6 million light-years, which is 80 times the diameter of the Milky Way galaxy, and a light output 2 trillion times that of the Sun.

Brightest object   The most luminous object in the sky is the quasar HS 1946 + 7658, which is at least 1.5×10^{15} times more luminous than the Sun. This quasar has a red shift of 3.02 and is therefore at a distance of about 12.4 billion light-years from Earth.

Brightest galaxy   The brightest galaxy (or galaxy in the process of forming) is IRAS F10214 + 4724, which was detected as a faint source by IRAS (Infra Red Astronomy Satellite) in 1983. IRAS F10214 + 4724 is 4.7×10^{14} times more luminous than the Sun and has a red shift of 2.286, equivalent to a distance of 11.6 billion light-years.

Farthest visible object   The remotest object visible to the naked eye is the Great Galaxy in Andromeda (magnitude 3.47), known as Messier 31. It was first observed by Simon Marius (Germany; 1570–1624). Messier 31 is a rotating spiral nebula at a distance of about 2,310,000 light-years from Earth.

   Under ideal conditions, Messier 33, the Spiral in Triangulum (magnitude 5.79), can be glimpsed by the naked eye at a distance of 2,530,000 light-years.

STARS

Nearest star   The closest star other than the Sun is the very faint Proxima Centauri, discovered in 1915, which is 4.225 light-years away.

The nearest star visible to the naked eye is the southern hemisphere binary Alpha Centauri (4.35 light-years away), which has an apparent magnitude of −0.27.

Largest star   The M-class supergiant Betelgeuse (Alpha Orionis—the top left star of Orion) is 310 light-years away. It has a diameter of 400 million miles, about 500 times greater than the Sun's diameter, and is surrounded by a gas halo up to 530 billion miles in diameter.

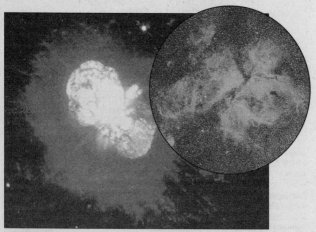

Eta Carinae, the most massive star, was also among the brightest stars in the middle of the last century, although it has since faded and is no longer visible to the naked eye. An optical image of the Carina Nebula, as seen by the Hubble Space Telescope after it was repaired in 1993, shows Eta Carinae at the center. (*Science Photo Library/Royal Observatory and Science Photo Library/Space Telescope Science Institute/NASA*)

Heaviest star   Eta Carinae, 9,100 light-years away in the Carina Nebula, is estimated to be 150–200 times more massive than the Sun.

Smallest star   Neutron stars, which may weigh three times as much as the Sun, have diameters of only 6–19 miles. Although black holes are pointlike sources, their distortion of local space–time means that they appear as black stars, with a diameter of 37 miles for one weighing 10 times the mass of the Sun.

Lightest star   The white dwarf companion to the millisecond pulsar PSR B1957 + 20 has a mass only 0.02 that of the Sun and is being evaporated away by the fast-spinning pulsar.

Brightest star If all the stars could be viewed at the same distance, Eta Carinae would be the brightest, with a total luminosity 6,500,000 times that of the Sun. However, the *visually* brightest star viewed through a telescope is the hypergiant Cygnus OB2 No. 12, which is 5,900 light-years away. It has an absolute visual magnitude of –9.9 and is therefore visually 810,000 times brighter than the Sun.

Brightest star seen from Earth Sirius A (Alpha Canis Majoris), 8.64 light-years away, is the brightest star in the sky, with an apparent magnitude of –1.46. It has a mass 2.14 times the mass of the Sun and is visually 24 times brighter.

SUPERNOVA!

The brightest supernova ever seen is believed to be SN 1006, seen near Beta Lupi in April 1006. It flared for two years and attained an estimated magnitude of –9 to –10. The remnant is believed to be the radio source G.327.6 + 14.5, nearly 3,000 light-years away.

Faintest star GD 165B, the brown dwarf candidate companion to the white dwarf GD 165A, which is 117 light-years away, is the faintest star. It has a luminosity 10,000 times less than that of the Sun and a visual brightness 8 million times less. It was discovered in September 1988.

Youngest stars The youngest stars appear to be two protostars known collectively as IRAS–4 buried deep in dust clouds in the nebula NGC 1333, which is 1,100 light-years away. These protostars will not blaze forth as full-fledged stars for at least another 100,000 years.

Longest star name Torcularis Septentrionalis is the name applied to the star Omicron Piscium in the constellation Pisces.

Slowest pulsar The pulsar that has the slowest spin-down rate, and is therefore the most accurate stellar clock, is PSR 1855 + 09, at only .00000000000000000021 revolutions per second.

Fastest pulsar For pulsars whose spin rates have been accurately measured, the fastest-spinning is PSR B1937 + 214. It is in the constellation Vulpecula, 11,700 light-years away, and has a pulse period of 1.5578064916 milliseconds, which is equivalent to a spin rate of 641.9282546 revolutions per second.

Black holes The first object to be tentatively identified as a black hole (a star that has undergone complete gravitational collapse) is the binary-star X-ray source Cygnus X–1, which was discovered in December 1972.
The likeliest black hole candidate is the central star of the star system

V404, which is 5,000 light-years away in the constellation Cygnus. This star first showed a possible black hole signature, which was observed by the Ginga satellite, in May 1989. In September 1991, its mass was firmly established as being at least six times the mass of the Sun and possibly as much as eight to 15 times.

Largest constellation Hydra (the Sea Serpent) covers 1302.844 square degrees, or 3.16 percent of the whole sky, and contains at least 68 stars visible to the naked eye (magnitude 5.5 or brighter). The constellation Centaurus (Centaur), which ranks ninth in area, contains at least 94 such stars.

Zodiacal Virgo is the largest, with an area of 1,294.428 square degrees. Taurus has the most bright stars, with 125 down to magnitude 6.

Smallest constellation Crux Australis (Southern Cross) has an area of only 0.16 percent of the sky, or 68.477 square degrees, compared with the 41,252.96 square degrees of the whole sky.

Zodiacal Of the zodiacal constellations, the smallest is Capricornus (Capricorn), with an area of 413.947 square degrees.

THE SOLAR SYSTEM

Largest model of the solar system The biggest scale model of the solar system was developed by the Lakeview Museum of Arts and Sciences in Peoria, IL and inaugurated in April 1992.

THE SUN

Largest object in the solar system The Sun is classified as a yellow dwarf type G2, but its mass of two octillion tons is 332,946.04 times the mass of Earth and represents over 99 percent of the total mass of the solar system. The Sun's diameter is 865,040 miles, and its density is 1.408 times that of water or a fourth of Earth's density.

The Sun has a central temperature of about 15,400,000 K (32,650,000°F) and a core pressure of 3.68×10^{12} pounds per square inch. It uses up about 4.4 million tons of hydrogen per second, but despite this rate of consumption it will be 10 billion years old when it finally exhausts its energy supply (about 5 billion years from now). The luminous intensity of the Sun is 2.7 octillion candela.

Greatest Earth–Sun distance Because Earth's orbit is elliptical, its distance from the Sun varies. At aphelion, the outermost point of the orbit, Earth is 94,509,200 miles from the Sun, compared with 91,402,600 miles at perihelion, the closest point.

Largest sunspot To be visible to the *protected* naked eye, a sunspot must cover about 1/2,000th of the Sun's disc, or 0.5 billion square miles. The largest sunspot ever recorded was in the Sun's southern hemisphere on

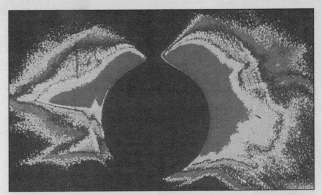

The nearest star is the Sun. Its corona—the outermost region of its atmosphere is only visible to the naked eye during a total solar eclipse. (*Spectrum Colour Library*)

April 8, 1947. Its area was about 7 billion square miles with an extreme longitude of 187,000 miles and an extreme latitude of 90,000 miles. Sunspots appear dark because they are more than 2,700°F cooler than the rest of the Sun's surface temperature of 9,939°F.

Most sunspots In October 1957, a smoothed sunspot count showed 263, the highest recorded index since records started in 1755.

Longest-lasting sunspot In 1943, one sunspot persisted for 200 days, from June to December.

PLANETS

Largest planet Jupiter, with an equatorial diameter of 88,846 miles and a polar diameter of 83,082 miles, is the largest of the nine major planets, with a mass 317.828 times, and a volume 1,323.3 times, that of Earth. It also has the shortest period of rotation; Jupiter's day is 9 hr. 50 min. 30.003 sec. long at the equator.

Smallest planet The discovery of Pluto by Clyde William Tombaugh (U.S.) at the Lowell Observatory, Flagstaff, AZ was announced on March 13, 1930. The planet has a diameter of 1,442 miles.

Coldest planet Although the surface temperature of Pluto is not known, its surface composition suggests that the temperature must be similar to the value of −391°F measured for Neptune's moon Triton, the lowest observed surface temperature of any natural body in the solar system.

Hottest planet Venus has an estimated surface temperature of 864°F, based on measurements taken from the Russian *Venera* and U.S. *Pioneer* surface probes.

Outermost planet The Pluto-Charon system orbits at a mean distance from the Sun of 3.674 billion miles.

The remotest solar system object in terms of distance at perihelion is the Kuiper Belt object 1994 ES_2—discovered by David Jewitt (Great Britain) and Jane Luu (U.S.) in 1994—which has the largest noncometary mean distance from the Sun of 4.208 billion miles and is 4.208 billion miles from the Sun at perihelion.

Uranus is the faintest planet that can be seen without a telescope. This picture is an artist's impression of the view of Uranus from Miranda, one of its 15 satellites. (*Spectrum Colour Library*)

Nearest planet to Earth Venus is, at times, only 26 million miles inside Earth's orbit, compared with Mars's closest approach of 35 million miles outside Earth's orbit.

Fastest planet Mercury, which orbits the Sun at an average distance of 35,983,100 miles, has a period of revolution of 87.9686 days, thus giving the highest average speed in orbit of 107,030 MPH.

Highest surface feature By far the highest and most spectacular surface feature of any planet is Olympus Mons (formerly Nix Olympica) in the Tharsis region of Mars. It has a diameter of 310–370 miles and an estimated height of 16 miles, making it more than $2\frac{1}{2}$ times as tall as Mt. Everest.

Brightest planet Viewed from Earth, the brightest of the five planets normally visible to the naked eye (Jupiter, Mars, Mercury, Saturn and Venus) is Venus, with a maximum magnitude of –4.4.

Faintest planet Uranus, with a magnitude of 5.5, can be seen with the naked eye under certain conditions. The faintest of the nine planets as seen from Earth is Pluto (magnitude 15.0), which can only be viewed through a telescope.

Densest planet Earth is the densest planet, with an average density 5.515 times that of water.

Least dense planet Saturn has an average density only about one-eighth of Earth's density or 0.685 times the density of water.

Greatest conjunction The most dramatic recorded conjunction of the seven principal members of the solar system besides Earth (Sun, Moon, Mercury, Venus, Mars, Jupiter and Saturn) occurred on February 5, 1962 when 16° covered all seven during an eclipse in the Pacific area. The next notable conjunction will take place on May 5, 2000.

SATELLITES

Largest satellite The largest and heaviest satellite is Ganymede (Jupiter III), which is 2.017 times as heavy as Earth's moon and has a diameter of 3,273 miles.

Smallest satellite Of satellites whose diameters have been measured, the smallest is Deimos, the irregularly shaped outermost moon of Mars, which has an average diameter of 7.8 miles.

Most satellites Of the 61 satellites in the solar system, 18 belong to Saturn.

Fewest satellites Earth and Pluto have only one satellite each and Mercury and Venus have none.

Shortest planet-satellite distance Phobos orbits Mars at a distance of 5,287 miles from the planet's center.

Longest planet–satellite distance Jupiter's outer satellite Sinope circles the planet at 14,700,000 miles from its center.

Newest satellite The most recently discovered satellite is the Saturnian satellite Pan, which was found on *Voyager 2* photographs taken during the close approach in August 1981. It has a diameter of only about 12 miles and orbits within the 200-mile Encke gap in the A ring.

ASTEROIDS

Largest asteroid The largest asteroid, and the first ever discovered (by G. Piazzi in Palermo, Sicily on January 1, 1801), is 1 Ceres, with an equatorial diameter of 596 miles.

Smallest asteroid $1993KA_2$ is the smallest known asteroid, with a diameter of about 16 feet.

CLOSE!

The asteroid $1994XM_1$, which measures 33 feet in diameter, was discovered by James Scotti (U.S.) on December 9, 1994, only 14 hours before it passed within 62,000 miles of Earth.

Brightest asteroid   The brightest asteroid is 4 Vesta with an absolute magnitude of 3.16.

Faintest asteroid   The faintest asteroid is $1993KB_2$, whose absolute magnitude of 29 makes it the faintest object ever detected.

Nearest to the Sun   The Apollo asteroid 3200 Phaethon (discovered in 1993) is only 12,980,000 miles from the Sun at perihelion.

Farthest from the Sun   The Kuiper belt object 1993 SB is 4.839 billion miles away from the Sun at aphelion.

THE MOON

Earth's closest neighbor in space and its only natural satellite is the Moon, which has an average diameter of 2,159.3 miles and a mass of 8.1×10^{19} tons, or 0.0123 of Earth's mass. Its density is 3.344 times the density of water. The Moon orbits at a mean distance from Earth of 238,854.5 miles center-to-center, and the orbital period (sidereal month) is 27.321661 days, giving an average orbital velocity of 2,289 MPH.

Shortest Earth–Moon distance   In this century, the closest approach to Earth by the Moon (the smallest perigee) was 221,441 miles center-to-center on January 4, 1912.

Longest Earth–Moon distance   On March 2, 1984, the Moon was 252,718 miles from Earth, the farthest distance (largest apogee) this century.

Largest crater   Only 59 percent of the Moon's surface is directly visible from Earth because it is in "captured rotation," i.e., the period of rotation is equal to the period of orbit. The largest wholly visible crater is the walled plain Bailly, towards the Moon's south pole, which is 183 miles across, with walls rising to 14,000 feet. The Orientale Basin, partly on the averted side, measures more than 600 miles in diameter.

Deepest crater   The Newton Crater has a floor estimated to be 23,000–29,000 feet below its rim and 14,000 feet below the level of the plain outside.

Highest mountains   In the absence of a sea level, lunar altitudes are measured relative to an adopted reference sphere with a radius of 1,080 miles.

DID YOU KNOW?

An eclipse of the Moon can have a totality of up to 107 minutes.

The next eclipse of this length is expected to occur on July 16, 2000.

CAROLYN'S COMETS

Some of the most exciting moments of Carolyn Shoemaker's life took place in the middle of the night while she sat on a dark, freezing-cold mountaintop, eating Oreo cookies. She didn't know those moments when they came, though. It wasn't until later, while studying telescope photographs in a well-lit, warm lab, that she'd point a finger and say, "I think I've got something here."

Carolyn Shoemaker's astronomy career took off after her children left home and she began assisting her husband, geological astronomer Eugene Shoemaker. Once a month, they'd drive all night to get to Palomar Mountain, 500 miles from their Arizona home. They'd set up their telescope and pray for clear skies.

(Terence Dickinson)

Shoemaker soon realized she had a talent for seeing asteroids and comets that others missed. One fateful night, the photographs the Shoemakers and partner David Levy took were accidentally ruined, and they had no choice but to set up their equipment again under cloudy conditions. A rip in the clouds revealed Jupiter, and the picture that resulted showed something phenomenal: a comet like a string of pearls in the sky, on a collision course with the big planet. "To our great pleasure, the largest telescopes in the world— and the Hubble, which is out of the world—were trained on our comet."

Most comets discovered

Carolyn Shoemaker has discovered 32 comets, more than any living astronomer. All 32 comets bear her name; no other astronomer in history has matched this achievement.

Nowadays, a photograph of Comet Shoemaker-Levy 9 hangs over the Shoemakers' bed. Photographs of asteroids they've discovered and named for family members have been known to appear under the Christmas tree. And Carolyn Shoemaker's personal record now stands at 32 comets and some 800 asteroids.

As a child, Shoemaker read L. Frank Baum's *Wizard of Oz* books and dreamed of having a magic belt, like Dorothy's, to fly through space. When she grew up, she became a pilot. "It's fun having a bird's eye view of everything. It's not so much the speed or flight, but that picture of life you get." Pictures of space continue to intrigue her: "I have an ever-increasing awareness of how big space is and how much there is out there. The universe is full of chaos, even if it looks peaceful to us."

On this basis, the highest elevation is 26,000 feet for the highlands north of the Korolev Basin, on the far side of the Moon.

Highest temperature   When the Sun is overhead, the temperature on the lunar equator reaches 243°F (31°F above the boiling point of water).

Lowest temperature   At sunset, the temperature at the lunar equator is 58°F, and after nightfall it sinks to −261°F.

ECLIPSES

Earliest recorded eclipse   There appears to be no evidence for ancient descriptions of eclipses before the partial eclipse observed in Nineveh in Assyria on June 15, 763 B.C. The first definite description of a total eclipse comes from Chu-fu, China, for an eclipse observed on July 17, 709 B.C.

Longest eclipse   The maximum possible duration of an eclipse of the Sun is 7 min. 31 sec. The longest of recent date was on June 20, 1955 (7 min. 8 sec.), west of the Philippines, although it was clouded out along most of its track.

Eclipse durations can be artificially extended when observers are airborne. On June 30, 1973, a total eclipse of the Sun was stretched to 74 minutes for observers aboard a Concorde that took off from Toulouse, France and stayed in the Moon's shadow over the Atlantic from 10:51 to 12:05 GMT before landing in Chad.

Most eclipses in a year   The greatest number of eclipses possible in a year is seven, as in 1935, when there were five solar and two lunar eclipses. In 1982, there were four solar and three lunar eclipses.

Fewest eclipses in a year   The lowest possible number of eclipses in one year is two, both of which must be solar, as in 1944 and 1969.

Most eclipses in one place   The only recent example of three total solar eclipses occurring at a single location was at a point 44° N, 67° E in Kazakhstan, east of the Aral Sea. These took place on September 21, 1941, July 9, 1945, and February 25, 1952.

COMETS

Brightest comets   The brightest comets are thought to be either the Curls Comet of 1862 or the Ikeya-Seki Comet of 1965.

Brightest periodical comet   Appearances of Halley's Comet, which has a period of 76 years, have been traced back to 467 B.C. It was first depicted in the Nuremburg Chronicle of A.D. 684.

Largest comet   The tail of the brilliant Great Comet of 1843 trailed for 205 million miles. The bow shock wave of Holmes Comet of 1892 once measured 1.5 million miles in diameter.

Longest period   The longest period computed for a comet is 1,550 years, for Comet McNaught-Russell, equivalent to a mean distance from the Sun of 12 billion miles.

Shortest period The periodic comet that returns most frequently is the increasingly faint Encke's Comet, first identified in 1786. It has an orbital period of 1,198 days (3.28 years) and has the closest approach to the Sun (30.8 million miles at perihelion, when its speed is 158,000 MPH.)

Closest approach to Earth On July 1, 1770, Lexell's Comet, traveling at 86,100 MPH relative to the Sun, came within 745,000 miles of Earth. Earth is believed to have passed through the tail of Halley's Comet on May 19, 1910.

METEORITES

Oldest meteorite The Krähenberg meteorite has been dated at 4.6 billion ± 20 million years, which is just within the initial period of solar system formation.

Largest meteorite The largest known meteorite was found in 1920 at Hoba West, near Grootfontein in Namibia. It is a block nine feet long by eight feet wide, estimated to weigh 65 tons.

The largest meteorite exhibited in a museum is the "Cape York" meteorite, weighing 68,085 pounds, now on display in the Hayden Planetarium in New York City. It was found in 1897 by the expedition of Cmdr. Robert Edwin Peary (U.S.) near Cape York, Greenland, where it was known to the Inuits as the Abnighito.

Greatest explosion There was an explosion of 10–15 megatons in the basin of the Podkamennaya Tunguska River, 40 miles north of Vanavar, in Siberia, Russia, on June 30, 1908. The blast devastated an area of 1,500 square miles and the shock was felt as far away as 625 miles. The most recent theory is that this explosion was caused by the total disintegration at an altitude of 33,000 feet of a 98-foot-diameter stony asteroid traveling at hypersonic velocity.

Largest crater It is estimated that some 2,000 asteroid–Earth collisions have occurred in the last 600 million years, and 102 collision sites or astroblemes have been identified.

In 1962, a crater 150 miles in diameter and half a mile deep in Wilkes Land, Antarctica was attributed to a meteorite. Such a crater could have been created by a meteorite weighing 14.33 billion tons striking at 44,000 MPH.

There is a craterlike formation or astrobleme 275 miles in diameter on the eastern shore of Hudson Bay, Canada.

The largest and best-preserved crater that was definitely formed by an asteroid is Coon Butte (or Barringer Crater), discovered in 1891 near Canyon Diablo, Winslow, AZ. It is 4,150 feet in diameter and now about 575 feet deep, with a parapet rising 130–155 feet above the surrounding plain. It has been estimated that an iron–nickel mass of some 2.2 million tons and with a diameter of 200–260 feet gouged out this crater *c.* 25,000 B.C.

Largest tektite The largest tektite of which details have been published weighed seven pounds and was found in 1932 at Muong Nong, Saravane Province, Laos. It is now in the Louvre Museum, Paris, France.

Largest meteor shower The greatest shower on record occurred on the night of November 16–17, 1966, when the Leonid meteors (which recur every 33¼ years) were visible between western North America and eastern Russia. It was calculated that meteors passed over Arizona at a rate of 2,300 per minute for a period of 20 minutes starting at 5 A.M. on November 17, 1966.

THE EARTH

The earth is approximately 4.54 billion years old. Its surface area is estimated to be 196,937,400 square miles and its volume about 259.875 billion cubic miles.

The earth's mass is 6.6 sextillion tons and its density is 5.515 times the density of water. The period of axial rotation, i.e., the true sidereal day, is 23 hr. 56 min. 4.0989 sec., mean time.

The earth is not a perfect sphere, but is flattened slightly at the poles. Its largest diameter is the equatorial diameter (7,926.3803 miles), which is 26.5757 miles larger than the polar diameter of 7,899.8046 miles.

There is also a slight ellipticity of the equator, since its major diameter at longitude 14.96° W is 456 feet longer than its minor axis.

The greatest departures from the reference ellipsoid are a protuberance of 240 feet in the area of Papua New Guinea and a depression of 344 feet south of Sri Lanka, in the Indian Ocean.

The greatest circumference of the earth is 24,901.458 miles at the equator, compared with 24,859.731 miles at any meridian.

FEATURES AND DIMENSIONS

OCEANS

The area of the earth covered by oceans and seas (the hydrosphere) is estimated to be 139,782,000 square miles or 70.98 percent of the total surface. The mean depth of the hydrosphere is 12,234 feet and the volume 323,870,000 cubic miles, compared with 8,400,000 cubic miles of fresh water. The total weight of the water is estimated to be 1.41 quintillion tons, or 0.024 percent of the earth's total weight.

Largest ocean   The Pacific Ocean, excluding adjacent seas, represents 45.9 percent of the world's oceans and covers 64,186,300 square miles. Its average depth is 12,925 feet.

Deepest ocean   The deepest part of the ocean was pinpointed in 1951 by the British Survey Ship *Challenger* in the Mariana Trench in the Pacific Ocean. On January 23, 1960, the manned U.S. Navy bathyscaphe *Trieste* descended 35,813 feet to the bottom. Data obtained in 1984 by the survey vessel *Takuyo* of the Hydrographic Department, Japan Maritime Safety Agency, using a narrow multi-beam echo sounder, produced a figure of 35,839 feet ± 33 feet.

A one-kilogram (2.2-pound) ball of steel dropped into the water above the Mariana Trench would take nearly 64 minutes to fall to the seabed, where hydrostatic pressure is over 18,000 pounds per square inch.

United States   Defining U.S. waters as within 200 nautical miles of any U.S. territory (Economic Exclusive Zone [EEZ]), the deepest point in American waters is Challenger D in the Mariana Trench in the Pacific Ocean. Challenger D is 35,838 feet deep, 170 nautical miles southwest of Guam at 11° 22.4′ N, 142° 35.5′ E.

Smallest ocean   The Arctic Ocean covers 5,105,700 square miles. Its average depth is 3,407 feet.

Largest sea   The South China Sea has an area of 1,148,500 square miles.

Remotest spot from land   The world's most distant point from land is a spot in the South Pacific, 47° 30′ S, 120° W, which is 1,600 miles from Pitcairn Island, Ducie Island and Cape Dart, Antarctica. Centered on this spot is a circle of water with an area of 8,041,200 square miles—about a million square miles larger than Russia, the world's largest country.

Largest bay   The largest bay measured by shoreline length is Hudson Bay, Canada, which has a shoreline of 7,623 miles and an area of 476,000 square miles. Measured by area, the Bay of Bengal, in the Indian Ocean, is larger, at 839,000 square miles.

Largest gulf   The Gulf of Mexico covers 596,000 square miles. Its shoreline extends 3,100 miles from Cape Sable, FL to Cabo Catoche, Mexico.

Longest fjord The Nordvest Fjord arm of the Scoresby Sound in eastern Greenland extends inland 195 miles from the sea.

Highest seamount The highest submarine mountain, or seamount, was discovered in 1953 near the Tonga Trench, between Samoa and New Zealand in the South Pacific. It rises 28,500 feet from the seabed, with its summit 1,200 feet below the surface.

Most southerly ocean The most southerly part of any of the world's oceans is located at 85° 34' S, 154° W, at the snout of the Robert Scott Glacier, 305 miles from the South Pole.

Lowest sea temperature The temperature of water at the surface of the White Sea can be as low as 28°F.

Highest sea temperature In the shallow areas of the Persian Gulf, the surface temperature can reach 96°F in summer.

The highest temperature recorded in the ocean is 759°F in a hot spring 300 miles off the west coast of the United States, measured in 1985 by an American research submarine.

Clearest sea The Weddell Sea, 71° S, 15° W off Antarctica, has the clearest water of any sea. A Secchi Disk one foot in diameter was visible to a depth of 262 feet on October 13, 1986, as measured by Dutch researchers at the German Alfred Wegener Institute. Such clarity is comparable to the clarity of distilled water.

STRAITS

Longest straits The Tatarskiy Proliv or Tartar Straits, between Sakhalin Island and the Russian mainland, run 500 miles from the Sea of Japan to Sakhalinsky Zaliv.

Broadest straits The broadest *named* straits in the world are the Davis Straits between Greenland and Baffin Island, Canada, with a minimum width of 210 miles. The Drake Passage, a deep waterway between the Diego Ramirez Islands, Chile and the South Shetland Islands, is 710 miles across.

Narrowest straits The narrowest navigable straits are between the Aegean island of Euboea and the mainland of Greece. The gap is only 135 feet wide at Khalkis.

WAVES

Highest wave The highest officially recorded sea wave was calculated at 112 feet from trough to crest; it was measured during a 68-knot hurricane by Lt. Frederic Margraff (U.S.N.) from the U.S.S. *Ramapo*, traveling from Manila, Philippines to San Diego, CA on the night of February 6–7, 1933. The highest instrumentally measured wave was 86 feet high, and was recorded by the British ship *Weather Reporter* in the North Atlantic on December 30, 1972 at Lat. 59° N, Long. 19° W.

GUESS WHAT?

Q. WHAT WAS THE DEEPEST DIVE BY A SUBMARINE?

A. LOOK IN "SHIPS" (TRANSPORT)

On July 9, 1958, a landslide caused a 100-MPH wave to wash 1,720 feet high along the fjord-like Lituya Bay in Alaska.

Highest seismic wave The highest tsunami was triggered by an underwater landslide that struck the island of Lanai in Hawaii *c*. 105,000 years ago. It deposited sediment up to an altitude of approximately 1,230 feet.

The highest tsunami in modern times appeared off Ishigaki Island, Ryukyu Chain on April 24, 1771. It was possibly 278 feet high, and it tossed an 830-ton block of coral more than 1.3 miles inland.

Most deadly tsunami The worst tsunami in the United States occurred on September 8, 1900 in Galveston, TX, killing more than 5,000 people.

CURRENTS

Greatest ocean current Based on measurements taken in 1982 in the Drake Passage, between Chile and Antarctica, the Antarctic Circumpolar Current or West Wind Drift Current was found to be flowing at a rate of 4.3 billion cubic feet per second. Results from computer modeling in 1990 estimate a higher figure of 6.9 billion cubic feet per second.

Strongest currents In Nakwakto Rapids, Slingsby Channel, British Columbia, Canada (Lat. 51° 05′ N, Long. 127° 30′ W), the flow rate may reach 16 knots.

United States The current ebbs at seven knots on the coast of Alaska in Chatham Strait, Pt. Kootzhahoo at Pt. Bridge. The strongest current on the east coast of the United States is at St. Johns River in Pablo Creek, FL, where the current ebbs at 5.2 knots.

TIDES

Greatest tide The greatest tides occur in the Bay of Fundy, which divides the peninsula of Nova Scotia, Canada from Maine and the Canadian province of New Brunswick.

Burncoat Head in the Minas Basin, Nova Scotia, has the greatest mean spring range, at 47 ft. 6 in. A range of 54 ft. 6 in. was recorded at springs in Leaf Basin, in Ungava Bay, Quebec, Canada in 1953.

Least tide Tahiti, in the mid-Pacific, experiences virtually no tide.

Highest and lowest tide The highest and lowest tide in the United States is at Sunrise, AK on Turnagain Arm islet. Its range is 33.3 feet.

CONTINENTS

Largest continent Of the earth's surface, only about 57,151,000 square miles (29.02 percent) is land above water, with a mean height of 2,480 feet above sea level. The Eurasian landmass is the largest, with an area (including islands) of 20,700,000 square miles.

The Afro-Eurasian landmass, which is separated artificially by the Suez Canal, covers an area of 32,700,000 square miles.

There is strong evidence that about 300 million years ago, the earth's land surface comprised a single primeval continent of 60 million square miles, now termed Pangaea. This supercontinent is believed to have split about 190 million years ago, during the Jurassic period, into two supercontinents—Laurasia (Eurasia, Greenland and North America) and Gondwana (Africa, Arabia, India, South America, Oceania and Antarctica).

Smallest continent The Australian mainland has an area of 2,941,526 square miles.

Land farthest from the sea The point of land remotest from the sea is at Lat. 46° 16.8′ N, Long. 86° 40.2′ E in the Dzungarian Basin, which is in the Xinjiang Uygur autonomous region in the far northwest of China. It is at a straight-line distance of 1,645 miles from the nearest open sea—Baydaratskaya Guba to the north (Arctic Ocean), Feni Point to the south (Indian Ocean) and Bohai Wan to the east (Yellow Sea).

Largest peninsula The world's largest peninsula is Arabia, with an area of about 1.25 million square miles.

United States The Alaskan peninsula is the longest in the United States, with a length of 471 miles. The longest in the conterminous 48 states is the Florida peninsula, at 383 miles.

ISLANDS

Largest island Discounting Australia, which is usually regarded as a continental landmass, the largest island in the world is Greenland, with an area of about 840,000 square miles.

Sand The largest sand island in the world is Fraser Island, Queensland, Australia, with a sand dune 75 miles long.

Freshwater The largest island surrounded mostly by fresh water (18,500 square miles) is the Ilha de Marajó in the mouth of the River Amazon, Brazil.

Inland The world's largest inland island (i.e., land surrounded by rivers) is Ilha do Bananal, Brazil (7,700 square miles). The largest island in a lake is Manitoulin Island (1,068 square miles) in the Canadian section of Lake Huron.

Remotest island Bouvet Island (Bouvetøya), an uninhabited Norwegian dependency in the South Atlantic, is about 1,050 miles north of the nearest land, the coast of Queen Maud Land in Antarctica.

The remotest inhabited island is Tristan da Cunha in the South Atlantic.

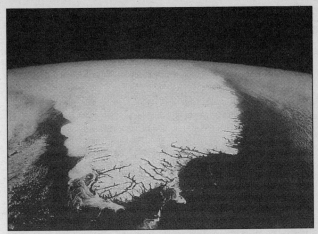

Greenland, the world's largest island, provides a spectacular view from space. (*Ann Ronan/Image Select*)

The 38-square-mile island was evacuated in 1961 because of volcanic activity, but 198 islanders returned in November 1963. The nearest inhabited land is the island of St. Helena, which is 1,315 nautical miles to the northeast.

Northernmost land The islet of Odaaq Ø, 100 feet across and 0.8 miles north of Kaffeklubben Ø off Pearyland, Greenland, is 438.9 miles from the North Pole.

Southernmost land The South Pole, unlike the North Pole, is on land. The polar ice cap drifts 33 feet per year away from the geographic pole along the 40th meridian west of Greenwich. The original Amundsen–Scott South Polar station was built at an altitude of 9,370 feet in 1957, but it could not withstand the severe conditions and was replaced in 1975.

Greatest archipelago The greatest archipelago is the crescent of more than 17,000 islands, 3,500 miles long, that forms Indonesia.

Highest rock pinnacle The world's highest rock pinnacle is Ball's Pyramid, near Lord Howe Island in the Pacific, which is 1,843 feet high but has a base axis of only 660 feet.

Largest atoll The largest atoll in the world is Kwajalein in the Marshall Islands, in the central Pacific Ocean. Its slender coral reef 176 miles long encloses a lagoon of 1,100 square miles.

The atoll with the largest land area is Christmas Atoll, in the Line Islands in the central Pacific Ocean. It has an area of 251 square miles, of which 124 square miles is land.

ROCKS

Oldest rock   The age of the earth is generally considered to be about 4.54 billion years, but no rocks this old have been found, presumably because geological processes have destroyed them. The greatest reported age for any scientifically dated rock is 3.962 billion years in the case of the Acasta Gneisses, found approximately 200 miles north of Yellowknife, Northwest Territories, Canada.

Older minerals that are not rocks have also been identified. Zircon crystals discovered in the Jack Hills, 430 miles north of Perth, Australia, were found to be 4.276 billion years old. These are the oldest fragments of the earth's crust discovered so far.

Largest rock   The largest exposed monolith in the world is Ayers Rock, known to Aborigines as Uluru, which rises 1,143 feet above the surrounding desert plain in Northern Territory, Australia. It is 1.5 miles long and a mile wide.

La Gran Piedra, a volcanic plug located in the Sierra Maestra, Cuba, has been estimated to weigh 67,632 tons.

Longest natural arch   The sandstone Landscape Arch in the Arches National Park, 25 miles north of Moab, UT, spans 291 feet and is set about 100 feet above the canyon floor. In one place erosion has narrowed it to six feet wide. The Rainbow Bridge, also in Utah, is only 270 feet long but more than 22 feet wide and rises 290 feet in elevation.

DEPRESSIONS

Deepest depression   The deepest depression so far discovered is the bedrock of the Bentley subglacial trench, Antarctica at 8,326 feet below sea level. The greatest submarine depression is an area of the northwest Pacific floor that has an average depth of 15,000 feet.

The deepest exposed depression on land is the shore surrounding the Dead Sea, now 1,310 feet below sea level. The deepest point on the bed of this saltiest of all lakes is 2,388 feet below sea level.

The deepest part of the bed of Lake Baikal in Russia is 3,875 feet below sea level.

United States   The lowest-lying area in the United States is in Death Valley, CA at 282 feet below sea level.

ANCIENT!

The oldest rocks in the United States are the Morton Gneisses, scattered over an area of 50 miles from New Ulm to Renville Co., MN. These rocks were dated at 3.6 billion years using the uranium–lead dating method.

LONGEST REEF

The Great Barrier Reef off Queensland, northeastern Australia is 1,260 miles long. It is not actually a single reef, but consists of thousands of separate reefs. Large areas of the central section of the reef—approximately between Cooktown and Proserpine—have been devastated by the crown-of-thorns starfish (*Acanthaster planci*).

Largest depression   The world's largest exposed depression is the Caspian Sea basin in Azerbaijan, Russia, Kazakhstan, Turkmenistan and Iran. It is more than 200,000 square miles, of which 143,550 square miles is lake area. The chief land area of the depression is the Prikaspiyskaya Nizmennost, lying around the northern third of the lake and stretching inland for a distance of up to 280 miles.

CAVES

Longest cave   The most extensive cave system in the world is in Mammoth Cave National Park, KY. Explorations by many groups of cavers have revealed that interconnected cave passages beneath the Flint, Mammoth Cave and Toohey ridges make up a system with a total mapped length that is now 348 miles.

Largest cave   The world's largest cave chamber is the Sarawak Chamber, Lubang Nasib Bagus, in the Gunung Mulu National Park, Sarawak, Malaysia. Its length is 2,300 feet, its average width is 980 feet, and it is not less than 230 feet high at any point. It would be large enough to hold 7,500 buses.

Longest underwater cave   The Nohoch Nah Chich cave system in Quintana Roo, Mexico has 24.53 miles of mapped passages. Exploration of the system, which began in November 1987, has been carried out by the CEDAM Cave Diving Team under the leadership of Mike Madden (U.S.)

Longest dive into a cave   The longest dive into a single flooded cave passage is 13,300 feet into the Doux de Coly, Dordogne, France by Olivier Issler (Switzerland) on April 4, 1991.

Deepest descent into a cave   The world depth record was set by the Groupe Vulcain in the Gouffre Jean Bernard, France at 5,256 feet in 1989. However, this cave, explored via multiple entrances, has never been entirely descended, so the "sporting" record for the greatest descent into a cave is recognized as 4,947 feet in the Shakta Pantjukhina in the Caucasus Mountains of Georgia by a team of Ukrainian cavers in 1988.

Longest stalactite   The longest known stalactite in the world is a wall-supported column extending 195 feet from roof to floor in the Cueva de Nerja, near Málaga, Spain.

IN THE
BEGINNING
THERE WAS
DREAMTIME . . .

when the earth was flat and void, without light or darkness, and Nature awaited the coming of godlike heroes to give it form and life . . . .

Ayers Rock rises mysteriously out of barren land in Australia's Northern Territory. From the summit, 1,143 feet above the desert plain, it is easy to see how this massive monolith came to play such a prominent part in aboriginal culture. To the Aborigines of the Pitjatjantjara and Yankunytjatjara tribes, each feature of Uluru, as it is known in their language, is the work or embodiment of one of the 10 mythical beings who appeared at the end of the Dreamtime. Aborigines still gather in the caves at the base of the rock to hold sacred ceremonies and paint their Dreamtime legends.

At 1.5 miles long and 1 mile wide, with a circumference of 5.6 miles, Uluru is the world's largest rock and an awe-inspiring sight. A mystical aura seems to surround the rock, and as the sun moves around it, it changes color from vivid red to lilac, blue, pink and brown. Its smooth, steep walls rise at an angle of 80°, making it very difficult for vegetation to take root; plaques on the rock commemorate tourists who have likewise failed to scale its mighty sides.

At the base of Ayers Rock, however, life is abundant. When it rains, water cascades down the rock and collects in pools at the bottom. Here, dingos, kangaroos, birds, reptiles and other animals come to drink, and trees and shrubs thrive. A tiny amount of water leaks through cracks in the hard sandstone on the way down, weakening the subsurface layer and gradually forcing the outer layers to peel off. This weathering process has resulted in strange formations, many of which figure in aboriginal legend. For example, a boulder near the northeast face is a Mala, one of the Hare-

Wallaby People who lived at Uluru but who were mostly destroyed by the devilish dingo, Kulpunya, himself represented by a slab of rock.

Ayers Rock is slowly decreasing in size as layers of the hard crust break off, although its form alters little and its formidable beauty endures. For the Aborigines, to whom the rock belongs, Uluru is unlikely to diminish in importance; it will always symbolize the mystery of creation, life rising out of the desert land.

Largest rock

The world's largest exposed monolith is Ayers Rock, known to the Aborigines as Uluru, which rises 1,143 feet above the surrounding desert plain in Northern Territory, Australia. It is 1.5 miles long and a mile wide.

The view from the 1,143-foot-high summit of Ayers Rock. (*Gamma/ Kactus Foto*)

The Brain is the result of years of weathering. Legend has it that pockmarks in the rock were made when enemy tribes threw spears at the tribes who lived there during the Dreamtime. (*Denise Duncan*)

The rock looms over desert oaks, which to the Aborigines represent an invading army of Poisonous Snake-People. (*Spectrum Colour Library*)

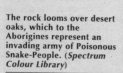

Uluru sprawls across the desert land. (*Spectrum Colour Library*)

The longest freehanging stalactite in the world is one 33 feet long in the Gruta do Janelão, in Minas Gerais, Brazil.

Tallest stalagmite   The tallest known stalagmite in the world is one in the Krásnohorská cave, near Rožňava in Slovakia, which is generally thought to be about 105 feet tall.

The tallest cave column is considered to be the Flying Dragon Pillar, 128 feet high, in Daji Dong, Guizhou, China.

Deepest cave   The deepest cave in the United States is Lechuguilla Cave in Carlsbad Caverns, Carlsbad, NM, which currently measures 1,571 feet deep and over 68 miles long.

MOUNTAINS

Highest mountain   Mt. Everest, a peak in the eastern Himalayas on the Tibet–Nepal border, was discovered to be the world's highest mountain in March 1856 by the Survey Department of the Government of India, from theodolite readings taken in 1849 and 1850. Its height was computed to be 29,002 feet, although recent satellite measurements put it at 29,029 feet.

The mountain whose summit is farthest from the earth's center is the Andean peak of Chimborazo (20,561 feet), 98 miles south of the equator in Ecuador. Its summit is 7,057 feet further from the earth's center than the summit of Mt. Everest.

The highest island mountain in the world is Puncak Jaya in Irian Jaya, Indonesia. A survey by the Australian Universities' Expedition in 1973 yielded a height of 16,023 feet.

United States   The highest mountain in the United States is Mt. McKinley in Alaska, with a highest point of 20,320 feet. McKinley, so named in 1896, was called Denali (Great One) in the Athabascan language of Native North Americans. The highest mountain in the 48 conterminous states is Mt. Whitney in California, with a highest point of 14,494 feet.

Tallest mountain   Measured from its submarine base in the Hawaiian Trough to its peak, the tallest mountain in the world is Mauna Kea (White Mountain), on the island of Hawaii, with a total height of 33,480 feet, of which 13,796 feet are above sea level.

Longest mountain range   The submarine Mid-Ocean Ridge extends 40,000 miles from the Arctic Ocean to the Atlantic Ocean, around Africa, Asia and Australia, and under the Pacific Ocean to the west coast of North America. Its highest point is 13,800 feet above the base ocean depth.

Land   The longest land mountain range is the Andes of South America, which is approximately 4,700 miles long.

Highest land mountain range   The Himalaya-Karakoram range contains 96 of the world's 109 peaks of over 24,000 feet.

Longest line of sight   Vatnajökull (6,952 feet), Iceland has been seen by re-fracted light from the Faeroe Islands 340 miles away.

HIGHEST ALTITUDES IN THE U.S. BY STATE

State *	Highest point	Elevation (ft.)
Alaska	Mt. McKinley	20,320
California	Mt. Whitney	14,494
Colorado	Mt. Elbert	14,433
Washington	Mt. Rainier	14,410
Wyoming	Gannett Peak	13,804
Hawaii	Mauna Kea	13,796
Utah	Kings Peak	13,528
New Mexico	Wheeler Peak	13,161
Nevada	Boundary Peak	13,140
Montana	Granite Peak	12,799
Idaho	Borah Peak	12,662
Arizona	Humphreys Peak	12,633
Oregon	Mt. Hood	11,239
Texas	Guadalupe Peak	8,749
South Dakota	Harney Peak	7,242
North Carolina	Mt. Mitchell	6,684
Tennessee	Clingmans Dome	6,643
New Hampshire	Mt. Washington	6,288
Virginia	Mt. Rogers	5,729
Nebraska	Johnson Township	5,426
New York	Mt. Marcy	5,344
Maine	Mt. Katahdin	5,267
Oklahoma	Black Mesa	4,973
West Virginia	Spruce Knob	4,861
Georgia	Brasstown Bald	4,784
Vermont	Mt. Mansfield	4,393
Kentucky	Black Mountain	4,139
Kansas	Mt. Sunflower	4,039
South Carolina	Sassafras Mountain	3,560
North Dakota	White Butte	3,506
Massachusetts	Mt. Greylock	3,487
Maryland	Blackbone Mountain	3,360
Pennsylvania	Mt. Davis	3,213
Arkansas	Magazine Mountain	2,753
Alabama	Cheaha Mountain	2,405
Connecticut	Mt. Frissell	2,380
Minnesota	Eagle Mountain	2,301
Michigan	Mt. Arvon	1,979
Wisconsin	Timms Hill	1,951
New Jersey	High Point	1,803
Missouri	Taum Sauk Mount	1,772
Iowa	Sec. 29, T 100N, R 41W	1,670
Ohio	Campbell Hill	1,549
Indiana	Franklin Township	1,257
Illinois	Charles Mound	1,235
Rhode Island	Jerimoth Hill	812
Mississippi	Woodall Mountain	806
Louisiana	Driskill Mountain	535
Delaware	Ebright Road	442
Florida	Sec. 30, T 6N, R 20W	345

* Pete Allard, Jim Grace, Shaun Lacher, David Sandway and Dennis Stewart reached each high point of the 48 conterminous states in a record time of 30 days 10 hours 51 minutes and 55 seconds, July 1–31, 1991. They hiked a total of 253 miles and drove 17,284 miles during the trip.

United States   In Alaska, Mt. McKinley (20,320 feet) has been sighted from Mt. Sanford (16,237 feet), a distance of 230 miles.

Greatest plateau   The most extensive high plateau in the world is the Tibetan Plateau in Central Asia. Its average altitude is 16,000 feet and its area is 715,000 square miles.

Sheerest wall   Mt. Rakaposhi (25,550 feet) rises 3.72 vertical miles from the Hunza Valley, Pakistan in 6.2 horizontal miles with an overall gradient of 31°.

The 3,200-foot-wide northwest face of Half Dome, Yosemite, CA is 2,200 feet high and does not depart more than 7° from the vertical.

Highest sea cliffs   The cliffs on the north coast of Moloka'i, HI near Umilehi Point descend 3,300 feet to the sea at an average inclination of more than 55°.

Highest halites   Along 725 miles of the northern shores of the Gulf of Mexico there are 330 subterranean "mountains" of salt, some of which rise more than 60,000 feet from bedrock. Above ground they appear as low salt domes.

VALLEYS

Deepest valley   The Yarlung Zangbo valley is 16,650 feet deep where it turns through the Himalayas in eastern Tibet, before the river changes its name to the Brahmaputra. The peaks of Namche Barwa (25,436 feet) and Jala Peri (23,891 feet) are just 13 miles apart, with the Yarlung Zangbo River in between, at an elevation of 8,000 feet.

Largest gorge   The Grand Canyon on the Colorado River in north-central Arizona extends from Marble Gorge to the Grand Wash Cliffs, a distance of 277 miles. It averages 10 miles in width and is one mile deep. The submarine Labrador Basin canyon, between Greenland and Labrador, Canada, is about 2,150 miles long.

Deepest canyon   A canyon or gorge is generally defined as a valley with steep rock walls and a considerable depth in relation to its width. The Grand Canyon (see above) has the characteristic vertical sections of wall, but is much wider than its depth. The Vicos Gorge in the Pindus mountains of northwest Greece is 2,950 feet deep and only 3,600 feet between its rims.

United States   The deepest canyon in the United States is Kings Canyon, East Fresno, CA, which runs through Sierra and Sequoia National Forests. The deepest point, which measures 8,200 feet, is in the Sierra National Park Forest section of the canyon.

Deepest submarine canyon   The submarine canyon 25 miles south of Esperance, Western Australia is 6,000 feet deep and 20 miles wide.

DEEPEST VALLEY

For many years, the Yarlung Zangbo in eastern Tibet was known to be among the deepest valleys in the world. Its inaccessibility meant that its depth could not be directly measured—until 1993, when, after 10 years of trying, explorer Richard Fisher obtained the permits he needed to visit the area. British botanist Francis Kingdon Ward explored the Yarlung Zangbo at the beginning of the century, but no other Westerners were able to do so until Fisher led his expedition there.

With a group of fellow Americans, plus Chinese and Tibetan colleagues and Minba and Loba tribal co-explorers, Fisher set off into the unknown. The result was clear-cut: the discovery of the deepest valley on earth.

With soaring peaks on either side of the Yarlung Zangbo, measurements were extremely difficult to take, but the conclusion was that the valley is 16,650 feet deep near the Tibet–India border. The peaks of Namche Barwa (25,436 feet) and Jala Peri (23,891 feet) are 13 miles apart, and the Yarlung Zangbo River flows between them at an elevation of 8,000 feet.

Richard Fisher says the Yarlung Zangbo is the only chasm he has encountered that compares with the Grand Canyon for sheer beauty. Fisher adds, "The Yarlung Zangbo is so vast and diverse that it must contain many mysteries yet to be discovered."

(Richard D. Fisher)

> ## Deepest valley
> The Yarlung Zangbo valley is 16,650 feet deep where it turns through the Himalayas in eastern Tibet, before the river changes its name to the Brahmaputra.

WATERFALLS

Highest waterfall The highest waterfall (as opposed to vaporized "bridal-veil fall") in the world is the Salto Angel (Angel Falls) in Venezuela, on a branch of the Carrao River, an upper tributary of the Caroni, with a total drop of 3,212 feet; the longest single drop is 2,648 feet.

United States The tallest continuous waterfall in the United States is Ribbon Falls in Yosemite National Park, CA, with a drop of 1,612 feet. This is a seasonal waterfall and is generally dry from late July to early September.

Yosemite Falls, also in Yosemite National Park, has the greatest *total* drop at 2,425 feet, but actually consists of three distinct waterfalls. These are the Upper (1,430 feet), Middle (675 feet) and Lower falls (320 feet).

Largest waterfall On the basis of average annual flow, the greatest waterfall in the world is the Boyoma Falls in Zaïre, with 600,000 cusec.

The waterfall with the greatest peak flow ever was the Guaíra (Salto das Sete Quedas) on the Alto Paraná River between Brazil and Paraguay, which on occasions reached a peak rate of 1.75 million cusec, until the completion of the Itaipú Dam gates in 1982.

Widest waterfall The Khône Falls in Laos are 6.7 miles wide and 50–70 feet high, with a flood flow of 1.5 million cusec.

Depending on the criteria used to pinpoint the ends of the Nile and the Amazon, the Nile could be considered the world's longest river. Above is a fairly familiar Egyptian Nile scene; the inset shows the Blue Nile at Tissiat Falls in Ethiopia, a country better known for its lack of water. (*Spectrum Colour Library*)

RIVERS

Longest rivers   The two longest rivers in the world are the Nile, flowing into the Mediterranean, and the Amazon, flowing into the South Atlantic. Which one is longest is more a matter of definition than of simple measurement.

The Amazon has several mouths that widen toward the sea, so that the exact point where the river ends is uncertain. If the Pará estuary (the most distant mouth) is counted, its length is approximately 4,195 miles.

The length of the Nile watercourse, as surveyed before the loss of a few miles of meanders due to the formation of Lake Nasser behind the Aswan High Dam, was 4,145 miles.

United States   The Mississippi is 2,348 miles long. It flows from its source at Lake Itasca, MN through 10 states before reaching the Gulf of Mexico. The entire Mississippi River system, including eastern and western tributaries, flows through 25 states.

Shortest rivers   As with the longest river, two rivers could be considered the shortest named rivers. The Roe River, which flows into the Missouri River near Great Falls, MT, is fed by a large freshwater spring. It has two forks, measuring 201 feet (East Fork Roe River) and 58 feet (North Fork Roe River). The D River, in Lincoln City, OR, connects Devil's Lake to the Pacific. Its length is officially quoted as 120 ± 5 feet.

Largest river basin   The Amazon basin covers about 2,720,000 square miles. It has countless tributaries and subtributaries, including the Madeira, which at 2,100 miles is the longest tributary in the world.

Longest estuary   The Ob, in northern Russia, is 550 miles long. It is up to 50 miles wide, and is also the widest river that freezes solid.

Largest delta   The delta created by the Ganges and Brahmaputra in Bangladesh and West Bengal, India covers an area of 30,000 square miles.

United States   The Mississippi River delta has an area of about 10,100 square miles.

Greatest flow   The Amazon discharges an average of 4.2 million cusec into the Atlantic Ocean, increasing to more than 7 million cusec in full flood. The flow of the Amazon is 60 times greater than the flow of the Nile.

Largest submarine river   In 1952, a 190-mile-wide submarine river, known as the Cromwell Current, was discovered flowing eastward below the surface of the Pacific for 4,000 miles along the equator. In places it flows at depths of up to 1,300 feet. Its volume is 1,000 times the volume of the Mississippi.

Largest subterranean river   In August 1958, a crypto-river (or concealed river), tracked by radioisotopes, was discovered flowing under the Nile. Its mean annual flow was calculated to be 20 trillion cubic feet, or six times the flow of the Nile.

Longest waterway The longest transcontinental waterway is 6,637 miles long and links the Beaufort Sea in northern Canada with the Gulf of Mexico in the United States. It starts at Tuktoyaktuk on the Mackenzie River and ends at Port Eads on the Mississippi delta.

Largest swamp The world's largest tract of swamp is the Pantanal, in the states of Mato Grosso and Mato Grosso do Sul, Brazil. It is about 42,000 square miles in area.

Largest marsh The Everglades is a vast plateau of subtropical saw-grass marsh in southern Florida, covering 2,185 square miles. Fed by water from Lake Okeechobee, the Everglades is the largest subtropical wilderness in the continental United States.

Largest river bore At spring tides, the bore (wave of tidal water) on the Qiantong Jiang in China reaches a height of up to 25 feet and a speed of 13–15 knots. It can be heard advancing at a range of 14 miles.

The annual downstream flood wave on the Mekong, in southeast Asia, sometimes reaches a height of 46 feet.

Two views of the world's largest swamp, the Pantanal in Brazil. The swamp has many rivers with pronounced meanders. (*Jacana/P. Wild*)

LAKES

Largest lake   The Caspian Sea (in Azerbaijan, Russia, Kazakhstan, Turkmenistan and Iran) is the largest inland sea or lake. It is 760 miles long and covers 143,550 square miles. Its maximum depth is 3,360 feet and the surface is 93 feet below sea level.

United States   The largest lake entirely within the United States is Lake Michigan, with a surface area of 22,300 square miles, a length of 307 miles, a breadth of 118 miles and a maximum depth of 923 feet. Both Lake Superior and Lake Huron have larger areas, but they straddle the border between Canada and the United States.

Deepest lake   Lake Baikal in Siberia, Russia is 385 miles long and 20–46 miles wide. The deepest part of the lake, the Olkhon Crevice, is 5,371 feet deep.

United States   Crater Lake, a 6-mile-long lake in the Cascade Mountains of Oregon, is 1,932 feet deep at its deepest point, and has an average depth of 1,500 feet. Crater Lake has no inlets or outlets; it is filled by precipitation.

Highest lake   The highest navigable lake in the world is Lake Titicaca in Peru and Bolivia. The 100-mile-long lake is 12,506 feet above sea level, has a maximum depth of 1,214 feet, and covers 3,200 square miles.

There are higher lakes in the Himalayas, but most are temporary glacial lakes only. A survey of the area carried out in 1984 showed a lake at a highest-ever height of 17,762 feet, named Panch Pokhri, which was one mile long.

Largest freshwater lake   Measured by surface area, Lake Superior is the largest freshwater lake. It covers 31,800 square miles, of which 20,700 square miles are in Minnesota, Wisconsin and Michigan and 11,100 square miles are in Ontario, Canada.

The freshwater lake with the greatest volume is Lake Baikal in Siberia, Russia, with an estimated volume of 5,500 cubic miles. (See DEEPEST LAKE.)

Largest lagoon   Lagoa dos Patos, near the seashore in Rio Grande do Sul, Brazil, is 174 miles long and extends over 3,803 square miles, separated from the Atlantic Ocean by long sand strips. It has a maximum width of 44 miles.

Largest underground lake   The surface of the lake in the Drachenhauchloch cave, near Grootfontein, Namibia, is 217 feet underground, and its depth is 276 feet.

United States   The Lost Sea in the Craighead Caverns, Sweetwater, TN is 300 feet underground and covers 4$\frac{1}{2}$ acres.

Largest lake in a lake   The largest lake inside another lake is Manitou Lake (41.09 square miles) on the world's largest lake island, Manitoulin Island (1,068 square miles), in the Canadian part of Lake Huron. The lake itself contains a number of islands.

DESERTS

Largest desert   The Sahara in North Africa stretches 3,200 miles from east to west at its widest point. From north to south it is 800–1,400 miles long, and it covers about 3,579,000 square miles.

United States   The Mojave Desert is the largest in the United States. It covers approximately 15,000 square miles.

Largest sand dunes   The world's highest measured sand dunes are those in the Saharan sand sea of Isaouane-N-Tifernine of east-central Algeria. They have a wavelength of three miles and are as high as 1,525 feet.

The largest desert in the world, the Sahara, stretches into 11 countries. In Algeria (above), vehicles are dwarfed by the surrounding features. To the east, in Libya (center and top), the temperature reached a world record 136°F in the shade in 1922. (*Gamma/E. Bonnier; Gamma/Beziau-Boisberrange*)

ICE

It is estimated that 5,250,000 square miles, or 9.7 percent of the earth's land surface, is permanently glaciated. The Antarctic ice sheet accounts for 86 percent of this and the Greenland ice sheet for 11 percent.

Longest glacier   The Lambert Glacier, which drains about a fifth of the East Antarctic ice sheet, is up to 40 miles wide and, with its seaward extension, the Amery Ice Shelf, it measures at least 440 miles long.

Fastest glacier   The fastest-moving major glacier is the Columbia Glacier, between Valdez and Anchorage, AK, which travels an average of 65 feet per day.

Thickest ice   The greatest recorded thickness of ice is 2.97 miles, measured by radio echo soundings from a U.S. Antarctic research aircraft at 69° 56' 17" S, 135° 12' 9" E, 270 miles from the coast of Wilkes Land, Antarctica on January 4, 1975.

Deepest permafrost   A permafrost of more than 4,500 feet was reported from the upper reaches of the Viluy River, Siberia, Russia in February 1982.

Largest iceberg   A tabular iceberg 208 miles long and 60 miles wide was sighted 150 miles west of Scott Island, in the South Pacific Ocean, by the U.S.S. *Glacier* on November 12, 1956.

Tallest iceberg   In 1958, the U.S. icebreaker *East Wind* reported a 550-foot-high iceberg off western Greenland.

Most southerly arctic iceberg   An arctic iceberg was sighted in the Atlantic by a U.S.N. weather patrol at Lat. 28° 44' N (approximately the same latitude as Miami, FL), Long. 48° 42' W, in April 1935.

Most northerly antarctic iceberg   A remnant of an antarctic iceberg was seen in the Atlantic by the ship *Dochra* at Lat. 26° 30' S (approximately the same latitude as Rio de Janeiro, Brazil), Long. 25° 40' W, on April 30, 1894.

NATURAL PHENOMENA

EARTHQUAKES

It is estimated that each year there are some 500,000 detectable seismic or microseismic disturbances, of which 100,000 can be felt and 1,000 cause damage.

Strongest earthquake   The most commonly used measure of the size of an earthquake is its surface magnitude (M_s), based on amplitudes of surface waves, usually at a period of 20 seconds. The largest reported magnitudes on this scale, known as the Richter scale, are about 8.9, but the scale does not properly represent the size of the very largest earthquakes, above M_s about 8, for which it is better to use the concept of seismic moment, M_o, devised by K. Aki in 1966.

Moment can be used to derive a "moment magnitude," M_w, first used by Hiroo Kanamori in 1977. The largest recorded earthquake on the M_w scale is the Chilean shock of May 22, 1960, which had $M_w = 9.5$, but measured only 8.3 on the M_s scale.

United States The strongest earthquake in American history, measuring 8.4 on the Richter scale and 9.2 on the M_w scale, was near Prince William Sound, AK (80 miles east of Anchorage) on March 27, 1964. It killed 131 people and caused an estimated $750 million in damage; it also caused a tsunami 50 feet high that traveled 8,445 miles at 450 MPH. The town of Kodiak was destroyed, and tremors were felt in California, Hawaii and Japan.

Deadliest earthquake The greatest estimated death toll in an earthquake is the 830,000 fatalities in the Shaanxi, Shanxi and Henan provinces of China on February 2, 1556.

Most destructive earthquake The greatest physical devastation was in the earthquake on the Kanto plain, Japan, on September 1, 1923 (Mag. $M_s = 8.2$). In Tokyo and Yokohama, 575,000 dwellings were destroyed. The official total of people killed and missing in this quake and the resultant fires was 142,807.

United States The insured property loss of the Los Angeles earthquake of January 17, 1994 amounts to $2.5 billion. It is estimated that the overall loss could reach $20 billion, making it the third most expensive disaster ever for insurers. The earthquake measured 7.5 on the Richter scale.

VOLCANOES

Greatest explosion The greatest explosion in historic times occurred on August 27, 1883, with an eruption of Krakatoa, an island (then 18 square miles) in the Sunda Strait, between Sumatra and Java, in Indonesia. The explosion, which was about 26 times as powerful as the largest hydrogen bomb ever tested, wiped out 163 villages, and 36,380 people were killed by the wave it caused. Pumice was thrown 34 miles high and dust fell 3,313 miles away 10 days later. The explosion was recorded four hours later on

ERUPTION!

The ejecta in the Taupo eruption in New Zealand c. A.D. 130 has been estimated at 33 billion tons of pumice moving at one time at 400 MPH. It flattened 6,200 square miles. Less than 20 percent of the 15.4 billion tons of pumice carried up into the air in this most violent of all documented volcanic events fell within 125 miles of the vent.

The southernmost active volcano is Mt. Erebus, in Antarctica.
(*Jacana/J.-P. Ferrero*)

the island of Rodrigues, 2,968 miles away, as "the roar of heavy guns," and was heard over one-thirteenth of the surface of the globe.

Deadliest volcano   Volcanic activity in Tambora, Sumbawa, Indonesia in April 1815 killed about 92,000 people.

United States   The most deaths from a volcanic eruption in the United States was 60 people, on May 18, 1980 from the eruption of Mt. St. Helens, WA.

Greatest volume of discharge   The total volume of matter discharged in the eruption of Tambora, a volcano on the Indonesian island of Sumbawa, April 5–10 1815, was 36–43 cubic miles. A crater five miles in diameter was formed and the height of the island was lowered from 13,450 feet to 9,350 feet. More than 92,000 people were killed in the eruption, or died as a result of the subsequent famine.

Longest lava flow   The longest lava flow in historic times was a mixture of ropey lava and blocky lava resulting from the eruption of Laki in 1783 in southeast Iceland, which flowed 40½–43½ miles. The largest known prehistoric flow is the Roza basalt flow in North America c. 15 million years ago, which had an unsurpassed length (190 miles), area (15,400 square miles) and volume (300 cubic miles).

Largest active volcano   Of the 1,343 active volcanoes (many of which are submarine), Mauna Loa in Hawaii is the largest. It has the shape of a broad, gentle dome 75 miles long and 31 miles wide (above sea level), with lava flows that occupy more than 1,980 square miles of the island. It has a total volume of 10,200 cubic miles, of which 84.2 percent is below sea level. Its caldera or volcano crater, Mokuaweoweo, measures four square miles and is 500–600 feet deep. Mauna Loa rises 13,680 feet and has averaged one eruption every 4½ years since 1843, although none have occurred since 1984.

The only active volcano in the conterminous 48 states is Mt. St. Helens, located near Seattle, WA. There have been 25 registered eruptions over the past decade, the last on February 14, 1991. Mt. St. Helens was 9,677 feet high before its 1980 eruption; it now stands at 8,364 feet.

Highest active volcano   The highest volcano regarded as active is Ojos del Salado, at a height of 22,595 feet, on the frontier between Chile and Argentina.

Northernmost volcano   Beeren Berg (7,470 feet), on the island of Jan Mayen in the Greenland Sea, erupted on September 20, 1970, and the island's 39 inhabitants had to be evacuated.

Southernmost volcano   The most southerly active volcano is Mt. Erebus (12,447 feet), on Ross Island in Antarctica.

Largest volcano crater   The world's largest caldera or volcano crater is that of Toba, north-central Sumatra, Indonesia, covering 685 square miles.

AVALANCHES

Greatest avalanche   The greatest natural avalanches occur in the Himalayas, but they are rarely observed and no estimates of their volume have been published. It was estimated that 120 million cubic feet of snow fell in an avalanche in the Italian Alps in 1885.

United States   The 250-MPH avalanche triggered by the Mt. St. Helens eruption in Washington State on May 18, 1980 was estimated to measure 96 billion cubic feet.

GEYSERS

Tallest geyser   The Waimangu geyser in New Zealand erupted to a height of more than 1,500 feet in 1903. In August of that year, one eruption killed four people. Although the ground in the area is still hot, Waimangu itself has not been active since late 1904.

The tallest active geyser is the Steamboat Geyser in Yellowstone National Park, WY. In the 1980s, this geyser erupted at intervals ranging from 19 days to more than four years, although there were occasions in the 1960s when it erupted as frequently as every 4–10 days. Its maximum height is 195–380 feet.

WEATHER

The meteorological records given below relate mainly to the last 150–170 years, since data before that time is sparse and often unreliable.

The longest continuous observations have been maintained at the Rad-cliffe Observatory, Oxford, England since 1814, and on a daily basis since 1874, though discontinuous records have enabled the Chinese to assert that 903 B.C. was a very bad winter.

Lowest ozone levels   Ozone levels reached a record low between October 9 and 14, 1993 over the South Pole, when an average figure of 91 Dobson units (DU) was recorded. The minimum level needed to shield the earth from solar ultraviolet radiation is 300 DU.

Most equable temperature   Short period   The location with the most equable recorded temperature over a short period is Garapan, on Saipan in the Mariana Islands. From 1927 to 1935, the lowest temperature recorded was 67.3°F on January 30, 1934 and the highest was 88.5°F on September 9, 1931, giving an extreme range of 21.2°F.

Long period   Between 1911 and 1990, the Brazilian offshore island of Fernando de Noronha had a minimum temperature of 63.9°F on February 27, 1980 and a maximum of 90.0°F on March 3, 1968, December 25, 1972 and April 17, 1973, giving an extreme range of 26.1°F.

Greatest temperature range   The greatest recorded temperature ranges are around the Siberian "cold pole" in the east of Russia. Temperatures in Verkhoyansk (67° 33′ N, 133° 23′ E) have ranged 188 degrees, from –90°F to 98°F.

The greatest temperature variation recorded in a day is 100 degrees (a fall from 44°F to –56°F) in Browning, MT on January 23–24, 1916.

The most freakish rise was 49 degrees in two minutes in Spearfish, SD, from –4°F at 7:30 A.M. to 45°F at 7:32 A.M. on January 22, 1943.

Highest shade temperature   The highest shade temperature ever recorded is 136°F at Al'Aziziyah, Libya on September 13, 1922.

Hottest place   On an annual mean basis, with readings taken over a 6-year period from 1960 to 1966, the temperature at Dallol, in Ethiopia, was 94°F.

At Marble Bar, Western Australia (maximum temperature 120.5°F), 160 consecutive days with maximum temperatures of 100°F or higher were recorded between October 31, 1923 and April 7, 1924. At Wyndham, also in Western Australia, the temperature reached 90°F or more on 333 days in 1946.

United States   The highest temperature ever recorded in the United States was 134°F at Greenland Ranch, Death Valley, CA on July 10, 1913. In Death Valley, maximum temperatures of over 120°F were recorded on 43 consecutive days, between July 6 and August 17, 1917.

The highest annual mean temperature in the United States is 78.2°F at Key West, FL.

Driest place   The annual mean rainfall on the Pacific coast of Chile between Arica and Antofagasta is less than 0.004 inches.

United States   In 1929, no precipitation was recorded for Death Valley, CA. Currently, the driest state is Nevada, with an annual rainfall of only nine inches.

Longest drought   The Atacama Desert, in northern Chile, experiences virtually no rain, although several times a century a squall may strike a small area of it.

DID YOU KNOW?

The most intense drought in the United States lasted 57 months, from May 1952 to March 1957, in western Kansas. The Drought Severity Index reached a lowest point ever of –6.2, in September 1956. Below –4.0 on this index indicates extreme drought conditions.

Most sunshine   The annual average at Yuma, AZ is 91 percent of the possible hours of sunshine (a mean of 4,055 hours out of 4,456 possible hours in a year).

St. Petersburg, FL recorded 768 consecutive sunny days from February 9, 1967 to March 17, 1969.

Lowest screen temperature   A record low of –128.6°F was registered at Vostok, Antarctica (alt. 11,220 feet) on July 21, 1983.

The coldest permanently inhabited place is the village of Oymyakon, Siberia, Russia, where the temperature reached –90°F in 1933, and an unofficial –98°F has also been published more recently.

United States   The lowest temperature ever recorded in the United States was –79.8°F on January 23, 1971 in Prospect Creek, AK.

The lowest temperature in the conterminous states was –69.7°F in Rogers Pass, MT on January 20, 1954.

Coldest place   Polyus Nedostupnosti (Pole of Inaccessibility), Antarctica, at 78° S, 96° E, is the coldest location in the world, with an extrapolated annual mean of –72°F.

The coldest measured mean is –70°F, at Plateau Station, Antarctica.

United States   Langdon, ND had 41 days below 0°F, from November 11, 1935 to February 20, 1936. Langdon also holds the record for most consecutive days below 32°F, with 92 days from November 30, 1935 to February 29, 1936.

International Falls, MN has an annual mean temperature of 36.5°F, the lowest in the United States.

Wettest place   By average annual rainfall, the wettest place in the world is Mawsynram, in Meghalaya State, India, with 467½ inches per year.

United States   The wettest state is Louisiana, with an annual rainfall of 56 inches.

Most rainy days   Mt. Wai-'ale-'ale (5,148 feet), Kauai, HI has up to 350 rainy days per year.

Greatest rainfall A record 73.62 inches of rain fell in 24 hours in Cilaos (alt. 3,940 feet), Réunion, Indian Ocean on March 15 and 16, 1952. This is equal to 8,327 tons of rain per acre.

For a calendar month, the record is 366 inches, at Cherrapunji, Meghalaya, India in July 1861.

The 12-month record was also set at Cherrapunji, with 1,041.8 inches between August 1, 1860 and July 31, 1861.

United States In the United States, the 24-hour record is 19 inches in Alvin, TX, on July 25–26, 1979. Over a 12-month period, 739 inches fell in Kukui, Maui, HI from December 1981 to December 1982. The greatest annual rainfall in the conterminous states is 184.56 inches, in Wynoochee Oxbow, WA in 1931.

Cumulonimbus clouds have been observed at a record height of 68,000 feet in the tropics. These clouds are always dark at the bottom, indicating rain, snow or hail, and they are often associated with thunder and lightning. (*Jacana/ P. Pilloud*)

Longest-lasting rainbow A rainbow was continuously visible for six hours over Sheffield, England on March 14, 1994.

Worst flood damage As of August 10, 1993 it was reported that an estimated $12 billion in property and agricultural damage had been caused by the great Midwest flood of 1993. The flood affected nine states and covered an area estimated at twice the size of New Jersey.

Deadliest flood The most deaths from a flood in the United States was more than 2,000 people, in Johnstown, PA on May 31, 1889. The water formed a wall 20–30 feet high, rushing through the valley on the way to Johnstown at a rate of 15 MPH.

Greatest flood In 1993, scientists reported the discovery of the largest freshwater flood in history. It occurred *c.* 18,000 years ago when an ancient ice dam lake in the Altay Mountains in Siberia, Russia broke and allowed the water to pour out. The lake was estimated to be 75 miles long and 2,500 feet deep, and the main flow of water was probably about 1,600 feet deep and traveling at 100 MPH.

Windiest place Commonwealth Bay, George V Coast, Antarctica, where gales reach 200 MPH, is the world's windiest place.

Highest surface wind speed A surface wind speed of 231 MPH was recorded on Mt. Washington (6,288 feet), NH on April 12, 1934.

The fastest speed at a low altitude was registered on March 8, 1972 at the U.S.A.F. base in Thule, Greenland, when a peak speed of 207 MPH was recorded. The fastest speed measured to date in a tornado is 280 MPH in Wichita Falls, TX on April 2, 1958.

COSTLIEST HURRICANES IN U.S. HISTORY

Year	Hurricane	Area	Losses (in millions)
1992	Andrew	Florida, Louisiana	$46,500
1989	Hugo	Georgia to Virginia	$4,195
1992	Iniki	Hawaii	$1,600
1979	Frederic	Florida to New York	$752
1983	Alicia	Texas	$675
1991	Bob	New Jersey to Maine	$620
1985	Elena	Gulf region	$543
1965	Betsy	Gulf region	$515
1985	Gloria	North Carolina to Maine	$418
1970	Celia	Texas	$309

Source: Insurance Information Institute

Deadliest hurricane The greatest number of fatalities from an American hurricane is an estimated 6,000 deaths on September 8, 1900 in Galveston Island, TX.

Costliest hurricane Hurricane Andrew hit southern Florida on August 24, 1992, crossed the Gulf of Mexico and caused further destruction in Louisiana. The hurricane killed 76 people, left approximately 258,000 people homeless and caused an estimated $46.5 billion in damages, making it the most costly hurricane ever in the United States.

Fastest hurricane winds The fastest sustained winds in a hurricane in the United States measured 200 MPH, with 210-MPH gusts, on August 17–18, 1969, when Hurricane Camille hit the Mississippi–Alabama coast at Pass Christian, MS. Hurricane Camille also had the greatest storm surge in the United States.

Fastest-moving hurricane   The greatest forward speed by a hurricane in the United States was in excess of 60 MPH, with an average speed of 58 MPH, for the Great New England Hurricane on September 21, 1938, when it struck central Long Island at Babylon, NY. The hurricane continued on to landfall at Milford, CT.

Deadliest tornado   The most deaths from one tornado in the United States is 695, on March 18, 1925 in Missouri, Illinois and Indiana. This tornado also ranks first as the tornado with the longest continuous track on the ground, 219 miles; first with a 3.5-hour continuous duration on the ground; first in total area of destruction, covering 164 square miles; first in dimensions, with the funnel sometimes exceeding one mile wide; and third in forward speed, reaching a maximum of 73 MPH and averaging 62 MPH.

Most tornadoes   The state with the most tornadoes recorded in a year is Texas, with 232 in 1967.

Highest waterspout   On May 16, 1898, the highest waterspout was observed off Eden, New South Wales, Australia. A theodolite reading from the shore gave its height as 5,014 feet. It was about 10 feet in diameter.

Heaviest hailstones   The heaviest hailstones on record, weighing up to $2\frac{1}{4}$ pounds, reportedly killed 92 people in the Gopalganj district of Bangladesh on April 14, 1986.

United States   The heaviest hailstone in the United States weighed 1.671 pounds and had a circumference of 17.5 inches and a diameter of 5.62 inches. It fell in Coffeyville, KS on September 3, 1970.

Greatest snowfall   A total of $1,224\frac{1}{2}$ inches of snow fell over a 12-month period from February 19, 1971 to February 18, 1972 at Paradise, Mt. Rainier, WA.

The record for a single snowstorm is 189 inches at Mt. Shasta Ski Bowl, CA, February 13–19, 1959, and for a 24-hour period, the record snowfall is 78 inches, at Mile 47 Camp, Cooper River Division, AK on February 7, 1963.

The greatest depth of snow on the ground was 37 ft. 7 in. in Tamarac, CA in March 1911.

Highest clouds   The highest standard cloud form is cirrus, averaging 29,500 feet, but the rare nacreous or mother-of-pearl formation may reach nearly 80,000 feet.

The cloud form with the greatest vertical range is cumulonimbus, which has been observed to reach a height of nearly 68,000 feet in the tropics.

Lowest clouds   The lowest cloud form is stratus, which occurs below 1,500 feet.

Coldest atmosphere temperature   The lowest temperature ever recorded in the atmosphere is –279°F at an altitude of 56 miles. This is in the region of noctilucent cloud formation in the mesosphere.

Most thunder-days   In Tororo, Uganda an average of 251 days of thunder per year was recorded for the 10-year period 1967–76.

Most times struck by lightning Ex-park ranger Roy C. Sullivan was struck by lightning seven times. His attraction for lightning began in 1942, when he lost his big toenail. Sullivan was hit again in July 1969 (lost eyebrows), in July 1970 (left shoulder seared), on April 16, 1972 (hair set on fire), on August 7, 1973 (hair set on fire again and legs seared), and on June 5, 1976 (ankle injured), and he was sent to Waynesboro Hospital, Waynesboro, VA with chest and stomach burns on June 25, 1977 after being struck while fishing.

Foggiest place Sea-level fogs—with visibility less than 0.56 miles—persist for weeks on the Grand Banks, Newfoundland, Canada. The average is more than 120 days of fog per year.

United States Cape Disappointment, WA has an average of 2,552 hours (or 106 complete days) of heavy fog per year.

Largest mirage The biggest mirage on record was sighted in the Arctic at 83° N 103° W by Donald B. MacMillan in 1913. This type of mirage, known as the Fata Morgana, appeared as the same "hills, valleys, snow-capped peaks extending through at least 120 degrees of the horizon" that Peary had misidentified as Crocker Land six years earlier.

On July 17, 1939, a mirage of the mountain Snaefellsjökull (4,744 feet) on Iceland was seen from the sea at a distance of 335–350 miles.

Highest pressure The highest barometric pressure ever recorded was 32 inches at Agata, Siberia, Russia (alt. 862 feet) on December 31, 1968.

United States The highest barometric pressure recorded in the United States was 31.43 inches in Barrow, AK on January 3, 1970. The highest in the conterminous states was 31.40 inches, in Helena, MT on January 9, 1962.

Lowest pressure The lowest sea-level barometric pressure was 25.69 inches in Typhoon Tip, 300 miles west of Guam, Pacific Ocean, at Lat. 16° 44′ N, Long. 137° 46′ E, on October 12, 1979.

United States The lowest barometric pressure recorded in the United States was 26.35 inches for the 1935 Labor Day Hurricane, which crossed the U.S. coastline at Matecumbe Key, FL at 10:00 P.M. on September 2, 1935.

GEMS AND PRECIOUS METALS

AMBER

Largest piece of amber *Burma Amber* weighs 33 lb. 10 oz. and is located in the Natural History Museum, London, England.

DIAMONDS

Largest diamond   *The Cullinan*, weighing 3,106 carats, was found on January 26, 1905 in the Premier Mine, Pretoria, South Africa. It was later cut into 106 polished diamonds and produced the largest cut fine quality colorless diamond, weighing 530.2 carats.

The largest known single piece of rough diamond still in existence weighs 1,462 carats and is retained by De Beers Central Selling Organization in London, England.

Largest cut diamond   The 545.67-carat gem known as the *Unnamed Brown* was made from a 775.5-carat rough into a fire rose cushion cut. The stone was found at the Premier Diamond Mine and designed by master cutter Gabi Tolkowsky. The *Unnamed Brown* was the forerunner to the *Centenary Diamond*, the world's largest flawless top color modern fancy cut diamond at 273.85 carats.

Smallest cut diamond   A 0.0000743-carat diamond fashioned by Pauline Willemse at Coster Diamonds B.V., Amsterdam, Netherlands, 1991–94, is 0.0063–0.0067 inches in diameter and 0.0043 inches high—smaller than the average grain of sand.

Highest-priced diamond   Many polished diamond sales are considered private transactions, and the prices paid are not disclosed. An 11-sided pear-shaped mixed-cut diamond of 101.84 carats was bought at Sotheby's, Geneva, Switzerland on November 14, 1990 for $12,760,000.

The highest price paid for a rough diamond was $10 million for a 255.1-carat stone from Guinea, by the William Goldberg Diamond Corporation

The largest flawless fancy cut diamond, the *Centenary Diamond*, was found at the Premier Diamond Mine in South Africa and designed by master cutter Gabi Tolkowsky. (*De Beers*)

in partnership with the Chow Tai Fook Jewelery Co. Ltd. of Hong Kong, in March 1989.

The record per carat is $926,315 for a 0.95-carat fancy purplish-red stone sold at Christie's, New York on April 28, 1987.

EMERALDS

Largest cut emerald   An 86,136-carat natural beryl was found in Carnaiba, Brazil in August 1974. It was carved by Richard Chan in Hong Kong and valued at £718,000 ($1,120,080) in 1982.

Largest emerald crystal   The largest single emerald crystal of gem quality, weighing 7,025 carats, was found in 1969 at the Cruces Mine, Gachala, Colombia. It is now privately owned.

Highest-priced emerald   The highest price paid for a single lot of emeralds was $3,080,000, for an emerald and diamond necklace made by Cartier, London, England in 1937 (a total of 12 stones weighing 108.74 carats), which was sold at Sotheby's, New York on October 26, 1989.

The highest price for a single emerald is $2,126,646, for a 19.77-carat emerald and diamond ring made by Cartier in 1958, which was sold at Sotheby's, Geneva, Switzerland on April 2, 1987. This also represented the record price per carat for an emerald, at $107,569.

GOLD

Largest mass of gold   The 7,560-ounce *Holtermann Nugget*, found in 1872 in the Beyers & Holtermann Star of Hope mine, Hill End, New South Wales, Australia, contained 220 pounds of gold in a 630-pound slate slab.

Largest pure gold nugget   The *Welcome Stranger*, found at Moliagul, Victoria, Australia in 1869, yielded 2,248 troy ounces of pure gold from 2,280¹/₄ ounces.

JADE

Largest piece of jade   A single lens of nephrite jade weighing 636 tons was found in the Yukon Territory of Canada in July 1992. It is owned by Yukon Jade Ltd.

OPALS

Largest opal   The largest gem-quality white opal was 26,350 carats, found in July 1989 at the Jupiter Field at Coober Pedy in South Australia. It has been named *Jupiter-Five* and is in private ownership.

Largest black opal   A stone found on February 4, 1972 at Lightning Ridge, New South Wales, Australia produced a finished gem of 1,520 carats, called the *Empress of Glengarry*. It measures 4³/₄ by 3¹/₈ by ⁵/₈ inches, and is owned by Clive Heard of Sydney, Australia.

Largest rough black opal   The largest gem-quality uncut black opal was also found at Lightning Ridge, on November 3, 1986. After cleaning, it weighs 1,982.5 carats and measures 4 by $2^5/_8$ by $2^1/_2$ inches. It has been named *Halley's Comet* and is owned by a team of opal miners known as The Lunatic Hill Syndicate.

PEARLS

Largest pearl The 14-lb.-1-oz. *Pearl of Lao-tze* was found at Palawan, Philippines on May 7, 1934 in the shell of a giant clam. This $9^1/_2$-inch-long by $5^1/_2$-inch-diameter pearl was bought at auction on May 15, 1980 in San Francisco, CA by Peter Hoffman and Victor Barbish for $200,000.

Largest abalone pearl A baroque abalone pearl measuring $2^3/_4$ by 2 by $1^1/_8$ inches and weighing 469.13 carats was found at Salt Point State Park, CA in May 1990. It is owned by Wesley Rankin and is called the *Big Pink*.

Largest cultured pearl A $1^1/_2$-inch round, 138.25-carat cultured pearl weighing 1 ounce was found near Samui Island, off Thailand, in January 1988. It is owned by the Mikimoto Pearl Island Company, Japan.

Highest-priced pearl La Régente, an egg-shaped pearl weighing 302.68 grains and formerly part of the French crown jewels, was sold at Christie's, Geneva, Switzerland on May 12, 1988 for $864,280.

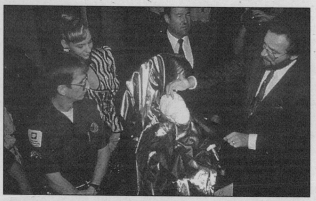

The world's largest pearl, the *Pearl of Lao-tze*. The San Francisco Gem Laboratory appraised it in 1984 and estimated its retail replacement value to be $40–42 million. (*Gamma/Sander/Liaison*)

PLATINUM

Largest platinum nugget The largest nugget of platinum ever found weighed 340 ounces and was discovered in the Ural Mountains in Russia in 1843. It was melted down shortly after its discovery.

The largest surviving platinum nugget, the *Ural Giant*, weighs 277 ounces and is currently in the custody of the Diamond Foundation in the Kremlin, Moscow, Russia.

RUBIES

Largest star ruby   The *Eminent Star* ruby, believed to be of Indian origin, is the largest ruby, at 6,465 carats. It is an oval cabochon with a six-ray star, and measures 4¼ by 3⅝ by 2¼ inches. It is owned by Kailash Rawat of Eminent Gems Inc. of New York.

Highest-priced ruby   A ruby and diamond ring made by Chaumet, in Paris, France, weighs 32.08 carats and was sold at Sotheby's, New York on October 26, 1989 for $4,620,000. The record per carat is $227,300 for a ruby ring with a stone weighing 15.97 carats, which was sold at Sotheby's, New York on October 18, 1988.

SAPPHIRES

Largest star sapphire   The 9,719.5-carat gem *The Lone Star* was cut in London, England in November 1989 and is now owned by Harold Roper.

Highest-priced sapphire   A step-cut stone of 62.02 carats was sold as part of a sapphire and diamond ring at Sotheby's, St. Moritz, Switzerland on February 20, 1988 for $2,791,723.

TOPAZ

Largest topaz   The rectangular cushion-cut 22,892.5-carat *American Golden Topaz*, with 172 facets and 5⅞ inches in overall width, has been on display at the Smithsonian Institution, Washington, D.C. since May 4, 1988.

SCIENCE & TECHNOLOGY

ELEMENTS

SUBATOMIC PARTICLES

Heaviest particle   The heaviest particle whose existence is accepted is the neutral weak gauge boson, the $Z°$, of mass 91.19 GeV and lifetime 2.64×10^{-25} seconds, the shortest lifetime of any particle.

Lightest particle   The photon and the theoretically predicted graviton are both expected to have as close to zero mass as is possible within current cosmological models.

Most stable particle   Experiments indicate that the lifetime of the most likely decay mode of a proton (to a positron and a neutral pion) has a lower limit of 3.1×10^{32} years.

Least stable particle   The shortest-lived subatomic particle is the boson ($Z°$), with a lifetime of 2.64×10^{-25} seconds.

THE ELEMENTS

Of the 111 known elements, the first 94 exist naturally. At room temperature the elements comprise 2 liquids, 11 gases and 85 known solids. Elements 85, 87 and 101 to 111 would also be solid at room temperature if they could be obtained in a coherent form.

Rarest natural element   Only 0.0056 ounces of astatine (At) is present in the earth's crust; the isotope astatine 215 (At 215) accounts for only 1.6×10^{-10} ounces. The least abundant element in the atmosphere is the radioactive gas radon (Rn), with a volume of 6×10^{-18} parts by volume.

Most common element   Hydrogen (H) accounts for over 90 percent of all known matter in the universe and 70.68 percent by mass in the solar system.

The commonest element in the earth's atmosphere is nitrogen (N), which is present at 78.08 percent by volume (75.52 percent by mass), and iron (Fe) is the most common element in the earth itself, accounting for 36 percent of the planet's mass.

Newest element   Element 111, provisional name unununium (literally one-one-one; Uuu), was discovered on a 3-atom basis in December 1994 at the Gesellschaft für Schwerionenforschung, Darmstadt, Germany by a joint German, Russian, Slovakian and Finnish team. Element 110, provisional name ununnilium (Uun), was discovered only a month earlier in the same laboratory.

Highest and lowest density   *Solid*   The densest solid at room temperature is osmium (Os) at 0.8161 pounds per cubic inch. The least dense element at room temperature is the metal lithium (Li) at 0.01927 pounds per cubic

Scientists recognize particles by their electronic signatures. These are shown graphically by computers in displays like this one. (*Science Photo Library/P. Loiez, CERN*)

inch, although the density of solid hydrogen at its melting point of −434.546°F is only 0.00315 pounds per cubic inch.

Gas The densest gas at NTP (Normal Temperature and Pressure, 0°C and one atmosphere) is radon (Rn) at 0.6274 pounds per cubic foot. The lightest gas is hydrogen (H) at 0.005612 pounds per cubic foot.

Highest melting and boiling points Metallic tungsten or wolfram (W) melts at 6,177°F. The graphite form of carbon (C) sublimes directly to vapor at 6,699°F and can only be obtained as a liquid above a temperature of 8,546°F and a pressure of 100 atmospheres.

Lowest melting and boiling points Helium (He) cannot be obtained as a solid at atmospheric pressure. The minimum pressure necessary is 24.985 atmospheres at −458.275°F. Helium also has the lowest boiling point, at −458.275°F. For metallic elements, mercury (Hg) has the lowest melting and boiling points, at −37.892°F and 673.92°F respectively.

Purest element In April 1978, P.V.E. McClintock of the University of Lancaster, Lancaster, England reported success in obtaining the isotope helium 4 (He-4) with impurity levels at less than two parts in 10^{15}.

Hardest element The carbon (C) allotrope diamond has a Knoop value of 8,400.

Highest and lowest thermal expansion The metal with the highest expansion is cesium (Cs), at 94×10^{-5} per degree C, while the diamond allotrope of carbon (C) has the lowest expansion at 1.0×10^{-6} per degree C.

Most ductile element One ounce of gold (Au) can be drawn to a length of 43 miles.

Highest tensile strength Boron (B) has the highest tensile strength, at 5.7 GPa 8.3×10^5 lbf/in.[2].

Strongest pure metal The strongest pure metal appears to be iridium (Ir) with a typical tensile strength of 550 MPa (8.0×10^4 lbf/in.[2]) although values as high as 2.5 GPa (3.6×10^5 lbf/in.[2]) have been reported for hot drawn wire.

Shortest and longest liquid ranges Based on the differences between melting and boiling points, the element with the shortest liquid range (on the Celsius scale) is the inert gas neon (Ne), at only 2.542 degrees (from −248.594°C to −246.052°C [−415.469°F to −410.894°F]). The radioactive element neptunium (Np) has the longest liquid range, at 3,453 degrees (from 637°C to 4,090°C [1,179°F to 7,394°F]).

Most toxic element The severest restriction placed on any element in the form of a radioactive isotope is 2.4×10^{-16} g/m³ in air for thorium 228 (Th-228) or radiothorium. The most severely restricted nonradioactive element is beryllium, with a threshold limit value in air of only 2 g/m³.

ISOTOPES

Most and fewest isotopes There are at least 2,570 isotopes, and cesium (Cs) has the most, with 37. The greatest number of stable isotopes is 10, for the metallic element tin (Sn). Hydrogen (H) has the fewest accepted isotopes, with just three.

Lightest and heaviest isotopes The lightest nuclide is hydrogen 1 (H-1) or protium, and the heaviest is unununium 272 (Uuu-272).

Most and least stable isotopes The most stable radioactive isotope is the double-beta decaying tellurium 128 (Te-128), with a half-life of 1.5×10^{24} years. Lithium 5 (Li-5) is the least stable, with a lifetime of 4.4×10^{-22} seconds.

CHEMICAL EXTREMES

Strongest acid The strongest super acid is an 80 percent solution of antimony pentafluoride in hydrofluoric acid (fluoroantimonic acid HF: SbF_5). This solution has not been measured directly, but even a 50 percent solution is 10^{18} times stronger than concentrated sulfuric acid.

Bitterest substance The bitterest-tasting substances are based on the denatonium cation and have been produced commercially as benzoate and saccharide. Taste detection levels are as low as one part in 500 million, and a dilution of one part in 100 million will leave a lingering taste.

Sweetest substance Talin from katemfe (*Thaumatococcus daniellii*), discovered in West Africa, is 6,150 times as sweet as a one percent sucrose solution.

Smelliest substance The most evil of the 17,000 smells so far classified may be a matter of opinion, but ethyl mercaptan (C_2H_5SH) and butyl selenomercaptan (C_4H_9SeH) are pungent claimants, each with a smell reminiscent of a combination of rotting cabbage, garlic, onions, burned toast and sewer gas.

Most powerful nerve gas Ethyl S-2-diisopropylaminoethylmethylphosphonothiolate or VX, developed at the Chemical Defense Experimental Establishment, Porton Down, England in 1952, is 300 times more powerful than the phosgene ($COCl_2$) used in World War I. The lethal dosage is 10 mg-minute per cubic meter airborne or 0.3 mg orally.

DID YOU KNOW?

The most lethal man-made chemical is TCDD (2, 3, 7, 8-tetrachlorodibenzo-p-dioxin), the most dangerous of the 75 known dioxins, which is 150,000 times more deadly than cyanide.

Most absorbent substance "H-span" or Super Slurper, composed of one-half starch derivative and one-fourth each of acrylamide and acrylic acid, can, when treated with iron, retain water 1,300 times its own weight.

Most refractory substance The most refractory substance is tantalum carbide ($TaC_{0.88}$), which melts at 7,214°F.

Most heat-resistant substance The existence of a complex material known as NFAARr or Ultra Hightech Starlite was announced in April 1993. Invented by Maurice Ward (Great Britain), it can temporarily resist plasma temperature (18,032°F).

Highest superconducting temperature In April 1993, bulk superconductivity with a transition to zero resistance at −221.3°F was achieved at the Laboratorium für Festkörperphysik, Zurich, Switzerland, in a mixture of oxides of mercury, barium, calcium and copper, $HgBa_2Ca_2Cu_3O_{1+x}$ and $HgBa_2CaCu_2O_{6+x}$.

Least dense solids Silica aerogels are composed of tiny spheres of bonded silicon and oxygen atoms, joined into long strands separated by pockets of air. In February 1990, the lightest of these aerogels, with a density of only five ounces per cubic foot, was produced at Lawrence Livermore Laboratory in California. The main use will be in space to collect micrometeoroids and the debris present in comets' tails.

Longest index The 12th collective index of *Chemical Abstracts*, completed in December 1992, contains 35,137,626 entries in 215,880 pages and 115 volumes and weighs 544 pounds. It provides references to 3,052,700 published documents in the field of chemistry.

PHYSICAL EXTREMES

Highest temperature   The highest temperature produced in a laboratory is 920,000,000°F on May 27, 1994, in the Tokamak Fusion Test Reactor at the Princeton University Plasma Physics Laboratory, Princeton, NJ using a deuterium-tritium plasma mix (see GREATEST FUSION POWER).

Hottest flame   The hottest-burning substance is carbon subnitride (C_4N_2), which, at one atmosphere pressure, can produce a flame calculated to reach 9,010°F.

Lowest temperature   Absolute zero, 0 K on the Kelvin scale, corresponds to −459.67°F. The lowest temperature ever reached is 2.8×10^{-10}K in a nuclear demagnetization device at the Low Temperature Laboratory, Helsinki University of Technology, Finland, announced in February 1993.

SLIPPERY!

The most efficient lubricant is Tufoil, manufactured by Fluoramics Inc. of Mahwah, NJ. It has a coefficient of friction of .029.

Highest pressure   A sustained laboratory pressure of 170 GPa (11,000 tons per square inch) was achieved in the giant hydraulic diamond-faced press at the Carnegie Institution's Geophysical Laboratory, Washington, D.C. and reported in June 1978.

Using dynamic methods and impact speeds of up to 18,000 MPH, momentary pressures of 7,000 GPa (540,000 tons per square inch) were reported in the United States in 1958.

Highest vacuum   In January 1991, K. Odaka and S. Ueda of Japan reported having obtained a vacuum of 7×10^{-16} atmospheres in a stainless steel chamber.

Lowest friction   The lowest coefficient of static and dynamic friction of any solid is 0.03, for Hi-T-Lube with an MOS2 burnished (B) exterior. The 0.03 result was achieved by sliding Hi-T-Lube (B) against Hi-T-Lube (B). This material was developed for NASA in 1965 by General Magnaplate Corp., Linden, NJ and has been used on many space projects.

Highest velocity   The highest velocity at which any solid visible object has been projected is 93 miles per second (334,800 MPH) in the case of a plastic disc at the Naval Research Laboratory, Washington, D.C., in August 1980.

Most magnetic substance   The most magnetic substance is neodymium iron boride ($Nd_2Fe_{14}B$) with a maximum energy product (the highest energy that a magnet can supply when operating at a particular operating point) of up to 280 kJ per cubic meter.

Strongest magnetic field   The strongest continuous field strength achieved was a total of 35.3 ± 0.3 teslas at the Francis Bitter National Magnet Laboratory, Massachusetts Institute of Technology, Cambridge, MA, on May 26, 1988, employing a hybrid magnet with holmium pole pieces.

Weakest magnetic field   The weakest magnetic field measured is one of 8×10^{-15} teslas in the heavily shielded room at the same laboratory. It is used for research into the very weak magnetic field generated in the heart and brain.

Most powerful electric current   If they were fired simultaneously, the 4,032 capacitors comprising the Zeus capacitor at the Los Alamos Scientific Laboratory, NM would produce, for a few microseconds, twice as much current as that generated anywhere else on earth.

Highest voltage   The highest potential difference obtained in a laboratory was 32 ± 1.5 million volts by the National Electrostatistics Corporation, Oak Ridge, TN on May 17, 1979.

Brightest light   The brightest artificial sources are laser pulses generated at the Los Alamos National Laboratory in New Mexico, announced in March 1987. An ultraviolet flash lasting one picosecond (1×10^{-12} seconds) is intensified to a power of 5×10^{15} watts.

The most powerful searchlight ever developed was one produced during World War II by the General Electric Company Ltd. at the Hirst Research Center in London, England. It had a consumption of 600 kW and a maximum beam intensity of 2.7 billion candles from its parabolic mirror (diameter 10 feet).

Highest measured frequency   The highest *directly* measured frequency is a visible yellow-green light at 520.2068085 terahertz (a terahertz being a million million hertz) for the o-component of the 17–1 P (62) transition line of iodine-127.

The highest measured frequency determined by precision metrology is a green light at 582.491703 terahertz for the b_{21} component of the R (15) 43–0 transition line of iodine-127.

Smallest hole   Holes with a diameter of 3.16 Å (3.16×10^{-10} m) were produced on the surface of molybdenum disulphide by Dr. Wolfgang Henkl of the University of Munich, Germany and Dr. John Maddocks of the University of Sheffield, England, using a chemical method involving a mercury drill. The holes were drilled on July 17, 1992 at the University of Munich.

Longest echo   The longest echo in any building is one of 15 seconds following the closing of the door of the Chapel of the Mausoleum, Hamilton, Scotland, built 1840–55.

SCIENTIFIC INSTRUMENTS

Largest scientific instrument   The Large Electron–Positron (LEP) storage ring at CERN, Geneva, Switzerland is 12½ feet in diameter and 17 miles in circumference.

Finest balance   The Sartorius Model 4108, manufactured in Göttingen, Germany, can weigh objects of up to 0.018 ounces to an accuracy of 3.5×10^{-10} ounces, equivalent to little more than ¹/₆₀th of the weight of the ink on this period.

Oldest measures   The oldest known measure of weight is the *beqa* of the Amratian period of Egyptian civilization *c.* 3800 B.C., found at Naqada, Egypt. The weights are cylindrical, with rounded ends, and weigh 6.65–7.45 ounces.

Smallest thermometer   Dr. Frederich Sachs, a biophysicist at the State University of New York at Buffalo, developed an ultra-microthermometer for measuring the temperature of single living cells. The tip is one micron in diameter, about ¹/₅₀th the diameter of a human hair.

Largest barometer   An oil-filled barometer, of overall height 42 feet, was constructed by Allan Mills and John Pritchard of the Department of Physics and Astronomy, University of Leicester, Leicester, England in 1991. It attained a standard height of 40 feet (at which pressure mercury would stand at 2½ feet).

Smallest microphone   Prof. Ibrahim Kavrak of Bogazici University, Istanbul, Turkey developed a microphone for a new technique of pressure measurement in fluid flow in 1967. It has a frequency response of 10 Hz–10 kHz and measures 0.06 by 0.03 inches.

Finest cut   The $13 million large optics diamond turning machine at the Lawrence Livermore National Laboratory, California was reported in June 1983 to be able to sever a human hair 3,000 times lengthwise.

Thinnest glass   The thinnest glass, type D263, has a minimum thickness of 0.00098 inches and a maximum thickness of 0.00137 inches. It is made by Deutsche Spezialglas AG, Grünenplan, Germany for use in electronic and medical equipment.

Largest sheet of glass   The biggest sheet of glass ever manufactured was one of 540 square feet, or 65 ft. 7 in. by 8 ft. 2¼ in., exhibited by the Saint Gobain Co. in France at the *Journées Internationales de Miroiterie* in March 1958.

FERMILAB

PARTICLE ACCELERATOR

An aerial view of Fermilab (Fermi National Accelerator Laboratory) in Batavia, IL, showing the 4-mile-circumference ring, which houses the world's highest-energy particle accelerator—the Tevatron. (*Fermilab Visual Media Services*)

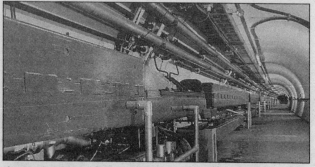

The tunnel of the Main Accelerator at Fermilab. The upper ring of conventional magnets comprises the fourth stage of particle acceleration. The particle beam can then be injected into the Tevatron, which is composed of superconducting magnets, designed to accelerate the protons to energies approaching 1 TeV (1×10^{12} eV)—almost the speed of light. (*Fermilab Visual Media Services*)

The Collider Detector at Fermilab weighs approximately 5,000 tons and stands more than three stories tall. It is used to detect and measure the particles produced in collisions between protons and antiprotons. (*Gamma/Fermilab/Liaison*)

Largest blown glass vessel   A bottle standing 7 ft. 8 in. tall with a capacity of about 188 gallons was blown at Wheaton Village, Millville, NJ on September 26–27, 1992 by a team led by glass artist Steve Tobin. The attempt was made during the "South Jersey Glass Blast," part of a celebration of the local glassmaking heritage.

Sharpest objects   The sharpest manufactured objects are glass micropipette tubes whose beveled tips have an outer diameter of 0.02 μm and an 0.01-μm inner diameter. The latter is 6,500 times thinner than a human hair. The tubes are used in intracellular work on living cells.

Smallest optical prism   A glass prism with 0.001-inch sides—barely visible to the naked eye—was created at the National Institute of Standards and Technology laboratories in Boulder, CO in 1989.

Most powerful microscope   The scanning tunneling microscope (STM) invented at the IBM Zürich research laboratory, Switzerland, in 1981 has a magnification of 100 million times and a resolution of $^1/_{100}$th the diameter of an atom (3×10^{-10} m), making it the world's most powerful microscope.

Most powerful laser   The "Nova" laser at the Lawrence Livermore National Laboratory, California produces laser pulses capable of generating 100×10^{12} W of power, much of which is delivered to a target the size of a grain of sand in 1×10^{-9} seconds. For this instant, that power is 200 times greater than the combined output of all the electrical generating plants in the United States. The laser itself is 300 feet long and about three stories high.

Most powerful particle accelerator   The world's highest-energy "atom-smasher" is the 1.25-mile-diameter proton synchroton "Tevatron" at the Fermi National Accelerator Laboratory (Fermilab) near Batavia, IL. On January 3, 1987 a center of mass energy of 1.8 TeV (1.8×10^{12} eV) was achieved by colliding beams of protons and antiprotons.

Fastest centrifuge   The highest rotary speed ever achieved is 4,500 MPH by a tapered 6-inch carbon fiber rod in a vacuum at Birmingham University, Birmingham, England, reported in January 1975.

Heaviest magnet   The heaviest magnet is in the Joint Institute for Nuclear Research at Dubna, near Moscow, Russia, in the 10 GeV synchrophasotron measuring 196 feet in diameter and weighing 42,000 tons.

Largest electromagnet   The octagonal electromagnet in the L3 detector, an experiment on LEP (Large Electron–Positron collider), consists of 7,055 tons of low carbon steel yoke and 1,213 tons of aluminum coil. Thirty thousand amperes of current flow through the aluminum coil to create a uniform magnetic field of five kilogauss. The total weight of the magnet, including the frame, coil and inner support tube, is 7,810 tons, and it is composed of more metal than is contained in the Eiffel Tower.

MATHEMATICS

In dealing with large numbers, scientists use the notation of 10 raised to various powers to eliminate a profusion of zeros. For example, 19,160,000,000,000 miles would be written as 1.916×10^{13} miles. Similarly, a very small number, for example 0.0000154324 grams, would be written as 1.54324×10^{-5} grams.

Largest numbers   The largest lexicographically accepted named number in the system of successive powers of 10 is the centillion, first recorded in 1852. It is the hundredth power of a million, or 1 followed by 600 zeros.

GUESS WHAT?

Q. HOW LONG IS THE LONGEST WORD IN ENGLISH?

A. LOOK IN "WORDS" (ARTS & ENTERTAINMENT)

Highest prime number   The highest known prime number was discovered by David Slowinski and Paul Gage at Cray Research Inc. in Eagan, MN in January 1994, while they were conducting tests on a CRAY C90 Series supercomputer. This prime number has 258,716 digits, enough to fill over 21 pages of *The Guinness Book of Records*. In mathematical notation it is expressed as $2^{859,433} - 1$, which denotes two multiplied by itself 859,433 times, minus one. Numbers expressed in this form are known as Mersenne prime numbers, named after Father Marin Mersenne, a 17th-century French monk who spent years searching for prime numbers of this type.

The largest known twin primes are $1,706,595 \times 2^{11,235} - 1$ and $1,706,595 \times 2^{11,235} + 1$, found on August 6, 1989 by a team in Santa Clara, CA.

Lowest composite number   The lowest nonprime or composite number (excluding 1) is 4.

Lowest and highest perfect numbers   A number is said to be perfect if it is equal to the sum of its divisors other than itself, e.g., $1 + 2 + 4 + 7 + 14 = 28$. The lowest perfect number is 6 ($= 1 + 2 + 3$).

The highest known perfect number is $(2^{859,433} - 1) \times 2^{859,433}$. It has a total of 517,430 digits (enough to fill over 41 pages of *The Guinness Book of Records*), and it is derived from the largest known Mersenne prime (see HIGHEST PRIME NUMBER).

Newest mathematical constant   The study of turbulent water, the weather and other chaotic phenomena has revealed the existence of a new universal constant, the Feigenbaum number. Named after its discoverer, Mitchell Feigenbaum (U.S.), it equals approximately 4.669201609102990.

THE MARGINAL LEGACY

Fermat's Last Theorem is the Mount Everest of mathematics. It says that although a perfect square can be the sum of two other perfect squares (for example, $5^2 = 3^2 + 4^2$), a perfect cube is never the sum of two perfect cubes, and so on; whatever the value of n, the equation $x^n + y^n = z^n$ has no solution in whole numbers.

Pierre de Fermat (1601–65) was a magistrate, and a wonderful amateur mathematician. He inspired centuries of hopeless searching when he wrote the theorem in a notebook, adding, "I have found an admirable proof of this theorem, but the margin is too narrow to contain it."

Since Fermat's death in 1665, hundreds of mathematicians, from famous professionals to enthusiastic amateurs, have tried, but failed, to prove his theorem. In 1908, a German mathematician named Wolfskehl left a prize of 100,000 marks for the first proof of Fermat's Last Theorem; the value of the prize vanished in the inflation of the 1930s, but for a while Wolfskehl's well-publicized generosity produced a deluge of false arguments.

The mathematician Edmund Landau even had a standard form produced, for replying to the countless correspondents who naively claimed to have proved Fermat's Last Theorem. It read: "On page____, lines ____ to ____, you will find a mistake." The forms were filled in by Landau's graduate students.

On June 23, 1993, it was announced that Professor Andrew Wiles, British-born professor of mathematics at Princeton University, had finally solved Fermat's Theorem. He had been intrigued by the problem since he first came across it as a child, and, fearing that someone else would find the solution first—mathematicians can be extremely competitive—or that his efforts would be laughed at, he worked in secret for eight years to produce a solution.

Unfortunately, Wiles soon admitted that there was a gap in his proof. However, the news at the start of 1995 was that Professor Wiles had filled the gap and was writing up his proof, which is several hundred pages long. This could be the end of the story—except that as with all important mathematics, one step forward prepares the way for further steps into the unknown.

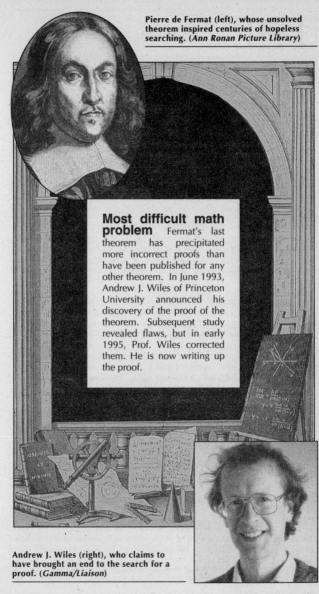

Pierre de Fermat (left), whose unsolved theorem inspired centuries of hopeless searching. (*Ann Ronan Picture Library*)

Most difficult math problem

Fermat's last theorem has precipitated more incorrect proofs than have been published for any other theorem. In June 1993, Andrew J. Wiles of Princeton University announced his discovery of the proof of the theorem. Subsequent study revealed flaws, but in early 1995, Prof. Wiles corrected them. He is now writing up the proof.

Andrew J. Wiles (right), who claims to have brought an end to the search for a proof. (*Gamma/Liaison*)

WRONG!

In 1897, the General Assembly of Indiana put forward the least accurate version of *pi* when it enacted Bill No. 246, stating that *pi* was *de jure* 4.

Most difficult math problem   Fermat's last theorem has precipitated more incorrect proofs than have been published for any other theorem. Pierre de Fermat inspired centuries of hopeless searching when he wrote the theorem in a notebook, adding, "I have found an admirable proof of this theorem, but the margin is too narrow to contain it." In June 1993, Andrew J. Wiles of Princeton University announced his discovery of the proof of the theorem. Subsequent study revealed flaws, but in early 1995, Prof. Wiles corrected them. He is now writing up the proof.

Most-proved theorem   A book published in 1940 entitled *The Pythagorean Proposition* contained 370 different proofs of Pythagoras' theorem.

Longest proof   The proof of the classification of all finite simple groups is spread over more than 14,000 pages in nearly 500 papers in mathematical journals, contributed by more than 100 mathematicians over a period of more than 35 years.

Most prolific mathematician   Leonard Euler (Switzerland; 1707–83) was so prolific that his papers were still being published for the first time more than 50 years after his death. His collected works have been printed bit by bit since 1910 and will eventually occupy more than 75 large volumes.

Oldest mathematical puzzle   "As I was going to St. Ives, I met a man with seven wives. Every wife had seven sacks, every sack had seven cats, every cat had seven kits. Kits, cats, sacks and wives, how many were going to St. Ives?"

Apart from slight differences in wording, this is identical to a puzzle found in the Rhind papyrus, an Egyptian scroll bearing mathematical tables and problems, copied by the scribe Ahmes *c.* 1650 B.C.

Most accurate version of pi   The most decimal places to which *pi* (π) has been calculated is 2,260,321,336 by brothers Gregory Volfovich and David Volfovich Chudnovsky, on their homemade supercomputer m zero, in New York City in the summer of 1991.

COMPUTING

Fastest computer   The fastest general-purpose vector-parallel computer is the CRAY Y-MP C90 supercomputer, with two gigabytes (gigabyte = one billion bytes) of central memory and with 16 CPUs (central processing units), giving a combined peak performance of 16 gigaflops (gigaflop = one billion flops [floating point operations] per second).

Several suppliers market "massively parallel" computers which, with enough processors, have a theoretical aggregate performance exceeding that of a C90, though the performance on real-life applications can often be less. This is because it may be harder to harness effectively the power of a large number of small processors than a small number of large ones.

Fastest chip The world's fastest microprocessor is the Alpha AXP 21164, developed by Digital Equipment Corporation of Maynard, MA. It can run at a speed of 300 MHz.

Largest computer network The Internet is accessed by 60 million users on 3,864,000 computers in 81 countries. It is estimated that by 2003, 5 billion people worldwide will be on the Internet.

Fastest transistor A transistor capable of switching 230 billion times per second was announced by the University of Illinois at Urbana–Champaign in October 1986. The devices were made of indium gallium arsenide and aluminum gallium arsenide and were developed in collaboration with General Electric Company.

Smallest modem The smallest modem is the SRM-3A, which is 2.4 inches long, 1.2 inches wide, and 0.8 inches high, and weighs 1.1 ounces. It is currently manufactured by RAD Data Communications Ltd. of Tel Aviv, Israel.

Smallest robot The world's smallest robot is the "Monsieur" microbot, developed by the Seiko Epson Corporation of Japan in 1992. The light-sensitive robot measures less than 0.06 cubic inches, weighs 0.05 ounces and is made of 97 separate watch parts (equivalent to two ordinary watches). Capable of speeds of 0.4 inches per second for about five minutes when charged, the "Monsieur" has earned a design award at the International Contest for Hill-Climbing Micromechanisms.

POWER

Oldest water mill The water mill with the oldest continuous commercial use is at Priston Mill near Bath, England, first mentioned in A.D. 931 in a charter to King Athelstan (924/5–939). The mill is driven by the Conygre Brook.

Oldest steam engine The oldest steam engine in working order is the Smethwick Engine, dating from 1779. Designed by James Watt (1736–1819) and built by the Birmingham Canal Company, the pump originally had a 24-inch bore and a stroke of eight feet. It worked on the canal locks at Smethwick, England until 1891. The engine was presented to the

Birmingham Museum of Science and Industry in 1960 and is regularly steamed for the public.

Largest steam engine The largest ever single-cylinder steam engine was designed by Matthew Loam of Cornwall, England and built by the Hayle Foundry Co. in 1849 for land draining at Haarlem, Netherlands. The cylinder was 12 feet in diameter and each stroke lifted 16,140 gallons of water.

Most efficient steam engine The most efficient steam engine recorded was Taylor's engine, built by Michael Loam for United Mines of Gwennap, England in 1840. It registered only 1.7 pounds of coal per horsepower per hour.

Greatest fusion power The highest power rating attained is 10.7 megawatts in the Tokamak Fusion Test Reactor (TFTR) at the Princeton University Plasma Physics Laboratory, Princeton, NJ on November 2, 1994 (see HIGHEST TEMPERATURE).

Largest generator A turbo generator of 1,450 MW (net) is being installed at the Ignalina atomic power station in southern Lithuania.

Largest power plant The most powerful power station is currently the Itaipu power station on the Paraná River near the Brazil–Paraguay border. Opened in 1984, the station has now attained its ultimate rated capacity of 13,320 MW.

Largest transformers The world's largest single-phase transformers are rated at 1,500,000 kVA. Eight of these are in service with the American Electric Power Service Corporation. Of these, five step down from 765 to 345 kV.

Longest transmission lines The longest span between pylons of any power line is 17,638 feet, across the Ameralik Fjord near Nuuk, Greenland. Built and erected by A.S. Betonmast of Oslo, Norway in 1991–92 as part of the 132 kV line serving the 45 MW Buksefjorden Hydro Power Station, the line weighs 42 tons.

Highest transmission lines The transmission lines across the Straits of Messina, Italy have towers of 675 feet (Sicily side) and 735 feet (Calabria side), 11,900 feet apart.

Highest-voltage transmission lines The highest voltages carried on a DC are 1,330 kV over a distance of 1,224 miles on the DC Pacific Inter-Tie in the United States, which stretches from approximately 100 miles east of Portland, OR to a location east of Los Angeles, CA.

The highest voltages carried on a 3-phase AC are 1,200 kV in Russia over a distance greater than 1,000 miles. The first section carries the current from Siberia to the province of North Kazakhstan, while the second takes the current from Siberia to Ural.

Biggest blackout The greatest power failure in history struck seven northeastern U.S. states and Ontario, Canada on November 9–10, 1965. About 30 million people in 80,000 square miles were plunged into darkness. Two people died as a result of the blackout. In New York City the power failed at 5:27 P.M. and was not fully restored for 13½ hours.

Largest nuclear reactor   The largest single nuclear reactor in the world is the Ignalina station, Lithuania, which came fully on line in January 1984 and has a net capacity of 1,380 MW.

Largest nuclear power station   The power station in Fukushima, Japan has 10 reactors and a net output of 8,814 MW.

The largest nuclear power complex in the United States is in Wintersburg, AZ. The three Palo Verde units (unit one: 1,235 MW; unit two: 1,235 MW; and unit three: 1,245 MW) have a net summer capability of 3,715 MW.

The largest unit in the country is found in Bay City, TX. The South Texas 1 unit has a capability of 1,251 MW; the South Texas 2 unit's capability is 1,250 MW.

Largest solar power plant   In terms of nominal capacity, the largest solar electric power facility in the world is the Harper Lake Site (LSP 8 and 9) in the Mojave Desert, California run by UC Operating Services. These two solar electric generating stations (SEGS) have a nominal capacity of 160 MW (80 MW each). The station site covers 1,280 acres.

Largest wind generators   The $55 million Boeing Mod-5B wind generator in Oahu, HI produces 3,200 kW with its 320-foot rotors when the wind reaches 32 MPH.

At year-end 1994, wind turbine capacity in the United States was 7,220 kW. Over 91.2 percent of the wind systems are located in California.

Largest turbines   The largest hydraulic turbines are 32 feet in diameter with a 449-ton runner and a 350-ton shaft. Rated at 815 MW (equivalent to 1.1 million hp), they were installed by Allis-Chalmers at the Grand Coulee Dam Third Powerplant in Washington State.

Smallest turbine   A self-sustaining gas turbine with compressor and turbine wheels measuring just two inches and an operating speed of 50,000 revolutions per minute was built by Geoff Knights of London, England.

Largest battery   The 10 MW lead-acid battery in Chino, CA has a design capacity of 40 MW/h. It is currently used at an electrical substation for leveling peak demand loads. This $13 million project is a cooperative effort by Southern California Edison Company Electric Power Research Institute and International Lead Zinc Research Organization Inc.

ENGINEERING

Strongest alloy   Carbon-manganese steel music wire measuring 0.004 inches wide has a required tensile strength in the range of 3.40–3.78 GPa (4.93×10^5 to 5.48×10^5 lbf/in.^{2}).

THE CASE AGAINST WORKING WEEKENDS...

When Graham Coates stepped into the elevator at his workplace in Brighton, England on Saturday, May 24, 1986, he simply meant to go to the third floor. He had no idea he would not emerge until the 3-day weekend was over.

"The elevator ground to a halt and the doors did not open. I waited and pressed the buttons again. I jumped up and down, but nothing happened. Then I pressed the alarm button."

As Coates began to shout at the top of his lungs, he realized the further irony of his situation: the business next door was a radio station whose employees worked out of soundproof studios.

"I decided I would have to live with it until it was over or go out of my mind. There was no way anyone would notice I was missing; I lived with my parents at the time, and they were used to me staying out for the whole weekend.

"I was wearing a digital watch that beeped every hour on the hour. It was driving me mad, so I turned it off. I had a part-time job at a pub, and as time passed, I started thinking about what I would be doing if I weren't in the elevator: serving pints and talking to customers. I became

(*Dick Milligan © Guinness Publishing*)

Longest incarceration in an elevator

Graham Coates of Brighton, England established an involuntary record when he was trapped in an elevator for 62 hours in Brighton, May 24–27, 1986.

terribly thirsty. I started to imagine that I had poured myself a beer. When Sunday came, I thought about the marvelous lunch the pub owner prepared. I had nothing to eat for the 62 hours, and I was starving. I ended up sleeping most of the time.

"Early Tuesday morning, I heard noises in the building. I shouted for about 10 minutes, and finally the company's vice-president heard me. He called the elevator manufacturer and they explained how to lower the elevator manually.

"After 62 hours of incarceration, I was cold, tired and weak. I had to take several weeks off work to recover, and I suffered headaches for some time.

"Occasionally, I have flashbacks when I get into elevators. Now I only use them if they have telephones installed."

Largest blast furnace   The no. 5 furnace at the Cherepovets works in Russia has a volume of 5,500 cubic meters.

Largest catalytic cracker   The Bayway Refinery plant in Linden, NJ had a fresh feed rate of 5.25 million gallons per day in 1994. The Bayway Refining Company is a wholly-owned subsidiary of Tosco Corporation of Stamford, CT.

Longest conveyor belt   The longest single-flight conveyor belt is 18 miles long. It is in Western Australia and was installed by Cable Belt Ltd. of Camberley, England.

Most powerful gantry crane   The 92.3-foot-wide Rahco gantry crane at the Grand Coulee Dam Third Powerplant in Washington State was tested to lift a load of 2,460 tons in 1975. It lowered a 1,972-ton generator rotor with an accuracy of 1.32 inches.

Tallest mobile crane   The 890-ton Rosenkranz K10001, with a lifting capacity of 1,100 tons, and a combined boom and jib height of 663 feet, is carried on 10 trucks, each limited to a length of 75 ft. 8 in. and an axle weight of 130 tons. It can lift 33 tons to a height of 525 feet.

Greatest load raised   The heaviest lifting operation in engineering history was the raising of the entire 1-mile-long offshore Ekofisk complex in the North Sea, Great Britain, after subsidence of the seabed. The complex consists of eight platforms weighing 44,090 tons. During August 17–18, 1987 it was raised 21 ft. 4 in. by 122 hydraulic jacks requiring a computer-controlled hydraulic system.

Most powerful diesel engines   Five 12RTA84 type diesel engines have been constructed by Sulzer Brothers of Winterthur, Switzerland, for container-ships built for the American President Lines. Each 12-cylinder power unit gives a maximum continuous output of 57,000 bhp at 95 revolutions per minute.

Largest earthmover   The giant wheeled loader developed for open-air coal mining in Australia by SMEC, a consortium of 11 manufacturers in Tokyo, Japan, is 55 feet long, weighs 198 tons, and has rubber tires 11½ feet in diameter. The bucket has a capacity of 671 cubic feet.

Fastest elevators   The fastest domestic passenger elevators in the world are in the 70-story, 971-foot-tall Yokohama Landmark Tower in Yokohama, Japan, opened to the public on July 16, 1993. Designed and built by Mitsubishi Electric Corporation of Tokyo, the lifts operate at 28 MPH, taking passengers from the second floor to the 69th floor observatory in 40 seconds.

Much higher speeds are achieved in the winding cages of mine shafts. A hoisting shaft 6,800 feet deep, owned by Western Deep Levels Ltd. in South Africa, winds at speeds of up to 41 MPH. Otitis media (popping of the ears) presents problems above even 10 MPH.

Longest incarceration in an elevator   Graham Coates of Brighton, England established an involuntary record when he was trapped in an elevator in Brighton for 62 hours, May 24–27, 1986.

The end of the line at the Teléferico Mérida in Venezuela—the highest and longest cable car in the world. Passengers travel from Mérida City to the summit of Pico Espejo, a rise of 10,250 feet. (*Spectrum Colour Library*)

Longest escalator   The 4-section outdoor escalator at Ocean Park, Hong Kong has an overall length of 745 feet and a total vertical rise of 377 feet.

Shortest escalator   The ultimate in pampering for weary shoppers is the escalator at Okadaya More's shopping mall at Kawasaki-shi, Japan. It has a vertical height of 32.83 inches and was installed by Hitachi Ltd.

Longest moving sidewalks   The moving sidewalks installed in 1970 in the Neue Messe Center, Düsseldorf, Germany measure 738 feet between comb plates.

Escalator riding   The record distance traveled on a pair of up and down escalators is 133.18 miles, by David Beattie and Adrian Simons at Top Shop in London, England, July 17–21, 1989. They each completed 7,032 circuits.

Longest ropeway   The COMILOG installation, built in 1959–62 for the Moanda manganese mine in Gabon, extends for 47 miles. It has 858 towers and 2,800 buckets, with 96 miles of wire rope running over 6,000 idler pulleys.

Highest cable car   The highest and longest passenger-carrying aerial ropeway in the world is the *Teléferico Mérida* in Venezuela, from Mérida City (5,379 feet) to the summit of Pico Espejo (15,629 feet), a rise of 10,250 feet. The ropeway is in four sections, involving three car changes in the 8-mile ascent in one hour. The fourth span is 10,070 feet long.

Largest forging   The largest forging on record is one of a 225-ton, 55-foot-long generator shaft, forged by the Bethlehem Steel Corporation of Pennsylvania in October 1973.

Most powerful forklifts Kalmar LMV of Sweden in 1991 manufactured three counterbalanced forklift trucks capable of lifting loads of up to 99 tons at a load center of 90.5 inches. They were built to handle the Libyan Great Manmade River Project, comprising two separate pipelines, one 620 miles long running from Sawir to the Gulf of Sirte and the other 557 miles from Tazirbu to Benghazi, Libya.

Largest lathe A 126-foot-long, 460-ton giant lathe was built by Waldrich Siegen of Germany in 1973 for the South African Electricity Supply Commission at Rosherville.

Largest nuts The largest nuts ever made weigh five tons each with an outside diameter of 52 inches and a 25-inch thread. Known as "Pilgrim Nuts," they are manufactured by Pilgrim Moorside Ltd. of Oldham, England for use on the columns of a large forging press.

Longest pipeline Natural gas The longest natural gas pipeline in the world is the TransCanada pipeline, which transported a record 2.2 billion cubic feet of gas over 8,562 miles of pipe in 1994.

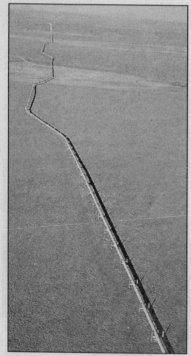

A section of the Trans-Alaskan oil pipeline, passing across the Alaskan Arctic tundra. The pipeline runs 800 miles from Prudhoe Bay on the north coast to Valdez on the south coast. (*Science Photo Library/W. Bacon***)**

Oil   The longest crude oil pipeline in the world is the Interprovincial Pipe Line Inc. installation, which spans the North American continent from Edmonton, Alberta, Canada through Chicago, IL to Montreal, Quebec, a distance of 2,367 miles. Along the length of the pipe, 82 pumping stations maintain a flow of 1.6 million gallons of oil per day.

Most expensive pipeline   The total cost of the Alaska oil pipeline, running 800 miles from Prudhoe Bay to Valdez, is $9 billion. The pipe is 48 inches in diameter and its capacity is 2.1 million barrels per day.

Most powerful presses   The world's two most powerful production machines are forging presses in the United States. The Loewy closed-die forging press, owned and operated by the Wyman-Gordon Company at North Grafton, MA, weighs 10,438 tons and stands 108 ft. 2½ in. high. It has a rated capacity of 50,000 tons and became operational in October 1955. A press of similar weight, height and rated capacity operates at the plant of the Aluminum Company of America in Cleveland, OH.

The greatest press force of any sheet metal forming press is 116,840 tons for a QUINTUS fluid cell press delivered by ASEA to BMG AG in Munich, Germany in January 1986.

Largest radar installation   The largest of the three installations in the U.S. Ballistic Missile Early Warning System (BMEWS) is near Thule, in Greenland, 931 miles from the North Pole. It was completed in 1960 at a cost of $500 million.

Largest rope   A coir fiber launching rope with a diameter of 47 inches was made in 1858 for the British liner *Great Eastern* by John and Edwin Wright of Birmingham, England. It consisted of four strands, each of 3,780 yarns.

Wire ropes   The longest wire ropes are the four made at British Ropes Ltd., Wallsend, England, each measuring 15 miles long. They are 1.3 inches in diameter, weigh 120 tons each, and were ordered by the CEGB for use in the construction of the 2,000 MW cross-Channel power cable.

Molten steel on the production line at Nippon, the world's largest steel producer. (*Gamma/K. Kurita*)

Largest steel producer   The Nippon Steel Corporation of Japan produced 30.52 million tons of crude steel in the year ending March 1992, compared with 31.959 million tons in 1991. It now has 37,388 employees, compared with 51,441 in 1988.

United States   The largest producer of steel in the United States is USX Corporation, of Pittsburgh, PA, which produced 11.7 million tons of raw steel in 1994. The annual sales figure for the U.S. Steel Group of USX was $6.1 billion and the number of employees for the year was 21,300.

Top-spinning   The duration record for spinning a clock-balance wheel by unaided hand is 5 min. 26.8 sec., by Philip Ashley, 16, of Leigh, England on May 20, 1968. The record using 36 inches of string with a 7¼-ounce top is 58 min. 20 sec., by Peter Hodgson in Southend-on-Sea, England on February 4, 1985.

A team of 25 from the Mizushima Plant of Kawasaki Steel Works in Okayama, Japan spun a giant top 6 ft. 6¾ in. tall and 8 ft. 6¼ in. in diameter, weighing 793.6 pounds, for 1 hr. 21 min. 35 sec. on November 3, 1986.

Largest wind tunnel   The largest test section of the NASA Ames Research Center wind tunnel in Mountain View, Palo Alto, CA measures 80 by 120 feet and is powered by six 22,500 horsepower motors, giving a top speed of 110 knots.

MINES AND DRILLING

Deepest penetration into the earth   A geological exploratory drilling near Zapolarny in the Kola Peninsula of Arctic Russia, begun in 1970, was reported in April 1992 to have surpassed a depth of 40,230 feet. The target of 49,212 feet was expected to be reached in 1995.

The deepest penetration made into the ground by human beings is in the Western Deep Levels Mine at Carletonville, Transvaal, South Africa, where a record depth of 11,749 feet was attained on July 12, 1977. The virgin rock temperature at this depth is 131°F.

GUESS WHAT?

Q.   WHAT WAS THE LONGEST DRIVE ON A SINGLE TANK OF GAS?

A.   LOOK IN "DRIVING" (TRANSPORT)

Shaft sinking   The one-month (31-day) world record is 1,251 feet for a standard shaft 26 feet in diameter at Buffelsfontein Mine, Transvaal, South Africa, in March 1962.

Deepest ocean drilling In 1993, the Ocean Drilling Program's vessel *JOIDES Resolution* drilled 6,926 feet into the seabed in the eastern equatorial Pacific. The deepest site at which drilling has been conducted is 23,077 feet below the surface on the western wall of the Mariana Trench, Pacific Ocean, by the Deep Sea Drilling Project's vessel *Glomar Challenger*.

Deepest ice-core drilling The deepest borehole in ice was reported in July 1993 to have reached the bottom of the Greenland ice sheet at a depth of 10,018 feet after five years' drilling by American researchers.

Fastest drilling The most footage drilled in one month is 34,574 feet, in June 1988 by Harkins & Company Rig Number 13 during the drilling of four wells in McMullen County, TX.

Coal shoveling The record for filling a 1,120-pound hopper with coal is 26.83 seconds, by Brian McArdle at the Fingal Valley Festival in Fingal, Tasmania, Australia on March 5, 1994. The record by a team of two, also set at the Fingal Valley Festival on March 5, 1994, is 15.01 seconds, by Brian McArdle and Rodney Spark, both of Middlemount, Queensland, Australia.

Deepest water bore The Stensvad Water Well 11-W1 is 7,320 feet deep, and was drilled by the Great Northern Drilling Co. Inc. in Rosebud County, MT in October–November 1961.

Deepest steam well The Thermal Power Co. geothermal steam well, begun in Sonoma County, CA in 1955, is down to 9,029 feet.

OIL

Largest oil producer Saudi Arabia produced 8,147,000 barrels per day in 1994. The United States was the second-largest producer, with 6,627,000 barrels per day.

Largest oil importer In 1994, the United States imported 8,916,000 barrels per day of crude oil and its by-products. Saudi Arabia was the leading supplier, providing 1,402,000 barrels per day, which represented 15.7 percent of U.S. imports.

U.S. CRUDE OIL IMPORTS

(January–December 1994)

Country	Barrels per day
Saudi Arabia	1,402,000
Venezuela	1,317,000
Canada	1,231,000
Mexico	985,000
Nigeria	637,000

U.S. Department of Energy

OPEC countries supplied the United States with 4,232,000 barrels per day, or 47.4 percent of the total, while Persian Gulf countries supplied 1,778,000 barrels per day, or 19.9 percent.

Largest refinery   The Petroleos de Venezuela S.A. refinery in Judibana, Falcón, Venezuela, operated by the Lagoven subsidiary of Petroleos, produced 530,000 barrels of crude oil per day in 1991.

United States   The largest refinery in the United States is Amoco Oil Co.'s Texas City, TX refinery, which has a capacity of 433,000 barrels per day.

Largest oil tanks   The five ARAMCO 1½-million-barrel storage tanks at Ju'aymah, Saudi Arabia are 72 feet tall with a diameter of 386 feet and were completed in March 1980.

Heaviest platform   The *Pampo* in the Campos Basin off Rio de Janeiro, Brazil was built and is operated by Petrobrás. Opened in the 1970s, it weighs 26,560 tons, covering 32,292 square feet, and processes 30,000 barrels per day. The platform operates at a height of 377 feet from the seabed.

Tallest platform   In December 1993, the "Auger" tension leg platform was installed in the Gulf of Mexico. Designed and engineered by Shell Oil

A closer view of a Saudi refinery. (*Gamma/L. Van Der Stockt*)

Company, it set a new water depth record for a drilling and production platform, extending 2,860 feet from seabed to surface.

Greatest oil gusher   The greatest wildcat ever recorded blew at Alborz No. 5 well, near Qum, Iran on August 26, 1956. The uncontrolled oil gushed to a height of 170 feet at 120,000 barrels per day at a pressure of 9,000 pounds per square inch. It was closed after 90 days' work by B. Mostofi and Myron Kinley of Texas.

Worst oil spill   A marine blow-out beneath the drilling rig *Ixtoc I* in the Gulf of Campeche, Gulf of Mexico on June 3, 1979 produced a slick that reached 400 miles by August 5, 1979. It was eventually capped on March 24, 1980 after a loss of 505,600 tons.

On January 19, 1991, Iraqi president Saddam Hussein ordered the pumping of Gulf crude oil from Kuwait's Sea Island terminal and from seven large tankers into the Persian Gulf. Provisional estimates put the loss at 6–8 million barrels.

The *Exxon Valdez* struck a reef in Prince William Sound, AK on March 24, 1989, spilling 10 million gallons of crude. The slick spread over 2,600 square miles.

NATURAL GAS

Largest gas producer   Russia produced 22.4 trillion cubic feet of natural gas in 1993. In 1994, the United States produced 18.857 trillion cubic feet.

Largest gas deposit   Eventual production at Urengoi, Russia totals 261.6 billion cubic yards per year through six pipelines from proved reserves of 9.156 trillion cubic yards.

Greatest gas fire   The biggest gas fire burned at Gassi Touil in the Algerian Sahara from noon on November 13, 1961 to 9:30 A.M. on April 28, 1962. The pillar of flame rose 450 feet and the smoke 600 feet. It was eventually extinguished by Paul Neal ("Red") Adair of Houston, TX, using 550 pounds of dynamite. His fee was reported to be about $1 million plus expenses.

CLOCKS AND WATCHES

Most accurate clock   A commercially available atomic clock manufactured by Hewlett-Packard of Palo Alto, CA was unveiled in December 1991. Designated the HP 5071A primary frequency standard with cesium II technology, the device, costing $54,000 and about the size of a desktop computer, is accurate to one second in 1.6 million years.

Oldest clock   The faceless clock, dating from 1386, or possibly earlier, at Salisbury Cathedral in England was restored in 1956, having struck the hours for 498 years and ticked more than 500 million times.

Largest clock   The astronomical clock in the Cathedral of St.-Pierre, Beauvais, France was constructed between 1865 and 1868. It contains 90,000 parts and is 40 feet high, 20 feet wide and nine feet deep.

Largest clock face The clock face on the floral clock constructed at Matsubara Park, Toi, Japan on June 18, 1991 is 101 feet in diameter.

Highest clock The highest two-sided clock is at the top of the Morton International Building, Chicago, IL. It is 580 feet above street level.

Largest sundial Designed by Arata Isozaki of Tokyo, Japan as the centerpiece of the Walt Disney World Co. headquarters in Orlando, FL, the largest sundial has a base diameter of 122 feet and is 120 feet high, with a gnomon (projecting arm) of the same length.

GUESS WHAT?

Q. HOW MUCH DID THE MOST EXPENSIVE NECKLACE COST?

A. LOOK IN "ANTIQUES" (ARTS & ENTERTAINMENT)

Most expensive clock The highest price paid for any clock is $1,540,000 for a rare "Egyptian Revival" clock made by Cartier in 1927. Designed as an ancient Egyptian temple gate, with figures and hieroglyphs, the exotic clock is made of mother-of-pearl, coral and lapis lazuli. It was sold at Christie's, New York on April 24, 1991 to a private bidder.

Longest pendulum The longest pendulum measures 73 ft. 9¾ in. and is part of the water-mill clock installed by the Hattori Tokeiten Co. in the Shinjuku NS building in Tokyo, Japan in 1983.

United States The longest pendulum in the United States is a reconstruction of Foucault's experiment. It swings from a cable 90 feet long and 23 feet above the heads of visitors to the Convention Center in Portland, OR and weighs 900 pounds.

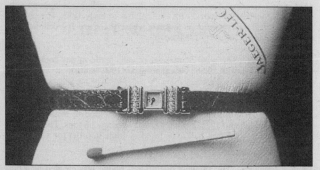

Smallest Watch **A jeweled wristwatch by Jaeger le Coultre of Switzerland, makers of the world's smallest watches. (*Gamma*)**

Largest watch A Swatch 531 ft. 6 in. long and 65 ft. 7½ in. in diameter was made by D. Tomas Feliu and set up on the site of the Bank of Bilbao building, Madrid, Spain, December 7–12, 1985.

Heaviest watch The Eta watch on the Swiss pavilion at Expo 86 in Vancouver, British Columbia, Canada, May–October 1986, weighed 38.5 tons and stood 80 feet high.

Smallest watches Jaeger le Coultre of Switzerland produces the smallest watches. Equipped with a 15-jeweled movement, they measure just over half an inch long and ³⁄₁₆ inch wide. Movement and case weigh under a quarter of an ounce.

Most expensive watch The record price paid for a watch is SFr4.95 million ($3,315,000) at Habsburg Feldman, Geneva, Switzerland on April 9, 1989 for a Patek Philippe Calibre '89. This watch has 1,728 separate parts.

Most complex astronomical watch The entirely mechanical Planetarium Copernicus, made by Ulysse Nardin of Switzerland, is the only wristwatch that indicates the time of day, date, phases of the moon, and astronomical position of the sun, Earth, the moon and the planets known in Copernicus' day. It also represents the Ptolemaic universe, showing the astrological "aspects" at any given time.

TELEPHONES AND FAXES

Most telephones The country with the greatest number of phones is the United States, with 148,084,000 as of March 1994. Monaco has the most telephones per head of population, with 1,994 per 1,000.

Most mobile phones The country with the most cellular telephone subscribers is the United States, with 24.1 million in early 1995. The country with the greatest penetration is Sweden, where there are 167 cellular telephone subscribers for every 1,000 people.

Most phone calls The greatest number of calls made in any country is in the United States, with 502.85 billion per year (1992 figure).

Largest telephone The world's largest operational telephone was exhibited at a festival on September 16, 1988 to celebrate the 80th birthday of Centraal Beheer, an insurance company based in Apeldoorn, Netherlands. It was 8 ft. 1 in. high and 19 ft. 11 in. long, and weighed 3.8 tons. The handset, which was 23 ft. 5 in. long, had to be lifted by crane in order for a call to be made.

Smallest telephone The smallest operational phone was created by Zbigniew Rózanek of Pleszew, Poland in 1992. It measured 2⅝ by ¾ by 1⅛ inches.

United States The smallest operational telephone in the United States was created by Jeff Smith of GTE Northwest, Everett, WA in 1988 and measured 4⅛ by ¾ by 1½ inches.

Busiest telephone route The busiest international phone route is between the United States and Canada. In 1993, there were 4.1 billion minutes of two-way traffic between the two countries.

Busiest telephone exchange GPT (GEC Plessey Telecommunications Ltd.) demonstrated the ability of the "System X" telephone exchange to handle 1,558,000 calls in an hour through one exchange in Beeston, Nottingham, England on June 27, 1989.

Longest telephone cable The world's longest submarine telephone cable is ANZCAN, which runs for 9,415 miles from Port Alberni, Canada to Auckland, New Zealand and Sydney, Australia via Fiji and Norfolk Island. It cost $379 million and was inaugurated by Queen Elizabeth II in November 1984.

Most expensive telephone card The highest price paid for a phone card was for the first card issued in Japan. It changed hands in January 1992 for $42,000.

Longest fiber optics transmission The longest transmission distance at a data rate of 20 gigabits per second over a fiber path containing repeaters is 78,000 miles. This was achieved using a recirculating fiber loop at the BT laboratories in Martlesham, England and was reported in September 1994. (*Science Photo Library/A. Hart-Davis*)

Morse code The highest recorded speed at which anyone has received Morse code is 75.2 words per minute—over 17 symbols per second. This was achieved by Ted R. McElroy of the United States in a tournament at Asheville, NC on July 2, 1939.

The fastest speed recorded for hand-key transmitting is 175 symbols a minute by Harry A. Turner of the U.S. Army Signal Corps at Camp Crowder, MO on November 9, 1942.

Largest fax machine Manufactured by WideCom Group Inc. of Mississauga, Ontario, Canada, the "WIDEFax 36" is able to scan, print and copy documents of up to 36 inches.

PLEASE HOLD!

The switchboard in the Pentagon, Washington, D.C. has 34,500 lines and handles over 1 million calls per day through 200,000 miles of telephone cable. Its busiest day ever was June 6, 1994—the 50th anniversary of D-Day—when there were 1,502,415 calls.

Smallest fax machine The Real Time Strategies Inc. hand-held device Pagentry combines various functions including the transmission of messages to facsimile machines. It measures 3 by 5 by ¾ inches and weighs five ounces.

Most expensive telegram Alberto Bolaffi of Turin, Italy paid $68,500 for the congratulatory telegram sent by Soviet premier Nikita Khrushchev to Yuri Gagarin on April 12, 1961 after Gagarin became the first man in space, at Sotheby's, New York on December 11, 1993.

Longest fiber optics transmission The longest transmission distance at a data rate of 20 gigabits per second over a fiber path containing repeaters is 78,000 miles. This was achieved using a recirculating fiber loop at the BT laboratories in Martlesham, England and was reported in September 1994.

TELESCOPES

Largest telescope The Keck telescope on Mauna Kea, HI has a 394-inch mirror, made up of 36 segments fitted together to produce the correct curve. Each segment is 72 inches in aperture. An active support system holds each segment in place and focuses the images. A twin Keck telescope is to be set up close to the first. When they are completed, Keck I and Keck II will be able to work together as an interferometer. Theoretically, they would be able to see a car's headlights separately from a distance of 15,500 miles.

The largest telescope of the century should be the VLT (Very Large Telescope) being planned by the European Southern Observatory. It will consist of four 26-ft.-8-in. telescopes working together, providing a light-grasp equal to a single 52-ft.-6-in. mirror. The chosen site is Cerro Paranal in northern Chile. It is hoped that the telescope will be completed by 2000.

DID YOU KNOW?

The oldest existing observatory building is the "Tower of the Winds" used by Andronichus of Cyrrhus in Athens, Greece *c.* 100 B.C., and equipped with sundials and clepsydra (water clock).

Largest reflector   The largest single-mirror telescope now in use is the 19-ft.-8-in. reflector on Mount Semirodriki, near Zelenchukskaya, Russia, at an altitude of 6,830 feet, completed in 1976.

United States   The largest single-mirror telescope in the United States is the 200-inch Hale reflector at Mount Palomar, CA, completed in 1948.

Largest infrared reflector   The UKIRT (United Kingdom Infrared Telescope) on Mauna Kea, HI has a 147-inch mirror. It is so good that it can be used for visual work as well as infrared.

Largest metal-mirror reflector   A 72-inch reflector was made by the third Earl of Rosse, and set up at Birr Castle, Ireland in 1845. The mirror was made of speculum metal (an alloy of copper and tin). With it, Lord Rosse discovered the spiral forms of the galaxies. The reflector was last used in 1909.

Largest multiple-mirror telescope   The MMT (Multiple-Mirror Telescope) at the Whipple Observatory at Mount Hopkins, AZ uses six 72-inch mirrors together, giving a light-grasp equal to a single 176-inch mirror.

Largest solar telescope   The McMath solar telescope at Kitt Peak, AZ has a 6-ft.-11-in. primary mirror; the light is sent to it via a 32° inclined tunnel from a coelostat (rotatable mirror) at the top end.

Largest submillimeter telescope   The James Clerk Maxwell telescope on Mauna Kea, HI has a 49-ft.-3-in. paraboloid primary, and is used for studies of the submillimeter part of the electromagnetic spectrum (0.01–0.03 inches).

Largest refractor   A 62-foot-long refractor completed in 1897 is situated at the Yerkes Observatory, Williams Bay, WI and belongs to the University of Chicago, IL. Although nearly 100 years old, the 40-inch refractor is still in full use on clear nights.

Largest radio dish   The world's largest radio telescope is the partially-steerable ionospheric assembly built over the natural bowl at Arecibo, Puerto Rico, completed in November 1963. The reflector dish is 1,000 feet in diameter and covers 18½ acres suspended 426 feet under a 600-ton triangular platform.

Largest radio installation   The largest radio installation is the Australia Telescope, which includes dishes at Parkes (210 feet in diameter), Siding

An aerial view of the largest dish radio telescope in the world, located in a natural crater in the mountains of Puerto Rico. (*Science Photo Library/Dr. S. Shostak*)

Spring (72 feet) and Culgoora (also 72 feet). There are links with tracking stations at Usuada and Kashima, Japan, and with the TDRS (Tracking and Data Relay Satellite), which is in a geosynchronous orbit. This is equivalent to a radio telescope with an effective diameter of 2.16 Earth diameters (17,102 miles).

United States The VLA (Very Large Array) of the U.S. National Science Foundation is Y-shaped, with each arm 13 miles long and with 27 mobile antennae (each 82 feet in diameter) on rails. It is 50 miles west of Socorro in the Plains of San Augustin, NM. It was completed on October 10, 1980.

Largest Schmidt telescope A Schmidt telescope uses a spherical mirror with a correcting plate and can cover a very wide field with a single exposure. The largest is the 6-ft.-6¾-in. instrument at the Karl Schwarzschild Observatory in Tautenberg, Germany. It has a clear aperture of 52¾ inches with a 78¾-inch mirror, focal length 13 feet. It was brought into use in 1960.

Largest space telescope The largest is the $2.1 billion NASA Edwin P. Hubble Space Telescope, which weighs 12 tons and is 43 feet in overall length,

W O W !

I T'S E. T.

C A L L I N G

Extraterrestrials have been caricatured in hundreds of different ways since H.G. Wells' classic *The War of the Worlds* was published in 1898. Are they hostile creatures with menacing ray guns and long tentacles? Or are they 4-foot-tall bald bipeds who have magical healing powers and can fly through the air?

Robert Dixon, Director of the Ohio SETI Program at Ohio State University in Columbus, Ohio—the longest-running full-scale search for extraterrestrial life—doesn't choose to have any conception of an alien's physical appearance. But he does believe in the validity of the search for life on other worlds. "We don't really think in terms of visual images of aliens," Dixon says. "We simply want an answer to the question, 'Are we alone?'"

(Philip Barnhart)

Dixon's questions may have been answered in 1977. The Ohio State radio telescope picked up a signal that Dixon describes as "unmistakably strong … it bore all the right earmarks of being extraterrestrial." Dubbed the "Wow!" signal because of a comment written in the margins of the computer printout by one of the staff scientists, the signal was at least one lunar distance away from Earth at a time when no publicly known satellites were near the source.

Unfortunately, the real origin of the "Wow!" signal will probably never be traced, as it came and went in only a fleeting moment. Dixon and his team have tried to reach that frequency countless times, but to no avail. Nevertheless, the Ohio SETI Program refuses to give up hope, and, undaunted by naysayers, it continues its 22-year mission. "Some people think the whole search is baloney," Dixon shrugs. "But once a signal is found, it means something is out there—and it becomes the plum of the century."

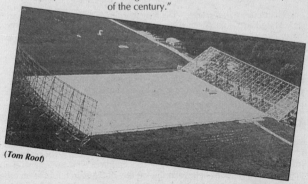

(Tom Root)

with a 94½-inch reflector. It was placed in orbit at 381 miles altitude by a U.S. space shuttle on April 24, 1990.

Highest observatory   The high-altitude observatory in Denver, CO is at 14,100 feet and was opened in 1973. The main instrument is a 24-inch reflector.

Lowest observatory   In the "observatory" at Homestake Mine, SD, the "telescope" is a tank of cleaning fluid (perchloro-ethylene), which contains chlorine, and can trap neutrinos from the sun. The installation is 1.1 miles below ground level, in the shaft of a gold mine; the detector has to be at this depth, otherwise the experiments would be confused by cosmic rays.

Oldest planetarium   The ancestor of the modern planetarium is the rotatable Gottorp Globe, built by Andreas Busch in Denmark about 1660. It was 34 ft. 7 in. in circumference, and is now preserved in St. Petersburg, Russia. The stars were painted on the inside.

The first modern planetarium was opened in 1923 in Jena, Germany; it was designed by Walther Bauersfelt of the Carl Zeiss company.

United States   The Adler Planetarium in Chicago, IL, which opened on May 12, 1930, is the oldest planetarium in the United States. Its dome is 68 feet in diameter and it seats 450 people.

Largest planetarium   The planetarium at the Ehime Prefectural Science Museum, Niihama City, Japan has a dome with a diameter of 98 ft. 5 in. Up to 25,000 stars can be displayed, and viewers can observe space as it would look from other planets.

United States   The Kelly Space Voyager Planetarium in Charlotte, NC is the largest planetarium in the United States. Completed in October 1991, it has a dome 78½ feet in diameter. The facility has 307 seats.

The American Museum–Hayden Planetarium, New York City has a dome diameter of 75 ft. 2 in., but has the largest seating capacity of any planetarium in the United States, with 650 seats.

Longest extraterrestrial search   The longest-running full-scale SETI (search for extraterrestrial intelligence) project is the Ohio SETI Program at Ohio State University in Columbus, OH, which has searched the universe for extraterrestrial radio signals for 22 years, beginning in 1973.

Largest extraterrestrial search   The most comprehensive search for extraterrestrial life is Project Phoenix (originally NASA SETI), which is conducted by the SETI Institute of Mountain View, CA. The project—

GUESS WHAT?

Q.   How big is the largest revolving globe?

A.   Look in "Big Deals" (Human Achievements)

---

presently stationed in New South Wales, Australia, where the team is utilizing the 210-foot Parkes antenna—intends to listen for extraterrestrial radio signals from the neighborhoods of approximately 1,000 nearby sunlike stars by the year 2000.

SPACE FLIGHT

Highest rocket velocity   The fastest escape velocity from Earth was 34,134 MPH, achieved by the ESA *Ulysses* spacecraft, powered by an IUS–PAM upper stage after deployment from the Space Shuttle *Discovery* on October 7, 1990, en route to an orbit around the poles of the Sun via a flyby of Jupiter.

Most powerful rocket   The NI booster of the former USSR, first launched from the Baikonur Cosmodrome at Tyuratam, Kazakhstan on February 21, 1969, had a thrust of 5,200 tons but exploded at takeoff + 70 seconds. Its current booster, *Energya*, first launched on May 15, 1987 from the Baikonur Cosmodrome, has a thrust of 3,900 tons. It is capable of placing 116 tons into low Earth orbit. Four strap-on boosters powered by single RD-170 engines burning liquid oxygen and kerosene were used.

Most powerful rocket engine   The most powerful rocket engine was built in the former USSR by Scientific Industrial Corporation of Energetic Engineering in 1980. The engine has a thrust of 900 tons in open space and 830 tons at Earth's surface. The RD-170 burns liquid oxygen and kerosene.

Earliest satellite   The first artificial satellite, *Sputnik 1*, was put into orbit by an intercontinental ballistic missile from the Baikonur Cosmodrome, Kazakhstan on the night of October 4, 1957. It reached an altitude of between 142 miles (perigee or nearest point to Earth) and 588 miles (apogee or furthest point from Earth) and a velocity of more than 17,750 MPH. It weighed 184.3 pounds, with a diameter of 22¾ inches; its lifetime is believed to have been 92 days, ending on January 4, 1958.

Largest objects orbited   The 440-pound U.S. RAE (Radio Astronomy Explorer) B, or *Explorer 49*, launched on June 10, 1973, was the largest object orbited, with antennae 1,500 feet from tip to tip. The heaviest object orbited is the *Saturn V* third stage of the *Apollo 15* spacecraft, which, prior to translunar injection into parking orbit, weighed 310,000 pounds. The longest object ever placed in space is the SEDS-2 mini-satellite space tether system, which had a final deployed length of 12.38 miles, and is used to connect and deploy a mini-satellite system.

First spacecraft to reach the moon   The first direct hit on the moon was achieved at 2 min. 24 sec. after midnight (Moscow time) on September 14, 1959, by the Soviet space probe *Lunar II*, near the Mare Serenitatis.

First extraterrestrial vehicle   The first wheeled vehicle to land on the moon was the unmanned *Lunokhod I*, which began its Earth-controlled travels

The most powerful rocket is *Energya,* seen here in a hangar at Baikonur Cosmodrome in Kazakhstan with the space shuttle *Buran* on its back. (*Science Photo Library/Novosti Press Agency*)

on November 17, 1970. It moved a total of 6.54 miles on gradients up to 30° in the Mare Imbrium and did not break down until October 4, 1971. The lunar speed and distance records were set by the manned *Apollo 16* Rover, driven by John Young, at 11.2 MPH downhill and 22.4 miles.

Closest approach to the sun by a spacecraft The research spacecraft *Helios B* approached within 27 million miles of the sun, carrying both U.S. and German instrumentation, on April 16, 1976.

Remotest man-made object *Pioneer 10*, launched from Cape Canaveral, FL, crossed the mean orbit of Pluto on October 17, 1986 at a distance of 3.67 billion miles from Earth.

Earliest manned spaceflight The earliest manned spaceflight was by Cosmonaut Flight Major (later Col.) Yuri Alekseyevich Gagarin (1934–68) in *Vostok 1* on April 12, 1961. Takeoff was from the Baikonur Cosmodrome, Kazakhstan at 6:07 GMT and the landing was near Smelovka, in the Saratov region of Russia, 108 minutes later. Col. Gagarin landed separately from his spacecraft, by parachute. The maximum altitude during *Vostok 1*'s 25,394½-mile flight was listed at 203 miles, with a maximum speed of 17,560 MPH.

DID YOU KNOW?

The first photographic images of the hidden side of the moon were collected by the Soviet *Lunar III* from 6:30 A.M. on October 7, 1959 from a range of up to 43,750 miles, and transmitted to Earth from a distance of 292,000 miles.

United States On May 5, 1961, aboard *Mercury 3*, Cdr. Alan B. Shepard, Jr. (U.S.N.) became the first American to pilot a spaceflight. The suborbital flight, which lasted 15 min. 28 sec., covered 302 miles and reached an altitude of 116.5 miles.

John H. Glenn was the first American to orbit Earth. His flight aboard *Mercury 6* (*Friendship 7*) was launched at 9:47 A.M. EST on February 20, 1962 and splashed down into the Atlantic Ocean at 2:43 P.M. EST that same day. Glenn completed three orbits of Earth and traveled approximately 81,000 miles.

First woman in space The first woman to orbit Earth was Junior Lt. (now Lt.-Col. Eng.) Valentina Vladimirovna Tereshkova (b. March 6, 1937), who was launched in *Vostok 6* from the Baikonur Cosmodrome, Kazakhstan at 9:30 A.M. GMT on June 16, 1963, and landed at 8:20 A.M. on June 19, after a flight of 2 days 22 hr. 50 min., during which she completed over 48 orbits (1,225,000 miles) and passed momentarily within three miles of *Vostok 5*.

United States The first American woman in space was Sally Ride, who was launched in the U.S. space shuttle *Challenger STS–7* on June 18, 1983, and returned to Earth on June 24. Eileen Marie Collins was the first woman to pilot a space shuttle, when she navigated *Discovery* for mission *STS-63*, February 3–11, 1992.

Longest manned spaceflight Dr. Valeriy Polyakov (Russia) was launched to *Mir* aboard *Soyuz TM-18* on January 8, 1994. He landed in *Soyuz TM-20* on March 22, 1995, after a spaceflight lasting 438 days 18 hr. The longest spaceflight by a woman was 169 days 5 hr. 21 min. 20 sec. by Yelena Kondakova (Russia), who was launched to *Mir* aboard *Soyuz TM-20* on October 3, 1994, and landed in the same spacecraft on March 22, 1995. She is also the woman with the most space experience.

Under the FAI Category P for aerospacecraft, the longest spaceflight is by mission *STS-67* aboard *Endeavour*, with seven crew members, which lasted 15 days 13 hr. 32 min., March 2–18, 1995.

Shortest manned spaceflight Cdr. Alan B. Shepard, Jr. (U.S.N.) made a spaceflight aboard *Mercury 3* on May 5, 1961. His suborbital mission lasted 15 min. 28 sec.

Fastest spaceflight The fastest speed at which humans have traveled is 24,791 MPH, when the command module of *Apollo 10*, carrying Col. (now Brig. Gen.) Thomas Patten Stafford (U.S.A.F.), Cdr. Eugene Andrew Cernan (U.S.N.) and Cdr. (now Capt.) John Watts Young (U.S.N.), reached this maximum value at the 75.7-mile altitude interface on its trans-Earth round-trip flight on May 26, 1969.

A model of the 8-wheel-drive Lunokhod 1, the first extraterrestrial vehicle, which moved a total of 6.54 miles on the Moon. (*Science Photo Library/Novosti Press Agency*)

Most expensive space project The total cost of the U.S. manned space program is estimated to have exceeded $85 billion by the spring of 1995, with the NASA shuttle program costing more than $50 billion.

Most journeys Capt. John Watts Young (U.S.N. ret.) completed his sixth spaceflight on December 8, 1983, when he relinquished command of *Columbia STS 9/Spacelab* after a space career of 34 days 19 hr. 41 min. 53 sec. Young flew *Gemini 3, Gemini 10, Apollo 10, Apollo 16, STS 1* and *STS 9*. The most by a woman is four, by Shannon Lucid (*STS 419, 31, 45* and *58*).

Most time in space Valeriy Polyakov, a physician and research cosmonaut, has the most accumulated time in space, with a total of 16,312:36 hours (nearly 680 days) in two missions (August 29, 1988–April 27, 1989 and January 8, 1994–March 22, 1995). The most experienced female space traveler is Yelena Kondakova (Russia), who has spent 169 days 5 hr. 21 min. 20 sec. in space (See LONGEST MANNED SPACEFLIGHT).

United States   Gerald P. Carr, Edward G. Gibson and William R. Pogue, the most experienced U.S. astronauts, manned the longest American flight, aboard *Skylab 4*, which was launched November 16, 1973 and splashed down February 8, 1974, after 84 days 1 hr. 15 min. 31 sec. in space. Shannon Lucid is the woman in the United States with the most space experience, with 34 days 22 hr. 52 min.

Oldest astronaut   The oldest astronaut of the 325 people in space (to April 3, 1995) was Vance DeVoe Brand (U.S.; b. May 9, 1931), age 59, while on the space shuttle mission aboard the *Columbia STS 35*, December 2–10, 1990. The oldest woman was Shannon Lucid (U.S.), age 50 yr. 278 days, on takeoff of the space shuttle mission *Columbia STS 58* in October 1993.

Youngest astronaut   Major (later Lt.-Gen.) Gherman Stepanovich Titov (b. September 11, 1935) was 25 yr. 329 days old when launched in *Vostok 2* on August 6, 1961. The youngest woman in space was Valentina Tereshkova, age 26. (See FIRST WOMAN IN SPACE.)

United States   The youngest American astronaut was Sally Ride (b. May 26, 1951), who on June 18, 1983, aged 32 yr. 23 days, was launched aboard *Challenger STS 7*.

Largest crew   The largest crew on a single space mission was eight, launched on October 30, 1985 on *Challenger 9 STS 61A*, the 22nd shuttle mission, which carried the German *Spacelab D1* laboratory. The mission, commanded by Henry Warren "Hank" Hartsfield, lasted 7 days 44 min. 51 sec. The greatest number of women in a space crew is three (of seven) on *Columbia STS 40* in June 1991.

Most people in space   The greatest number of people in space at any one time was 13, by the crews of the 7-person American mission *STS-67* aboard *Endeavour*, and the combined Russian teams *Soyuz TM-20* and *Soyuz TM-21*, each of which consisted of three crew members (one American). From March 14 to March 18, 1995, all parties were in space and conducting joint scientific experiments.

Farthest person from Earth   The greatest distance from Earth attained by humans was when the crew of the *Apollo 13* were at apocynthion (i.e., their furthest point) 158 miles above the lunar surface, and 248,655 miles from Earth's surface, at 1:21 A.M. EST on April 14, 1970. The crew were Capt. James Arthur Lovell, Jr. (U.S.N.), Fred Wallace Haise, Jr. and John L. Swigert.

WHOOSH!

The fastest solar system speed of approximately 158,000 MPH is reached by the NASA–German *Helios B* solar probe each time it reaches the perihelion of its solar orbit.

The total cost of the U.S. manned space program is estimated to have exceeded $85 billion by the spring of 1995, with the NASA shuttle program costing some $50 billion. (*NASA/Image Select, Gamma/NASA/Liaison and Gamma/Wells/Liaison*)

DID YOU

KNOW?

Capt. Eugene Cernan and

Dr. Harrison Hagen "Jack"

Schmidt spent 74 hr. 59

min. on the surface of the

Moon during the *Apollo 17*

mission, which took

12 days 13 hr. 51 min.

on December 7–19, 1972.

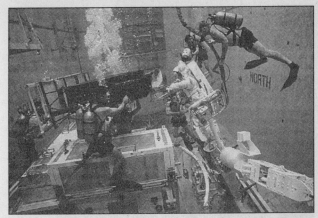

The demands of space travel require huge amounts of training. Above, astronauts prepare for flight *STS 61*. (*NASA/Image Select, Gamma/NASA/Liaison and Gamma/Wells/Liaison*)

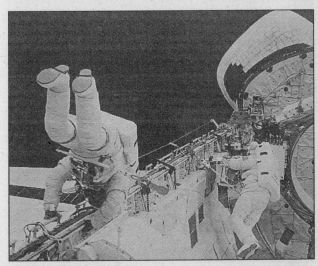

Gregory Harbaugh and Mario Runco Jr. engage in extravehicular activity, or walking in space, outside *Endeavour* on January 17, 1993, during shuttle flight *STS 54*. (*NASA/Image Select, Gamma/NASA/Liaison and Gamma/Wells/Liaison*)

The shuttle is normally associated with missions into space, but a dramatic 1982 photograph shows it in a very different setting. (*NASA/Image Select, Gamma/NASA/Liaison and Gamma/Wells/Liaison*)

Most isolated human being The farthest any human has been removed from the nearest living fellow human is 2,233.2 miles, in the case of the command module pilot Alfred M. Worden on the U.S. *Apollo 15* lunar mission of July 30–August 1, 1971, while David Scott and James Irwin were at Hadley Base exploring the surface.

Longest spacewalk The longest spacewalk was 8 hr. 29 min., by Pierre Thuot, Rick Hieb and Tom Akers of *Endeavour STS 49* on May 13, 1992. The longest spacewalk by a woman lasted 7 hr. 49 min., by Kathryn Thornton (U.S.) of *Endeavour STS 49* on May 14, 1992.

LOOK, NO HANDS!

Capt. Bruce McCandless II (U.S.N.), from the space shuttle *Challenger,* was the first to engage in untethered extravehicular activity, at an altitude of 164 miles above Hawaii, on February 7, 1984.

Most spacewalks Russian cosmonaut Aleksandr Serebrov completed a record ninth spacewalk on October 22, 1993. The mission was carried out to check the orbiting *Mir* space station.

United States During the 11-day *Endeavour* shuttle mission to repair the Hubble Telescope, Lt. Col. Thomas Akers made his fifth spacewalk, the most by any U.S. astronaut. Akers had logged 29 hr. 40 min. walking in space by December 7, 1993. Dave Scott also made five spacewalks, during *Apollo* missions *9* and *15* in 1969 and 1971.

First person on the moon   Neil Alden Armstrong, command pilot of the *Apollo 11* mission, became the first human to set foot on the moon, on the Sea of Tranquility, at 02:56 and 15 seconds GMT on July 21, 1969. He was followed out of the lunar module *Eagle* by Col. Edwin Eugene "Buzz" Aldrin, Jr. (U.S.A.F.) while the command module *Columbia*, piloted by Lt. Col. Michael Collins (U.S.A.F.), orbited above.

Most flights by a shuttle   As of May 6, 1994, *Discovery* had flown the most times, with 18 missions.

Greatest spaceflight disaster   The greatest published number to perish in any of the 179 attempted spaceflights (to April 3, 1995) is seven, aboard the *Challenger 51L* on January 28, 1986, when an explosion occurred 73 seconds after liftoff, at a height of 47,000 feet. *Challenger* broke apart under extreme aerodynamic overpressure.

BUILDINGS & STRUCTURES

ORIGINS

Oldest human structure In January 1960, Dr. Mary Leakey discovered what may be the footings of a windbreak built 1.75 million years ago in the Olduvai Gorge, Tanzania. The site consists of a rough circle of loosely piled lava blocks associated with artifacts and bones on a work-floor.

United States Samples taken from the remains of a circular structure near Akron, OH in 1992 confirmed that it was a Native American hunting camp 11,000 years ago.

Oldest freestanding structures The megalithic temples of Mgarr, Skorba and Ggantija in Malta date from *c.* 3250 B.C., three and a half centuries before the first Egyptian pyramid.

Oldest wooden structure The oldest extant wooden buildings in the world are the Pagoda, Chumanar Gate and Temple of Horyu (Horyu-ji) in Nara, Japan, dating from *c.* A.D. 670.

The Nara Todaiji temple in Nara, Japan, approximately 1,300 years old, is one of the oldest wooden buildings still standing. (*Photo: Spectrum Colour Group*)

BUILDINGS FOR LIVING

Oldest habitation   The remains of 21 huts containing hearths or pebble-lined pits and delimited by stake-holes, found in October 1965 at the Terra Amata site in Nice, France, are thought to belong to the Acheulian culture of approximately 400,000 years ago.

Northernmost habitation   The Danish scientific station set up in 1952 in Pearyland, Greenland is more than 900 miles north of the Arctic Circle and is manned every summer.

Southernmost habitation   The United States' Amundsen–Scott South Polar Station was completed in 1957 and replaced in 1975.

CASTLES

Oldest castle   The castle at Gomdan, Yemen originally had 20 stories and dates from before A.D. 100.

Largest ancient castle   Hradčany Castle, Prague, Czech Republic dates from the ninth century and covers 18 acres.

Tallest sand castle   A sand castle 21 ft. 6 in. high, constructed only with hands, buckets and shovels, was made by a team led by Joe Maize, George Pennock and Ted Siebert at Harrison Hot Springs, British Columbia, Canada on September 26, 1993. Their "Christmas Tree" sand castle was made to look even more authentic by the addition of gifts.

Longest sand castle   A sand castle measuring 5.2 miles long was made by staff and pupils of Ellon Academy, near Aberdeen, Scotland, on March 24, 1988.

PALACES

Largest palace   The Imperial Palace (Gugong) in the center of Beijing, China covers a rectangle of 3,150 by 2,460 feet, an area of 178 acres. The outline survives from the construction of the third Ming emperor, Yongle (1402–24), but most of the five halls and 17 palaces are from the 18th century.

The Palace of Versailles, 14 miles southwest of Paris, France, has a fa-

---

GUESS WHAT?

Q.   WHAT IS THE LARGEST STRUCTURE BUILT BY ANIMALS?

A.   LOOK IN "ANIMALS" (LIVING WORLD)

The illuminated ice construction in St. Paul, MN was the latest in the city's century-long line of record-breaking ice palaces. (*Photo: Gamma/ B. Pugliano/Liaison*)

cade 1,902 feet long, with 375 windows. The building, completed in 1682 for Louis XIV (1643–1715), occupied over 30,000 workmen under the supervision of Jules Hardouin-Mansert (1646-1708).

Residential   Istana Nurul Iman, the palace of the Sultan of Brunei in the capital Bandar Seri Begawan, completed in January 1984 at a reported cost of $350 million, is the largest residence in the world, with 1,788 rooms and 257 bathrooms. The underground garage accommodates the sultan's 110 cars.

Largest ice palace   The ice palace built by TMK Construction Specialties for the St. Paul, MN Winter Carnival in January 1992 used 18,000 blocks of ice weighing 10.8 million pounds, stood 166 ft. 8 in. tall, and covered an area the size of a football field, making it the largest ice construction ever.

Largest snow palace   The largest snow construction was a snow palace with a volume of 3,658,310.2 cubic feet and a height of 99 ft. 5 in. unveiled on February 8, 1994 at Asahikawa, Hokkaido, Japan.

Largest moat   From plans drawn by French sources, it appears that the moats surrounding the Imperial Palace in Beijing measure 162 feet wide and have a total length of 10,800 feet.

HOUSING

According to the National Association of Realtors, as of December 31, 1994, the median price of existing homes sold in the 136 largest metropolitan areas in the United States is $109,800, and for new homes the median price is $132,000. The metropolitan area with the highest median price is Honolulu, HI, at $360,000.

Largest house The 250-room Biltmore House in Asheville, NC is owned by George and William Cecil, grandsons of George Washington Vanderbilt II (1862–1914). The house was built between 1890 and 1895 on an estate of 119,000 acres, at a cost of $4.4 million; it is now valued at $5.5 million, with 12,000 acres.

Largest gingerbread house A gingerbread house 52 feet high and 32 feet square was built by David Sunken and Roger A. Pelcher of the Bohemian Club of Des Moines, IA and 100 volunteers on December 2, 1988. The house was made of 2,000 sheets of gingerbread and 1,650 pounds of icing.

Most expensive house The most expensive private house ever built is the Hearst Ranch in San Simeon, CA. It was built 1922–39 for William Randolph Hearst (1863–1951), at a total cost of over $30 million. It has more than 100 rooms, a 104-foot-long heated swimming pool, an 83-foot-long assembly hall and a garage for 25 limousines. The house was originally maintained by 60 servants.

Largest nonpalatial residence St. Emmeram Castle, Regensburg, Germany, valued at more than $177 million, contains 517 rooms with a floor space of 231,000 square feet. Only 95 rooms are used by the family of the late Prince Johannes von Thurn und Taxis.

Longest continuous house construction Winchester House in San Jose, CA was under construction for 38 years. The original house was an eight-room farmhouse with separate barn on the 161-acre estate of Oliver Winchester. Sarah Winchester, widowed in 1886, consulted a psychic in Boston, who told her that she alone could balance the ledger for those killed by Winchester firearms by never stopping construction of the estate. Mrs. Winchester moved to California, where she transformed the farmhouse into a mansion, which now has 13 bathrooms, 52 skylights, 47 fireplaces, 10,000 windows, 40 staircases, 2,000 doorways and closets opening into blank walls, secret passageways, trapdoors, three $10,000 elevators and more. The constant remodeling of the house was intended to confuse the resident ghosts.

Most durable resident Virginia Hopkins Phillips of Onancock, VA lived in the same house from her birth in 1891 until a few months before her death at age 102 in 1993.

Camping out The silent Indian *fakir* Mastram Bapu ("contented father") remained on the same spot by the roadside in the village of Chitra for 22 years, from 1960 to 1982.

Pole sitting Modern records do not come close to that of St. Simeon the Younger (*c.* A.D. 521–97), called Stylites, a monk who spent his last 45 years on top of a stone pillar on the Hill of Wonders, near Antioch, Syria. His achievement is the longest-standing record in *The Guinness Book of Records*.

Living standards at the tops of poles can vary widely. Mellissa Sanders lived in a shack measuring six feet by seven feet at the top of a pole in Indianapolis, IN, from October 26, 1986 to March 24, 1988, a total of 516 days.

Rob Colley stayed in a 180-gallon barrel at the top of a 43-foot pole in

The Hearst Ranch in San Simeon, CA cost more than $30 million to build, making it the world's most expensive private house. (*Spectrum Colour Group*)

TOP DECK

The time: March 3, 1995.

The place: World Trade Center, Boston, MA.

The attractions: furniture, shingles, toilets, and the Wonder Knife (which can slice a hammer head).

But the real center of attention was Bryan Berg, a junior at Iowa State University's architecture school, who once again achieved a Guinness record: an 83-story house of cards. Berg learned to build card houses from his grandfather and improved his skills in his living room under challenges from his brother. He built his first Guinness skyscraper in 1992, after buying out entire card departments of discount stores. For the last three years he's been called upon to break his own record with new structures, and has succeeded grandly. The nation's TV networks are already jockeying for the privilege of airing his next record attempt—but Berg has no definite plans.

Why not? The problem, it seems, is knocking the houses down. "I'd like to build a house in a museum, where people could see it and I could visit it. That way I could see how long it would stand." But, as Berg learned back home in his living room, everybody loves to knock a card house down. So, Berg decided to prove a point about how sturdy his towers are. "I got a huge fan and aimed it at the audience. It whipped everybody's hair straight back. Then I aimed it at the tower. Just a few cards flew off. Then we got out the rubber bands. They just bounced off. So I started tearing cards off the outside. They're just there so I don't have to see the internal structure bending under the load of the tower. Finally, I pulled off about a fifth of the corner, took my hand and went whap."

Down went the tower. Up leaped the crowd. "They rushed the barricade," recalls the astonished Berg, "and carried off every single card— 27,000 of them. It blows my mind."

Tallest house of cards   The greatest number of stories achieved in building freestanding houses of standard playing cards is 83, to a height of 16 feet, by Bryan Berg of Spirit Lake, IA on February 24 and March 3, 1995. No adhesives may be used in such houses.

Dartmoor Wildlife Park, near Plymouth, England, for 42 days 35 min. from August 13 to September 24, 1992.

Tallest house of cards   The greatest number of stories achieved in building freestanding houses of standard playing cards is 83, to a height of 16 feet, by Bryan Berg of Spirit Lake, IA on February 24 and March 3, 1995. No adhesives may be used in such houses.

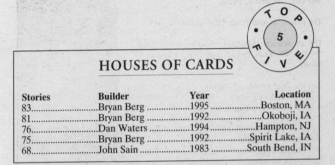

HOUSES OF CARDS

Stories	Builder	Year	Location
83	Bryan Berg	1995	Boston, MA
81	Bryan Berg	1992	Okoboji, IA
76	Dan Waters	1994	Hampton, NJ
75	Bryan Berg	1992	Spirit Lake, IA
68	John Sain	1983	South Bend, IN

Tallest apartment building   The 1,127-foot John Hancock Center in Chicago, IL is 100 stories high; floors 44–92 are residential.

The tallest purely residential apartment house is Lake Point Tower, Chicago, IL, which has 879 units consisting of 70 stories, standing 639 feet high.

HOTELS

Oldest hotel   The Hoshi Ryokan at the village of Awazu, Japan dates from A.D. 717, when Garyo Hoshi built an inn near a hot water spring that was said to have miraculous healing powers. The waters are still celebrated for their recuperative effects, and the Ryokan now has 100 bedrooms.

Largest hotel   The MGM Grand Hotel/Casino/Theme Park in Las Vegas, NV consists of four 30-story towers on a 112-acre site. The hotel has 5,009 rooms with suites of up to 6,000 square feet, and the complex also includes a 15,200-seat movie theater and a 33-acre theme park. The complex was started in 1991 and opened officially in December 1993. Its total cost was $1 billion.

Largest hotel chain   With its acquisition of Holiday Inns Worldwide in February 1991, Bass plc, Great Britain's largest brewing company, took ownership of the world's largest hotel chain. The company now owns, manages and franchises 1,645 hotels totaling 327,059 rooms in 52 countries.

United States   The largest hotel operator as of December 31, 1993, based on number of rooms, was Holiday Inns Worldwide, which operates 279,581 rooms.

Largest lobby The lobby at the Hyatt Regency, San Francisco, CA is 350 feet long and 160 feet wide, and with its 170-foot ceiling is as tall as a 17-story building.

Tallest hotel Measured from the main entrance to the top, the 73-story Westin Stamford in Raffles City, Singapore "topped out" in March 1985 at 742 feet tall. However, the Westin at the Renaissance Center in Detroit, MI is 748 feet tall when measured from the rear entrance.

Most expensive room The Galactic Fantasy Suite in the Nassau Marriott Resort and Crystal Palace Casino in the Bahamas can be rented for $25,000 per night, although the casino's big spenders are usually allowed to stay there free. The price includes a robot named Ursula who explains all the suite's high-tech toys, including a Lucite piano that produces images as well as music, a rotating sofa and bed, and a thunder and lightning sound and light show.

Most mobile hotel The 3-story brick Hotel Fairmount (built 1906) in San Antonio, TX, which weighs 1,600 tons, was moved on 36 dollies with pneu-

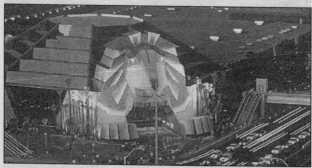

The MGM lion greets visitors to the MGM Grand, the world's largest hotel, in Las Vegas, NV. The MGM Grand also encompasses a theme park and an expansive casino. (*Gamma/E. Sanders/Liaison*)

MOST EXPENSIVE HOTEL ROOM

The Galactic Fantasy Suite at the Nassau Marriott Resort and Crystal Palace Casino in the Bahamas was designed by Diane Sepler. The bi-level, 2-bedroom, 2-bathroom suite is furnished in white, chrome, and silver to create a 23rd-century experience. High-tech toys, such as a crystal-clear Lucite grand piano that creates moving art as it plays, are explained by Ursula the robot (she also hands guests a towel as they step out of the shower). In the living room, a 6-foot-long tropical aquarium, home to a stingray, eels and lionfish, faces a dramatic ocean view. Works of art are projected onto a screen that can also be used as an over-sized television. When they are tired of playing with their toys, guests can retire to the first-floor bedroom with its huge rotating bed or to a rhinestone-studded bed on the second floor.

(*DJS Marketing Group*)

matic tires a distance of approximately five blocks and over a bridge, which had to be reinforced. The move, by Emmert International of Portland, OR, took six days, March 30–April 4, 1985, and cost $650,000.

Largest fumigation   During the restoration of the Mission Inn complex in Riverside, CA, June 28–July 1, 1987, Fume Masters Inc. of Riverside carried out the largest fumigation ever conducted to rid the buildings of termites. More than 350 tarpaulins, each weighing up to 350 pounds, were used to completely cover the 70,000-square-foot site and buildings—domes, minarets, chimneys and balconies, some of which were more than 100 feet high.

BUILDINGS FOR WORKING

Largest construction project   The Madinat Al-Jubail Al-Sinaiyah project in Saudi Arabia is the largest public works project in modern times. Construction started in 1976 on an industrial city covering 250,705 acres. At the peak of construction, nearly 52,000 workers from 62 countries were employed.

Largest demolition project   The biggest building ever demolished by explosives was the 21-story Traymore Hotel, Atlantic City, NJ on May 26, 1972 by Controlled Demolition Inc. of Towson, MD. This 600-room hotel had a volume of 6.5 million cubic feet.

The tallest structure ever demolished by explosives was the Matla Power Station chimney, Kriel, South Africa, on July 19, 1981. It stood 902 feet tall and was brought down by the Santon (Steeplejack) Co. Ltd. of Manchester, England.

Fifteen members of the Aurora Karate Do demolished a 7-room house in Prince Albert, Saskatchewan, Canada in 3 hr. 9 min. 59 sec. using only feet and bare hands on April 16, 1994.

Tallest scaffolding   Regional Scaffolding and Hoisting Co. Inc. of Bronx, NY erected scaffolding with a height of 650 feet and a volume of 4.8 million cubic feet around the New York City Municipal Building in 1988. The work required 12,000 scaffold frames and 20,000 aluminum planks, and was in place until 1992.

Scaffold erecting   David McBride and Tom Stirling of Turner Plus Eight Ltd., Glasgow, Scotland built a 2-story scaffold measuring 65 ft. 7 in. by 16 ft. 5 in. by 3 ft. 3 in. in 25 min. 53 sec. on March 31, 1995.

Largest industrial building   Asia Terminals Ltd.'s container freight station at the Kwai Chung containerport in Hong Kong is the largest industrial building that is one discrete structure. The building was completed in 1994 and has a total area of 9,320,867 square feet on 15 levels. It measures 906 by 958 feet, with a height of 359 ft. 3 in. The entire area of each floor is directly accessible by 46-foot container trucks, and the building includes 16.67 miles of roadway and 2,609 container truck parking bays.

RECORD BRICKER

"The average bricklayer lays 1,200 bricks a day," says Sammy Joe Wingfield. To set his record, he laid 1,048 bricks in one hour.

Bricklaying
Sammy Joe Wingfield of Arlington, TN laid 1,048 bricks in 60 minutes on May 20, 1994. The record was set under the normal working conditions of an average bricklayer.

Wingfield comes from a long line of bricklayers. "When I was about 19 years old, I was really fast, but kind of sloppy. I was kind of smart-mouthed, too, and I told them, "I'm going to be in *The Guinness Book of Records* one day!"

"When we were growing up, my brothers and cousins and I would race all the time. Laying bricks came easy to me. I was faster than everybody. Finally my wife checked out the Book and I said, 'I can beat that.' "

He started counting his bricks as he worked, and realized he was up to 16 bricks a minute. "Nobody'd believe me if I told them I counted 1,000 bricks an hour, but I was doing it."

Wingfield broke the record with ease, and under difficult conditions. "I did it just like a bricklayer who gets up and goes to work each morning. The ground wasn't level, and I used queen-size bricks, which weigh about three pounds." He set his record without help, lifting his own bricks and spreading his own mortar.

What's more, Wingfield actually built the wall of a house in the process. "It's still standing," he says with pride. It should be: Wingfield has helped build 500 or 600 houses in his career.

"The guy who lives in the house now isn't all that impressed," Wingfield reports. "But for me, the builder, it's an honor."

WHAT A DUMP!

The average New Yorker generates 6–7 pounds of garbage daily. New York City as a whole produces approximately 14,000 tons of garbage per day, collected six days a week—that's 4,368,000 tons each year. So where does all of this waste go?

The garbage from New York City's five boroughs (Brooklyn, Queens, Staten Island, the Bronx and Manhattan) is taken to Fresh Kills landfill in Staten Island, the largest garbage dump in the world. The task of the New York City Department of Sanitation is not only to collect and transport the garbage, but also to ensure sanitary conditions and a clean environment.

Lucian Chalfen, the Department of Sanitation's Assistant Commissioner for Public Affairs, claims that in spite of the bulk of garbage, Fresh Kills is one of the neatest landfills in the United States. "There's nary a rodent in Fresh Kills," he points out. "But we do have over 50,000 seagulls."

Chalfen describes the painstaking process of dealing with the waste once it's collected: "We use what we call a double-lock system. We have a boom machine and skimmer boats that operate like a vacuum, cleaning the waterways before and after the boats carrying the garbage come in. Once the garbage is dropped, we process and cover it with soil all in the same day."

The New York City Department of Sanitation handles all residential and institutional garbage for the Big Apple. It's also responsible for collecting recyclables such as newspapers, magazines, cardboard and plastic, and paying private processors by the ton to manage the actual recycling.

The fun doesn't end there, Chalfen explains. "We also pick up the manure from the New York City Police Department's 100 horses. We almost prefer it to normal garbage because it degrades quickly and is good for the soil."

Largest garbage dump Reclamation Plant No. 1, Fresh Kills, Staten Island, NY, opened in March 1948, is the world's largest sanitary landfill. The facility covers 3,000 acres and is estimated to process 4,368,000 tons of garbage per year, or 14,000 tons a day, six days a week.

Bricklaying Sammy Joe Wingfield of Arlington, TN laid 1,048 bricks in 60 minutes on May 20, 1994. The record was set under the normal working conditions of an average bricklayer.

Hod carrying Russell Bradley of Worcester, England carried bricks weighing 361 lb. 9 oz. up a ladder of the minimum specified length of 12 feet on January 28, 1991 at Worcester City Football Club. The hod weighed 94 lb. 13 oz., and Bradley was therefore carrying a total weight of 456 lb. 6 oz.

Largest brickworks The London Brick Co. Ltd. plant in Stewartby, England, established in 1898, now covers 221 acres and has a weekly production capacity of 6 million bricks and brick equivalent.

Largest commercial building In terms of floor area, the largest commercial building in the world under one roof is the flower auction building Bloemenveiling Aalsmeer (VBA) in Aalsmeer, Netherlands. The floor surface of the building measures 7.6 million square feet.

The world's largest building in terms of volume is the Boeing Company's main assembly plant in Everett, WA, at 196,476,000 cubic feet on completion in 1968. Subsequent expansion programs increased the volume to 472 million cubic feet, with a further increase in volume of 50 percent completed in 1993 in preparation for production of the new 777 airliner. The site covers 1,025 acres.

Largest wooden buildings Between 1942 and 1943, 16 wooden blimp hangars for Navy airships were built at various locations throughout the United States. They measure 1,040 feet long, 150 ft. 4 in. high at the crown and 296 ft. 6 in. wide at the base. There are only nine remaining—two each in Tillamook, OR, Moffett Field and Santa Ana, CA and Lakehurst, NJ, and one in Elizabeth City, NC.

Largest kitchen An Indian government field kitchen set up in April 1973 in Ahmadnagar, Maharashtra, then a famine area, provided 1.2 million subsistence meals daily.

Longest stairway The service staircase for the Niesenbahn funicular near Spiez, Switzerland rises to 7,759 feet. It has 11,674 steps and a banister.

Tallest spiral staircase The staircase on the outside of the Bòbila Almirall chimney in Tarrasa, Spain, built by Mariano Masana Ribas in 1956, is 207 feet high and has 217 steps.

DIZZY!

The spiral staircase in the Mapco–White County Coal Mine, Carmi, IL is 1,103 feet deep and has 1,520 steps. It was installed by Systems Control, Inc. in May 1981.

Largest garbage dump   Reclamation Plant No. 1, Fresh Kills, Staten Island, NY, opened in March 1948, is the world's largest sanitary landfill. The facility covers 3,000 acres and is estimated to process 4,368,000 tons of garbage per year, or 14,000 tons a day, six days a week.

Largest gas tanks   In Fontaine-l'Evêque, Belgium, disused mines have been adapted to store up to 17.6 billion cubic feet of gas at normal pressure.

The largest conventional gas tank is the one in Simmering, Vienna, Austria, completed in 1968, with a height of 275 feet and a capacity of 10.6 million cubic feet.

Largest refuse electrical generation plants   The South Meadow, Hartford County, CT plant and the Refuse and Coal Plant in Franklin County, OH, both with a capacity of 90 MW, are the two biggest refuse electrical generation plants in the United States.

Largest sewage works   The Stickney Water Reclamation Plant (formerly the West–Southwest Sewage Treatment Works) in Stickney, IL began operation in 1939 on a 570-acre site and serves an area containing 2,200,000 people. Its 651 employees treated an average of 773 million gallons of waste per day in 1994.

OFFICES

Largest administrative building   The largest ground area covered by any office building is that of the Pentagon, in Arlington, VA. Built to house the offices of the U.S. Defense Department, it was completed on January 15, 1943 and cost an estimated $83 million. Each of the outermost sides is 921 feet long, and the perimeter of the building is about 4,610 feet. Its five stories enclose a floor area of 149.2 acres. The corridors total 17.5 miles in length, and there are 7,754 windows to be cleaned. There are 23,000 people working in the building.

Largest office building   The complex with the largest rentable space is the World Trade Center in New York City, with a total of 12 million square feet of rentable space available in seven buildings, including 4.37 million square feet in each of the twin towers. Each tower has 99 elevators and 43,600 windows containing 600,000 square feet of glass. There are 50,000 people working in the complex and 70,000 visitors daily.

Tallest office building   The 110-story Sears Tower, national headquarters of Sears, Roebuck & Co. on Wacker Drive, Chicago, IL, rises to 1,454 feet. The addition of two TV antennae brought the total height to 1,707 feet. Construction started in August 1970, and the building was "topped out" on May 4, 1973. The tower has a gross area of 4.5 million square feet, is served by 104 elevators and has 16,100 windows.

Tallest indoor waterfall   The waterfall in the lobby of the International Center Building, Detroit, MI measures 114 feet tall and is backed by 9,000 square feet of marble.

BUILDINGS FOR ENTERTAINMENT

STADIUMS

Largest stadium   The open Strahov Stadium in Prague, Czech Republic was completed in 1934 and could accommodate 240,000 spectators for mass displays of up to 40,000 gymnasts.

Largest in use   The Maracanã Municipal Stadium in Rio de Janeiro, Brazil has a normal capacity of 205,000, of whom 155,000 can be seated. A crowd of 199,854 was accommodated for the World Cup soccer final between Brazil and Uruguay on July 16, 1950. A dry moat 10 feet wide and more than five feet deep separates players from spectators.

United States   The largest stadium in the United States is Michigan Football Stadium, Ann Arbor, MI, which has a seating capacity of 102,501. The largest crowd ever to attend an event there was 106,851 for the Michigan vs. Ohio State game on September 11, 1993. Ohio State won 27–23.

Largest covered stadium   The Aztec Stadium, Mexico City, opened in 1968, has a capacity of 107,000 for soccer, although a record attendance of 132,274 was achieved for boxing on February 20, 1993. Nearly all seats are under cover.

Largest indoor stadium   The $173-million 273-foot-tall Louisiana Superdome in New Orleans, LA, covering 13 acres, was completed in May 1975. Its maximum seating capacity for conventions is 97,365, or 76,791 for football.

Largest roof   The transparent acrylic "marquee" roof over the Munich Olympic Stadium, Germany measures 914,940 square feet in area, resting on a steel net supported by masts.
   The largest roofspan in the world is 787 ft. 4 in. for the major axis of the elliptical Texas Stadium, completed in 1971 in Irving, TX.

DID YOU KNOW?

The retractable roof covering the SkyDome, Toronto, Ontario, Canada, completed in June 1989, covers eight acres, spans 674 feet at its widest point and rises to 282 feet.

Largest dome   The Louisiana Superdome, New Orleans, LA has a diameter of 680 feet.

Largest air-supported building   The 80,638-capacity octagonal Pontiac Silverdome Stadium, Pontiac, MI is 522 feet wide and 722 feet long. The 10-

The translucent roof of the Pontiac Silverdome Stadium is supported by five pounds of air pressure per square foot.
(*Gamma/Caputo/Liaison*)

acre translucent Fiberglas roof is 202 feet high and is supported by compressed air. Geiger-Berger Associates of New York City were the structural engineers.

RESORTS

Largest amusement resort Disney World is set in 30,000 acres of Orange and Osceola counties, 20 miles southwest of Orlando in central Florida. It was opened on October 1, 1971 after a $400 million investment.

Most attended amusement resort Disneyland at Anaheim, CA (opened 1955) had received more than 350 million visitors by the end of 1994.

Largest recreational beach Virginia Beach, VA has 28 miles of beachfront on the Atlantic and 10 miles of estuary frontage on Chesapeake Bay. The area covers 310 square miles with 147 hotel properties and 2,323 campsites.

Longest entertainment pier The world's longest entertainment pier is Southend Pier in Southend-on-Sea, England. The original wooden pier was opened in 1830; the present iron pier is 1.34 miles long and was opened on July 8, 1889. In 1949–50, the pier had a peak 5.75 million visitors.

Most entertainment piers Atlantic City, NJ had seven piers, built from 1898 to 1912. Currently only four remain.

Largest casino Foxwoods Resort Casino in Ledyard, CT includes a total gaming area of 193,000 square feet. There are 3,854 slot machines, 234 table games and 3,500 bingo seats.

Largest naturist resort Domaine de Lambeyran, near Lodève in southern France, covers 840 acres. The Helio-Marin Center at Cap d'Agde, also in southern France, is visited by around 250,000 people per year.

United States   The largest naturist colony in the United States in terms of total acreage is Oaklake Trails, Tulsa, OK, which covers 418 acres. Club Paradise, Land O'Lakes, FL, had 70,000 visitors in 1993.

Largest maze   The largest maze ever constructed was the stegosaurus made in a cornfield at Lebanon Valley College, Annville, PA. It was 500 feet long, covered an area of 126,000 square feet, and was in existence for two months between September and November 1993.

Permanent   The largest permanent maze is the hedge maze in Ruurlo, Netherlands, which has an area of 94,080 square feet. It was created from beech hedges in 1891.

The maze with the greatest path length is at Longleat, Warminster, England. It was opened on June 6, 1978 and has 1.69 miles of paths flanked by 16,180 yew trees.

The oldest datable representation of a labyrinth is on a clay tablet from Pylos, Greece *c.* 1220 B.C.

Tallest fountain   The fountain in Fountain Hills, AZ, built at a cost of $1.5 million for McCulloch Properties Inc., can reach 625 feet when all three pumps are on and weather conditions are favorable.

FAIRS

Largest fair   The Louisiana Purchase Exposition in St. Louis, MO in 1904 covered 1,271.76 acres and was attended by 19,694,855 people. Events of the 1904 Olympic Games were staged in conjunction with the fair.

Largest exhibition center   The International Exposition Center in Cleveland, OH is situated on a 188-acre site adjacent to Hopkins International Airport in a building that measures 2.5 million square feet. An indoor terminal provides direct rail access and parking for 10,000 cars, and the Center accommodates 200 different events each year.

Largest marquee   A marquee covering an area of 188,350 square feet (4.32 acres) was erected by the firm of Deuter of Augsburg, Germany for the 1958 "Welcome Expo" in Brussels, Belgium.

Largest Ferris wheel   The Cosmoclock 21 in Yokohama City, Japan is 344½ feet high and 328 feet in diameter, with 60 eight-seat gondolas. It features illumination by laser beams and acoustic effects by synthesizers. The 60 arms holding the gondolas serve as second hands for the 42½-foot-long electric clock mounted at the hub.

United States The tallest Ferris wheel in the United States is the Texas Star at Fair Park in Dallas, TX, built in 1985. It is 212 ft. 6 in. high, with 44 gondolas and a seating capacity of 244 riders. It operates during the annual State Fair of Texas.

Largest swing A glider swing 30 feet high was constructed by Kenneth R. Mack, Langenburg, Saskatchewan, Canada for Uncle Herb's Amusements in 1986. The swing is capable of taking its four riders 25 feet off the ground.

Tallest scarecrow "Stretch II," constructed by the Speers family of Paris, Ontario, Canada and a crew of 15 at the Paris, Ontario Fall Fair on September 2, 1989, measured 103 ft. 6¾ in. tall.

Largest bonfire Residents and off-duty firefighters from Workington, England lit a bonfire 122 ft. 6 in. high, with an overall volume of 250,700 cubic feet, on November 5, 1993.

ROLLER COASTERS

Oldest operating roller coaster *Rutschebahnen* (Scenic Railway) Mk.2 was constructed at the Tivoli Gardens, Copenhagen, Denmark, in 1913. This coaster opened to the public in 1914, and has remained open ever since.

United States The oldest operating roller coaster in the United States is the *Zippin Pippin*, constructed at Libertyland Amusement Park, Memphis, TN in 1915.

Greatest drop The 4-inversion *Steel Phantom*, opened in April 1991 at Kennywood Amusement Park, West Mifflin, PA, has a second vertical drop of 225 feet into a natural ravine, with a design speed of 80 MPH. Sharing the record for the greatest drop is *Desperado*—a non-inversion coaster

---

ROLL 'EM!

The *Dragon Khan* at Port Aventura, Salou, Spain has the greatest number of loops/inversions of any complete-circuit multi-element coaster. It was designed by Bollinger and Mabillard of Mothey, Switzerland. Riders are turned upside-down eight times over the 4,166-ft.-2-in. track.

---

at Buffalo Bill's Resort and Casino, Primadonna Resorts Complex, Jean, NV. *Desperado*'s first vertical drop plunges 225 feet; this ride also has a design speed of 80 MPH (See TALLEST ROLLER COASTER).

Longest roller coaster The *Ultimate* at Lightwater Valley Theme Park in Ripon, England has a run of 1.42 miles.

United States   *The Beast* at Kings Island, Cincinnati, OH has a run of 1.40 miles, including 800 feet of tunnels and a 540-degree banked helix.

GUESS WHAT?

Q. HOW FAST IS THE FASTEST VEHICLE ON RAILS?

A. LOOK IN "TRAINS" (TRANSPORT)

Tallest roller coaster   The tallest complete-circuit roller coaster is *Desperado* (See GREATEST DROP) at Buffalo Bill's Casino, NV. It features a lift height of 209 feet.

Most roller coasters   Cedar Point Amusement Park in Sandusky, OH offers a choice of two wood and nine steel track coasters.

The world's largest bonfire, built in Workington, England, is closely watched by firefighters just in case anything goes wrong. The temperature at the heart of the bonfire was estimated to be 9,900°F. (*Richard Graham*)

BARS AND RESTAURANTS

Largest bar The largest beer-selling establishment in the world is the Mathäser, Bayerstrasse 5, Munich, Germany, where daily sales reach 84,470 pints. It was established in 1829, demolished in World War II and rebuilt by 1955. It seats 5,500 people.

Tallest bar The bar at Humperdink's Seafood and Steakhouse in Irving, TX is 25 ft. 3 in. high with two levels of shelving containing over 1,000 bottles. The lower level has four rows of shelves approximately 40 feet across and can be reached from floor level. The upper level, which has five rows of shelves, is reached by climbing a ladder.

Longest bar The longest permanent continuous bar is the 405-ft.-10-in.-long counter in the Beer Barrel Saloon at Put-in-Bay, South Bass Island, OH, opened in 1989. The bar is fitted with 56 beer taps and surrounded by 160 bar stools. Longer temporary bars have been erected, notably for beer festivals.

Largest night club Gilley's Club (formerly Shelly's) on Spencer Highway, Houston, TX, built in 1955, was extended in 1971 and now has a seating capacity of 6,000 under one roof covering four acres.

Lowest night club The Minus 206 in Tiberias, Israel, on the shores of the Sea of Galilee, is 676 feet below sea level.

Largest restaurant The Royal Dragon (Mang Gorn Luang) restaurant in Bangkok, Thailand, opened in October 1991, can seat 5,000 customers served by a staff of 1,200. In order to cover the 8.35-acre service area more quickly, the employees wear roller skates.

Highest restaurant The restaurant in the Chacaltaya ski resort, Bolivia is at an altitude of 17,519 feet.

Largest restaurant chain McDonald's Corporation of Oak Brook, IL licensed and owned 15,205 restaurants in 79 countries as of December 31, 1994. Worldwide sales in 1994 were $26 billion.

SHOPPING CENTERS

Largest shopping center The $1.1 billion West Edmonton Mall in Alberta, Canada covers 5.2 million square feet on a 121-acre site and encompasses over 800 stores and services as well as 11 major department stores. Parking is provided for 20,000 cars, and more than 500,000 shoppers visit the mall each week.

United States The largest shopping center and entertainment complex in the United States is the Mall of America in Bloomington, MN, which covers 4.2 million square feet. It contains 350 stores, eight night clubs, and a 7-acre amusement park. There are parking spaces for 12,750 cars, and approximately 750,000 people shop there every week.

Largest wholesale center The Dallas Market Center on Stemmons Freeway, Dallas, TX covers nearly 6.9 million square feet in five buildings. The

Anything from polishing up your golf to practicing your breaststroke is possible at the world's largest shopping center, West Edmonton Mall, Alberta, Canada. Then again, you could always shop at the huge 121-acre site. (*West Edmonton Mall*)

whole complex covers 175 acres and houses some 2,580 permanent showrooms displaying merchandise of more than 30,000 manufacturers. The center attracts 800,000 buyers each year to its 40 annual markets and trade shows.

Longest mall   The £40 million ($68 million) shopping center in Milton Keynes, England is 2,133 feet long.

BUILDINGS FOR WORSHIP

Oldest church   The oldest standing church in the United States is the Newport Parish Church, commonly known as St. Luke's, in Isle of Wight County, VA, four miles south of Smithfield, VA. The church was built *c.* 1632 and was originally called Warrisquioke Parish Church. Its present name was instituted in 1957.

Oldest synagogue   The oldest synagogue in the United States is Touro Synagogue, Newport, RI. Construction was started in 1759 and completed in 1763.

Largest temple   The largest religious structure ever built is Angkor Wat ("City Temple"), enclosing 402 acres in Cambodia. It was built to the Hindu god Vishnu by the Khmer King Suryavarman II in the period A.D. 1113–50. Its curtain wall measures 4,199 by 4,199 feet and its population, before it was abandoned in 1432, was 80,000. The whole complex of 72 major monuments, begun *c.* A.D. 900, extends over 15 by 5 miles.

Highest temple   The Rongbu temple, between Tingri and Shigatse in Tibet, is at an altitude of *c.* 16,750 feet, just 25 miles from Mt. Everest. It contains nine chapels, and is inhabited by lamas and nuns.

Largest cathedrals   The Gothic cathedral church of the Episcopal Diocese of New York, St. John the Divine, in New York City, has a floor area of 121,000 square feet and a volume of 16,822,000 cubic feet. The cornerstone was laid on December 27, 1892, but work on the building stopped in 1941. Work was restarted in earnest in July 1979, but is still not finished. The nave is the longest in the world at 601 feet, with a vaulting 124 feet in height.

The cathedral covering the largest area is that of Santa Mariá de la Sede in Sevilla (Seville), Spain. It was built in Spanish Gothic style between 1402 and 1519, and is 414 feet long, 271 feet wide and 100 feet high to the vault of the nave.

Smallest cathedral   The Christ Catholic Church, Highlandville, MO, consecrated in July 1983, measures 14 by 17 feet and seats 18 people.

Largest church   The church of the Basilica of Our Lady of Peace (Notre Dame de la Paix) in Yamoussoukro, Ivory Coast was completed in 1989. It has a total area of 100,000 square feet, with seating for 7,000 people. Including its golden cross, it is 519 feet high.

The elliptical Basilica of St. Pio X at Lourdes, France was completed in 1957. It is 660 feet long and has a capacity of 20,000 under its giant span arches.

Longest   The crypt of the underground Civil War Memorial Church in the Guadarrama Mountains, 28 miles from Madrid, Spain, is 853 feet long. It took 21 years (1937–58) to build, at a reported cost of $392 million, and is surmounted by a cross 492 feet tall.

Largest synagogue   Temple Emanu-El on Fifth Avenue at 65th Street, New York City, was completed in September 1929. It has a frontage of 150 feet on Fifth Avenue and 253 feet on 65th Street. The sanctuary proper can accommodate 2,500 people, and the Beth-El Chapel seats 350. When all facilities are in use, more than 6,000 people can be accommodated.

Largest mosque   The area of the Shah Faisal Mosque, near Islamabad, Pakistan, is 46.87 acres, with a covered area of 1.19 acres. It can accommodate 100,000 worshippers in the prayer hall and the courtyard, and a further 200,000 people in the adjacent grounds.

Tallest minaret   The minaret of the Great Hassan II Mosque, Casablanca, Morocco measures 656 feet. The cost of construction of the mosque was $540 million.

Tallest spire The tallest cathedral spire in the world is that of the Protestant Cathedral of Ulm in Germany. The building is early Gothic and was begun in 1377. The tower, in the center of the west facade, was not finally completed until 1890 and is 528 feet high.

The world's tallest church spire is that of the Chicago Temple of the First Methodist Church on Clark Street, Chicago, IL. The building consists of a 22-story skyscraper (erected in 1924) surmounted by a parsonage at 330 feet, a "Sky Chapel" at 400 feet and a steeple cross at 568 feet above street level.

WALLS, WINDOWS AND DOORS

Longest wall The Great Wall of China has a main-line length of 2,150 miles. Completed during the reign of Qin Shi Huangdi (221–210 B.C.), it has a further 1,780 miles of branches and spurs. Its height varies from 15 feet to 39 feet and it is up to 32 feet thick. A survey report from China in 1985 stated that the wall's total length was once 6,200 miles.

Thickest walls Ur-nammu's city walls at Ur (now Muqayyar, Iraq), destroyed by the Elamites in 2006 B.C., were 88 feet thick and made of mud brick.

SLAM!

The door of the laser target room at Lawrence Livermore National Laboratory, CA weighs 360 tons and is up to eight feet thick. It was installed by Overly Manufacturing Company.

Longest fence The dingo-proof wire fence enclosing the main sheep areas of Australia is six feet high, one foot underground and stretches for 3,437 miles. The Queensland state government discontinued full maintenance in 1982.

Tallest fences The world's tallest fences are security screens 65 feet high erected by Harrop-Allin of Pretoria, South Africa in November 1981 to protect fuel depots and refineries at Sasolburg from rocket attack.

Largest windows The windows in the Palace of Industry and Technology at Rondpoint de la Défense, Paris, France have an extreme width of 715 feet and a maximum height of 164 feet.

Oldest stained glass window The oldest complete stained glass window in the world is in the Cathedral of Augsburg, Germany. It represents the Prophets and dates from the second half of the 11th century.

Pieces of stained glass dated before A.D. 850, some possibly even to the seventh century, excavated by Prof. Rosemary Cramp, were set into a window of that date in the nearby St. Paul's Church, Jarrow, Ireland.

United States   The oldest figured stained glass window in the United States is in Christ Church, Pelham Manor, NY and was designed by William Jay Bolton and John Bolton in 1843.

Largest stained glass window   The window of the Resurrection Mausoleum in Justice, IL measures 22,381 square feet in 2,448 panels and was completed in 1971.

The Basilica of Our Lady of Peace (Notre Dame de la Paix) at Yamoussoukro, Ivory Coast contains a number of stained glass windows covering a total area of 80,000 square feet.

Tallest stained glass window   The back-lit glass mural installed in 1979 in the atrium of the Ramada Hotel, Dubai is 135 feet high.

Window cleaning   Gerald Follis of Lurgan, Northern Ireland cleaned three standard 42½-by-47-inch office windows with an 11¾-inch-long squeegee and two gallons of water in 9.1 seconds on April 16, 1994 at the Citybus Guinness World of Records Weekend in Belfast.

United States   Keith Witt of Amarillo, TX cleaned three standard 42½-by-47-inch office windows with an 11¾-inch-long squeegee and two gallons of water in 10.13 seconds on January 31, 1992 at the International Window Cleaning Association convention in San Antonio, TX.

Largest doors   The four doors in the Vehicle Assembly Building near Cape Canaveral, FL have a height of 460 feet.

BRIDGES

Oldest bridge   The oldest datable bridge still in use is the slab stone single-arch bridge over the River Meles in Izmir, Turkey, which dates from *c*. 850 B.C.

Busiest bridge   The Howrah Bridge across the river Hooghly in Calcutta, India carries 57,000 vehicles per day and an incalculable number of pedestrians across its 1,500-foot-long, 72-foot-wide span.

Fastest bridge building   A team of British soldiers from 21 Engineer Regiment, based in Nienburg, Germany, constructed a bridge across a 26-foot gap using a 5-bay single-story MGB (medium-girder bridge) in a time of 7 min. 12 sec. in Hameln, Germany on November 3, 1992. Future times will be slower following the introduction of new rules.

Bridge sale   The largest antique ever sold was London Bridge, in England in March 1968. Ivan F. Luckin of the Court of Common Council of the

The Seto-Ohashi bridge is the world's longest road and rail bridge, with an overall length of 43,374 feet. It links Honshu, Japan's main island, with the smaller island of Shikoku. (*Gamma/K. Kurita*)

Corporation of London sold it to the McCulloch Oil Corporation of Los Angeles, CA for £1,029,000 ($2,469,600). The 11,800 tons of facade stonework were reassembled at a cost of $7.2 million at Lake Havasu City, AZ and rededicated on October 10, 1971.

Longest cable suspension bridge The world's longest bridge span is the main span of the Humber Estuary Bridge, Humberside, England, at 4,626 feet. The towers are 533 ft. 1⅝ in. tall and are 1⅜ inches out of parallel to allow for the curvature of the earth. Including its two side spans, the bridge stretches 1.37 miles. It was completed on July 18, 1980.

Cable-stayed The Pont de Normandie in Le Havre, France has a cable-stayed main span of 2,808 feet. It was opened to traffic on January 20, 1995.

The Mackinac Straits Bridge between Mackinac City and St. Ignace, MI is the longest suspension bridge between anchorages (1.58 miles), and has an overall length, including approaches, of five miles.

United States The longest suspension bridge in the United States is the Verrazano-Narrows Bridge, completed in 1964, which measures 4,260 feet. The bridge spans Lower New York Bay and connects Staten Island to Brooklyn.

Suspension bridge walking Donald H. Betty of Lancaster, PA has walked over 46 suspension bridges, including the 13 longest in the world.

Longest cantilever bridge The Quebec Bridge over the St. Lawrence River in Canada has the longest cantilever truss span of any in the world—1,800 feet between the piers and 3,239 feet overall. It carries a railroad track and two roadways.

United States The longest cantilever bridge in the United States is the John Barry Bridge, in Chester, PA. It spans the Delaware River and measures 1,644 feet.

NO BRIDGE TOO FAR

Donald H. Betty needs some inside information on Japan. "I want to know if the Kanmon Strait Bridge between Honshu and Kyushu has a pedestrian walkway." If not, Betty will have to convince authorities to close down a lane and let him walk the giant bridge. Once he does, he will have walked across the 14 longest suspension bridges in the world.

Getting credit for the first 13 crossings as well as for numerous shorter suspension bridges has been a struggle and a triumph. "If you want to cross the Golden Gate, all you have to do is fly to San Francisco and start walking." But bridges without walkways, including those in Portugal, Venezuela, and Mackinac Island, Michigan, have been tricky. "I used a knee injury to get handicapped status, and crossed the Verrazano-Narrows Bridge during the New York Marathon. In Turkey, armed guards came with me when I crossed two bridges over the Bosporus Strait that run between two continents."

In his early years, Betty worked for Bethlehem Steel before becoming a mechanical engineer. "Once you get steel in your blood, it stays there. I developed a tremendous feeling for people who designed these bridges, and the bravery and death-defying acts of the people who built them."

His aim? To keep on going until he's crossed the 21 longest existing bridges, as well as the four big bridges now under construction in Denmark (to be finished in 1996), Sweden (1997), Hong Kong (1998), and Kobe, Japan (1999).

During more than 20 years of bridge walking, Betty has developed some rituals. "I always lie down in the middle of the bridge and take a vertical shot of the tower. People ask, 'What's that man doing lying there?' It doesn't bother me. I get spectacular pictures. On the bridge, I pick up the coins people throw out of their cars for good luck. I have pennies from everywhere."

Suspension bridge walking

Donald H. Betty of Lancaster, PA has walked over 46 suspension bridges, including the 13 longest in the world.

The Royal Gorge suspension bridge in Colorado is a record 1,053 feet above water. (*Spectrum Colour Library; Joan S. Betty*)

PLASTIC FANTASTIC!

The reinforced plastic bridge at the Aberfeldy Golf Club, Aberfeldy, Scotland has a main span 206 ft. 8 in. long and an overall length of 370 ft. 9 in.

Longest covered bridge   The covered bridge in Hartland, New Brunswick, Canada measures 1,282 feet overall. It was completed in 1899.

Longest floating bridge   The Second Lake Washington Bridge, Seattle, WA has a total length of 12,596 feet and a floating section that measures 7,518 feet. It was completed in August 1963.

Longest railroad bridge   The 43,374-foot-long Seto-Ohashi double-deck road and rail bridge links Kojima, Honshu with Sakaide, Shikoku, Japan.

United States   The Huey P. Long Bridge, Metairie, LA has a railroad section 23,235 feet long, including approach roads. It has a 3-span trestle: 529 feet, 790 feet and 531 feet, followed by a single span of 531.5 feet. It was completed on December 16, 1935.

Longest bridging   The Second Lake Pontchartrain Causeway was completed on March 23, 1969, joining Mandeville and Metairie, LA. It has a length of 126,055 feet.

Longest concrete arch bridge   The Jesse H. Jones Memorial Bridge, which spans the Houston Ship Canal in Texas, measures 1,500 feet.

Longest steel arch bridge   The New River Gorge Bridge, near Fayetteville, WV, has a span of 1,700 feet.

Longest stone arch bridge   The 3,810-foot-long Rockville Bridge, north of Harrisburg, PA, has 48 spans containing 216,050 tons of stone. It was completed in 1901.

Widest long-span bridge   The 1,650-foot Sydney Harbor Bridge, Sydney, Australia is 160 feet wide. It carries two electric overhead railroad tracks, eight road lanes, and bicycle and pedestrian lanes.

Highest bridge   The suspension bridge in the Royal Gorge in Colorado is 1,053 feet above the Arkansas River. It has a main span of 880 feet and was constructed in six months, ending on December 6, 1929.

Highest railroad bridge   The Mala Reka viaduct of Yugoslav Railways at Kolašin on the Belgrade–Bar line is 650 feet high. It consists of steel spans mounted on concrete piers.

Highest road bridge   The road bridge at the highest altitude in the world, 18,380 feet, is the 98.4-foot-long Bailey Bridge, built by an Indian Army team in August 1982 near Khardung-La, in Ladakh, India.

Tallest bridge towers   The towers of the Golden Gate Bridge, which connects San Francisco and Marin Co., CA, stand 745 feet above the water. The bridge has an overall length of 8,966 feet.

Longest railway viaduct   The rock-filled Great Salt Lake Railroad Trestle, carrying the Southern Pacific Railroad 11.85 miles across the Great Salt Lake, UT, was opened as a pile and trestle bridge on March 8, 1904, but converted to rock fill in 1955–60.

Longest ancient aqueduct   The aqueduct of Carthage in Tunisia ran 87.6 miles from the springs of Zaghouan to Djebel Djougar. It was built by the Romans during the reign of Publius Aelius Hadrianus (A.D. 117–138), also known as Hadrian. In 1895, 344 arches still survived. Its original capacity has been calculated at 7 million gallons per day.

Longest modern aqueduct   The California State Water Project aqueduct, completed in 1974, has a total length of 826 miles, of which 385 miles is canalized.

Tallest aqueduct   The tallest of the 109 arches of the Aguas Livres aqueduct, built in Lisbon, Portugal, 1729–48, is 213 feet high.

MASTS AND TOWERS

Tallest mast   The tallest-ever structure in the world was the guyed Warszawa Radio mast in Konstantynow, Poland. Prior to its fall during renovation work on August 10, 1991, it was 2,120 feet tall. The mast was put into operation on July 22, 1974. It was designed by Jan Polak and weighed 606 tons.

The world's tallest structure is now a stayed television transmitting tower 2,063 feet tall, between Fargo and Blanchard, ND. It was built at a cost of about $500,000 for Channel 11 of KTHI-TV in 30 days (October 2 to November 1, 1963) by 11 men from Hamilton Erection, Inc. of York, SC.

Tallest tower   The tallest building and freestanding tower (as opposed to a guyed mast) in the world is the $63 million CN Tower in Toronto, Ontario, Canada, which rises to 1,815 ft. 5 in. Excavation began on February 12, 1973 for the erection of the 143,300-ton reinforced, post-tensioned concrete structure, which was completed on April 2, 1975. The 416-seat

---

GUESS WHAT?

Q. HOW TALL WAS THE WORLD'S TALLEST CAKE?

A. LOOK IN "FOOD AND DRINK" (HUMAN ACHIEVEMENTS)

restaurant revolves in the Sky Pod at 1,150 feet, from which diners can see hills 75 miles away.

Tallest LEGO tower A 72.6-foot-tall LEGO tower was built at "La Belle Etoile" shopping center in Luxembourg on September 4, 1994, by the supermarket CACTUS SA.

Largest cooling tower The cooling tower adjacent to the nuclear power plant in Uentrop, Germany is 590 feet tall and was completed in 1976.

Tallest water tower The Waterspheroid in Edmond, OK, built in 1986, rises to a height of 218 feet, and has a capacity of 500,000 gallons. The tower was manufactured by Chicago Bridge and Iron Na-Con Inc.

Tallest chimney The Ekibastuz, Kazakhstan coal power plant No. 2 stack is 1,377 feet tall. The chimney tapers from 144 feet in diameter at the base to 46 ft. 7 in. at the top, and it weighs 53,600 tons.

Most massive chimney The 1,148-foot chimney at Puentes de Garcia Rodriguez, northwest Spain, built by M.W. Kellogg Co. for Empresa Nacional

The CN Tower in Toronto, Canada is the world's tallest building and the tallest freestanding tower. (*Spectrum Colour Library*)

TALLEST
TOTEM POLE

Tallest totem pole

A 180-ft.-3-in.-tall pole known as the *Spirit of Lekwammen* (lekwammen = land of the winds) was raised on August 4, 1994, in Victoria, British Columbia, Canada before the Commonwealth Games took place there. It was a Spirit of Nations project developed by Richard Krentz of Campbell River, British Columbia, and took nine months to carve.

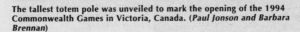

The tallest totem pole was unveiled to mark the opening of the 1994 Commonwealth Games in Victoria, Canada. (*Paul Jonson and Barbara Brennan*)

de Electricidad S.A., contains 556,247 cubic feet of concrete and 2.9 million pounds of steel and has an internal volume of 6.7 million cubic feet.

Tallest flagpole   The flagpole at Panmunjon, North Korea, near the border with South Korea, is 525 feet high and flies a flag 98 ft. 6 in. long.

United States   The tallest flagpole in the United States was trimmed from a Douglas fir and erected at the 1915 Panama–Pacific International Exposition in San Francisco, CA. It stood 299 ft. 7 in. tall and weighed 52 tons.

The tallest unsupported flagpole in the world is the 282-foot-tall steel pole, weighing 120,000 pounds, that was erected on August 22, 1985 at the Canadian Expo 86 exhibition in Vancouver, British Columbia. The flagpole supports a hockey stick 205 feet long.

Tallest totem pole   A 180-ft.-3-in.-tall pole known as the *Spirit of Lekwammen* (lekwammen = land of the winds) was raised on August 4, 1994 in Victoria, British Columbia, Canada before the Commonwealth Games took place there. It was a Spirit of Nations project developed by Richard Krentz of Campbell River, British Columbia, and took nine months to carve.

Tallest lighthouse   The 348-foot steel tower near Yamashita Park in Yokohama, Japan has a power of 600,000 candelas and a visibility range of 20 miles.

The lights with the greatest range are the ones 1,089 feet above the ground on the Empire State Building, New York City. Each of the 4-arc mercury bulbs is visible 80 miles away on the ground and 300 miles away from aircraft.

CANALS AND LOCKS

Longest ancient canal   The Grand Canal of China was begun in 540 B.C. and not completed until A.D. 1327, when it extended (including canalized river sections) for 1,107 miles. The estimated work force *c*. A.D. 600 reached 5 million on the Bian section.

Longest modern canal   The Belomorsko-Baltiyskiy Canal from Belomorsk to Povenets, Russia is 141 miles long and has 19 locks. It was completed with the use of forced labor in 1933. The canal cannot accommodate ships of more than 16 feet in draft.

The world's longest big-ship canal is the Suez Canal linking the Red Sea with the Mediterranean, opened on November 17, 1869. It is 100.8 miles long from the Port Said lighthouse to Suez Roads, and ranges from 984 feet to 1,198 feet wide. It took 10 years and a work force of 1.5 million people to build the canal; 120,000 workers died during construction.

United States   The longest canal in the United States is the Erie Barge Canal, connecting the Hudson River at Troy, NY with Lake Erie at Buffalo, NY. It is 365 miles long, 150 feet wide and 12 feet deep.

Busiest ship canal   The Kiel Canal, linking the North Sea with the Baltic Sea in Germany, has more than 40,000 transits each year. The busiest in terms of tonnage of shipping is the Suez Canal, with 423,723,000 gross registered tons in the fiscal year 1994.

Longest irrigation canal   The Karakumsky Canal stretches 745 miles from Haun-Khan to Ashkhabad, Turkmenistan. The course length is 500 miles.

Largest canal system   The seawater cooling system associated with the Madinat Al-Jubail Al-Sinaiyah construction project in Saudi Arabia brings 388 million cubic feet of seawater per day to cool the industrial establishment.

Longest artificial seaway   The St. Lawrence Seaway is 189 miles long along the New York State–Ontario border from Montreal to Lake Ontario. It enables ships up to 728 feet long and weighing up to 29,100 tons to sail 2,342 miles from the North Atlantic up the St. Lawrence estuary and across the Great Lakes to Duluth, MN. The project opened on April 25, 1959.

Largest lock   The Berendrecht lock, which links the River Scheldt with docks at Antwerp, Belgium, is the largest sea lock in the world. First used in April 1989, it has a length of 1,640 feet, a width of 223 feet and a sill level of 44 feet. Each of its four sliding lock gates weighs 1,770 tons.

Deepest lock   The deepest lock in the United States is the John Day dam lock on the River Columbia, in Oregon and Washington, completed in 1963. It can raise or lower barges 113 feet and is served by a 1,100-ton gate.

Highest lock elevator   The lock elevator at Ronquières on the Charleroi–Brussels Canal, Belgium rises to 225 feet. Two 236-wheeled caissons, each able to carry 1,500 tons, take 22 minutes to cover the 4,698-foot-long inclined plane.

Largest cut   The Corinth Canal, Greece, opened in 1893, is 3.93 miles long, 26 feet deep, 81 feet wide at the surface and has an extreme depth of cutting of 259 feet.

DAMS AND RESERVOIRS

Most massive dam   Measured by volume, the largest dam is at the Sobradinho hydroelectric power station on the São Francisco River, Bahia, Brazil. Completed in 1983, the dam has a volume of 44.5 billion cubic yards, an area of 1,622 square miles, and is 217 miles long. It was constructed by the Companhia Hidro Elétrica do São Francisco.

Largest concrete dam   The Grand Coulee Dam on the Columbia River, WA was begun in 1933 and completed in 1942. The dam has a crest length of 4,173 feet, is 550 feet high, and contains 285 million cubic feet (21.5 million tons) of concrete.

The largest levees are those alongside the Mississippi. They were seriously damaged during extensive flooding in the summer of 1993. (*Gamma/Holbrooke/Liaison*)

Highest dam   The 1,098-foot-high Rogun earth-filled dam across the river Vakhsh, Tadzhikistan has a crest length of only 1,975 feet but a volume of 92.9 million cubic yards. The dam was constructed between 1981 and 1987.

United States   The embankment–earthfill Oroville Dam, spanning the Feather River in California, is the United States' highest dam, reaching 754 feet. It was completed in 1968.

Strongest dam   The 803-foot-high Sayano-Shushenskaya Dam on the River Yenisey, Russia is designed to bear a load of 20 million tons from a fully filled reservoir of 41 billion cubic yards capacity. Although completed, this dam is not yet operational.

Longest dam   The Kiev Dam across the Dnieper, Ukraine, completed in 1964, has a crest length of 25.6 miles.

Largest tidal barrier   The Oosterscheldedam, a storm-surge barrier in the southwestern corner of the Netherlands, has 65 concrete piers and 62 steel gates, and covers a total length of 5½ miles. It was opened by Queen Beatrix on October 4, 1986.

Largest levees   The most massive levees ever built were the Mississippi River levees, begun in 1717 but vastly augmented by the federal government after the disastrous floods of 1927. They extended for 1,732 miles along the main river from Cape Girardeau, MO to the Gulf of Mexico and comprised more than a billion cubic yards of earthworks. Levees on the tributaries comprised an additional 2,000 miles. Much of the area suffered from extensive flooding in the summer of 1993, which caused serious damage to the levees.

Longest breakwater   The granite South Breakwater protecting the Port of Galveston, TX is 6.74 miles long.

Largest reservoir   The largest man-made reservoir in terms of volume is the Bratskoye reservoir, on the Angara River in Siberia, Russia, with a volume of 40.6 cubic miles and an area of 2,111 square miles. It extends for 372 miles with a width of 21 miles. It was filled in 1961–67.

The world's largest artificial lake measured by surface area is Lake Volta, Ghana, formed by the Akosombo Dam, completed in 1965. By 1969, the lake had filled to an area of 3,275 square miles, with a 4,500-mile shoreline.

United States   The largest wholly artificial reservoir in the United States is Lake Mead in Nevada. It was formed by the Hoover Dam, which was completed in 1936. The lake has a capacity of 1,241,445 million cubic feet and a surface area of 28,255,000 acre-feet.

Largest waterwheel   The Mohammadieh Noria wheel at Hamah, Syria has a diameter of 131 feet and dates from Roman times.

TUNNELS

Longest tunnel   The longest tunnel of any kind is the New York City West Delaware water-supply tunnel, begun in 1937 and completed in 1944. It has a diameter of $13\frac{1}{2}$ feet and runs for 105 miles from the Rondout Reservoir into the Hillview Reservoir in Yonkers, NY.

DID YOU KNOW?

The Channel Tunnel is the longest undersea tunnel. It runs under the English Channel between Folkestone, England and Calais, France, and was opened on May 6, 1994. The length of each twin rail tunnel is 31.03 miles and the diameter 24 ft. 11 in. The undersea section of the tunnel is 23.6 miles long.

Longest rail tunnel   The 33.46-mile-long Seikan Rail Tunnel was bored to 787 feet beneath sea level and 328 feet below the seabed of the Tsugaru

Strait between Tappi Saki, Honshu, and Fukushima, Hokkaido, Japan. The underwater section is 14¹/₂ miles long.

United States   The longest railroad main-line tunnel in the United States is the Moffat Tunnel, which cuts through a 6.2-mile section of the Rocky Mountains in Colorado. Tunnel construction was completed in 1928.

Longest subway tunnel   The Moscow Metro Kaluzhskaya underground railroad line from Medvedkovo to Bittsevsky Park is 23¹/₂ miles long and was completed in early 1990.

Longest road tunnel   The 10.14-mile-long 2-lane St. Gotthard road tunnel from Göschenen to Airolo, Switzerland opened to traffic on September 5, 1980.

United States   The longest road tunnel in the United States is the 1.69-mile long twin Eisenhower Memorial Tunnel on Interstate 70 under the Continental Divide in Colorado. The westbound bore was opened to traffic on March 8, 1973, while the eastbound became open full-time on February 29, 1980.

Largest road tunnel   The largest-diameter road tunnel in the world is the one blasted through Yerba Buena Island, San Francisco, CA. It is 77 ft. 10 in. wide, 56 feet high and 540 feet long. More than 250,000 vehicles pass through on its two decks every day.

Deepest road tunnel   The Hitra Tunnel in Norway, which links the mainland to the island of Hitra, reaches a depth of 866 feet below sea level. It is 3¹/₂ miles long and has three lanes. The tunnel was opened in December 1994.

Longest hydroelectric irrigation tunnel   The 51¹/₂-mile-long Orange–Fish Rivers tunnel, South Africa, was bored between 1967 and 1973. The lining to a minimum thickness of nine inches gave a completed diameter of 17 ft. 6 in.

The Majes dam project in Peru involves 60.9 miles of tunnels for hydroelectric and water-supply purposes. The dam is at an altitude of 13,780 feet.

Largest sewerage tunnel   The Chicago Water Reclamation District Tunnel and Reservoir Project (TARP) in Illinois, also known as the "Deep Tunnel," will have 131 miles of sewerage tunneling when it is complete. It is divided into a pollution control section and a flood control section. As of May 1995, 75.4 miles were in operation and 18 miles were under construction. The estimated cost of the total project, including the three 41-billion-gallon total capacity reservoirs, is $3.7 billion.

Longest bridge-tunnel   The Chesapeake Bay bridge-tunnel extends 17.65 miles from the Eastern Shore region of the Virginia Peninsula to Virginia Beach, VA. It was opened to traffic on April 15, 1964. The longest bridged section is Trestle C (4.56 miles long) and the longest tunnel section is the Thimble Shoal Channel Tunnel (1.09 miles).

Longest and largest canal-tunnel The Rove Tunnel on the Canal de Marseille au Rhône in the south of France was completed in 1927 and is 23,359 feet long, 72 feet wide and 37 feet high. Built to be navigated by seagoing ships, it was closed in 1963 following a collapse and has not been reopened.

Oldest navigable tunnel The Malpas tunnel on the Canal du Midi in southwest France was completed in 1681 and is 528 feet long. Its completion enabled vessels to navigate from the Atlantic Ocean to the Mediterranean Sea via the river Garonne to Toulouse and via the Canal du Midi to Sète.

Longest unsupported tunnel The longest unsupported example of a machine-bored tunnel is the Three Rivers water tunnel, 5.82 miles long with a 10-ft.-6-in. diameter, constructed for the city of Atlanta, GA from April 1980 to February 1982.

MONUMENTS

Tallest monument The stainless-steel Gateway to the West arch in St. Louis, MO, completed on October 28, 1965, is a sweeping arch spanning 630 feet and rising to 630 feet. The arch cost $29 million and was designed in 1947 by Finnish-American architect Eero Saarinen.

Tallest menhir The 330-ton Grand Menhir Brisé in Locmariaquer, Brittany, France originally stood 59 feet high, but it is now in four pieces.

Largest trilithons The largest trilithons are at Stonehenge, Salisbury Plain, England, with single sarsen blocks weighing more than 50 tons. The blocks would have required at least 550 men to drag them up a 9-degree gradient. The earliest stage of construction at the site has been dated to 2800 B.C.

PYRAMIDS

Largest pyramid The largest pyramid, and the largest monument ever constructed, is the Quetzalcóatl at Cholula de Rivadabia, 63 miles southeast of Mexico City. It is 177 feet tall and its base covers an area of nearly 45 acres. Its total volume has been estimated at 4.3 million square yards.

The largest single block in pyramid-building is from the Third Pyramid (Pyramid of Mycerinus) at El Gizeh, Egypt and weighs 320 tons.

Oldest pyramid The Djoser step pyramid in Saqqara, Egypt dates from *c.* 2630 B.C. It was constructed by Imhotep (Djoser's royal architect) to a height of 204 feet.

Largest ziggurat The Ziggurat of Choga Zambil, 18.6 miles from Haft Tepe, Iran, had an outer base 344 by 344 feet, and the fifth "box," nearly 164 feet above, measured 92 by 92 feet.

STATUES AND COLUMNS

Tallest monumental column   Constructed 1936–39, the tapering column that commemorates the Battle of San Jacinto (April 21, 1836), on the bank of the San Jacinto River near Houston, TX, is 570 feet tall, 47 feet square at the base, and 30 feet square at the observation tower, which is topped by a star weighing 220 tons.

Tallest columns   The 36 fluted pillars of Vermont marble in the colonnade of the Education Building, Albany, NY are 90 feet tall. Their base diameter is 6 ft. 6 in.

Load-bearing   The tallest load-bearing stone columns are in the Hall of Columns of the Temple of Amun at Karnak, Egypt. They are 69 feet tall and were built in the 19th dynasty during the reign of Rameses II *c.* 1270 B.C.

Tallest floodlights   The tallest lighting columns are the four made by Petitjean & Cie of Troyes, France and installed by Taylor Woodrow at Sultan Qaboos Sports Complex, Muscat, Oman. They stand 208 ft. 4 in. high.

Tallest obelisk   The Washington Monument in Washington, D.C. stands 555 ft. 5⅛ in. high. It was built to honor George Washington (1732–99).

Largest obelisk   The obelisk of Tuthmosis III, brought from Aswan, Egypt by Emperor Constantius in the spring of A.D. 357, was repositioned in the Piazza San Giovanni in Laterano, Rome on August 3, 1588. Once 118 ft. 1 in. tall, it now stands 107 ft. 7 in. and weighs 502 tons.

An unfinished obelisk, probably commissioned by Queen Hatshepsut *c.* 1490 B.C., *in situ* at Aswan, Egypt is 136 ft. 10 in. long and weighs 1,287 tons.

Tallest statue   A bronze statue of Buddha 394 feet high was completed in Tokyo, Japan in January 1993. It is 115 feet wide and weighs 1,100 tons. The statue took seven years to make, and was a joint Japanese–Taiwanese project.

United States   The Statue of Liberty, originally named Liberty Enlightening the World, is the tallest statue in the United States. Designed and built in France to commemorate the friendship of the two countries, the 152-foot statue was shipped to New York City, where its copper sheets were assembled. President Grover Cleveland accepted the statue for the United States on October 28, 1886.

Largest LEGO statue   The sculpture of the Native American chief Sitting Bull, at the Legoland Park, Billund, Denmark, is 25 feet tall. The largest statue ever constructed from LEGO, it required 1.5 million bricks, individually glued together to withstand the weather.

CEMETERIES AND TOMBS

Largest cemetery   Ohlsdorf Cemetery in Hamburg, Germany covers an area of 990 acres, with 969,969 burials and 403,263 cremations as of December 31, 1994. It has been in continuous use since 1877.

The largest monolithic obelisk in the world, weighing 502 tons, is the "skewer" or "spit" of Tuthmosis III in Rome, Italy.

United States The largest cemetery in the United States is Arlington National Cemetery, situated on the Potomac River in Virginia. It covers 612 acres, and more than 200,000 members of the armed forces are buried there.

Tallest cemetery The permanently illuminated Memorial Necrópole Ecumênica, located in Santos, near São Paulo, Brazil, is 10 stories high, occupying an area of 4.4 acres. Construction started in March 1983 and the first burial was on July 28, 1984.

Largest crematorium The Nikolo-Arkhangelskiy Crematorium, east Moscow, Russia has seven twin cremators. It was completed in March 1972 and covers an area of 519 acres.

Largest artificial mound The gravel mound on the summit of Nemrud Dagi, Malatya, Turkey measures 197 feet tall and covers 7.5 acres. It was built as a memorial to the Seleucid King Antiochus I (r. 69–34 B.C.).

Largest tomb The Mount Li tomb, the burial place of Qin Shi Huangdi, the First Emperor of Qin, was built during his reign, 221–210 B.C. and is situated 25 miles east of Xianyang, China. The two walls surrounding the grave measure 7,129 by 3,195 feet and 2,247 by 1,896 feet respectively. Several pits in the tomb contained a vast army of an estimated 8,000 terracotta soldiers and horses that are life-size and larger.

Largest mass tomb A tomb housing 180,000 World War II dead in Okinawa, Japan was enlarged in 1985 to accommodate another 9,000 bodies thought to be buried on the island.

Grave digging It is recorded that Johann Heinrich Karl Thieme, sexton of Aldenburg, Germany, dug 23,311 graves during a 50-year career. In 1826, his understudy dug *his* grave.

TRANSPORT

SHIPS

Oldest vessel A pinewood dugout found in Pesse, Netherlands was dated to *c.* 6315 B.C. ± 275 years. It is now in the Provincial Museum, Assen.

An 18-inch-long paddle was found in England in 1948. It has been dated to *c.* 7600 B.C. and is now in the Cambridge Museum of Archaeology, Cambridge, England.

Oldest boat A 27-foot-long, 2½-foot-wide wooden eel-catching canoe dated to *c.* 4490 B.C. was discovered at Tybrind Vig on the Baltic island of Fünen.

Oldest paddle wheeler The *Skibladner* has been continuously operated since 1856. It was built in Motala, Sweden, has had two major refits, and continues to ply Lake Mjøsa in Norway.

Longest canoe The "Snake Boat" *Nadubhagóm*, 135 feet long, from Kerala, southern India, has a crew of 109 rowers and nine "encouragers."

Heaviest wooden ship The *Richelieu*, 333 ft. 8 in. long and weighing 9,548 tons, was launched in Toulon, France on December 3, 1873.

Longest wooden ship The New York-built *Rochambeau* (1867–72), formerly the *Dunderberg*, measured 377 ft. 4 in. overall.

Largest human-powered ship The giant ship *Tessarakonteres*, a 3-banked catamaran galley with 4,000 rowers, built for Ptolemy IV *c.* 210 B.C. in Alexandria, Egypt, measured 420 feet, with up to eight men to an oar of 38 cubits (57 feet) in length.

Largest and most powerful tugs The *Nikolay Chiker* (SB-135) and *Fotiy Krylov* (SB-134) were commissioned in 1989 and built by Hollming Ltd. of Finland for V/O Sudoimport, in the former USSR. They have 25,000 bhp, are capable of 291 tons bollard pull at full power, and measure 325 feet long and 64 feet wide. *Fotiy Krylov* is reported to be under charter to the Tsavliris Group of Companies of Piraeus, Greece, and may for a time have been named *Tsavliris Giant*.

Most powerful icebreakers The *Rossiya* and its sister ships *Sovetskiy Soyuz* and *Oktyabryskaya Revolutsiya* are the most powerful icebreakers in the world. The *Rossiya* weighs 28,000 tons, is 460 feet long, and is powered by 75,000 hp nuclear engines. It was built in Leningrad (now St. Petersburg), Russia and completed in 1985.

Most powerful dredger The 468.2-foot-long *Prins der Nederlanden*, weighing 10,586 gross tons, can dredge up 22,400 tons of sand from a depth of 115 feet via two suction tubes in less than an hour.

Largest propeller The largest propeller is a triple-bladed screw of 36 ft. 1 in. diameter made by Kawasaki Heavy Industries, Japan, and delivered

A Russian icebreaker forges its way through Antarctica. The most powerful icebreakers are three Russian sister ships of 28,000 tons, built in 1985. (*Gamma/F. Lochon*)

on March 17, 1982 for the 233,787-ton bulk carrier *Hoei Maru* (now renamed *New Harvest*).

Largest hydrofoil The 212-foot-long *Plainview* (347 tons full-load) naval hydrofoil was launched by the Lockheed Shipbuilding and Construction Co. at Seattle, WA on June 28, 1965. It has a service speed of 57.2 MPH.

TANKERS

Largest tanker The largest ship of any kind and the largest oil tanker is *Jahre Viking*, formerly the *Happy Giant*, which weighs 622,534 tons deadweight. The tanker measures 1,471 feet long overall, with a beam of 225 ft. 11 in., and a draft of 80 ft. 9 in. It was lengthened by Nippon Kokan in 1980 by adding a midship section of 265 ft. 8 in.

Largest wreck The 354,043-ton deadweight very large crude carrier (VLCC) *Energy Determination* blew up and broke in two in the Straits of Hormuz on December 12, 1979. Its hull value was $58 million.

Largest wreck removal In 1979, Smit Tak International removed the remains of the French tanker *Betelgeuse*, weighing 120,000 tons, from Bantry Bay, Republic of Ireland. The exercise took 20 months.

Most massive collision On December 16, 1977, 22 miles off the coast of southern Africa, the tanker *Venoil* (330,954 deadweight tons) struck its sister ship *Venpet* (330,869 deadweight tons).

CARGO VESSELS

Largest cargo vessel The largest ship carrying dry cargo is the Norwegian ore carrier *Berge Stahl*, 402,082.6 tons deadweight, built in South Korea for the Norwegian owner Sig Bergesen. It has a length of 1,125 feet, a beam measuring 208 feet and was launched on November 5, 1986.

Largest containership   American President Lines built five ships in Germany—*President Adams, President Jackson, President Kennedy, President Polk* and *President Truman*—that were termed post-Panamax, being the first container vessels too large to travel through the Panama Canal. They are 902.69 feet long and 129.29 feet abeam; the maximum beam for the Panama transit is 106 feet. These vessels have a quoted capacity of 4,340 TEU (standard length 20 feet—Equivalent Unit containers).

Although of smaller registered tonnage, *Dresden Express*, built in South Korea in 1991 for the German Hapag-Lloyd company, is longer at 964 feet, and has a quoted capacity of 4,422 TEU. The greatest capacity is that of *NYK Altair* at 4,812 TEU, delivered in December 1994, and *NYK Vega*, delivered in February 1995.

Largest barges   The largest RoRo (roll-on, roll-off) ships are five 730-foot-long barges that are operated by Crowley American Transport of Jacksonville, FL.

Largest ferry   The largest car and passenger ferry is the 59,914 gross registered tonnage *Silja Europa*, which entered service in 1993 between Stockholm, Sweden and Helsinki, Finland. Operated by the Silja Line, the ferry is 662 feet long and 107 feet abeam, and can carry 3,000 passengers, 350 cars and 60 trucks.

Largest rail ferries   The world's biggest international rail ferries, *Klaipeda, Vilnius, Mukran* and *Greifswald*, operate on the Baltic Sea between the ports of Mukran, Germany and Klaipeda, Lithuania. The ferries were built in Wismar, Germany and are 625 feet long, 301.4 feet broad and 13,104 tons deadweight. Each of the 2-deck ferries can carry 103 standard railcars measuring 48.65 feet long and weighing up to 84 tons. The ferries can cover a distance of 273 nautical miles (314.2 miles) in 17 hours.

Fastest ferry   The twin-hulled, wave-piercing Sea Cats constructed by International Catamarans of Hobart, Tasmania, Australia were first launched in 1990. They have a cruising speed of 35 knots and are capable of 42 knots. Each one can carry 432 passengers and 80 cars.

SUBMARINES

Largest submarines   The launch of the first Russian Typhoon class submarine at the covered shipyard at Severodvinsk in the White Sea was announced on September 23, 1980. The submarines are believed to have a dive displacement of 29,211 tons, to measure 562.7 feet overall and to be armed with 20 SS-NX-20 missiles with a range of 4,800 nautical miles, each

---

DEEPEST DIVE

The U.S. Navy deep submergence vessel *Sea Cliff* (DSV 4), 30 tons, commissioned in 1973, reached a depth of 20,000 feet in March 1985.

MISSION
WATER BEETLE!

In 1991, retired Royal Air Force diving officer William G. Smith set out to raise funds for St. Richard's Hospital, Chichester, England by building the world's smallest fully functional submarine. Smith spent two years applying his technical expertise to the construction of the vessel in his garage, and easily achieved his fundraising objectives. Dubbed *Water Beetle*, the 9-ft.-8-in. yellow submarine was first tested in a swimming pool. *Water Beetle* achieved an 80-foot dive in June 1993, and acquired a 4.8-hp diesel engine in the summer of 1994. After spending some time on display in a museum in Shoreham, England, the vessel will be used to locate wreckage off the Sussex coast.

Smallest submarine William G. Smith of Bognor Regis, England constructed a fully functional submarine only 9 ft. 8 in. long, 3 ft. 9 in. wide and 4 ft. 8 in. high. It can reach depths of around 100 feet and remain underwater for four hours.

KEY:

A. Diesel engine
B. Electric motor/generator
C. Heat exchanger
D. Tri-plate rudder
E. Skids (with shock absorbers)
F. Relay unit (motor control)
G. Marker buoy (retractable)
H. Clutch unit
I. Anchor box
J. Pressure regulator
K. Isolation valve
L. External control switch

M. Exhaust valve
N. Strobe light
O. Pressure relief valve
P. Directional hydrophone
Q. Compass
R. Main switching panel
S. Hydroplane & rudder control
T. Auto-ascent circuit
U. Motor control unit
V. CB radio
W. Viewing ports
X. External ballast release
Y. Back rest/ high level seat
Z. Battery compartments

WATER BEETLE: Performance statistics

Propulsion: 4.8-hp diesel engine (surface)
1.25-hp electric motor (underwater)

Speed: Surface–5 knots (conservative estimate)
Submerged–3 knots

Underwater duration: At least 4 hours using 3-hp air cyls.
(This can be increased by the use of 2 additional external cyls.)

Maximum depth: As applicable to scuba divers and subject to
the same physiological considerations, but nominally 100 feet.

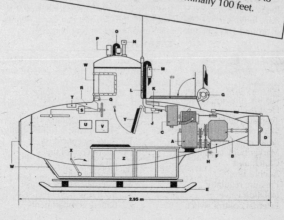

2.95 m

with seven warheads. By late 1987, two others built in St. Petersburg, Russia (formerly Leningrad, USSR) were operational, each deploying 140 warheads.

United States   The largest submarines in the U.S. Navy are of the Ohio class. Each of the nine ships in active service has a displacement of 18,700 tons. At 560 feet, they are the longest submarines in the fleet, and also have the largest crew, at 165.

Smallest submarine   William G. Smith of Bognor Regis, England constructed a fully functional submarine only 9 ft. 8 in. long, 3 ft. 9 in. wide and 4 ft. 8 in. high. It can reach depths of around 100 feet and remain underwater for four hours.

Fastest submarine   The Russian Alpha class nuclear-powered submarines had a reported maximum speed of 45 knots plus (51.8 MPH) and were believed to be able to dive to 2,500 feet. It is thought that only one now remains in service, used for testing purposes.

Longest submarine patrol   The longest submerged and unsupported patrol made public is 111 days, by HM Submarine *Warspite* in the South Atlantic, November 25, 1982–March 15, 1983. It sailed 30,804 nautical miles.

Fastest human-powered submarine   The fastest speed attained by a human-powered propeller submarine is 5.94 knots, by *F.A.U-Boat*, designed and built by the Florida Atlantic University Ocean Engineering Department, Boca Raton, FL, on March 8, 1994. The vessel used a 2-blade high aspect ratio propeller propulsion system, and was crewed by Karl Heeb, Charles Callaway and William Fay.

Nonpropeller   The fastest speed attained by a human-powered nonpropeller submarine is 2.9 knots, by *SubDUDE* on August 21, 1992. The submarine was designed by the Scripps Institution of Oceanography, University of California, San Diego and used a horizontal oscillating foil propulsion system. The crew consisted of Kimball Millikan, pilot; Ed Trevino, athlete; and team leader Kevin Hardy.

WARSHIPS

Largest aircraft carriers   The warships with the largest full-load displacement are the Nimitz class U.S. Navy aircraft carriers U.S.S. *Nimitz, Dwight D. Eisenhower, Carl Vinson, Theodore Roosevelt, George Washington* and *Abraham Lincoln*, the last two of which displace 114,240 tons. The ships are 1,092 feet in length overall, with 4½ acres of flight deck, and have a speed well in excess of 30 knots. They have to be refueled after about 900,000 miles of steaming. Their full complement of personnel is 5,986.

Largest battleships   The Japanese battleships *Yamato* (completed on December 16, 1941 and sunk southwest of Kyushu, Japan by U.S. planes on April 7, 1945) and *Musashi* (sunk in the Philippine Sea on October 24, 1944) were the largest battleships ever commissioned; each one had a full-load displacement of 81,545 tons. With an overall length of 863 feet, a beam of 127 feet and a full-load draft of 35½ feet, they mounted nine 18.1-

inch guns in three triple turrets. Each gun weighed 181.5 tons and was 75 feet long, firing a 3,200-pound projectile.

United States The largest battleships were the U.S.S *Missouri*, an Iowa class battleship, and the U.S.S *Wisconsin*, 887 feet long; both have a full-load displacement of 64,400 tons. The ships were commissioned in 1944 and recommissioned in 1986 and 1988 respectively, following major refits. Armaments included nine 16-inch guns used in the Gulf War in 1991 and capable of firing 2,700-pound projectiles a distance of 23 miles. Both ships have now been withdrawn from service.

DID YOU KNOW?

The greatest number of landings on an aircraft carrier in one day was 602, achieved by Marine Air Group 6 of the United States Pacific Fleet Air Force aboard the U.S.S. *Matanikau* on May 25, 1945 between 8 A.M. and 5 P.M.

Fastest armed vessel A U.S. Navy hovercraft, the 78-foot-long 110-ton test vehicle SES-100B, achieved a speed of 91.9 knots (105.8 MPH), on January 25, 1980. (See FASTEST HOVERCRAFT.)

Fastest destroyers The fastest speed attained by a destroyer was 45.25 knots (51.83 MPH) by the 3,120-ton French destroyer *Le Terrible* in 1935. It was built in Blainville, France and was powered by four Yarrow small-tube boilers and two Rateau geared turbines, giving100,000 shp. It was removed from the active list at the end of 1957.

United States The fastest destroyers in the U.S. Navy arsenal are the Spruance class and Kidd class ships, which attain a maximum speed of 33 knots (38 MPH).

PASSENGER VESSELS

Fastest turnaround The largest liner under the British flag, MV *Queen Elizabeth II*, set a "turnaround" record of 3 hr. 18 min. in New York City on December 14, 1993.

Largest passenger liner The largest in current use, and the longest ever, is the *Norway*, 76,049 tons and 1,035 ft. 7½ in. long, with a capacity of 2,022 passengers and 900 crew. It was built as the *France* in 1960 and renamed after purchase in June 1979 by Norwegian Knut Kloster. It normally cruises in the Caribbean and is based at Miami, FL. Work undertaken during an extensive refit in 1990 increased the number of passenger decks to 11. Its draft is 34½ feet and its speed is 18 knots.

Largest riverboat The world's largest inland boat is the 382-foot *Mississippi Queen*, designed by James Gardner of London, England. The vessel was commissioned on July 25, 1976 in Cincinnati, OH and is now in service on the Mississippi River.

Largest yacht *Royal* The Saudi Arabian royal yacht *Abdul Aziz* is 482 feet long. Built in Denmark and completed in 1984 at Vospers Yard, Southampton, England, it was estimated in September 1987 to be worth more than $100 million.

Nonroyal The largest private (nonroyal) yacht is the *Alexander*, a former ferry converted to a private yacht in 1986, at 400 feet overall.

Largest passenger hydrofoil Three 185-ton Supramar PTS 150 Mk III hydrofoils carry 250 passengers at 40 knots across the Öre Sound between Malmö, Sweden and Copenhagen, Denmark. They were built by Westermoen Hydrofoil Ltd. of Mandal, Norway.

Message in a bottle The longest recorded interval between drop and pickup is 73 years. A message thrown from from the SS *Arawatta* out of Cairns, Queensland, Australia on June 9, 1910 in a lotion bottle was found on Moreton Island, Queensland on June 6, 1983.

SAILING SHIPS

Oldest active sailing ship The oldest active square-rigged sailing vessel in the world is the restored SV *Maria Asumpta* (formerly the *Ciudad de Inca*), built near Barcelona, Spain in 1858. It is 98 feet long overall and weighs 142.3 tons. Restored in 1981–82, it is operated by The Friends of *Maria Asumpta* of Lenham, England.

Largest sailing ship The *France II*, weighing 5,806 gross tons, was launched at Bordeaux, France in 1911. The ship was a steel-hulled, 5-masted barque with a hull measuring 418 feet overall. It was wrecked off New Caledonia on July 12, 1922.

Largest in service The 357-foot-long *Sedov* was built in 1921 in Kiel, Germany. It is 48 feet wide, with a displacement of 6,300 gross registered tons (4,267.2 tons) and a sail area of 45,123 square feet.

Longest sailing ship The French-built *Club Med I* is 613 feet long with five aluminum masts. The polyester sails have an area of 3,013 square feet and are computer-controlled. The ship is operated as a Caribbean cruise vessel for 425 passengers bound for Club Med. With its small sail area and powerful engines it is really a motor-sailer. A sister ship, *Club Med II*, is now being commissioned.

Largest junk The seagoing *Zheng He*, flagship of Admiral Zheng He's 62 treasure ships, *c.* 1420, had a displacement of 3,472 tons and a length variously estimated up to 538 feet. It is believed to have had nine masts.

Largest sails The largest spars ever carried were those in HM Battleship *Temeraire*, completed at Chatham, England on August 31, 1877 and broken up in 1921. The fore and main yards measured 115 feet long. The foresail contained 5,100 feet of canvas weighing 2.23 tons, and the total sail area was 25,000 square feet.

Tallest mast The *Velsheda*, a J-class sailing vessel, is the tallest known single-masted yacht in the world. Measured from heel fitting to the mast truck, it is 169$\frac{1}{4}$ feet high. Built in 1933, it has a displacement of 160 tons and supports a sail area of 7,500 square feet.

OCEAN CROSSINGS

Earliest Atlantic crossing The earliest crossing of the Atlantic by a power vessel, as opposed to an auxiliary-engined sailing ship, was a 22-day voyage begun in April 1827, from Rotterdam, Netherlands, to the West Indies, by the *Curaçao*. It was a 127-foot wooden paddle boat of 490.5 tons, built as the *Calpe* in Dover, England in 1826 and purchased by the Dutch government for a West Indian mail service.

The earliest Atlantic crossing entirely under steam (with intervals for de-

Destriero, the powerboat that crossed the Atlantic in record time, and its crew. (***Gamma Sport***)

salting the boilers) was by HMS *Rhadamanthus*, from Plymouth, England to Barbados in 1832.

The earliest crossing under continuous steam power was by the condenser-fitted packet ship *Sirius* (787 tons) from Queenstown (now Cobh), Ireland to Sandy Hook, NJ, in 18 days 10 hr., from April 4 to April 22, 1838.

Fastest Atlantic crossing Under the rules of the Hales Trophy or "Blue Riband," which recognizes the highest average speed rather than the shortest duration, the record is held by the 222-foot Italian powerboat *Destriero*, with an average speed of 53.09 knots between the Nantucket Light Buoy and Bishop Rock Lighthouse, Isles of Scilly, Great Britain, August 6–9, 1992, in a time of 58 hr. 34 min. 4 sec.

Fastest Pacific crossing The fastest crossing from Yokohama, Japan to Long Beach, CA—4,840 nautical miles (5,567.64 miles)—took 6 days 1 hr. 27 min. (June 30 to July 6, 1973) by the containership *Sea-Land Commerce* (56,353 tons), at an average speed of 33.27 knots (38.31 MPH).

San Francisco to Boston Richard B. Wilson and Bill Biewenga sailed from San Francisco to Boston via Cape Horn in 69 days 19 hr. 44 min. They left San Francisco in the 53-foot trimaran *Great American II* on January 27 and arrived in Boston on April 7, 1993.

Longest solo ocean row Peter Bird spent 304 days 14 hr. nonstop rowing at sea during a transpacific voyage that began on May 12, 1993 and ended prematurely on March 12, 1994.

Fastest circumnavigation Peter Blake (New Zealand) and Robin Knox-Johnson (Great Britain) won the Jules Verne Trophy when they arrived back in France on April 1, 1994, after circling the globe nonstop in 74 days 22 hr. 17 min. in the catamaran *Enza*.

MERCHANT SHIPPING

Shipbuilding Worldwide production completed in 1994, excluding naval auxiliaries, nonpropelled vessels, the U.S. Reserve Fleet, vessels restricted to harbor or river/canal service, and vessels of less than 100 gross registered tonnage, was 19 million gross registered tonnage. Japan completed 8.6 million gross registered tonnage (45 percent of the world total) in 1994.

The world's leading shipbuilder in 1994 was Hyundai Heavy Industries Co. Ltd. of South Korea, which completed 34 ships of 2.21 million gross tons.

Largest ship owner The Japanese NYK Group's fleet of owned vessels totaled 11,921,701 gross tonnage on February 1, 1995.

United States The largest shipping owner and operator in the United States is Exxon Corporation, whose fleets of owned/managed and chartered tankers in 1987 totaled a daily average of 10.42 million deadweight tons.

Largest fleet The largest merchant fleet in the world at the end of 1994 was the one sailing under the flag of Panama, with a fleet totaling 64.2 million gross tonnage.

Fastest shipbuilding The fastest times for building complete ships of more than 10,000 tons were achieved at Kaiser's Yard, Portland, OR during World War II. The yard completed 2,742 Liberty ships starting on September 27, 1941. In 1942, No. 440, named *Robert E. Peary*, had its keel laid on November 8, was launched on November 12, and was operational after 4 days 15½ hr. on November 15.

Fastest riveting The world record for riveting is 11,209 rivets in nine hours, by John Moir at the Workman Clark Ltd. shipyard, Belfast, Northern Ireland in June 1918. His peak hour was his seventh, with 1,409 rivets, an average of nearly 23½ per minute.

PORTS

Largest port The Port of New York and New Jersey has a navigable waterfront of 755 miles (295 miles in New Jersey), stretching over 92 square miles, with a total berthing capacity of 391 ships at a time. The total warehouse floor space covers 422.4 acres.

Busiest port The busiest port and largest artificial harbor is in Rotterdam, Netherlands. It covers 38 square miles, with 76 miles of quays, and handled 324 million tons of cargo in 1994.

Although the port of Hong Kong handles less tonnage than Rotterdam in total seaborne cargo, it is the world's leading containerport, and is now handling 1 million TEUs per month.

United States The busiest port in the United States is South Louisiana, LA, which handled 193,796,104 U.S. tons of cargo in 1993.

Containers wait to be loaded onto ships at Rotterdam, the world's busiest port. (*Gamma/M. Deville*)

REMARKABLE RIVETING

During World War I, in late 1917 and early 1918, German submarines sank an alarming number of British ships, causing anxiety about the speed of British shipbuilding. From this concern came the idea of a competition to break the record for the fastest rate of riveting.

On June 5, 1918, at the Belfast shipyard of Workman, Clark and Co. Ltd., John Moir eclipsed the record by driving in 11,209 $7/8$-inch rivets on the double-bottom floor of a standard ship in nine hours. In the seventh hour, Moir beat his own 1-hour record by driving in 1,409 rivets—an average of almost $3\frac{1}{2}$ per minute. In his best minute, he drove in 26.

Moir beat his nearest rival, John Lowry at Harland & Wolff, by more than 4,000 rivets. His achievement earned him expressions of gratitude from all over Great Britain, including telegrams from King George V and Prime Minister Lloyd George. One correspondent even wrote a congratulatory poem: "Well done brave Mr. Moir,/As you are honoured by the King/On your rivetting achievement,/Allow me now your praises ring . . ."

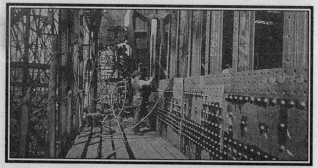

(Ulster Folk & Transport Museum, Harland and Wolff Collection)

Fastest riveting The world record for riveting is 11,209 rivets in nine hours, by John Moir at the Workman Clark Ltd. shipyard, Belfast, Northern Ireland in June 1918.

	NUMBER OF RIVETS	ACCUMULATING TOTALS
1ST HOUR	1167	1167
2ND ..	1101	2268
3RD ..	1071	3339
4TH ..	1187	4526
5TH ..	1267	5793
6TH ..	1328	7121
7TH ..	1409	8530
8TH ..	1276	9806
9TH ..	1403	11209
TOTAL		

Largest dry dock With a maximum shipbuilding capacity of 1.2 million deadweight tons, the Daewoo Okpo No. 1 Dry Dock, Koje Island in South Korea measures 1,740 feet long by 430 feet wide and was completed in 1979. The dock gates, 46 feet high and 33 feet thick at the base, are the world's most massive.

HOVERCRAFT

Fastest hovercraft The 78-foot-long 110-ton U.S. Navy test hovercraft SES-100B attained a speed of 91.9 knots (105.8 MPH) on January 25, 1980 on the Chesapeake Bay Test Range, MD.

Largest hovercraft The SRN4 Mk III, a British-built civil hovercraft, weighs 341 tons and can carry 418 passengers and 60 cars. It is 185 feet long and can travel at over 65 knots. ⋅

Longest hovercraft journey Under the leadership of David Smithers, the British Trans-African Hovercraft Expedition traveled 5,000 miles through eight West African countries in a Winchester class SRN6, between October 15, 1969 and January 3, 1970.

Highest hovercraft The highest altitude reached by a hovercraft was on June 11, 1990 when *Neste Enterprise* and her crew of 10 reached the navigable source of the Yangzi River, China at 16,050 feet.

The greatest altitude at which a hovercraft is operating is on Lake Titicaca, Peru, where since 1975 an HM2 Hoverferry has been hovering 12,506 feet above sea level.

MODEL BOATS

Longest model boat run Members of the Lowestoft Model Boat Club crewed a radio-controlled scale model boat on August 17–18, 1991 at The Dome, Doncaster Leisure Park, Doncaster, England and set a 24-hour distance record of 111.18 miles.

24-hour run David and Peter Holland of Doncaster, England, of the Conisbrough and District Modelling Association, crewed a 28-inch-long scale model boat of the trawler *Margaret H* continuously on one battery for 24 hours, and recorded a distance of 33.45 miles, at The Dome, Doncaster Leisure Park, Doncaster, England, August 15–16, 1992.

BICYCLES

Longest bicycle The longest true tandem bicycle (i.e., without a third stabilizing wheel) was designed and built by Terry Thessman of Pahiatua, New Zealand. It measures 72.96 feet long and weighs 340 pounds. It was ridden by four riders a distance of 807 feet on February 27, 1988. Turning corners proved to be a problem.

Smallest bicycle The world's smallest-wheeled ridable bike has wheels 0.76 inches in diameter. Its constructor, Neville Patten of Gladstone, Queensland, Australia, rode it for a distance of 13 ft. 5½ in. on March 25, 1988.

The smallest ridable bicycle in terms of length was built by Jacques Puyoou of Pau, Pyrénées-Atlantiques, France, whose tandem is 14.1 inches long. The bicycle has been ridden by him and Madame Puyoou.

Largest bicycle The largest bicycle as measured by the front-wheel diameter is "Frankencycle," built by Dave Moore of Rosemead, CA and first ridden by Steve Gordon of Moorpark, CA, on June 4, 1989. The wheel diameter is 10 feet and the bicycle itself is 11 ft. 2 in. high.

Largest tricycle The Dillon Colossal Tricycle was designed by Arthur Dillon. It has rear wheels 11 feet in diameter, constructed by David Moore, and a front wheel 5 ft. 10 in. high.

Longest wheelie David Robilliard set a record of 5 hr. 12 min. 33 sec. at the Beau Sejour Leisure Centre, St. Peter Port, Guernsey, Channel Islands on May 28, 1990.

Underwater tricycling A team of 32 divers pedaled a distance of 116.66 miles in 75 hr. 20 min. on a standard tricycle at Diver's Den, Santa Barbara, CA on June 16–19, 1988.

HUMAN-POWERED VEHICLES

Fastest human-powered vehicle The world speed records for human-powered vehicles (HPVs) over a 200-meter (656.2-foot) flying start (single rider) are 65.484 MPH by Fred Markham at Mono Lake, CA on May 11, 1986 and 62.92 MPH (multiple riders) by Dave Grylls and Leigh Barczewski at the Ontario Speedway, CA, on May 4, 1980.

The 1-hour standing start (single rider) record is held by Pat Kinch, riding *Kingcycle Bean*, averaging a speed of 46.96 MPH on September 8, 1990 at Millbrook Proving Ground, Bedford, England.

Fastest water cycle The men's 6,562-foot (single rider) record is 12.84 MPH, by Steve Hegg in *Flying Fish* off Long Beach, CA on July 20, 1987.

UNICYCLES

Tallest unicycle The tallest unicycle ever mastered is 101 ft. 9 in. tall. It was ridden by Steve McPeak (with a safety wire suspended by an overhead crane) for a distance of 376 feet in Las Vegas, NV in October 1980.

Smallest unicycle Peter Rosendahl (Sweden) rode a unicycle with a wheel diameter of one inch, with no attachments or extensions fitted, a distance of 12 feet in Las Vegas, NV on March 25, 1994.

One hundred miles Takayuki Koike of Kanagawa, Japan set a unicycle record for 100 miles in 6 hr. 44 min. 21.84 sec. on August 9, 1987 (average speed 14.83 MPH).

Longest unicycle journey Akira Matsushima (Japan) unicycled 3,260 miles from Newport, OR to Washington, D.C. from July 10 to August 22, 1992.

Unicycling backwards Ashrita Furman (U.S.) rode backwards for a distance of 53.17 miles at Forest Park, Queens, NY on September 16, 1994.

Fastest unicycle sprint Peter Rosendahl set a sprint record for 100 meters (328.1 feet) of 12.11 seconds (18.47 MPH) in Las Vegas, NV on March 25, 1994.

MOTORCYCLES

In January 1993, it was estimated that there were 4,001,000 registered motorcycles in the United States.

Longest motorcycle Gregg Reid of Atlanta, GA designed and built a Yamaha 250-cc motorcycle that measures 15 ft. 6 in. long and weighs 520 pounds. It is street legal and has been insured.

Smallest motorcycle Simon Timperley and Clive Williams of Progressive Engineering Ltd., Ashton-under-Lyne, England designed and constructed a motorcycle with a 4.25-inch wheelbase, a seat height of 3.75 inches and a wheel diameter of 0.75 inches for the front and 0.95 inches for the back. The bike was ridden 3.2 feet.

SPEED

Fastest speeds On July 14, 1990, Dave Campos (U.S.), rode a 23-foot-long streamliner called *Easyriders*, powered by two 91-cubic-inch Ruxton Harley-Davidson engines, to set AMA and FIM absolute speed records with an overall average of 322.150 MPH on Bonneville Salt Flats, UT. Campos completed the faster run at an average of 322.870 MPH.

The fastest time for a single run over 440 yards from a standing start is 6.19 seconds, by Tony Lang (U.S.) riding a supercharged Suzuki at Gainesville, FL in 1994.

The highest terminal velocity recorded at the end of a 440-yard run from a standing start is 231.24 MPH, by Elmer Trett (U.S.) at Virginia Motorsports Park, Petersburg, VA in 1994.

Fastest production road machine The 151-hp 1-liter Tu Atara Yamaha Bimota 6th edition EI has a road-tested top speed of 186.4 MPH.

Simon Timperley and Clive Williams of Progressive Engineering Ltd., Ashton-under-Lyne, England designed and constructed the world's smallest motorcycle.

RIDING

Longest motorcycle ride   Jari Saarelainen (Finland) rode his Honda Gold Wing 1,500-cc motorcycle over 67,109 miles through 43 countries. He set off from Helsinki, Finland on December 1, 1989 and returned 742 days later on December 12, 1991.

Jim Rogers and Tabitha Estabrook traveled 57,022 miles on two motorcycles, covering six continents. They set off from New York in March 1990 and returned in November 1991.

Trans-Americas ride   Kurt Nerlich and Hans Shirmer traveled 67,000 miles (55,400 by motorcycle) around the Americas (North, South and Central) in 27 months from July 1954 to September 1956. Travel to and through Central and South America was much more primitive then than it is today.

Longest scooter ride   The longest time a motor scooter has been kept in nonstop motion is 1,001 hours. A Kinetic Honda DX 100 cc, ridden by Har Parkash Rishi, Amarjeet Singh and Navjot Chadha, covered a distance of

19,241 miles at Traffic Park, Pune, Maharashtra, India between April 22 and June 3, 1990.

Largest pyramid The Army Service Corps, Indian Army established a record with a pyramid of 93 men on nine motorcycles. The pyramid was held together by muscle and determination only, with no straps, harnesses or other aids. It traveled a distance of 328 yards at Gill Stadium, Bangalore, India on July 19, 1994.

GUESS WHAT?

Q. HOW FAST CAN THE FASTEST INSECT MOVE?

A. LOOK IN "INSECTS" (LIVING WORLD)

Longest wheelie Yasuyuki Kudō covered 205.7 miles nonstop on the rear wheel of his Honda TLM 220 R 216-cc motorcycle at the Japan Automobile Research Institute, Tsukuba, Japan on May 5, 1991.

United States The United States record was set by Doug Domokos (U.S.) on the Alabama International Speedway, Talladega on June 27, 1984. He covered 145 miles nonstop on the rear wheel of his Honda XR 500. He stopped only when the gasoline ran out.

Fastest wheelie The highest speed attained on a rear wheel of a motorcycle is 157.87 MPH, by Jacky Vranken (Belgium) on a Suzuki GSXR 1100 at St. Truiden Military Airfield, Belgium on November 8, 1992.

Wall of death The greatest endurance feat on a "wall of death" was 7 hr. 0 min. 13 sec., by Martin Blume, Berlin, Germany on April 16, 1983. He rode over 12,000 laps on the 33-foot-diameter wall on a Yamaha XS400, averaging 30 MPH for the 181½ miles.

Most on one machine The record for the most people on a single machine is 46 members of the Illawarra Mini Bike Training Club, New South Wales, Australia. They rode on a 1,000-cc motorcycle and traveled a distance of one mile on October 11, 1987.

Ramp jumping The longest distance ever achieved by a motorcycle long-jumping is 251 feet, by Doug Danger on a 1991 Honda CR500 at Loudon, NH on June 22, 1991.

AUTOMOBILES

PRODUCTION

The total number of vehicles constructed worldwide in 1994 was a record 51,745,907. The peak year for production of automobiles was also 1994, when 36,289,127 cars were produced.

Largest manufacturer The largest manufacturer of motor vehicles and parts (and the largest manufacturing company) is General Motors Corporation of Detroit, MI. In 1994, General Motors produced 8,420,000 cars worldwide; 4,500,000 of them were made in the U.S. It has on average

The largest single automobile plant in the world is the Volkswagenwerk in Wolfsburg, Germany. (*Gamma/B. Edelbajt*)

750,000 employees. The company's highest annual income was $155 billion in 1994.

Largest plant   The largest single automobile plant in the world is the Volkswagenwerk in Wolfsburg, Germany, with 60,000 employees and a capacity for producing 4,000 vehicles every week (208,000 per year). The factory buildings cover 371 acres and the whole plant covers 1,878 acres, with 46 miles of rail sidings.

United States   The largest automobile plant in the United States is the Nissan Motor Manufacturing Corp.'s Smyrna, TN plant. It had a capacity of 450,000 cars and compact pickup trucks at the end of 1994. The plant covers an area of 5.1 million square feet.

Longest in production   A total of 21,220,000 Volkswagen "Beetles" have been built since 1937. Two production lines continue to produce the car—Puebla, Mexico and São Paulo, Brazil.

The Morgan 4/4, built by the Morgan Motor Car Co. of Malvern, England (founded 1910), celebrated its 59th birthday on December 27, 1994. There is still a waiting list of 6–8 years to buy this model.

United States   The oldest mass-production model still being made is the Chrysler Imperial, which was in production from 1926 to 1984 and 1990–present. The luxury model Cadillac Fleetwood has been in continuous production since 1936.

Largest car   Of cars produced for private use, the largest was the Bugatti Royale type 41, of which only six were assembled at Molsheim, France by the Italian Ettore Bugatti. First built in 1927, this machine has an

License plate No. 9 was sold at a Hong Kong government auction for HK$13 million—over eight times the value of the Rolls-Royce it was assigned to. (*Emperor Group*)

SMASH!

In a career lasting 40 years until his retirement in 1993, stuntman Dick Sheppard of Gloucester, England wrecked 2,003 cars.

8-cylinder engine of 12.7-liter capacity, and measures over 22 feet long. The hood is over seven feet long.

Longest car A 26-wheeled limo measuring 100 feet long was designed by Jay Ohrberg of Burbank, CA. It had many special features, including a swimming pool, a diving board and a king-sized water bed. It was designed so that it could be driven as one piece, or changed to bend in the middle.

Largest engine The largest engine capacity of a production car is 13.5 liters, for the U.S. Pierce-Arrow 6–66 Raceabout of 1912–18, the U.S. Peerless 6–60 of 1912–14, and the Fageol of 1918.

Most powerful car The most powerful current production car is the McLaren F1 6.1; it develops in excess of 627 BHP.

Heaviest car The heaviest car recently in production (up to 25 were made annually) appears to be the Soviet-built Zil–41047 limousine with a 12.72-foot wheelbase. It weighs 7,352 pounds (3.7 tons).
   A "stretched" Zil (two or three made annually) was used by former USSR President Mikhail Gorbachev until December 1991. It weighed 6.6

Since 1937, approximately 21,220,000 Volkswagen "Beetles" have been turned out. The car is still manufactured on two production lines—in Puebla, Mexico and São Paulo, Brazil. (*Gamma/J.L. Bulcao*)

tons and was made of 3-inch armor-plated steel. The 8-cylinder, 7-liter engine guzzled fuel at a rate of six miles per gallon.

Lightest car Louis Borsi of London, England has built and driven a 21-pound car with a 2.5-cc engine. It is capable of 15 MPH.

Smallest street-legal car The smallest registered street-legal car in the United States has an overall length of 88¾ inches and a width of 40½ inches. It was built by Arlis Sluder and is now owned by Jeff Gibson.

Most expensive car The most expensive car ever built was the U.S. Presidential 1969 Lincoln Continental Executive delivered to the U.S. Secret Service on October 14, 1968. It has an overall length of 21 ft. 6¼ in. with a 13-ft.-4-in. wheelbase, and with the addition of 2.2 tons of armor plate, weighs six tons (12,000 pounds). The estimated cost of research, development and manufacture was $500,000, but it is rented at $5,000 per year. Even if all four tires were shot out it could travel at 50 MPH on inner rubber-edged steel discs.

Used The greatest confirmed price paid is $15 million, including commission, for the 1931 Bugatti Type 41 Royale Sports Coupé by Kellner, sold to the Meitec Corporation of Japan, completed on April 12, 1990.

Most inexpensive car The cheapest car of all time was the 1922 Red Bug Buckboard, built by the Briggs & Stratton Co. of Milwaukee, WI, listed at $125–$150. It had a 62-inch wheelbase and weighed 245 pounds. Early models of the King Midget cars were sold in kit form for self-assembly for as little as $100 in 1948.

Longest parade of cars A parade of 2,223 Corvettes traveled from the Bloomington Gold Corvette Show in Springfield, IL to Athens, IL and back again on June 25, 1994.

Most expensive license plate License plate No. 9 was sold at a Hong Kong government auction for HK$13 million (approximately $1.7 million) in March 1994 to Albert Yeung Sau-Shing. "Nine" sounds like the word "dog" in Chinese, and the purchase was considered lucky because 1994 was the Year of the Dog.

Tire supporting The greatest number of tires supported in a freestanding lift is 96, by Gary Windebank of Romsey, England in February 1984. The total weight was 1,440 pounds. The tires used were Michelin XZX 155 × 13.

SPEED

Fastest land vehicle The *official* 1-mile land-speed record is 633.468 MPH, set by Richard Noble on October 4, 1983 over the Black Rock Desert, NV in his 17,000-pound-thrust Rolls-Royce Avon 302 jet-powered *Thrust 2*, designed by John Ackroyd.

Fastest rocket-engined vehicle The fastest speed attained by any wheeled land vehicle is 631.367 MPH by *The Blue Flame*, a rocket-powered

4-wheeled vehicle driven by Gary Gabelich (U.S.) on the Bonneville Salt Flats, UT on October 23, 1970. Gabelich momentarily exceeded 650 MPH. The car was powered by a liquid natural gas/hydrogen peroxide rocket engine developing a thrust of up to a maximum 22,000 pounds.

The fastest reputed land speed figure in one direction is 739.666 MPH, or Mach 1.0106, by Stan Barrett (U.S.) in the *Budweiser Rocket*, a rocket-engined 3-wheeled car, at Edwards Air Force Base, CA on December 17, 1979. This published speed of Mach 1.0106 is not officially sanctioned by the U.S.A.F. because the Digital Instrument Radar was not calibrated or certified. The radar information was not generated by the vehicle directly but by an operator aiming a dish using a TV screen.

Fastest piston-engined car   The fastest speed measured for a wheel-driven car is 432.692 MPH by Al Teague in *Speed-O-Motive/Spirit of '76* at Bonneville Salt Flats, UT on August 21, 1991 over the final 132 feet of a mile run (av. 425.230 MPH for the whole mile).

Fastest diesel-engined car   The prototype 3-liter Mercedes C 111/3 attained 203.3 MPH in tests on the Nardo Circuit, southern Italy, October 5–15, 1978, and in April 1978 averaged 195.4 MPH for 12 hours, thus covering a world record 2,344.7 miles.

Fastest steam car   On August 19, 1985 Robert E. Barber broke the 79-year-old record for a steam car driving No. 744, *Steamin' Demon*, built by the Barber-Nichols Engineering Co., which reached 145.607 MPH at Bonneville Salt Flats, UT.

Fastest road car   Various revved-up track cars have been licensed for road use but are not normal production models.

The fastest speed ever attained by a standard production car is 217.1 MPH for a Jaguar XJ220, driven by Martin Brundle at the Nardo Circuit, Italy on June 21, 1992.

The highest road-tested acceleration reported for a street-legal car is 0–60 MPH in 3.07 seconds for a Ford RS200 Evolution, driven by Graham Hathaway at the Boreham Proving Ground, Essex, England on May 25, 1994.

DRIVING

Six-continent drive   The fastest drive taking in all the continents except Antarctica, with a total distance driven of more than an equator's length (24,901 miles), is one of 39 days 7 hr. 55 min. by Navin Kapila, Man Badahur, and Vijay Raman, driving a Contessa Classic. They left New Delhi, India on November 22, 1991, and returned to the same place on December 31, 1991.

Amphibious circumnavigation   The only circumnavigation by an amphibious vehicle was by Ben Carlin (Australia) in the amphibious jeep *Half-Safe*. He completed the last leg of the Atlantic crossing (the English Channel) on August 24, 1951. He arrived back in Montreal, Canada on May 8, 1958, having completed a circumnavigation of 39,000 miles over land and 9,600 miles by sea and river. He was accompanied on the transatlantic stage by his ex-wife Elinore (U.S.) and on the long transpacific stage (Tokyo, Japan to Anchorage, AK) by Broye Lafayette De-Mente (U.S.).

One-year drive   The greatest distance ever covered in one year is 354,257 miles, by two Opel Rekord 2-liter passenger sedans, both of which covered this distance between May 18, 1988 and the same date in 1989 without any major mechanical breakdowns. The vehicles were manufactured by the Delta Motor Corporation, Port Elizabeth, South Africa, and were driven on tar and gravel roads in the Northern Cape by a team of company drivers from Delta.

Trans-Americas drive   Garry Sowerby (Canada), with Tim Cahill (U.S.) as co-driver and navigator, drove a 1988 GMC Sierra K3500 4-wheel-drive pickup truck powered by a 6.2-liter V8 Detroit diesel engine from Ushuaia, Tierra del Fuego, Argentina to Prudhoe Bay, AK, a distance of 14,739 miles, in a total elapsed time of 23 days 22 hr. 43 min. from September 29 to October 22, 1987. The vehicle and team were surface-freighted from Cartagena, Colombia to Balboa, Panama so as to bypass the Darién Gap.

Layne Hall, the oldest known driver, with his New York State driver license, which shows his date of birth as March 15, 1880. Hall drove a 1962 Cadillac until his death in 1990.

Oldest car to cross the United States   Raymond H. Carr drove across the United States in a 1902 Northern, the oldest car ever to make the trip. Traveling at 15–20 MPH, Carr left San Diego, CA on May 8, 1994 and arrived at Jekyll Island, GA on May 31, 1994.

Highest mileage   The highest recorded mileage for a car is 1,536,278 miles as of January 15, 1995, for a 1963 Volkswagen Beetle owned by Albert Klein of Pasadena, CA. The highest recorded mileage for a car with the original gasoline motor without an overhaul is 624,050 miles to April 12, 1995 for a 1979 Cadillac DeVille owned by Don Champion of Louisville, KY.

Longest fuel range   The greatest distance driven without refueling on a single fill-up in a standard vehicle (38.2 gallons carried in factory-optional twin fuel tanks) is 1,691.6 miles, by a 1991 Toyota LandCruiser diesel station wagon. Driven by Ewan Kennedy with Ian Lee (observer) from Nyngan, New South Wales, Australia to Winton, Queensland, Australia and back from May 18 to May 21, 1992, the car averaged 37.3 MPH, giving 44.2 MPG.

The greatest distance traveled by an unmodified production car on the contents of a standard fuel tank is 1,338.1 miles, giving 75.94 MPG. Stuart Bladon and Robert Procter drove the length of Great Britain, July 26–28, 1992, from John o' Groat's to Land's End, and returned to Scotland driving an Audi 100 TD1 diesel car. The fuel of the 17.62-gallon fuel tank ran out after 35 hr. 18 min.

Driving in reverse   Charles Creighton and James Hargis of Maplewood, MO drove their Model A Ford 1929 roadster in reverse for 3,340 miles from New York to Los Angeles, CA, from July 26 to August 13, 1930 without once stopping the engine. They arrived back in New York in reverse on September 5, having completed 7,180 miles in 42 days.

Brian "Cub" Keene and James "Wilbur" Wright drove their Chevrolet Blazer 9,031 miles in reverse in 37 days (August 1–September 6, 1984) through 15 states and Canada. Though the name of the car, "Stuck in Reverse," was prominently displayed, law-enforcement officers in Oklahoma refused to believe it and insisted they drive in reverse reverse—i.e., forward—out of the state.

The highest average speed attained in any nonstop reverse drive exceeding 500 miles was achieved by Gerald Hoagland, who drove a 1969 Chevrolet Impala 501 miles in 17 hr. 38 min. at Chemung Speed Drome, NY, July 9–10, 1976, to average 28.41 MPH.

Longest battery-powered car journey   David Turner and Tim Pickhard of Turners of Boscastle Ltd., Cornwall, England traveled 875 miles from Land's End to John o' Groat's in a Freight Rover Leyland Sherpa, powered by a Lucas electric motor, December 21–25, 1985.

Two-side-wheel driving   Car   Bengt Norberg of Äppelbo, Sweden drove a Mitsubishi Colt GTi-16V on two side wheels nonstop for a distance of 192.873 miles in a time of 7 hr. 15 min. 50 sec. He also achieved a distance of 27.842 miles in one hour at Rattvik Horse Track, Sweden on May 24, 1989.

Sven-Erik Söderman (Sweden) achieved a speed of 102.14 MPH over a 100-meter (328.1-foot) flying start on two wheels of an Opel Kadett at

HAZARDOUS!

It was reported that a 75-year-old male driver received 10 traffic tickets, drove on the wrong side of the road 4 times, committed 4 hit-and-run offenses and caused 6 accidents, all within 20 minutes, in McKinney, TX on October 15, 1966.

Mora Siljan Airport, Mora, Sweden on August 2, 1990. Söderman achieved a record speed for the flying kilometer at 152.96 km/h (95.04 MPH) at the same venue on August 24, 1990.

Truck   Sven-Erik Söderman drove a Daf 2800 7.5-ton truck on two wheels for a distance of 6.73 miles at Mora Siljan Airport, Mora, Sweden on May 19, 1991.

Bus   Bobby Ore (Great Britain) drove a double-decker bus a distance of 810 feet on two wheels at North Weald Airfield, England on May 21, 1988.

Longest wheelie   Steve Murty, driving a Pirelli High Performer, established the record for the longest wheelie in a truck, covering 1,794.9 feet at the National Power Sports Festival in Blackpool, England on June 28, 1991.

GUESS WHAT?

Q.   Where was the largest car wash held?

A.   Look in "Fantastic Events" (Human Achievements)

Most durable driver   Goodyear Tire and Rubber Co. test driver Weldon C. Kocich drove 3,141,946 miles from February 5, 1953 to February 28, 1986, thus averaging 95,210 miles per year.

Oldest drivers   Layne Hall (b. December 24/25, 1884 or March 15, 1880) of Silver Creek, NY was issued a New York State driver's license valid until his birthday in 1993, when, based on his date of birth on the license, he would have been 113 years old. He died, however, on November 20, 1990, at age 105 (according to the death certificate).

Mrs. Maude Tull of Inglewood, CA, who took to driving at age 91 after her husband died, was issued a license renewal on February 5, 1976 when she was 104.

Driving tests   The easiest tests are those in Egypt, in which the ability to drive 19.64 feet forward and the same in reverse has been deemed sufficient. In 1979, it was reported that an accurate reversing test had been added.

Mrs. Fannie Turner (b. 1903) of Little Rock, AR passed the *written* test for drivers on her 104th attempt in October 1978.

Most parking tickets   Mrs. Silvia Matos of New York City set what must be a world record in unpaid parking tickets, totaling $150,000. She collected the 2,800 tickets between 1985 and 1988, but authorities were unable to collect any money; she registered her car under 19 addresses and 36 license plates and could not be found.

SPECIALIZED VEHICLES

Largest automotive land vehicle   "Big Muskie" was built by Bucyrus Erie for the Central Ohio Coal Co.'s Muskingum site, OH. It is a 13,200-ton walking dragline (a machine that removes dirt from coal) but it is no longer in use as it is too expensive to run.

Longest land vehicle   The Arctic Snow Train owned by Steve McPeak (U.S.) has 54 wheels and is 572 feet long. It was built by R.G. Le Tourneau Inc. of Longview, TX for the U.S. Army. Its gross train weight is 441 tons, with a top speed of 20 MPH, and it was driven by a crew of six when used as an "overland train" for the military. It generates 4,680 shp and has a fuel capacity of 7,832 gallons. McPeak undertook all repairs, including every flat tire, single-handedly in often sub-zero temperatures in Alaska.

Heaviest load   On July 14–15, 1984, John Brown Engineers & Contractors BV moved the Conoco Kotter Field production deck with a roll-out weight of 325 tons for the Continental Netherlands Oil Co. of Leidsenhage, Netherlands.

AMBULANCES

Largest ambulances   The 59-foot-long articulated Alligator Jumbulances Marks VI, VII, VIII and IX, operated by the ACROSS Trust, convey the sick and handicapped on vacations and pilgrimages across Europe. They are built by Van Hool of Belgium with Fiat engines, cost $350,000 and carry 44 patients and staff.

BUSES

Longest buses   The articulated DAF Super CityTrain buses of Zaire have room for 110 seated passengers and 140 "strap-hangers" in the first trailer, and 60 seated and 40 "strap-hangers" in the second, for a total of 350. The buses are 105.64 feet long and weigh 32 tons empty.

Rigid   The longest rigid single bus is 49 feet long and carries 69 passengers. It was built by Van Hool of Belgium.

Largest bus fleet   The 10,364 single-deck buses in São Paulo, Brazil make up the world's largest bus fleet.

Longest bus route   Run by Expreso Internacional Ormeño S.A., the regular scheduled 6,003-mile-long service between Caracas, Venezuela and Buenos Aires, Argentina takes 214 hours, with a 12-hour stopover in Santiago, Chile and a 24-hour stopover in Lima, Peru.

United States   The longest scheduled bus route currently in use in the United States is operated by Greyhound from Chicago to San Francisco. It runs once per day, is 2,294 miles long, and takes 51 hr. 49 min. to complete, employing seven drivers, with no change of bus.

Greatest passenger volume   The city with the greatest passenger volume in the United States as of December 1992 was New York City, with unlinked passenger trips of 636.7 million for buses and 1.32 billion for trains. In 1992, the city with the highest aggregate for passenger miles traveled was also New York City, where riders logged approximately 1.9 billion miles.

CAMPERS

Largest camper   In 1990, Sheik Hamad Bin Hamdan Al Nahyan of Abu Dhabi, United Arab Emirates built a 2-wheeled, 5-story vehicle measuring 66 feet long, 39 feet wide and 39 feet high. Weighing 120 tons, it comprises 8 bedrooms, 8 bathrooms, 4 garages and water storage for 6,340 gallons.

DID YOU KNOW?

The Marion 8-caterpillar crawler, used for conveying Saturn V rockets to their launch pads at Cape Canaveral, FL, measures 131 ft. 4 in. by 114 feet. The loaded train weight is 9,000 tons. The windshield wiper blades are 42 inches long and are the largest in the world.

Longest camper journey   Harry B. Coleman and Peggy Larson set off in a Volkswagen Camper on August 20, 1976. They traveled continuously until April 20, 1978, covering 143,716 miles through 113 countries.

Fastest camper   A Roadster camper towed by a 1990 Ford EA Falcon, driven by Charlie Kovacs, achieved 126.76 MPH at Mangalore Airfield, Seymour, Victoria, Australia on April 18, 1991.

FIRE ENGINES

Greatest pumping capacity   The fire appliance with the greatest pumping capacity is the 860-hp 8-wheel Oshkosh firetruck, which weighs 66 tons and is used for aircraft and runway fires. It can discharge 50,200 gallons of foam through two turrets in just 2 min. 30 sec.

Fastest fire vehicle   On November 2, 1982, John Griffiths drove a Jaguar XJ-12, 5.3-liter, 4-door sedan "Project Thrust Fire Control Vehicle" at a speed of 130.57 MPH at Black Rock Desert, Gerlach, NV.

Fire pumping   The greatest gallonage stirrup-pumped by a team of eight in an 80-hour charity pump is 37,898 gallons, by firefighters at the Knaresborough Fire Station in Knaresborough, England, June 25–28, 1992.

Fire pump handling   The longest unaided tow of a fire appliance in excess of 1,120 pounds in 24 hours on a closed circuit is 223 miles, by a 32-man team of the Dublin Fire Brigade with a 1,144-pound fire pump, Dublin, Ireland, June 20–21, 1987.

GO-KARTS

Highest go-kart mileage   The highest mileage recorded in 24 hours on an outdoor circuit by a 4-man team is 1,018 miles, on a 1-mile track at the Erbsville Kartway, Waterloo, Ontario, Canada, September 4–5, 1983. The 5-hp 140-cc Honda-engined kart was driven by Owen Nimmo, Gary Ruddock, Jim Timmins and Danny Upshaw.

The highest mileage recorded in 24 hours on an indoor track by a 4-man team driving 160-cc karts is 883.9 miles, at the Welsh Karting Centre, Cardiff, Wales on November 26, 1993. The drivers were Ian O'Sullivan, Paul Marram, Richard Jenkins and Michael Watts.

Six-hour drive   The record distance achieved in six hours in the 100-cc non-gearbox category is 249.117 miles, by Zack Dawson of Ridgecrest, CA at the Mesa Marin Raceway in Bakersfield, CA on April 9, 1993.

LAWN MOWERS

Widest lawn mower   The widest gang mower in the world is the 5-ton 60-foot-wide 27-unit "Big Green Machine" used by the turf farmer Jay Edgar Frick of Monroe, OH. It mows an acre in 60 seconds.

Longest lawn mower drive   Ian Ireland of Harlow, England drove an Iseki SG15 power lawn mower 3,034 miles between Harlow and Southend Pier, England, August 13–September 7, 1989. He was assisted by members of 158 Round Table, Luton, England and raised over £15,000 ($26,250) to aid the Leukemia Research Fund.

MODEL CARS

Smallest car   Nippondenso of Kariya, Japan created a motorized scale model car of Toyota's first passenger car, the 1936 Model AA Sedan. The model is 1,000 times as small as the actual car; it measures 0.189 inches long, 0.068 inches wide, and 0.068 inches high. The motor (the coil of which is only 0.0394 inches in diameter) drives the front wheels, with the power delivered from an external source through a copper wire that enters via the roof. The car has a top speed of 0.011 MPH.

Longest drive   A Scalextric Jaguar XJ8 ran nonstop for 866 hr. 44 min. 54 sec. and covered a distance of 1,771.2 miles from May 2 to June 7, 1989. The event was organized by the Rev. Bryan G. Apps and church members of Southbourne, Bournemouth, England.

24-hour slot car race   On September 4–5, 1994, H.O. Racing and Hobbies of San Diego, CA achieved a distance of 375.079 miles for a 1:64 scale car. On July 5–6, 1986, the North London Society of Model Engineers team at the ARRA club in Southport, England achieved a 24-hour distance record of 305.949 miles for a 1:32 scale car, a Rondeau M482C Group C Sports car built by Ian Fisher. This was under the rules of the B.S.C.R.A. (British Slot Car Racing Association).

Longest slot car track   The longest slot car track measures 958 feet and was built at Mallory Park Circuit, Leicester, England on November 22, 1991. One car successfully completed a full lap.

SNOW PLOWS

Largest snow-plow blade   A blade measuring 50.25 feet long and four feet high, with a clearing capacity of 1,095 cubic feet in one pass, was made by Aero Snow Removal Corporation of New York, NY in 1992 for operation at JFK International Airport.

SNOWMOBILES

Longest snowmobile ride   John W. Outzen of Derry, NH (expedition organizer and leader), with Andre, Carl and Dennis Boucher, traveled 10,252.3 miles across North America, from Anchorage, AK to Dartmouth, Nova Scotia, Canada, in 62 days (56 riding days) from January 2 to March 3, 1992 on four Arctic Cat Panther Deluxe Snowmobiles.

Tony Lenzini of Duluth, MN drove his 1986 Arctic Cat Cougar snowmobile a total of 7,211 miles in 60 riding days between December 28, 1985 and March 20, 1986.

SOLAR-POWERED VEHICLES

Fastest solar-powered land vehicle   The fastest speed attained by a solely solar-powered land vehicle is 48.71 MPH, by Molly Brennan driving the General Motors *Sunraycer* at Mesa, AZ on June 24, 1988. The fastest speed of 83.88 MPH using solar/battery power was achieved by Star Micronics' solar car *Solar Star*, driven by Manfred Hermann on January 5, 1991 at Richmond R.A.A.F. Base, Richmond, Australia.

TANKS

Heaviest tank   The heaviest tank ever constructed was the German Panzer Kampfwagen Maus II, which weighed over 210 tons. By 1945, it had reached only the experimental stage and was not developed further.

The heaviest operational tank used by any army was the 83-ton 13-man French Char de Rupture 2C bis of 1922. It carried a 155-mm howitzer and had two 250-hp engines giving a maximum speed of 8 MPH.

United States   The heaviest tank in the United States Army is the M1A1 Abrams, which weighs 67 tons when combat loaded, is 32 ft. 3 in. long, and can reach a maximum speed of 41.5 MPH.

Most heavily armed tank   The most heavily armed tank since 1972 is the Soviet T-72, which has a 4⅞-inch high-velocity gun and is the only rocket-gun tank with explosive reactive armor.

Fastest tank   The fastest tracked armored reconnaissance vehicle is the British Scorpion, which can reach 50 MPH with a 75 percent payload.

The American experimental tank M1936, built by J. Walter Christie, was clocked at 64.3 MPH during official trials in Great Britain in 1938.

Most tanks produced   The greatest production of any tank was that of the Soviet T-54/55 series, of which more than 50,000 were built between 1954 and 1980 in the USSR alone, with further production in the one-time Warsaw Pact countries and China.

ZOOM!

The highest speed recorded on ice is 247.93 MPH by the rocket-powered sled *Oxygen*, driven by Sammy Miller on Lake George, NY on February 15, 1981.

TAXIS

Largest taxi fleet   Mexico City has a taxi fleet of 60,000 taxis, including regular taxis, communal fixed-route taxis and airport taxis.

United States   The city with the largest taxi fleet in the United States is New York City, which on January 1, 1994 had 11,787 registered yellow medallion cabs and 40,000 licensed drivers serving an estimated 226 million passengers yearly. In addition, there are approximately 30,000 For Hire Vehicle (FHV) cabs serving out of 600 bases stationed throughout the city's five boroughs.

TAXI!

The longest taxicab ride on record is one of 14,414 miles at a cost of 70,000 FIM (approximately $16,000). Mika Lehtonen and Juhani Saramies left Nokia, Finland on May 2, 1991, traveling through Scandinavia down to Spain, and arrived back in Nokia on May 17, 1991.

Most durable taxi driver   Carmen Fasanella was continuously licensed as a taxicab owner and driver in the Borough of Princeton, NJ for 68 yr. 243 days, from February 1, 1921 to November 2, 1989.

TRACTORS

Largest tractor   The $459,000 U.S. Department of Agriculture Wide Tractive Frame Vehicle, completed by Ag West of Sacramento, CA in June 1982, measures 33 feet between its wheels, which are designed to run on permanent paths, and weighs 24.5 tons.

Tractor-pulling   The sport of tractor-pulling was put on a national U.S. championship basis in 1967 at Bowling Green, OH, where the winner was "The Purple Monster" built and driven by Roger E. Varns. Today there are 12 classes, ranging up to "12,200 pounds unlimited."

Longest tractor journey   The Young Farmers Group of Devon, England left their native country on October 18, 1990 in one tractor and supporting trailer, and drove overland to Zimbabwe, a total of 14,500 miles, arriving on March 4, 1991.

TROLLEYS

Oldest trolley   Motor cars 1 and 2 of the Manx Electric Railway date from 1893. They run regularly on the 17¾-mile railroad between Douglas and Ramsey, Isle of Man, Great Britain.

Most extensive trolley system   By early 1991, St. Petersburg, Russia had the most extensive trolley system, with 2,402 cars on 64 routes and 429.13 miles of track.

Longest trolley journey   The longest trolley journey now possible is from Krefeld St. Tönis to Witten Annen Nord, Germany. With luck at the eight interconnections, the 65.5-mile trip can be completed in five and a half hours.

TRUCKS

Largest truck   The Terex Titan 33–19 manufactured by General Motors Corporation and now in operation at Westar Mine, British Columbia, Canada has a loaded weight of 604.7 tons and a capacity of 350 tons. When tipped, its height is 56 feet. The 16-cylinder engine delivers 3,300 hp. The fuel tank holds 1,300 gallons.

Most powerful truck   Les Shockley of Galena, KS drove his Jet Truck *ShockWave*, powered by three Pratt & Whitney jet engines developing 36,000 hp, to a record speed of 256 MPH in 6.36 seconds over a quarter-mile from a standing start on June 4, 1989 at Autodrome de Monterrey, Mexico. He set a further record for the standing mile at 376 MPH at Paine Field, Everett, WA on August 18, 1991.

WRECKERS

Most powerful wrecker   The Twin City Garage and Body Shop's 22.7-ton, 36-foot-long International M6-23 "Hulk" 1969 is stationed at Scott City, MO. It can lift in excess of 325 tons on its short boom.

SERVICES

Largest filling station The largest concentration of pumps is 204—96 of them Tokheim Unistar (electronic) and 108 Tokheim Explorer (mechanical)—in Jeddah, Saudi Arabia.

Highest filling station The highest filling station in the world is at Leh, Ladakh, India, at 12,001 feet, operated by the Indian Oil Corporation.

Largest garage The largest private garage is one of two stories built outside Bombay, India for the private collection of 176 cars owned by Pranlal Bhogilal.

The KMB Overhaul Center, operated by the Kowloon Motor Bus Co. (1933) Ltd., Hong Kong, is the world's largest multistory service center. Built expressly for double-decker buses, it has four floors occupying more than 11.6 acres.

Largest tires Goodyear Tire & Rubber Co. manufactures 12-foot-diameter tires for giant dump trucks. The tires weigh 12,500 pounds each and cost $74,000.

Longest skid marks The skid marks made by the jet-powered *Spirit of America*, driven by Norman Craig Breedlove, after the car went out of control at Bonneville Salt Flats, UT, on October 15, 1964, were nearly six miles long.

Longest tow Great Britain's Automobile Association used a Land Rover to tow a replica Model T Ford van 4,995 miles, starting in Ascot, England on May 4, 1993 and ending up in Widmerpool, England on May 12, 1993.

ROADS

Greatest length of road The United States has more miles of road than any other country, with 3,880,151 miles of graded road. The state with the most miles of road is Texas, with 305,951 miles, while Hawaii has the fewest, with 4,099 miles.

Longest driveable road The Pan-American Highway, from northwest Alaska to Santiago, Chile, then eastward to Buenos Aires, Argentina, terminating in Brasilia, Brazil, is over 15,000 miles long. There is, however, a small incomplete section in Panama and Colombia known as the Darién Gap.

United States The longest highway solely in the United States is US-20, which runs 3,370 miles from Boston, MA to Newport, OR. The longest

Above is just half of the Monumental Axis, the world's widest road, in Brasilia, the capital of Brazil. The road, which opened in April 1960, runs for 1½ miles and is 820.2 feet wide. (*Gamma/E. Soderstrom*)

highway in the interstate system is I-90, 3,107 miles from Boston, MA to Seattle, WA.

Worst exit to miss The longest distance between controlled access exits in the United States is 51.1 miles from Florida Turnpike exit 193 (Yeehaw Junction, FL) to exit 244 (Kissimmee, FL). The longest distance on any interstate highway is 37.7 miles from I-80 exit 41 (Knolls, UT) to exit 4 (Bonneville Speedway, UT).

Highest trail The highest trail in the world is an 8-mile stretch of the Gangdise between Khaleb and Xinji-fu, Tibet, which in two places exceeds 20,000 feet.

Highest road The highest road in the world is in Kyardungla Pass, at an altitude of 18,650 feet. This is one of three passes of the Leh-Manali road completed in 1976 by the Border Roads Organization, New Delhi, India; motor vehicles were able to use it from 1988 on.

Lowest road The lowest road is along the Israeli shores of the Dead Sea at 1,290 feet below sea level.

Widest road The Monumental Axis runs for 1½ miles from the Municipal Plaza to the Plaza of the Three Powers in Brasilia, the capital of Brazil. The dual 6-lane boulevard, opened in April 1960, is 820.2 feet wide.

Highest traffic volume The most heavily traveled stretch of road is Interstate 405 (San Diego Freeway), in Orange County, CA, which has a rush-hour volume of 25,500 vehicles on a 0.9-mile stretch between Garden Grove Freeway and Seal Beach Boulevard.

Highest traffic density The territory with the highest traffic density in the world is Hong Kong. In 1992, there were 418 vehicles per mile of serviceable road, giving a density of 4.53 yards per vehicle.

Longest traffic jam On February 16, 1980, a traffic jam stretching northwards from Lyons 109.3 miles towards Paris, France was reported. A record traffic jam was reported for 1.5 million cars crawling bumper-to-bumper over the East–West German border on April 12, 1990.

Longest street The longest designated street in the world is Yonge Street, running north and west from Toronto, Ontario, Canada. The first stretch, completed on February 16, 1796, ran 34 miles. Its official length, now extended to Rainy River on the Ontario–Minnesota border, is 1,178.3 miles.

Narrowest street The world's narrowest street is in the village of Ripatransone in the Marche region of Italy. It is called *Vicolo della Virilita* ("Virility Alley") and is 16.9 inches wide.

Shortest street The title for "The Shortest Street in the World" is claimed by the town of Bacup, England, where Elgin Street measures just 17 feet.

Steepest street Baldwin Street, Dunedin, New Zealand has a maximum gradient of 1 in 1.266.

United States The crookedest and steepest street in the United States is Lombard Street, San Francisco, CA. It has eight consecutive 90-degree turns of 20-foot radius.

RAILROADING

TRAINS

Fastest train The fastest speed attained by a railed vehicle is 6,121 MPH, or Mach 8, by an unmanned rocket sled over the 9½-mile-long rail track at White Sands Missile Range, NM on October 5, 1982.

The fastest speed recorded on any national rail system is 320.2 MPH by the French SNCF high-speed train TGV (*Train à Grande Vitesse*) Atlantique between Courtalain and Tours on May 18, 1990. The TGV Sud-Est was brought into service on September 27, 1981. TGV Atlantique and Nord services now run at up to 186 MPH. The fastest point-to-point schedule is between Paris and St. Pierre des Corps, near Tours. The 144 miles are covered in 55 minutes—an average of 157 MPH. The Eurostar service from London to Paris also runs at 186 MPH on the French side of the Channel. New Series 500 trains for Japan's JR West rail system are also designed to run at 186 MPH in regular service.

United States The fastest train in the United States is the Amtrak X2000, which has a maximum speed of 156 MPH. The train completed its demonstration run between Washington, D.C. and New York on February 1, 1993. The Swedish-built passenger train will travel the New York–Washington corridor and the New Haven-to-Boston route in 1997.

Fastest steam locomotive The highest speed ever ratified for a steam locomotive was 125 MPH over 1,320 feet, by the LNER 4–6–2 No. 4468 *Mallard* (later numbered 60022), which hauled seven coaches weighing 267.9 tons down Stoke Bank, near Essendine, England on July 3, 1938. Driver Joseph

A train on the Trans-Siberian railway winds its way through Russia. (*Gamma/Le Figaro Magazine*)

Duddington was at the controls with Fireman Thomas Bray. The engine suffered some damage to the middle big-end bearing.

Most powerful steam locomotive   In terms of tractive effort, the most powerful steam locomotive was No. 700, a triple-articulated or triplex 6-cylinder 2–8–8–8–4 engine built by the Baldwin Locomotive Works in 1916 for the Virginian Railway. It had a tractive force of 166,300 pounds when working compound and 199,560 pounds when working simple.

Strongest rail carrier   The 36-axle "Schnabel" has a capacity of 838 tons, measures 301 ft. 10 in. long, and was built for a U.S. railroad by Krupp, Germany in March 1981.

The heaviest load ever moved on rails is the 11,971-ton Church of the Virgin Mary (built in 1548 in the village of Most, Czech Republic), which was obstructing coal operations. In October–November 1975, it was moved 2,400 feet at 0.0013 MPH over four weeks, at a cost of $17 million.

CHOO-CHOO!

The largest operating steam locomotive is Union Pacific RR *Challenger* type 4–6–6–4 No. 3985, built by the American Locomotive Co. in 1943. In working order, with tender, it weighs 543.2 tons.

Longest and heaviest train   On August 26–27, 1989, a 4½-mile-long train weighing 77,720 tons (excluding locomotives) made a run on the 3-ft.-6-in.-gauge Sishen–Saldanha railroad in South Africa. Carrying the largest number of cars ever recorded, the train consisted of 660 cars each loaded to 105 tons gross, a tank car, and a caboose. It was moved by nine 50 kV electric and seven diesel-electric locomotives distributed along the train. The train traveled a distance of 535 miles in 22 hr. 40 min.

United States   The longest and heaviest freight train on record was about four miles long. It comprised 500 coal motor cars with three 3,600-hp diesels pulling and three more in the middle; the total weight was nearly 47,040 tons. The train traveled on the Iaeger, WV-to-Portsmouth, OH stretch of 157 miles on the Norfolk and Western Railway on November 15, 1967.

Longest passenger train   A train belonging to the National Belgium Railway Company measured 1,895 yards long, consisted of 70 coaches, and had a total weight of over 2,800 tons. The train was powered by one electric locomotive and took 1 hr. 11 min. 5 sec. to complete the 38.5-mile journey from Ghent to Ostend on April 27, 1991.

TRACKS

Longest track   The world's longest run without change of train is one of 5,864½ miles on the Trans-Siberian line from Moscow to Nakhodka, Russia, on the Sea of Japan. There are 97 stops on the journey, which is scheduled to take 8 days 4 hr. 25 min.

Longest straight track   United States   The longest straight track in the United States is 78.86 miles on CSX Railroad, between Wilmington and Hamlet, NC.

Widest and narrowest gauge   The widest in standard use is 5 ft. 6 in. This width is used in Spain, Portugal, India, Pakistan, Bangladesh, Sri Lanka, Argentina and Chile.

The narrowest gauge on which public services are operated is 10¼ inches on the Wells Harbor (0.7 miles) and Wells–Walsingham Railways (four miles) in Norfolk, England.

DID YOU KNOW?

The Commonwealth Railways Trans-Australian line over the Nullarbor Plain, from Mile 496 between Nurina and Loongana, Western Australia to Mile 793 between Ooldea and Watson, South Australia, is 297 miles dead straight, although it is not level.

Highest line   At 15,806 feet above sea level, the standard gauge (4 ft. 8½ in.) track on the Morococha branch of the Peruvian State Railways at La Cima is the highest in the world.

Lowest line   The Seikan Tunnel, which crosses the Tsugaro Strait between Honshu and Hokkaido, Japan, reaches a depth of 786 feet below sea level. The tunnel was opened on March 13, 1988 and is 33½ miles long.

Steepest railway   The Katoomba Scenic Railway in the Blue Mountains of New South Wales, Australia is 1,020 feet long, with a gradient of 1 in 0.82. A 220-hp electric winding machine hauls the car by twin steel cables of 22-mm diameter. The ride takes about 1 min. 40 sec., and the railway carries about 420,000 passengers a year.

Greatest length of railroad   As of 1993, the United States had 168,964 miles of road (route miles) operated for all classes of track. There were 123,738 miles of class I track (freight only) and 45,226 miles of non-class I track operated. There was a total of 186,288 miles of track owned by class I railroads, including sidings and yards.

Steepest gradient   The world's steepest gradient worked by adhesion is 1 in 11, between Chedde and Servoz on the meter-gauge SNCF Chamonix line, France.

Busiest system   The railroad carrying the largest number of passengers is the East Japan Railway Co., which in 1993 carried 16,700,000 passengers daily, providing it with a revenue of $19.5 billion.

Spike driving   In the World Championship Professional Spike Driving Competition, held at the Golden Spike National Historic Site in Utah, Dale C. Jones, 49, of Lehi, UT, drove six 7-inch railroad spikes in a time of 26.4 seconds on August 11, 1984. He incurred no penalty points under the official rules.

TRAIN TRAVEL

Most countries in 24 hours   The greatest number of countries traveled through entirely by train in 24 hours is 11, by Alison Bailey, Ian Bailey, John English and David Kellie, May 1–2, 1993. Their journey started in Hungary and continued through Slovakia, the Czech Republic, Austria, Germany, back into Austria, Liechtenstein, Switzerland, France, Luxembourg, Belgium and the Netherlands, where they arrived 22 hr. 10 min. after setting off.

Most miles traveled   John E. Ballenger of Dunedin, FL logged 76,485 miles of unduplicated rail routes in North and South America.

United States   James J. Brady of Wilmington, OH traveled through 442 out of 498 stations in the U.S. over 21,485 unduplicated miles of track from February 11 to March 11, 1984.

Most miles in one week   Andrew Kingsmell and Sean Andrews of Bromley, England and Graham Bardouleau of Crawley, England traveled 13,105 miles on the French National Railway System in 6 days 22 hr. 38 min., November 28–December 5, 1992.

Longest train ticket   A train ticket 111 ft. 10½ in. long was issued to Ronald, Norma and Jonathan Carter for journeys traveled on British Rail, February 15–23, 1992.

Fastest handpumped railcars   A speed of 20.58 MPH for a 984-foot course was achieved by a 5-man team (one pusher, four pumpers) at Rolvenden, England, August 21, 1989, recording a time of 32.61 seconds.

STATIONS

Largest station   Grand Central Terminal, Park Avenue and 42nd Street, New York City, was built 1903–13. It covers 48 acres on two levels, with 41 tracks on the upper level and 26 on the lower. On average, there are more than 550 trains and 200,000 commuters daily, in addition to the 500,000 people who walk through the terminal daily to visit the shops and restaurants or greet travelers boarding or getting off trains.

Highest station   Condor station in Bolivia is situated at 15,705 feet on the meter-gauge Rio Mulato-to-Potosi line.

Grand Central Terminal, the world's largest railroad station, in New York City. (*Image Select*)

Largest waiting rooms The four waiting rooms in Beijing Station, Chang'an Boulevard, Beijing, China, which were opened in September 1959, have a total standing capacity of 14,000.

Longest railroad platform The Kharagpur platform in West Bengal, India measures 2,733 feet long.

Largest freight yard Bailey Yard in North Platte, NE covers 2,850 acres and has 260 miles of track. It handles an average of 108 trains and some 8,500 freight cars every day.

MODEL TRAINS

Longest run A standard Life-Like BL2 HO scale electric train pulled six 8-wheel coaches for 1,207.5 hours without stopping, from August 4 to September 23, 1990, and covered a distance of 909.5 miles. The event was organized by Ike Cottingham and Mark Hamrick of Mainline Modelers of Akron, OH.

24-hour run The 7¼-inch-gauge model steam locomotive "Peggy" covered 167.7 miles in 24 hours at Weston Park Railway, Weston Park, England, June 17–18, 1994.

Smallest model railroad   A miniature model railroad with a scale of 1:1,400 was made by Bob Henderson of Gravenhurst, Ontario, Canada. The engine runs on a 4½-volt battery and measures ⁵⁄₁₆ of an inch overall.

SUBWAY SYSTEMS

Most extensive subway system   The most extensive underground railway system is the London Underground, England, with 254 miles of route, of which 86 miles is bored tunnel and 20 miles is "cut and cover." The system is operated by a staff of 17,000; there are 270 stations, and 3,955 cars form a fleet of 547 trains. Passengers made 735 million journeys in 1993–94.

The New York City subway system has 469 stations, 277 of which are underground. (*Gamma/C. Edinger/Liaison*)

Most stations   The subway system with the most stations in the world is the Metropolitan Transportation Authority/New York City Transportation Authority subway (first section opened on October 27, 1904). The network covers 238 route miles, comprising 469 subway stations. In 1994, it served an average of 3.5 million passengers per day, plus an additional 3,611,000 in student population.

Traveling the New York subway   The record time for traveling the whole system is 26 hr. 21 min. 08 sec., set by Kevin Foster (U.S.), October 25–26, 1989.

DID YOU KNOW?

The worst subway accident in the United States occurred on November 1, 1918, in Brooklyn, NY, when a BRT Line train derailed on a curve on Malbone St. in the Brighton Beach section. There were 97 fatalities on the scene, and five more people died later from injuries sustained in the crash.

Busiest subway system   Greater Moscow Metro (opened 1935) in Russia had as many as 3.3 billion passenger journeys per year at its peak—although the figure has now declined to 2.5 billion. It has 3,500 railcars and a workforce of 25,000. There are 141 stations and 140 miles of track.

Longest subway platform   The State Street Center subway platform on "The Loop" in Chicago, IL measures 3,500 feet long.

AIRCRAFT AND FLIGHT

First power-driven flight   The first controlled and sustained power-driven flight occurred near Kill Devil Hill, Kitty Hawk, NC, at 10:35 A.M. on December 17, 1903, when Orville Wright (1871–1948) flew the 12-hp chain-driven *Flyer I* for a distance of 120 feet at an airspeed of 30 MPH, a ground speed of 6.8 MPH, and an altitude of 8–12 feet for about 12 seconds, watched by his brother Wilbur (1867–1912) and five other observers. *Flyer I* is now exhibited in the National Air and Space Museum at the Smithsonian Institution, Washington, D.C.

First jet aircraft flight   The first flight by an airplane powered by a turbojet engine was made by the Heinkel He 178, piloted by Captain Erich Warsitz, at Marienehe, Germany on August 27, 1939. It was powered by a Heinkel He S3b engine weighing 834 pounds (as installed with long tailpipe) designed by Dr. Hans Pabst von Ohain.

United States   The U.S.-built Bell XP59A, using Whittle-designed engines, first flew at Muroc, CA on October 1, 1942. The first U.S.-built operational jet aircraft was the Lockheed P-80, which first flew on January 8, 1944.

First transatlantic flight   The first crossing of the North Atlantic by air was made by Lt.-Cdr. (later Rear Admiral) Albert Cushion Read and his crew (Stone, Hinton, Rodd, Rhoads and Breese) in the 84-knot U.S. Navy/Curtiss flying boat NC-4 from Trepassey Harbor, Newfoundland, Canada, via the Azores, to Lisbon, Portugal, May 16–27, 1919. The whole flight of 4,717 miles, originating from Rockaway Air Station, Long Island, NY on May 8, took 53 hr. 58 min., terminating at Plymouth, England on May 31.

FILL 'ER UP!

The Sky Harbor Air Service line crew refueled a 1975 Cessna 310 (N29HH) with 102.7 gallons of 100 octane avgas in 3 min. 42 sec. on July 5, 1992. The plane had landed at Cheyenne Airport in Wyoming during an around-the-world air race.

Nonstop The first nonstop transatlantic flight was achieved 18 days later. The pilot, Capt. John Williams Alcock, and navigator, Lt. Arthur Whitton Brown, left Lester's Field, St. John's, Newfoundland, Canada at 4:13 P.M. GMT on June 14, 1919, and landed at Derrygimla Bog near Clifden, Republic of Ireland, at 8:40 A.M. GMT, June 15, having covered a distance of 1,960 miles in their Vickers Vimy, powered by two 360-hp Rolls-Royce Eagle VIII engines.

Solo The first solo transatlantic flight was achieved by Capt. Charles Augustus Lindbergh, who took off in his 220-hp Ryan monoplane *Spirit of St. Louis* at 12:52 P.M. GMT on May 20, 1927 from Roosevelt Field, Long Island, NY. He landed at 10:21 P.M. GMT on May 21, 1927 at Le Bourget Airfield, Paris, France. His flight of 3,610 miles lasted 33 hr. 29½ min. and he won a prize of $25,000. The *Spirit of St. Louis* is now in the National Air and Space Museum at the Smithsonian Institution, Washington, D.C.

First transpacific flight The first nonstop flight across the Pacific was by Major Clyde Pangborn and Hugh Herndon in the Bellanca cabin monoplane *Miss Veedol*. They took off from Sabishiro Beach, Japan and covered the distance of 4,558 miles to Wenatchee, WA in 41 hr. 13 min., October 3–5, 1931.

Fred Finn, Rolls-Royce and Concorde. Finn has flown a record 707 times on the Concorde. (*Fred Finn*)

Circumnavigational flights Circumnavigation of the globe requires the aircraft to pass through two antipodal points, covering a minimum distance of 24,859.73 miles.

First without refueling Richard G. "Dick" Rutan and Jeana Yeager, in their specially constructed aircraft *Voyager*, designed by Dick's brother Burt Rutan, flew from Edwards Air Force Base, CA, December 14–23, 1986. Their flight took 9 days 3 min. 44 sec. and they covered a distance of 24,987 miles, averaging 115.65 MPH. The plane, with a wingspan of 110 ft. 10 in., was capable of carrying 1,240 gallons of fuel weighing 8,934 pounds.

HEAVY FLYING

Air Foyle, a British charter company, and Antonov, a Ukrainian aircraft design company, set the record for carrying the heaviest single piece of cargo by air when they transported a 136.7-ton generator from Düsseldorf, Germany to New Delhi, India on September 22, 1993. The aircraft used was the Ukrainian An-124 Ruslan, the largest commercially available aircraft in the world, which is designed exclusively for heavy and oversize cargo. Air Foyle explains the background:

Preparing for takeoff (above) and the route taken (facing page). (BMS)

"The generator was urgently needed at Dadri Combined Cycle Power Plant, the largest such plant in India. Siemens, one of the world's leading electrical and electronic engineering companies, was asked to provide the generator. Time was of the essence; a sea voyage would have taken too long and been followed by a lengthy overland journey into the heart of India.

Because the cargo was so large, it was escorted by police from the Siemens factory in Mülheim to Düsseldorf. The journey started at 11 P.M., since the cargo took up most of the road in some places. It then took over 10 hours to complete the loading operation. During the flight itself, six refueling stops were necessary.

In India, there were still further problems to be overcome. An alternative route had to be found because there were bridges on the original route that could not support the weight of the loaded truck."

Air Foyle is used to this type of challenge. With Antonov, they once held the record for the largest single piece of cargo, and they set the record for the greatest cargo consignment in one plane in 1991 when they took a total of 154.3 tons of equipment in the Ruslan from Spain to New Caledonia.

Heaviest commercial cargo Ukrainian aircraft designer Antonov and British charter company Air Foyle set the record for carrying the heaviest single piece of cargo, by flying a 136.7-ton power plant generator from Düsseldorf, Germany to New Delhi, India on September 22, 1993.

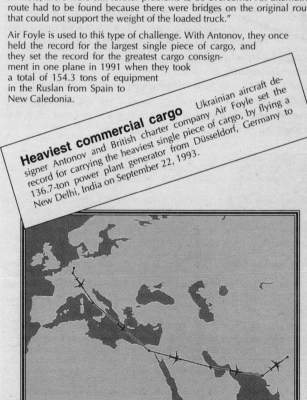

The pilot flew from a cockpit measuring 5 ft. 7 in. by 1 ft. 10 in. and the off-duty crew member occupied a cabin 7 ft. 6 in. by 2 feet. *Voyager* is in the National Air and Space Museum at the Smithsonian Institution, Washington, D.C.

First circumpolar   Capt. Elgen M. Long, 44, achieved the first circumpolar flight in a twin-engined Piper PA-31 Navajo, from November 5 to December 3, 1971. He covered 38,896 miles in 215 flying hours.

Oldest   Fred Lasby completed a solo around-the-world flight at the age of 82 in his single-engined Piper Comanche. He left Fort Meyers, FL on June 30, 1994, flew a distance of 23,218 miles with 21 stops, and arrived back at Fort Meyers on August 20, 1994.

First supersonic flight   The first supersonic flight was achieved on October 14, 1947, by Capt. (later Brig. Gen.) Charles "Chuck" Elwood Yeager, over Edwards Air Force Base, Muroc, CA, in a Bell XS-1 rocket plane (*Glamorous Glennis*—named after Yeager's wife) at Mach 1.015 (670 MPH) at an altitude of 42,000 feet. The XS-1 is now in the National Air and Space Museum at the Smithsonian Institution, Washington D.C.

AIRCRAFT

Largest wingspan   The $40-million Hughes H4 Hercules flying boat (*Spruce Goose*) had a wingspan of 319 ft. 11 in. and measured 218 ft. 8 in. long. The 8-engined 213-ton aircraft was raised 70 feet into the air in a test run of 3,000 feet, piloted by Howard Hughes, off Long Beach Harbor, CA, on November 2, 1947, but after this it never flew again.

Among current aircraft, the Ukrainian Antonov An-124 has a span of 240 ft. 5³/₄ in. The U.S.A.F. C-5B cargo plane has a wingspan of 222 ft. 8¹/₂ in., the greatest for any United States military aircraft.

Heaviest aircraft   The Ukrainian Antonov An-225 *Mriya* has the highest standard maximum takeoff weight, at 660 tons (1,322,750 pounds). This aircraft lifted a payload of 344,579 pounds to a height of 40,715 feet on March 22, 1989. The flight was achieved by Capt. Aleksandr Galunenko and his crew of seven pilots.

Most capacious aircraft   The Aero Spacelines Super Guppy, a converted Boeing C-97, has a cargo hold with a usable volume of 49,790 cubic feet and a maximum takeoff weight of 87.5 tons. Its wingspan is 156 ft. 3 in. and its length 141 ft. 3 in. Its cargo compartment is 108 ft. 10 in. long with a cylindrical section 25 feet in diameter.

Heaviest commercial cargo   Ukrainian aircraft designer Antonov and British charter company Air Foyle carried out the heaviest commercial air cargo movement, by taking three transformers weighing 47.4 tons each and other equipment from Barcelona, Spain to Nouméa, New Caledonia (Pacific), January 10–14, 1991. The total weight carried in the An-124 *Ruslan* was 154.3 tons.

Air Foyle and Antonov also set the record for carrying the heaviest single piece of cargo, by flying a 136.7-ton power plant generator from Düsseldorf, Germany to New Delhi, India on September 22, 1993. Again, the aircraft used was the Ukrainian An-124 *Ruslan*. Because of the huge weight, the plane had to make six refueling stops during the 5,600-mile flight.

Smallest aircraft The smallest biplane ever flown was the *Bumble Bee Two*, designed and built by Robert H. Starr of Arizona. It was 8 ft. 10 in. long, with a wingspan of 5 ft. 6 in., and weighed 396 pounds empty. The fastest speed it attained was 190 MPH. On May 8, 1988, after flying to a height of approximately 400 feet, it crashed, and was totally destroyed.

Bombers   Heaviest The former Soviet 4-jet Tupolev Tu-160 has a maximum takeoff weight of over 600,270 pounds.

Longest The Boeing B-52G is the longest bomber in the U.S.A.F. at 160 ft. 11 in. The B-52H has the greatest thrust of a bomber in the U.S. fleet, at 136,000 pounds, and the greatest unrefueled range of over 8,800 miles.

Fastest The world's fastest operational bombers include the French Dassault Mirage IV, which can fly at Mach 2.2 (1,450 MPH) at 36,000 feet.

The American variable-geometry or "swing-wing" General Dynamics FB-111A has a maximum speed of Mach 2.5, and the Soviet swing-wing Tupolev Tu-22M has an estimated over-target speed of Mach 2.0 but could be as fast as Mach 2.5.

AIRLINERS

Oldest jet airliner According to the British-based aviation information and consultancy service company Airclaims, a first-generation Douglas DC-8 jet airliner built in 1959 was still being used in May 1994 as a flying operating room for emergency surgery.

Largest jet airliner The highest-capacity jet airliner is the Boeing 747-400, which entered service with Northwest Airlines on January 26, 1989. It has a wingspan of 211 ft. 5 in., a range exceeding 8,000 miles and a capacity for up to 567 passengers. The original Boeing 747 "Jumbo Jet" has a capacity of 385 to 560 passengers and a maximum speed of 602 MPH. Its wingspan is 195 ft. 5 in. and its length 231 ft. 10 in. The plane entered service on January 22, 1970.

Greatest passenger load The greatest passenger load carried by any single commercial airliner was 1,088 during *Operation Solomon*, which began on May 24, 1991 when Ethiopian Jews were evacuated from Addis Ababa to Israel on an El Al Boeing 747 El Al. This figure includes two babies born during the flight.

Most flights by a propeller-driven airliner General Dynamics (formerly Convair) reported in March 1994 that some of its CV-580 turboprop airliners had logged over 150,000 flights, typically averaging no more than 20 minutes, in short-haul operations.

Most flights by a jet airliner A survey of aging airliners or so-called "geriatric jets" published in *Flight International* magazine in April 1994 reported a McDonnell Douglas DC-9 still in service that had logged 95,939 flights in less than 28 years.

The most hours recorded by a jet airliner still in service is 94,804 hours in less than 25 years, reported for a Boeing 747 in the same issue of *Flight International* (see above).

AIRLINES

Oldest airline Koninklijke-Luchtvaart-Maatschappij NV (KLM), the national airline of the Netherlands, was established on October 7, 1919. It opened its first scheduled service (Amsterdam–London, England) on May 17, 1920.

Chalk's International Airline has been flying amphibious planes from Miami, FL to the Bahamas since July 1919. The founder, Albert "Pappy" Chalk, flew planes from 1911 to 1975.

BUSY!

The city-pair with the highest international scheduled passenger traffic is London/Paris. More than 3 million passengers fly between the two cities annually, or more than 4,100 each way each day (although London-bound traffic is greater than that bound for Paris).

Largest airline The Russian state airline Aeroflot was instituted on February 9, 1923. In its last complete year of formal existence (1990) it employed 600,000 (more than the top 18 U.S. airlines put together) and flew 139 million passengers, with 20,000 pilots, along 620,000 miles of domestic routes across 11 time zones.

Since the breakup of the Soviet Union, the company that carries the greatest number of passengers is American Airlines, with 81,093,687 in 1994. The German airline Lufthansa has the longest route network, covering 585,000 miles.

Busiest airline system The country with the busiest airline system is the United States, where the total number of passengers for air carriers in scheduled domestic operations exceeded 481.3 million in 1994.

SCHEDULED FLIGHTS

Longest scheduled flight The longest nonstop scheduled flight currently operating is one of 7,969 miles by joint operation between South African Airways and American Airlines for the flight from New York to Johannesburg, South Africa. In terms of time taken the longest is 15 hr. 30 min. for the flight from Los Angeles, CA to Hong Kong with Delta Air Lines.

Shortest scheduled flight Using Britten-Norman Islander twin-engined 10-seat transports, Loganair has been flying between the Orkney Islands of

Westray and Papa Westray, Great Britain since September 1967. Though scheduled for two minutes, in favorable wind conditions the flight was once completed in 58 seconds by Capt. Andrew D. Alsop. The check-in time for the 2-minute flight is 20 minutes.

Fastest circumnavigation The fastest time for a circumnavigation on scheduled flights is 44 hr. 6 min., by David J. Springbett of Taplow, England, January 8–10, 1980. His route took him from Los Angeles, CA eastwards via London, Bahrain, Singapore, Bangkok, Manila, Tokyo and Honolulu, over a 23,069-mile course. A minimum distance of 22,858.8 miles (the length of the Tropic of Cancer or Capricorn) must be flown.

NONSTOP!

The longest nonstop flight by a commercial airliner was one of 11,951 miles from Auckland, New Zealand to Le Bourget, Paris, France in 21 hr. 46 min., June 17–18, 1993 by the Airbus Industrie A340–200. It was the return leg of a flight that had started at Le Bourget the previous day.

Antipodal points Brother Michael Bartlett of London, England traveled around the world on scheduled flights, taking in exact antipodal points, in a time of 66 hr. 38 min. from June 10 to June 13, 1993. Leaving from London, he flew via Tokyo, Japan and Auckland, New Zealand to Palmerston, also in New Zealand, and then traveled by car to Ti Tree Point. He later changed planes at Madrid airport, Spain (the point exactly opposite Ti Tree Point on the other side of the world). His journey took him a distance of 25,861 miles.

He also achieved a record time for flying around the world on scheduled flights, but just taking in the airports closest to antipodal points, when he flew via Shanghai, China and Buenos Aires, Argentina in a time of 58 hr. 44 min. On this trip he started and finished at Zürich, Switzerland and traveled a distance of 25,816 miles, February 13–16, 1995.

Most flights in 24 hours Brother Michael Bartlett made 42 scheduled passenger flights with Heli Transport of Nice, France between Nice, Sophia Antipolis, Monaco and Cannes in 13 hr. 33 min. on June 13, 1990.

SPEED

Official airspeed record Capt. Eldon W. Joersz and Major George T. Morgan, Jr. flew at 2,193.2 MPH in a Lockheed SR-71A "Blackbird" near Beale Air Force Base, CA over a 15½-mile course on July 28, 1976.

Fastest fixed-wing aircraft The U.S. North American Aviation X-15A-2, powered by a liquid oxygen and ammonia rocket-propulsion system, first flew (after modification from the X-15A) on June 25, 1964. The landing speed was momentarily 242 MPH. The fastest speed attained was 4,520 MPH (Mach 6.7) when piloted by Major William J. Knight, U.S.A.F., on October 3, 1967.

The space shuttle *Columbia*, commanded by Capt. John Young (U.S.N.) and piloted by Capt. Robert L. Crippen (U.S.N.), was launched from the Kennedy Space Center, Cape Canaveral, FL on April 12, 1981. *Columbia* broke all records in space by a fixed-wing craft, with 16,600 MPH at main engine cutoff. After reentry from 75.8 miles, experiencing temperatures of 3,920°F, it glided home weighing 107 tons, and with a landing speed of 216 MPH, on Rogers Dry Lake, CA on April 14, 1981.

Fastest jet   The U.S.A.F. Lockheed SR-71, a reconnaissance aircraft, was first flown in its definitive form on December 22, 1964. It was reportedly capable of attaining an altitude ceiling of close to 100,000 feet. The jet has a wingspan of 55.6 feet, is 107.4 feet long, and weighs 85 tons at takeoff. Its reported range at Mach 3 was 2,982 miles at 78,750 feet.

Fastest airliner   The Tupolev Tu-144, first flown on December 31, 1968, reportedly reached Mach 2.4 (1,600 MPH), but normal cruising speed was Mach 2.2. Scheduled services began on December 26, 1975, flying freight and mail.

The supersonic BAC/Aérospatiale Concorde, first flown on March 2, 1969, cruises at up to Mach 2.2 (1,450 MPH) and became the first supersonic airliner used in passenger service on January 21, 1976. The New York–London, England record is 2 hr. 54 min. 30 sec., set on April 14, 1990.

Fastest biplane   The fastest is the Italian Fiat CR42B, with a 1,010-hp Daimler-Benz DB601A engine, which attained 323 MPH in 1941. Only one was built.

Fastest piston-engined aircraft   On August 21, 1989, in Las Vegas, NV, the *Rare Bear*, a modified Grumman Bearcat F8F piloted by Lyle Shelton, set the FAI-approved world record for a 3-km run of 528.3 MPH.

Fastest propeller-driven aircraft   The fastest propeller-driven aircraft in use is the former Soviet Tu-95/142 "Bear" with four 14,795 hp engines driving 8-blade counter-rotating propellers with a maximum level speed of Mach 0.82 (575 MPH).

Fastest coast-to-coast flight   The record aircraft time from coast to coast (Los Angeles to Washington, D.C.) is 68 min. 17 sec. by Lt. Col. Ed Yeilding, pilot, and Lt. Col. J.T. Vida, reconnaissance systems officer, aboard the SR-71 Blackbird spy plane on March 6, 1990. The Blackbird was refueled over the Pacific Ocean at 27,000 feet before starting a climb to above 80,000 feet, heading east from the California coastline and crossing the finish line near Salisbury, MD. This is the first (and only) time that a sonic boom has traveled uninterrupted from coast to coast across the continental United States.

Fastest transatlantic flight   Major James V. Sullivan (U.S.) and Major Noel F. Widdifield (U.S.) flew eastwards across the Atlantic in 1 hr. 54 min. 56.4 sec. in a Lockheed SR-71A "Blackbird" on September 1, 1974. The average speed, slowed by refueling from a KC-135 tanker aircraft, for the New York–London stage of 3,461.53 miles was 1,806.96 MPH.

Solo   On March 12, 1978, Capt. John J.A. Smith flew from Gander, Newfoundland, Canada to Gatwick, London, England in 8 hr. 47 min. 32 sec., in a Rockwell Commander 685 twin-turboprop. He achieved an average speed of 265.1 MPH.

Fastest London–New York flight   The record time from central London, England to downtown New York City by helicopter and Concorde is 3 hr. 59 min. 44 sec., and for the return, 3 hr. 40 min. 40 sec., both by David J. Springbett and David Boyce, February 8–9, 1982.

Fastest circumnavigational flight   The fastest flight under the FAI rules, which permit flights that exceed the length of the Tropic of Cancer or Capricorn (22,858.8 miles), was that of the westbound flight of 32 hr. 49 min. 3 sec. by an Air France Concorde (Capt. Claude Delorme and Capt. Jean Boyé) from Lisbon, Portugal via Santo Domingo, Acapulco, Honolulu, Guam, Bangkok and Bahrain, October 12–13, 1992.

GUESS WHAT?

Q.   WHO IS THE MOST SEASONED SPACE TRAVELER?

A.   LOOK IN "SPACE FLIGHT" (SCIENCE & TECHNOLOGY)

Fastest climb   Heinz Frick of British Aerospace took a Harrier GR5 powered by a Rolls-Royce Pegasus 11-61 engine from a standing start to 39,370 feet in 2 min. 6.63 sec. above the Rolls-Royce test center in Filton, England on August 15, 1989.

Aleksandr Fedotov (USSR) flew a Mikoyan E 266M (MiG-25) aircraft to establish the fastest time-to-height record on May 17, 1975. He reached 114,830 feet in 4 min. 11.7 sec. after takeoff from Podmoscovnoe, Russia.

United States   The fastest time-to-height record for a United States aircraft is to 62,000 feet in 2 min. 2.94 sec., by Major Roger J. Smith (U.S.A.F.), in an F-15 Eagle on January 19, 1975.

DURATION RECORDS

Longest flight The longest flight on record is 64 days 22 hr. 19 min. 5 sec., set by Robert Timm and John Cook in the Cessna 172 *Hacienda*. They took off from McCarran Airfield, Las Vegas, NV just before 3:53 P.M. local time on December 4, 1958 and landed at the same airfield just before 2:12 P.M. on February 7, 1959. They covered a distance equivalent to six times around the world, being refueled without any landings.

PERSONAL AVIATION RECORDS

Oldest and youngest passengers Airborne births are reported every year. The oldest person to fly was Mrs. Jessica S. Swift (b. Anna Stewart, September 17, 1871), age 110 yr. 3 mo. She flew from Vermont to Florida in December 1981.

Oldest pilot Stanley Wood (1896–1994) of Shoreham-by-Sea, England was still taking the controls of aircraft at the age of 96; the last occasion was when he flew a Piper Cherokee Warrior on June 7, 1993. His first solo flight had been an unofficial one during World War I, which means that his flying career spanned more than 80 percent of the history of aviation.

Most flying hours *Pilot* John Edward Long (U.S.) logged 60,269 hours of flight time as a pilot between May 1933 and April, 1995. This adds up to almost seven years.

Evelyn Bryan Johnson holds the women's record, having logged 53,050 hours in flight as a pilot and flight instructor since 1945.

Passenger The record for a supersonic passenger is held by Fred Finn, who has made 707 Atlantic crossings on Concorde. He commutes regularly from New Jersey to London, England, and had flown a total distance of 11,023,000 miles by the end of March 1995.

Most planes flown James B. Taylor, Jr. (1897–1942) flew 461 different types of powered aircraft during his 25 years as an active experimental test and demonstration pilot for the U.S. Navy and a number of American aircraft manufacturers.

Most transatlantic flights Between March 1948 and his retirement on September 1, 1984, Flight Service Manager Charles M. Schimpf logged a total of 2,880 Atlantic crossings—a rate of 6.4 per month.

Most experienced passenger Edwin A. Shackleton of Bristol, England has flown as a passenger in 538 different types of aircraft. His first flight was in March 1943 in D.H. Dominie R9548; other aircraft have included helicopters, gliders, microlights, gas and hot-air balloons.

Longest airplane ticket A ticket 39 ft. 4½ in. long was issued for $4,500 to Bruno Leunen of Brussels, Belgium in December 1984 for a 53,203-mile trip on 80 airlines with 109 layovers.

Plane pulling David Huxley single-handedly pulled a British Airways Concorde weighing 116 tons a distance of 469 ft. 2 in. across the tarmac at Sydney Airport, Australia on October 20, 1994.

Edwin Shackleton of Bristol, England has flown as a passenger in 538 different types of aircraft. This hot-air balloon took him on flight number 459. (*Charles Breton*)

A team of 59 Qantas personnel pulled a Boeing 747 weighing 226 tons a distance of 328 feet in 62.1 seconds at Perth Airport, Australia on October 22, 1988.

Wing walking   Roy Castle flew on the wing of a Boeing Stearman airplane for 3 hr. 23 min. on August 2, 1990, taking off from Gatwick, England and landing at Le Bourget, near Paris, France.

AIRPORTS

Largest airport   The $3.6 billion King Khalid International Airport outside Riyadh, Saudi Arabia covers an area of 87 square miles (55,040 acres). It was opened on November 14, 1983. The Hajj Terminal at the $4.76 billion King Abdul-Aziz Airport near Jeddah, Saudi Arabia is the world's largest roofed structure, covering 370 acres.

PLANES,
PASSENGERS
AND

PIZZA

Working at O'Hare International Airport, the world's busiest airport, does lend itself to horror stories, says Lisa Howard, Director of Public Relations for the Chicago Department of Aviation. In a meeting of almost epic proportions, Howard met with Jenny Bradley of Heathrow Airport, London, England to exchange tales of airport chaos.

Howard told Bradley that O'Hare has 500 cots on standby, in case weather conditions ground flights and the hotels get booked up. Recently, these cots came in handy when flights were canceled due to fog. "We had an all-out slumber party at the airport with hundreds of people," Howard recalled. "We provided everyone with travel kits that included toothbrushes, toothpaste, etc. One mother needed baby formula, so someone from the airport had to run out and find some."

Meanwhile, across the Great Pond, Heathrow Airport faces an even graver concern. "Jenny told me her major worry was the terrorist bombings. I said to her that we didn't know we had it so good over here."

One emergency O'Hare will never have is a food shortage. Each year, 4.2 million cups of soda pop, as it's still called in Chicago, and 500,000 glasses of wine are consumed at the airport's restaurants and cafes. And every day travelers take a bite out of 9,600 slices of Chicago's world-famous thick crust pizza.

As for shipping food, the airport transports 20,000 pounds of seafood each week in the bellies of the jets. "We even transport cows," Ms. Howard reports. "Though I'm not sure where the workers stick the airbill."

"When I first started at O'Hare, there were lots of farms all around the airport. Next to us was the Old Orchard golf course, which I remember because I used to play golf there. Of course it's all been replaced by terminals and runways now."

Joan Winters, a secretary at O'Hare
from 1957 to 1994

(Peter Schulz, Chicago Department of Aviation)

Busiest airport   O'Hare International Airport, Chicago, IL had a total of 66,488,269 passengers and 883,062 aircraft movements in 1994. This represents, on average, a takeoff or landing every 37 seconds.

VISIBILITY!

The control tower at Denver International Airport, Denver, CO is 327 feet tall, giving air traffic controllers an unobstructed 3-mile view.

Terminal Opened on September 21, 1980, the terminal at Hartsfield Atlanta International Airport, GA has floor space covering 5.7 million square feet (approximately 131 acres) and is still expanding. In 1994, the terminal serviced 54,093,051 passengers using 182 gates, although it has a capacity for 70 million.

Busiest airport O'Hare International Airport, Chicago, IL had a total of 66,488,269 passengers and 883,062 aircraft movements in 1994. This represents, on average, a takeoff or landing every 37 seconds.

Heathrow Airport, London, England handles more international traffic than any other airport, with 44,250,000 international passengers in 1994, but it is only the fourth busiest airport overall (see LARGEST AIRPORT).

The busiest landing area ever was Bien Hoa Air Base, South Vietnam, which handled approximately 1,019,437 takeoffs and landings in 1970.

Heliport The heliport at Morgan City, LA, owned and operated by Petroleum Helicopter Inc., is one of a string used by helicopters flying energy-related offshore operations into the Gulf of Mexico. The heliport is spread over 52 acres and has pads for 48 helicopters. The world's largest helipad was at An Khe, South Vietnam, during the Vietnam war. It covered an area of 1¼ by 1¾ miles and could accommodate 434 helicopters.

Highest landing field The highest is La Sa (Lhasa) Airport, Tibet, People's Republic of China, at 14,315 feet.

Lowest landing field The lowest landing field is El Lisan on the east shore of the Dead Sea, 1,180 feet below sea level, but during World War II BOAC Short C-class flying boats operated from the surface of the Dead Sea at 1,292 feet below sea level.

The world's lowest international airport is Schiphol, Amsterdam, Netherlands, at 15 feet below sea level.

Longest runway The runway at Edwards Air Force Base on the west side of Rogers dry lakebed at Muroc, CA measures 39,104 feet, or 7.4 miles, long. The *Voyager* aircraft, taking off on its around-the-world unrefueled flight, used 14,200 feet of the 15,000-foot-long main base concrete runway.

Civil The runway at Pierre van Ryneveld Airport, Upington, South Africa is 3.04 miles long. It was constructed in five months from August 1975 to January 1976.

Largest hangar Hangar 375 ("Big Texas") at Kelly Air Force Base, San Antonio, TX, completed on February 15, 1956, has four doors each 250 feet wide, 60 feet high, and weighing 681 tons. The high bay is 2,000 by 300 by 90 feet in area and is surrounded by a 44-acre concrete apron. It is the largest freestanding hangar in the world.

GUESS WHAT?

Q. WHICH COUNTRY HAS THE LARGEST AIR FORCE?

A. LOOK IN "ARMED FORCES" (HUMAN WORLD)

HELICOPTERS

Fastest helicopter Under FAI rules, the world's speed record for helicopters was set by John Trevor Eggington with co-pilot Derek J. Clews, who averaged 249.09 MPH over Somerset, England on August 11, 1986 in a Westland Lynx company demonstrator helicopter.

Largest helicopter The former Soviet Mil Mi-12 was powered by four 6,500-hp turboshaft engines and had a span of 219 ft. 10 in. over its rotor tips, with a length of 121 ft. 4½ in. It weighed 114 tons. The aircraft was demonstrated in prototype form at the Paris Air Show but never entered formal service.

The largest rotorcraft was the Piasecki Heli-Stat, which used four Sikorsky S-58 airframes attached to a Goodyear ZPG-2 airship. Powered by four 1,525-hp piston engines, it was 343 feet long, 111 feet high and 149 feet wide. It first flew in October 1985 in Lakehurst, NJ, but was destroyed in a crash on July 1, 1986.

Smallest helicopter The single-seat Seremet WS-8 ultralight helicopter was built in Denmark in 1976. It had a 35-hp engine, a rotor diameter of 14 ft. 9 in. and an empty weight of 117 pounds.

Highest helicopter altitude Jean Boulet flew an Aérospatiale SA315B Lama at 40,820 feet over Istres, France on June 21, 1972.

The highest recorded landing was at 24,600 feet, during SA315B demonstrations in the Himalayas in 1969.

Longest hover Doug Daigle, Brian Watts and Dave Meyer of Tridair Helicopters, together with Rod Anderson of Helistream, Inc. of California, maintained a continuous hovering flight in a 1947 Bell 47B model for 50 hr. 50 sec. from December 13 to December 15, 1989.

Greatest load lifted On February 3, 1982 at Podmoscovnoe in the USSR, a Mil Mi-26 heavy-lift helicopter crewed by G.V. Alfeurov and L.A. Indeyev lifted a total mass of 6,560 feet.

Longest helicopter flight Under FAI rules, the record for the longest unrefueled nonstop flight was set by Robert Ferry, flying a Hughes YOH-6A, over a distance of 2,213.1 miles from Culver City, CA to Ormond Beach, FL in April 1966.

First helicopter circumnavigation   H. Ross Perot, Jr. and Jay Coburn made the first helicopter circumnavigation in *Spirit of Texas* in 29 days 3 hr. 8 min. 13 sec., September 1–30, 1982 from Dallas, TX.

The first solo around-the-world flight in a helicopter was completed by Dick Smith (Australia) on July 22, 1983. Taking off from and returning to the Bell Helicopter Facility at Fort Worth, TX, in a Bell Model 206L, LongRanger III, Smith began his flight on August 5, 1982 and covered 35,258 miles.

GYROCOPTERS

Speed, altitude and distance records   Wing-Cdr. Kenneth H. Wallis (Great Britain) holds the straight-line distance record of 543.27 miles, set in his WA-116/F gyrocopter on September 28, 1975 with a nonstop flight from Lydd, England to Wick, Scotland. On July 20, 1982, flying from Boscombe Down, England, he established a new altitude record of 18,516 feet in his WA-121/Mc gyrocopter.

Wing-Cdr. Wallis also flew his WA-116/F/S gyrocopter, with a 60-hp Franklin aero-engine, to a record speed of 120.3 MPH over a 1.86-mile straight course at Norfolk, England on September 18, 1986.

AIRSHIPS

Largest airship   The 235-ton German *Hindenburg* (LZ 129) and its sister ship *Graf Zeppelin II* (LZ 130) each had a length of 803 ft. 10 in. and a capacity of 7,062,100 cubic feet. The *Hindenburg* first flew in 1936 and the *Graf Zeppelin II* in 1938.

Nonrigid   The largest nonrigid airship ever constructed was the U.S. Navy ZPG 3-W, which had a capacity of 1.5 million cubic feet, a length of 403 feet, a diameter of 85.1 feet and a crew of 21. It first flew on July 21, 1958 but crashed into the sea in June 1960.

Longest flight   The longest recorded flight by an airship (without refueling) is 264 hr. 12 min. by a U.S. Navy Goodyear-built ZPG-2 class ship (Cdr. J.R. Hunt, U.S.N.) that flew 9,448 miles, leaving from South Weymouth Naval Air Station, MA on March 4, 1957 and landing in Key West, FL, on March 15.

The FAI-accredited straight-line distance record for airships is 3,967.1 miles, set by the German *Graf Zeppelin* LZ 127, captained by Dr. Hugo Eckener, October 29–November 1, 1928.

From November 21 to November 25, 1917, the German *Zeppelin* (L 59) flew from Yambol, Bulgaria to a point south of Khartoum, Sudan and returned, covering a minimum of 4,500 miles.

Greatest passenger load   The most people ever carried in an airship was 207, in the U.S. Navy *Akron* in 1931. The transatlantic record is 117, carried by the German *Hindenburg* in 1937. This airship exploded into a fireball at Lakehurst, NJ on May 6, 1937.

The largest airship currently certified for the public transport of passengers is the 221-ft.-5-in.-long Sentinel 1000 of 353,100-cubic-foot capacity, built by Westinghouse Airships, Inc. Its maiden flight was on June 26, 1991.

HELIUM BALLOONING

First transatlantic crossing Col. Joe Kittinger (U.S.A.F.) became the first person to complete a solo transatlantic crossing by balloon. On September 14, 1984, Kittinger lifted off from Caribou, ME in the 101,000-cubic-foot helium-filled balloon *Rosie O'Grady* and completed a distance of 3,543 miles before landing at Montenotte, near Savóna, Italy 86 hours later on September 18, 1984.

Longest balloon flight The record distance traveled by a balloon is 5,208.68 miles, by the Raven experimental helium-filled balloon *Double Eagle V* (capacity 399,053 cubic feet) from November 9 to November 12, 1981. The journey started at Nagashima, Japan and ended at Covello, CA. The crew for this first manned balloon crossing of the Pacific Ocean was Ben L. Abruzzo, Rocky Aoki (Japan), Ron Clark and Larry M. Newman.

Richard Abruzzo and Troy Bradley set the FAI endurance and distance records for a gas and hot-air balloon in *Team USA*. They crossed the Atlantic Ocean from Bangor, ME to Ben Slimane, Morocco, a distance of 3,318.2 miles, in 144 hr. 16 min., September 16–22, 1992.

Highest balloon altitude *Unmanned* The highest altitude attained by an unmanned balloon was 170,000 feet, by a Winzen balloon with a 47.8 million-cubic-foot capacity, launched at Chico, CA in October 27, 1972.

Manned The highest altitude reached in a manned balloon is an unofficial 123,800 feet by Nicholas Piantanida (1933–66) of Bricktown, NJ, from Sioux Falls, SD on February 1, 1966. He landed in a cornfield in Iowa but did not survive.

The official record (closed gondola) is 113,740 feet by Cdr. Malcolm D. Ross (U.S.N.R.) and the late Lt. Cdr. Victor A. Prother (U.S.N.), in an ascent from the deck of the U.S.S. *Antietam* over the Gulf of Mexico on May 4, 1961 in a balloon of 12 million-cubic-foot capacity.

Scientists Harold Froelich and Keith Lang of Minneapolis, MN made an unplanned ascent in an open gondola, without pressure suits or goggles, to an altitude of 42,126 feet on September 26, 1956. During the 6½-hour flight they measured a temperature of –72°F.

Largest balloon The largest balloon ever built had an inflatable volume of 70 million cubic feet and stood 1,000 feet tall. It was unmanned, and was manufactured by Winzen Research Inc. (now Winzen Engineering Inc.) of South St. Paul, Minnesota. The balloon did not get off the ground and was destroyed at launch on July 8, 1975.

HOT-AIR BALLOONING

Largest mass ascent On August 15, 1987, 128 participants at the Ninth Bristol International Balloon Festival in Bristol, England made the greatest mass ascent of hot-air balloons from a single site within one hour.

First Atlantic crossing   Richard Branson (Great Britain) and his pilot, Per Lindstrand (Great Britain), were the first to cross the Atlantic in a hot-air balloon, July 2–3, 1987. They ascended from Sugarloaf, ME and covered the distance of 3,075 miles to Limavady, Northern Ireland in 31 hr. 41 min.

First Pacific crossing   Richard Branson and Per Lindstrand crossed the Pacific in the *Virgin Otsuka Pacific Flyer* from the southern tip of Japan to Lac la Matre, Yukon, northwestern Canada, January 15–17, 1991 in a 2.6 million-cubic-foot capacity hot-air balloon (the largest ever flown) to set FAI records for duration (46 hr. 15 min.) and distance (great circle 4,768 miles).

Highest hot-air balloon ascent   Per Lindstrand (Great Britain) achieved the altitude record of 64,997 feet in a Colt 600 hot-air balloon over Laredo, TX on June 6, 1988.

Most passengers in a balloon   The balloon *Super Maine*, with a capacity of 2.6 million cubic feet, was built by Tom Handcock of Portland, ME. Tethered, it rose to a height of 50 feet with 61 passengers on board on February 19, 1988.

The Dutch balloonist Henk Brink made an untethered flight of 656 feet in the 850,000-cubic-foot capacity Nashua Number One, carrying a total of 50 passengers and crew. The flight, on August 17, 1988, began from Lelystad Airport, Netherlands, lasted 25 minutes, and reached an altitude of 228 feet.

Most to jump from a balloon   On September 12, 1992, a record 15 people all parachuted from a hot-air balloon over the Somerset/Devon county line, England. The same group made a similar ascent on October 1, 1992, when a record 10 people jumped simultaneously from a height of 6,000 feet.

First flight over Mount Everest   Two balloons—*Star Flyer 1*, piloted by Chris Dewhirst and with cameraman Leo Dickinson, and *Star Flyer 2*, piloted by Andy Elson with cameraman Eric Jones (all British)—achieved the first overflight of the summit of Mt. Everest on October 21, 1991. The two 240,000-cubic-foot balloons had the highest recorded launch of a hot-air balloon at 15,536 feet and the highest recorded touch-down of a hot-air balloon at 16,200 feet.

MODEL AIRCRAFT

Highest model aircraft flight   Maynard L. Hill (U.S.), flying a radio-controlled model, established the world record for altitude of 26,919 feet on September 6, 1970.

Fastest model aircraft   The overall speed record is 245.84 MPH by a model flown on control lines by Leonid Lipinski (USSR) on December 6, 1971. The record for a radio-controlled model is 242.91 MPH, set by Walter Sitar (Austria) on June 10, 1977.

Longest model aircraft flight   Gianmaria Aghem (Italy) holds the closed-circuit distance record, with 769.9 miles, achieved on July 26, 1986.

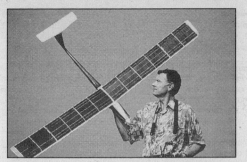

Jean-Pierre Schiltknecht with his record-breaking solar-driven model aircraft.

The longest flight in a straight line to a nominated landing point was 306.44 miles, by Peter Garoni (Australia), from Balladonia to Border Village, Western Australia in 6 hr. 30 min. on May 18, 1994.

The record duration flight is one of 33 hr. 39 min. 15 sec. by Maynard Hill, with a powered model, October 1–2, 1992.

An indoor model with a wound rubber motor, designed by Robert Randolph (U.S.), set a duration record of 55 min. 6 sec. on December 5, 1993.

Jean-Pierre Schiltknecht flew a solar-driven model aircraft for a duration of 10 hr. 43 min. 51 sec. at Wetzlar, Germany on July 10, 1991.

Largest model glider   In January 1990, *Eagle III*, a radio-controlled glider weighing 14 lb. 8 oz. with a wingspan of 32 ft. 6 in., was designed and constructed by Carlos René Tschen and Carlos René Tschen Jr. of Colonia San Lázaro, Guatemala.

Smallest model aircraft   The smallest to fly is one weighing 0.004 ounces, powered by an attached horsefly and designed by insectonaut Don Emmick of Seattle, WA. On July 24, 1979 an Emmick flew for five minutes at Kirkland, WA.

Largest paper aircraft   The largest flying paper airplane, with a wingspan of 40 ft. 6 in., was constructed by a team of engineers from BP Chemicals Ltd. and flown in Filton, England on June 24, 1994. It was launched indoors and flew 77 ft. 4 in.

Longest paper aircraft flight   The level flight duration record for a hand-launched paper aircraft is 18.80 seconds, by Ken Blackburn in a hangar at John F. Kennedy International Airport, New York City on February 17, 1994.

A paper plane was reported by "Chick" C.O. Reinhart to have flown 1¼ miles from a tenth-story office window at 60 Beaver Street, New York City across the East River to Brooklyn in August 1933, helped by a thermal from a coffee-roasting plant.

An indoor distance of 193 feet was recorded by Tony Felch at the La Crosse Center, La Crosse, WI on May 21, 1985.

ARTS &
ENTERTAINMENT

ART

PAINTINGS

Largest painting   The largest-ever painting measures 72,437 square feet after allowing for shrinkage of the canvas. It is made up of brightly colored squares with a "Smiley" face superimposed, and was painted by students of Robb College in Armidale, Australia, aided by local schoolchildren and students from neighboring colleges. The canvas was completed by its designer, Australian artist Ken Done, and unveiled at the University of New England at Armidale on May 10, 1990.

Most valuable painting   The "Mona Lisa" (*La Gioconda*) by Leonardo da Vinci (1452–1519) in the Louvre, Paris, France, was assessed for insurance purposes at $100 million for its move to Washington, D.C. and New York City for exhibition from December 14, 1962 to March 12, 1963. However, insurance was not purchased because the cost of the closest security precautions was less than that of the premiums. It was painted *c.* 1503–07 and measures 30.5 by 20.9 inches.

Most prolific painter   Pablo Picasso (1881–1973) was the most prolific of all painters in a career that lasted 78 years. It has been estimated that Picasso produced about 13,500 paintings or designs, 100,000 prints or engravings, 34,000 book illustrations and 300 sculptures or ceramics. The complete body of his work has been valued at over $800 million.

La Gioconda or the "Mona Lisa" is so valuable that insuring it is impractical; it is also arguably the most expensive object ever stolen. (*AKG London*)

Finest standard paintbrush The finest standard brush sold is the 000 in Series 7 by Winsor and Newton, known as a "triple goose." It is made of 150–200 Kolinsky sable hairs weighing 0.000529 ounces.

GALLERIES

Largest art gallery Visitors would have to walk 15 miles to cover all of the 322 galleries of the Winter Palace and the neighboring Hermitage in St. Petersburg, Russia. The galleries house nearly 3 million works of art and objects of archaeological interest.

The Hermitage in St. Petersburg, Russia, along with the neighboring Winter Palace, houses nearly 3 million works of art and archaeological finds. (*Gamma/Shone*)

The J. Paul Getty Museum has the largest budget for acquisitions of any museum. (*Gamma/J. C. Francolon*)

Most heavily endowed gallery The J. Paul Getty Museum in Malibu, CA was established with an initial $1.4 billion budget in January 1974 and now has an annual budget of $180 million for acquisitions to stock its 38 galleries.

MOSAICS

Largest mosaic The mosaic on the walls of the central library of the Universidad Nacional Autónoma de México in Mexico City is the largest in the world. The two largest of the four walls measure 12,949 square feet, and the scenes on each represent the pre-Hispanic past.

MURALS

Oldest mural In 1961, clay relief leopards were discovered by James Malaart on manmade walls at level VII at Catal Hüyük in southern Anatolia, Turkey. They date from *c.* 6200 B.C.

Largest mural *Planet Ocean*, by the artist Wyland, measures 105 feet high and 1,220 feet long (128,000 square feet). It is painted on the Long Beach Arena, CA and was completed on May 4, 1992.

POSTERS

Largest poster A poster measuring 236,119 square feet was made by the Community Youth Club of Hong Kong on October 26, 1993. The poster followed the theme of the International Year of the Family, and was displayed at Victoria Park, Hong Kong.

SCULPTURE

Oldest sculpture An animal head carved on a woolly rhinoceros vertebra from Tolbaga, Siberia is thought to be 34,860 years old. The oldest stone figurine is a 31,790-year-old serpentine female statuette from Galgenberg, Austria. About 32,000 years ago, several ivory figurines of humans and animals were deposited in Hohler Stein, Geissenklösterle and Vogelherd caves in southern Germany. Remarkably, these are generally more sophisticated and more animated than the sculpture of subsequent periods.

Largest sculpture The mounted figures of Jefferson Davis (1808–89), Gen. Robert E. Lee (1807–70) and Gen. Thomas "Stonewall" Jackson (1824–63) cover 1.33 acres on the face of Stone Mountain, near Atlanta, GA. They are 90 feet high. Roy Faulkner was on the mountain face for 8 yr. 174 days with a thermo-jet torch, working with sculptor Walker Kirtland Hancock and other helpers, from September 12, 1963 through March 3, 1972.

Sand sculptures The longest sand sculpture ever made was the 86,535-ft.-6-in.-long sculpture named "The GTE Directories Ultimate Sand Castle" built by more than 10,000 volunteers at Myrtle Beach, SC on May 31, 1991.
  The tallest was the "Invitation to Fairyland," which was 56 ft. 2 in. high, and was built by 2,000 local volunteers in Kaseda, Japan on July 26, 1989 under the supervision of Gerry Kirk (U.S.) and Shogo Tashiro (Japan).

HERD OF BUFFALO?

NOW HEAR THIS . . .

"Buffalo were as big as mastodons when they came over the Bering Strait," explains sculptor Robert Berks. His buffalo is much, much larger.

For five days, Berks stood on a 400-foot overlook at Wyoming's Wind River Basin, using a walkie-talkie to direct a tractor as it dropped straw and spread red dye over a $1/2$-mile by $1/3$-mile area—all to create one giant picture of a buffalo. But the record doesn't end there.

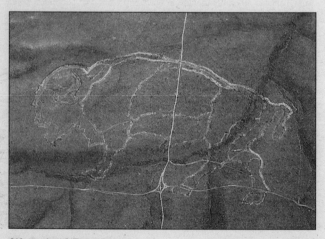

Berks plans to make the drawing permanent by laying down stone over the straw lines, each 50 feet wide. Then the drawing will be filled in with weather vanes the size and shape of buffalo. How many buffalo will that be? "One thousand," says Berks. "The size of a herd in the old days. They say you could hear them coming for three days in advance." You'll be able to hear Berks's buffalo, too. Special tubing in the construction of the weather vanes allows them to make a sound like real buffalo.

No project is too ambitious for Robert Berks, who has been an artist and sculptor since he was a child. He sold his first portrait at age nine (he bought a pair of racing skates with the money) and went on to become the sculptor of many of the 20th century's most notable monuments, including the giant head of John F. Kennedy in the Kennedy Center in Washington, D.C., the statue of Albert Einstein outside the National Academy of Sciences, Washington D.C. and the original sculpture of Abraham Lincoln that President Bill Clinton keeps in the Oval Office. "I'm 73," he says, "but I feel like 45. My best work is yet to come."

Largest ground figures   *Modern*   The painted straw representation of Will the Great Buffalo in northeast Wyoming, completed by Robert Berks in September 1993, is half a mile long.

Largest ground figures   In the Nazca Desert, 185 miles south of Lima, Peru, there are straight lines (one more than seven miles long), geometric shapes, and outlines of plants and animals that were drawn on the ground some time between 100 B.C. and A.D. 600. They were first detected from the air *c.* 1928 and have been described as the world's longest works of art.

Modern   The painted straw representation of Will the Great Buffalo in northeast Wyoming, completed by Robert Berks in September 1993, is half a mile long.

Largest hill figures   A 330-foot-tall figure was found on a hill above Tarapacá, Chile in August 1968.

Largest hillside caricature   A temporary 492-foot-tall caricature of British Prime Minister John Major was created on a hillside near Ditchling Beacon, England in July 1994. Dubbed the Grey Man of Ditchling, the figure was made with 11 tons of chalk.

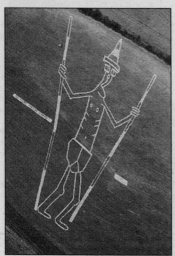

A caricature of British Prime Minister John Major sprawls across a hillside near Ditchling Beacon, England. (*Spectrum Colour Library*)

HIGHEST PRICES

Most expensive painting   On May 15, 1990, *Portrait of Dr. Gachet* by Vincent Van Gogh was sold for $82.5 million at Christie's, New York City. The painting depicts Van Gogh's physician and was completed only weeks before the artist's suicide in 1890. The buyer was later identified as Ryoei Saito, Japan's second-largest paper manufacturer.

20th-century   The record bid at auction for a 20th-century painting is $47.8 million for a self-portrait by Pablo Picasso, *Yo Picasso* (1901), at Sotheby's, New York City on May 9, 1989.

Living artist   The highest price paid at auction for a work by a living artist is $20.68 million for *Interchange*, an abstract by the American painter Willem de Kooning, at Sotheby's, New York City on November 8, 1989. Painted in 1955, it was bought by Japanese dealer-collector "Mountain Tortoise."

Most expensive miniature   The record price is £352,000 ($621,632), paid by the Alexander Gallery of New York at Christie's, London, England on November 7, 1988 for a 2¹/₈-inch-high miniature of George Washington. It was painted by the Irish-American miniaturist John Ramage in 1789.

Most expensive print   The record price for a print at auction was £561,600 ($786,000) for a 1655 etching of *Christ Presented to the People* by Rembrandt (1606–69) at Christie's, London on December 5, 1985.

Most expensive drawing   On November 14, 1990, at Christie's, New York City, an anonymous buyer paid $8.36 million for the pen-and-ink scene *Jardin de Fleurs*, drawn by Vincent Van Gogh in Arles, France in 1888.

Most expensive poster   The record price for a poster is £68,200 (*c.* $93,000) for an advertisement for the 1895 Glasgow exhibition by Charles Rennie Macintosh, sold at Christie's, London on February 4, 1993.

Most expensive sculpture   The record price for a sculpture at auction is £6.82 million ($12 million) at Sotheby's, London on December 7, 1989 for a bronze garden ornament, *The Dancing Faun*, made by the Dutch-born sculptor Adrien de Vries (1545/6–1626). London dealer Cyril Humpris bought the figure from a couple who had paid £100 ($240) for it in the 1950s and in whose garden it had stood undiscovered for 40 years.

The highest price paid for the work of a sculptor during his lifetime is $1,265,000 at Sotheby's, New York City on May 21, 1982 for the 75-inch-long elmwood *Reclining Figure* by Henry Moore (Great Britain; 1898–1986).

United States   The highest price paid at auction for a sculpture by an American sculptor is $4.4 million for *Coming Through the Rye*, by Frederic Remington (1861–1909), at Christie's, New York City on May 25, 1989.

ANTIQUES

HIGHEST PRICES

All prices quoted are inclusive of the buyer's premium, and all records were set at public auction unless otherwise stated.

Art nouveau   The highest auction price for any piece of art nouveau is $1.78 million for a standard lamp in the form of three lotus blossoms by the Daum Brothers and Louis Majorelle of France, sold at Sotheby's, New York City on December 2, 1989.

Armor   The highest auction price paid for a suit of armor was £1,925,000 ($3,657,000), by B.H. Trupin (U.S.) on May 5, 1983 at Sotheby's, London, England, for a suit made in Milan by Giovanni Negroli in 1545 for Henri II of France. It came from the Hever Castle Collection in Kent, England.

Blanket   A Navajo Churro hand-spun serape dated *c.* 1852 sold for $115,500 at Sotheby's, New York City on October 22, 1983.

Bottle   A rare Korean Punch'ong bottle was sold at Christie's, New York City on November 17, 1993 for $376,500.

Box   A Cartier jeweled vanity case, set with a fragment of an ancient Egyptian stela, was sold at Christie's, New York City for $189,500 on November 17, 1993.

Carpet   On June 9, 1994, a Louis XV Savonnerie carpet was sold at Christie's, London to Djanhanguir Riahi for £1,321,000 ($2,113,600).
   The Spring carpet of Khusraw, made for the audience hall of the Sassanian palace at Ctesiphon, Iraq, was the most expensive carpet ever made. It comprised about 7,000 square feet of silk and gold thread, and was encrusted with emeralds. The carpet was cut up as booty by looters in A.D. 635, and from the known realization value of the pieces, must have had an original value of *c.* $170 million.

Ceramics   The highest auction price for any ceramic is £3.74 million ($6.4 million) for a Chinese Tang dynasty (A.D. 618–906) horse sold by the British Rail Pension Fund and bought by a Japanese dealer at Sotheby's, London, on December 12, 1989.

Furniture   The highest price ever paid for a single piece of furniture is £8.58 million ($15 million) at Christie's, London, on July 5, 1990 for the 18th-century Italian "Badminton Cabinet" owned by the Duke of Beaufort. It was bought by Barbara Piasecka Johnson of Princeton, NJ.

United States   The highest price ever paid for a single piece of American furniture is $12.1 million by dealer Israel Sack at Christie's, New York City on June 3, 1989 for a mahogany desk-cum-bookcase, made in the 1760s.

Glass   The auction record is £520,000 ($1,175,200) for a Roman glass cage-cup of *c.* A.D. 300, measuring seven inches in diameter and four inches in height, sold at Sotheby's, London, on June 4, 1979 to Robin Symes.

Gun   An 1873 .45 caliber Colt single-action army revolver, Serial No. 1, was sold for $242,000 at Christie's New York City on May 14, 1987.

Helmet   The highest price ever paid for an item of headwear is $66,000 by the Alaska State Museum at an auction in New York City in November 1981 for a native North American Tlingit Kiksadi ceremonial frog helmet dating from *c.* 1600.

Jewelry   The world's largest jewelry auction, which included a Van Cleef and Arpels 1939 ruby and diamond necklace, realized over $50 million when the collection belonging to the Duchess of Windsor (1896–1986) was sold at Sotheby's, Geneva, Switzerland on April 3, 1987.

A Harry Winston diamond necklace was bought for $4.40 million at Sotheby's, New York City on April 14, 1994 by Saudi Arabian businessman Ahmed Fitahi.

Music box The highest price paid for a music box is £20,900 ($22,990) for a Swiss example made for a Persian prince in 1901 and sold at Sotheby's, London, on January 23, 1985.

Playing cards The highest price for a deck of playing cards is $143,352, paid by the Metropolitan Museum of Art, New York City at Sotheby's, London, on December 6, 1983. The cards, dating from around 1470–85, constituted the oldest known *complete* hand-painted set.

The highest price paid for a single card was $7,450 for a card dated 1717, which was used as currency in Canada. It was sold by the dealer Yasha Beresiner to Lars Karlson (Sweden) in October 1990.

Silver The record for silver is $3,386,440 for a Hanover chandelier from the collection of M. Hubert de Givenchy, sold at Christie's, Monaco on December 4, 1993.

Surgical instrument The record price paid for a surgical instrument was $34,848 for a mid-19th-century German mechanical chain saw sold at Christie's, London, on August 19, 1993.

Tapestry The highest auction price for a tapestry is £638,000 ($1,124,794), paid by Swiss dealer Peter Kleiner at Christie's, London, on July 3, 1990 for a fragment of a rare Swiss example woven near Basle in the 1430s.

Teddy Girl (left), the most expensive teddy bear. Right, Bob Henderson, the bear's original owner, with his brother Charles and Teddy Girl in 1910.

Teddy bear A Steiff bear named Teddy Girl was sold for £110,000 ($171,578), more than 18 times the estimate, by Christie's, London on December 5, 1994 to Japanese businessman Yoshihiro Sekiguchi. The bear was made in 1904, only a year after Steiff made the first jointed plush teddy bear, and had a particularly well documented history.

Toy   An antique toy was sold for $231,000 to an anonymous telephone bidder at Christie's, New York City on December 14, 1991. The work is a hand-painted tinplate replica of the "Charles" hose reel, a piece of firefighting equipment pulled by two firemen, measuring 15 by 23 inches and built around 1870 by George Brown & Co. of Forestville, CT.

LANGUAGE

Commonest language   Chinese is spoken by an estimated 1 billion people. The so-called "common language" (*putonghua*) is the standard form of Chinese, with a pronunciation based on that of Beijing.

Most widespread language   English is spoken by an estimated 800 million people; more generous estimates put the figure at 1.5 billion. Of these, some 350 million are native speakers, 220 million of whom are in the United States.

Greatest concentration of languages   About 845 of the world's 3,950 languages and dialects are spoken in India. Papua New Guinea has many isolated valleys, resulting in the greatest concentration of separate languages in the world. Each of the estimated 869 languages has about 4,000 speakers.

Most complex language   The following extremes of complexity have been noted: the Ample language of Papua New Guinea has the most verb forms, with over 69,000 finite forms and 860 infinitive forms of the verb; Haida, a North American Indian language, has the most prefixes, with 70; Tabassaran, a language of Daghestan, Azerbaijan, uses the most noun cases, 48;

Jubilee Day in Papua New Guinea, the territory with the greatest concentration of separate languages in the world. (*Spectrum Colour Library*)

and Inuit uses 63 forms of the present tense, with simple nouns having as many as 252 inflections.

Fewest irregular verbs The artificial language Esperanto, with no irregular verbs, was first published by its inventor, Dr. Ludwig Zamenhof of Warsaw, Poland, in 1887. It is now estimated (by textbook sales) to have a million speakers worldwide. The even earlier interlanguage Volapük, invented by Johann Martin Schleyer (1831–1912), also has absolutely regular configuration.

Most irregular verbs According to *The Morphology and Syntax of Present-day English* by Prof. Olu Tomori, English has 283 irregular verbs, 30 of which are formed merely by adding prefixes.

Rarest sounds The rarest speech sound is probably that written "ř" in Czech and termed a "rolled post-alveolar fricative." In the southern Bushman language !xo, there is a click articulated with both lips, which is written θ. This sound, essentially a kiss, is termed a "velaric ingressive bilabial stop." In some contexts the "l" sound in the Arabic word *Allah* is pronounced uniquely in that language.

Commonest sound No language is known to be without the vowel "a" (as in the English word "father").

Largest vocabulary The English language contains about 616,500 words plus another 400,000 technical terms, the most in any language, but it is doubtful if any individual speaker uses more than 60,000. William Shakespeare, for instance, employed a vocabulary of only *c.* 33,000 words.

Greatest linguist Dr. Harold Williams (1876–1928), a journalist of New Zealand, was reputed to speak 58 languages and many dialects fluently.

Living The greatest living linguist is Ziad Fazah (Brazil; b. July 10, 1954), who speaks and writes 58 languages. He was tested in a live interview in

Athens, Greece on July 30, 1991, when he surprised members of the audience by talking to them in their various native tongues.

Alexander Schwartz of New York City *worked* with 31 languages as a translator for the United Nations between 1962 and 1986.

Longest debate Together with staff and friends, students at St. Andrews Presbyterian College in Laurinburg, NC debated the motion "There's no place like home" for 517 hr. 45 min., April 4–26, 1992. The aim of the debate was to increase awareness of the problems of being homeless.

ALPHABET

Earliest alphabetic writing A clay tablet of 32 cuneiform letters was found at Ugarit (now Ras Sharma), Syria, and dated to *c*. 1450 B.C.

Oldest letter The letter "O" has not changed in shape since its adoption in the Phoenician alphabet *c*. 1300 B.C.

Newest letters The newest letters to be added to the English alphabet are "j" and "v," which are of post-Shakespearean use (*c*. 1630). Formerly they were used only as variants of "i" and "u."

Longest alphabet The language with the most letters in its alphabet is Cambodian, with 74.

Shortest alphabet Rotokas of central Bougainville Island, Papua New Guinea, has the fewest letters, with 11 (a, b, e, g, i, k, o, p, ř, t and u).

Most and fewest consonants The language with the greatest number of distinct consonantal sounds was Ubykh, with 80–85. Ubykh speakers migrated from the Caucasus to Turkey in the 19th century and the language is now obsolete. The language with the fewest consonants is Rotokas, which has only six.

Most and fewest vowels The language with the most vowels is Sedang, a central Vietnamese language with 55 distinguishable vowel sounds. The Caucasian language Abkhazian has the fewest, with two.

Smallest letters Scanning tunneling microscope (STM) techniques pioneered in April 1990 by physicists Donald Eigler and Erhard Schweizer at IBM's Almaden Research Center in San Jose, CA have allowed single atoms of various elements to be manipulated to form characters and pictures.

WORDS

Longest word A compound "word" of 195 Sanskrit characters (which transliterates into 428 letters in the Roman alphabet) describes the region near Kanci, Tamil Nadu, India. The word appears in a 16th-century work by Tirumalāmbā, Queen of Vijayanagara.

English The longest word in the *Oxford English Dictionary* is *pneumonoultramicroscopicsilicovolcanoconiosis*, which has 45 letters and allegedly means "a lung disease caused by the inhalation of very fine silica dust." It is, however, described as "factitious" by the editors of the dictionary.

Longest scientific name   The systematic name for *deoxyribonucleic acid* (DNA) of the human mitochondria contains 16,569 nucleotide residues and is thus *c.* 207,000 letters long. It was published in key form in *Nature* on April 9, 1981.

Longest palindromes   The longest palindromic word (a word that reads the same backward or forward) is *saippuakivikauppias* (19 letters), which is Finnish for "a dealer in lye." The longest in English is *tattarrattat*, with 12 letters, which appears in the *Oxford English Dictionary*.

Some baptismal fonts in Greece and Turkey bear the circular 25-letter inscription NIψON ANOMHMATA MH.M.ONAN OψIN, meaning "wash (my) sins not only (my) face."

GUESS WHAT?

Q.   WHAT IS THE LONGEST COMPANY NAME?

A.   LOOK IN "COMMERCE" (BUSINESS & LAW)

Longest anagrams   The longest nonscientific English words that can form anagrams are the 17-letter transpositions *representationism* and *misrepresentation*. The longest scientific transposals are *hydroxydesoxycorticosterone* and *hydroxydeoxycorticosterones*, with 27 letters.

Longest abbreviation   The initials S.K.O.M.K.H.P.K.J.C.D.P.W.B. stand for the Syarikat Kerjasama Orang-orang Melayu Kerajaan Hilir Perak Kerana Jimat Cermat Dan Pinjam-meminjam Wang Berhad. This is the Malay name for The Cooperative Company of the Lower State of Perak Government's Malay People for Money Savings and Loans Ltd., in Teluk Anson, Perak, West Malaysia (formerly Malaya). The abbreviation for the abbreviation is Skomk.

Shortest abbreviation   The 55-letter full name of Los Angeles (El Pueblo de Nuestra Señora la Reina de los Angeles de Porciuncula) is abbreviated to L.A., or 3.63 percent of its length.

Longest acronym   The longest acronym is NIIOMTPLABOPARMBET-ZHELBETRABSBOMONIMONKONOTDTEKHSTROMONT with 56 letters (54 in Cyrillic) in the *Concise Dictionary of Soviet Terminology, Institutions and Abbreviations (1969)*, meaning: the Laboratory for Shuttering, Reinforcement, Concrete and Ferroconcrete Operations for Composite-monolithic and Monolithic Constructions of the Department of the Technology of Building-Assembly Operations of the Scientific Research

LONGEST WORDS

Japanese[1]	Chi-n-chi-ku-ri-n (12 letters) *a very short person (slang)*
Spanish	Superextraordinarisimo (22) *extraordinary*
French	Anticonstitutionnellement (25) *anticonstitutionally*
Italian	Precipitevolissimevolmente (26) *as fast as possible*
Portuguese	Inconstitucionalissimamente (27) *with the highest degree of unconstitutionality*
Icelandic	Haecstaréttarmálaflutningsmaður (29 Icelandic letters, transliterating as 31) *supreme court barrister*
Russian	Ryentgyenoelyektrokardiografichyeskogo (33 Cyrillic letters, transliterating as 38) *of the X-ray electrocardiographic*
Hungarian	Megszentségtelenithetetlenségeskedéseitekért (44) *for your unprofanable actions*
Dutch[2]	Kindercarnavalsoptochtvoorbereidingswerkzaamheden (49) *preparation activities for a children's carnival procession*
Mohawk[3]	Tkanuhstasrihsranuhwe'tsraaksahsrakaratattsrayeri' (50) *the praising of the evil of the liking of the finding of the house is right*
Turkish[2]	Cekoslovakyalılastırabilemediklerimizlerdenmisiniz (50) *"are you not of that group of persons that we were said to be unable to Czechoslovakianize?"*
German[2,4]	Donaudampfschiffahrtselektrizitaetenhauptbetriebswerkbauunterbeamtengesellschaft (80) *The club for subordinate officials of the head office management of the Danube steamboat electrical services (name of a prewar club in Vienna)*
Swedish[2]	Nordöstersjökustartilleriflygspaningssimulatoranläggningsmaterielunderhållsuppföljningssystemdiskussionsinläggsförberedelsearbeten (130) *Preparatory work on the contribution to the discussion on the maintaining system of support of the material of the aviation survey simulator device within the northeast part of the coastartillery of the Baltic*

[1] *Patent applications sometimes harbor long compound "words." An extreme example is one of 13 kana (Japanese syllabary) which transliterates to the 40-letter Kyūkitsürohekimenfuchakunenryosekisanryo meaning "the accumulated amount of fuel condensed on the wall face of the air intake passage."*

[2] *Agglutinative words are limited only by imagination and are not found in standard dictionaries. The first 100-letter such word was published in 1975 by the late Eric Rosenthal in Afrikaans.*

[3] *Lengthy concatenations are a feature of Mohawk.*

[4] *The longest dictionary word in everyday usage is Rechtsschutzversicherungsgesellschaften (39) meaning "insurance companies which provide legal protection."*

DRUNK ON WORDS!

Zozzled. Looped. Beerified. Lit. You can't rightfully describe Paul Dickson as any of those, but you might say, to quote another old verbophile, that he's "in-ebriated with the exuberance of his own verbosity"— that is to say, drunk on his favorite thing, words.

"The point is not to celebrate drunkenness, which is a social evil," states Dickson. "The idea is to show how the English language is versatile, flexible, phenomenal, gleeful." He's done that all right, more than 2,000 times over—that's the number of synonyms he's compiled for the word "drunk" —and the record grows each time Dickson talks to another person from another region, researches another era of history), or quizzes another bartender.

(Russell Mott)

When not tickling what he calls "the soft underbelly of *The Guinness Book of Records*"—the language section—with new synonyms to add to the list, Dickson hunts down baseball terms for his 5,000-entry Dickson Baseball Dictionary, and works on other wordy books; he has more than 20 to his credit. "It would be just a hobby if I sold insurance or cut hair or did some other respectable job," smiles Dickson. Though he laughs about his chosen career, he's in quite respectable company. "Through the years many people have made their own drunk lists. Benjamin Franklin, Edmund Wilson, and H. L. Mencken all had lists. I collected those and added many more to them. It's almost a tradition. And every generation adds new words. It's like a huge snowball rolling down a hill."

So what word—or group of words—is in second place? "Synonyms for crazy," Dickson claims. "My favorite ones come out of a belt of the U.S. from West Virginia to Texas." He starts running through his favorites: "Crooked as a West Virginia mountain goat. One taco short of a combination platter. One sandwich shy of a picnic . . ."

Institute of the Organization for Building Mechanization and Technical Aid of the Academy of Building and Architecture of the USSR.

Most meanings   The most overworked word in English is "set," to which Dr. Charles Onions (1873–1965) of Oxford University Press gave 58 uses as a noun, 126 uses as a verb and 10 uses as a participial adjective.

Most synonyms   There are more synonyms for being intoxicated than for any other condition or object in the English language. *Dickson's Word Treasury,* compiled by Paul Dickson of Garrett Park, MD, and published in 1992, lists 2,660 synonyms for this condition.

PERSONAL NAMES

Oldest name   The oldest surviving personal name belongs to a predynastic king of Upper Egypt *ante* 3050 B.C., who is represented by the hieroglyphic sign for a scorpion. It was suggested that the name should be read as Sekhen.

Longest personal name   The longest name to appear on a birth certificate is for Rhoshandiatellyneshiaunneveshenk Koyaanisquatsiuth Williams, born to Mr. and Mrs. James Williams in Beaumont, TX on September 12, 1984. On October 5, 1984, Mr. Williams filed an amendment that expanded his daughter's first name to 1,019 letters and her middle name to 36 letters.

Most first names   A. Lindup-Badarou of Truro, England, formerly known as A. Hicks, had a total of 3,530 first names as of March 1995.

Shortest family names   The commonest single-letter surname is "O," which is prevalent in Korea. Every other letter, except "Q," has been traced as a surname in U.S. telephone books by A. Ross Eckler.

Commonest family name   The commonest surname in the English-speaking world is Smith. There are an estimated 2,382,509 Smiths in the United States.

Most contrived name   In the United States, the determination to derive commercial or other benefit from being the last listing in the local telephone book has resulted in self-given names starting with up to nine

"Z's"—an extreme example being Zachary Zzzzzzzzzra in the San Francisco book.

PLACE-NAMES

Longest place-name   The official name for Bangkok, the capital city of Thailand, is Krungthep Mahanakhon. However, the full name is Krungthep Mahanakhon Bovorn Ratanakosin Mahintharayutthaya Mahadilokpop Noparatratchathani Burirom Udomratchanivet Mahasathan Amornpiman Avatarnsathit Sakkathattiyavisnukarmprasit (167 letters), which in its most scholarly transliteration emerges with 175 letters.

The longest place-name now in use is Taumatawhakatangihangakoauauotamateaturipukakapikimaungahoronukupokaiwhenuakitanatahu, the unofficial 85-letter version of the name of a hill (1,002 feet above sea level) in the Southern Hawke's Bay district of North Island, New Zealand. The Maori translation means "The place where Tamatea, the man with the big knees, who slid, climbed and swallowed mountains, known as landeater, played his flute to his loved one."

MOUTHFUL!

The longest place-name recognized by the United States Board on Geographic Names belongs to Nunathloogagamiutbingoi Dunes in the Bethel borough of Alaska. The dunes are three miles long and are located on the southeast coast near the Nunivak Islands, one mile north of Cape Mendon Hall.

Shortest place-name   The shortest place-names consist of just single letters, and examples can be found in various countries around the world. There was once a town called "6" in West Virginia.

Most spellings   The spelling of the Dutch town of Leeuwarden has been recorded in 225 versions since A.D. 1046.

LITERATURE

Oldest book   The oldest handwritten book still intact is a Coptic Psalter dated to about 1,600 years ago, found in 1984 at Beni Suef, Egypt.

Oldest mechanically printed work   The oldest surviving printed work is the Dharani scroll or *sutra* from wooden printing blocks found in the foundations of the Pulguk Sa pagoda, Kyongju, South Korea on October 14, 1966. It has been dated to no later than A.D. 704.

The earliest mechanically printed full-length book is thought to be the 42-line-per-page Gutenberg Bible, printed in Mainz, Germany *c.* 1454 by Johann Henne zum Gensfleisch zur Laden, called "zu Gutenberg."

The earliest exactly dated printed work is the Psalter completed on August 14, 1457 by Johann Fust and Peter Schöffer, who had been Gutenberg's chief assistant.

Smallest book The smallest marketed bound printed book is printed on 22-gsm paper and measures $1/25$ by $1/25$ inches. It contains the children's story *Old King Cole!* and was published in 85 copies in March 1985 by The Gleniffer Press of Paisley, Scotland. The pages can be turned only by using a needle.

Largest publication The *Yongle Dadian* (the great thesaurus of the Yongle reign) comprises 22,937 manuscript chapters (370 of which still survive) in 11,095 volumes. It was written by 2,000 Chinese scholars between 1403 and 1408.

TALL TALE!

The novel *Tokuga-Wa Ieyasu* by Sohachi Yamaoka has been serialized in Japanese daily newspapers since 1951. Now completed, it would require nearly 40 volumes if published.

Largest dictionary *Deutsches Wörterbuch*, started by Jacob and Wilhelm Grimm in 1854, was completed in 1971 and consists of 34,519 pages and 33 volumes.

English language The 20-volume *Oxford English Dictionary* comprises 21,728 pages. The first edition was published between 1884 and 1928. The second edition, published in March 1989, defines a total of 616,500 word-forms, with 2,412,400 illustrative quotations and approximately 350 million letters and figures. The longest entry in the second edition is for the verb *set*, with over 75,000 words of text.

United States The largest English-language dictionary in the United States is *Webster's Third New International Dictionary Unabridged*, published in 1986 by Merriam-Webster, Inc. It defines 470,000 word-forms, with 9,370 illustrative quotations and approximately 60 million letters and numerics. The longest entry is for the verb *turn*, with over 5,500 words of text.

Largest encyclopedia The Chinese *Yongle Dadian* (See LARGEST PUBLICATION) was the largest encyclopedia ever compiled.

Currently, the largest encyclopedia is *La Enciclopedia Universal Ilustrada Europeo-Americana* (J. Espasa & Sons, Madrid and Barcelona), totaling 105,000 pages, with an annual supplement since 1935. The encyclopedia comprises 165.2 million words. The number of volumes in the set in August 1983 was 104, and the price $2,325.

MAPS

Oldest map A clay tablet depicting the river Euphrates flowing through northern Mesopotamia (Iraq) dates to *c.* 2250 B.C. The earliest printed map in the world is one of western China dated to 1115.

Largest map The largest permanent, 2-dimensional map measures 49,000 square feet and was painted by students of O'Hara Park School, Oakley, CA in the summer of 1992.

Relief The Challenger relief map of British Columbia, Canada, measuring 6,080 square feet, was designed and built in the period 1945–52 by the late George Challenger and his son Robert. It is now on display at the Pacific National Exhibition in Vancouver, British Columbia.

Smallest map In 1992, Dr. Jonathon Mamin of IBM's Zurich laboratory used sudden electrical impulses to create a map of the Western Hemisphere from atoms. The map has a scale of one trillion to one, and a diameter of about one micron or ¹/₁₀₀th the diameter of a human hair.

HIGHEST PRICES

Most expensive atlas The highest price paid for an atlas is $1,925,000 for a version of Ptolemy's *Cosmographia* dating from 1492, which was sold at Sotheby's, New York City on January 31, 1990.

Most expensive book The highest price paid for any book is £8.14 million ($11.9 million) for the 226-leaf manuscript *The Gospel Book of Henry the Lion, Duke of Saxony* at Sotheby's, London on December 6, 1983. The book, which measures 13¹/₂ by 10 inches, was illuminated *c.* 1170 by the monk Herimann at Helmershansen Abbey, Germany with 41 full-page illustrations.

Printed Tokyo booksellers Maruzen Co. Ltd. paid $5.39 million for an Old Testament (Genesis to the Psalms) Gutenberg Bible printed in 1455 in Mainz, Germany at Christie's, New York City on October 22, 1987.

Most expensive broadsheet On June 13, 1991, Donald J. Scheer of Atlanta, GA paid $2,420,000 for one of the 24 known copies of the Declaration of Independence, printed by John Dunlap in Philadelphia, PA in 1776.

Most expensive manuscript *United States* On December 16, 1992, a manuscript written by Abraham Lincoln was sold for $1.54 million. The 1-page script is the earliest surviving formulation of his "house divided" doctrine, written in the winter of 1857 or 1858. The manuscript was bought by Seth Kaller of Kaller Historical Documents.

Musical The auction record for a musical manuscript is $4,394,500 at Sotheby's, London, on May 22, 1987 for a 508-page bound volume measuring 8¹/₂ by 6¹/₂ inches and containing nine complete symphonies in Mozart's hand. The manuscript is owned by Robert Owen Lehman and is on deposit at the Pierpont Morgan Library in New York City.

The record price paid for a single musical manuscript is £1.1 million (*c.* $2 million), paid at Sotheby's, London, on December 6, 1991 for the autograph copy of the Piano Sonata in E minor, opus 90, by Ludwig van Beethoven (1770–1827).

DID YOU KNOW?

An illustrated manuscript by Leonardo da Vinci known as the "Codex Hammer," in which da Vinci predicted the invention of the submarine and the steam engine, was sold for a record $30.8 million at Christie's, New York City on November 11, 1994. The buyer was Bill Gates (See RICHEST MEN). It is the only da Vinci manuscript in private hands.

DIARIES AND LETTERS

Longest-kept diary   Col. Ernest Loftus of Harare, Zimbabwe began his daily diary on May 4, 1896 at age 12 and continued it until his death on July 7, 1987 at the age of 103 yr. 178 days. George C. Edler of Bethesda, MD kept a handwritten diary continuously from September 20, 1909 until his death in 1987, a total of 78 years.

Longest and most letters   From July 1961 until the death of his bedridden wife, Mitsu, in March 1985, Uichi Noda wrote her 1,307 letters, amounting to 5 million characters, during his overseas trips. These letters have been published in 25 volumes totaling 12,404 pages.

Rev. Canon Bill Cook and his fiancée/wife Helen of Diss, England exchanged 6,000 love letters during their 4¼-year separation from March 1942 to May 1946.

Shortest correspondence   While Victor Marie Hugo was on vacation in 1862, he became anxious to know how his new novel *Les Misérables* was selling. The message he sent his publisher, Hurst and Blackett, was "?"; he received the reply "!"

Longest sustained correspondence   Mrs. Ida McDougall of Tasmania, Australia and Miss R. Norton of Sevenoaks, England were pen pals for 75 years from November 11, 1904 until Mrs. McDougall's death on December 24, 1979.

Most expensive autograph letter   The highest price ever paid on the open market for a single signed autograph letter was $748,000 on December 5, 1991 at Christie's, New York City for a letter written by Abraham Lincoln on January 8, 1863 defending the Emancipation Proclamation. It was sold to Profiles in History of Beverly Hills, CA.

Most presidential signatures The only known document that bears eleven U.S. presidential signatures is a letter sent by President Franklin Delano Roosevelt to Richard C. Corbyn, then of Dallas (now of Amarillo), TX, dated October 26, 1932. It was subsequently signed by Herbert Hoover, Harry S. Truman, Dwight D. Eisenhower, Gerald Ford, Lyndon Johnson, Jimmy Carter, Ronald Reagan, George Bush and Bill Clinton. Richard Nixon's first signature was signed with an auto-pen but he later re-signed it.

Most Christmas cards The greatest number of personal Christmas cards sent by an individual is believed to be 62,824, by Werner Erhard of San Francisco, CA in December 1975.

Christmas card exchange Frank Rose of Burnaby, British Columbia, Canada and Gordon Loutet of Lake Cowichan, British Columbia have exchanged the same Christmas card every year since 1929.

Warren Nord of Mesa, AZ and Thor (Tut) Andersen (d. September 11, 1988) of Ashtabula, OH exchanged the same Christmas card every year from 1930 to 1987.

BEST-SELLING BOOKS

Most copies sold The world's best-selling and most widely distributed book is the Bible, with an estimated 2.5 billion copies sold, 1815–1975. By the end of 1993, the whole Bible had been translated into 337 languages; 2,062 languages have translations of at least one book of the Bible. The oldest publisher of bibles is the Cambridge University Press, which began with the Geneva version in 1591.

Excluding noncopyright books, such as the Bible and the Koran, the world's all-time best-selling book is *The Guinness Book of Records*, first published in October 1955 by the Guinness Brewery and edited by Norris Dewar McWhirter and his twin brother Alan Ross McWhirter. Global sales in 37 languages reached 77 million in April 1995.

Studying the Bible, one of the world's best-selling and most widely distributed books. (*Gamma/R. Gaillarde*)

Most weeks on the best-seller list The longest duration on the *New York Times* best-seller list (founded 1935) was *The Road Less Traveled* by M. Scott Peck, which had its 598th week on the list as of April 14, 1995. Over 5 million copies of the book, which is published by Touchstone (a division of Simon & Schuster), are currently in print.

Slowest-selling book David Wilkins's translation of the New Testament from Coptic into Latin was published by Oxford University Press (OUP) in 1716 in a printing of 500 copies. Selling an average of one every 20 weeks, it remained in print for 191 years.

GUESS WHAT?

Q. How small is the smallest writing?

A. Look in "Fantastic Feats" (Human Achievement)

AUTHORS

Most prolific author A lifetime output of 72–75 million words has been calculated for Charles Harold St. John Hamilton, alias Frank Richards (1876–1961). In his peak years (1915–26) he wrote up to 80,000 words a week for the boys' school weeklies *Gem* (1907–39), *Magnet* (1908–40) and *Boys' Friend* (1895–1927), published in Great Britain.

Novels The greatest number of novels published by one author is 1,020, by Brazilian novelist José Carlos Ryoki de Alpoim Inoue (b. July 22, 1946). He writes science fiction, Westerns and thrillers.

Top-selling fiction author The world's top-selling writer of fiction is Agatha Christie (1890–1976), whose 78 crime novels have sold an estimated 2 billion copies in 44 languages. Agatha Christie also wrote 19 plays and 6 romantic novels under the pseudonym Mary Westmacott. Royalty earnings from her works are estimated to be worth $4.25 million per year.

Brazilian author Jorge Amado (b. August 10, 1912) has had his 32 novels published in 48 different languages in 60 countries. His first book, *O País do Carnaval*, appeared in 1931; his most recent book, *A Descoberta da América pelos Turcos*, was published in 1994.

Highest-paid author per word In 1958, Deborah Schneider of Minneapolis, MN wrote 25 words to complete a sentence in a competition for the best slogan for Plymouth cars. She beat about 1.4 million other entrants to win a prize of $500 every month for life. Based on normal life expectancy, she should collect $12,000 per word. No known anthology includes Schneider's prose, but it is in her safe deposit box at her bank, "Only to be opened after death," because the company feared complaints from other disgruntled contestants.

Oldest author   Alice Pollock of Haslemere, England published her first book, *Portrait of My Victorian Youth* (Johnson Publications), in March 1971 at age 102 yr. 8 mo.

Most pseudonyms   The *Dictionary of Pseudonyms* by I.F. Masanov, published in Moscow in 1960, lists 325 different pen names for Russian humorist Konstantin Arsenievich Mikhailov (b. 1868). The names, which range from Ab. to Z, were mostly abbreviations of his real name.

Longest poem   The longest poem ever published was the Kirghiz folk epic *Manas*, which appeared in printed form in 1958 but has never been translated into English. According to the *Dictionary of Oriental Literatures*, this 3-part epic runs to about 500,000 lines.

English language   A poem on the life of King Alfred by John Fitchett (1766–1838) of Liverpool, England ran to 129,807 lines and took 40 years to write. His editor, Robert Riscoe, added the concluding 2,585 lines.

Longest literary gestation   In 1629, Jean Bolland, an ecclesiastical historian, began a chronicle of the saints' lives (*Acta Sanctorum*) following an original idea by the priest Héribert Rosweyde. He arranged the work according to saints' feast days; during his lifetime Bolland completed the first two parts, *January* and *February*. The work was continued after his death by a group of Belgian Jesuits known as Bollandists. An introduction for December was published in 1940 and there are now 67 folio volumes of the completed *Acta Sanctorum*.

PUBLISHERS AND PRINTERS

Largest printer   The largest printer in 1994 was Bertelsmann in Germany. In 1993, the company had sales of $10,956 million with profits of $289 million. It employed 14,696 people.

United States   The largest printer in the United States is R.R. Donnelley & Sons Co. of Chicago, IL. The company, founded in 1864, has 200 manufacturing facilities, offices, service centers and subsidiaries in 20 countries. In 1994, Donnelly had 36,500 employees worldwide, and turned out $4.9 billion worth of work.

The largest printer under one roof is the United States Government Printing Office (founded 1861) in Washington, D.C. Encompassing 34.4 acres of floor space, the central office processes an average of 1,464 print orders daily, and uses 93.2 million pounds of paper annually.

Highest printings   It is believed that in the United States, Van Antwerp Bragg and Co. printed some 60 million copies of the 1879 edition of *The McGuffey Reader*, compiled by Henry Vail in the pre-copyright era for distribution to public schools.

Oldest publisher   Cambridge University Press has a continuous history of printing and publishing since 1584. The University received a Royal Letters Patent to print and sell all manner of books on July 20, 1534.

United States The firm of Williams and Wilkins (formerly Lea and Febiger) of Malvern, PA has a continuous history of publishing since 1785.

Most prolific publisher At its peak in 1989, Progress Publishers (founded in 1931 as the Publishing Association of Foreign Workers in the former USSR) of Moscow, Russia printed over 750 titles in 50 languages annually.

Fastest publishing Two thousand bound copies of *The Book Fair Book*, published by the Zimbabwe International Book Fair Trust and printed by Print Holdings (Pvt) Ltd., were produced from raw disk in 5 hr. 23 min. at the Zimbabwe International Book Fair in Harare on August 5, 1993. The time for 1,000 copies was 4 hr. 50 min., and Braille, large print, CD-ROM, and audiotape formats were produced simultaneously.

BOOKSTORES AND LIBRARIES

Largest bookstore The bookstore with the most titles and the longest shelving (30 miles) in the world is W. & G. Foyle Ltd. of London, England. First established in 1904 in a small store, the company now has a site of 75,825 square feet.

The most capacious individual bookstore in the world measured by square footage is the Barnes & Noble Bookstore at 105 Fifth Avenue at 18th Street, New York City. It covers 154,250 square feet and has 12.87 miles of shelving.

Oldest library The first library in America was established at Harvard University in 1638. The first subscription library in the country was the Philadelphia Library Company in 1731. The first library in America that meets the definition of a modern public library was established in Peterboro, NH, on April 9, 1833. The original collection contained 700 books.

Largest library The United States Library of Congress (founded on April 24, 1800) in Washington, D.C. contains 107,824,509 items, including 16,448,469 books in the classified collections and 91,376,040 items in the nonclassified collections. The library has 532 miles of shelving and employs 4,701 people.

Nonstatutory The largest nonstatutory library—not funded or operated by the state—is the New York Public Library (founded 1895) on Fifth Avenue, New York City with a floor space of 525,276 square feet and 172 miles of shelving, plus an underground extension with the capacity for an

---

OVERDUE!

A book on febrile diseases (London, 1805, by Dr. J. Currie) was checked out in 1823 from the University of Cincinnati Medical Library and returned December 7, 1968 by the borrower's great-grandson, Richard Dodd. The calculated fine of $2,264 was waived.

---

additional 84 miles. Its collection, including 82 branch libraries, contains 4.6 million volumes and 38 million items of research material.

Public The largest public library in the United States is the Harold Washington Library Center, Chicago, IL, which opened on October 7, 1991. The 10-story, 756,640-square-foot building contains 70.85 miles of bookshelves and cost $144 million. The collection includes 1.6 million books, 9,513 periodical titles, and more than 5 million microforms, recordings and other items.

University The largest university library in the United States is believed to be Harvard University Library, in Cambridge, MA, which consists of at least 90 separate libraries and a total of 12,877,360 volumes.

Most overdue book A book in German on the Archbishop of Bremen, published in 1609, was borrowed from Sidney Sussex College, Cambridge, England by Colonel Robert Walpole, 1667–68. It was found by Prof. Sir John Plumb in the library at Houghton Hall, Norfolk, England and returned 288 years later. No fine was charged.

MUSEUMS

Oldest museum The world's oldest museum is the Ashmolean in Oxford, England, built between 1679 and 1683 and named after the collector Elias Ashmole (1617–92).

Largest museum The Smithsonian Institution comprises 16 museums containing over 140 million items and has over 6,000 employees.

The American Museum of Natural History in New York City (founded in 1869) comprises 23 interconnected buildings in an 18-acre park. The buildings of the museum and the planetarium contain 1.2 million square feet of floor space, accommodating more than 30 million artifacts and specimens. Its exhibits are viewed by more than 3 million visitors each year.

Most popular museum The highest attendance on a single day for any museum is over 118,437 on April 14, 1984 at the Smithsonian's National Air and Space Museum, Washington, D.C., opened in July 1976. The record-setting day required the doors to be temporarily closed.

NEWSPAPERS

In 1994, the total number of morning and evening newspapers published in the United States was 1,538, with a total circulation of 59,024,805. There were 889 Sunday newspapers with a circulation of 62,643,379. The peak year for U.S. newspapers was 1910, when there were 2,202.

Most newspaper readers The country with the most newspaper readers is Sweden, where 580 newspapers are sold for every 1,000 people.

Highest circulation The highest circulation for any newspaper in the world was for *Komsomolskaya Pravda* (founded 1925), the youth paper of the former Soviet Communist Party; it reached a peak daily circulation of 21,975,000 copies in May 1990.

The 8-page weekly newspaper *Argumenty i Fakty* (founded 1978) of Moscow, Russia attained a figure of 33,431,100 copies in May 1990, when it had an estimated readership of over 100 million.

DID YOU KNOW?

The highest circulation for any *currently* published newspaper is that of *The Yomiuri Shimbun*, founded 1874, which publishes morning and evening editions. The combined daily circulation was 14,567,000 in January 1995.

United States The highest-circulation daily newspaper in the United States is the *Wall Street Journal* (founded 1889), published by Dow Jones & Co. As of March 31, 1994, circulation was 1,854,901 copies.

Oldest newspaper A copy exists of a news pamphlet published in Cologne, Germany in 1470. The oldest existing newspaper is the Swedish official journal *Post och Inrikes Tidningar* (founded 1645), published by the Royal Swedish Academy of Letters. The oldest existing commercial newspaper is the *Haarlems Dagblad/Oprechte Haarlemsche Courant*, published in Haarlem, Netherlands, first issued as the *Weeckelycke Courante van Europa* on January 8, 1656. A copy of issue No. 1 survives.

United States The oldest continuously published newspaper in the United States is the *Hartford Courant*, established by Thomas Greene on October 29, 1764. Originally a weekly 4-page newspaper, it became a daily newspaper in 1836. Its current circulation figures are 230,724 daily and 320,851 Sunday papers, as of April 1995.

Largest newspaper The most massive single issue of a newspaper was the September 14, 1987 edition of the Sunday *New York Times*, which weighed 12 pounds and contained 1,612 pages.

The largest page size ever used was 55.9 by 39.2 inches for the June 14, 1993 edition of *Het Volk*, which was published in Gent, Belgium.

Smallest newspaper The *Daily Banner* of Roseberg, OR had an original page size of 3 by 3¾ inches. It retailed at 25 cents per month, and issues dated February 1 and 2, 1876 survive.

Longest editorship Sir Etienne Dupuch of Nassau, Bahamas was editor-in-chief of *The Tribune* from April 1, 1919 to 1972, and a contributing editor until his death on August 23, 1991—a total of 72 years.

Most Pulitzer prizes The *New York Times* has won 69 Pulitzer prizes, more than any other news organization.

Most durable feature Mary MacArthur of Port Appin, Scotland has contributed a regular feature to *The Oban Times and West Highland Times* since 1926.

SORRY!

The *Hartford Courant* issued an apology to Thomas Jefferson, 193 years late. In 1800, the newspaper ran a vehement editorial opposing his election as president, and expounding on the ways in which the country would be irrevocably damaged as a result. In 1993, the *Courant* finally admitted the error of its judgment with a formal apology, and the words: "It's never too late to admit a mistake."

Most durable advertiser The Jos Neel Co., a clothing store in Macon, GA (founded 1880), ran an ad in the *Macon Telegraph* in the upper-left-hand corner of page 2A every day, February 22, 1889–August 16, 1987.

Most widely syndicated columnist Ann Landers appears in over 1,200 newspapers with an estimated readership of 90 million.

COMIC STRIPS

Earliest comic strip "The Yellow Kid" appeared for the first time in the *New York Journal* on October 18, 1896.

Most durable comic strip The longest-lived newspaper comic strip is "The Katzenjammer Kids" (Hans and Fritz), created by Rudolph Dirks and first published in the *New York Journal* on December 12, 1897. The strip—still running as of April 13, 1995, and currently drawn by cartoonist Hy Eisman—has been taken over by King Features Syndicate and is now syndicated in approximately 50 newspaper publications.

Political cartoons Ranan R. Lurie (U.S.) is the world's most widely syndicated political cartoonist. As of June 1995, his work was published in 102 countries in 1,098 newspapers with a circulation of 102 million copies.

PEANUTS!

"Peanuts" by Charles Schulz of Santa Rosa, CA, first published in October 1950, currently appears in 2,300 newspapers in 68 countries and 26 languages, making it the most widely syndicated comic strip.

PERIODICALS

Oldest periodical The oldest continuing periodical in the world is *Philosophical Transactions of the Royal Society*, published in London, England, which first appeared on March 6, 1665.

United States The oldest continuously published periodical in the United States is *The Old Farmer's Almanac*, started in Massachusetts by Robert Thomas, a teacher and amateur astronomer, in 1792.

Largest circulations The total dispersal through noncommercial channels by Jehovah's Witnesses of *The Truth that Leads to Eternal Life*, published by the Watchtower Bible and Tract Society of New York City on May 8, 1968, reached 107,651,627 in 117 languages by April 1995.

The world's highest-circulation periodical is *TV Guide*, with a circulation of 14,037,062 as of December 31, 1994.

In its 46 basic international editions, *Reader's Digest* (established February 1922) circulates more than 28 million copies monthly in 18 languages, including a U.S. edition of more than 15 million copies. *Parade*, the syndicated color magazine, is distributed with a record 352 U.S. newspapers every Sunday, and as of April 17, 1995, had a peak circulation of 37.614 million, the highest for any magazine.

Largest consumer magazine The January 1992 issue of *Hong Kong Toys* ran to 1,356 pages. Published by the Hong Kong Trade Development Council, it retails for HK$100 (about $12.50).

Most advertising pages The greatest number of pages of advertisements sold in a single issue of a periodical is 829.54 by the October 1989 issue of *Business Week*.

CROSSWORD PUZZLES

Largest published crossword puzzle In July 1982, Robert Turcot of Québec, Canada compiled a crossword puzzle comprising 82,951 squares. It contained 12,489 clues across, 13,125 down, and covered 38.28 square feet.

PUZZLED!

In May 1966, a Fijian woman informed *The Times* of London that she had just completed their crossword puzzle No. 673, published in the April 4, 1932 issue. The problem wasn't that the puzzle was fiendishly difficult—it was in an edition that had been used to wrap a package, and had subsequently lain uncompleted for 34 years.

Most prolific crossword compiler Roger F. Squires of Ironbridge, England composes 38 published puzzles single-handedly each week. His total output to September 1995 was over 46,000 puzzles.

Fastest crossword puzzle solution The fastest recorded time for completing *The Times* (London) crossword puzzle under test conditions is 3 min. 45 sec., by Roy Dean of Bromley, England, on December 19, 1970.

MUSIC

Highest and lowest voices   Before this century, the extremes were a staccato E in *alt altissimo* (e^4) by Ellen Beach Yaw in Carnegie Hall, New York City on January 19, 1896, and an A$_2$ (55 Hz [cycles per second]) by Kasper Foster (1617–73).

Madeleine Marie Robin (1918–60), the French operatic coloratura, could produce and sustain the B above high C in the Lucia mad scene in Donizetti's *Lucia di Lammermoor*. Ivan Rebroff, the Russian singer, has a voice that extends easily over four octaves, from low F to high F, one and a quarter octaves above C. Dan Britton of Branson, MO can produce the note E-flat$_3$ (18.84 Hz).

The highest note put into song is g^4, occurring in Mozart's *Popoli di Tessaglia*. The lowest vocal note in the classical repertoire is in Mozart's *Die Entführung aus dem Serail* in Osmin's aria, which calls for a low D (73.4 Hz).

Fastest rapper   Rebel X.D. of Chicago, IL rapped 674 syllables in 54.9 seconds at the Hair Bear Recording Studio, Alsip, IL on August 27, 1992.

SONGS

Oldest song   The *shaduf* chant has been sung since time immemorial by irrigation workers on the Nile water mills (or *saqiyas*) in Egypt.

The oldest known harmonized music performed today is the English song *Sumer is icumen in*, which dates from *c*. 1240.

Oldest national anthem   The words of the *Kimigayo* of Japan date from the ninth century, although the music was written in 1881. The oldest music belongs to the anthem of the Netherlands, *Vilhelmus*, which was written

The world's biggest guitar bash took place in Vancouver, Canada in 1994. (*Music West*)

c. 1570. Of the 11 wordless national anthems, the oldest is that of Spain, dating from 1770.

Shortest national anthems The anthems of Japan, Jordan and San Marino each have only four lines.

Longest rendering of a national anthem *God Save the King* was played non-stop 16 or 17 times by a German military band on the platform of Ra-thenau railroad station, Brandenburg, Germany on the morning of February 9, 1909. The reason was that King Edward VII was struggling to put on a German field-marshal's uniform inside the train before he could emerge.

Most renditions of the national anthem Susan R. Jeske sang the *Star-Spangled Banner* live at 17 official events in California, attended by ap-proximately 60,000 people, within a 24-hour period, July 3–4, 1992. She traveled to the functions by automobile, helicopter and boat.

Most frequently sung songs The most frequently sung songs in English are *Happy Birthday to You* (based on the original *Good Morning to All*), by Kentucky-born Sunday school teachers Mildred Hill and Patty Smith Hill of New York (written in 1893 and under copyright from 1935 to 2010); *For He's a Jolly Good Fellow* (originally the French *Malbrouk*), known at least as early as 1781; and *Auld Lang Syne* (originally the Strathspey *I Fee'd a Lad at Michaelmass*), some words of which were written by Scottish poet Robert Burns (1759–96).

Most successful songwriters In terms of number-one singles, the most suc-cessful songwriters are John Lennon (1940–80) and Paul McCartney (b. June 18, 1942). McCartney is credited as writer on 32 number-one hits in the United States to Lennon's 26 (with 23 co-written), whereas Lennon au-thored 29 British number-ones to McCartney's 28 (25 co-written).

Oldest hymns The music and parts of the text of a hymn in the *Oxyrhynchus Papyri* from the second century are the earliest known hymnody. The earliest exactly datable hymn is the *Heyr Himna Smiður* (*Hear, the Maker of Heaven*) from 1208 by the Icelandic bard and chieftain Kolbeinn Tumason (1173–1208).

Longest published hymn *Sing God's Song*, a hymn by Carolyn Ann Aish of Inglewood, New Zealand, is 754 verses or 3,016 lines long, with an addi-tional 4-line refrain to each verse.

Most prolific hymnist Frances (Fanny) Jane van Alstyne (née Crosby, 1820–1915) of the United States wrote 8,500 hymns.

Oldest choral society The oldest active choral society in the United States is the Old Stoughton Musical Society of Stoughton, MA, founded in 1786.

Largest choir Excluding "sing-alongs" by stadium crowds, the greatest choir was one of 60,000 that sang in unison as a finale to a choral contest held among 160,000 participants in Breslau, Germany on August 2, 1937.

INSTRUMENTS

Largest organ   The largest and loudest musical instrument ever constructed is the now only partially functional Auditorium Organ in Atlantic City, NJ. Completed in 1930, this instrument had two consoles (one with seven manuals and another movable one with five), 1,477 stop controls and 33,112 pipes, ranging in tone from $\frac{1}{5}$ inch to the 64-foot tone. It had the volume of 25 brass bands, with a range of seven octaves.

The world's largest fully functional organ is the 6-manual 30,067-pipe Grand Court Organ installed in the Wanamaker Department Store, Philadelphia, PA in 1911 and enlarged between then and 1930. The organ has a 64-foot tone gravissima pipe.

Loudest organ stop   The Ophicleide stop of the Grand Great in the Solo Organ in the Atlantic City Auditorium is operated by a pressure of water $3\frac{1}{2}$ pounds per square inch and has a pure trumpet note of ear-splitting volume, more than six times the volume of the loudest locomotive whistles.

Grandest piano   The grandest weighed 1.4 tons and was 11 ft. 8 in. long. It was made by Chas H. Challen & Son Ltd. of London, England in 1935. Its longest bass string measured 9 ft. 11 in., with a tensile strength of 33 tons.

Most expensive piano   On March 26, 1980, a non-pianist paid $390,000 for a *c.* 1888 Steinway grand piano sold by the Martin Beck Theater at Sotheby Parke Bernet, New York City.

GUESS WHAT?

Q.   WHAT IS THE DIAMETER OF THE LARGEST BALL OF STRING?

A.   LOOK IN "BIG DEALS" (HUMAN ACHIEVEMENT)

Largest pan pipes   Simon Desorgher and Lawrence Casserley created pan pipes consisting of five contrabass pipes, each four inches in diameter, with lengths of 19 inches, 16 inches, 14 inches, 12 inches and 10 inches respectively, and five bass pipes of 2-inch diameter with lengths of 9.5 inches, 8 inches, 7 inches, 6 inches and 5 inches.

Largest brass instrument   A contrabass tuba standing $7\frac{1}{2}$ feet tall, with 39 feet of tubing and a bell 3 ft. 4 in. across, was constructed for a world tour by the band of American composer John Philip Sousa, *c.* 1896–98.

Largest movable stringed instrument   A pantaleon with 270 strings stretched over 50 square feet was used by George Noel in 1767.

Largest double bass   A double bass measuring 14 feet tall was built in 1924 in Ironia, NJ by Arthur K. Ferris. It weighed 1,301 pounds with a sound box eight feet across, and had leather strings totaling 104 feet. Its low notes could be felt rather than heard.

Master violin-maker Christian Urbista of Cordes, France built the world's largest cello, which is potentially playable by someone with a record-breaking reach. (*Gamma/J. F. Laberine*)

Double bass playing   Eighteen musicians played a double bass simultaneously (seven bowing, five fingering and five plucking) in a rendition of Strauss's *Perpetuum Mobile* at the studios of the BBC's *Record Breakers* television show on September 28, 1991.

Largest playable guitar   Students of Shakamak High School in Jasonville, IN made a guitar measuring 38 ft. 2 in. tall, 16 feet wide and weighing 1,865 pounds. It was unveiled on May 17, 1991 when, powered by six amplifiers, it was played simultaneously by six people from the school.

Acoustic   A guitar 28 ft. 5 in. long and 3 ft. 2 in. deep is on display at the Stradivarium exhibition in The Exploratory, Bristol, England. Its dimensions were enlarged from the proportions of a Stradivarius classical guitar. When the guitar is played, its five strings resonate impressively.

Most expensive guitar   A Fender Stratocaster belonging to legendary rock guitarist Jimi Hendrix (1942–70) was sold by his former drummer Mitch Mitchell to an anonymous buyer for £198,000 ($338,580) at Sotheby's, London on April 25, 1990.

Guitar marathon   On May 7, 1994, a gathering of 1,322 guitarists played "Taking Care of Business" in unison for 68 min. 40 sec., in an event organized by Music West of Vancouver, Canada.

Most valuable violin   The highest price paid at auction for a violin is £902,000 ($1.7 million) for the 1720 "Mendelssohn" Stradivarius. It was sold to a mystery buyer at Christie's, London on November 21, 1990.

Largest cello   Master violin-maker Christian Urbista of Cordes, France worked for a thousand hours to build the world's largest playable cello. The instrument stands 24.4 feet tall and is made of pine, maple, beech and plane.

Most valuable cello   The highest auction price for a cello is £682,000 (approximately $1.2 million) at Sotheby's, London on June 22, 1988 for a Stradivarius known as "The Cholmondeley," which was made in Cremona, Italy *c.* 1698.

Largest drum   A drum with a 13-foot diameter was built by the Supreme Drum Co., London, England and played at the Royal Festival Hall, London on May 31, 1987.

Largest drum kit   A drum kit consisting of 308 pieces—153 drums, 77 cymbals, 33 cowbells, 12 hi-hats, 8 tambourines, 6 wood blocks, 3 gongs, 3 bell trees, 2 maracas, 2 triangles, 2 rain sticks, 2 bells, 1 ratchet, 1 set of chimes, 1 xylophone, 1 afuche, and 1 doorbell—was built by Dan McCourt of Pontiac, MI in 1994.

Most drums played   Four hundred separate drums were played in 20.50 seconds by Carl Williams at the Alexander Stadium, Birmingham, England on October 4, 1992.

Longest alphorn   An alphorn 154 ft. 8 in. long (excluding mouthpiece) and weighing 227 pounds was completed by Swiss-born Peter Wutherich, of

Boise, ID in December 1989. The diameter at the bell is 24½ inches and the sound takes 105.7 milliseconds to emerge from the bowl after entry into the mouthpiece.

Highest and lowest notes   The extremes of orchestral instruments (excluding the organ) range from a handbell tuned to g^5 (6,272 cycles per second, or 6,272 Hz) to the sub-contrabass clarinet, which can reach C_4 (16.4 Hz). The highest note on a standard pianoforte is c^4 (4,186 Hz), which is also the violinist's limit. In 1873, a sub-double bassoon able to reach B_4 (14.6 Hz) was constructed, but no surviving specimen is known.

The extremes for the organ are g^6 (12,544 cycles per second, or 12,544 Hz) and C_5 (8.12 Hz), obtainable from ¾-inch and 64-foot pipes respectively.

BELLS

Oldest bell   The tintinnabulum found in the Babylonian Palace of Nimrod in 1849 by Austen Henry Layard dates from *c.* 1100 B.C.

Tower   The oldest tower bell is in St. Benedict Church, Rome, Italy. It bears the date "anno domini millesimo sexagesimo IX" (1069).

United States   The oldest bell in the United States is located at St. Stephens Episcopal Church in East Haddam, CT. The bell was cast in Spain in 815 A.D. and shipped to the United States in 1834.

Heaviest bell   The Tsar Kolokol, cast by Russian brothers I.F. and M.I. Motorin on November 25, 1735 in Moscow, weighs 222.6 tons, measures 22 feet in diameter and is 20 feet high. The bell was cracked in a fire in 1737 and a fragment, weighing 12.91 tons, was broken from it. The bell has stood unrung on a platform in the Kremlin in Moscow since 1836 with the broken section alongside.

The heaviest bell still in use is the Mingun bell in Mandalay, Myanmar, which was cast late in the reign of King Bodawpaya (1782–1819). It weighs 101 tons and has a diameter of 16 ft. 8½ in. at the lip. The bell is struck by a teak boom from the outside. The heaviest swinging bell in the world is the Petersglocke in the southwest tower of Cologne Cathedral, Germany. It was cast in 1923, has a diameter of 11 ft. 1¾ in., and weighs 28 tons.

Heaviest peals   The heaviest ring in the United States is that of 10 bells cast in 1963 for the Washington National Cathedral, Washington, D.C.

DING DONG!

The total bell weight of 13 bells cast in 1938–39 for the Anglican Cathedral in Liverpool, England is 18.5 tons, of which Emmanuel, the tenor bell note A, weighs 9,195 pounds.

The total bell weight is 13,682 pounds—the heaviest bell weighs 3,588 pounds.

Largest carillon   The largest carillon (minimum of 23 bells) in the world is the Laura Spelman Rockefeller Memorial Carillon in Riverside Church, New York City, with 74 bells weighing 114 tons. The bourdon, giving the note lower C, weighs 20.5 tons and is the largest tuned bell in the world.

ORCHESTRAS

Oldest orchestra   The oldest existing symphony orchestra, the Gewandhaus Orchestra of Leipzig, Germany, was established in 1743. Originally known as the Grosses Concert and later as the Musikübende Gesellschaft, it took its current name in 1781.

United States   The oldest orchestra in the United States is the Philharmonic-Symphony Society of New York, which was founded by Ureli Corelli Hill in 1842.

Largest orchestra   On June 17, 1872, Johann Strauss the younger (1825–99) conducted an orchestra of 987 pieces supported by a choir of 20,000, at the World Peace Jubilee in Boston, MA. The number of first violinists was 400.

On December 14, 1991, the 2,000-piece "Young People's Orchestra and Chorus of Mexico," consisting of 53 youth orchestras from Mexico plus musicians from Venezuela and the former USSR, gave a classical concert conducted by Fernando Lozano and others at the Magdalena Mixhiuca Sports Center, Mexico City.

Bottle orchestra   The Brighton Bottle Orchestra—consisting of Terry Garoghan and Peter Miller—performed a musical medley on 444 Gordon's Gin bottles at the Brighton International Festival, England on May 21, 1991. It took 18 hours to tune the bottles, and about 10 times the normal rate of puff (90 breaths per minute) to play them. There was no risk of intoxication, as the bottles were filled with water.

Most prolific conductor   The Austrian conductor Herbert von Karajan, principal conductor of the Berlin Philharmonic Orchestra for 35 years prior to his retirement in 1989, made over 800 recordings of all the major works.

Longest-serving conductor   Dr. Aloys Fleischmann conducted the Cork Symphony Orchestra (Cork, Republic of Ireland) for 58 seasons, ending in 1991–92.

United States   The Chicago Symphony Orchestra was directed by Frederic Stock from 1905 until his death in 1942, a total of 37 seasons.

Largest band   The most massive band ever assembled was one of 20,100 players at the Ulleyaal Stadium, Oslo, Norway from Norges Musikkorps Forbund bands on June 28, 1964.

Largest one-man band Rory Blackwell, of Starcross, England, aided by his double left-footed perpendicular percussion-pounder, plus his 3-tier right-footed horizontal 22-pronged differential beater, and his 12-outlet bellow-powered horn-blower, played 108 different instruments (19 melody and 89 percussion) simultaneously in Dawlish, England on May 29, 1989. He also played 314 instruments in a single rendition in 1 min. 23.07 sec., also in Dawlish, on May 27, 1985.

Largest marching band The largest marching band was one of 6,017 people, including 927 majorettes and standard-bearers. On June 27, 1993 the band marched 3,084 feet at Stafsberg Airport, Hamar, Norway, under the direction of Odd Aspli, Chairman of Hamar County Council.

Longest musical march Members of Marum, a Dutch marching band, walked 46.7 miles from Assen to Marum, Netherlands on May 9, 1992. Of the 60 people who started, 52 managed to complete the march in 13 hr. 50 min.

Musical chairs The largest game started with 8,238 participants, and ended with Xu Chong Wei on the last chair. It was held at the Anglo-Chinese School, Singapore on August 5, 1989.

Baton twirling The greatest number of complete spins done between tossing a baton into the air and catching it is 10, by Donald Garcia, on December 9, 1986. The women's record is eight spins, by Danielle Novakowski, in South Bend, IN on July 24, 1993.

CONCERTS

Classical concert An estimated record 800,000 attended a free open-air concert by the New York Philharmonic conducted by Zubin Mehta, on the Great Lawn of Central Park, New York City on July 5, 1986, as part of the Statue of Liberty Weekend.

Paul McCartney attracted record-breaking numbers to his concert at the Maracanã Stadium in Rio de Janeiro on April 21, 1990. (*Gamma/A. Sassaki*)

Rock/pop festival Steve Wozniak's 1983 U.S. Festival in San Bernardino, CA attracted an audience of 725,000.

Solo performer The largest *paying* audience ever attracted by a solo performer was an estimated 180,000–184,000 in the Maracanã Stadium, Rio de Janeiro, Brazil to hear Paul McCartney on April 21, 1990. Rod Stewart's *free* concert at Copacabana Beach, Rio de Janeiro, Brazil on New Year's Eve, 1994 reportedly attracted an audience of 3.5 million.

The Grateful Dead played 2,263 concerts from 1965 through 1994. (*Ken Friedman © Grateful Dead Productions, Inc.*)

Most successful concert tour The Rolling Stones' 1989 "Steel Wheels" North American tour earned an estimated $310 million and was attended by 3.2 million people in 30 cities.

Most rock concerts performed The Grateful Dead, originally known as the Warlocks, performed 2,263 documented rock concerts, 1965–94. They have played live in front of an estimated 25 million Deadheads and have played approximately 553 different songs and jams.

Most durable musicians The Romanian pianist Cual Delavrancea (1887–1991) gave her last public recital, receiving six encores, at the age of 103. The longest international career in the history of Western music is held by Polish pianist Mieczyslaw Horszowski (1892–1993), who played for Emperor Franz-Joseph in Vienna, Austria in 1899 and was still playing in 1989.

The world's oldest active musician is Jennie Newhouse (b. July 12, 1889) of High Bentham, England, who has been the regular organist at the Church of St. Boniface in Bentham since 1920.

Most successful concert series Michael Jackson sold out for seven nights at Wembley Stadium, London, England in the summer of 1988. The stadium has a capacity of 72,000, so a total of 504,000 people saw Jackson perform July 14–16, 22–23, and August 26–27, 1988.

Largest concert On July 21, 1990, Potsdamer Platz, straddling East and West Berlin, was the site of the largest single rock concert in terms of participants and organization ever staged. Roger Waters' production of Pink Floyd's "The Wall" involved 600 people performing on a stage measuring 551 by 82 feet at its highest point. An estimated 200,000 people gathered for the symbolic building and demolition of a wall made of 2,500 Styrofoam blocks.

Clapping The duration record for continuous clapping (sustaining an average of 160 claps per minute, audible at 120 yards) is 58 hr. 9 min. by V. Jeyaraman of Tamil Nadu, India, February 12–15, 1988.

Rod Stewart's free New Year's Eve concert in Rio de Janeiro attracted 3.5 million people. (*Pepsi International*)

COMPOSERS

Most prolific composer Georg Philipp Telemann (1681–1767) of Germany composed 12 complete sets of services (one cantata every Sunday) for a year, 78 services for special occasions, 40 operas, 600 to 700 orchestral suites, 44 passions, plus concertos, sonatas and other chamber music.

Longest symphony The symphony *Victory at Sea*, written by Richard Rodgers (1902–79) and arranged by Robert Russell Bennett in 1952 for the NBC television series of the same name, lasted 13 hours.

Longest solo piano composition The longest continuous nonrepetitious piano piece ever published is *The Well-Tuned Piano* by La Monte Young, first presented by the Dia Art Foundation at the Concert Hall, Harrison St., New York City on February 28, 1980. The piece lasted 4 hr. 12 min. 10 sec.

Longest silence The longest interval between the known composition of a piece by a major composer and its performance in the manner intended is from March 3, 1791 until October 9, 1982, in the case of Mozart's *Organ*

Piece for a Clock, a fugue fantasy in F minor (K 608), arranged by the organ builders Wm. Hill & Son and Norman & Beard Ltd. at Glyndebourne, England.

OPERA

Longest opera   *The Heretics* by Gabriel von Wayditch (1888–1969), a Hungarian-American, is orchestrated for 110 pieces and lasts 8½ hours. The longest commonly performed opera is *Die Meistersinger von Nürnberg* by Richard Wagner (1813–83) of Germany. A normal uncut performance of this opera entails 5 hr. 15 min. of music.

Shortest opera   *The Sands of Time* by Simon Rees and Peter Reynolds was first performed by Rhian Owen and Dominic Burns on March 27, 1993 at The Hayes, Cardiff, Wales; it lasted for 4 min. 9 sec. An even shorter performance, lasting only 3 min. 34 sec., was directed by Peter Reynolds at BBC Television Centre, London, England on September 14, 1993.

Largest opera house   The Metropolitan Opera House, Lincoln Center, New York City was completed in 1966 at a cost of $45.7 million. It has a standing and seating capacity of 4,065 with 3,800 seats in an auditorium 451 feet deep. The stage is 230 feet wide and 148 feet deep.
   The Teatro della Scala (La Scala) in Milan, Italy shares with the Bolshoi Theatre in Moscow, Russia the distinction of having the greatest number of tiers—six.

Longest aria   The longest single aria, in the sense of an operatic solo, is Brünnhilde's immolation scene in Wagner's *Götterdämmerung*. It has been timed at 14 min. 46 sec.

Oldest opera singers   The tenor Hugues Cuénod (b. June 26, 1902) sang the part of Emperor Altoum in *Turandot* at the Metropolitan Opera House, New York City on March 10, 1988 at age 85. Danshi Toyotake (b. Yoshie Yokota, 1891–1989) of Hyogo, Japan sang *Musume Gidayu* (traditional Japanese narrative) for 91 years from the age of seven. Her professional career spanned 81 years.

Most curtain calls   On February 24, 1988, Luciano Pavarotti received 165 curtain calls and was applauded for 1 hr. 7 min. after singing the part of Nemorino in Gaetano Donizetti's *L'Elisir d'amore* at the Deutsche Oper in Berlin, Germany.

Oldest opera company   The oldest continuously performing opera company in the United States is the Metropolitan Opera Company of New York City; its first season was in 1883.

Longest operatic encore   The Austro-Hungarian emperor Leopold II (r. 1790–92) ordered an encore of the entire opera *Il Matrimonio Segreto* by Cimarosa at its premiere in 1792.

RECORDED SOUND

Oldest recordings   The oldest existing recording was made in 1878 by Augustus Stroh, but it remains on the mandrel of his machine and has never been played.

The oldest playable record is believed to be an engraved metal cylinder made by Frank Lambert in 1878 or 1879 and voicing the hours on the clock. The recording is owned by Aaron Cramer of New York City.

Smallest recorder   In April 1983, Olympic Optical Industry Co. of Japan marketed a micro-cassette recorder measuring $4^1/_5$ by 2 by $^1/_2$ inches and weighing 4.4 ounces.

Smallest cassette   The NT digital cassette made by the Sony Corporation of Japan for use in dictating machines measures just $1^1/_5$ by $^4/_5$ by $^1/_5$ inches.

Smallest functional record   Six titles of $1^5/_{16}$-inch diameter were recorded by HMV's studio in Hayes, England on January 26, 1923 for Queen Mary's Doll House. Some 92,000 of these miniature records were pressed, including 35,000 of *God Save the King*.

Largest record store   HMV opened the world's largest record store at 150 Oxford Street, London, England on October 24, 1986. Its selling area measures 36,684 square feet.

TOP RECORDING ARTISTS

Most successful solo recording artist   Although no independently audited figures have ever been published for Elvis Presley (1935–77), he had over 170 hit singles and over 80 top-selling albums starting in 1956. Aretha Franklin is the female solo artist with the most million-selling singles, with 14 between 1967 and 1973.

Most successful group   The singers with the greatest sales of any group were the Beatles. The group, from Liverpool, England, comprised George Harrison, John Lennon, Paul McCartney and Ringo Starr. The all-time Beatles sales have been estimated by EMI at over a billion discs and tapes.

Most gold, platinum, and multiplatinum discs   The only *audited* measure of gold, platinum and multiplatinum singles and albums within the United States is certification by the Recording Industry Association of America (RIAA), introduced on March 14, 1958.

The Rolling Stones have the most certified gold discs for any group, with 39 (34 albums, 5 singles). The group with the most multiplatinum albums is the Beatles, with 12.

In August 1992, following new audit figures, the estate of Elvis Presley was presented with 60 gold and 50 platinum discs, making him the most certified recording artist ever. The female solo artist to receive the most gold discs is Barbra Streisand, with 43 (36 albums, 7 singles).

Elvis Presley earned 60 gold and 50 platinum discs, more than any other recording artist. (*London Features International*)

Most recordings A set of 180 compact discs containing the complete authenticated works of Mozart was produced by Philips Classics for release in 1990/91 to commemorate the bicentennial of the composer's death. The complete set comprises over 200 hours of music and would occupy 6½ feet of shelving.

Most Grammy Awards An all-time record 31 awards to an individual (including a special Trustees' award presented in 1967) have been won since 1958 by the Hungarian-born British conductor Sir Georg Solti (b. Budapest, Hungary, October 12, 1912). The most won by a solo pop performer is 17, by Stevie Wonder. The most won by a pop group is eight, by the Fifth Dimension. The largest shared Grammy Award is 46, by the Chicago Symphony. The greatest number won in one year is eight, by Michael Jackson, in 1984.

BIGGEST SELLERS

Singles The greatest seller of any phonograph record to date is *White Christmas* by Irving Berlin, recorded by Bing Crosby on May 29, 1942. North American sales alone reached 170,884,207 copies by June 30, 1987.

The highest claim for any rock record is an unaudited 25 million for *Rock Around the Clock*, copyrighted in 1953 by James E. Myers under the name Jimmy DeKnight and Max C. Freedman and recorded on April 12, 1954 by Bill Haley and the Comets.

Albums The best-selling album of all time is *Thriller* by Michael Jackson, with global sales of over 47 million copies to date. The best-selling album

Bill Haley and the Comets recorded "Rock Around the Clock," the best-selling rock record, in 1954. (*London Features International*)

by a group is Fleetwood Mac's *Rumours* with over 21 million sales by May

1990.

Whitney Houston by Whitney Houston, released in 1985, is the best-selling debut album of all time. It has sold over 14 million copies, including over 9 million in the United States, 1 million in Great Britain, and a further million in Canada.

Classical album The best-selling classical album is *In Concert*, with sales of five million to date. It was recorded by José Carreras, Placido Domingo and Luciano Pavarotti at the 1990 Soccer World Cup Finals in Rome, Italy.

THE CHARTS

U.S. singles Singles record charts were first published by *Billboard* on July 20, 1940, when the No. 1 single was *I'll Never Smile Again* by Tommy Dorsey sung by Frank Sinatra. *Near You* by Francis Craig stayed at the No. 1 spot for 17 weeks in 1947.

The Beatles have had the most No. 1 singles (20), Conway Twitty the most Country No. 1's (40) and Aretha Franklin the most Rhythm and Blues No. 1's (20). Elvis Presley has had the most hit singles on *Billboard*'s Hot 100, with 149 from 1956 to January 1983.

Bing Crosby's *White Christmas* spent a total of 86 weeks on the charts between 1942 and 1962, while *Tainted Love* by Soft Cell stayed on the charts for 43 *consecutive* weeks from January 1982.

The Beatles had 15 No. 1 albums, the record for the United States.
(*London Features International*)

Albums   *Billboard* first published an album chart on March 24, 1945, when the No. 1 was *King Cole Trio* featuring Nat "King" Cole (1919–65). *South Pacific* was No. 1 for 69 weeks (nonconsecutive) from May 1949. *Dark Side of the Moon* by Pink Floyd enjoyed 741 weeks on the *Billboard* charts to October 1988.

The Beatles had the most No. 1 albums (15), Elvis Presley was the most successful male soloist (9), and Simon and Garfunkel was the top duo with 3. Elvis Presley has had the most hit albums, with 92 from 1956 to September 1992.

The woman with the most No. 1 albums (7), and most hit albums in total (43 between 1963 and July 1994), is Barbra Streisand.

Number one in most countries   Madonna reached No. 1 in 28 countries with her album *True Blue*, which sold over 17 million copies.

GUESS WHAT?

Q. WHERE WAS THE GREATEST SNOWFALL?

A. LOOK IN "WEATHER" (EARTH & SPACE)

The album *In Concert* by the three tenors—Luciano Pavarotti, José Carreras and Placido Domingo—is the best-selling classical album in the world. (*Gamma/Kemnerly/Liaison*)

ALL-TIME TOP U.S. SINGLES

Title	Artist	Year	Weeks at No. 1
I'll Make Love to You	Boyz II Men	1994	14
I Will Always Love You	Whitney Houston	1992	14
End of the Road	Boyz II Men	1992	13
Don't Be Cruel/Hound Dog	Elvis Presley	1956	11
I Swear	All-4-One	1994	11
Cherry Pink and Apple Blossom White	Perez Prado	1955	10
Sincerely	The McGuire Sisters	1955	10
Singing the Blues	Guy Mitchell	1956	10
Physical	Olivia Newton-John	1981	10
You Light Up My Life	Debby Boone	1977	10

Radio Research, Inc.

DANCING

Largest dance An estimated 48,000 people took part in a Birdie Dance held during the 1994 Oktoberfest-Zinzinnati in Cincinnati, OH on September 17, 1994.

Longest dance The most taxing marathon dance staged as a public spectacle was by Mike Ritof and Edith Boudreaux, who logged 214 days 12 hr. 28½ min. to win $2,000 at Chicago's Merry Garden Ballroom, Belmont and Sheffield, IL, August 29, 1930–April 1, 1931. Rest periods were progressively cut from 20 to 10 to 5 to zero minutes per hour, with 10-inch steps and a maximum of 15 seconds for closure of eyes.

The longest distance ever danced by one person was 13.1 miles, by Elizabeth Ursic, who tap-danced the Arizona Half Marathon in Tempe, AZ on January 10, 1993.

BRAVO!

Dame Margot Fonteyn and Rudolf Nureyev received 89 curtain calls after a performance of *Swan Lake* at the Vienna Staatsoper, Austria in October 1964.

Rosie Radiator led an ensemble of 12 tap dancers through the streets of San Francisco, CA in a routine covering 9.61 miles on July 11, 1994.

Ballet   *Fastest entrechat douze*   In the *entrechat*, the starting and finishing position each count as one, so that in an *entrechat douze* there are five crossings and uncrossings. This feat was performed by Wayne Sleep for the British Broadcasting Corporation *Record Breakers* TV program on January 7, 1973. He was in the air for 0.71 seconds.

Grands jetés   On November 28, 1988, Wayne Sleep completed 158 *grands jetés* along the length of Dunston Staiths, Gateshead, England in two minutes.

Most turns   The greatest number of spins called for in classical ballet choreography is 32 *fouettés rond de jambe en tournant* in *Swan Lake* by Piotr Ilyich Tchaikovsky (1840–93). Delia Gray (Great Britain) achieved 166 such turns during the Harlow Ballet School's summer workshop at The Playhouse, Harlow, England on June 2, 1991.

Most successful ballroom dancers   The professional ballroom dancing champions Bill and Bobbie Irvine won 13 world titles between 1960 and 1968.

Oldest ballroom dancer   The oldest competitive ballroom dancer was Albert J. Sylvester (1889–1989) of Corsham, England, who retired at age 94.

United States   The oldest competitive ballroom dancer in the United States is Lorna S. Lengfeld, who was still competing at age 90.

Longest conga line   The Miami Super Conga, held in conjunction with Calle Ocho—a party to which Cuban-Americans invite the rest of Miami for a celebration of life together—consisted of 119,986 people. The event was held on March 13, 1988.

Largest country line dance   A total of 2,578 people danced to the "Boot Scootin' Boogie" in Lebanon, TN on July 30, 1994.

Longest dancing dragon   On April 17, 1994, 2,180 people brought to life a dancing dragon measuring 5,114 ft. 10 in. from nose to tail. The dragon danced on a bridge linking Macau with the island of Taipa.

Fastest flamenco dancer   Solero de Jerez attained 16 heel taps per second in Brisbane, Australia in September 1967.

Lowest limbo dancer   Dennis Walston, alias King Limbo, passed under a flaming bar that was just six inches off the floor in Kent, WA on March 2, 1991.

Roller skates   The record for a performer on roller skates is $4^7/_{10}$ inches, achieved by Syamala Gowri in Hyderabad, Andhra Pradesh, India on May 10, 1993.

Square dance calling   Alan Covacic called for 26 hr. 2 min. for the Wheelers and Dealers Square Dance Club at Halton Royal Air Force Base, Aylesbury, England, November 18–19, 1988.

Tap   Fastest tap dancer   The fastest rate ever measured for tap dancing is 32 taps per second, by Stephen Gare of Sutton Coldfield, England at the Grand Hotel, Birmingham, England on March 28, 1990.

United States   The fastest rate measured for a tap dancer in the United States is 28 taps per second, by Michael Flatley of Palos Park, IL on May 9, 1989.

Most taps   Roy Castle achieved one million taps in 23 hr. 44 min. at the Guinness World of Records exhibition, London, England, October 31–November 1, 1985.

Most tap dancers in a single routine   On August 21, 1994, 6,252 tap dancers tapped through a single routine outside Macy's department store at 34th Street and Sixth Avenue, New York City.

THEATER

Oldest indoor theater   The Teatro Olimpico in Vicenza, Italy was designed in the Roman style by Andrea di Pietro, alias Palladio (1508–80). It was begun three months before his death and finished in 1583. The theater is preserved today in its original form.

Largest theater   The Perth Entertainment Center, Western Australia is the largest theater measured by capacity. It was completed in November 1976 and has 8,003 seats. The stage area is 12,000 square feet.

United States   The highest-capacity theater currently in use on Broadway is the Gershwin Theater, with 1,933 seats. Designed by Ralph Alswang, the theater opened on November 28, 1972.

Amphitheater   The Flavian amphitheater or Colosseum of Rome, Italy, completed in A.D. 80, covers five acres and has a capacity of 87,000. It has a maximum length of 612 feet and a maximum width of 515 feet.

Smallest theater   The smallest regularly operated professional theater in the world is the Piccolo in Juliusstrasse, Hamburg, Germany. It was founded in 1970 and has a maximum capacity of 30 seats.

Largest stage   The largest stage in the world is the Hilton Theater at the Reno Hilton, Reno, NV, which measures 175 by 241 feet. The stage has three main elevators each capable of raising 1,200 performers (40 tons), two 62½-foot-circumference turntables and 800 spotlights.

Longest runs   The longest continuously running show is *The Mousetrap* by Agatha Christie. This thriller opened on November 25, 1952 at the Ambassadors Theatre, London, England (capacity 453) and moved after 8,862 performances to the St. Martin's Theatre next door on March 25, 1974.

The 17,256th performance was on May 9, 1994, and the box office total was £20 million ($36 million) from more than 9 million attenders.

The Vicksburg Theater Guild, Vicksburg, MS has been playing the melodrama *Gold in the Hills* by J. Frank Davis discontinuously but every season since 1936.

Revue The greatest number of performances of any theatrical presentation is 47,250 (to April 1986) in the case of *The Golden Horseshoe Revue*, a show staged at Disneyland, Anaheim, CA. It started on July 16, 1955 and closed on October 12, 1986 after being seen by 16 million people.

DID YOU KNOW?

Hamlet is the longest of Shakespeare's 37 plays. Written in 1604, it has 4,042 lines or 29,551 words. The longest of Shakespeare's 1,277 speaking parts is the role of Hamlet, with 11,610 words.

Musicals The off-Broadway musical show *The Fantasticks* by Tom Jones and Harvey Schmidt opened on May 3, 1960, and celebrated its 35th anniversary on May 3, 1995. As of that date, the show had been performed a record 14,488 times at the Sullivan Street Playhouse, Greenwich Village, New York City.

Most ardent theatergoer Dr. H. Howard Hughes, Prof. Emeritus of Texas Wesleyan College, Fort Worth, TX attended 6,136 shows in the period 1957–87.

Greatest loss The greatest loss sustained by a theatrical show was by the American producers of the Royal Shakespeare Company's musical *Carrie*, which closed after five performances on Broadway on May 17, 1988 at a cost of $7 million.

Tony Awards Harold Prince has won 13 Tonys—the awards of the American Theater Wing—the most for any individual. Prince has won a total of 6 awards as a producer and 7 as a director.

Three plays share the record for most Tonys, with five: *A Man for All Seasons* (1962), *Who's Afraid of Virginia Woolf?* (1963) and *Amadeus* (1981).

The only person to win five Tonys in starring roles is Julie Harris, in *I Am a Camera* (1952), *The Lark* (1956), *Forty Carats* (1969), *The Last of Mrs. Lincoln* (1973) and *The Belle of Amherst* (1977).

One-man shows The longest run of one-man shows is 849, by Victor Borge (Denmark) in his *Comedy in Music* from October 2, 1953 through January 21, 1956 at the Golden Theater, Broadway, New York City.

The world aggregate record for one-man shows is 1,700 performances of *Brief Lives* by Roy Dotrice (Great Britain), including 400 straight at the Mayfair Theatre, London, England ending on July 20, 1974. He was on

stage for more than 2½ hours per performance of this 17th-century mono-
logue and required 3 hours for makeup and 1 hour for removal of makeup,
thus totaling 40 weeks in the chair.

Most durable performer Kanmi Fujiyama played the lead role in 10,288
performances by the comedy company Sochiku Shikigeki from November
1966 to June 1983.

Most durable understudy On March 12, 1994, Nancy Seabrooke, age 79,
retired from the company of *The Mousetrap* in London, England after having understudied the part of "Mrs. Boyle" for 15 years or 6,240 performances.

Greatest advance sales The musical *Miss Saigon*, produced by Cameron
Mackintosh and starring Jonathan Pryce and Lea Salonga, opened on
Broadway in April 1991 after generating record advance sales of $36 mil-
lion.

Most roles The greatest recorded number of theatrical, film and television
roles portrayed is 3,389 since 1951 by Jan Leighton (U.S.).

Theatrical roles Kanzaburo Nakamura performed in 806 Kabuki titles
from November 1926 to January 1987. Since each title in this classical
Japanese theatrical form lasts 25 days, he gave 20,150 performances.

Longest chorus lines The longest chorus line in performing history numbered up to 120 in some of the early *Ziegfeld Follies*. In the finale of *A Chorus Line* on the night of September 29, 1983, when it broke the record as
the longest-running Broadway show ever, 332 top-hatted "strutters" performed on stage.

On March 28, 1992 at the Swan Center, Eastleigh, England, 543 mem-
bers of the castof *Showtime News*, a production by Hampshire West
Guides, performed a routine choreographed by professional dancer Sally
Horsley.

Largest arts festival The Edinburgh Fringe Festival is held annually in Edinburgh, Scotland (instituted in 1947). In 1993, its record year, 582 groups
gave 14,108 performances of 1,643 shows between August 15 and September 4. Nigel Tantrum of East Kilbride, Scotland attended a record 169 separate performances at the 1994 Edinburgh Festival.

Fashion shows The greatest distance covered by a model on a catwalk is
83.1 miles, by Eddie Warke at Parke's Hotel, Dublin, Republic of Ireland,
September 19–21, 1983. The record by female models is 71.1 miles, by
Roberta Brown and Lorraine McCourt on the same occasion.

Fastest magician Eldon D. Wigton, alias Dr. Eldoonie, performed 225 different tricks in two minutes in Kilbourne, OH on April 21, 1991.

PHOTOGRAPHY

Oldest photograph In 1827, Joseph Niépce used a camera obscura to take a photograph of the view from the window of his home. The photo is now in the Gernsheim Collection at the University of Texas, Austin, TX.

Most expensive photograph A photograph by Alfred Stieglitz of the hands of his wife, Georgia O'Keeffe, called *Georgia O'Keeffe–A Portrait with Symbol*, was sold at Christie's, New York City on October 8, 1993 for a record $398,500.

CAMERAS

Largest camera The largest and most expensive industrial camera ever built is the 30-ton Rolls-Royce camera now owned by BDC Holdings Ltd. of Derby, England. It was commissioned in 1956, and measures 8 ft. 10 in. high, 8¼ feet wide and 46 feet long. The lens is a 63-inch f16 Cooke Apochromatic.

A pinhole camera was created from a Portakabin unit measuring 34 by 9½ by 9 feet by photographers John Kippen and Chris Wainwright at the National Museum of Photography, Film and Television in Bradford, England on March 25, 1990. The unit produced a direct positive measuring 33 feet by 4 ft. 2 in.

Largest lens The National Museum of Photography, Film and Television, Bradford, England displays the largest lens, made by Pilkington Special Glass Ltd., St. Asaph, Wales. Its dimensions are: focal length 333 inches, diameter 54 inches, weight 474 pounds. Its focal length allows writing on the museum's walls to be read from a distance of 40 feet.

The largest camera lens is on display at the National Museum of Photography, Film & Television, Bradford, England. (*N.M.P.F.T*)

Fastest camera   A camera built for research into high-power lasers by The Blackett Laboratory of Imperial College of Science and Technology, London, England registers images at a rate of 33 billion per second. The fastest production camera is currently the Imacon 675, made by Hadland Photonics Ltd. of Bovington, England, at up to 600 million frames per second.

Camera auction   The record total for any camera auction is £296,043 ($503,000) for a collection of "spy," subminiature and detective cameras sold at Christie's, London, England on December 9, 1991.

The highest auction price for a camera is $58,727 for a gold camera custom-made for Sultan Abdul Aziz of Morocco in 1901. It was sold at Christie's, London, England on November 25, 1993.

Longest negative   On May 6, 1992, Thomas Bleich of Austin, TX produced a negative measuring 23 ft. 4$\frac{1}{2}$ in. by 10$\frac{1}{2}$ inches using a 10$\frac{1}{2}$-inch focal length Turner-Reich lens and Kodak No. 10 Cirkut Camera. The photograph was a portrait of 3,500 concert attendants in Austin.

CLICK!

Apart from cameras built for espionage and intracardiac surgery, the smallest that has been marketed is the circular Japanese "Petal" camera, with a diameter of 1.14 inches and a thickness of 0.65 inches. It has a focal length of 0.47 inches.

CINEMA

FILMS

Earliest film   The earliest motion pictures were made by Louis Aimé Augustin Le Prince (1842–90), who was attested to have achieved dim moving outlines on a whitewashed wall at the Institute for the Deaf, Washington Heights, New York City as early as 1885–1887. The oldest surviving film (sensitized 2$\frac{1}{8}$-inch-wide paper roll) is from his camera; it was taken of the garden of his father-in-law, Joseph Whitley, in early October 1888, in Roundhay, England at 10 to 12 frames per second.

Earliest feature film   The world's first full-length feature film was *The Story of the Kelly Gang*, made in Melbourne, Australia in 1906. Produced on a budget of £450, this biography of the notorious armored bushranger Ned Kelly (1855–80) ran for 60–70 minutes and opened at the Melbourne Town Hall on December 26, 1906. It was produced by the local theatrical company J. and N. Tait.

Earliest "talkie" The earliest sound-on-film motion picture was made by Eugene-Augustin Lauste, who patented his process on August 11, 1906 and produced a workable system using a string galvanometer in 1910 in Benedict Road, London, England. The earliest public presentation of sound on film was by the Tri-ergon process at the Alhambra Theater, Berlin, Germany on September 17, 1922.

United States The earliest screening of a sound-on-picture motion picture in the United States for a paying audience was at the Rivoli Theater in New York City on April 15, 1923. The first all-talking motion picture was Warner Brothers' *Lights of New York*, shown at the Strand Theater, New York City on July 6, 1928.

India produces more feature-length films than any other country. (*Gamma/Bartholomew/Liaison*)

Country with largest output India produces more feature-length films than any other country, with an average of 930 produced every year and more than 26,000 released since 1913.

United States In the United States, 420 films were released in 1995; 491 were produced in 1988, the most in a year since 1968.

Most expensive film The most expensive film ever produced was Universal's *Waterworld* (U.S., 1995), directed by Kevin Reynolds and starring Kevin Costner and Dennis Hopper, which cost $175 million. Extraordinary special effects and schedule overruns contributed to the huge costs.

In terms of real costs adjusted for inflation, the most expensive film ever made was *Cleopatra* (U.S., 1963), whose $44 million budget would be equivalent to over $200 million in 1993.

Most expensive film rights   The highest price ever paid for film rights was $9.5 million, announced on January 20, 1978 by Columbia, for *Annie*, the Broadway musical by Charles Strouse.

Longest film   The longest film commercially released in its entirety was Edgar Reitz's 25-hr.-32-min. *Die Zweite Heimat* (Germany, 1992), premiered in Munich, September 5–9, 1992.

Highest box office gross   As of April 21, 1995, Universal's *Jurassic Park* had earned $912.8 million ($356.8 million in North America; $556 million elsewhere).

Annual   In 1994, domestic box-office receipts in the United States were $5.4 billion, an all-time high.

Batman Returns (Warner Brothers) set an opening-day record of $16.1 million on June 19, 1992. On June 12, 1993, *Jurassic Park* shattered the single-day record, with a final domestic gross of $17.6 million.

Foreign language   The highest-grossing foreign language film in the United States is Alfonso Arau's *Like Water for Chocolate*, which had a final domestic gross of $21.7 million as of April 21, 1995.

Largest film premiere   *A Few Good Men*, starring Tom Cruise, Demi Moore and Jack Nicholson, was released simultaneously in over 50 countries by Columbia Pictures in December 1992.

Largest loss   It cost a total $124,053,994 to produce, promote and distribute *Last Action Hero* (Columbia; U.S., 1993). The film, starring Arnold Schwarzenegger, is estimated to have earned $44 million worldwide, creating a resounding loss of some $80 million.

GUESS WHAT?

Q. WHICH COMPANY REPORTED THE WORST TRADING LOSS?

A. LOOK IN "COMMERCE" (BUSINESS & LAW)

Highest earnings   Jack Nicholson stood to receive up to $60 million for playing "The Joker" in Warner Brothers' $50 million *Batman*, through a percentage of the film's receipts in lieu of salary.

Most durable series   The longest series of films is the 103 features made in Hong Kong about the 19th-century martial arts hero Huang Fei-Hong, starting with *The True Story of Huang Fei-Hong* (1949) and continuing through *Once Upon a Time in China 5* (1995). The most durable continuing series with the same star is Shockiku Studios of Japan's 46 *Tora-San* comedy films, featuring Kiyoshi Atsumi (b. 1929) in a Chaplinesque role from August 1969 to December 1992.

HORRORS

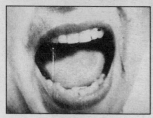

Psycho, 1960. (Kobal Collection)

The first influential horror films were produced in Germany shortly before World War I. In the 1920s, the U.S. was making films with such well-known titles as *Dr. Jekyll and Mr. Hyde, The Hunchback of Notre Dame* and *The Phantom of the Opera*. A decade later, *Dracula, Frankenstein* and *King Kong* were terrifying audiences around the globe. The peak year for horror film production was 1972, when 189 films were made, 83 of them U.S. productions.

William Peter Blatty, author of *The Exorcist* (1973), has grossed more than any other novelist in film history. The total amount earned by Blatty is not known, but he received 40 percent of the gross profits—in North American rentals alone, *The Exorcist* has grossed over $89 million.

Created by Irish writer Bram Stoker (1847–1912), Dracula is the most frequently portrayed character in horror films. Appearances of the Count, or his near relatives, outnumber those of his closest rival, Frankenstein's monster, by 161 to 117.

The shower scene in *Psycho* (1960), with its distinctive music, is probably one of the most memorable in horror film history. The scene involved 70 camera set-ups for 45 seconds of edited footage and took seven days to shoot.

Winona Ryder in *Bram Stoker's Dracula*, 1994. (*Kobal Collection*)

Bela Lugosi in *Dracula*, 1931. (*Kobal Collection*)

Max von Sydow in *The Exorcist*, 1973. (*Kobal Collection*)

Brad Pitt in *Interview with the Vampire*, 1994. (*Kobal Collection*)

Most profitable series   The most successful movie series is the 18 James Bond films, from *Dr. No* (1962) starring Sean Connery to *License to Kill* (1989) with Timothy Dalton. The series grossed over $1 billion worldwide.

Largest studios   The largest complex of film studios in the world is the one at Universal City, Los Angeles, CA. The back lot contains 479 buildings and there are 31 sound stages on the 420-acre site.

Largest studio stage   The 007 stage at Pinewood Studios, Buckinghamshire, England was designed by Michael Brown for producer Albert R. Broccoli and set creator Ken Adam. It was built in 1976 for the James Bond film *The Spy Who Loved Me*. It measures 336 by 139 by 41 feet and can accommodate 1.2 million gallons of water, a full-scale 672,000-ton oil tanker and 3 scaled-down nuclear submarines.

Largest film set   Veniero Colosanti and John Moore designed a Roman Forum measuring 1,312 by 754 feet for Samuel Bronston's production of *The Fall of the Roman Empire* (1964). It was built on a 55-acre site outside Madrid, Spain. It took 1,100 workmen seven months to lay the surface of the Forum with 170,000 cement blocks, erect 22,000 feet of concrete stairways, 601 columns and 350 statues, and construct 27 full-size buildings.

Largest number of extras   It is believed that over 300,000 extras appeared in the funeral scene of Sir Richard Attenborough's *Gandhi* (1982).

Most expensive prop   The highest price paid at auction for a film prop is $275,000 at Sotheby's, New York City on June 28, 1986 for James Bond's Aston Martin DB5 from *Goldfinger* (Great Britain, 1964).

Longest directorial career   The directorial career of King Vidor lasted for 67 years, beginning with the 2-reel comedy *Hurricane in Galveston* (1913) and culminating in another short, a documentary called *The Metaphor* (1980).

Oldest director   The Dutch director Joris Ivens (1898–1989) made the Franco-Italian co-production *Une Histoire de Vent* in 1988 at age 89. He made his directorial debut with the Dutch film *De Brug* in 1928. Hollywood's oldest director was George Cukor, who made his 50th and final film, MGM's *Rich and Famous*, in 1981 at age 81.

Youngest director   The film *Lex the Wonderdog*, a thriller of canine detection, was written, produced, and directed by Sydney Ling (b. 1959) when he was 13 years old. Ling was therefore the youngest-ever director of a professionally made feature-length film.

Most successful director   Steven Spielberg is the most successful filmmaker ever, with seven movies in the all-time top 10. Collectively, his films have grossed more than $2.17 billion. *Schindler's List*, Spielberg's masterful and moving portrayal of the Holocaust, won him his first "Best Director" Oscar.

Entertainment Salaries

Entertainer	Gross annual income
Steven Spielberg	$165,000,000
Pink Floyd	56,000,000
Oprah Winfrey	53,000,000
Eagles	52,000,000
Barbra Streisand	52,000,000
Rolling Stones	50,000,000
Bill Cosby	34,000,000
David Copperfield	29,000,000
Harrison Ford	27,000,000
Barney the Dinosaur (Creator: S. Leach; Publisher: R. Leach)	25,000,000

Forbes, 1994

Oldest performer   The oldest screen performer in a speaking role was Jeanne Louise Calment (b. 1875–*fl.* April 1995), who portrayed herself in the 1990 Canadian film *Vincent and Me*. Calment is the oldest living person and the last living person to have known Vincent van Gogh.

Most durable performers   The record for the longest screen career is 83 years, held by German actor Curt Bois (1900–91), who made his debut in *Der Fidele Bauer* at age eight; one of his most recent films is *Wings of Desire* (1988). American actress Helen Hayes (1900–93) first appeared on screen at age 10 in *Jean and the Calico Doll*, with much of her later work being for television. Her last screen role was in *Divine Mercy, No Escape* (1988) in a career lasting 78 years. The most enduring star of the big screen was Lillian Gish (1893–1993—although her birthdate is usually given as 1896). She made her debut in *An Unseen Enemy* (1912), and her last film in a career spanning 75 years was *The Whales of August* (1987).

Most generations of screen actors   There are four generations of screen actors in the Redgrave family. Roy Redgrave made his screen debut in 1911 and continued to appear in Australian films until 1920. His son, Sir Michael Redgrave, married actress Rachel Kempson, and their two daughters Vanessa and Lynn and son Corin are all actors. Vanessa's two daughters, Joely and Natasha, and Corin's daughter Jemma, are also actresses.

Most portrayed character   The character most frequently recurring on the screen is Sherlock Holmes, created by Sir Arthur Conan Doyle (1859–1930). The Baker Street sleuth has been portrayed by some 75 actors in over 211 films since 1900.

In horror films, the character most often portrayed is Count Dracula, created by the Irish writer Bram Stoker (1847–1912). Representations of the Count or his immediate descendants outnumber those of his closest rival, Frankenstein's monster, by 161 to 117.

Most films seen   Gwilym Hughes of Dolgellau, Wales had seen 22,118 films on video by March 29, 1995. He saw his first film in 1953.

Most costumes   The largest number of costumes used for any one film was 32,000 for the 1951 film *Quo Vadis*.

Most costume changes   Elizabeth Taylor changed costume 65 times in *Cleopatra* (1963). The costumes were designed by Irene Sharaff and cost $130,000.

The film that won the most Oscars in 1995 was *Forrest Gump*, with six awards out of 13 nominations: best picture; best director (Robert Zemeckis); best actor (Tom Hanks); best adapted screenplay; best editing; and best visual effects. (*London Features International/Gregg De Guire*)

Most expensive costume   Constance Bennett's sable coat in *Madame X* was valued at $50,000. The most expensive costume designed and made specially for a film was Edith Head's mink-and-sequin dance costume worn by Ginger Rogers in *Lady in the Dark*. It cost Paramount $35,000. The ruby slippers, a personal prop worn by Judy Garland in the 1939 film *The Wizard of Oz*, were sold on June 2, 1988 to a mystery buyer at Christie's, New York City for $165,000.

Highest-paid stunt performer   Stuntman Dar Robinson was paid $100,000 for the 1,000-foot leap from the CN Tower, Toronto, Canada in November 1979 for *High Point*. His parachute opened just 300 feet above the ground.

Oscar winners   Walt Disney (1901–66) won more Oscars—the awards of the Academy of Motion Picture Arts and Sciences, instituted on May 16, 1929—than any other person. The physical count comprises 20 statuettes and 12 other plaques and certificates, including posthumous awards.

The only person to win four Oscars in starring roles is Katharine Hepburn, for *Morning Glory* (1932/33), *Guess Who's Coming to Dinner* (1967), *The Lion in Winter* (1968) and *On Golden Pond* (1981). She has been nominated 12 times. Edith Head (1907–81) won eight individual awards for costume design.

The film with the most awards is *Ben Hur* (1959) with 11. The film with the most nominations was *All About Eve* (1950) with 14. It won 6 awards.

The film that won the most awards in 1995 was *Forrest Gump* with six awards out of 13 nominations: best picture; best director (Robert Zemeckis); best actor (Tom Hanks); best adapted screenplay; best editing; and best visual effects.

Youngest winners   The youngest winner in competition was Tatum O'Neal, who was 10 when she received the award in 1974 for Best Supporting Actress in *Paper Moon* (1973). Shirley Temple was awarded an honorary Oscar at age five in 1934.

Oldest winner   The oldest recipient of an Oscar was Jessica Tandy, who won Best Actress for *Driving Miss Daisy* in 1990 at the age of 80.

MOVIE THEATERS

Largest movie theater audience   China had mainland attendance figures of 14 billion in 1991, compared with a peak of 21.8 billion in 1988.

DID YOU KNOW?

The largest movie theater in the world is the Radio City Music Hall, New York City, opened on December 27, 1932, with 5,945 (now 5,874) seats. Kinepolis, the first eight screens of which opened in Brussels, Belgium in 1988, is the world's largest theater complex. It has 24 screens and a total seating capacity of 7,000.

Biggest screen The largest permanently installed theater screen was opened on April 20, 1984. It has an area of 96 by 70½ feet and is located at the Keong Emas Imax Theatre, Taman Mini Park, Jakarta, Indonesia. The Six Flags Great America Pictorium, Gurnee, IL, opened in 1979, has a screen of equal size, but it is 3D. A temporary screen measuring 297 by 33 feet was used at the 1937 Paris Exposition in France.

VIDEO

Best-selling video The world's best-selling video is Walt Disney's animated feature *Aladdin*, which was released in North America in October 1993 and had sold over 41 million copies worldwide through May 1, 1995. The best-selling video in North America is Walt Disney's *Lion King*, released in 1994, which had sold 26 million copies on that continent through May 1, 1995.

Fastest video production Tapes of the Royal Wedding of Prince Andrew and Sarah Ferguson on July 23, 1986 were produced by Thames Video Collection. Live filming ended with the departure of the honeymoon couple from Chelsea Hospital by helicopter at 4:42 P.M. The first fully edited and packaged VHS tapes were purchased 5 hr. 41 min. later at the Virgin Megastore on Oxford Street, London, England at 10:23 P.M.

RADIO

First wireless station The first permanent wireless installation was constructed on the Isle of Wight, Great Britain, by Marconi's Wireless Telegraph Co. Ltd., in November 1897.

Most durable programs *Rambling with Gambling*, the early morning program on WOR, New York City, was first broadcast in March 1925 and celebrated its 21,881st show on April 30, 1995. The show has been hosted by three generations of the Gambling family: John B. Gambling (1925–59), John A. Gambling (1959–present) and John R. Gambling (1985–present). The show currently airs six days a week, year-round.

The Grand Ole Opry has broadcast continuously from November 28, 1925 to May 8, 1995, and celebrates its 70th anniversary on November 28, 1995.

The weekly sports report "The Tenpin Tattler" was first broadcast on WCFL, Chicago, IL on August 24, 1935. Sixty years or 3,100 broadcasts later, it continues on WGN, Chicago with the original host, Sam Weinstein, who is the longest continuing host of a program.

Longest continuous radio broadcast Radio Telefis Eireann transmitted an unedited reading of *Ulysses* by James Joyce for 29 hr. 38 min. 47 sec. on July 16–17, 1982.

Most hours broadcast per week Larry King's radio and television programs were broadcast a combined 36 hours per week from 1985 through May 27,

1994. From May 30, 1994 through the present, King's television show has aired simultaneously on radio and television six hours per week in 200 countries.

Most radio stations   The United States has more radio broadcasting stations than any other country. As of May 8, 1995, there were 11,811 authorized broadcast stations, made up of 4,911 AM stations, 5,150 commercial FM stations and 1,750 FM educational stations.

GUESS WHAT?

Q. WHERE IS THE WORLD'S LARGEST RADIO DISK?

A. LOOK IN "TELESCOPES" (SCIENCE & TECHNOLOGY)

Largest audience   Surveys carried out in over 100 countries showed that, in 1994, the global estimated audience for the British Broadcasting Corporation World Service was 133 million regular listeners—greater than any other international broadcaster. The World Service is now broadcast in 41 languages.

Largest response   The largest recorded response to a radio show occurred June 21–27, 1993, when FM Osaka 85.1 in Osaka, Japan received a total of 8,091,309 calls in response to a phone-in lottery. The prize was 100,000 yen (around $1,500), and a chance to win it was offered for a 20-minute period every hour, for 10 hours each day. The maximum call count in one day of phone-ins (3 hr. 20 min.) was 1,540,793 on June 23, 1993.

Biggest radio prize   Mary Buchanan, 15, won a prize of $25,000 for 40 years (or $1 million) on WKRQ Cincinnati on November 21, 1980.

Most assiduous radio ham   The late Richard C. Spenceley of KV4AA in St. Thomas, VI built his contacts (QSOs) to a record level of 48,100 in 365 days in 1978.

TELEVISION

At the end of 1992, there were 1,125 commercial and educational licensed television stations in the United States.

First public demonstration of television   John Logie Baird of Scotland gave a demonstration on January 27, 1926 using a development of the mechanical scanning system patented by Paul Gottlieb Nipkow on January 6, 1884.

Most durable shows   The most durable TV show is NBC's *Meet the Press*, first transmitted on November 6, 1947 and broadcast weekly since September 12, 1948. As of April 17, 1995, 2,391 shows had been broadcast.

The last televised broadcast of the *Joe Franklin Show* aired in August 1993. Starting in 1951, Franklin hosted 31,015 episodes of the show and conducted 309,136 interviews.

Stock Market Observer is the longest-running television show in terms of total hours of air time. Since August 1967, it has broadcast more than 39,779 hours of New York Stock Exchange floor trading.

Most episodes   Since 1949, over 150,000 individual episodes of the TV show *Bozo the Clown*, by Larry Harmon Pictures, have been aired daily on 150 stations in the United States and abroad.

Most hours on camera   The greatest number of hours on camera on U.S. national television is 10,394 hours by the TV personality Hugh Downs in 48 years up to April 7, 1995.

Most spinoffs   The U.S. television series with the most spinoffs is *Star Trek*, which has evolved into a total of five syndicated programs: *Star Trek* (1966–69), *Star Trek* animated cartoon (1973–75), *Star Trek: The Next Generation* (1987–94), *Star Trek: Deep Space Nine* (1993–present) and *Star Trek: Voyager* (1995–present). *Star Trek* has also spawned seven feature films.

Greatest audience   On January 30, 1994, 134.4 million viewers watched Super Bowl XXVIII.

The program that attracted the highest-ever rating share was the "Goodbye, Farewell and Amen" final episode of *M*A*S*H*, transmitted by CBS on February 28, 1983 to 60.3 percent of all households in the United States. It was estimated that some 125 million people tuned in, taking a 77 percent share of all viewing.

Most watched show   *Baywatch*, with an estimated weekly audience of 2,396,839,980 people throughout 103 countries, claims to be the most

***Baywatch* is broadcast on every continent except Antarctica. (© 1994 All American TV, Inc.)**

widely watched television show in the world. The show is viewed in every continent except Antarctica.

Highest rated talk show   *The Oprah Winfrey Show*, with Oprah Winfrey as host, has led all talk shows in ratings for a record eight consecutive seasons spanning 1986–94.

Most expensive television rights   In November 1991, it was reported that a group of U.S. and European investors, led by CBS, had paid $8 million for the television rights to *Scarlett*, the sequel to Margaret Mitchell's *Gone With the Wind*, written by Alexandra Ripley.

Most Emmy Awards   The most Emmys won by any individual is 16, by television producer Dwight Arlington Hemion. He also holds the record for most nominations, with 37. *Sesame Street* (PBS) has won the most awards for a series, with 58 between 1970 and 1995. *Cheers* has received the most nominations, with 117 (winning 27) between 1983 and 1993. The most Emmys awarded to a miniseries was 9, to *Roots* (ABC) in 1977. In 1977, *Eleanor and Franklin: The White House Years* (ABC) received the most Emmys, 11, for a television movie. Columbia Broadcasting System (CBS) holds the record for most Emmys won by a network in a single season, with 44, 1973–74.

Most expensive TV production   *War and Remembrance* was the most expensive TV production ever, costing $110 million. This 14-episode miniseries was aired by ABC in two parts in November 1988 and March 1989, and won the 1989 Emmy award for best mini-series. Shooting took three years to complete.

Biggest TV program sale   The greatest number of episodes of any TV program ever sold was 1,144 episodes of *Coronation Street* by Granada Television to CBKST Saskatoon, Saskatchewan, Canada, on May 31, 1971. This constituted 20 days 15 hr. 44 min. of continuous viewing.

The Oprah Winfrey Show had the highest ratings of any talk show for eight consecutive seasons, 1986–94. (*Stephen Green © 1994, Harpo Production, Inc.*)

ENGAGE!

STAR TREK EXPLORES A NEW RECORD

The original *Enterprise* from *Star Trek* (© 1992 Paramount Pictures)

The original *Star Trek* science fiction series, created in 1966 by Gene Roddenberry, was canceled after three seasons and reached a peak rating of only 52. Nearly 30 years, five television series and seven profitable films later, *Star Trek* continues to go where no one has gone before.

Each year, *Star Trek* conventions draw thousands of "Trekkies" who listen to guest speakers, watch show outtakes and purchase untold billions of dollars worth of merchandising, ranging from Vulcan pointy ears to telephones in the shape of the show's famed ship, the *U.S.S. Enterprise*. There are no fewer than 18 *Star Trek*-related fan clubs in the United States, the largest of which, "Star Trek: The Official Fan Club," boasts 50,000 members.

From a technological standpoint, the original *Star Trek* (1966–69) was ahead of its time in predicting innovations, presenting concepts that are commonplace items in the 1990s: desktop computers, CD-ROMs and MRI machines. The second show, *Star Trek: The Next Generation* (1987–94), depicted time continuum disruptions, a holodeck room—in which people and places could be realistically recreated—and even an *Enterprise* that could separate into two crafts in an emergency.

Although *Star Trek: The Next Generation* aired its last television episode in 1994, its ongoing mission has traveled at warp speed to the big screen with *Star Trek: Generations*.

The film starred Patrick Stewart as the stalwart Captain Jean-Luc Picard and featured characters from the original series—most prominently, William Shatner as the fearless Captain James T. Kirk. Currently, two hit shows remain on first run syndicated television: *Star Trek: Deep Space Nine*, headed by Avery Brooks as Commander Benjamin Cisko; and *Star Trek: Voyager*, starring Kate Mulgrew as Captain Kathryn Janeway.

The cast of *Star Trek: The Next Generation* (© 1992 Paramount Pictures)

With *Star Trek* television shows, films, videos, books, games, comics, merchandising and even CD-ROM and Internet projects constantly bombarding the market, it's safe to say that Gene Roddenberry's brainchild will live long and prosper.

The cast of *Star Trek* (© 1992 Paramount Pictures)

Most spinoffs   The U.S. television series with the most spinoffs is *Star Trek*, which has evolved into a total of five syndicated programs: *Star Trek* (1966–69), *Star Trek* animated cartoon (1973–75), *Star Trek: The Next Generation* (1987–94), *Star Trek: Deep Space Nine* (1993–present) and *Star Trek: Voyager* (1995–present). *Star Trek* has also spawned seven feature films.

Most prolific TV scriptwriter The most prolific television writer in the world was the Rt. Hon. Lord Willis (1918–92). He created 41 series, 37 stage plays and 39 feature films, and had 29 plays produced. His total output since 1942 was estimated to be 20 million words.

Most prolific TV producer The most prolific producer in television history was game show producer Mark Goodson. Goodson produced over 39,000 episodes totaling more than 21,240 hours of airtime.

Aaron Spelling has produced more than 2,993.5 TV episodes totaling 2,576.5 hours of air time.

Largest TV set The Sony Jumbo Tron color TV screen at the Tsukuba International Exposition '85 near Tokyo, Japan in March 1985 measured 80 by 150 feet.

Smallest TV set The Seiko TV-Wrist Watch, launched on December 23, 1982 in Japan, has a 1.2-inch screen and weighs only 2.8 ounces. Including the receiver unit and headphones, the entire black and white system, costing 108,000 yen ($1,038), weighs only 11.3 ounces.

The smallest single-piece set is the Casio-Keisanki TV-10, weighing 11.9 ounces with a 2.7-inch screen, launched in Tokyo in July 1983.

The smallest and lightest color set is the Casio CV-1, launched by the Casio Computer Co. Ltd. of Japan in 1992, with dimensions of 2.4 by 0.9 by 3.6 inches, weighing, with batteries, only six ounces. It has a screen size of 1.4 inches and retails in Japan for 40,000 yen (about $350).

ADVERTISING

TELEVISION

Highest TV advertising rate The highest TV advertising rate was $2.2 million per minute for ABC network prime time during the transmission of Super Bowl XXIX on January 29, 1995, watched by 120 million viewers.

Shortest TV commercial An advertisement lasting only four frames (there are 30 frames in a second) was aired on KING-TV's *Evening Magazine* on November 29, 1993. The ad was for Bon Marche's Frango candies, and cost $3,780 to make.

Fastest production A 30-second TV advertisement for Reebok Insta-PUMP shoes, starring Emmitt Smith of the Dallas Cowboys, was created, filmed and aired during Super Bowl XXVII on January 31, 1993. Filming continued until the beginning of the fourth quarter, editing began in the middle of the third quarter, and the finished product was aired during the commercial break at the 2-minute warning of the fourth quarter.

Longest-running commercial characters Jan Miner appeared in U.S. TV commercials as "Madge the Manicurist" from 1965 to 1991, and Dick Wilson, alias "Mr. Whipple," from 1964 to 1989.

NEST FULL OF EMMYS

If there were a TV Olympics, *Sesame Street* would win the gold medal. With 58 Emmy awards (the runner-up, *The Mary Tyler Moore Show*, earned 29), the show holds the record for endurance, achievement, and, most would agree, contagious charm. And it stars the biggest bird around.

Caroll Spinney has filled Big Bird's shoes—literally—since the 8-foot-2-inch puppet was created by Jim Henson. "I'm 61," says Spinney, "but Big Bird will always be six years old." *Sesame Street* owes much of its success to the Muppets, and to a carefully conceived approach to sharing basic concepts with young children. "It's a combination of the right people doing the right thing, with so much humor and thought," explains Spinney. If a bit of adult attitude informs this preschool program, that's all to the good. "We make a deliberate attempt to keep the parent in the room. If a parent can sit and chuckle and talk about the show, the child gets more out of it and learns more."

To become Big Bird, Spinney stands inside Big Bird's legs and reaches his right arm high to control Big Bird's head, which is essentially a hand puppet. "Big Bird has all the sweetness and compassion and confusion of a child who's learning to read or roller-skate." Big Bird's charm has taken him to the White House during five administrations (Nixon, Ford, Carter, Reagan and Bush)—and Hillary Rodham Clinton came to *Sesame Street* to meet him. "We'll make it to a 35th anniversary with this show, that's certain. *Sesame Street* doesn't get old."

Most Emmy Awards
Sesame Street (PBS) has won the most awards for a series, with 58 between 1970 and 1995.

(Big Bird © Jim Henson Productions, Inc.)

SIGNS

Highest advertising sign   The highest advertising sign is the logo "I" at the top of the 73-story, 1,017-foot-tall First Interstate World Center building, Los Angeles, CA.

Most visible advertising sign   The electric Citroën sign on the Eiffel Tower, Paris, France was switched on on July 4, 1925, and could be seen 24 miles away. It was in six colors with 250,000 bulbs and 56 miles of electric cables. The letter "N" in "Citroën" measured 68 ft. 5 in. high. The whole apparatus was dismantled in 1936.

Largest and tallest freestanding advertising sign   The sign at the Hilton Hotel and Casino in Las Vegas, NV was completed in December 1993. Its two faces had a total area of 82,328 square feet and it was 362 feet high when completed, but it was damaged in a storm on July 18, 1994, and part of it fell down. Even after this, it is still both the largest and tallest sign.

Largest advertising sign   The largest advertisement on a building measured 41,756 square feet and was erected to promote Emirates, the international airline of the United Arab Emirates. It was located along the M4 motorway, near Chiswick, England, and was displayed November 1992–January 1993.

Airborne   Reebok International Ltd. of Massachusetts flew a banner from a single-seater plane that read "Reebok Totally Beachin." The banner measured 50 feet high and 100 feet long, and was flown for four hours each day between March 13–16 and 20–23, 1990, in Daytona Beach, FL.

Animated   Topsy the Clown, outside the Circus Circus Hotel, Reno, NV, is 127 feet tall and weighs over 45 tons, with 1.4 miles of neon tubing. Topsy's smile measures 14 feet across.

Billboard   The billboard for the Bassat Ogilvy Promotional Campaign for Ford España is 475 ft. 9 in. long and 49 ft. 3 in. high. It is sited at Plaza de Toros Monumental de Barcelona, Barcelona, Spain, and was installed on April 27, 1989.

Largest illuminated advertising signs   A sign measuring 210 feet by 55 feet was built for Marlboro cigarettes at Hung Hom, Kowloon, Hong Kong in May 1986. It contains 35,000 feet of neon tubing and weighs approximately 126 tons.

Longest   The longest illuminated sign measures 197 by 66 feet. It is lit by 62 400-W metal-halide projectors and was erected by Abudi Signs Industry Ltd. in Ramat Gan, Israel. A larger such sign, measuring 171 by 138 feet, was displayed throughout 1988 on the Australian Mutual Provident Building in Sydney, New South Wales, Australia. The sign, reading "1788–1988," consisted of 4.26 miles of LUMENYTE fiber optics.

Neon   The longest neon sign is the letter "M" installed on the Great Mississippi River Bridge, Old Man River in Memphis, TN. It is 1,800 feet long and is made up of 200 high-intensity lamps.

An interior-lit fascia advertising sign in Clearwater, FL completed by the Adco Sign Corp. in April 1983 measured 1,168 ft. 6½ in. long.

CIRCUS

Oldest circus The oldest permanent circus building is Cirque d'Hiver (originally Cirque Napoléon), which opened in Paris, France on December 11, 1852.

Largest circus The traveling circus tent of Ringling Bros. and Barnum & Bailey, used on tours in the United States from 1921 to 1924, covered 91,415 square feet. It consisted of a round top 200 feet in diameter with five middle sections each 60 feet wide.

Largest circus audience An audience of 52,385 attended the Ringling Bros. and Barnum & Bailey circus at the Superdome, New Orleans, LA on September 14, 1975. The largest audience in a tent was 16,702 (15,686 paid), also for Ringling Bros. and Barnum & Bailey, in Concordia, KS on September 13, 1924.

Aerial acts The highest trapeze act was performed by Ian Ashpole (Great Britain) at a height of 16,420 feet, suspended from a hot-air balloon between St. Neots and Newmarket, England on May 16, 1986. Janet May Klemke (U.S.) performed 305 1-arm planges at Medina Shrine Circus, Chicago, IL on January 21, 1938. Angela Revelle performed the first single-heel hang on a swinging bar in Australia in 1977.

Flexible pole The first and only publicly performed quadruple back somersault on the flexible pole was accomplished by Maksim Dobrovitsky (USSR) of the Yegorov Troupe at the International Circus Festival of Monte Carlo in Monaco on February 4, 1989.

Corina Colonelu Mosoianu (Romania) is the only person to have performed a triple full twisting somersault, at Madison Square Garden, New York City, on April 17, 1984.

Flying return trapeze A flying return trapeze act was first performed by Jules Léotard (France) at Cirque Napoléon, Paris, France on November 12, 1859. A triple back somersault on the flying trapeze was first performed by Lena Jordan (Latvia) to Lewis Jordan (U.S.) in Sydney, Australia in April 1897. The back somersault record is a quadruple back, by Miguel Vasquez (Mexico) to Juan Vasquez at Ringling Bros. and Barnum & Bailey Circus, Tucson, AZ on July 10, 1982. The greatest number of consecutive triple back somersaults is 135, by Jamie Ibarra (Mexico) to Alejandro Ibarra, between July 23 and October 12, 1989, at various locations in the United States.

High diving Col. Harry A. Froboess (Switzerland) jumped 394 feet into the Bodensee from the airship *Graf Hindenburg* on June 22, 1936.

The greatest height reported for a dive into an air bag is 326 feet, by stuntman Dan Koko, who jumped from the top of Vegas World Hotel and Casino onto a 20 by 40 by 14-foot target on August 13, 1948.

High wire   A 7-person pyramid (three layers) was achieved by the Great Wallendas (Germany) at Wallenda Circus in 1947. The highest high-wire feat (ground supported) was at a height of 1,350 feet by Philippe Petit (France) between the towers of the World Trade Center, New York on August 7, 1974.

Horseback riding   The record for consecutive somersaults on horseback is 23, by James Robinson (U.S.) at Spalding & Rogers Circus, Pittsburgh, PA in 1856. Willy, Beby, and Rene Fredianis (Italy) performed a 3-high column at Nouveau Cirque, Paris, France in 1908, a feat not since emulated. "Poodles" Hanneford (Ireland; b. England) holds the record for running leaps on and off, with 26 at Barnum & Bailey Circus, New York in 1915.

Human pyramid   The weight record is 1,700 pounds, when Tahar Douis supported 12 members of the Hassani Troupe (three levels in height) at the BBC TV studios, Birmingham, England on December 17, 1979. The height record is 39 feet, when Josep-Joan Martinez Lozano of the Colla Vella dels Xiquets mounted a 9-high pyramid in Valls, Spain on October 25, 1981.

Plate spinning   The greatest number of plates spun simultaneously is 108, by Dave Spathaky of London, England for the Tarm Pai Du television program in Thailand on November 23, 1992.

Boom!

The first human cannonball was Eddie Rivers (U.S.), billed as "Lulu," who was shot from a Farini cannon at Royal Cremorne Music Hall, London, England in 1871. Emanuel Zacchini (Italy) was fired 175 feet from a cannon in the United States in 1940.

Stilt-walking   *Speed*   Roy Luiking covered 328 feet on 1-foot-high stilts in 13.01 seconds in Didam, Netherlands on May 28, 1992.

Over a long distance, the fastest stilt-walker was M. Garisoain of Bayonne, France, who in 1892 walked the 4.97 miles from Bayonne to Biarritz on stilts in 42 minutes, an average speed of 7.10 MPH.

Distance   Joe Bowen walked 3,008 miles on stilts from Los Angeles, CA to Bowen, KY, February 20–July 26, 1980.

Tallest and heaviest stilts   Eddy Wolf ("Steady Eddy") of Loyal, WI mastered stilts measuring 40 ft. 9½ in. from ground to ankle and weighing 57 pounds each when he walked a distance of 25 steps without touching his safety handrail wires on August 3, 1988.

Teeter board   The Shanghai Acrobats achieved a 6-person-high unaided column (with only one person on each level) in Shanghai, China in 1993.

Trampoline   Marco Canestrelli (U.S.) performed a septuple twisting back somersault to bed at Ringling Bros. and Barnum & Bailey Circus, St. Petersburg, FL in January 1979. He also managed a quintuple twisting back somersault to a 2-high column, to Belmonte Canestrelli at Ringling Bros. and Barnum & Bailey Circus, New York City, in March 1979. Richard Tisson (France) did a triple twisting triple back somersault in Berchtesgaden, Germany in June 1981.

Traveling amusement park   The largest traveling amusement park or carnival in the United States is Amusements of America, which encompasses a route of over 19,000 miles, with a yearly attendance in excess of 8 million people.

Wild animal presentations   Willy Hagenbeck (Germany) worked with 70 polar bears in a presentation at the Paul Busch Circus, Berlin, Germany in 1904. The greatest number of lions mastered and fed in a cage by an unaided lion-tamer was 40, by "Captain" Alfred Schneider in 1925. Clyde Raymond Beatty (U.S.) handled 43 "cats" (lions and tigers) simultaneously in 1938, and was the featured attraction at every show he appeared in for more than 40 years.

BUSINESS & LAW

COMMERCE

Oldest industry   Flint knapping, which involves the production of chopping tools and hand axes, dates from 2.5 million years ago in Ethiopia. The earliest evidence of trading in exotic stone and amber dates from *c.* 28,000 B.C. in Europe.

Oldest company   The oldest existing documented company is Stora Kopparbergs Bergslags of Falun, Sweden, which has been in continuous operation since the 11th century. It is first mentioned in historical records from 1288, when a bishop bartered an eighth share in the enterprise, and it was granted a charter in 1347.

Family business   The Hoshi Ryokan, a hotel in Japan, dates back to A.D. 717 and has been run as a family business for 46 generations.

Largest manufacturing company   General Motors Corporation of Detroit, MI has operations throughout the world and a workforce of 692,800. Its assets in 1994 were $198.6 billion, with sales totaling $155.0 billion and a net profit of $4.99 billion.

Longest company name   The longest company name on the Index registered under the British Companies Acts is "The Only Ordinary People Trying to Impress the Big Guys with Extra Ordinary Ideas, Sales, Management, Creative Thinking and Problem Solving Consultancy Company Ltd.," Company number 2660603.

Shortest company names   The shortest company names on the Index are D Ltd., E Ltd., H Ltd., Q Ltd., X Ltd. and Y Ltd.

Largest employer   On March 31, 1992, Indian Railways had 1,654,066 employees.

Greatest sales   The *Fortune 500* list of leading industrial corporations in April 1995 was headed by General Motors Corporation of Detroit, MI, with sales of $155.0 billion for 1994.

Greatest corporate profit   The American Telephone and Telegraph Co. (AT&T) made a net profit of $7.6 billion in 12 months from October 1, 1981 to September 30, 1982.

Greatest loss   In 1992, General Motors reported an annual net trading loss of $23.5 billion. The bulk of this figure was, however, due to a single charge of some $21 billion for employees' health costs and pensions and was disclosed because of new U.S. accounting regulations.

Largest corporate takeover bid   On October 24, 1988, the Wall Street leveraged buyout firm Kohlberg Kravis Roberts (KKR) bid $21 billion, or $90 a share, for RJR Nabisco Inc., the tobacco, food and beverage company. By

December 1, 1988, the bid, led by Henry Kravis, had reached $109 per share, to total $25 billion.

Biggest bankrupt On September 3, 1992, newspaper heir Kevin Maxwell became the world's biggest bankrupt following the death of his father, Robert Maxwell (1923–91), with debts of £406.8 million (*c.* $813.6 million).

Corporate The biggest corporate bankruptcy in terms of assets was $35.9 billion, filed by Texaco in 1987.

Largest public auction In 1995, the Federal Communications Commission (FCC) raised $7.7 billion for the U.S. Treasury by auctioning off 99 licenses to provide advanced digital communication services. The auction, conducted by Kennedy-Wilson International, ended on March 13, after three months of bidding. Sprint Corp. and three partner companies put in the highest bid of $2.11 billion for 29 markets.

Greatest barter deal In July 1984, 30 million barrels of oil, valued at $1.71 billion, were exchanged for 10 Boeing 747s for the Royal Saudi Airline.

Largest banks The largest commercial bank is the Dai-Ichi Kangyo Bank Ltd. of Japan, with assets on March 31, 1993 of $427.1 billion.

The largest commercial bank in the United States is Citibank of New York City, with total assets of $250.5 billion and deposits of $155.7 billion for the 1994 fiscal year.

The International Bank of Reconstruction and Development, generally known as World Bank, is the largest multilateral development bank. Based in Washington, D.C., the bank had total assets of $170 billion for the 1994 fiscal year.

Most branches The State Bank of India had 12,704 outlets on April 1, 1994 and assets of $36 billion.

Most cash machines The United States had 109,080 ATM (automated teller machine) cash machines as of September 1, 1994. Bank America in San Francisco, CA had 5,700 cash machines, the most of any city in the U.S.

Oldest bank The oldest bank in continuous operation in the United States is The Bank of New York, founded in 1834.

Largest piggy bank Penny the Pig, the largest piggy bank in the United States, measures 6 ft. 11 in. high and 17 ft. 2 in. long. It was created by Mary Ann Spanagel and Coldwell Banker Real Estate of Pittsburgh, PA.

Charity fund-raising The greatest recorded amount raised by a charity walk or run is $Cdn24.7 million by Terry Fox of Canada, who, with an artificial leg, ran from St. John's, Newfoundland to Thunder Bay, Ontario in 143 days, April 12–September 2, 1980. He covered 3,339 miles.

Largest charity food bank The South Plains Food Bank's Breedlove Dehydration Plant in Lubbock, TX can dehydrate 28 million pounds of surplus fruit and vegetables per year, enough to produce 30,000 meals per day.

The Breedlove Dehydration Plant in Lubbock, TX is the largest charity food bank in the United States. (*Jim Watkins, Lubbock Avalanche Journal*)

Largest distillers   The world's most profitable distilling company, and the largest blender and bottler of Scotch whiskey, is United Distillers, the liquor company of Guinness plc. United Distillers made a profit of £915 million ($1.5 billion) in 1994.

Largest drug store chains   The world's largest chain of drug stores is Rite Aid Corporation of Camp Hill, PA, which in 1994 had 2,834 branches throughout the United States. The Walgreen Co. of Deerfield, IL has fewer stores, but a larger volume of sales, totaling $9.2 billion in 1994.

Largest food company   The world's largest food company is the Swiss-based Nestlé, with sales in 1994 totaling SFr56.9 billion ($43.5 billion).

Largest grocery chain   The single largest operator of supermarkets and food stores in the United States is Kroger Co. of Cincinnati, OH, with sales of $23.0 billion as of December 31, 1994. The company also has the most stores in the United States, with 2,126.

Largest insurance companies   The company with the highest volume of insurance in force is the Metropolitan Life Insurance Co. of New York City, with $1.27 trillion at year end 1994. The Prudential Insurance Company of America of Newark, NJ has the greatest volume of consolidated assets, totaling $212 billion in 1994.

The largest single insurance association is Blue Cross and Blue Shield of Chicago, IL. As of December 31, 1994, it had a membership of 65.2 million and paid out benefits totaling $71.4 billion.

Largest insurance policies   The largest life insurance policy ever issued was for $100 million, bought by a major American entertainment corporation on the life of a leading American entertainment industry figure. The policy was sold in July 1990 by Peter Rosengard of London, England and was placed by Shel Bachrach of Albert G. Ruben & Co. Inc. of Beverly Hills,

HIGHEST
OFFICE RENTS

If you've ever wondered about the costs of renting in a high-rise, look no further. The table on page 384 gives a rundown of the twenty locations where you will pay most dearly for the privilege of working. Property is priciest in Tokyo, where it costs nearly three times as much to rent an office as it does in midtown New York City.

Above: Exchange Square, home of the Hong Kong Stock Exchange. (*Spectrum Colour Library*)

Above: Inner central Tokyo—top of the list. (*Spectrum Colour Library*)

New York, midtown to downtown—
14th and 28th respectively on the
list. (*Image Select*)

Right: Ho Chi Minh City, Vietnam—
18th on the list, above Rome, Sydney
and downtown New York. (*Spectrum
Colour Library*)

Left: Offices for rent in the West
End of London. (*Spectrum Colour
Library*)

Congestion on
Dadabhoy Naoroji
Road, Bombay.
(*Spectrum Colour
Library*)

LOCATION OF OFFICES	RENT AS QUOTED LOCALLY, DECEMBER 1994	EQUIVALENT NET ANNUAL RENT IN $/SQ. FT.	SERVICE CHARGE	PROPERTY TAX	TOTAL ANNUAL OCCUPATION COST IN $/SQ. FT.
1. Tokyo—Inner central	¥40,000 tsubo p.m.	$143.38	15%	N/A	$164.13
2. Hong Kong	HK$888.64 sq.ft. p.m.	$137.34	6%	6%	$152.51
3. Bombay	US$960 sq.m. p.a.	$145.38	4%	N/A	$151.48
4. London—West End	£42.50 sq.ft. p.a.	$66.30	15%	52%	$111.09
5. London—City	£32.50 sq.ft. p.a.	$50.70	20%	78%	$100.43
6. Beijing	US$950 sq.m. p.a.	$88.17	6%	1%	$94.52
7. Shanghai	US$864 sq.m. p.a.	$80.18	6%	1%	$85.96
8. Tokyo—Outer central	¥17,400 tsubo p.a.	$61.42	22%	N/A	$74.88
9. Paris	Fr3300 sq.m. p.a.	$60.76	12%	8%	$72.73
10. New Delhi	US$460 sq.m. p.a.	$69.65	4%	N/A	$72.71
11. Singapore	S$7.48 sq.ft. p.m.	$45.02	18%	18%	$61.12
12. Guangzhou	US$590 sq.m. p.a.	$54.76	9%	1%	$60.08
13. Mexico City	US$45 sq.m. p.m.	$55.69	7%	N/A	$59.60
14. New York—Midtown	US$47.25 sq.ft. p.a.	$39.03	22%	29%	$59.00
15. Hanoi	US$45 sq.m. p.a.	$50.12	16%	N/A	$57.91
16. Frankfurt	DM62.50 sq.m. p.m.	$47.63	13%	1%	$54.48
17. Taipei	NT$2300 ping p.m.	$44.35	13%	2%	$51.14
18. Ho Chi Minh City	US$38 sq.m. p.a.	$42.32	16%	N/A	$50.12
19. Prague	DM55 sq.m. p.a.	$43.31	9%	N/A	$47.24
20. Rome	Lit600,000 sq.m. p.a.	$37.46	20%	N/A	$43.23

p.m. = per month; p.a. = per year

Richard Ellis

CA and Richard Feldman of the Feldman Agency, East Liverpool, OH with nine insurance companies to spread the risk.

The highest payout on a single life was reported on November 14, 1970 to be some $18 million to Linda Mullendore, widow of an Oklahoma rancher. Her murdered husband had paid $300,000 in premiums in 1969.

Marine insurance   The largest marine insurance loss was approximately $836 million for the Piper Alpha Oil Field in the North Sea. On July 6, 1988, a leak from a gas compression chamber underneath the living quarters ignited and triggered a series of explosions that blew Piper Alpha apart. Of the 232 people on board, only 65 survived.

The largest sum claimed for consequential losses was approximately $1.7 trillion against owning, operating and building corporations and Claude Phillips, resulting from the 55-million-gallon oil spill from MT *Amoco Cadiz* on the Brittany coast, France on March 16, 1978.

Longest pension   Millicent Barclay was born on July 10, 1872, three months after the death of her father, Col. William Barclay, and became eligible for a Madras Military Fund pension to continue until her marriage. She died unmarried on October 26, 1969, having drawn the pension every day of her life of 97 yr. 3 mo.

Largest landowner   The United States government has a holding of 728.8 million acres.

Most expensive land   The most expensive piece of property ever recorded was the land around the central Tokyo retail food store Mediya Building in the Ginza district, which was quoted in October 1988 by the Japanese National Land Agency at 358.5 million yen ($248,000) per square foot.

Most expensive offices   The highest rentals in the world for prime offices, according to *World Rental Levels* by Richard Ellis of London, England, were in Tokyo, Japan at $143.38 per square foot per annum (December 1994) compared with a peak of $206.68 in June 1991. With added service charges and rates this increased to $163.13 per square foot (December 1994) and $225.34 in June 1991.

Largest retailer   The largest retailer in the United States is Wal-Mart, Inc. of Bentonville, AR, with unaudited 1994 sales of $82.5 billion and an unaudited 1994 net income of $2.7 billion reported on January 31, 1995. As of May 1, 1995, Wal-Mart had 2,648 retail locations and employed 600,000 people. Wal-Mart was founded by Sam Walton in Rogers, AR in 1962.

DID YOU KNOW?

Woolworth Corporation operated 8,629 stores worldwide as of January 28, 1995. Frank Winfield Woolworth opened his first store, "The Great Five Cent Store," in Utica, NY on February 22, 1879.

Largest rummage sale   The Cleveland Convention Center, Cleveland, OH White Elephant Sale (instituted 1933), held October 18–19, 1983, raised $427,935.21. The greatest amount of money raised at a one-day sale was $214,085.99 at the 62nd one-day rummage sale organized by the Winnetka Congregational Church, Winnetka, IL on May 12, 1994.

Savings and loan association   The world's biggest lender is the Japanese government-controlled House Loan Corporation.

United States   The largest savings and loan association (S&L) in the United States is Home Savings and Loan FSB, in Irwindale, CA. As of March 1995, the company had total assets of $53.7 billion and total deposits of $41.7 billion.

Largest soft drink company   The largest beverage company in the world is PepsiCo of Purchase, NY, with total sales for 1994 of $28.5 billion, compared with $16.2 billion for the Coca-Cola company of Atlanta, GA. Coca-Cola is, however, the world's most popular soft drink, with sales in 1994 of over 540 million drinks per day, representing an estimated 46 percent of the world market.

PERSONAL WEALTH

Richest man   Much of the wealth of the world's monarchs represents national rather than personal assets. The least fettered and most monarchical is HM Sir Muda Hassanal Bolkiah Mu'izzaddin Waddaulah of Brunei. *Fortune* magazine reported in June 1993 that his fortune was $37 billion.

Richest woman   Her Majesty Queen Elizabeth II is asserted by some to be the wealthiest woman in the world, and *The Sunday Times* of London, England estimated in April 1993 that she had assets worth £6.75 billion ($11.7 billion). However, few of her assets under the perpetual succession of the Crown are personal or disposable, and her personal wealth was estimated at £500 million ($900 million). An alternative estimate published by the British magazine *The Economist* in January 1992 placed her personal wealth at much closer to £150 million ($270 million).

GUESS WHAT?

Q. HOW MUCH HAS THE MOST SUCCESSFUL JOCKEY EARNED?

A. LOOK IN "HORSE RACING" (SPORTS)

Richest families   It has been tentatively estimated that the combined value of the assets nominally controlled by the Du Pont family, which has about 1,600 members, may be $150 billion. The family arrived in the United States from France on January 1, 1800.

Fund manager George Soros earned at least $1.1 billion in 1993, according to *Financial World*'s list of the highest-paid individuals on Wall Street. (*Rex Features/The Times*)

A more conclusive claim is for the Walton retailing family, worth an estimated $23.5 billion.

Youngest millionaire   The youngest self-made millionaire was the American child film actor Jackie Coogan (1914–84), who co-starred with Charlie Chaplin in *The Kid*, made in 1921.

Youngest billionaire   The youngest of the 101 billionaires reported in the United States in 1992 was William Gates, cofounder of Microsoft, whose *MS/DOS* operating system runs on an estimated 72 million of the United States' 90 million personal computers. Gates was 20 when he set up his company in 1976 and was a billionaire by 31.

Highest incomes   The largest incomes derive from the collection of royalties per barrel by rulers of oil-rich sheikhdoms who have not formally revoked personal entitlement. Sheikh Zayid ibn Sultan an-Nuhayan (b. 1918), head of state of the United Arab Emirates, arguably has title to some $9 billion of the country's annual gross national product.

LOADED!

The richest private individual is Warren Buffett of Omaha, NE, who owns 42 percent of Berkshire Hathaway. *Forbes* magazine listed his net worth as $8.3 billion in October 1993. Taikichiro Mori of Japan (1904–93) was estimated to have assets of $10 billion during 1991.

HONEST!

In May 1994, Howard Jenkins of Tampa, FL, a 31-year-old roofing company employee, discovered that $88 million had been mistakenly transferred into his account. Although he initially withdrew $4 million, his conscience got the better of him and he returned the $88 million in full.

Highest salary Fund manager George Soros earned at least $1.1 billion in 1993, according to *Financial World*'s list of the highest-paid individuals on Wall Street.

Highest personal tax levy The highest recorded personal tax levy is one for $336 million on 70 percent of the estate of Howard Hughes.

Largest golden handshake *Business Week* magazine reported in May 1989 that the largest "golden handshake" ever given was one of $53.8 million, to F. Ross Johnson, who left RJR Nabisco as chairman in February 1989.

Largest dowry In 1929, Don Simón Iturbi Patiño (1861–1947), the Bolivian tin millionaire, bestowed $39 million on his daughter, Elena Patiño. His total fortune was at one time estimated to be worth $607.5 million.

Largest single bequests American publisher Walter Annenberg announced on March 12, 1991 that he would be leaving his art collection, worth $1 billion, to the Metropolitan Museum of Art in New York City.

The largest single cash bequest was the $500 million gift, announced on December 12, 1955, to 4,157 educational and other institutions from the Ford Foundation (established 1936) of New York.

Highest lottery sales In the 1994 fiscal year (July 1–June 30), the United States Lottery netted record total sales of $33,882,158,000 in North America.

The state with the highest recorded lottery sales is Texas, with $2,681,260,000 in the 1994 fiscal year (July 1–June 30).

Largest lottery jackpot The largest U.S. lottery jackpot was $118,800,000, shared by ten ticket-holders, in California, on April 17, 1991.

The highest payout for one ticket was shared by Leslie Robbins and Colleen DeVries of Fond du Lac, WI. The two won $111,200,000 in the Powerball lottery on July 7, 1993; each will receive an annual net sum of $1,500,000 for twenty years.

PAPER MONEY

Oldest paper money The world's earliest bank notes (*banco-sedler*) were issued in Stockholm, Sweden in July 1661. The oldest survivor is a 5-daler note dated December 6, 1662.

Largest paper money   The 1-guan note of the Chinese Ming Dynasty issue of 1368–99 measured 9 by 13 inches.

Smallest paper money   The smallest national note ever issued was the 10-bani note of the Ministry of Finance of Romania, in 1917. Its printed area measured 1¹/₁₆ by 1¹/₂ inches.

Highest values   The highest value ever issued by the U.S. Federal Reserve System is a note for $100,000, bearing the head of Woodrow Wilson (1856–1924), which is only used for transactions between the Federal Reserve and the Treasury Department.

The highest-value notes in circulation are U.S. Federal Reserve $10,000 bank notes, bearing the head of Salmon P. Chase (1808–73). In 1969, it was announced that no further notes higher than $100 would be issued, and only 345 $10,000 bills remain in circulation or unretired.

Most expensive paper money   On February 14, 1991, Richard Lobel paid £240,350 ($478,900) including buyer's premium, on behalf of a consortium, at Phillips, London, England, for a single lot of bank notes. The lot consisted of a cache of British military notes that were found in a vault in Berlin, Germany, and contained more than 17 million notes.

Largest paper money collection   Chris Boyd of New Malden, England has accumulated bank notes from 204 different countries since he started collecting in 1990.

CHECKS AND COINS

Largest check   An internal U.S. Treasury check for $4,176,969,623.57 was drawn on June 30, 1954.

The largest check in terms of physical dimensions measured 70 by 31 feet. It was presented by InterMortgage of Leeds, England to Yorkshire Television's 1992 Telephone Appeal on September 4, 1992, and had a value of £10,000 ($19,000).

GUESS WHAT?

Q. WHAT WAS THE HIGHEST PRICE FOR ANTIQUE SILVER?

A. LOOK IN "ANTIQUES" (ARTS & ENTERTAINMENT)

Most expensive coin collection   The highest price paid for a coin collection was $25,235,360 for a collection of U.S. and colonial coins that had been donated to Johns Hopkins University, Baltimore, MD. The sales were made at a series of four auctions held November 28–29, 1979 and March 25–26, 1981 at the Bowers & Ruddy Galleries in Wolfeboro, NH. The col-

DEAN'S DEXTROUS DEEDS

Coin snatching is a skill that requires great patience, perfect balance, strong arms, and big hands. Build a stack of coins on your forearm near your elbow, bring your hand forward quickly, and catch as many of the coins as you can in the same hand. Is it as simple as it sounds?

Dean Gould of Felixstowe, England caught a record 328 out of 482 British 10-pence coins (roughly the same size and weight as an American quarter) on April 6, 1993. Gould used a highly intricate stack of coins, consisting of 13 linked columns. "The interlocking stacking method was developed in the mid-1980s," he says. "It was a turning point for big catches—it makes the coins stay together better.

The technique has to be perfect, from the way the coins balance to how I stand and the speed of the catch," Gould explains. "Stacking the coins takes 20 minutes. The wider the stack, the better, provided it's within your hand span."

Why does he do it? "It was an ambition of mine to get into *The Guinness Book of Records*. I chose coin snatching because it was something I was good at as a boy. I always wanted to be the best at something."

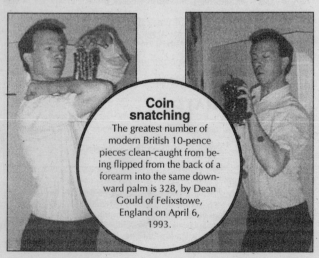

Coin snatching
The greatest number of modern British 10-pence pieces clean-caught from being flipped from the back of a forearm into the same downward palm is 328, by Dean Gould of Felixstowe, England on April 6, 1993.

lection was put together by members of the Garrett family between 1860 and 1942.

Column of coins The most valuable column of coins was worth 39,458 Irish pounds ($55,063) and stood 6 ft. 2 in. high. It was built by St. Brigid's Family and Community Centre in Waterford, Ireland on November 20, 1993.

Pile of coins The most valuable pile of coins had a total value of $126,463.61 and consisted of 1,000,298 coins of various denominations. It was constructed by the YWCA of Seattle, King County, WA in Redmond, WA on May 28, 1992.

Line of coins The most valuable line of coins was made up of 1,724,000 quarters with a value of $431,000. It was 25.9 miles long, and was laid at

---

COINS

Oldest
Electrum staters of King Gyges of Lydia, Turkey, *c.* 670 B.C.[1]

Earliest dated
Samian silver tetradrachm struck in Zankle (now Messina), Sicily, dated year 1, *viz.* 494 B.C.

Heaviest
Swedish 10-daler copper plate, 1644, 43 lb. $7^{1}/4$ oz.
Gold: Islamic 1,000-muhur, 32 lb., minted in Agra, 1613.[2]

Lightest
Nepalese silver $^{1}/4$ jawa *c.* 1740, 14,000 to the oz.

Most valuable
Set: $3,190,000 for the King of Siam Proof Set, a set of 1804 and 1834 U.S. coins that had once been given to the King of Siam, purchased by Iraj Sayah and Terry Brand at Superior Galleries, Beverly Hills, CA on May 28, 1990. Included in the set of nine coins was the 1804 silver dollar, which had an estimated value of about $2,000,000.

Individual: $1,500,000 for the U.S. 1907 Double Eagle Ultra High Relief $20 gold coin, sold by MTB Banking Corporation of New York to a private investor on Jul. 9, 1990.

[1] *Chinese uninscribed "spade" money of the Zhou dynasty has been dated to c. 770 B.C.*
[2] *The largest coinlike medallion was completed on Mar. 21, 1986 for the World Exposition in Vancouver, British Columbia, Canada, Expo 86—a $1,000,000 gold piece. Its dimensions were 37.5 in. diameter and $^{3}/4$ in. thick and it weighed 365 lb. 15 oz., or 5,337 oz. (troy) of gold.*

the Atlanta Marriott Marquis Hotel, GA by members of the National Exchange Club on July 25, 1992.

Longest   The longest line of coins had a total length of 30.38 miles and comprised 1,886,975 2-pence coins. It was laid by the Friends of the Samaritans at the Great Park, Windsor, England on August 16, 1992.

Coin snatching   The greatest number of modern British 10-pence pieces clean-caught from being flipped from the back of a forearm into the same downward palm is 328, by Dean Gould of Felixstowe, England on April 6, 1993.

Coin balancing   On March 16, 1993, Mohammad Irshadullah Hamidi of Muzaffarpur, India stacked a pyramid of 870 coins on the edge of a coin freestanding vertically on the base of another coin that was on a table.

The tallest single column of coins ever stacked on the edge of a coin was made up of 253 Indian 1-rupee pieces on top of a vertical 5-rupee coin, by Dipak Syal of Yamuna Nagar, India on May 3, 1991. He also balanced 10 1-rupee coins and 10 10-paise coins alternately horizontally and vertically in a single column on May 1, 1991.

Most valuable hoard   The most valuable hoard of coins was one of about 80,000 aurei found in Brescello near Modena, Italy in 1714, and believed to have been deposited *c.* 37 B.C.

Mints   *Largest*   The U.S. Treasury mint was built 1965–1969 on Independence Mall, Philadelphia and covers 11½ acres, with an annual production capacity on a 3-shift 7-day week of 12 billion coins.

Fastest   The Graebner Press high-speed stamping machine can produce coins at a rate of 42,000 per hour. The record production for coins was in 1982, when 19.5 billion were produced between the Philadelphia and Denver mints.

Smallest issuing   The single-press mint belonging to the Sovereign Military Order of Malta, the City of Rome, is housed in one small room and has issued proof coins since 1961.

STOCK EXCHANGES

Oldest stock exchange   The stock exchange in Amsterdam, Netherlands was founded in 1602 with dealings in printed shares of the United East India Company of the Netherlands in the Oude Zijds Kapel.

Largest stock exchange   The largest in trading volume in 1994 was the New York Stock Exchange, with $2,454.2 billion.

New York Stock Exchange   The market value of stocks listed on the New York Stock Exchange reached an all-time high of $5 trillion on May 4, 1995.

The record day's trading was 608,148,710 shares on October 20, 1987.

The largest stock trade in the history of the New York Stock Exchange was a 48,788,800-share block of Navistar International Corporation stock sold at $10 per share on April 10, 1986.

The highest price paid for a seat on the New York Stock Exchange was $1.15 million in 1987. The lowest 20th-century price was $17,000, in 1942.

Closing prices　As of June 5, 1995, the highest index figure on the Dow Jones Industrial average of selected stocks at the close of a day's trading was 4,476.55.

The Dow Jones Industrial average, which reached 381.71 on September 3, 1929, plunged 30.57 points on October 29, 1929, on its way to the Depression's lowest point of 41.22 on July 8, 1932. The largest decline in a day, 508 points (22.6 percent), occurred on October 19, 1987.

The total lost in security values from September 1, 1929 to June 30, 1932 was $74 billion. The greatest paper loss in a year was $210 billion in 1974.

The record daily increase, on October 21, 1987, was 186.84 points, to 2,027.85.

Largest flotation　The £5.2 billion ($9.9 billion) sale of the 12 regional British electricity companies to 5.7 million stockholders at the end of 1990 was the largest in stock market history.

The earlier flotation of British Gas plc in 1986 had an equity offer that produced the higher sum of £7.75 billion ($10.85 billion), but to only 4.5 million stockholders.

Most valuable company　The greatest market value of any corporation as of year end 1994 was $92.3 billion for General Electric Co., of Fairfield, CT.

Greatest stockholders attendance　In April 1961, a total of 20,109 stockholders attended the annual general meeting of the American Telephone and Telegraph Co. (AT&T), thereby setting a world record.

Longest-serving current member　As of June 1995, the longest-serving current member of the New York Stock Exchange was David Granger, who became a member on February 4, 1926.

GOLD!

The highest closing spot price for gold on the Commodities Exchange (COMEX) in New York City was $875 per fine ounce on January 21, 1980.

Largest rights issue The largest recorded rights issue was one of £921 million ($1.57 billion) by Barclays Bank, Great Britain, announced on April 7, 1988.

Highest silver price The highest closing spot price for silver on the Commodities Exchange (COMEX) in New York City was $50.35 per fine ounce on January 18, 1980.

Highest par value The highest denomination of any share quoted in the world is a single share in Moeara Enim Petroleum Corporation, worth 165,000 Dutch florins ($75,500) on April 22, 1992.

POSTAL SERVICES

Largest mail service The country with the largest mail service in the world is the United States. Its population mailed 177.1 billion letters and packages during the 1994 fiscal year. The U.S. Postal Service employs 728,944 people and has the world's largest civilian vehicle fleet of 200,000 cars and trucks. The average number of letters and packages per capita was 675. There are 39,372 post offices in the U.S.

Most post offices The country with the greatest number of post offices is India, with 144,829 in 1988.

POSTAGE STAMPS

Earliest
Put on sale May 6, 1840. 1 d Penny Black of Great Britain, Queen Victoria, 68,158,080 printed.

U.S.
Put on sale in New York City Jul. 1, 1847. 5-cent red-brown Benjamin Franklin, 3,712,200 issued, and 10-cent black George Washington, 891,000 issued.

Earliest adhesive stamp
Earliest adhesive stamps were those used for local delivery by the *City Dispatch Post,* established in New York City Feb. 15, 1842.

Highest price (auction)

SFr 3,400,000 ($2,400,000), including buyer's premium. Penny Black, May 2, 1840 cover, bought at Harmers, Lugano, Switzerland, on behalf of a Japanese buyer on May 23, 1991.

£203,500 ($350,000), including buyer's premium, for a philatelic item. Bermuda 1854 Perot Postmasters' Stamp affixed to a letter, 1d red on bluish wove paper, sold by Christie's Robson Lowe, London, England on Jun. 13, 1991.

U.S.

$1.1 million (including buyer's premium). "Curtiss Jenny" plate block of four 24-cent stamps from 1918 with inverted image of an airplane, bought by an unnamed American executive at Christie's, New York on Oct. 12, 1989.

Largest purchase

$11 million. Marc Haas collection of 3,000 U.S. postal and pre-postal covers to 1869 by Stanley Gibbons International Ltd. of London, England in August 1979.

Largest (special)

$9^3/_4 by 2^3/_4 in. Express Delivery of China, 1913.

U.S.

3^3/_4 by 2 in. 1865 newspaper stamps.

Largest (standard)

6.3 by 4.33 in. Marshall Islands 75-cent issued Oct. 30, 1979.

U.S.

^1/_11 by 1^5/_11 in. 5-cent blue and carmine Air Beacon issued Jul. 25, 1928, and 2-cent black and carmine George Rogers Clark issued Feb. 25, 1929.

Smallest

0.31 by 0.37 in. 10-cent and 1-peso Colombian State of Bolivar, 1863–66.

Highest denomination

$10,000. Documentary and Stock Transfer stamps, 1952–58.

U.S.

$100. Indian Maiden, 1895–97.

Lowest denomination

3,000 pengö of Hungary. Issued 1946 when 604.5 trillion pengö = 1 cent.

U.S.

^1/_2 cent. Earliest sepia Nathan Hale, 1925; George Washington, 1932; Benjamin Franklin, 1938 and 1954.

Rarest

Unique examples include British Guiana 1-cent black on magenta, 1856 (last on the market in 1980) and Swedish 3-skilling-banco yellow color error, 1855.

The Swedish 3-skilling-banco yellow color error of 1855 is one of the world's rarest stamps. (*David Feldman SA*)

Stamp licking John Kenmuir of Hamilton, Scotland licked and affixed 393 stamps in four minutes at the BBC TV studios on September 26, 1990.

AGRICULTURE

FISHERIES

Leading fishing nation United Nations Food and Agricultural Organization figures for 1990 (the last year for which comparable data is available) showed the world's leading fishing nation to be China, with a total catch of 13.44 million tons. The United States was in fifth place with 6.57 million tons out of a worldwide total of 108.86 million tons, down from a worldwide 112 million tons in 1989.

Most valuable catch The record value for a catch by a single trawler is $473,957, from a 41,776-ton catch by the Icelandic vessel *Videy* at Hull, England on August 11, 1987. The greatest catch ever recorded from a single throw is 2,724 tons, by the purse seine-net boat M/S *Flømann* from Hareide, Norway in the Barents Sea on August 28, 1986. It was estimated that more than 120 million fish were caught in this shoal.

BREWERIES AND VINEYARDS

Oldest brewer Weihenstephan Brewery, Freising, near Munich, Germany, was founded in A.D. 1040.

Oldest vat   The oldest vat still in use is at Hugel et Fils (founded 1639), Riqueweihr, Haut-Rhin, France. Twelve generations of the family have used it since 1715.

Oldest vintners   The world's oldest champagne firm is Ruinart Père et Fils, founded in 1729. The oldest cognac firm is Augier Frères & Cie, established in 1643.

Largest brewer   The largest single brewing organization in the world is Anheuser-Busch Inc. of St. Louis, MO, with 13 breweries in the United States. In 1994, the company sold 2.74 billion gallons, the greatest annual volume ever produced by a brewing company in a year. One of its brands, Budweiser, is the top-selling beer in the world, with 1.271 billion gallons sold in 1993.

The company's St. Louis plant covers 100 acres. The completion of modernization projects in 1994 gave the plant an annual capacity of 412 million gallons.

The largest brewery on a single site is Coors Brewing Co. of Golden, CO, where 587 million gallons were produced in 1994. At the same location is the world's largest aluminum can manufacturing plant, with a capacity of more than 4 billion cans annually.

Largest vineyard   The vineyard that extends over the Mediterranean slopes between the Pyrenees and the Rhône in the *départements* Gard, Hérault, Aude and Pyrénées-Orientales, France covers an area of 2,075,685 acres.

Largest wine cellars   The cellars of the Ko-operatieve Wijnbouwers Vereniging (KWV), Paarl, Cape Province, in the center of the wine-growing district of South Africa, cover an area of 54 acres and have a capacity of 32 million gallons.

United States   The Cienega Winery of the Almaden Vineyards in Hollister, CA covers four acres and can house 37,300 oak barrels containing 1.83 million gallons of wine.

Largest vat   "Strongbow," used by H.P. Bulmer Ltd., the English cidermakers, measures 64½ feet in height and 75½ feet in diameter, with a capacity of 1.95 million gallons.

The largest wooden winecask in the world is the Heidelberg Tun, completed in 1751, in the cellar of the Friedrichsbau, Heidelberg, Germany. Its capacity is 58,570 gallons.

Largest vine   A grapevine planted in 1842 at Carpinteria, CA yielded more than 9.9 tons of grapes in some years, and averaged 7.7 tons per year until it died in 1920.

FARMS

Largest farms   The *kolkhozy* (collective farms) in the former USSR were reduced in number from 235,500 in 1940 to 26,900 in 1988 and represented a total cultivated area of 417.6 million acres. Units of over 60,000 acres were not uncommon.

Fine wines

The Ko-operatieve Wijnbouwers Vereniging (KWV) in Paarl, Cape Province, in the center of South Africa's wine-growing district, has wine cellars that cover an area of 54 acres and have a capacity of 32 million gallons. More than 100 different natural wines, as well as a wide range of brandies and fortified wines, are produced here for the world market.

In the Cathedral Cellar (facing page), a cool, peaceful sanctuary with a soaring barrel-vaulted roof, exquisite chandeliers and an imposing row of huge wooden vats, KWV honors its long tradition of making fine wines. The cellar was given its name by Dutch poet Antonie Donkersloot, who proclaimed, "This is indeed a cathedral of wine!"

In an adjoining cellar are five huge vats—the largest collection of such massive vats in one place. A person is dwarfed by these monsters (below).

Wine connoisseurs will be pleased to know that guided tours are available, but you don't have to be a wine lover to appreciate the beauty and tranquility of the largest wine cellars in the world.

(KWV)

Largest wine cellars

The cellars of Ko-operatieve Wijnbouwers Vereniging (KWV), Paarl, Cape Province, South Africa cover 54 acres and have a capacity of 32 million gallons.

The pioneer farm owned by Laucidio Coelho near Campo Grande, Mato Grosso, Brazil covered 3,358 square miles and supported 250,000 head of cattle at the time of the owner's death in 1975.

Largest cattle ranch The Anna Creek cattle ranch in South Australia, owned by the Kidman family, comprises 11,600 square miles. The biggest component is Strangway, at 5,500 square miles.

Largest egg farm The Agrigeneral Company L.P. in Croton, OH has 4.8 million hens laying 3.7 million eggs daily.

Largest community garden The project operated by the City Beautiful Council and the Benjamin Wegerzyn Garden Center in Dayton, OH comprises 1,173 plots, each measuring 812 square feet.

Largest hop farm The world's leading hop growers are John I. Haas Inc., with farms in Oregon, Washington, Tasmania and Australia, covering a total net area of 5,940 acres. The largest field covers 1,385 acres near Toppenish, WA.

Largest mushroom farm Moonlight Mushrooms Inc. founded a farm in 1937 in a disused limestone mine near Worthington, PA. It now employs over 1,106 people who work in a maze of underground galleries 156 miles long, producing over 54 million pounds of mushrooms per year.

Largest rice farm Clearwater Rice Inc. in Clearbrook, MN is a wild rice (Zizania aquatica) farm covering 2,000 acres. In 1986, it yielded 577,000 pounds, its largest amount to date.

Largest sheep ranch Commonwealth Hill, South Australia grazes between 50,000 and 70,000 sheep, along with 24,000 uninvited kangaroos, in an area of 4,080 square miles enclosed by 138 miles of dog-proof fencing. The head count on Sir William Stevenson's 40,970-acre Lochinver station in New Zealand was 127,406 on January 1, 1993.

Largest sheep move In 1886, 27 horsemen moved a flock of 43,000 sheep 40 miles from Barcaldine to Beaconsfield station, Queensland, Australia.

Largest turkey farm The farms of Bernard Matthews plc of Norfolk, England produce 10 million turkeys per year and employ a staff of 2,500. The largest farm, in North Pickenham, England, produces 1 million turkeys.

Combine harvesting Philip Baker of West End Farm, Merton, Bicester, England harvested 182.5 tons of wheat in eight hours using a Massey Ferguson MF 38 combine on August 8, 1989. On August 9, 1990, an international team from CWS Agriculture, led by estate manager Ian Hanglin, harvested 394.73 tons of wheat in eight hours from 108.72 acres at Cockayne Hatley Estate, Sandy, England. The equipment consisted of a Claas Commandor 228 combine fitted with a Shelbourne Reynolds SR 6000 stripper head.

Bale rolling Michael Priestley and Marcus Stanley of Heckington Young Farmers Club rolled a 3-ft.-11-in.-wide cylindrical bale over a 164-foot course in 18.06 seconds at the Lincolnshire Federation of Young Farmers' Clubs annual sports day in Sleaford, England on June 25, 1989.

Baling A rick of 40,400 bales of straw was built between July 22 and September 3, 1982 by Nick and Tom Parsons with a gang of eight at Cuckoo Pen Barn Farm, Birdlip, England. It measured 150 by 30 by 60 feet high and weighed some 784 tons. The team baled, hauled and ricked 24,200 bales in seven consecutive days, starting on July 22.

Svend Erik Klemmensen of Trustrup, Djursland, Denmark baled 220 tons of straw in 9 hr. 54 min. using a Hesston 4800 baling machine on August 30, 1989.

The largest farms in the world are the *kolkbozy* (collective farms) in Russia—some units cover as much as 60,000 acres. (*Rex Features/Sipa Press/Laski*)

Plowing The fastest recorded time for plowing an acre by the United Kingdom Society of Ploughmen rules is 9 min. 49.88 sec., by Joe Langcake at Hornby Hall Farm, Brougham, England on October 21, 1989. He used a case IH 7140 Magnum tractor and a Kverneland four-furrow plow.

The greatest area plowed with a 6-furrow plow to a depth of nine inches in 24 hours is 173 acres, by Richard Gaisford and Peter Gooding of Wiltshire Young Farmers, using a Case IH tractor and a Lemken plow, at Manor Farm, Pewsey, England, September 25–26, 1990.

Field to loaf The fastest time for producing 13 loaves of bread (a baker's dozen) from growing wheat is 12 min. 11 sec., by representatives from the villages of Clapham and Patching in England on August 23, 1992. They used 13 microwave ovens. Using a traditional baker's oven to bake the bread, the record time is 19 min. 45 sec., by a team organized by John Haynes of millers Read Woodrow in Alpheton, England on September 19, 1992.

Largest grain elevator The single-unit elevator operated by the C-G-F Grain Co. in Wichita, KS consists of a triple row of storage tanks, 123 on each side of the central loading tower or "head house." The unit is 2,717 feet long and 100 feet wide. Each tank is 120 feet high, with an inside diameter of 30 feet, giving a total storage capacity of 20 million bushels of wheat.

The largest collection of grain elevators are the 23 at Thunder Bay, Ontario, Canada, on Lake Superior, with a total capacity of 103.9 million bushels.

CATTLE

Leading cattle producer   India was the world's leading cattle farming nation in 1993, with an estimated 271.3 million head out of a worldwide total of 1.05 billion head.

The leading producer of milk in 1994 was the United States, with 154 billion pounds. As of January 1, 1995, there were 103.3 million head of cattle farmed in the United States. The leading cattle producer was Texas, with 15.1 million head.

Largest cattle breed   The heaviest breed of cattle is the Chianini, which was brought to the Chiana Valley in Italy from the Middle East in pre-Roman times. Four types of the breed exist, the largest of which is the Val di Chianini, found on the plains and low hills of Arezzo and Siena. Bulls average 5 ft. 8 in. at the forequarters and weigh 2,865 pounds (compare with 1,873 pounds for cows), but Chianini oxen have been known to attain heights of 6 ft. 2¾ in. The sheer expense of feeding such huge cattle has put the breed under threat of extinction in Italy, but farmers in North America, Mexico and Brazil are still enthusiastic buyers of the breed.

Heaviest bovine   A Holstein–Durham cross named Mount Katahdin, exhibited by A.S. Rand of Maine from 1906 to 1910, frequently weighed in at an even 5,000 pounds. He was 6 ft. 2 in. at the shoulder with a 13-foot girth, and died in a barn fire *c.* 1923.

Smallest cattle breed   The smallest breed of domestic cattle is the Ovambo of Namibia. Bulls and cows average 496 pounds and 353 pounds respectively.

India has the world's largest stock of cattle, with an estimated 271.3 million head in 1993—more than a quarter of the world total. (*Rex Features*)

MOST EXPENSIVE LIVESTOCK

Species		Price
Cattle	Joe's Pride (Beefalo); bought by Beefalo Cattle Co., Calgary, Canada, Sept. 9, 1974	$2,500,000
Sheep	Collinsville stud JC&S 43; bought by Willogoleche Pty. Ltd., 1989 Adelaide Ram Sales, South Australia	$358,750
Goat	Angora buck; bought by Elliott Brown Ltd., Waipu, New Zealand, Jan. 25, 1985	$79,000
Pig	Bud (cross-bred barrow); bought by E.A. Bud Olson and Phil Bonzio, Mar. 5, 1983	$56,000
Horse	Farceur (Belgian stallion); bought by C.G. Good, Ogden, IA, Oct. 16, 1917	$47,000

Oldest bovine Big Bertha, a Dremon owned by Jerome O'Leary of Blackwatersbridge, County Kerry, Republic of Ireland, died less than three months short of her 49th birthday, on December 31, 1993.

Most reproductive cow On April 25, 1964, a cow named Lyubik gave birth to seven calves in Mogilev, Byelarus. A case of five live calves at one birth was reported in 1928 by T.G. Yarwood of Manchester, England. The lifetime breeding record is 39 in the case of Big Bertha.

Heaviest calf The heaviest recorded live birth weight for a calf is 225 pounds for a British Friesian cow at Rockhouse Farm, Bishopston, Wales in 1961.

Lightest calf The lowest live birthweight for a calf is nine pounds, for a Holstein heifer called Christmas, born on December 25, 1993 on Mark and Wendy Theuringer's farm in Hutchinson, MN.

Highest milk yields In 1994, the United States produced 154 billion pounds of cow's milk. As of April 1995, the state producing the most cow's milk was California, with a monthly total of 2.1 billion pounds. The highest lifetime yield of milk for a single cow is 465,224 pounds, by the unglamorously named cow No. 289 owned by M.G. Maciel & Son of Hanford, CA, to May 1, 1984.

The greatest recorded yield for one lactation (maximum 365 days) is 59,298 pounds in 1993 by the Holstein cow Robthom Suzet Paddy, owned by Mark Thomson of Springfield, MO. Suzet also has the world record for protein yield for 365 days, at 2,038 pounds.

The highest reported milk yield in a day is 241 pounds, by a cow named Urbe Blanca in Cuba on or about June 23, 1982.

Hand-milking of cows Joseph Love of Kilifi Plantations Ltd., Kenya milked 117 gallons from 30 cows on August 25, 1992.

United States The record for hand-milking is 88.2 gallons, by Andy Faust at Collinsville, OK in 1937 in 12 hours.

Highest butterfat yields   The world record lifetime yield is 16,370 pounds, by the Holstein Breezewood Patsy Bar Pontiac in 3,979 days.

The record for 365 days is 3,126 pounds, by Roybrook High Ellen, a Holstein owned by Yashuhiro Tanaka of Tottori, Japan.

Largest cheese producer   The United States produces the most cheese, with a total of 6.73 billion pounds in 1994.

Highest cheese consumption   The most avid cheese-eaters are the French, with an annual average of 43.6 pounds per person.

United States   In 1994, consumption in the United States stood at 7 billion pounds, an annual per-person cheese consumption of 27 pounds, or just over a half-pound of cheese per week.

GOATS

Largest goat   A British Saanen named Mostyn Moorcock, owned by Pat Robinson of Ewyas Harold, England, reached a weight of 400 pounds (shoulder height 44 inches and overall length 66 inches). He died in 1977 at age four.

Oldest goat   A Golden Guernsey–Anglo Nubian cross named Naturemade Aphrodite (1975–93), belonging to Katherine Whitwell of Moulton, New-market, England, died on August 23, 1993 aged 18 yr. 1 mo. Aphrodite was bred for 10 consecutive years, during which time she reared 26 kids, including five sets of triplets and one set of quads.

Most reproductive goat   According to the British Goat Society, at least one or two cases of quintuplets are recorded annually out of the 10,000 goats registered, but some breeders only record the females born.

On January 14, 1980, a nanny goat named Julie, owned by Galen Cowper of Nampah, ID, gave birth to septuplets, but all seven died, along with the mother.

Highest milk yield   In 1977, Osory Snow-Goose, owned by Mr. and Mrs. G. Jameson of Leppington, New South Wales, Australia, produced 7,714 pounds in 365 days.

PIGS

Largest producer   The world's leading producer of hogs in 1993 was China, with 384.2 million head from a world total of 754.1 million. As of March 1, 1995, there were 58.4 million head of pigs and hogs farmed in the United States. The leading state was Iowa with 14.2 million head.

Largest pig   A Poland–China hog named Big Bill was so obese that his belly dragged along the ground. Bill weighed an astonishing 2,552 pounds just before he was put to sleep after suffering a broken leg in an accident en route to the Chicago World's Fair for exhibition in 1933. Other statistics included a shoulder height of five feet and a length of nine feet. At the request of his owner, W.J. Chappall, this prized possession was mounted and put on display in Weekly County, TN until 1946, when the exhibit was acquired by a traveling carnival. On the death of the carnival's proprietor his family reportedly donated Big Bill to a museum, but no trace has been found of him since.

Smallest pig After 10 years of experimentation with Vietnamese pot-bellied pigs, Stefano Morini of St. Golo d'Enza, Italy developed the Mini Maialino. Piglets of this breed weigh 14 ounces at birth and 20 pounds at maturity.

Largest litter The highest recorded number of piglets in one litter is 37, farrowed on September 21, 1993 by Sow 570, a Meishan cross Large White–Duroc at Mr. and Mrs. M.P. Ford's Eastfield House Farm, Melbourne, England. Of the 36 piglets that were born alive, 33 survived.

Highest birth weight The average birth weight for a piglet is three pounds. A Hampshire–Yorkshire sow belonging to Rev. John Schroeder of Mountain Grove, MO farrowed a litter of 18 on August 26, 1979. Five were stillborn, including one male that weighed 5 lb. 4 oz.

The highest recorded weight for a piglet at weaning (eight weeks) is 81 pounds for a boar, one of a litter of nine farrowed on July 6, 1962 by the Landrace gilt Manorport Ballerina 53rd, alias "Mary," and sired by a Large White named Johnny at Kettle Lane Farm, West Ashton, England.

POULTRY

Largest poultry producer In 1994, the United States was the largest producer of chicken meat, or broiler, with a total of 32.53 billion pounds. The most produced by a state was 4.86 billion pounds, by Arkansas. The leading egg producer is China, where an estimated 215 billion were laid in 1993. United States egg production in 1994 was 73.87 billion eggs. The state with the highest production was California, with 6.6 billion eggs.

Largest chicken The heaviest breed of chicken is the White Sully, developed by Grant Sullens of West Point, CA. The largest recorded chicken was Big Snow, a rooster weighing 23 lb. 3 oz. on June 12, 1992, with a chest girth of 2 ft. 9 in. and standing 1 ft. 5 in. at the shoulder. Owned and bred by Ronald Alldridge of Deuchar, Queensland, Australia, Big Snow died of natural causes on September 6, 1992.

Most reproductive chicken A White Leghorn, No. 2988, laid 371 eggs in 364 days in an official test conducted by Prof. Harold V. Biellier ending on August 29, 1979 at the College of Agriculture, University of Missouri.

CHOLESTEROL!

In July 1971, a hen's egg was reported by Diane Hainsworth of Hainsworth Poultry Farms, Mount Morris, NY to have nine yolks. A hen's egg in Kyrgyzstan was also reported to have nine yolks in August 1977.

The highest recorded annual average per bird for a flock is 315 eggs in 52 weeks (August 1991–August 1992) from 5,997 free-range ISA Brown layers, owned by Vernon Weicle of Park Farm, Heol-y-Cyw, Penwed, Wales.

Most reproductive duck   An Aylesbury duck that belonged to Annette and Angela Butler of Princes Risborough, England laid 457 eggs in 463 days, including an uninterrupted run of 375 in as many days. The duck died on February 7, 1986. Another duck of the same breed, owned by Edmond Walsh of Gormanstown, Republic of Ireland, laid eggs every year right up to her 25th birthday. She died on December 3, 1978 at age 28 yr. 6 mo.

Largest chicken egg   A Black Minorca laid a 5-yolked egg of nearly 12 ounces, measuring 12¼ inches around the long axis and nine inches around the short, at Mr. Stafford's Damsteads Farm, Mellor, Lancashire, England in 1896.

Heaviest chicken egg   A White Leghorn in Vineland, NJ laid an egg weighing 16 ounces, with double yolk and double shell, on February 25, 1956.

Heaviest goose egg   An egg weighing 24 ounces and measuring 13½ inches around the long axis with a maximum circumference of 9½ inches around the short axis was laid on May 3, 1977 by a white goose named Speckle, owned by Donny Brandenberg of Goshen, OH. The average weight is 10–12 ounces.

Egg shelling   Two kitchen hands, Harold Witcomb and Gerald Harding, shelled 1,050 dozen eggs in a 7¼-hour shift at Bowyers, Trowbridge, England on April 23, 1971.

Egg dropping   The greatest height from which fresh eggs have been dropped (to the ground) and remained intact is 700 feet, by David Donoghue from a helicopter on August 22, 1994 on a golf course in Blackpool, England.

Longest chicken flight   Sheena, a barnyard bantam owned by Bill and Bob Knox, flew 630 ft. 2 in. at Parkesburg, PA on May 31, 1985.

Chicken plucking   Ernest Hausen (1877–1955) of Fort Atkinson, WI died undefeated after 33 years as champion chicken plucker. On January 19, 1939 he was timed at 4.4 seconds.

Turkey plucking   Vincent Pilkington of Cootehill, County Cavan, Republic of Ireland killed and plucked 100 turkeys in 7 hr. 32 min. on December 15, 1978. His record for a single turkey is 1 min. 30 sec. in Dublin on November 17, 1980.

Heaviest dressed turkey   A stag named Tyson, reared by Philip Cook of Leacroft Turkeys Ltd., Peterborough, England, had a dressed weight of 86 pounds. It won the annual "heaviest turkey" competition held in London, England on December 12, 1989 and was auctioned for charity for a record £4,400 ($7,480).

SHEEP

Largest sheep producer   The world's leading producer of sheep is Australia, with a total of 147.1 million head in 1993. As of January 1, 1995, there were 8.9 million head of sheep farmed in the United States. The leading state was Texas, with 1.7 million head.

Largest sheep   A Suffolk ram named Stratford Whisper 23H weighed 545 pounds and stood 43 inches tall in March 1991. It is owned by Joseph and Susan Schallberger of Boring, OR.

Smallest sheep   The Ouessant, from the Ile d'Ouessant, Brittany, France, weighs 29–35 pounds and stands 18–20 inches at the withers.

Oldest sheep   A crossbred sheep owned by Griffiths & Davies of Dolclettwr Hall, Taliesin, Wales gave birth to a healthy lamb in the spring of 1988 at the grand old age of 28, after lambing successfully more than 40 times. She died on January 24, 1989 just one week before her 29th birthday.

Largest litter   A Finnish Landrace ewe owned by the D.M.C. Partnership of Feilding, Manawatu, New Zealand gave birth to eight lambs (five rams and three ewes) at a single birth on September 4, 1991. On December 2, 1992, a Charolais ewe owned by Graham and Jo Partt of Wem, England also gave birth to eight lambs, seven of which survived.

Heaviest lamb   A lamb weighing 38 pounds was born at Clearwater, Sedgwick County, KS in 1975, but neither lamb nor ewe survived. Another lamb of the same weight was born on April 7, 1975 on the Gerald Neises Farm, Howard, SD but died soon afterwards.

Lightest lamb   A ewe named Texel (one of twins) weighing 1 lb. 15¾ oz. was born on March 28, 1991 at the farm owned by Verner and Esther Jensen in Rødekro, Denmark. This record was equaled on June 8, 1991 by a badger-faced Welsh mountain lamb named Lyle (also a twin) at Thorpe Park, England.

Sheep's survival   On March 24, 1978, Alex Maclennan found one ewe still alive after he dug out 16 sheep buried in a snowdrift for 50 days near the River Skinsdale on Mrs. Tyser's Gordonbush Estate in Sutherland, Scotland. In the aftermath of a snowstorm the sheep's hot breath creates airholes in the snow and the animals gnaw their own wool for protein, enabling them to survive in a snowdrift for a considerable length of time.

Sheep to shoulder   At the International Wool Secretariat Development Center, Ilkley, England, a team of eight using commercial machinery produced a sweater—from shearing sheep to the finished article—in 2 hr. 28 min. 32 sec. on September 3, 1986.

Fine spinning   The longest thread of wool, hand-spun and plied to weigh 0.35 ounces, was 1,815 ft. 3 in. long, and was achieved by Julitha Barber of Bull Creek, Western Australia, at the International Highland Spin-In, Bothwell, Tasmania, Australia on March 1, 1989.

Sheep shearing   The fastest speed for sheep shearing in a working day was by Alan McDonald, who machine-sheared 805 lambs in nine hours (averaging 40.2 seconds per lamb) at Waitnaguru, New Zealand on December 20, 1990. The hand-shearing record is 353 lambs in nine hours, by Peter Casserly of Christchurch, New Zealand on February 13, 1976.

Longest fleece   A Merino wether found on K.P. & B.A. Reynolds Company's Willow Springs Station, South Australia in November 1990 produced 65 pounds of wool from a fleece 25 inches long, representing a 7-year growth.

LAW

LEGISLATION AND LITIGATION

Oldest statute   The oldest surviving judicial code is the code of King Ur-Nammu, from the third dynasty of Ur, Iraq, *c.* 2250 B.C.

Most inexplicable legislation   A judge of the Court of Session of Scotland once nominated the following law as his candidate for most confusingly worded law: "In the Nuts (unground), (other than ground nuts) Order, the expression nuts shall have reference to such nuts, other than ground nuts, as would but for this amending Order not qualify as nuts (unground) (other than ground nuts) by reason of their being nuts (unground)."

Most protracted litigation   A controversy over the claim of the Prior and Convent (now the Dean and Chapter) of Durham Cathedral in England to administer the diocese during a vacancy in the See grew fierce in 1283. The dispute, with the Archbishop of York, flared up again in 1672 and 1890; an attempt in November 1975 to settle the issue, then 692 years old, was unsuccessful. Neither side admits the legitimacy of writs of appointment issued by the other, even though identical persons are named.

Longest trial   The longest civil case heard before a jury is *Kemner* vs. *Monsanto Co.*, which concerned an alleged toxic chemical spill in Sturgeon, MO in 1979. The trial started on February 6, 1984, at St. Clair County Court House, Belleville, IL before Circuit Judge Richard P. Goldenhersh, and ended on October 22, 1987. The testimony lasted 657 days, following which the jury deliberated for two months. The residents of Sturgeon were awarded $1 million nominal compensatory damages and $16,280,000 punitive damages, but these awards were overturned by the Illinois Appellate Court in June 1991 because the jury in the original trial had not found that any damage had resulted from the spill.

Greatest damages   *Civil damages*   The largest damages awarded in legal history were $11.12 billion to Pennzoil Company against Texaco Inc., as a result of Texaco's allegedly unethical tactics in January 1984 in attempting to break up a merger between Pennzoil and Getty Oil Company. The verdict was handed down in Houston, TX on December 10, 1985. An out-of-court settlement of $5.5 billion was reached after a 48-hour negotiation on December 19, 1987.

The largest damages awarded against an individual were $2.1 billion. On July 10, 1992, Charles H. Keating, Jr., the former owner of Lincoln Savings and Loan of Los Angeles, CA, was ordered by a federal jury to pay this sum to 23,000 small investors who were defrauded by his company. On July 8, 1993, Keating was sentenced to 12¹/₂ years in prison.

Personal injury   Model Marla Hanson was awarded $78,183,000 on September 29, 1987 after her face was slashed with razors in New York City in June 1987. The award was uncontested and included $4 million in punitive damages. The three men convicted and sentenced to 5–15 years in prison had no assets, but Hanson was entitled to 10 percent of their post-prison earnings.

The compensation for the disaster on December 2–3, 1984 at the Union Carbide Corporation plant in Bhopal, India was set at $470 million. The Supreme Court of India passed the order for payment on February 14, 1989 after a settlement between the corporation and the Indian government, which represented the interests of more than 500,000 claimants. On March 27, 1992, the Bhopal Court put the death toll at more than 4,000, with 20,000 injured and the number of claimants rising to 600,000.

Sexual harassment   The record award in a sexual harassment case was $7.1 million to Rena Weeks, a former secretary at the law firm Baker & McKenzie in Palo Alto, CA, against Martin Greenstein, a partner in the firm, on September 2, 1994. The firm said that it would appeal.

Best-attended trial   The greatest attendance at any trial was at that of Major Jesús Sosa Blanco, age 51, for an alleged 108 murders. At one point in the 12¹/₂-hour trial (5:30 P.M. to 6 A.M., January 22–23, 1959), 17,000 people were present in the Havana Sports Palace, Cuba. The defendant was found guilty and was executed on February 18, 1959.

Most viewed trial   Between January 24 and June 2, 1995, a daily average of 5.5 million Americans watched live coverage of the O. J. Simpson trial on three major cable networks. Simpson, a pro football Hall of Famer and actor, was on trial for the murder of his ex-wife, Nicole Brown Simpson, and waiter Ronald Goldman on June 12, 1994.

Greatest compensation for wrongful imprisonment   Robert McLaughlin, 29, was awarded $1,935,000 in October 1989 for wrongful imprisonment for a murder in New York City in 1979 which he did not commit. He had been sentenced to 15 years in prison and had actually served six years, from 1980 to 1986, when he was released after his foster father succeeded in showing the authorities that he had had nothing to do with the crime.

Largest divorce settlement   The largest publicly declared settlement, achieved in 1982 by the lawyers for Soraya Khashoggi, was £500 million ($950 million) plus property from her husband Adnan Khashoggi.

Largest alimony suit   Belgian-born Sheika Dena Al-Fassi filed the highest-ever alimony claim of $3 billion against her former husband, Sheik Mohammed Al-Fassi of the Saudi Arabian royal family, in Los Angeles, CA in February 1982. Attorney Marvin Mitchelson, explaining the size of the settlement claim, alluded to the Sheik's wealth, which included 14 homes in Florida alone and numerous private aircraft. On June 14, 1983, the claimant was awarded $81 million and declared she would be "very very happy" if she were able to collect.

Largest patent violation case   Litton Industries Inc. was awarded $1.2 billion in damages from Honeywell Inc. on August 31, 1993. A jury in Los Angeles, CA decided that Honeywell had violated a Litton patent covering airline navigation systems.

DID YOU KNOW?

Thomas Alva Edison (1847–1931) had the most patents, with 1,093 either on his own or jointly. They included the microphone, the motion-picture projector and the incandescent electric lamp.

Highest costs   The Blue Arrow trial, involving the illegal support of the company's shares during a rights issue in 1987, is estimated to have cost approximately £35 million (*c.* $60 million). The trial at the Old Bailey, London, England lasted a year and ended on February 14, 1992 with four of the defendants being convicted. Although they received suspended prison sentences, they were later cleared on appeal.

United States   The McMartin Preschool case in Los Angeles, CA is estimated to have cost $15 million. The trial, concerning the alleged abuse of children at the school in Manhattan Beach, CA, had begun with jury selec-

The trial of O.J. Simpson has fascinated a record number of television viewers. (*AP/WorldWide Photos*)

tion on April 20, 1987 and resulted in the acquittal on January 18, 1990 of the two defendants on 52 counts of child molestation and conspiracy.

Oldest will   The oldest written will dates from 2061 B.C. It was carved on the walls of the tomb of Nek'ure, the son of the Egyptian pharaoh Khafre, and indicated that Nek'ure would bequeath 14 towns, two estates and other property to his wife, another woman and three children.

Shortest will   The shortest valid will consists of four characters in Hindi meaning "All to son." It was written by Bimla Rishi of Delhi, India and is dated February 9, 1995.

Longest will   The will of Frederica Evelyn Stilwell Cook (U.S.) was proved in London, England on November 2, 1925. It consisted of four bound volumes containing 95,940 words, primarily concerning some $100,000 worth of property.

COMMITMENT!

The longest lease, on a plot for a sewage tank adjoining Columb Barracks, Mullingar, Ireland, was signed on December 3, 1868 for 10 million years.

Most codicils   The largest number of codicils (supplements modifying the details) to a will admitted to probate is 21, in the case of the will of J. Paul Getty. The will was dated September 22, 1958 and had 21 codicils dating from June 18, 1960 through March 11, 1976. Getty died on June 6, 1976.

Most durable judge   The oldest recorded active judge was Judge Albert R. Alexander of Plattsburg, MO. He was enrolled as a member of the Clinton County Bar in 1926, and was later the magistrate and probate judge of Clinton County until his retirement at age 105 yr. 8 mo. on July 9, 1965.

Narrowest margin   Judge Clarence Thomas was elected to the Supreme Court in 1991 by the narrowest margin ever recorded, 52 votes to 48.

Youngest judge   No collated records on the ages of judicial appointments exist. However, David Elmer Ward had to wait until he reached the legal age of 21 before taking office after nomination in 1932 as judge of the County Court in Fort Myers, FL.

Muhammad Ilyas passed the examination enabling him to become a civil judge in July 1952 at the age of 20 yr. 9 mo., although formalities such as medicals meant that it was not until eight months later that he started work as a civil judge in Lahore, Pakistan.

Most lawyers   In the United States there were an estimated 896,172 resident and active lawyers as of June 1995, or one lawyer for every 290 people.

CRIME

Largest criminal organizations   There are believed to be more than 250,000 members of Chinese triad societies worldwide, but they are fragmented into many groups that often fight each other and compete in disputed areas. Hong Kong alone has some 100,000 members.

In terms of profit, the largest syndicate in organized crime is the Mafia or La Cosa Nostra. The Mafia consists of some 3,000 to 5,000 individuals in 25 "families" federated under "The Commission," with an annual turnover in illegal activities that was estimated by *U.S. News & World Report* in December 1982 at $200 billion, and a profit estimated in March 1986 by U.S. District Attorney Rudolph Giuliani at $75 billion.

In terms of numbers, the Yamaguchi-gumi gang of the *yakuza* in Japan is the largest, with 30,000 members. There are some 90,000 *yakuza* or gangsters altogether, in more than 3,000 groups. On March 1, 1992, Japan instituted new laws to combat their activities, which include drug trafficking, smuggling, prostitution and gambling.

Most assassinations   The country with the most leaders assassinated in modern times is Russia, where, between 1718 and 1918, four Tsars and two heirs apparent were assassinated. There were also many other assassination attempts that did not succeed.

The target of the highest number of *failed* assassination attempts on an individual head of state in modern times was Charles de Gaulle, president of France from 1958 to 1969. He was reputed to have survived no fewer than 31 plots against his life between 1944 and 1966, although some plots were foiled and did not culminate in actual physical attacks.

Most murders committed   It was established at the trial of Behram, the Indian Thug, that he had strangled at least 931 victims with his yellow and white cloth strip or *ruhmal* in the Oudh district between 1790 and 1840. An estimated 2 million Indians were strangled by Thugs during the reign of the Thugee cult from 1550 until its final suppression by the British raj in 1853.

Twentieth century   A total of 592 deaths was attributed to one Colombian bandit leader, Teófilo ("Sparks") Rojas, between 1948 and his death in an ambush near Armenia, Colombia on January 22, 1963. Some sources attribute 3,500 slayings to him during *La Violencia* of 1945–62.

United States   The greatest mass murder committed in the United States was the Happy Land fire, which resulted in the deaths of 87 individuals. The fire was set by 36-year-old Julio Gonzalez, on March 25, 1990 at an illegal New York City social club, The Happy Land, in revenge for being thrown out of the club after an argument with a former girlfriend, Lydia Feliciano, who worked at the club. Feliciano was one of six survivors.

Greatest mass arrest   The greatest mass arrest reported in a democratic country was of 15,617 demonstrators on July 11, 1988, rounded up by

South Korean police to ensure security in advance of the 1988 Olympic Games in Seoul.

Most lynchings   The worst year in the 20th century for lynchings in the United States was 1901, with 130 lynchings, of which 125 were of blacks and five were of whites. The first year with no reported cases was 1952. The date on which lynchings were last reported was June 21, 1964, in Philadelphia, MS. Three men—two white (Michael Schwerner and Andrew Goodman) and one black (James Chaney)—were murdered in the Neshoba County town.

Greatest mass poisoning   On May 1, 1981, an 8-year-old boy became the first of more than 600 victims of the Spanish cooking oil scandal. On June 12, it was discovered that the cause of his death was the use of "denatured" industrial oil from rape-seed. The trial of 38 defendants, including the manufacturers, Ramón and Elías Ferrero, lasted from March 30, 1987 to June 28, 1988. The 586 counts on which the prosecution demanded jail sentences totaled 60,000 years.

Biggest robbery   The robbery of the Reischbank following Germany's collapse in April–May 1945 was described by the Pentagon in Washington as "an unverified allegation." However, the book *Nazi Gold* by Ian Sayer and Douglas Botting, published in 1984, finally revealed full details and estimated the total haul at what were then current values as £2.5 billion ($3.75 billion).

The government of the Philippines announced on April 23, 1986 that it had succeeded in identifying $860.8 million salted away since 1965 by former President Ferdinand Edralin Marcos and his wife Imelda. The total wealth taken by the couple was believed to be $5–$10 billion.

Art   It is arguable that the *Mona Lisa*, though never appraised, is the most valuable object ever stolen. The painting disappeared from the Louvre, Paris, France on August 21, 1911. It was recovered in Italy in 1913, when Vincenzo Perugia was charged with its theft.

Bank   During the extreme civil disorder prior to January 22, 1976 in Beirut, Lebanon, a guerrilla force blasted the vaults of the British Bank of the Middle East in Bab Idriss and cleared out safe deposit boxes with contents valued by former Finance Minister Lucien Dahdah at $50 million and by another source at an "absolute minimum" of $20 million.

Jewels   The greatest recorded theft of jewels was from the Carlton Hotel, Cannes, France on August 11, 1994. Gems with an estimated value of Fr250 million ($48 million) were stolen from the jewelry store by a 3-man gang. A security guard was seriously injured during the raid.

Largest object stolen by a single person   On a moonless night at dead calm high water on June 5, 1966, at Wolfe's Cove, St. Lawrence Seaway, Canada, N. William Kennedy, armed with only a sharp ax, slashed free the mooring lines of the 10,640-ton SS *Orient Trader*, owned by Steel Factors Ltd. of Ontario. The vessel drifted to a waiting blacked-out tug, thus escaping the ban on any shipping movements during a violent wildcat waterfront strike. It then sailed for Spain.

Greatest hijacking ransom   The government of Japan paid $6 million to aircraft hijackers for a JAL DC-8 and 38 hostages at Dacca Airport, Bangladesh on October 2, 1977. Six convicted criminals were also exchanged. The Bangladesh government had refused to sanction any retaliatory action.

Greatest kidnapping ransom   Historically, the greatest ransom paid was that for Atahualpa by the Incas to Francisco Pizarro in 1532–33 at Cajamarca, Peru. It constituted a hall full of gold and silver, worth some $1.5 billion on today's market. Pizarro did not keep his side of the bargain; he murdered Atahualpa instead of returning him.

The greatest ransom ever reported in modern times was 1,500 million pesos ($60 million) for the release of the brothers Jorge and Juan Born of the firm Bunge and Born, paid to the left-wing urban guerrilla group Montoneros in Buenos Aires, Argentina on June 20, 1975.

Largest narcotics haul   In terms of value, the greatest haul in a drug seizure was on September 28, 1989, when cocaine with an estimated street value of $6–7 billion was seized in a raid on a warehouse in Los Angeles, CA. The 22-ton haul was prompted by a tip-off from a local resident who had complained about heavy truck traffic and people leaving the warehouse "at odd hours and in a suspicious manner."

Largest narcotics operation   The bulkiest haul was 3,200 tons of Colombian marijuana in the 14-month-long "Operation Tiburon," carried out by the U.S. Drug Enforcement Administration and Colombian authorities. The arrest of 495 people and the seizure of 95 vessels was announced on February 5, 1982.

Greatest bank note forgery   The German Third Reich's forging operation, code name "Operation Bernhard," was engineered by Major Bernhard Krüger during World War II. It involved more than £130 million worth of British notes, which were produced by 140 Jewish prisoners at Sachsenhausen concentration camp.

Biggest bank fraud   The Banca Nazionale del Lavoro of Italy admitted on September 6, 1989 that it had been defrauded of a huge sum, later estimated to be in the region of $5 billion, with the disclosure that its branch in Atlanta, GA had made unauthorized loan commitments to Iraq. Both the bank's chairman, Nerio Nesi, and its director general, Giacomo Pedde, resigned following the revelation.

Biggest computer fraud   Between 1964 and 1973, 64,000 fake insurance policies were created on the computer of the Equity Funding Corporation in the United States, involving $2 billion.

Stanley Mark Rifkin was arrested in Carlsbad, CA by the FBI on November 6, 1978 and charged with defrauding a Los Angeles bank of $10.2 million by manipulation of a computer system. He was sentenced to eight years' imprisonment in June 1980.

Biggest maritime fraud   A cargo of 198,414 tons of Kuwaiti crude oil on the supertanker *Salem* at Durban was sold without title to the South African government in December 1979. The ship mysteriously sank off Senegal on

January 17, 1980, leaving the government to pay £148 million ($318.2 million) to Shell International, which owned the shipment.

FINES

Heaviest fine   A fine of $650 million was imposed on the U.S. securities firm of Drexel Burnham Lambert in December 1988 for insider trading. This figure represented $300 million in direct fines, with the balance to be put into an account to satisfy claims of parties who could prove they were defrauded by Drexel's actions.

The record for an individual is $200 million, which Michael Milken agreed to pay on April 24, 1990. In addition, he agreed to settle civil charges filed by the Securities and Exchange Commission. The payments were in settlement of a criminal racketeering and securities fraud suit brought by the U.S. government. On appeal, Milken's sentence was reduced to 33 mo. 26 days. He was released from prison on March 2, 1993, but was required to give 1,800 hours of community service.

CAPITAL PUNISHMENT

Largest hanging   The Nazi Feldkommandant simultaneously hanged 50 Greek resistance fighters as a reprisal measure in Athens, Greece on July 22, 1944.

The greatest number of people hanged from one gallows was 38 Sioux Indians, by William J. Duly outside Mankato, MN on December 26, 1862 for the murder of unarmed citizens.

Last public hanging   The last public hanging in the United States occurred in Owensboro, KY on August 14, 1936, when Rainey Bethea was hung in a field by the banks of the Ohio River. He was executed in the presence of a crowd of 10–15,000.

Most experienced executioners   The Sanson family of France supplied executioners through several generations, from 1688 to 1847. Charles-Henri Sanson, known as Monsieur de Paris, dispatched more than 3,000 victims, most of them in two years, 1793–94, including the king, Louis XVI, on January 21, 1793.

Longest stay on death row   Sadamichi Hirasawa (1893–1987) spent 39 years on death row in Sendai Jail, Japan. He was convicted in 1948 of poisoning 12 bank employees with potassium cyanide to effect a theft of $403, and died in prison at age 94.

United States   Howard Virgil Lee Douglas spent $17^1/_2$ years on death row, longer than any other person in American penal history. On May 15, 1991, he was resentenced to life in prison..

PRISON SENTENCES

Longest sentences   Chamoy Thipyaso, a Thai woman known as the queen of underground investing, and seven of her associates were each sentenced to serve 141,078 years in jail by the Bangkok Criminal Court, Thailand on July 27, 1989 for swindling the public through a multimillion-dollar deposit-taking business.

The longest sentence imposed on a mass murderer was 21 consecutive life sentences and 12 death sentences in the case of John Wayne Gacy, Jr., who killed 33 boys and young men between 1972 and 1978 in Illinois. He was sentenced by a jury in Chicago, IL on March 13, 1980, and executed on May 10, 1994.

Longest time served   Paul Geidel was convicted of second-degree murder on September 5, 1911 when he was a 17-year-old porter in a hotel in New York. He was released from the Fishkill Correctional Facility, Beacon, NY at age 85 on May 7, 1980, having served 68 yr. 8 mo. 2 days—the longest term in U.S. history.

Oldest prisoner   Bill Wallace spent the last 63 years of his life in Aradale Psychiatric Hospital, Ararat, Victoria, Australia. He had shot and killed a man at a restaurant in Melbourne, Victoria in December 1925, and having been found unfit to plead, was transferred to the responsibility of the Mental Health Department in February 1926. He remained at Aradale until his death on July 17, 1989, shortly before his 108th birthday.

PRISONS

Most expensive imprisonment   Spandau Prison, Berlin, Germany, originally built in 1887 for 600 prisoners, was used solely for the Nazi war criminal Rudolf Hess (April 26, 1894–August 17, 1987) for the last 20 years of his life. The cost of maintenance of the staff of 105 was estimated in 1976 to be $415,000 per year.

Longest escape   On December 15, 1923, Leonard T. Fristoe escaped from Nevada State Prison, where he was serving time for killing two sheriff's deputies. Fristoe was turned in by his son on November 15, 1969, in Compton, CA, having had 46 years of freedom under the name of Claude R. Willis.

Largest jailbreaks   On February 11, 1979, an Iranian employee of the Electronic Data Systems Corporation led a mob into Gasr Prison, Tehran, Iran in an attempt to rescue two Americans. Some 11,000 other prisoners took advantage of the situation and became part of history's largest-ever jailbreak. Although it was the Iranian employee's actions that allowed the actual jailbreak to happen, the plan to get the Americans out was masterminded by their employer, H. Ross Perot.

In September 1971, Raúl Sendic and 105 other Tupamaro guerrillas, plus five nonpolitical prisoners, escaped from a Uruguayan prison through a tunnel 298 feet long.

Highest prison population   Some human rights organizations have estimated that there are 20 million prisoners in China, or 1,677 per 100,000 population, although this figure is not officially acknowledged. Among countries for which statistics are available, the country with the highest per capita prison population is the United States, with 389 prisoners per 100,000 population.

OFF WITH THEIR HEADS!

Most experienced executioners The Sanson family of France supplied executioners through several generations, from 1688 to 1847. Charles-Henri Sanson, known as Monsieur de Paris, dispatched more than 3,000 victims, most of them in 1793–94.

Charles-Henri Sanson, known as Monsieur de Paris, has the unhappy distinction of having executed more people than anyone else in history; his total number of victims was over 3,000.

Born in 1739, Sanson was the son, grandson and great-grandson of executioners. He began assisting his father when he was 15 years old and eventually took over from him as chief executioner in 1778. When the guillotine replaced the sword as the method of beheading people, it was Sanson who performed the first execution by guillotine, on April 25, 1792, at the Place de Grève, Paris.

As the French Revolution developed and the period known as "The Terror" began, Sanson became such an expert with the guillotine that he could execute one person per minute. He kept records of the numbers he dealt with: "Seventeen persons were sentenced to death yesterday. I executed them this morning . . . The women were in a majority. Several of these women had their children in the carts." Another entry simply said, "Fifty-four victims."

Before his victims were buried, Sanson made the severed heads of some of them available to a young sculptor named Marie Grozholtz. She made effigies of famous people and became, on her marriage in 1795, Madame Tussaud.

Sanson's victims included the queen, Marie Antoinette, and the king, Louis XVI. It is said that Napoleon once asked Sanson if he would be prepared to execute him if necessary. He replied, "Sire, I executed Louis XVI!"

A.K.G London

HUMAN WORLD

GEOGRAPHY AND POPULATION

COUNTRIES

The world comprises 192 sovereign countries and 65 nonsovereign or other territories (dependencies of sovereign states, territories claimed in Antarctica, disputed and other territories), making a total of 257 as of June 1995.

Largest country   Russia has a total area of 6,592,800 square miles, or 11.5 percent of the world's total land area. It is 1.8 times the size of the United States, but had a population of 148,174,000 people in 1994, around 60 percent the size of the U.S. population.

Smallest country   The smallest independent country in the world is the State of Vatican City or Holy See (Stato della Città del Vaticano), which was made an enclave within the city of Rome, Italy on February 11, 1929. The enclave has an area of 108.7 acres.

Republic   The world's smallest republic is Nauru, just south of the equator in the western Pacific, which became independent on January 31, 1968. It has an area of 5,263 acres and a population of 10,200 (1994 estimate).

Colony   Gibraltar (since 1969, the City of Gibraltar) has an area of 1,440 acres. However, Pitcairn Island, the only inhabited island (55 people in late 1993) of a group of four islands in the South Pacific, has an area of 960 acres.

Flattest and most elevated country   The country with the lowest "high point" is Maldives, at eight feet above sea level. The country with the highest "low point" is Lesotho, where the egress of the Senqu (Orange) riverbed is 4,530 feet above sea level.

Largest political division   The Commonwealth, a free association of 51 independent states and their dependencies, covers an area of 11,797,193 square miles with a population of some 1.5 billion. Almost all member countries once belonged to the former British Empire.

Most border crossings   The most frequently crossed frontier is the border between the United States and Mexico. In the fiscal year 1993 (to September 1993), there were 475,489,103 crossings.

The country with the most land frontiers is China, with 16—Mongolia, Russia, North Korea, Hong Kong, Macau, Vietnam, Laos, Myanmar, India, Bhutan, Nepal, Pakistan, Afghanistan, Tajikistan, Kyrgyzstan and Kazakhstan. These extend for 14,900 miles.

The country with the largest number of maritime boundaries is Indonesia, with 19.

Longest boundary   The longest *continuous* boundary in the world is the border between Canada and the conterminous United States, which extends for 3,987 miles. The longest land boundary is the border between Chile and Argentina, which is 3,265 miles long.

Maritime   The maritime boundary between Greenland and Canada is 1,676 miles long.

Shortest boundary   The land frontier between Gibraltar and Spain at La Linea, closed between June 1969 and February 1985, measures one mile in length. Zambia, Zimbabwe, Botswana and Namibia, in Africa, almost meet at a single point on the Zambezi River.

Longest coastline   The country with the longest coastline is Canada, with 152,100 miles including islands.

DID YOU KNOW?

There are 319 national land boundaries in the world. The continent with the greatest number is Africa, with 109. The ratio of boundaries to area of land is greatest in Europe.

Shortest coastline   The sovereign country with the shortest coastline is Monaco, with 3½ miles, excluding piers and breakwaters.

Nearest and farthest capital cities   The nearest capitals of two neighboring countries are the Vatican City and Rome (Italy), as the Vatican is actually surrounded by Rome. The greatest distance between the capitals of coun-

---

GUESS WHAT?

Q.   WHERE IS THE REMOTEST INHABITED ISLAND?

A.   LOOK IN "ISLANDS" (EARTH & SPACE)

---

tries that share a common border is 2,600 miles, in the case of Moscow (Russia) and Pyongyang (Democratic People's Republic of Korea).

STATES

Largest state   The largest state in land area is Alaska, with 591,004 square miles. The largest of the 48 conterminous states is Texas, with 267,017 square miles of land.

Smallest state   The smallest state is Rhode Island, with 1,212 square miles.

Most populous state   The most populous state in the United States as of July 1, 1992 was California, with an estimated 30,867,000 people.

Least populous state   As of July 1, 1992, Wyoming had 466,000 people.

Longest coastline   Alaska is the state with the longest coastline; it measures 33,904 miles.

COUNTIES

As of July 1, 1995, there were 3,142 counties in the United States (in Alaska, counties are known as boroughs, and in Louisiana they are called parishes).

Largest county   The largest county in the lower 48 states is San Bernardino County, CA, with an area of 20,062 square miles. The biggest legally established county is the North Slope Borough of Alaska, at 87,860 acres.

Most and fewest counties   The state with the most counties is Texas, with 254, and the state with the fewest is Delaware, with three (Kent, New Castle and Sussex).

Most counties visited   Allen F. Zondlak of St. Clair Shores, MI visited all 3,142 counties and county equivalents in the United States, completing his travels in 1991.

CITIES AND TOWNS

Oldest town   The oldest walled town in the world is Arihā (Jericho), which was inhabited by perhaps 2,700 people as early as 7800 B.C. The settlement of Dolní Věstonice, Czech Republic has been dated to the Gravettian culture *c.* 27,000 B.C.

The oldest town of European origin in the United States is St. Augustine, St. John's County, FL. The town was founded on September 8, 1565, on the site of Seloy, by Pedro Menendez de Aviles. Its present population is 12,000.

Oldest city   The oldest capital city in the world is Damascus, Syria. It has been continuously inhabited since *c.* 2500 B.C.

United States   The oldest incorporated city is York, ME (present population 14,000), which received an English charter in March 1642, and was incorporated under the name Georgiana.

Most populous city   The United Nations *Prospects of World Urbanization 1992* lists Tokyo, Japan as the most populous, with a population of 25,000,000 in 1990. This is expected to increase to 28,000,000 by the year 2000.

United States   The most populous metropolitan area in the United States is that of New York City, with 18,087,251 residents.

Smallest incorporated place   The smallest incorporated place in the United States in 1990 was Valley Park, OK, with one resident.

Largest city In terms of area, the world's largest city (defined as a densely populated settlement) is Mount Isa, Queensland, Australia. The area administered by the City Council is 15,822 square miles.

Highest town The new town of Wenzhuan, founded in 1955 on the Qinghai–Tibet road north of the Tangla range, is the highest in the world, at 16,730 feet above sea level.

Highest capital city The highest capital in the world, before the domination of Tibet by China, was Lhasa, at an elevation of 12,087 feet above sea level. La Paz, administrative and *de facto* capital of Bolivia, stands at an altitude of 11,916 feet above sea level. Sucre, the legal capital of Bolivia, stands at 9,301 feet above sea level.

Farthest town from the sea The large town most remote from the sea is Urumqi (Wu-lu-mu-ch'i) in Xinjiang, the capital of China's Xinjiang Uygur Autonomous Region, at a distance of about 1,500 miles from the nearest coastline. Its population was estimated to be 1,160,000 in late 1990.

Highest settlement The settlement on the T'e-li-mo trail in southern Tibet is sited at an altitude of 19,800 feet.

The highest inhabited buildings in the world are those in the Indo-Tibetan border fort of Bāsisi by the Māna Pass (Lat. 31° 04′ N, Long. 79° 24′ E) at *c.* 19,700 feet.

In April 1961, a 3-room dwelling was discovered at 21,650 feet on Cerro Llullaillaco (22,057 feet), on the Argentina–Chile border. The dwelling is believed to date from the late pre-Columbian period *c.* 1480.

Lowest settlement The Israeli settlement of Ein Bokek on the shores of the Dead Sea is the lowest in the world, at 1,291 feet below sea level.

Northernmost settlement Ny Ålesund (78° 55′ N) is a coal mining settlement on King's Bay, Vest Spitsbergen in the Norwegian territory of Svalbard. Its population varies from around 25 in winter to nearly 100 in summer.

United States   The northernmost city in the United States is Barrow, AK (71° 17′ N).

Northernmost capital city   The northernmost capital is Reykjavik, Iceland (64° 08′ N). Its population was 100,855 in 1993.

Southernmost settlement   The world's southernmost village is Puerto Williams (population about 1,000) on the north coast of Isla Navarino, Tierra del Fuego, Chile, 680 miles north of Antarctica.

United States   The southernmost city in the United States is Hilo, HI (19° 43′ N).

Southernmost capital city   Wellington, the capital of New Zealand (41° 17′ S), had a population of 325,700 in 1991.

Administrative center   Port Stanley, Falkland (Malvinas) Islands (51° 43′ S), has a population of 1,643.

POPULATION

The world's population in 1995 was estimated to be 5.716 billion. At the beginning of the century, the population was 1.633 billion and in the year 2000 it is expected to be 6.159 billion. The average daily increase in the world's population is approximately 236,000, or an average of some 164 births per minute.

Most populous country   China had an estimated population of 1,192,300,000 in mid-1994 and a rate of natural increase of over 12.8 million per year or more than 35,000 per day. Its population is larger than that of the whole world 150 years ago.

Least populous country   The independent state with the smallest population is Vatican City or the Holy See, with 1,000 inhabitants in 1994.

Most sparsely populated territory   Antarctica became permanently occupied by relays of scientists from 1943 on. The population varies seasonally and reaches 2,000 at times.

Most houses   For comparison purposes, a dwelling unit is defined as a structurally separated room or rooms occupied by a private household of one or more people and having separate access or a common passageway to the street.
   The country with the most dwelling units is China, with 276,947,962 in 1990.

Most emigrants   More people emigrate from Mexico than from any other country, mainly to the United States. Wars or droughts periodically cause large upheavals in population; in late 1992, there were some 27 million refugees worldwide.

WORST DISASTERS IN THE WORLD

Type of Disaster	Number killed	Location	Date
Atomic Bomb	155,200	Hiroshima, Japan (including radiation deaths within year)	Aug. 6, 1945
Conventional Bombing[1]	c. 140,000	Tokyo, Japan	Mar. 10, 1945
Marine (Single Ship)	c. 7,700	Wilhelm Gustloff (28,542.1 tons) German liner torpedoed off Danzig by USSR submarine S-13 (only 903 survivors)	Jan. 30, 1945
Dam Burst[2]	c. 5,000	Machhu River Dam, Morvi, Gujarat, India	Aug. 11, 1979
Panic	c. 4,000	Chongquig, China, air raid shelter	Jun. 6, 1941
Smog	3,500–4,000	London, England	Dec. 4–9, 1952
Industrial (Chemical)	3,350	Union Carbide methylisocyanate plant, Bhopal, India	Dec. 2–3, 1984
Tunneling (Silicosis)	c. 2,500	Hawk's Nest hydroelectric tunnel, West Virginia	1931–35
Fire (Single building)[3]	1,670	The Theatre, Canton, China	May 1845
Explosion[4]	1,635	Halifax, Nova Scotia, Canada	Dec. 6, 1917
Mining[5]	1,549	Honkeiko Colliery (Benxihu), China (coal dust explosion)	Apr. 26, 1942
Riot	c. 1,400	Riots following arrest of woman selling contraband cigarettes, Taiwan	Mar. 1947
Tornado	c. 1,300	Shaturia, Bangladesh	Apr. 26, 1989
Mass Suicide[6]	960	Jewish Zealots, Masada, Israel	A.D. 73
Railway	>800	Bagmati River, Bihar, India	Jun. 6, 1981
Fireworks	>800	Dauphin's wedding, Seine, Paris, France	May 16, 1770
Aircraft (Civil)[7]	583	KLM-Pan Am Boeing 747 ground crash, Tenerife, Canary Islands, Spain	Mar. 27, 1977
Man-eating Animal	436	Champawat district, India, tigress shot by Col. Jim Corbett (died 1955)	1902–07
Terrorism	329	Bomb aboard Air-India Boeing 747, crashed into Atlantic southwest of Ireland. Sikh extremists suspected	Jun. 23, 1985
Road[8]	176	Gas tanker explosion inside Salang Tunnel, Afghanistan	Nov. 3, 1982
Offshore Oil Platform	167	Piper Alpha oil production platform, North Sea	Jul. 6, 1988
Submarine	130	Le Surcouf rammed by U.S. merchantman Thomas Lykes in Caribbean	Feb. 18, 1942

Elevator	105	Gold mine elevator at Vaal Reefs, South Africa fell 1,600 feet	May 11, 1995
Helicopter	61	Russian military helicopter carrying refugees shot down near Lata, Georgia	Dec. 14, 1992
Mountaineering	43	Lenin Peak, Tajikistan/Kyrgyzstan border (then USSR)	Jul. 13, 1990
Ski Lift (Cable car)	42	Cavalese resort, northern Italy	Mar. 9, 1976
Nuclear Reactor[9]	31	Chernobyl No. 4, Ukraine (then USSR)	Apr. 26, 1986
Yacht Racing	19	28th Fastnet Race—23 boats sunk or abandoned in Force 11 gale	Aug. 13–15, 1979
Space Exploration[10]	7	U.S. Challenger 51L Shuttle, Cape Canaveral, FL	Jan. 28, 1986
Nuclear Waste Accident[11]	?	Venting of plutonium extraction wastes, Kyshtym, Russia (then USSR)	c. Dec. 1957

[1] The number of civilians killed by the bombing of Germany has been put variously at 593,000 and "over 635,000," including some 35,000 deaths in the raids on Dresden, Germany from Feb. 13–15, 1945. Total Japanese fatalities were 600,000 (conventional) and 220,000 (nuclear).

[2] The dynamiting of a Yangtze Kiang dam at Huayuan Kou by the Kuomintang during the Sino-Japanese war in 1938 is reputed to have resulted in 900,000 deaths.

[3] More than 200,000 were killed in the sack of Moscow, as a result of fires started by the invading Tartars in May 1571. In the worst-ever hotel fire, 162 were killed in the Hotel Daeyungak, Seoul, South Korea, December 25, 1971. The worst circus fire killed 168 in Hartford, CT, Jul. 6, 1944.

[4] Some sources maintain that the final death toll was over 3,000, Dec. 6–7.

[5] The worst gold-mining disaster in South Africa was when 182 were killed in Kinross gold mine on Sep. 16, 1986.

[6] As reported by the historian Flavius Josephus (c. 37–100). In modern times, the greatest mass suicide was on Nov. 18, 1978 when 913 members of the People's Temple cult died of mass cyanide poisoning near Port Kaituma, Guyana. Some 7,000 Japanese committed suicide, many of them jumping off cliffs to their deaths, in July 1944 during the U.S. Marines' assault on the island of Saipan.

[7] The crash of JAL's Boeing 747, flight 123, near Tokyo on Aug. 12, 1985, in which 520 passengers and crew perished, was the worst crash involving a single plane in aviation history.

[8] Western estimates gave the number of deaths at c. 1,100. Latvia has the highest fatality rate in road accidents, with 34.7 deaths per 100,000 population, and Malta the lowest, with 1.6 per 100,000. The worst year for road deaths in the United States was 1972 (56,278).

[9] Explosion at 0123 hours local time. Thirty-one was the official Soviet total of immediate deaths. It is not known how many of the c. 200,000 people involved in the cleanup died in the five-year period following the disaster since no systematic records were kept. The senior scientific officer, Vladimir Chernousenko, who gave himself two to four years to live due to his exposure to radiation, put the death toll at between 7,000 and 10,000 in a statement on Apr. 13, 1991.

[10] In the greatest space disaster on the ground, 91 people were killed when an R-16 rocket exploded during fueling at the Baikonur Space Center, Kazakhstan, on Oct. 24, 1960.

[11] More than 30 small communities in a 460-square-mile area were eliminated from maps of the USSR in the years after the accident, with 17,000 people evacuated. A report released in 1992 indicated that 8,015 people had died over a 32-year period of observation as a direct result of discharges from the complex.

ON THE RECORD

TRI-STATE TWISTER

"It was dark and gloomy . . . Then the air was filled with 10,000 things. Boards, poles, cans, garments, stoves, whole sides of little frame houses, in some cases the houses themselves, were picked up and smashed to earth. And living things, too. A baby was blown from its mother's arms. A cow, picked up by the wind, was hurled into the village restaurant." (*The St. Louis Post-Dispatch*, March 19, 1925)

The United States' most lethal tornado first struck at 1:00 P.M. on March 18, 1925 in Ellington, MO. Traveling at a maximum speed of 73 MPH, the beast ripped through 13 towns in three states—Missouri, Illinois, and Indiana—and took a devastating toll on human life: 695 killed, 2,000 injured and 15,000 homeless.

The second town in the twister's path was Annapolis, MO. Eyewitness Edith LaPlant, then 13, recalls her mother's awestruck reaction: "She saw the funnel of the tornado and passed out. We wrapped a quilt around her to protect her. I held my baby sister tight."

Ms. LaPlant described how the tornado knocked out the window frames in the bedroom and pulled a fence out in the backyard. At one point, "the dinner dishes, which were still on the table, went flying in the air."

In a time span of only 3 hr. 18 min., the tornado wreaked havoc on 219 miles of the Midwest, until it finally blew itself out in Petersburg, IN at 4:18 P.M. "What a day of misery that was," Ms. LaPlant sums up. "We'll never forget that, no sir."

Deadliest tornado　　The most deaths from one tornado in the United States is 695, on March 18, 1925 in Missouri, Illinois and Indiana. This tornado also ranks first as the tornado with the longest continuous track on the ground, 219 miles; first with a 3.3-hour continuous duration on the ground; first in total area of destruction, covering 164 square miles; first in dimensions, with the funnel sometimes exceeding one mile wide; and third in forward speed, reaching a maximum of 73 MPH and averaging 62 MPH.

Most immigrants   The country that regularly receives the most legal immigrants is the United States. During fiscal year 1993 (October 1992–September 1993), an estimated 1,024,908 people legally entered the United States.

In fiscal year 1993, a total of 1,327,259 people were apprehended for immigration violations. The largest group by nationality were 1,269,294 from Mexico.

CROWDED!

The Portuguese province of Macau, with an estimated population of 416,000 (1994) in an area of 6.9 square miles, has a density of 60,290 people per square mile.

Most tourists   The World Tourism Organization reports that the most popular destination is France, which in 1994 received 60,639,000 foreign tourists. The country with the greatest receipts from tourism is the United States, with $60 billion in 1994. The biggest spenders on foreign tourism are Americans, who in the same year spent $43.1 billion abroad.

Most and fewest hospitals   The country with the greatest number of hospitals is China, with 63,101 in 1991. Nauru has the most hospital beds per person (250 for every 10,000 people) and Nepal and Bangladesh the fewest (3 per 10,000).

Highest and lowest death rates   The world's crude death rate—the number of deaths per 1,000 population of all ages—was an estimated 9.7 per 1,000, between 1985 and 1990. East Timor had a peak rate of 45.0 per 1,000, 1975–80. The lowest estimated rate for the period 1985–90 was 3.5 deaths per 1,000 for Bahrain.

Highest and lowest suicide rates   The country with the highest suicide rate is Sri Lanka, with a rate of 47 per 100,000 population in 1991. The country with the lowest recorded rate is Jordan, with just a single case in 1970 and hence a rate of 0.04 per 100,000.

Most marriages   The marriage rate for the Northern Mariana Islands in the Pacific Ocean is 31.2 per 1,000 population.

Most divorces   The country with the most divorces is the United States, with a total of 1,187,000 in 1993—a rate of 4.6 per 1,000 people. The all-time high rate was 5.3 per 1,000 people, in 1979 and 1981. The lowest rate on record was 0.7 per 1,000 people, in 1900.

Greatest gender ratio imbalance   There are an estimated 1,015 men in the world for every 1,000 women. The country with the largest recorded shortage of women is the United Arab Emirates, with an estimated 566 women for every 1,000 men. The country with the largest recorded shortage of men is Latvia, with an estimated 1,167 women for every 1,000 men.

Highest and lowest infant mortality rates   The world infant mortality rate—the number of deaths at ages under one year per 1,000 live births—in 1985–90 was 68 per 1,000 live births. The lowest of the latest recorded rates is 5 per 1,000 in Japan for the period 1985–90. The highest rate recently estimated is 172 per 1,000 in Afghanistan (1985–90).

United States   The infant mortality rate for the United States in 1993 was estimated to be 8.3 per 1,000 live births, or 33,300. Washington, D.C. had the highest infant mortality rate in 1993, with 18.5 percent, while New Hampshire had the lowest, with 4.8 percent.

Life expectancy   World life expectancy has risen from 46.4 years (1950–55) to 63.3 years (1985–90).
   The highest average life expectancy at birth is in Japan, with 82.1 years for women and 76.1 years for men in 1991. The lowest life expectancy at birth for the period 1985–90 is 39.4 years for men in Ethiopia and Sierra Leone, and 42.0 years for women in Afghanistan.

Highest and lowest birthrates   The crude birthrate—the number of births per 1,000 population—for the whole world was estimated to be 27 per 1,000 in the period 1985–90. The highest rate estimated by the United Nations for the period 1985–90 was 55.6 per 1,000 for Malawi. Excluding Vatican City, where the rate is zero, the lowest recorded rate was 9.5 per 1,000 for San Marino.

United States   The National Center for Health Statistics (NCHS) estimates that the United States' crude birthrate (the number of babies for every 1,000 people) is 15.7. Official statistics for 1993 show that California led with 589,685 births, while Wyoming had the fewest, with 6,662. The most live births registered in the United States in any year were 4,300,000 in 1957. The highest birthrate recorded after 1909, the first year official records were recognized, was 30.1 in 1910.

Highest and lowest natural increase   The rate of natural increase (crude birthrate minus crude death rate) for the whole world was estimated to be 17.3 (27.0 minus 9.7) per 1,000 in the period 1985–90, compared with a peak of 20.6 per 1,000 in 1965–70. The highest of the latest available recorded rates was 37.4 (43 minus 5.6) for Oman in 1985–90. The lowest rate of natural increase in any major independent country in recent times was in Hungary, which experienced a decline in the same period, with a figure of –1.7 per 1,000 (11.9 births and 13.6 deaths).

Most and fewest physicians   The country with the greatest number of physicians is China, which had 1,808,000 physicians in 1992, including those practicing dentistry and those practicing traditional Chinese medicine. The United States had 647,008 physicians as of January 1, 1993.
   Niger has the highest number of people per physician, with 54,472, while at the other extreme, in Italy there is one physician for every 225 people.

Largest religion   Christianity is the world's largest religion, with some 1.90 billion adherents in 1994, or 33.7 percent of the world's population. Of these, 1.06 billion were Roman Catholics. The largest non-Christian religion is Islam, with some 1.03 billion followers in 1994.

GENOCIDES AND MASSACRES

Most lives saved   The greatest number of people saved from extinction by one person is estimated to be nearly 100,000 Jews in Budapest, Hungary, July 1944–January 1945, by Swedish diplomat Raoul Wallenberg. After escaping an assassination attempt by the Nazis, he was imprisoned without trial in the Soviet Union. Officials claimed that Wallenberg died in Lubyanka Jail, Moscow on July 16, 1947, but sighting reports within the gulag system persisted for years after his disappearance. Wallenberg was made an Honorary Citizen of the United States in 1981.

Worst mass killings   Cambodia   As a percentage of a nation's total population the worst genocide appears to have taken place in Cambodia during the Khmer Rouge regime of Saloth Sar, alias Pol Pot. According to the foreign minister, Ieng Sary, more than a third of the 8 million Khmers were killed between April 17, 1975, when the Khmer Rouge captured Phnom Penh, and January 1979, when they were overthrown.

China   The greatest massacre ever imputed by the government of one sovereign nation to the government of another is that of 26.3 million Chinese during the regime of Mao Zedong (Tse-tung), 1949–May 1965. This accusation was made by an agency of the Soviet government in a radio broadcast on April 7, 1969.

The Walker Report, published by the U.S. Senate Committee of the Judiciary in July 1971, placed the parameters of the total death toll within China since 1949 between 32.25 and 61.7 million. An estimate of 63.7 million was published by *Le Figaro* Magazine, November 19–25, 1978.

Nazi Germany   The most extreme extermination campaign against a people was the Holocaust, the genocidal "Final Solution" (*End-lösung*) or-

The aftermath of the Oklahoma terrorist bombing at the Alfred P. Murrah Federal Building on April 19, 1995. (*Eric Draper/AP Photo*)

dered by Adolf Hitler, starting at the latest by the fall of 1941 and continuing into May 1945. Reliable estimates of the number of victims range from 5.1 million to 6 million Jews. At the SS death camp at Auschwitz-Birkenau in southern Poland, it is estimated that 1,350,000 Jews and 115,000 others were murdered, June 14, 1940–January 18, 1945. The greatest number killed in a day was 6,000.

Worst terrorist bombing The largest terrorist attack in the United States was the car bombing of the Alfred P. Murrah Federal Building in Oklahoma City, OK on April 19, 1995. The death toll was 168, including one rescue worker.

ECONOMICS

Largest budget The greatest governmental expenditure ever made by any country was $1.461 trillion by the United States government for the fiscal year 1994. The highest-ever revenue figure was $1.258 trillion in the same fiscal year.

The greatest fiscal surplus ever was $8,419,469,844 in the United States in 1947/48. The worst deficit was $290 billion in the U.S. fiscal year 1992.

Foreign aid The greatest foreign aid donor is the United States government, which gave a net total of $436.9 billion from July 1, 1945 through May 1, 1995.

The country receiving most U.S. aid in 1994 was Israel, with $4.57 billion for economic and military aid and loan guarantees.

Lowest taxation rates The sovereign countries with the lowest income tax in the world are Bahrain and Qatar, where the rate is zero, regardless of income. No tax is levied on the inhabitants of Sark in the Channel Islands, Great Britain.

United States The lowest income tax rate in United States history was 1 percent between 1913 and 1915.

Highest taxation rates The country with the highest taxation is Norway, where the highest rate of income tax in 1992 was 65 percent, although additional personal taxes make it possible to be charged in excess of 100 percent.

In Denmark, the highest rate of income tax is 68 percent, but a net wealth tax of 1 percent can result in tax of over 100 percent on income in extreme situations.

United States The highest income tax rate in United States history was implemented in 1944 by the Individual Tax Act with a 91 percent bracket. The current highest income tax bracket is 31 percent.

Balance of payments (current account) The record balance of payments deficit for any country for a calendar year is $167.1 billion in 1987 by the United States. The record surplus was Japan's $117.64 billion (the equivalent of 149 trillion yen) in 1992.

Largest national debt The United States has the world's largest national debt. By April 26, 1995, it reached $4.848 trillion, with net interest payments on the debt of $202.957 billion and gross interest payments of $296.278 billion.

Most foreign debt The country most heavily in overseas debt at the end of fiscal year 1994 was the United States, with over $654 billion.

Largest gross national product The gross national product of the United States was running at $6.7 trillion at the end of 1994.

Richest country The richest country in the world, according to the United Nations Statistical Division, is Liechtenstein, which in 1992 had an average gross national product per capita of $54,607. The per capita income for the United States was $25,774 as of December 31, 1994.

According to the Department of Commerce, in 1994, Connecticut enjoyed the highest per capita income level of any state ($29,402), while Mississippi continued to have the lowest ($15,838). Personal income in the United States averaged $21,809 per person for 1994 and set a record high of $5.6 trillion in the same year.

The median household income in the United States in 1994 was $31,241. Alaska enjoyed the highest level, at $42,931, while Mississippi had the lowest, at $22,191.

Poorest country Mozambique had the lowest gross national product per capita in 1991, with $70, although there are several countries for which the *World Bank Atlas* is not able to include data.

Largest gold reserves The country with the greatest monetary gold reserves is the United States, whose Treasury held 261.7 million fine troy ounces as of December 31, 1994. At $383.10 per fine ounce (December 30, 1994, New York Mercantile Exchange, COMEX division price), their value was $100.26 billion. The highest spot price for gold in 1994 was $395.90 per fine ounce.

The United States Bullion Depository at Fort Knox, near Louisville, KY, has been the main federal depository of U.S. gold since December 1936. Gold is stored in 446,000 standard mint bars of 400 troy ounces measuring 7 by 3⅝ by 1⅝ inches. Gold's peak price was $875 per fine ounce on January 21, 1980.

Worst inflation In Hungary in June 1946, the 1931 gold pengö was valued at 130 million trillion (1.3×10^{20}) paper pengös. Notes were issued for

"Egymillard billion" (one sextillion or 1×10^{21}) pengös on June 3 and withdrawn on July 11, 1946. Vouchers for 1 billion trillion (1×10^{27}) pengös were issued for taxation payment only.

The country with the worst inflation in 1993 was Moldova, where consumer prices rose by 2,707 percent.

The best-known and most frequently analyzed hyperinflationary episode occurred in Germany in 1923. The circulation of the Reichsbank mark on November 6 reached 400,338,326,350,700,000,000 and inflation was 755.7 billion times 1913 levels.

United States The United States Department of Labor measures changes in the Consumer Price Index (CPI) in 12-month periods ending in December. The Bureau of Labor Statistics first began keeping the CPI in 1913. Since then, the change of the greatest magnitude was a 20.4 percent increase for the 12-month period ending December 1918; the largest decline was −10.8 percent, in December 1921. The largest peacetime increase, recorded in December 1979, was 13.3 percent. Figures are based on the United States city average CPI for all urban consumers.

EMPLOYMENT

Largest labor union The Professionalniy Soyuz Rabotnikov Agro-Promyshlennogo Kompleksa (Agro-Industrial Complex Workers' Union) in the former Soviet Union had 15.2 million members in January 1993.

United States As of January 1994, the largest union in the United States was the National Education Association (NEA), which had 2.1 million members.

Smallest labor union The ultimate in small unions was the Jewelcase and Jewelry Display Makers Union (JJDMU), founded in 1894. It was dissolved on December 31, 1986 by its general secretary, Charles Evans. The motion was seconded by Fergus McCormack, its only other surviving member.

Longest strike The longest recorded strike ended on January 4, 1961, after 33 years. It concerned the employment of barbers' assistants in Copenhagen, Denmark.

Industrial The longest industrial strike was at the plumbing fixtures factory of the Kohler Co. in Sheboygan, WI, between April 1954 and October

---

MOUTHFUL!

The union with the longest name is the International Association of Marble, Slate and Stone Polishers, Rubbers and Sawyers, Tile and Marble Setters' Helpers and Marble, Mosaic and Terrazzo Workers' Helpers, or the IAMSSPRSTMSHMMTWH, of Washington, D.C.

1962. The strike is alleged to have cost the United Automobile Workers' Union about $12 million to sustain.

Lowest unemployment In Switzerland (population 6.6 million), the total number of unemployed in 1973 was reported to be 81.

United States The lowest unemployment average in the United States was 1.2 percent, or 670,000 people, in 1944 during World War II, based on a labor force aged 14 and older.

Highest unemployment The highest annual unemployment average in United States history was 24.9 percent, or 12,830,000 people, in 1933 during the Great Depression.

Longest working career Shigechiyo Izumi began work goading draft animals at a sugar mill at Isen, Tokunoshima, Japan in 1872. He retired as a sugar cane farmer in 1970 at the age of 105 after working for 98 years. (See HUMAN BEING, OLDEST PERSON.)

HEADS OF STATE AND ROYALTY

Of the world's 192 sovereign states, 146 are republics. The other 46 are headed by 1 emperor, 14 kings, 3 queens, 2 sultans, 1 grand duke, 2 princes, 3 emirs, an elected monarch, the Pope, a president chosen from and by 7 hereditary sheiks, a head of state currently similar to a constitutional monarch, and 2 nominal nonhereditary "princes" in one country. Queen Elizabeth II is head of state of the United Kingdom and 15 other commonwealth countries.

Oldest ruling house The Emperor of Japan, Akihito, is the 125th in line from the first Emperor, Jimmu Tenno or Zinmu, whose reign was traditionally from 660 to 581 B.C., but more probably dates from *c.* 40 B.C. to *c.* 10 B.C.

Longest reign The reign of Phiops II (also known as Pepi II), or Neferkare, a Sixth Dynasty pharaoh of Egypt, began *c.* 2281 B.C., when he was six years old, and is believed to have lasted for 94 years. Musoma Kanijo, although not a monarch, was chief of the Nzega district of western Tanganyika (now part of Tanzania), and reputedly reigned for more than 98 years, from 1864, when he was eight years old, until his death on February 2, 1963.

Current The King of Thailand, Bhumibol Adulyadej (Rama IX), is currently the world's longest-reigning monarch, having succeeded to the throne on June 9, 1946. The reign of the King of Cambodia, Norodom Sihanouk, has spanned a record 54 years, although he did not reign for more than 38 years from 1955 to 1993. During this time he filled various posts including Prime Minister and Foreign Minister and spent many years in exile in China. The longest-reigning queen is Queen Elizabeth II of the United

Kingdom, who succeeded to the throne on February 6, 1952 on the death of her father.

Shortest reign Crown Prince Luis Filipe of Portugal was fatally wounded at the same time that his father was assassinated in the streets of Lisbon on February 1, 1908. He was thus technically King of Portugal (Dom Luis III) for about 20 minutes.

The reign of the King of Cambodia, King Norodom Sihanouk, has spanned a record 54 years, although with a break of more than 38 years from 1955 to 1993. The photographs show him in France in 1946 and greeting supporters in Cambodia in 1993. (*Popperfoto/Romeo Gacao/AFP*)

Youngest king and queen King Mswati III of Swaziland was crowned on April 25, 1986 at age 18 yr. 6 days. The country with the youngest queen is Denmark, with Queen Margrethe II (b. April 16, 1940).

Most prolific royalty The most prolific monogamous "royal" was Prince Hartmann of Liechtenstein (1613–86), who had 24 children, of whom 21 were born alive, by Countess Elisabeth zu Salm-Reifferscheidt (1623–88). HRH Duke Roberto I of Parma (1848–1907) also had 24 children, but by two wives.

Highest post-nominal number The highest post-nominal number used to designate a member of a royal house was 75, briefly enjoyed by Count Heinrich LXXV Reuss zu Schleiz (1800–1801). All male members of this branch of the German family are called Heinrich and are successively numbered from I upwards.

Heaviest monarch In September 1976, 6-ft.-3-in.-tall King Taufa'ahau of Tonga recorded a weight of 462 pounds. In early 1993, he weighed 280 pounds.

Oldest and youngest heads of state The oldest head of state is Joaquín Balaguer (b. September 1, 1907), president of the Dominican Republic. The oldest monarch is King Taufa'ahau of Tonga (b. July 4, 1918). The youngest is King Mswati III of Swaziland (b. April 19, 1968).

First female presidents   Isabel Perón of Argentina became the world's first female president when she succeeded her husband following his death on July 1, 1974. She held office until she was deposed on March 24, 1976. President Vigdis Finnbogadottir of Iceland became the world's first democratically elected female head of state on June 30, 1980.

Largest gathering of world leaders   The summit segment of the United Nations Conference on Environment and Development, on June 12 and 13, 1992, was attended by 92 heads of state and heads of government. The summit had 103 participants altogether and was one of the meetings at the "Earth Summit," which was held in Rio de Janeiro, Brazil, June 3–14, 1992.

UNITED STATES GOVERNMENT

PRESIDENTS

Oldest president   Ronald Reagan was 69 yr. 349 days old when he took the oath of office. He was reelected at age 73.

Youngest president   Vice-President Theodore Roosevelt became president at age 42 yr. 10 mo. when President William McKinley was assassinated in 1901. The youngest president ever elected was John Fitzgerald Kennedy, who took the oath of office at age 43 yr. 236 days in 1961.

Longest and shortest terms of office   Franklin D. Roosevelt served in office for 12 yr. 39 days (1933–45). The shortest term in office was 32 days (March 4–April 4, 1841) by William Henry Harrison.

Longest and shortest inaugural speeches   William Henry Harrison's inaugural speech of 1841 lasted for two hours, making it the longest one ever. George Washington's second inaugural speech of March 4, 1793 was the shortest, lasting only 90 seconds.

Largest presidential gathering   On December 30, 1834, eight men who had been or would become president gathered together in the old House Chamber of the Capitol: ex-president John Quincy Adams; ex-president Andrew Jackson; Vice-President Martin Van Buren; Senator John Tyler; Senator James Buchanan; and Representatives James K. Polk, Millard Fillmore and Franklin Pierce.

Most handshakes   The record number of hands shaken by a public figure at an official function was 8,513, by President Theodore Roosevelt at a New Year's Day White House presentation in Washington, D.C. in 1907.

ELECTIONS

Largest popular majority   Since the introduction of the popular vote in presidential elections in 1872, the greatest majority won was 17,994,460 votes in 1972, when President Richard M. Nixon (Republican) defeated George S. McGovern (Democrat) with 47,165,234 votes to 29,170,774.

Smallest popular majority   The smallest popular majority was 7,023 votes in 1880, when President James A. Garfield (Republican) defeated Winfield Scott Hancock (Democrat) with 4,449,053 votes to 4,442,030.

Largest electoral college majority   Since 1872, the greatest electoral college majority was 515 votes in 1936 when President Franklin D. Roosevelt (Democrat) defeated Alfred M. Landon (Republican) with 523 votes to 8.

VICE-PRESIDENTS

Longest term of office   Five vice-presidents have served two full 4-year terms in office: John Adams (1789–97), Thomas R. Marshall (1913–1921), John Nance Garner (1933–41), Richard Nixon (1953–61) and George Bush (1981–89).

Youngest vice-president   The youngest man to become vice-president was John Cabell Breckinridge, who took office on March 4, 1857 at age 36 yr. 1 mo.

Oldest vice-president   Alben William Barkley took office on January 20, 1949 at age 71 yr. 40 days. He served a full 4-year term.

Longest-lived vice-president   John Nance Garner served under Franklin D. Roosevelt from 1933 to 1941. He was born in 1868 and died on November 7, 1967 at age 98.

GOVERNORS

Oldest governor   Walter S. Goodland became governor of Wisconsin in 1943, at age 84.

Youngest governor   Stevens T. Mason was 24 years old when he was elected governor of Michigan in 1835.

CONGRESS

Most expensive election   The Federal Election Commission reported on April 28, 1995 that the 1994 congressional campaign was the most expensive in history. Candidates spent a total of $724 million. Senate candidates spent $318 million and House candidates spent $406 million.

Longest congressional service   Carl Hayden (1877–1972; D-Arizona) holds the record for the longest congressional service, a total of 57 consecutive years (1912–1969), of which 42 years were spent as a senator and the remainder as a representative.

Longest-serving speaker   The longest time served by any speaker was 17 years, by Sam Rayburn (D-Texas). Rayburn served three terms: 1940–47, 1949–53, and 1955–61.

Shortest term   The shortest term of any speaker was one day, March 3, 1869, served by Theodore Medad Pomeroy (R-New York).

Oldest speaker   Sam Rayburn (D-Texas) was reelected speaker for the 87th Congress on January 3, 1961 at age 78 yr. 11 mo.

Youngest speaker   Robert Mercer Taliaferro Hunter (D-Virginia) was chosen speaker for the 26th Congress on December 2, 1839 at age 30 yr. 7 mo.

Longest-serving representative   The longest any representative has ever served is 53 yr. 2 mo., by Rep. Jamie L. Whitten (D-Mississippi). He began his career on November 4, 1941 and retired on January 3, 1995.

Youngest representative   The youngest man ever to serve in the House was William Charles Cole Claiborne (1775–1817; Jeffersonian Democrat-Tennessee), who, in contravention of the 25-year age requirement of the Constitution, was elected in August 1797 at age 22.

Oldest representative   The oldest man ever elected representative was Claude Denson Pepper (D-Florida), who was reelected on November 8, 1988 at age 88 yr. 2 mo.

Longest-serving senator   The longest any senator has ever served is 42 years, by Carl Trumbull Hayden (D-Arizona), who served in the Senate from 1927 to 1969. The current longest-serving member of the Senate is James Strom Thurmond (R-South Carolina). As of June 1995, Thurmond had served for 39 yr. 10 mo. He was originally elected as a Democrat in December 1954, but changed to the Republican Party in 1964.

Oldest senator   The greatest age at which anyone has been returned as a senator is 87 yr. 11 mo., the age at which Strom Thurmond (R-South Carolina) was reelected in November 1990.

Youngest senator   The youngest person ever elected senator was Brig. Gen. Armistead Thomson Mason (D-Virginia), who was elected on January 3, 1816 and was sworn in on January 22 at age 28 yr. 5 mo. 18 days. The youngest-ever senator was John Henry Eaton (D-Tennessee), who was appointed on September 5, 1818 and sworn in on November 16, at age 28 yr. 4 mo. 29 days.

Most roll calls   Senator William Proxmire (D-Wisconsin) did not miss a single one of the 9,695 roll calls from April 1966 to August 27, 1987. Rep. William H. Natcher (D-Kentucky) cast 18,401 consecutive roll call votes from January 6, 1954 through March 3, 1994.

Longest filibuster   The longest continuous speech in the history of the Senate was that by Senator Wayne Morse (D-Oregon) on April 24 and 25, 1953, when he spoke on the Tidelands oil bill for 22 hr. 26 min. without resuming his seat.

Interrupted only briefly by the swearing-in of a new senator, Senator Strom Thurmond (R-South Carolina) spoke against a civil rights bill for 24 hr. 19 min., August 28–29, 1957. The record at state level is 43 hours, by Texas State Senator Bill Meier, who spoke against nondisclosure of industrial accidents, in May 1977.

WORLD LEGISLATURES

PARLIAMENTS

Oldest legislative body   The Althing of Iceland was founded in A.D. 930. This body was abolished in 1800, but restored by Denmark to a consultative status in 1843 and a legislative status in 1874. The legislative assembly with the oldest *continuous* history is the Tynwald of the Isle of Man, Great Britain, which may have its origins in the late ninth century and possibly predates the Althing.

Largest legislative body   The National People's Congress of the People's Republic of China has 2,978 single-party members who are indirectly elected for a 5-year term.

Highest-paid legislators   The most highly paid of all the world's legislators are the Japanese. The prime minister has an annual salary of 38,463,360 yen ($343,000) including monthly allowances and bonuses. Members of the House of Representatives and the House of Councilors have annual salaries of 23,633,565 yen ($211,000) including bonuses.

Smallest quorum   The House of Lords in Great Britain has the smallest quorum, expressed as a percentage of members eligible to vote, of any legislative body in the world—less than one-third of 1 percent of 1,205 members. There need be only three peers present, including the lord chancellor or his deputy, to transact business.

Largest petition The largest petition on record was signed by 21,202,192 people, mainly from South Korea, between June 1, 1993 and October 31, 1994. They were protesting against the forced separation of families since the Korean war, and the division of the country into North and South Korea.

Longest membership The longest span as a legislator was 83 years, by József Madarász (1814–1915). He attended the Hungarian Parliament 1832–38 as *oblegatus absentium* (i.e., on behalf of an absent deputy), and was a full member 1848–50 and from 1861 until his death on January 31, 1915.

Longest speech Chief Mangosuthu Buthelezi, the Zulu leader, gave an address to the KwaZulu legislative assembly, March 12–29, 1993. He spoke on 11 of the 18 days, averaging nearly 2½ hours on each of those days.

The longest continuous speech made in the United Nations was one of 4 hr. 29 min. on September 26, 1960 by President Fidel Castro of Cuba.

Oldest treaty The oldest treaty still in force is the Anglo-Portuguese Treaty, which was signed in London, England on June 16, 1373.

Oldest constitution The world's oldest national constitution still in uninterrupted use is that of the United States of America, ratified by the necessary ninth state (New Hampshire) on June 21, 1788 and declared to be in effect on March 4, 1789.

Earliest women's suffrage In 1838, the Pitcairn Islands incorporated female suffrage in its constitution, although this was only *de facto* and not legally binding. The first legislature with female voters was that of the Territory of Wyoming in 1869, followed by that of the Isle of Man, Great Britain in 1881. The first country to have universal women's suffrage was New Zealand in 1893.

United States In 1920, the 19th Amendment to the Constitution granted nationwide suffrage to women.

ELECTIONS

Largest election The largest election began on May 20, 1991 for the Indian Lower House, which has 543 elective seats. A total of 315,439,908 people

---

GUESS WHAT?

Q. WHICH LETTER HAS THE MOST PRESIDENTIAL SIGNATURES?

A. LOOK IN "DIARIES AND LETTERS" (ARTS & ENTERTAINMENT)

cast their votes out of an eligible electorate of 488,678,993. The election was contested by 359 parties, and there were nearly 565,000 polling stations manned by 3 million people. A new government was formed under P.V. Narasimha Rao of the Congress (I) Party.

Closest election   On January 18, 1961 in Zanzibar (now part of Tanzania), the Afro-Shirazi Party won the general elections by a single seat, after the seat of Chake-Chake on Pemba Island was won by a single vote.

The narrowest recorded percentage win in an election was for the office of Southern District Highway Commissioner in Mississippi on August 7, 1979. Robert E. Joiner was declared the winner over W.H. Pyron, with 133,587 votes to 133,582. The loser thus obtained more than 49.999 percent of the votes.

Most decisive election   North Korea recorded a 100 percent turnout of electors and a 100 percent vote for the Workers' Party of Korea in the general election of October 8, 1962. An almost unanimous vote occurred in Albania on November 14, 1982, when a single voter spoiled national unanimity for the official (and only) candidates, who consequently obtained 99.99993 percent of the vote in a reported 100 percent turnout of 1,627,968.

Longest in power   In Mongolia, the Communists (Mongolian People's Revolutionary Party) have been in power since 1924, although only since July 1990 within a multiparty system. In February 1992, the term "People's Republic" was dropped from the official name of Mongolia.

Highest personal majority   The highest-ever personal majority for any politician was 4,726,112 by Boris Yeltsin, the people's deputy candidate for Moscow, in the parliamentary elections held in the former Soviet Union on March 26, 1989. Yeltsin received 5,118,745 votes out of the 5,722,937 that were cast in the Moscow constituency, his closest rival obtaining 392,633 votes. Benazir Bhutto achieved 98.48 percent of the vote in the Larkana-III constituency in the 1990 general election in Pakistan, with 94,462 votes. The next-highest candidate obtained just 718 votes.

Largest political party   The Chinese Communist Party, formed in 1920, had an estimated membership of 50,320,000 in 1991.

Largest field of candidates   There were 301 candidates running to represent one seat, that of Belgaum City, in the State Assembly (Vidhan Sabha) elections in Karnataka, India held on March 5, 1985.

Most coups   Statisticians contend that Bolivia, since it became a sovereign country in 1825, has had 191 coups. The latest was on June 30, 1984, when President Hernan Siles Zuazo was temporarily kidnapped from his official residence by more than 60 armed men masquerading as police officers.

PRIME MINISTERS AND HEADS OF STATE

Oldest prime minister   El Hadji Muhammadel Mokri, Grand Vizier of Morocco, died on September 16, 1957 at a reputed age of 116 Muslim (*Hijri*) years, equivalent to 112½ years.

CROOKED!

In the Liberian presidential election of 1927, President Charles D.B. King was returned with an officially announced majority of 234,000 over his opponent, Thomas J.R. Faulkner of the People's Party. President King thus claimed a "majority" more than 15½ times greater than the entire electorate.

The oldest age at first appointment was 81, in the case of Morarji Ranchhodji Desai of India (1896–1995) in March 1977. Philippe Pétain (1856–1951), although not prime minister, became "chief of state" of the French state on July 10, 1940 at age 84.

Currently, the oldest prime minister is Andreas Papandreou of Greece (b. February 5, 1919), who is now in his second term of office.

Youngest head of government   Dr. Mario Frick (b. May 8, 1965) became prime minister of Liechtenstein at age 28 on December 15, 1993.

Longest-serving prime minister   The longest-serving prime minister of a sovereign state is Khalifa bin Sulman al-Khalifa of Bahrain, who took office 1½ years before Bahrain became independent in August 1971.

Marshall Kim Il Sung was head of government or head of state of the Democratic People's Republic of Korea from August 25, 1948 until his death on July 8, 1994.

Woman   Indira Gandhi (1917–84) of India was prime minister for 15 years—in two spans, 1966–77 and 1980–84. Eugenia Charles (b. May 15, 1919) of Dominica is the current record holder; she took office when her Dominica Freedom Party won the elections in July 1980.

Most women in a cabinet   The greatest representation of women in a cabinet is in Sweden, where, following an election in September 1994, a new cabinet was formed containing 11 women out of a total 22 ministers.

HONORS, DECORATIONS AND AWARDS

Oldest order   The oldest honor known is the "Gold of Honor" for extraordinary valor, which was awarded in the 18th Dynasty *c.* 1440–1400 B.C. A representative statuette was found at Qan-el-Kebri, Egypt. The oldest true order is the Order of St. John of Jerusalem (the direct descendant of which is the Sovereign Military Order of Malta), legitimized in 1113.

Youngest awardees   Kristina Stragauskaite of Skirmantiskes, Lithuania was awarded a medal "For Courage in Fire" when she was just 4 yr. 252 days old. She had saved the lives of her younger brother and sister when a fire

LANDSLIDE

(Rex Features/Alfred)

When election time rolls around in the Larkana-III district of Pakistan, almost everyone expects a landslide victory. For Larkana-III is the constituency of Benazir Bhutto, Pakistan's 43-year-old prime minister. In December 1988, this remarkable politician became the first-ever female prime minister of a modern Islamic nation, receiving 96.71 percent of the votes cast in her district. Bhutto won by 80,250 votes; her nearest rival obtained only 1,979 votes.

Bhutto was dismissed because of allegations of corruption in August 1990, but in the election held two months later, she achieved an even more staggering 98.48 percent of the poll in her district, obtaining 94,462 votes. For the second time in two years, she had set a record for the greatest percentage of the vote in a free election. This time the next-highest candidate obtained only 718 votes, giving Bhutto a majority of 93,744. What made her achievement all the more remarkable was that her party lost the election, and she did not become prime minister at that time. In October 1993, Bhutto was elected once again, although without beating her record.

Educated at Harvard and Oxford, Bhutto has wealth, celebrity and aristocratic status. She has been in exile, has led her country back to democracy following a period of military dictatorship, and has always had to be vigilant. She believes that in 1981, while she was undergoing an operation, the military may have tried to have her killed. She was also the target of death threats after she declared a war on drugs. Benazir Bhutto does have her enemies, but she also has her very loyal followers, none more so than in her own district.

Highest personal majority Benazir Bhutto achieved 98.48 percent of the vote in the Larkana-III constituency in the 1990 general election in Pakistan, with 94,462 votes. The next-highest candidate received just 718 votes.

---

broke out on April 7, 1989 in the family's home while her parents were out. The award was decreed by the Presidium of the then Lithuanian Soviet Socialist Republic.

The youngest person to have received an official gallantry award is Julius Rosenberg of Winnipeg, Canada, who was given the Medal of Bravery on March 30, 1994 for stopping a black bear that attacked his 3-year-old sister on September 20, 1992. Aged five at the time of the incident, he saved his sister's life by growling at the bear.

VANITY!

The world record for raising statues to oneself was set by Joseph Stalin (1879–1953), leader of the Soviet Union, 1924–53. It is estimated that during the Stalin era there were c. 6,000 statues to him throughout the USSR and in Eastern Europe.

Most titles   The 18th Duchess of Alba (Alba de Tormes), Doña Maria del Rosario Cayetana Fitz-James Stuart y Silva, is five times a duchess, once a countess-duchess, once a viscountess, 17 times a marchioness, 19 times a countess, and 14 times a Spanish grandee.

Most valuable annual prize   The most valuable annual prize is the Louis Jeantet Prize for Medicine, which in 1995 was worth SFr2.1 million (equivalent to approximately $1,840,000). It was first awarded in 1986 and is intended to "provide substantial funds for the support of biomedical research projects."

Most statues   The man to whom the most statues have been raised is Buddha. The 20th-century champion is Vladimir Ilyich Ulyanov, alias Lenin (1870–1924), busts of whom have been mass-produced.

Most honorary degrees   The greatest number of honorary degrees awarded to any one individual is 130, given to Rev. Father Theodore M. Hesburgh, president of the University of Notre Dame, IN. These have been accumulated since 1954.

MILITARY AND DEFENSE

WAR

Oldest weapon   The oldest known offensive weapon is a broken wooden spear found in April 1911 in Clacton-on-Sea, England by S. Hazzledine

Warren. It is much beyond the limit of radiocarbon dating but is estimated to have been made before 200,000 B.C.

Longest continuous war The Thirty Years' War, between various European countries, was fought continuously from 1618 to 1648. The *Reconquista*—the series of campaigns in the Iberian Peninsula to recover the region from the Islamic Moors—began in the year 718 and continued intermittently until 1492, when Granada, the last Moorish stronghold, was finally conquered.

Bloodiest war World War II (1939–45) was by far the most costly war in terms of human life; the total number of fatalities, including battle deaths and civilians of all countries, is estimated to have been 56.4 million, assuming 26.6 million Soviet fatalities and 7.8 million Chinese civilians killed. The country that suffered most was Poland, with 6,028,000 or 17.2 percent of its population of 35.1 million killed.

In the Paraguayan war of 1864–70 against Brazil, Argentina and Uruguay, Paraguay's population was reduced from 1.4 million to 220,000 survivors.

Preparations are made on a B-52G bomber about to depart for the Gulf in one of the record-breaking long-range attacks in January 1991. (*Rex Features/J.M. Gubl*)

Civil The bloodiest civil war in history was the *Taiping* ("Great Peace") rebellion, which was a revolt against the Chinese Qing Dynasty between 1851 and 1864. According to the best estimates, the loss of life was some 20 million, including more than 100,000 killed by government forces in the sack of Nanjing, July 19–21, 1864.

Most costly war The material cost of World War II far transcended that of all the rest of history's wars put together and has been estimated at $1.5 trillion.

Bloodiest battles   It is difficult to compare the major battles of World Wars I and II because of the different time scales. The 142-day-long first battle of the Somme, France (July 1–November 19, 1916) produced an estimated total number of casualties of over 1.22 million; of these, 623,907 were Allied and the rest German. The greatest death toll in a battle has been estimated at *c.* 1,109,000 in the Battle of Stalingrad, USSR, ending with the German surrender on January 31, 1943 by Field Marshal Friedrich von Paulus (1890–1957). The Germans suffered 200,000 losses. The Soviet garrison commander was Gen. Vasiliy Chuikov; about 650,800 soldiers from the Soviet army were injured but survived. Additionally, only 1,515 civilians from a pre-war population of more than 500,000 were found alive after the battle. The final drive on Berlin, Germany by the Soviet army, and the battle for the city that followed, April 16–May 2, 1945, involved 3.5 million men, 52,000 guns and mortars, 7,750 tanks and 11,000 aircraft on both sides.

United States   The American Civil War (1861–65) was the bloodiest war ever fought on American soil. The war claimed 200,000 lives and left 469,000 wounded. The bloodiest battle was at Gettysburg, PA, July 1–3, 1863, when the Union reported 23,000 killed, wounded and missing, and the Confederacy approximately 28,000 killed, wounded and missing.

Greatest naval battles   *Modern*   The greatest number of ships and aircraft ever involved in a sea–air action was 231 ships and 1,996 aircraft in the Battle of Leyte Gulf, in the Philippines, during World War II. The battle raged from October 22 through October 27, 1944, with 166 Allied and 65 Japanese warships engaged, of which 26 Japanese and 6 U.S. ships were sunk. In addition, 1,280 U.S. and 716 Japanese aircraft were engaged. The greatest purely naval battle of modern times was the Battle of Jutland on May 31, 1916, during World War I, in which 151 British Royal Navy warships were involved against 101 German warships. The Royal Navy lost 14 ships and 6,097 men, and the German fleet lost 11 ships and 2,545 men.

GUESS WHAT?

Q.   WHAT IS THE LEADING CAUSE OF DEATH IN THE U.S.?

A.   LOOK IN "ILLNESS AND DISEASE" (HUMAN BEING)

Greatest invasion   The greatest invasion in military history was the Allied land, air and sea operation against the Normandy coast of France on D-Day, June 6, 1944. Thirty-eight convoys of 745 ships moved in during the first three days, supported by 4,066 landing craft, carrying 185,000 men, 20,000 vehicles and 347 minesweepers. The air assault comprised 18,000 paratroopers from 1,087 aircraft. The 42 available divisions had air support from 13,175 aircraft. Within a month 1.1 million troops, 200,000 vehicles and 840,000 tons of stores were landed. The Allied invasion of Sicily, July 10–12, 1943, involved the landing of 181,000 men in three days.

Airborne The largest airborne invasion was the British–American assault by three divisions (34,000 men), with 2,800 aircraft and 1,600 gliders, near Arnhem, Netherlands, on September 17, 1944.

Longest-range attacks The longest-range attacks in air history were those undertaken by seven B-52G bombers that took off from Barksdale Air Force Base, LA on January 16, 1991 to deliver air-launched cruise missiles against targets in Iraq shortly after the start of the Gulf War. Each bomber flew a distance of 14,000 miles, refueling four times in flight, with the round-trip mission lasting some 35 hours.

Greatest evacuation The greatest evacuation in military history was that carried out by 1,200 Allied naval and civilian craft from the beachhead at Dunkerque (Dunkirk), France, May 27–June 4, 1940. A total of 338,226 British and French troops were evacuated.

EVACUATE!

Following the Iraqi invasion of Kuwait in August 1990, Air India evacuated 111,711 Indian nationals who were working in Kuwait. Beginning on August 13, 488 flights took the expatriates back to India over a 2-month period.

Longest march The longest march in military history was the famous Long March by the Chinese Communists, 1934–35. In 368 days, of which 268 were days of movement, their force of some 100,000 covered 6,000 miles from Ruijin, in Jiangxi, to Yan'an, in Shaanxi. They crossed 18 mountain ranges and 24 rivers, and eventually reached Yan'an with only about 8,000 survivors, following continual rear guard actions against nationalist Kuomintang (KMT) forces.

Stretcher bearing The record for carrying a stretcher case with a 140-pound "body" is 167.86 miles in 49 hr. 2 min., April 29–May 1, 1993, achieved by two 4-man teams from the 85th CFB (Canadian Forces Base) Trenton in and around Trenton, Ontario, Canada.

Worst sieges The 880-day siege of Leningrad, USSR (now St. Petersburg, Russia) by the German army, from August 30, 1941 through January 27, 1944 was the worst siege in history. It is estimated that 1.3–1.5 million defenders and citizens died, including 641,000 people who died of hunger in the city and 17,000 civilians killed by shelling. More than 150,000 shells and 100,000 bombs were dropped on the city.

The longest recorded siege was in Azotus (now Ashdod), Israel, which according to Herodotus was besieged by Psamtik I of Egypt for 29 years, during the period 664–610 B.C.

Chemical warfare The greatest number of people killed in chemical warfare were the estimated 4,000 Kurds who died at Halabja, Iraq in March 1988 when President Saddam Hussein used chemical weapons against

Iraq's Kurdish minority in revenge for the support it had given to Iran in the Iran–Iraq war.

Biggest demonstration   A figure of 2.7 million was reported from China for a demonstration against the USSR in Shanghai, March 3–4, 1969 following border clashes.

ARMED FORCES

Largest armed force   The strength of China's People's Liberation Army in 1994 was estimated to be 2,930,000 troops (comprising land, sea and air forces), with reductions continuing. Its reserves number around 1.2 million.

Largest navy   The largest navy in terms of personnel is the United States Navy, with a total of 445,483 active-duty servicemen and servicewomen, plus 172,843 active-duty Marines. As of February 28, 1995, the navy's active strength included 7 nuclear-powered aircraft carriers, 5 conventionally powered aircraft carriers, 15 ballistic missile submarines, 84 nuclear attack submarines, 33 cruisers, 42 destroyers, 35 frigates, and 40 amphibious warfare ships.

Oldest army   The 80–90-strong Pontifical Swiss Guard in Vatican City was founded January 21, 1506. Its origins, however, predate 1400.

Largest army   The army of the People's Republic of China had a total strength of some 2.2 million in mid-1994.

Fernando Inchauste Montalvo was only five years old when he went to war with his father in 1935, in the conflict between Bolivia and Paraguay. In 1964, he experienced dramatic events of a happier nature, representing Bolivia in the 1964 Olympic Games and having the honor of carrying his country's flag.

Oldest soldier John B. Salling of the Army of the Confederate States of America was the last accepted survivor of the Civil War (1861–65). He died in Kingsport, TN on March 16, 1959, aged 113 yr. 1 day.

Youngest soldier Luís Alves de Lima e Silva, Marshal Duke of Caxias (August 25, 1803–May 7, 1880), Brazilian military hero and statesman, entered his infantry regiment at age five in 1808. He was promoted to captain in 1824 and made Duke in 1869.

Fernando Inchauste Montalvo, the son of a major in the Bolivian air force, went to the front with his father on his fifth birthday during the war between Bolivia and Paraguay (1932–35). He had received military training and was subject to military discipline.

Youngest conscripts In March 1976, President Francisco Macias Nguema of Equatorial Guinea decreed compulsory military service for all boys between the ages of seven and 14. The edict stated that parents refusing to hand over their sons would be "imprisoned or shot."

Tallest soldier Väinö Myllyrinne was conscripted into the Finnish army when he was 7 ft. 3 in.; he later grew to 8 ft. 3 in.

Largest mutiny During World War I, 56 French divisions, comprising some 650,000 men and their officers, refused orders on the Western front sector of General Robert Nivelle in April 1917 after the failure of his offensive.

Oldest air force The earliest autonomous air force is the Royal Air Force, which can be traced back to 1878, when the British War Office commissioned the building of a military balloon. Balloons had been used for military observation by both sides during the American Civil War (1861–65).

Largest air force The United States Army Air Corps (now the U.S. Air Force) had 79,908 aircraft in July 1944 and 2,411,294 personnel in March 1944. In mid-1994, the U.S. Air Force, including strategic missile forces, had 433,800 personnel and 5,900 aircraft (plus more in storage).

BOMBS

Heaviest bomb The heaviest conventional bomb ever used operationally was the Royal Air Force's *Grand Slam*, weighing 22,000 pounds and measuring 25 ft. 5 in. long, dropped on Bielefeld railroad viaduct, Germany on March 14, 1945.

In 1949, the United States Air Force tested a bomb weighing 42,000 pounds at Muroc Dry Lake, CA.

Nuclear The heaviest known nuclear bomb was the MK 17, carried by U.S. B-36 bombers in the mid-1950s. It weighed 42,000 pounds and was 24 ft. 6 in. long.

Most powerful thermonuclear device The most powerful thermonuclear device so far tested has a power equivalent to that of 57 megatons of TNT, and was detonated by the former USSR in the Novaya Zemlya area on October 30, 1961. The shock wave circled the world three times, taking 36 hr.

27 min. for the first circuit. The largest U.S. H-bomb tested was the 18–22 megaton *Bravo* at Bikini Atoll, Marshall Islands on March 1, 1954.

Largest nuclear weapons The most powerful ICBM (intercontinental ballistic missile) is the former USSR's SS–18 (Model 5), believed to be armed with ten 750-kiloton MIRVs (multiple independently targetable reentry vehicles). SS–18 ICBMs are located on both Russian and Kazakhstan territory—they are now controlled by the Commonwealth of Independent States.

GUNS

Largest gun A gun with a caliber of 31 inches and a barrel 94 ft. 8½ in. long was used by German forces in the siege of Sevastopol, USSR (now Russia) in July 1942. The whole gun was 141 feet long and weighed 1,481.5 tons, with a crew of 1,500. The range for an 8.9-ton projectile was 29 miles.

Heaviest gun The heaviest gun in the U.S. Army is the MK19-3 40mm automatic grenade launcher, which weighs 72.5 pounds and has both the greatest caliber and range of any U.S. Army weapon: about 1,650 yards at point targets, over 2,400 yards at area targets. The bullets can penetrate two inches into armor at 2,400 yards.

Greatest altitude The greatest altitude ever attained by a gun was achieved by the HARP (High Altitude Research Project) gun, consisting of two 16½-inch-caliber barrels fused in tandem into a single barrel 119 ft. 5 in. long and weighing 165 tons, at Yuma, AZ. On November 19, 1966, an 185-pound projectile was fired to an altitude of 112 miles or 590,550 feet.

Largest cannon The highest-caliber cannon ever constructed is the *Tsar Pushka* (King of Cannons), now housed in the Kremlin, Moscow, Russia. It was built in the 16th century with a bore of 35 inches and a barrel 17 ft. 6 in. long. It weighs 44 tons.

EDUCATION

Oldest university The oldest existing educational institution in the world is the University of Karueein, founded in A.D. 859 in Fez, Morocco.

United States The oldest college in the United States is Harvard College in Cambridge, MA, founded in 1636 as Newtowne College and renamed in 1638 after its first benefactor, John Harvard.

Largest university The largest existing university building in the world is the M. V. Lomonosov State University on the Lenin Hills, south of Moscow, Russia. It stands 787 ft. 5 in. tall, and has 32 stories and 40,000 rooms. It was constructed from 1949 to 1953.

Greatest enrollment The university with the greatest enrollment in the world is the State University of New York, which had 393,228 students at 64 campuses throughout the state in late 1994. The greatest enrollment at a university centered in one city is at the City University of New York, which had 213,000 students in late 1994. It has several campuses throughout the city.

Most graduates in family Mr. and Mrs. Harold Erickson of Naples, FL saw all of their 14 children—11 sons and 3 daughters—obtain university or college degrees between 1962 and 1978. All 14 children—10 sons and 4 daughters—of Mr. and Mrs. Robert Johnson of Edwards, MI also obtained degrees, between 1959 and 1983.

Youngest university student Michael Kearney started studying for an Associate of Science degree at Santa Rosa Junior College, Santa Rosa, CA in September 1990 at 6 yr. 7 mo.

Youngest graduate Michael Kearney became the youngest graduate in June 1994, at age 10 yr. 4 mo., when he obtained his BA in anthropology from the University of South Alabama.

Youngest doctorate On April 13, 1814, the mathematician Carl Witte of Lochau was made a Doctor of Philosophy of the University of Giessen, Germany at age 12.

Youngest college president The youngest president of a major college was Ellen Futter, who was appointed to head Barnard College, New York City in May 1981 at age 31.

Most schools China has the greatest number of primary schools, with 885,479 in 1992. San Marino has the lowest pupil-to-teacher ratio, with 5.3 children per teacher.

At general secondary level, India has the most schools, with 235,793 in

The country with the most primary schools is China. (*Gamma*)

1993, while San Marino has the best pupil-to-teacher ratio, with 5.8 pupils per teacher.

Most expensive school   The annual cost of keeping a pupil at the most expensive school in the United States for the academic year 1994/95 was $32,500 at the Oxford Academy (founded 1906), in Westbrook, CT.

Largest school   In 1992/93, Rizal High School, Pasig, Manila, Philippines had an enrollment of 16,535 regular students.

Most schools attended   Wilma Williams, now Mrs. R.J. Horton, attended 265 schools as a pupil from 1933 to 1943 when her parents were in show business traveling around the United States.

Most durable teacher   Medarda de Jesús León de Uzcátegui, alias La Maestra Chucha, has been teaching in Caracas, Venezuela for a total of 84 years. In 1911, when she was 12, she and her two sisters set up a school named *Modelo de Aplicación*. Since marrying in 1942, La Maestra Chucha has run her own school, which she calls the *Escuela Uzcátegui*, from her home in Caracas.

Highest endowment   The greatest single gift in the history of education was $500 million, to the U.S. public education system by Walter Annenburg in December 1993. The gift was intended to help fight violence in schools.

Highest lecture fee   Dr. Ronald Dante was paid $3,080,000 for giving a lecture on hypnotherapy at a 2-day course held in Chicago on June 1–2, 1986. He taught for eight hours each day, and thus earned $192,500 per hour.

HUMAN
ACHIEVEMENTS

FANTASTIC FEATS

Balloon release   A mass release of 1,592,744 balloons was staged by Disney Home Video at Longleat House, England on August 27, 1994.

Barrel rolling   The record for rolling a full 36-gallon metal beer barrel over a measured mile is 8 min. 7.2 sec., by Phillip Randle, Steve Hewitt, John Round, Trevor Bradley, Colin Barnes and Ray Glover of Haunchwood Collieries Institute and Social Club, Nuneaton, England on August 15, 1982.

A team of 10 people rolled a 140-pound barrel 150 miles in 30 hr. 31 min. in Chlumčany, Czech Republic, October 27–28, 1982.

Barrow pushing   A 1-wheeled barrow loaded with bricks weighing a gross 8,275 pounds was pushed a distance of 243 feet by John Sarich in London, Ontario, Canada on February 19, 1987.

Barrow racing   The fastest time attained in a 1-mile wheelbarrow race is 4 min. 48.51 sec., by Piet Pitzer and Jaco Erasmus at the Transvalia High School, Vanderbijlpark, South Africa on October 3, 1987.

Bathtub racing   The record for a 36-mile bathtub race is 1 hr. 22 min. 27 sec., by Greg Mutton at the Grafton Jacaranda Festival, New South Wales, Australia on November 8, 1987. Tubs are limited to 75 inches and 6-hp motors. The greatest distance for paddling a hand-propelled bathtub in

A new mass balloon release record is set at Longleat House, England on August 27, 1994. (*Mike Robertson © HCA Integrated Marketing*)

still water in 24 hours is 90.5 miles, by 13 members of Aldington Prison Officers Social Club, near Ashford, Kent, England, May 28–29, 1983.

Bed making The pair record for making a bed with one blanket, two
sheets, an under-sheet, an uncased pillow, one bedspread and "hospital"
corners is 14.0 seconds, by Sister Sharon Stringer and Nurse Michelle
Benkel of the Royal Masonic Hospital, London, England on November 26,
1993 at Canary Wharf, London, England.
   The record time for one person to make a bed is 28.2 seconds, by Wendy
Wall, 34, of Hebersham, Sydney, Australia on November 30, 1978.

Bed pushing A wheeled hospital bed was pushed 3,233 miles by a team of
nine employees of Bruntsfield Bedding Center, Edinburgh, Scotland, June
21–July 26, 1979.

Bed race The course record for a 10-mile bed race is 50 minutes, as established by the Westbury Harriers' 3-man bed team in Chew Valley, Avon,
England.

Beer coaster flipping Dean Gould of Felixstowe, England flipped a pile of
111 coasters (0.047-inch wood pulp board) through 180 degrees and caught
them all on January 13, 1993.

Beer keg lifting George Olesen raised a keg of beer weighing 138 lb. 11 oz.
above his head 737 times in six hours in Horsens, Denmark on May 1,
1994.

Beer stein carrying Duane Osborn covered a distance of 49 ft. 2½ in. in
3.65 seconds with five full steins in each hand in a contest in Cadillac, MI
on July 10, 1992.

Brick balancing John Evans of Marlpool, England balanced 66 bricks
(weighing a total of 296 lb. 4 oz.) on his head for 10 seconds in Cannock,
England on February 12, 1994.

Brick carrying The greatest distance achieved for carrying a 9-pound
brick in one ungloved hand using an uncradled downward pincer grip is 65
miles, by Paddy Doyle of Atherstone, England, around Ballycotton, Ireland, September 3–4, 1994. The women's record for carrying a 9-lb.-12-oz.
brick is 22.5 miles, by Wendy Morris of Walsall, England on April 28, 1986.

Brick lifting Russell Bradley of Worcester, England lifted 31 bricks laid
side by side off a table, raising them to chest height and holding them there
for two seconds, on June 14, 1992. The greatest weight of bricks lifted was

by Fred Burton of Cheadle, Staffordshire, England, who lifted 20 far heavier bricks weighing a total of 197 lb. 10¼ oz. on July 17, 1994, holding them for more than four seconds.

Bubble-gum blowing The greatest reported diameter for a bubble-gum bubble under the strict rules of this highly competitive activity is 23 inches, by Susan Montgomery Williams of Fresno, CA on July 19, 1994.

Carriage pushing The greatest distance covered in 24 hours while pushing a baby carriage is 350.23 miles, by 60 members of the Oost-Vlanderen branch of Amnesty International in Lede, Belgium on October 15, 1988. A 10-man team from the Royal Marines School of Music, Deal, England, with an adult "baby," covered a distance of 271.7 miles in 24 hours from November 22 to November 23, 1990.

Car washing Students from Carroll High School, Yakima, WA washed 3,844 cars in eight hours on May 7, 1983.

Cherry stem tying Al Gliniecki of Pensacola, FL tied 833 cherry stems into knots with his tongue in one hour on April 21, 1995.

Cigar box balancing Terry Cole of London, England balanced 220 unmodified cigar boxes on his chin for nine seconds on April 24, 1992.

Al Gliniecki beats his own record for cherry stem tying on April 21, 1995. (*Courtesy of Al Gliniecki*)

Crawling The longest continuous voluntary crawl (progression with one knee or the other in unbroken contact with the ground) on record is 31.5 miles, by Peter McKinlay and John Murrie, who covered 115 laps of an athletic track in Falkirk, Scotland, March 28–29, 1992. Over a 15-month period ending on March 9, 1985, Jagdish Chander crawled 870 miles from Aligarh to Jamma, India to propitiate his revered Hindu goddess, Mata.

Egg and spoon racing Dale Lyons of Meriden, England ran 26 mi. 385 yd. (the classic marathon distance) while carrying a dessert spoon with a fresh egg on it in 3 hr. 47 min. on April 23, 1990.

Egg hunt The greatest egg hunt on record in the United States involved 120,000 plastic and candy eggs at a community Easter egg hunt at Coquina Beach in Manatee, FL on March 23, 1991. The event, hosted by Meals on Wheels PLUS of Manatee, Inc., entertained 1,870 children.

Fire bucket brigade The longest fire company bucket brigade stretched over 11,471 feet, with 2,271 people passing 50 buckets along the complete course, at the Centennial Parade and Muster held in Hudson, NY on July 11, 1992.

Garbage collecting The greatest number of volunteers involved in collecting garbage in one location in one day is 50,405, on the coastline of Cali-

The largest human logo consisted of 30,000 men. Arthur S. Mole and John D. Thomas organized everyone so that the perspective was correct; the result is a near-perfect photograph. (*Mole & Thomas/Chicago Historical Society*)

fornia on October 2, 1993, in conjunction with the International Coast Cleanup.

Glass balancing   Terry Cole of Walthamstow, London succeeded in balancing 50 British pint glasses on his chin for 14 seconds on British television on October 6, 1994.

Gold panning   The fastest time for "panning" eight planted gold nuggets in a 10-inch-diameter pan is 7.55 seconds, by Don Roberts of Diamond Bar, CA in the 27th World Gold Panning Championship on April 16, 1989 in Dahlonega, GA.

The women's record is 10.03 seconds, by Susan Bryeans of Fullerton, CA at the 23rd World Gold Panning Championship on March 6, 1983 at Knott's Berry Farm, Buena Park, CA.

Grape catching   The greatest distance at which a grape thrown from level ground has been caught in the mouth is 327 ft. 6 in., by Paul J. Tavilla in East Boston, MA on May 27, 1991. The grape was thrown by James Deady.

Handshaking   Kang Ho Dong, a Korean wrestler, shook hands with 28,233 different people in eight hours at Expo '93 in Taejon, South Korea on August 22, 1993.

Hopscotch   The greatest number of games of hopscotch successfully completed in 24 hours is 390, by Ashrita Furman of Jamaica, NY, April 2–3, 1995.

Human centipede   The largest "human centipede" to move 98 ft. 5 in. (30 meters), with ankles firmly tied together, consisted of 1,537 students from Great Barr School, Birmingham, England, March 11, 1994. Nobody fell over in the course of the walk.

Human logo   The largest human logo ever made was the Human U.S. Shield consisting of 30,000 officers and men at Camp Custer, Battle Creek, MI on November 10, 1918.

Joke telling   Working on the premise that a joke must have a beginning, a middle and an end, Felipe Carbonell of Lima, Peru told 345 jokes in one hour on July 29, 1993. Mike Hessman of Columbus, OH told 12,682 jokes in 24 hours on November 16–17, 1992.

Kissing   Alfred A.E. Wolfram of New Brighton, MN kissed 8,001 people in eight hours at the Minnesota Renaissance Festival on September 15, 1990—one every 3.6 seconds.

GUESS WHAT?

Q. WHAT WAS THE LONGEST FLIGHT BY A PAPER AIRPLANE?

A. LOOK IN "MODEL AIRCRAFT" (TRANSPORT)

Kite flying The following records are recognized by *Kite Lines* Magazine:

Highest A record height of 31,955 feet was reached by a train of eight kites over Lindenberg, Germany on August 1, 1919.

The altitude record for a single kite is 12,471 feet, in the case of a kite flown by Henry Helm Clayton and A.E. Sweetland at the Blue Hill Weather Station, Milton, MA on February 28, 1898.

Longest The longest kite flown was 3,394 feet long. It was made and flown by Michel Trouillet and a team of helpers in Nîmes, France on November 18, 1990.

Largest The largest kite flown was 5,952 square feet. It was first flown by a Dutch team on the beach in Scheveningen, Netherlands on August 8, 1991.

Fastest The fastest speed attained by a kite was 120 MPH for a kite flown by Pete Di Giacomo in Ocean City, MD on September 22, 1989.

Most figure eights The greatest number of figure eights achieved with a kite in an hour is 2,911, by Stu Cohen in Ocean City, MD on September 25, 1988.

Most on a single line The greatest number of kites flown on a single line is 11,284, by Sadao Harada and a team of helpers in Sakurajima, Kagoshima, Japan in October 1990.

Longest duration The longest recorded kite flight is one of 180 hr. 17 min. by the Edmonds Community College team in Long Beach, WA, August 21–29, 1982. Managing the flight of this J-25 parafoil was Harry N. Osborne.

Knitting The world's fastest hand-knitter was Gwen Matthewman of Featherstone, England. She attained a speed of 111 stitches per minute in a test at Phildar's Wool Shop, Leeds, England on September 29, 1980.

The Exeter Spinners—Audrey Felton, Christine Heap, Eileen Lancaster, Marjorie Mellis, Ann Sandercock and Maria Scott—produced a sweater by hand from raw fleece in 1 hr. 55 min. 50.2 sec. on September 25, 1983 at British Broadcasting Corporation Television Centre, London, England.

Knot tying The fastest recorded time for tying the six Boy Scout Handbook knots (square knot, sheet bend, sheepshank, clove hitch, round turn and two half hitches, and bowline) on individual ropes is 8.1 seconds, by Clinton R. Bailey, Sr. of Pacific City, OR on April 13, 1977.

Ladder climbing A team of 10 firefighters from Royal Berkshire Fire & Rescue Service climbed a vertical height of 47.58 miles up a standard fire-service ladder in 24 hours in Reading, England, April 28–29, 1995.

Land rowing The greatest distance covered on a land rowing machine is 3,280 miles, by Rob Bryant of Fort Worth, TX, who "rowed" across the United States. He left Los Angeles, CA on April 2, 1990, reaching Washington, D.C. on July 30.

The greatest distance recorded in a rope slide, or death slide, as it is also known, is 5,730 feet, by Lance Corporal Peter Baldwin of the British Royal Marines and Stu Leggett of the Canadian School of Rescue Training, from the top of Mt. Gibraltar, near Calgary, Canada on August 31, 1994. The descent, some of which was done at speeds in excess of 100 MPH, took 36 seconds, but that tells only part of the story.

THE AMAZING ROPE TRICK

The whole event was a mammoth logistical exercise, and there were many problems to solve. Bad weather meant that the attempt had to be postponed for three days. It took two days to get all the supplies to the base camp, which was a 1½-hour walk from the nearest road. A helicopter had to be used to take the specially made rope to the start point at the top of Mt. Gibraltar, 8,470 feet above sea level. The setting-up period took longer than planned because the rope kept getting caught on trees and the weather fluctuated from snow to extreme heat. The nearest hospital was four hours away, so a helicopter was on standby just in case anything went wrong. As if this were not enough, a grizzly bear was seen not far away—a further worry that everyone could have done without.

Eventually, everything was ready and the all-clear was given. Baldwin and Leggett hurled themselves off the mountain, and just over half a minute later, after a bumpy ride, they were on *terra firma* again, albeit after hitting a tree and taking out its top branches near the end. The previous record of 1,202 feet, set by some of Baldwin's colleagues in Blackpool, England, had been smashed out of sight.

Longest rope slide

The greatest distance recorded in a rope slide is 5,730 feet, by Lance Corporal Peter Baldwin of the British Royal Marines and Stu Leggett of the Canadian School of Rescue Training, from the top of Mt. Gibraltar, near Calgary, Canada, down to level ground on August 31, 1994.

Above right: Adding finishing touches to the rope at the summit
Facing page bottom: Former athlete Kriss Akabusi (right), now a BBC television announcer, attending to camp duties
Facing page top: Last pose for the camera
Facing page center: Positioning the rope to be uncoiled; Mt. Gibraltar looms in the background
Above top left: Bringing in supplies to base camp
Above bottom left: Preparing to drop a weight to the ground after a test run *(Steve Lewis RN © Crown Copyright Department)*

CRACK!

The longest whip ever cracked (i.e., the end made to travel faster than the speed of sound) is one of 184 ft. 6 in., excluding the handle, wielded by Krist King of Pettisville, OH on September 17, 1991.

Leapfrogging   The greatest distance covered is 996.2 miles, by 14 students from Trancos dormitory at Stanford University, Stanford, CA. They started leapfrogging on May 16, 1991 and stopped 244 hr. 43 min. later on May 26.

Log rolling   The record number of International Championships won is 10, by Jubiel Wickheim of Shawnigan Lake, British Columbia, Canada, between 1956 and 1969.

Mantle of bees   Jed Shaner was covered by a mantle of an estimated 343,000 bees weighing an aggregate of 80 pounds in Staunton, VA on June 29, 1991.

Milk bottle balancing   The greatest distance walked by a person continuously balancing a milk bottle on the head is 70.16 miles, by Ashrita Furman in Jamaica, NY, August 1–2, 1993. It took him 18 hr. 46 min. to complete the walk.

Milk crate balancing   Terry Cole of Walthamstow, England balanced 29 crates on his chin for the minimum specified 10 seconds on May 16, 1994. John Evans of Marlpool, England balanced 91 crates (each weighing three pounds) on his head for 10 seconds in Guernsey, Channel Islands on May 9, 1995.

Needle threading   The record number of times that a strand of cotton has been threaded through a number 13 needle (eye $1/2$ by $1/16$ inches) in two hours is 20,675, achieved by Om Prakash Singh of Allahabad, India on July 25, 1993.

Oyster opening   Mike Racz opened 100 oysters in 2 min. 20.07 sec. in Invercargill, New Zealand on July 16, 1990.

Paper chain   A paper chain 36.69 miles long was made by 60 students from University College Dublin, Republic of Ireland, as part of UCD Science Day in Dublin, February 11–12, 1993. The chain consisted of nearly 400,000 links and was made over a period of 24 hours.

Paper clip chain   A chain of 190,400 paper clips was made by 60 students from Nanyang Technological University, Singapore on July 12, 1992. The chain was completed in 5 hr. 35 min. and measured 18,087.3 feet long.

Pass the parcel   In the largest game of pass the parcel, 3,464 people removed 2,000 wrappers in two hours from a parcel measuring 5 by 3 by feet at Alton Towers, Alton, England on November 8, 1992. The event was organized by Parcelforce International.

Pedal-boating Kenichi Horie of Kobe, Japan set a pedal-boating distance record of 4,660 miles, leaving Honolulu, HI on October 30, 1992 and arriving in Naha, Okinawa, Japan on February 17, 1993.

Pogo stick jumping The greatest number of jumps achieved is 177,737, by Gary Stewart at Huntington Beach, Los Angeles, CA, May 25–26, 1990. Ashrita Furman of Jamaica, NY set a distance record of 16 miles in 6 hr. 40 min. on October 8, 1993 in Gotemba, Japan.

Rope slide The greatest distance recorded in a rope slide is 5,730 feet, by Lance Corporal Peter Baldwin of the British Royal Marines and Stu Leggett of the Canadian School of Rescue Training, from the top of Mt. Gibraltar, near Calgary, Canada, down to level ground on August 31, 1994. Some of the descent was done at speeds in excess of 100 MPH.

Snowman The tallest snowman was built by eight residents of Saas-Fee, Switzerland. They spent 21 days building the 90-ft.-1-in.-tall snowman, which was completed on November 6, 1993.

Spitting The greatest recorded distance for spitting a cherry stone is 88 ft. 5½ in., by Horst Ortmann in Langenthal, Germany on August 29, 1992. The record for projecting a watermelon seed is 68 ft. 9⅛ in., by Lee Wheelis in Luling, TX on June 24, 1989.

United States Rick Krause of Flint, MI spat a cherry stone 72 ft. 7½ in. on July 2, 1988 at the International Cherry Pit Spitting Championship in Eau Claire, MI.

David O'Dell of Apple Valley, CA spat a tobacco wad 49 ft. 5½ in. at the 19th World Tobacco Spitting Championships held in Calico Ghost Town, CA on March 26, 1994.

GUESS WHAT?

Q. WHO HAS THE LARGEST FEET?

A. LOOK IN "HANDS AND FEET" (HUMAN BEING)

Standing The longest period on record that anyone has continuously stood is more than 17 years in the case of Swami Maujgiri Maharaj when performing the *Tapasya* or penance from 1955 to November 1973 in Shahjahanpur, Uttar Pradesh, India. When sleeping he would lean against a plank. He died at age 85 in September 1980.

Step-ups Terry Cole of Walthamstow, England completed 2,362 step-ups in one hour on April 5, 1995 using a 15-inch-high exercise bench.

Stone skipping The video-verified stone skipping record is 38 skips, achieved by Jerdone in Wimberley, TX on October 20, 1991.

Tailoring The fastest production of a 3-piece suit from sheep to finished article was 1 hr. 34 min. 33.42 sec., by 65 members of the Melbourne College of Textiles, Pascoe Vale, Victoria, Australia on June 24, 1982. Catching and fleecing took 2 min. 21 sec., and carding, spinning, weaving and tailoring occupied the remaining time.

Tightrope walking The oldest tightrope walker was "Professor" William Ivy Baldwin, who crossed the South Boulder Canyon in Colorado on a 320-foot wire with a 125-foot drop on his 82nd birthday on July 31, 1948.

Ashley Brophy of Neilborough, Victoria, Australia walked 7.18 miles on a wire 147.64 feet long and 32.81 feet above the ground in Adelaide, Australia on November 1, 1985 in 3½ hours.

The greatest drop over which anyone has walked on a tightrope is 10,335 feet above the French countryside, by Michel Menin of Lons-le-Saunier, France, on August 4, 1989.

STEADY!

The world tightrope endurance record is 205 days, by Jorge Ojeda-Guzman of Orlando, FL, on a wire 36 feet long and 35 feet above the ground. He was there from January 1 to July 25, 1993 and entertained onlookers by walking, balancing on a chair and dancing.

Typewriting The highest recorded speeds attained with a 10-word penalty per error on a manual machine are—five minutes: 176 WPM by Carole Forristall Waldschlager Bechen in Dixon, IL on April 2, 1959; one hour: 147 WPM by Albert Tangora (U.S.) on an Underwood Standard, October 22, 1923.

The official 1-hour record on an electric typewriter is 9,316 words (40 errors) on an IBM machine, giving a net rate of 149 WPM, by Margaret Hamma (later Dilmore) in Brooklyn, NY on June 20, 1941. In an official test in 1946, Stella Pajunas (later Garnand) attained a rate of 216 WPM on an IBM machine.

Gregory Arakelian of Herndon, VA set a speed record of 158 WPM, with two errors, on a personal computer in the Key Tronic World Invitational Type-off, which attracted some 10,000 entrants worldwide. He recorded this speed in a 3-minute test in the semifinal on September 24, 1991.

Mikhail Shestov of Fredriksberg, Denmark set a numerical record by typing spaced numbers from 1 to 795 in five minutes on October 14, 1993.

Les Stewart of Mudjimba Beach, Queensland, Australia had typed the numbers 1 to 860,000 in *words* on 17,090 quarto sheets as of April 30, 1995. His target is to become a "millionaire."

Unsupported circle An unsupported circle of 10,323 employees of the Nissan Motor Co. was formed at Komazawa Stadium, Tokyo, Japan on October 23, 1982.

Wine glass stacking   Alain Fournier of Montreal, Canada put in position and held 45 wine glasses in one hand on "Live! With Regis and Kathie Lee" on July 20, 1994.

Writing   Mechanical   In the mid-1950s, Horace Dall of Luton, England constructed a pantograph with a writing stylus made from a diamond fragment. With this he was able to engrave writing so small that an entire Bible would fit onto a pinhead.

In 1985, Thomas Newman used a film of silicon nitride to record text in the form of a dot-matrix pattern, each dot measuring only 60 atoms in width.

Yo-yo   Fast Eddy McDonald of Toronto, Canada completed 21,663 loops in three hours on October 14, 1990 in Boston, MA. McDonald also set the 1-hour speed record of 8,437 loops in Cavendish, Prince Edward Island, Canada on July 14, 1990.

MICROWRITING

The Guinness Book of Records has received many claims for miniature handwriting over the years. Brian J. Ford, an expert microscopist and a *Guinness Book* adviser, was not impressed with many of the results.

"Unfortunately, as size decreases, so does legibility," he says. "Some of them look like scribble when magnified. In some cases, we've been sent clear copies of what people said they wrote—but you'd never guess it from looking through the microscope!"

The best recent claims come from India and China.

Surendra Apharya of Jaipur, India wrote 1,749 characters (names of various countries, towns and regions) on a single grain of rice in May 1991. Xie Shui Lin of Jiangxi, China wrote 11,660 characters (speeches by Sir Winston Churchill) within the size of a definitive postage stamp, measuring 0.78 by 0.7 in., in October 1993. Finally, Pan Xixing of Wuxi, China wrote 395 characters (meaning "True friendship is like sound health, the value of which is seldom known until it be lost") on a human hair $^8/_{10}$ in. long in April 1995.

FLORIDA GLOBE-TROTTERS

Most-traveled couple Dr. Robert and Carmen Becker of East Northport, NY have visited all 192 sovereign countries and all but nine of the 65 nonsovereign or other territories.

They met in her hometown in France during World War II, when he was among Patton's troops. He went on to Germany, and when the war ended he came back to marry her. Bob and Carmen Becker have been running around together ever since. They planned to celebrate their 50th anniversary in June 1995 with a trip to two small islands north of Australia. Ashmore and Cartier are among the places the Beckers haven't been. And they can count the rest on their fingers.

The Beckers have visited all 192 sovereign countries and all but nine of the 65 nonsovereign countries and other territories. Imelda Marcos sang for them, and they were once introduced to Japanese royalty. Just a few small islands stand in the way of their truly covering the globe. "We both traveled as kids," says Carmen Becker. "We had to go back to some places after we were married so we could say we'd been there as a couple."

Both groan when asked to recall how many trips they've taken. "We have no idea," Mrs. Becker says. "We're still trying to prove we were on the Golan Heights. Of course we remember it; it was 1977. But we can't find the pictures!" Now retired, the couple spends time in their Florida home, sticking thumbtacks in their latest world map ("It all keeps changing!") and reminiscing. "I'm glad we did certain things when the world was more primitive. It's not as safe anymore."

Of all the places she's been, Mrs. Becker figures she could happily take up residence in French Polynesia, as a second choice to the U.S. Her husband, an archaeology enthusiast, remembers Australia most fondly, especially Ayers Rock. "Everywhere we go, everybody is hospitable, everybody likes us. If you're nice to people, they're nice to you."

So, how many times has the world's most-traveled couple lost their luggage? Only once, in Japan.

The Beckers have visited places as diverse as Thailand (bottom) and Guadeloupe (top). (*Robert and Carmen Becker; Images; Spectrum/HOA-QUI*)

ADVENTURE

Most-traveled person   John D. Clouse of Evansville, IN had visited all 192 sovereign countries and all but six of the 65 nonsovereign or other territories that existed in early 1995.

Couple   Dr. Robert and Carmen Becker of East Northport, NY have visited all of the sovereign countries and all but nine of the nonsovereign or other territories.

Longest walks   The greatest distance claimed for an around-the-world walker is 30,520 miles, by Arthur Blessitt of North Fort Meyers, FL, since December 25, 1969. He has been to all seven continents, including Antarctica, carrying a 12-foot cross and preaching throughout his walk. Steven Newman of Bethel, OH spent four years, April 1, 1983–April 1, 1987, walking 22,500 miles around the world (thus going at a faster rate than Blessitt), covering 20 countries and five continents.

Rick Hansen (Canada), who was paralyzed from the waist down in 1973 as a result of a car accident, wheeled his wheelchair 24,901.55 miles through four continents and 34 countries. He started his journey from Vancouver, British Columbia on March 21, 1985 and arrived back there on May 22, 1987.

DID YOU KNOW?

The highest unclimbed mountain is Kankar Punsum, the 67th highest mountain in the world (24,741 feet), on the Bhutan–Tibet border. The highest unclimbed summit is Lhotse Middle (27,605 feet), in the Khumbu district of the Nepal Himalaya. It is the 10th highest individually recognized peak in the world.

Trans-Americas   George Meegan (Great Britain) walked 19,019 miles from Ushuaia, in the southern tip of South America, to Prudhoe Bay in northern Alaska, taking 2,426 days from January 26, 1977 to September 18, 1983.

Trans-America   Sean Eugene McGuire (U.S.) walked 7,327 miles from the Yukon River, north of Livengood, AK to Key West, FL in 307 days, from June 6, 1978 to April 9, 1979. John Lees (Great Britain) walked 2,876 miles across the United States from City Hall, Los Angeles to City Hall, New York City in 53 days 12 hr. 15 min. (averaging 53.75 miles a day) between April 11 and June 3, 1972.

Trans-Canada Clyde McRae walked 3,764 miles from Halifax to Vancouver in 96 days, from May 1 to August 4, 1973.

MOUNTAINEERING

Climbing Mount Everest Everest (29,029 feet) was first climbed on May 29, 1953, when the summit was reached by Edmund Percival Hillary (New Zealand) and Sherpa Tenzing Norgay (formerly called Tenzing Khumjung Bhutia). The successful expedition was led by Col. Henry Cecil John Hunt.

Most conquests Ang Rita Sherpa has scaled Everest eight times, with ascents in 1983, 1984, 1985, 1987, 1988, 1990, 1992, and 1993, all without the use of bottled oxygen.

First solo Reinhold Messner (Italy) was the first to make the entire climb solo, on August 20, 1980. Messner and Peter Habeler (Austria) made the first ascent without bottled oxygen on May 8, 1978.

First woman Junko Tabei (Japan) reached the summit on May 16, 1975.

Oldest Ramon Blanco (Spain) was 60 years old when he reached the summit on October 7, 1993.

Most climbers The Mount Everest International Peace Climb, a team of American, Russian and Chinese climbers, led by James W. Whittaker (U.S.), put the greatest number of people on the summit, 20, on May 7–10, 1990.

Most in a day Nine separate expeditions (32 men and 8 women from the United States, Canada, Australia, Great Britain, Russia, New Zealand, Finland, Lithuania, India and Nepal) reached the summit on May 12, 1992.

Sea level to summit Timothy John Macartney-Snape (Australia) traversed Mt. Everest's entire altitude from sea level to summit. He set off on foot from the Bay of Bengal near Calcutta, India on February 5, 1990 and reached the summit of Mt. Everest on May 11, having walked approximately 745 miles.

Most summits Reinhold Messner scaled all 14 of the world's mountains of over 26,250 feet, all without oxygen. With his ascent of Kanchenjunga in 1982, he became the first person to climb the world's three highest mountains, having earlier reached the summits of Everest and K2.

Oldest mountain climber Ichijirou Araya (Japan) climbed Mt. Fuji (12,388 feet) at the age of 100 yr. 258 days on August 5, 1994.

Greatest walls The highest final stage in any wall climb is the one on the south face of Annapurna I (26,545 feet). It was climbed by the British expedition led by Christian John Storey Bonington, when, from April 2 to May 27, 1970, using 18,000 feet of rope, Donald Whillans and Dougal Haston scaled to the summit. The longest wall climb is on the Rupal-Flank from the base camp, at 11,680 feet, to the South Point, at 26,384 feet, of Nanga Parbat—a vertical ascent of 14,704 feet. This was scaled by the

POLAR CONQUEST

The first person to walk to both the North and South Poles was Robert Swan (Great Britain). He led the 3-man Footsteps of Scott expedition, which reached the South Pole on Jan. 11, 1986, and three years later he headed the 8-man Icewalk expedition, which arrived at the North Pole on May 14, 1989. Below are listed a selection of other firsts in polar conquest.

Both Poles

Category	Adventurers	Date
First to see both poles	Capt. Engeburth Gravning Amundsen and Oskar Wisting	May 12, 1926
First to visit both poles	Dr Albert Paddock Crary (U.S.), by aircraft and Sno Cat	Feb. 12, 1961
First Pole to Pole circumnavigation[1]	Sir Ranulph Fiennes and Charles Burton	Sep. 2, 1979–Aug. 29, 1982

South Pole

Category	Adventurers	Date
First to cross Antarctic Circle	Capt. James Cook, Lt. Tobias Furneaux and 193 crewmen, British Royal Navy	Jan. 17, 1773
First to sight antarctic ice shelf	Capt. Fabian Gottlieb Benjamin von Bellinshausen	Jan. 27, 1820
First to sight continent mainland	Capt. William Smith and Master Edward Bransfield, British Royal Navy	Jan. 27, 1820
First to reach the South Pole	Capt. Roald Engeburth Gravning Amundsen (Norway) and four others	11 A.M., Dec. 14, 1911
First to reach the South Pole solo	Erling Kagge (Norway)	Jan. 7, 1993
First crossing of continent	Dr. Vivian Ernest Fuchs (Great Britain) in a party of 12	1:47 P.M., Mar. 2, 1958
First crossing in a single season	Sir Ranulph Fiennes and Charles Burton	Oct. 28–Dec. 15, 1980

POLAR CONQUEST

North Pole

Category	Adventurers	Date
First to reach the North Pole[2]	Ralph Plaisted (U.S.), Walter Pederson, Gerald Pitzl, Jean Luc Bombardier	3 P.M. EST, Apr. 19, 1968
First to reach the North Pole solo[3]	Naomi Uemura (Japan)	4:45 A.M. GMT, May 1, 1978
First to ski to the North Pole	Dmitry Shparo and six members of a Soviet expedition	May 31, 1979
First to motorcycle to North Pole	Shinji Kazama (Japan) on a 200-cc motorcycle	Apr. 20, 1987
First crossing of continent	Wally Herbert, Maj. Ken Hedges, Allan Gill, Dr Roy Koerner	Feb. 21, 1968–May 29, 1969

[1] Fiennes and Burton reached the South Pole on Dec. 15, 1980 and the North Pole on Apr. 10, 1982. In all, they covered over 35,000 miles.
[2] The claims of the two Arctic explorers Dr. Frederick Albert Cook (1865–1940) and Cdr. Robert Edwin Peary (1856–1920) of the U.S. Naval Civil Engineering branch to have reached the North Pole are not subject to irrefutable proof, and several recent surveys have produced conflicting conclusions.
[3] Dr Jean-Louis Etienne was the first to reach the Pole solo and without dogs, on May 11, 1986 after 63 days.

Austro-German-Italian expedition led by Dr. Karl Maria Herrligkoffer in April 1970.

Highest bivouac Four Nepalese summiters bivouacked at more than 28,870 feet in their descent from the summit of Everest on the night of April 23, 1990. They were Ang Rita Sherpa, on his record-breaking sixth ascent of Everest; Ang Kami Sherpa; Pasang Norbu Sherpa; and Top Bahadur Khatri.

Human fly The longest climb on the vertical face of a building occurred on May 25, 1981, when Daniel Goodwin, 25, of California climbed a record 1,454 feet up the outside of the Sears Tower in Chicago, using suction cups and metal clips for support.

POLAR EXPLORATION

Longest sled journey The longest polar sled journey was undertaken by the International Trans-Antarctica Expedition (six members), who traveled a distance of about 3,750 miles by sled in 220 days, from July 27, 1989 (Seal Nunataks) to March 3, 1990 (Mirnyy). The expedition was accompanied by a team of 40 dogs, but a number of the dogs were flown out from one of the staging posts for a period of rest before returning to the Antarctic. The expedition was supported by aircraft throughout its duration.

The longest *totally self-supporting* polar sled journey ever made was one of 1,350 miles from Gould Bay to the Ross Ice Shelf by Sir Ranulph Fiennes and Dr. Michael Stroud from November 9, 1992 to February 11, 1993.

Arctic crossing The first crossing of the Arctic sea-ice was achieved by the British Trans-Arctic Expedition, which left Point Barrow, AK on February 21, 1968 and arrived at the Seven Island archipelago northeast of Spitzbergen, Svalbard, Norway 464 days later, on May 29, 1969. This involved a haul of 2,920 statute miles with a drift of 700 miles, compared with the straight-line distance of 1,662 miles. The team was made up of Wally Herbert (leader), Major Ken Hedges, RAMC, Allan Gill, Dr. Roy Koerner (glaciologist), and 40 huskies.

Antarctic crossing The first surface crossing of the Antarctic continent was completed at 1:47 P.M. on March 2, 1958, after a trek of 2,158 miles lasting 99 days from November 24, 1957, from Shackleton Base to Scott Base via the Pole. The crossing party of 12 was led by Dr. (later Sir) Vivian Ernest Fuchs (Great Britain).

The 2,600-mile trans-Antarctic leg from Sanae to Scott Base of the 1980–82 British Trans-Globe Expedition was achieved in 67 days and eight rest days, from October 28, 1980 to January 11, 1981, the expedition having reached the South Pole on December 15, 1980. The 3-man snowmobile team comprised Sir Ranulph Fiennes, Oliver Shepard and Charles Burton.

OCEAN EXPLORATION

Greatest ocean descent The record ocean descent was achieved in the Challenger Deep of the Mariana Trench, 250 miles southwest of Guam in the Pacific Ocean, when the Swiss-built U.S. Navy bathyscaphe *Trieste*, manned by Dr. Jacques Piccard (Switzerland) and Lt. Donald Walsh (U.S.N.), reached a depth of 35,813 feet on January 23, 1960. The descent took 4 hr. 48 min. and the ascent 3 hr. 17 min.

Deepest dive The record depth for the dangerous (and ill-advised) activity of breath-held diving is 410 feet, by Francisco "Pipin" Ferreras (Cuba) off Grand Bahama Island, on November 14, 1993. He was underwater for 2 min. 9 sec.

The record dive with scuba gear is 437 feet, by John J. Gruener and R. Neal Watson (U.S.) off Freeport, Grand Bahama on October 14, 1968.

The record dive utilizing gas mixtures was a simulated dive to a depth of 2,300 feet of seawater by Théo Mavrostomos as part of the HYDRA 10 operation at the Hyperbaric Center of Comex in Marseilles, France on November 20, 1992, during a 43-day dive. He was breathing "hydreliox" (hydrogen, oxygen and helium).

Arnaud de Nechaud de Feral performed a saturation dive of 73 days, October 9–December 21, 1989, in a hyperbaric chamber simulating a depth of 985 feet, as part of the Comex HYDRA 9 operation. He was breathing "hydrox," a mixture of hydrogen and oxygen.

Richard Presley spent 69 days 19 min. in an underwater module in a lagoon in Key Largo, FL, May 6–July 14, 1992. The test was carried out as part of a mission called Project Atlantis that explored the human factors of living in an undersea environment.

Longest submergence The *continuous* duration record (no rest breaks) with scuba gear is 212 hr. 30 min., by Michael Stevens of Birmingham,

HIGH ALTITUDE DIVING

Henri García of the Chilean *Expedición America* team dived at an altitude of 19,357 feet into a lagoon in the crater of Licancabur, a volcano on the border between Chile and Bolivia. García spent 1 hr. 8 min. exploring the lake at depths of 16–23 feet on January 16, 1995.

England in a Royal Navy tank at the National Exhibition Center, Birmingham, February 14–23, 1986.

Deepest underwater escapes The deepest underwater rescue ever achieved was of the *Pisces III*, in which Roger R. Chapman and Roger Mallinson were trapped for 76 hours when their vessel sank to 1,575 feet, 150 miles southeast of Cork, Ireland on August 29, 1973. It was hauled to the surface on September 1 by the cable ship *John Cabot* after work by *Pisces V*, *Pisces II* and the remote-control recovery vessel *Curv* (Controlled Underwater Recovery Vehicle).

The greatest depth from which an unaided escape without any equipment has been made is 225 feet, by Richard A. Slater from the rammed submersible *Nekton Beta* off Catalina Island, CA on September 28, 1970.

The record for an escape with equipment was by Norman Cooke and

Hamish Jones on July 22, 1987. During a naval exercise they escaped from a depth of 601 feet from the submarine HMS *Otus* in Bjornefjorden, off Bergen, Norway. They were wearing standard suits with a built-in life jacket, from which air expanding during the ascent passes into a hood over the escaper's head.

Deepest salvage   The greatest depth at which salvage has been carried out is 17,251 feet, in the case of a helicopter that crashed into the Pacific Ocean in August 1991 with the loss of four lives. The crew of the U.S.S. *Salvor* and personnel from East Port International managed to raise the wreckage to the surface on February 27, 1992 so that the authorities could try to determine the cause of the accident.

The deepest salvage operation ever achieved with divers was on the wreck of HM cruiser *Edinburgh*, sunk on May 2, 1942 in the Barents Sea off northern Norway, inside the Arctic Circle, in 803 feet of water. Over 32 days (September 7–October 7, 1981), 12 divers worked on the wreck in pairs, using a bell from the *Stephaniturm* (1,594 tons), under the direction of former British Royal Navy officer Michael Stewart. All of the 460 gold ingots were recovered, John Rossier being the first person to touch the gold.

Longest survival at sea   Tabwai Mikaie and Arenta Tebeitabu, two fishermen from the island of Nikunau in Kiribati, were found alive on May 12, 1992 after surviving for a record 177 days adrift at sea in their fishing boat, a 13-foot open dinghy.

Longest on a raft   The longest recorded survival alone on a raft is 133 days (4½ months) by Second Steward Poon Lim (b. Hong Kong) of Great Britain's Merchant Navy, whose ship, the SS *Ben Lomond*, was torpedoed in the Atlantic 565 miles west of St. Paul's Rocks at Lat. 00° 30′ N, Long. 38° 45′ W at 11:45 A.M. on November 23, 1942. He was picked up by a Brazilian fishing boat off Salinópolis, Brazil on April 5, 1943 and was able to walk ashore.

MARRIAGES

Longest engagement   The longest engagement on record was between Octavio Guillen and Adriana Martinez. They finally took the plunge after 67 years in June 1969 in Mexico City. Both were then 82 years old.

Most marriages   The greatest number of marriages contracted by one person in the monogamous world is 28, by former Baptist minister Glynn "Scotty" Wolfe of Blythe, CA, who first married in 1927. He is currently separated from his 28th wife and is hoping to marry again. He believes that he has had a total of 41 children.

The greatest number of monogamous marriages by a woman is 22, by Linda Lou Essex of Anderson, IN, who has married 15 different men since 1957. Her most recent marriage was in 1991, but that ended in divorce, like the others.

The record for bigamous marriages is 104, by a man using the name Giovanni Vigliotto, from 1949 to 1981 in 27 states and 14 countries. On March 28, 1983 in Phoenix, AZ, Vigliotto received a sentence of 28 years for fraud and six for bigamy, and was fined $336,000. He died in February 1991.

Oldest bride and bridegroom The oldest recorded bridegroom was Harry Stevens, age 103, who married Thelma Lucas, 84, at the Caravilla Retirement Home, Beloit, WI on December 3, 1984.

The oldest bride was Minnie Munro, age 102, who married Dudley Reid, 83, in Point Clare, New South Wales, Australia on May 31, 1991.

Youngest married couple In 1986, an 11-month-old boy was reportedly married to a 3-month-old girl in Aminpur, Bangladesh to end a 20-year feud between two families over a disputed farm.

Longest marriages The longest recorded marriages were both of 86 years. Sir Temulji Bhicaji Nariman and Lady Nariman were married from 1853, when they were five years old, until 1940, when Sir Temulji died in Bombay, India at the age of 91 yr. 11 mo. Lazarus Rowe of Greenland, NH and Molly Webber were married in 1743. He died first, in 1829, also after 86 years of marriage.

Golden weddings The greatest number of golden weddings in a family is 10. The six sons and four daughters of Joseph and Sophia Gresl of Mani-

Glynn "Scotty" Wolfe with his 28th wife, Evia, after their wedding on June 27, 1994. The couple are now separated, and Wolfe is planning to marry again. (*Courtesy of Glynn "Scotty" Wolfe*)

towoc, WI all celebrated golden weddings between April 1962 and September 1988; the six sons and four daughters of George and Eleonora Hopkins of Patrick County, VA all celebrated their golden weddings between November 1961 and October 1988; and the five sons and five daughters of Alonzo and Willie Alpharetta Cagle of McLennan County, TX all celebrated golden weddings between December 1971 and December 1993.

Wedding ceremonies The largest mass wedding ceremony was one of 20,825 couples officiated over by Sun Myung Moon of the Holy Spirit Association for the Unification of World Christianity in the Olympic Stadium in Seoul, South Korea on August 25, 1992. An additional 9,800 couples around the world took part in the ceremony through a satellite link.

Most ceremonies Richard and Carole Roble of South Hempstead, NY have married each other 55 times, starting in 1969. They have chosen a different location each time, including ceremonies in all 50 states.

Most expensive The wedding of Mohammed, son of Shaik Rashid Bin Saeed Al Maktoum, to Princess Salama in Dubai in May 1981 lasted seven days and cost an estimated $44 million. It was held in a stadium built especially for the occasion, accommodating 20,000 wedding guests.

Greatest attendance At the wedding of Aharon Mordechai Rokeah and Sara Lea Lemberger in Jerusalem, Israel on August 4, 1993, the attendance of the Belz Hasidic community was estimated to be 30,000.

JUGGLING

"Juggled" means the number of catches made equals twice the number of objects thrown.

"Flashed" means the number of catches made equals at least the number of objects thrown.

Most objects aloft 826 jugglers kept 2,478 objects in the air simultaneously, each person juggling at least three objects, in Glastonbury, England on June 26, 1994.

12 rings (flashed) Albert Lucas (U.S.), 1985; Anthony Gatto (U.S.), 1993.

8 clubs (flashed)   Anthony Gatto (U.S.), 1989.

11 balls (flashed)   Bruce Sarafian (U.S.), 1992.

10 balls (bounce juggled)   Tim Nolan (U.S.), 1988.

8 plates (flashed)   Enrico Rastelli (Italy), 1920s; Albert Lucas (U.S.), 1984. There is no existing proof that makes it clear whether the plates in Rastelli's historically accepted record were only flashed or actually juggled.

7 flaming torches (juggled)   Anthony Gatto (U.S.), 1989.

5 balls inverted   Bobby May (U.S.), 1953.

Ball spinning (on one hand)   François Chotard (France), 9 balls, 1990.

Basketball spinning   Bruce Crevier (U.S.), 18 basketballs (whole body), 1994.

Duration: 5 clubs without a drop   45 min. 2 sec., Anthony Gatto (U.S.), 1989.

Duration: 3 objects without a drop   Terry Cole (Great Britain), 11 hr. 4 min. 22 sec., 1995.

FOOD AND DRINK

Alcohol consumption   In 1993, Russia had the highest consumption of hard liquor per person, with an average of 8.0 pints of pure alcohol in that year. In the same year, the Czech Republic was the leading beer consumer, with 295.9 pints per person, and France headed the list for wine, with 134.2 pints per person in 1993.

Most alcoholic drink   When Estonia was independent, between the two World Wars, the Estonian Liquor Monopoly marketed 98 percent alcohol (196 proof) distilled from potatoes. In 31 states, Everclear, 190 proof or 95 percent alcohol by volume, is marketed by the American Distilling Co. "primarily as a base for home-made cordials."

Apple pie   The largest apple pie ever baked was made in a dish measuring 40 by 23 feet, by chef Glynn Christian, at Hewitts Farm, Chelsfield, England, August 25–27, 1982. Over 600 bushels of apples were included in the pie, which weighed 30,115 pounds.

Banana split   The longest banana split ever created measured 4.55 miles long, and was made by residents of Selinsgrove, PA on April 30, 1988.

Oldest beer   Physical evidence of beer dating from as far back as *c.* 3500 B.C. has been detected in the remains of a jug found at Godin Tepe, Iran in

1973 during an expedition by the Royal Ontario Museum, Canada. It was only in 1991 that the remains were analyzed, establishing that residues in deep grooves in the jug were calcium oxalate, also known as beerstone and still created in barley-based beers.

Strongest beer   Baz's Super Brew, brewed by Barrie Parish and on sale at The Parish Brewery, Somerby, England, has an alcohol volume of 23.0 percent.

United States   Samuel Adams Triple Bock, brewed by the Boston Beer Company, is 17.7 percent alcohol by volume.

Burrito   Montebello Town Center, Montebello, CA constructed a 3,960-pound burrito on September 16, 1994. The burrito consisted of eggs, refried beans, cheese, tomatoes, lettuce and salsa wrapped in a 3,055.4-foot-long tortilla.

Cake   Largest   The largest cake ever created weighed 128,238 lb. 8 oz., including 16,209 pounds of icing. It was made to celebrate the 100th birthday of Fort Payne, AL, and was in the shape of Alabama. The cake was prepared by a local bakery, EarthGrains, and the first cut was made by 100-year-old resident Ed Henderson on October 18, 1989.

Tallest   The tallest cake was 101 ft. 2½ in. high. It was created by Beth Cornell Trevorrow and her team of helpers at the Shiawassee County Fairgrounds, MI. The cake consisted of 100 tiers, and work was completed on August 5, 1990.

Oldest   The Alimentarium Food Museum in Vevey, Switzerland has on display the world's oldest cake, which was sealed and "vacuum-packed" in the grave of Pepionkh, who lived in ancient Egypt around 2200 B.C. The 4.3-inch-wide cake has sesame on it and honey inside, and was possibly made with milk.

Candy   The largest candy was a marzipan chocolate weighing 4,078 lb. 8 oz., made at the Ven International Fresh Market, Diemen, Netherlands, May 11–13, 1990.

Champagne cork flight   The longest flight of a cork from an untreated and unheated bottle four feet from level ground is 177 ft. 9 in., reached by Prof.

MEATY!

The largest meat pie on record weighed 19,908 pounds and was baked in Denby Dale, England on September 3, 1988 to mark the bicentennial of Denby Dale pie-making, their first pie having been made in 1788 to celebrate King George III's return to sanity.

Emeritus Heinrich Medicus, Rensselaer Polytechnic Institute, at the Woodbury Vineyards Winery, NY on June 5, 1988.

Champagne fountain The greatest number of stories achieved in a champagne fountain, successfully filled from the top and using traditional long-stem glasses, is 47 (height 25 ft. 9 in.), achieved by Moet et Chandon Champagne with 23,642 glasses at Caesars Palace, Las Vegas, NV, July 19–23, 1993.

Cheese The largest cheese ever created was a cheddar weighing 40,060 pounds, made March 13–14, 1988 at Simon's Specialty Cheese, Little Chute, WI. It was subsequently taken on tour in a specially designed, refrigerated "Cheesemobile."

Cherry pie The largest cherry pie on record weighed 37,740 lb. 10 oz. and contained 36,800 pounds of cherry filling. It measured 20 feet in diameter, and was baked by members of the Oliver Rotary Club in Oliver, British Columbia, Canada on July 14, 1990.

Chocolate model The largest chocolate model weighed 8,818 lb. 6 oz., and was in the shape of a traditional Spanish sailing ship. It was made by Gremi Provincial de Pastissería, Confitería i Bollería school, Barcelona in February 1991 and measured 42 ft. 8 in. by 27 ft. 10½ in. by 8 ft. 2½ in.

Cocktail The largest cocktail on record was a Finlandia Sea Breeze of 2,933 gallons, made at Maui Entertainment Center, Philadelphia, PA on August 5, 1994. It consisted of Finlandia vodka, cranberry juice, grapefruit juice and ice.

It took 10 hours to make the world's largest cocktail. "Everyone was pretty impressed with it," commented the organizers. "Now they're just trying to drink it." (*Scott Weiner/Retna © Ricky Blatstein*)

Cookie The largest cookie ever made was a chocolate chip cookie with an area of 1,001 square feet, made at Santa Anita Fashion Park in Arcadia, CA on October 15, 1993. It was 35 ft. by 28 ft. 7 in. and contained more than 3 million chocolate chips.

Crepe The largest crepe was 49 ft. 3 in. in diameter and one inch deep, and weighed 6,614 pounds. It was made and flipped in Rochdale, England on August 13, 1994.

Crepe tossing The greatest number of times a crepe has been tossed in two minutes is 349, by Dean Gould in Felixstowe, England on January 14, 1995.

Dish The largest item on any menu in the world is roasted camel, prepared occasionally for Bedouin wedding feasts. Cooked eggs are stuffed into fish, the fish stuffed into cooked chickens, the chickens stuffed into a roasted sheep's carcass and the sheep stuffed into a whole camel.

Doughnut The largest doughnut ever made weighed 3,739 pounds. It was 16 feet in diameter and 16 inches high in the center. The jelly doughnut was made by representatives from Hemstrought's Bakeries, Donato's Bakery and radio station WKLL-FM in Utica, NY on January 21, 1993.

Easter egg The heaviest chocolate Easter egg on record, and also the tallest, weighed 10,482 lb. 14 oz., and was 23 ft. 3 in. high. It was made by the staff of Cadbury Red Tulip at their factory in Ringwood, Victoria, Australia, and completed on April 9, 1992.

Most expensive spice Prices for wild ginseng from the Chan Pak Mountain area of China were reported in November 1979 to be as high as $23,000 per ounce in Hong Kong.

Hamburger The largest hamburger on record weighed 5,520 pounds and was 21 feet in diameter. The burger was made at the Outagamie County Fairgrounds, Seymour, WI on August 5, 1989.

Ice-cream sundae The largest ice-cream sundae weighed 54,914 lb. 13 oz., and was made by Palm Dairies Ltd. under the supervision of Mike Rogiani in Edmonton, Alberta, Canada on July 24, 1988. It consisted of 44,689 lb. 8 oz. of ice cream, 9,688 lb. 2 oz. of syrup and 537 lb. 3 oz. of topping.

Jell-O A 9,246-gallon watermelon-flavored pink Jell-O was made by Paul Squires and Geoff Ross at Roma Street Forum, Brisbane, Australia on February 5, 1981, in a tank supplied by Pool Fab.

Jelly bean jar The largest jar of jelly beans was 96 inches high and contained 378,000 jelly beans weighing a total of 2,910 pounds. The Disney Channel sponsored the jar, which was unveiled on October 14, 1992 at Westside Pavilion, Los Angeles, CA.

Kebab The longest kebab ever was one 2,889 ft. 3 in. long, made by the West Yorkshire Family Service Units, Trade Association of Asian Restaurant Owners, and National Power in Bradford, England on June 19, 1994.

GUESS WHAT?

Q. WHERE IS THE WORLD'S LARGEST RESTAURANT?

A. LOOK IN "BARS AND RESTAURANTS" (BUILDINGS & STRUCTURES)

Lasagne   The largest lasagne weighed 8,188 lb. 8 oz. and measured 70 feet by 7 feet. It was made by the Food Bank for Monterey County in Salinas, CA on October 14, 1993.

Most expensive liquor   A bottle of 50-year-old Glenfiddich Scotch was sold for a record price of 99,999,999 lire (approximately $71,200) to an anonymous Italian businessman at a charity auction in Milan, Italy. The postal auction was held over a 2-month period in 1992.

Loaf   The longest loaf on record was a Rosca de Reyes measuring 3,491 ft. 9 in. long, baked at the Hyatt Regency Hotel in Guadalajara, Mexico on January 6, 1991. If a consumer of the "Rosca," or twisted loaf, finds the embedded doll, that person has to host the Rosca party (held annually at Epiphany) the following year.

The largest pan loaf ever baked weighed 3,163 lb. 10 oz. and measured 9 ft. 10 in. by 4 ft. 1 in. by 3 ft. 7 in., by the staff of Sasko in Johannesburg, South Africa on March 18, 1988.

Lollipop   The largest lollipop was peppermint-flavored, and weighed 3,011 pounds. It was made by the staff of BonBon in Holme Olstrup, Denmark on April 22, 1994.

Milk shake   The largest milk shake was a chocolate one of 1,955.1 gallons, made by the Nelspruit and District Welfare Society and the Fundraising Five in Nelspruit, South Africa on March 5, 1994.

Noodle making   Simon Sang Koon Sung of Singapore made 8,192 noodle strings from a single piece of noodle dough in 59.29 seconds during the Singapore Food Festival on July 31, 1994. This is more than 138 noodles per second.

Omelet   The largest omelet in the world had an area of 1,383 square feet and contained 160,000 eggs. The omelet was cooked by representatives of Swatch in Yokohama, Japan on March 19, 1994.

Omelet making   The greatest number of 2-egg omelets made in 30 minutes is 427, by Howard Helmer at the International Poultry Trade Show held in Atlanta, GA on February 2, 1990.

Paella   The largest paella ever prepared measured 65 ft. 7 in. in diameter and was made by Juan Carlos Galbis and a team of helpers in Valencia, Spain on March 8, 1992. It was eaten by 100,000 people.

POP 'TIL
YOU DROP

"Egads!" fifth-grader Timmy Arvanetes exclaimed with joy when he heard the news. **"We're in** ***The Guinness Book of Records!"***

"There was a hot air popper in every classroom. We had them piled in the hallways. Anywhere we could find an outlet we plugged in a popper," Beauclerc Elementary School Principal Montelle A. Trammell recounts. "We even had to have school board electricians come in to do heavy re-wiring so we wouldn't overload the circuits."

As this Jacksonville, Florida elementary school popped to the top of the record book with the largest container of popcorn, a new precedent may have been set for having fun while learning. "This was also an educational experiment," Ms. Trammell explains. "Every class was responsible for tying the popcorn popping to the curriculum."

In English class, fifth-grader Debbie Brown had to find all of the words with "pop" in them. Eleven-year-old William Howard wrote a story about the experience. And Timmy Arvanetes said, "In math I learned dividing and multiplication by figuring out how much the box was full and how much came up the sides."

(Theresa Walsh/Beauclerc Elementary School)

The kids hardly ate any of the leftover popcorn, since most of it was donated to charities. Ms. Trammell tells of one unusual recipient of the popcorn: "One truck came and took bags of popcorn to a pig farm to feed the pigs. Some popcorn spilled off the truck and it was like a yellow brick road all of the way over to the pig farm."

Popcorn The largest container full of popcorn was one with 6,619.76 cubic feet of popped corn. It was 39 ft. 11½ in. long, 20 ft. 8½ in. wide and 8 feet high, and was filled at Beauclerc Elementary School in Jacksonville, FL over six days, October 6–11, 1994.

In 1989, Frank Garcia of GNS Spices discovered the hottest spice—the red "Savina" habanero—almost by accident. His company now grows it commercially. (*GNS Spices Inc.*)

Pastry The longest pastry in the world was a millefeuille (cream puff pastry) 3,403 feet long. It was made by employees of Pidy, a company based in Ypres, Belgium, September 4–5, 1992.

Pecan pie A pecan pie weighing 40,266 pounds and measuring 40 feet in diameter was baked on June 16, 1989 for the Pecan Festival in Okmulgee, OK.

The world's largest popcorn ball weighs in at 2,225 pounds. (*Le Spearman 1995*)

Pizza The largest pizza ever baked was one measuring 122 ft. 8 in. in diameter with an area of 11,816 square feet, made at Norwood Hypermarket, Norwood, South Africa on December 8, 1990.

Popcorn The largest container full of popcorn was one with 6,619.76 cubic feet of popped corn. The box was 39 ft. 11½ in. long, 20 ft. 8½ in. wide and 8 feet high, and was filled at Beauclerc Elementary School in Jacksonville, FL over a period of six days, October 6–11, 1994.

Popcorn ball A 2,225-pound popcorn ball was created in Sac County, IA on April 29, 1995. The Sac Economic Tourism and Development office organized the construction of the 6-foot-high popcorn ball, which 35 volunteers worked for 10 hours to complete.

Popsicle The world's largest popsicle was a vanilla, chocolate and nut one of 19,357 pounds, made by the staff of Augusto Ltd. in Kalisz, Poland, September 18–29, 1994.

Rice pudding The New York Guild of Chefs made a pot of rice pudding weighing 2,146.6 pounds in Manorhaven Park, NY on September 11, 1993. The finished pudding was enjoyed by 2,600 people.

Salami The longest salami on record was 68 ft. 9 in. long with a circumference of 25 inches, and weighed 1,492 lb. 5 oz. It was made by employees of A/S Svindlands Pølsefabrikk in Flekkefjord, Norway, July 6–16, 1992.

Sausage The longest continuous sausage on record was one of 28.77 miles, made by M & M Meat Shops in partnership with J.M. Schneider Inc. in Kitchener, Ontario, Canada on April 28–29, 1995.

Spice The hottest of all spices is believed to be the red "Savina" habanero, belonging to the genus *Capsicum*, developed by GNS Spices of Walnut, CA. A single dried gram will produce detectable "heat" in 719 pounds of bland sauce.

Strawberry bowl The largest bowl of strawberries ever picked had a net weight of 5,266 pounds. The strawberries were picked at Joe Moss Farms near Embro, Ontario, Canada and the bowl was filled at the Kitchener-Waterloo Hospital, also in Ontario, on June 29, 1993.

Strawberry shortcake A strawberry shortcake measuring 50 ft. 3 in. by 8 ft. was created by Biringer Farm Products at Westlake Center, Seattle, WA on July 22, 1994.

Wine Oldest It is thought that New Stone Age people may have been cultivating wine as early as 8000 B.C. Physical evidence of wine dating from *c.* 3500 B.C. has been detected in remains of a Sumerian jar found at Godin Tepe, Iran in 1973 during an expedition by the Royal Ontario Museum, Canada. In 1989, a large red stain in the jar was analyzed and found to contain tartaric acid, a chemical naturally abundant in grapes.

Most expensive £105,000 ($131,250) was paid for a bottle of 1787 Château Lafite claret, sold to Christopher Forbes (U.S.) at Christie's, London, England on December 5, 1985. The bottle was engraved with the initials of

Thomas Jefferson (1743–1826), "Th J"—a factor that greatly affected the bidding. In November 1986 its cork, dried out by exhibition lights, slipped, making the wine undrinkable.

The record price for a glass of wine is Fr8,600 ($1,447), for the first glass of Beaujolais Nouveau 1993 released in Beaune (from Maison Jaffelin), in the wine region of Burgundy, France. It was bought by Robert Denby at Pickwick's, a British pub in Beaune, on November 18, 1993.

Wine tasting   The largest ever reported was that staged by WQED on November 22, 1986 in San Francisco, CA. Some 4,000 tasters consumed 9,360 bottles of wine.

FEASTS AND CELEBRATIONS

Largest banquet   The largest feast was attended by 150,000 guests on the occasion of the renunciation ceremony of Atul Dalpatlal Shah, when he became a monk, in Ahmedabad, India on June 2, 1991.

Indoor   The greatest number of people served indoors at a single sitting was 18,000 municipal leaders at the Palais de l'Industrie, Paris, France on August 18, 1889.

Most restaurants visited   The world champion for eating out was Fred E. Magel of Chicago, IL, who over a period of 50 years dined out 46,000 times in 60 countries as a restaurant grader. He claimed that the restaurant that served the largest helpings was Zehnder's Hotel, Frankenmuth, MI. Mr. Magel's favorite dishes were South African rock lobster and mousse of fresh English strawberries.

Highest dinner party   The greatest altitude at which a formal meal has been held is 22,205 feet, at the top of Mt. Huascaran, Peru, when nine members of the Ansett Social Climbers from Sydney, Australia scaled the mountain on June 28, 1989 with a dining table, chairs, wine and a 3-course meal. At the summit they put on top hats and thermal evening attire for their dinner party, which was marred only by the fact that the wine turned to ice.

Largest party   The International Year of the Child children's party in Hyde Park, London, England, May 30–31, 1979 was attended by 160,000 children.

SIZZLER!

The record attendance at a 1-day barbecue was 44,158 at Warwick Farm Racecourse, Sydney, Australia on October 10, 1993. The greatest meat consumption at a barbecue was at the Lancaster Sertoma Club's Chicken Bar-B-Que in Lancaster, PA, on May 21, 1994; the participants ate 44,010 pounds of chicken in eight hours.

Birthday The world's biggest birthday party was attended by an estimated 100,000 people in Aberdeen, Scotland on July 24, 1994. It was held to celebrate the 200th birthday of Union Street, the main street in the city.

The biggest birthday party in the United States was attended by 75,000 people in Buffalo, NY on July 4, 1991, as part of the 1991 Friendship Festival, an annual event held every year to celebrate the national birthdays of the United States and Canada.

The largest birthday party held for someone who actually went to the party was attended by an estimated 35,000 people in Louisville, KY on September 8, 1979, to celebrate the 89th birthday of Col. Harland Sanders, the founder of Kentucky Fried Chicken.

Christmas The largest Christmas party ever staged was the one thrown by the Boeing Co. in the 65,000-seat Kingdome, Seattle, WA. The party was held in two parts on December 15, 1979, and a total of 103,152 people attended.

Teddy bear picnic The largest teddy bear picnic ever staged was attended by 18,116 bears together with their owners at Selsdon Park Hotel, Croydon, England on August 7, 1994.

BIG DEALS

Because of the infinite number of objects it is possible to collect, we can include only a small number of claims—those that in our experience reflect proven widespread interest.

We are more likely to consider claims for items accumulated on a personal basis over a significant period of time, made through established and recognized organizations, as these organizations are often in a better position to comment authoritatively in record terms.

Ax A steel ax 60 feet long, 23 feet wide and weighing 7.7 tons was designed and built by BID Ltd. of Woodstock, New Brunswick, Canada. The ax was presented to the town of Nackawic, also in New Brunswick, on May 11, 1991 to commemorate the town's selection as Forestry Capital of Canada for 1991.

Balloon sculpture The largest balloon sculpture was a reproduction of van Gogh's *Fishing Boats on the Beach of Les Saintes Maries*, made out of

25,344 colored balloons on June 28, 1992. Students from Haarlem Business School created the picture at a harbor in Ouddorp in the Netherlands.

Basket   A hand-woven maple basket measuring 48 by 23 by 19 feet was made by the Longaberger Company of Dresden, OH in 1990.

Beer cans   William B. Christiensen of Madison, NJ collected over 75,000 different cans from 125 different countries, colonies and territories.

Most expensive   A Rosalie Pilsner can sold for $6,000 in the United States in April 1981.

Beer labels   Jan Solberg of Oslo, Norway had collected 424,868 different beer labels from around the world as of June 1995.

Bench   The longest bench in the world, called "Big Benn," was made by Norimasa Yabuyamada of Toyama, Japan, between April and September, 1991. It was 24.93 feet long, 2.43 feet wide and 1.97 feet high.

Blanket   A hand-knitted, machine-knitted and crocheted blanket measuring a record 186,107.8 square feet was made by members of the Knitting and Crochet Guild worldwide, coordinated by Gloria Buckley of Bradford, England, and assembled at Dishforth Airfield, Thirsk, England on May 30, 1993.

Bottle   A bottle 10 ft. 2 in. tall and 11 ft. 6 in. in circumference was filled with Schweppes Lemonade in Melbourne, Australia on March 17, 1994 to celebrate 200 years of Schweppes.

Bottle caps   Starting in 1950, Helge Friholm of Søborg, Denmark amassed 73,823 different bottle caps from 179 countries.

Pyramid   A pyramid consisting of 362,194 bottle caps was constructed by a team of 11 led by Yevgeniy Lepechov in Chernigov, Kiev, Ukraine, November 17–22, 1990.

Bottle collections   George E. Terren of Southboro, MA had a collection of 31,804 miniature liquor bottles on May 31, 1993.

The record for beer is 4,145 unduplicated full bottles from 106 countries, collected by Ted Shuler of Germantown, TN.

Ron Werner of Bothell, WA has a collection of 6,352 different bottles from 71 countries, of which 3,235 are full.

David L. Maund of Upham, Hampshire, England had a collection of unduplicated miniature Scotch whiskey bottles amounting to 9,847 as of April 1993.

Christopher Weide of Jacksonville, FL had collected 6,510 different soda bottles as of August 1993.

Bowl   The largest one-piece wooden bowl was made by Dan Cunningham, David Tarleton and Scott Hare in Kamuela, HI in September 1990. The bowl took 2,978 man-hours to complete, and was constructed of monkeypod wood. It stands 6 ft. 7 in. tall, and its widest diameter is 5 ft. 9⅝ in. with a circumference of 18 ft. 1 in.

Can construction A 1:4 scale model of the Basilica di Sant'Antonio di Padova was built from 3,245,000 empty beverage cans in Padova (Padua), Italy by the charities AMNIUP, AIDO, AVIS and GPDS. The model, measuring 96 by 75 by 56 feet, was completed on December 20, 1992 after 20,000 hours of work.

Can pyramid Five adults and five children from Dunhurst School in Petersfield, England built a record-breaking pyramid of 4,900 cans in 25 min. 54 sec. on May 13, 1994.

Carpets and rugs *Largest* A 52,225-square-foot, 31.4-ton red carpet was laid on February 13, 1982, by the Allied Corporation, from Radio City Music Hall to the New York Hilton along the Avenue of the Americas, in New York City.

Most finely woven The most finely woven carpet known is a silk hand-knotted example with 4,224 knots per square inch, measuring 14 by 22 inches. It was made over a period of 22 months by the Kapoor Rug Corporation of Jaipur, India and completed in May 1993.

Chair The largest is the Washington Chair, a 53-ft.-4-in.-high replica of the chair George Washington sat in when he presided over the Constitu-

This diamond-encrusted wedding dress by Hélène Gainville is the most expensive in the world. (*Gamma/F. Darmigny*)

tional Convention in Philadelphia in 1787. Built by NSA and first displayed in Los Angeles, CA on December 9, 1988, the chair was designed to withstand earthquakes and 70-MPH winds.

Chandelier The world's largest chandelier was created by the Kookje Lighting Co. Ltd. of Seoul, South Korea. It is 39 feet high, weighs 11.8 tons and has 700 bulbs. Completed in November 1988, it occupies three floors of the Lotte Chamshil Department Store in Seoul.

Christmas cracker The largest functional Christmas cracker ever constructed was 150 feet long and 10 feet in diameter. It was made by Ray Price for Markson Sparks! of New South Wales, Australia and pulled at Westfield Shopping Town, Chatswood, Sydney, Australia on November 9, 1991.

Coasters The largest collection of coasters is owned by Leo Pisker of Langenzersdorf, Austria, who has collected 145,430 different coasters from 160 countries to date.

Credit cards The largest collection of valid credit cards to date is one of 1,384 (all different) by Walter Cavanagh of Santa Clara, CA. The cost of acquisition for "Mr. Plastic Fantastic" was zero, and he keeps the cards in

Carol McFadden (top) has a collection of 18,750 pairs of earrings mounted on display boards in her home.

the world's longest wallet—250 feet long, weighing 38 lb. 4 oz. and containing cards worth more than $1.6 million in credit.

Doll   The largest rag doll in the United States is 41 ft. 11 in. in total length, and was created by Apryl Scott at Autoworld in Flint, MI on November 20, 1990.

Dress   A wedding outfit created by Hélène Gainville with jewels by Alexander Reza is believed to be worth $7,301,587.20 precisely. The dress is embroidered with diamonds mounted on platinum and was unveiled in Paris, France on March 23, 1989.

Dress train   The world's longest wedding dress train measured 515 feet and was made by the Hansel and Gretel bridal outfitters of Guriskirchen, Germany in 1992.

Earrings   Carol McFadden of Oil City, PA had collected 18,750 different pairs of earrings as of January 1995.

Egg   The largest and most elaborate jeweled egg stands two feet tall and was fashioned from 37 pounds of gold, studded with 20,000 pink diamonds. Designed by British jeweler Paul Kutchinsky, the Argyle Library Egg took six British craftsmen 7,000 hours to create and has a price tag of £7 million ($12 million). It was unveiled on April 30, 1990 before going on display at the Victoria and Albert Museum, London, England.

Fabrics   Oldest   The oldest fabric, radiocarbon dated to 7000 B.C., was reported in July 1993 to have been discovered in southeastern Turkey. The

The Meisterstück Solitaire Royal fountain pen can be made to order by Montblanc for just $121,000. (*Montblanc*)

The largest flower pot—pictured here with one of its creators, Peter Start—measures 6.4 feet tall. (*P. Goff*)

semi-fossilized cloth, measuring roughly 3 by 1½ inches, was believed to be linen.

Most expensive The most expensive wool fabric is one manufactured by Fujii Keori Ltd. of Osaka, Japan that retailed at 3 million yen ($30,000) per meter in January 1989.

Fan A handpainted fan made of fabric and wood, measuring 18 ft. 5½ in. when unfolded and 9 ft. 6 in. high, was completed by Brajesh Shrivastava of Bhopal, India in 1994.

Fireworks The largest firework ever produced was *Universe I Part II*, exploded for the Lake Toya Festival, Hokkaido, Japan on July 15, 1988. The 1,543-pound shell was 54.7 inches in diameter and burst to a diameter of 3,937 feet.

Catherine wheel A self-propelled horizontal firework wheel measuring 47 ft. 4 in. in diameter, built by Florida Pyrotechnic Arts Guild, was displayed at the Pyrotechnics Guild International Convention in Idaho Falls, ID on August 14, 1992. It functioned for 3 min. 45 sec.

Flags *Oldest* The oldest surviving Stars and Stripes is preserved in the Bennington Historical Museum in Old Bennington, VT, and dates from the 18th century.

Largest The largest flag ever flown from a flagpole is a Brazilian national flag measuring 229 ft. 8 in. by 328 ft. 1 in., unfurled in Brasilia.

Float The world's largest float was 184 ft. 8 in. long. It was produced by the World of Dreams Foundation for the 169th St. Patrick's Day parade, Montreal, Quebec, Canada on March 14, 1993.

Four-leaf clover collection Norman W. Bright of Heber Springs, AR had collected 7,116 4-leaf clovers as of May 20, 1995.

Globe The revolving "Globe of Peace," built between 1982 and 1987 by Orfeo Bartolucci of Apecchi, Pesaro, Italy, is 33 feet in diameter and weighs 33 tons.

Greeting cards Craig Shergold of Carshalton, England was reported to have collected a record 33 million get-well cards by May 1991, when his mother pleaded for no more.

Gum wrapper chain The longest gum wrapper chain on record measured 12,105 feet long, and was made by Gary Duschl of Waterdown, Ontario, Canada between 1965 and 1994.

Jigsaw puzzles *Largest* The world's largest jigsaw puzzle measures 51,484 square feet and consists of 43,924 pieces. Assembled on July 8, 1992, it was devised by Centre Socio-Culturel d'Endoume in Marseilles, France and was designed on the theme of the environment.

A puzzle consisting of 204,484 pieces was made by BCF Holland b.v. of Almelo, Netherlands and assembled by students of the local Gravenvoorde School, from May 25 to June 1, 1991. The completed puzzle measured 1,036 square feet.

Louise J. Greenfarb, "The Magnet Lady," and part of her collection of 12,000 refrigerator magnets. (*Courtesy of Louise J. Greenfarb*)

Kettle   The largest antique copper kettle stood three feet high with a 6-foot girth and a 20-gallon capacity. It was built in Taunton, England, for the hardware merchants Fisher and Son *c.* 1800.

Knife   The penknife with the greatest number of blades is the Year Knife, made by cutlers Joseph Rodgers & Sons, of Sheffield, England, whose trademark was granted in 1682. The knife was made in 1822 with 1,822 blades, and a blade was added every year until 1973, when there was no further space. It was acquired by Britain's largest hand tool manufacturers, Stanley Works (Great Britain) Ltd. of Sheffield, England, in 1970.

Longest lei   A 14,550-foot paper flower lei was made by local citizens at the Hyatt Regency Waikiki, Honolulu, HI on December 19, 1992.

Matchstick model   Joseph Sciberras of Malta constructed an exact replica, including the interior, of St. Publius Parish Church, Floriana, Malta, consisting of over 3 million matchsticks. The model, made to scale, is 6½ by 6½ by 5 ft.

Parking meters   Lotta Sjölin of Solna, Sweden had a collection of 269 different parking meters as of May 1994.

Pencil   A pencil measuring 8.9 feet long and weighing 53 pounds was constructed by students at Huddersfield Technical College, Huddersfield, England for Cliffe School, Lightcliffe, England in 1995.

Pens   Vilma Valma Turpeinen of Tampere, Finland had collected 14,492 different pens as of April 29, 1992.

The most expensive writing pen is the Meisterstück Solitaire Royal fountain pen made by Montblanc. It is made of solid gold and is encased with 4,810 diamonds—the height in meters of Mont Blanc mountain. The pen can be made to order for £75,000 ($121,000), and takes a painstaking six months to make.

A Japanese collector paid Fr1.3 million ($2,340,000) in February 1988 for the "Anémone" fountain pen made by Réden, France. It was encrusted with 600 precious stones, including emeralds, amethysts, rubies, sapphires and onyx, and took skilled craftsmen over a year to complete.

Piñata   The world's biggest piñata measured 27 feet high and had a diameter of 30 feet, a circumference of 100 feet and a weight of 10,000 pounds. It was built in March 1990 for Carnaval Miami in Miami, FL.

Pottery   The largest thrown vase on record is one measuring 17 ft. 6 in. high (including a 4-ft.-3-in.-tall lid), weighing 1,322 lb. 12 oz. It was completed on June 1, 1991 by Faiarte Ceramics of Rustenberg, South Africa.

Terra-cotta flower pot   The world's largest terra-cotta flower pot measures 6.4 feet tall with a circumference of 17.1 feet. It was hand-built by Peter Start and Albert Robinson at The Plant Pottery, Barby, England in May 1985.

Quilt   In June 1994, the Saskatchewan Seniors' Association of Saskatchewan, Canada completed a quilt measuring 155 ft. 4½ in. by 82 ft. 8 in.

Refrigerator magnets   Louise J. Greenfarb of Spanaway, WA had collected 12,000 refrigerator magnets as of January 1995.

Rubber band ball   Philip J. Johns of Doncaster, England constructed a rubber band ball that weighed 850 pounds.

Scarf   The longest scarf ever knitted measured 20 miles 13 ft. long. It was knitted by residents of Abbeyfield Houses for the Abbeyfield Society in Potters Bar, England and was completed on May 29, 1988.

Shoes   Emperor Field Marshal Jean Fedor Bokassa of the Central African Empire (now Republic) commissioned pearl-studded shoes at a cost of $85,000 from the House of Berluti, Paris, France for his self-coronation on December 4, 1977.

The most expensive manufactured shoes are mink-lined golf shoes with 18-carat gold embellishments and ruby-tipped spikes made by Stylo Matchmakers International of Northampton, England, which retail for $23,000 per pair.

Emperor Field Marshal Jean Fedor Bokassa of the Central African Empire commissioned the world's most expensive shoes for his self-coronation at Bangui on December 4, 1977. *(Gamma/Abbas)*

Silver   The largest single pieces of silver are a pair of water jugs of 10,408 troy ounces (4.77 cwt) made in 1902 for the Maharaja of Jaipur (1861–1922). They are 5 ft. 3 in. tall, with a circumference of 8 ft. 1½ in., and have a capacity of 2,160 gallons. They are now in the City Palace, Jaipur, India. The silversmith was Gorind Narain.

Sofa   In April 1990, a 21-ft.-9-in.-long jacquard fabric sofa was specially manufactured by Mountain View Interiors of Collingwood, Ontario, Canada.

String ball   The largest ball of string on record is one 13 ft. 2½ in. in diameter, 41 ft. 6 in. in circumference, amassed by J.C. Payne of Valley View, TX between 1989 and 1991.

Table   The longest table was set up in Pesaro, Italy on June 20, 1988 by the U.S. Libertas Scavolini basketball team. It was 10,072 feet long and seated 12,000 people.

Tablecloth   The world's largest tablecloth is 1,502 feet long and 4½ feet wide, and was made by the Sportex division of Artex International in Highland, IL on October 17, 1990.

Tapestry and embroidery   The largest tapestry ever woven is the *History of Iraq*, with an area of 13,370.7 square feet. It was designed by the Yugoslavian artist Frane Delale and produced by the Zivtex Regeneracija Workshop in Zabok, Yugoslavia. The tapestry was completed in 1986 and it now adorns the wall of an amphitheater in Baghdad, Iraq.

Longest   The famous Bayeux tapestry, *Telle du Conquest, dite tapisserie de la reine Mathilde*, a hanging tapestry 19½ inches by 23 feet, depicts events of 1064–66 in 72 scenes and was probably worked in Canterbury, England, *c.* 1086. It was lost for 2½ centuries, from 1476 until 1724.

Embroidery   An 8-inch-deep, 1,338-foot-long embroidery of scenes from C.S. Lewis's *Narnia* children's stories was worked by Margaret S. Pollard of Truro, England to the order of Michael Maine. Its total area is about 937 square feet.

Ties   A collection of 10,453 ties accumulated by Bill McDaniel of Santa Maria, CA was sold to a museum in St. Augustine, FL in 1992.

Wallet   The most expensive wallet ever made is a platinum-cornered, diamond-studded crocodile creation made by Louis Quatorze of Paris and Mikimoto of Tokyo, selling in September 1984 for $84,000.

Yo-yo   A yo-yo measuring 10 ft. 4 in. in diameter and weighing 897 pounds was devised by J.N. Nichols (Vimto) Ltd. and made by engineering students at Stockport College, Stockport, England. It was suspended from a 187-foot crane in Wythenshawe, England on August 1, 1993, and "yo-yoed" about four times.

Zipper   The world's longest zipper was laid around the center of Sneek, Netherlands on September 5, 1989. The brass zipper, made by Yoshida (Netherlands) Ltd., is 9,353.56 feet long and consists of 2,565,900 teeth.

SPORTS & GAMES

GENERAL RECORDS

Fastest sport   The fastest projectile speed in any moving ball game is *c.* 188 MPH, in jai alai. This compares with 170 MPH (electronically timed) for a golf ball driven off a tee.

Youngest record breaker   The youngest age at which anybody has broken a nonmechanical world record is 12 yr. 298 days for Gertrude Ederle (U.S.), with 13 min. 19.0 sec. for women's 880-yard freestyle swimming, in Indianapolis, IN on August 17, 1919.

Oldest record breaker   Gerhard Weidner (Germany) set a 20-mile walk record on May 25, 1974, at age 41 yr. 71 days, thus becoming the oldest to set an official world record recognized by an international governing body.

Most records broken   Between January 24, 1970 and November 1, 1977, Vasiliy Alekseyev (USSR) broke 80 official world records in weightlifting.

Youngest champions   The youngest successful competitor in a world title event was a French boy, whose name is not recorded, who coxed the Netherlands' Olympic pair in the rowing competition at Paris, France on August 26, 1900. He was not more than 10 and may have been as young as seven.
   Fu Mingxia (China, b. August 16, 1978) won the women's world title for platform diving in Perth, Australia on January 4, 1991, at age 12 yr. 141 days.

Olympic   The youngest individual Olympic winner was Marjorie Gestring (U.S.), who took the springboard diving title at the age of 13 yr. 268 days at the Olympic Games in Berlin, Germany on August 12, 1936.

Oldest champion   Fred Davis (Great Britain; b. February 14, 1913) won the world professional billiards title in 1980, at age 67.

Heaviest sportsman   Professional wrestler William J. Cobb of Macon, GA, who in 1962 was billed as "Happy Humphrey," weighed 802 pounds. The heaviest player of any ball game was Bob Pointer, the 487-pound football tackle on the 1967 Santa Barbara (CA) High School team.

Longest-reigning champion   Jacques Barre (France) was a world champion for 33 years (1829–62) at court tennis.

Largest crowds   It is estimated that more than 10 million people see the annual Tour de France cycling race, which is spread over three weeks. The greatest number of live spectators for any 1-day sporting spectacle is the estimated 2.5 million who have lined the route of the New York City Marathon.

Stadium   A crowd of 199,854 attended the Brazil vs. Uruguay World Cup Finals deciding soccer game, in the Maracanã Municipal Stadium, Rio de Janeiro, Brazil on July 16, 1950.

Most participants   On May 15, 1988, an estimated 110,000 (including un-registered athletes) ran in the *Examiner* Bay-to-Breakers 7.6-mile race in San Francisco, CA.

Worst sports disaster   The stands at the Hong Kong Jockey Club racetrack collapsed and caught fire on February 26, 1918, killing an estimated 604 people.

AEROBATICS

World Championships   The former USSR has won the men's team compe-tition a record six times. The most victories in the men's individual champi-onship is two, by Petr Jirmus (Czechoslovakia), 1984 and 1986. In the women's event the record is also two titles, by Betty Stewart (U.S.), 1980 and 1982.

Longest inverted flight   The duration record is 4 hr. 38 min. 10 sec. by Joann Osterud (U.S.) from Vancouver to Vanderhoof, Canada on July 24, 1991.

Most loops   Joann Osterud achieved 208 outside loops in a "Supernova" Hyperbipe over North Bend, OR on July 13, 1989. On August 9, 1986, David Childs performed 2,368 inside loops in a Bellanca Decathalon over North Pole, AK.

AIR RACING

The first international airplane racing competition, the Bennett Trophy, was held in Rheims, France, August 22–28, 1909. In 1964, the sport was revived in the United States by Bill Stead, who staged the first National Championship Air Races (NCAR) at Reno, NV; this is now the premier air racing event in the United States.

NATIONAL CHAMPIONSHIP AIR RACES

Unlimited class   In this class the aircraft must use piston engines, be pro-peller-driven and be capable of pulling six *g*'s. The planes race over a 9.128-mile course marked with pylons.

Most titles   Darryl Greenmyer has won seven NCAR titles in the unlimited class, the top level of the sport: 1965–69, 1971 and 1977.

Fastest average speed (race)   Lyle Shelton won the 1991 NCAR title, setting the fastest average speed of 481.618 MPH in his "Rare Bear."

Fastest qualifying speed   The 1-lap NCAR qualifying record is 482.892 MPH, by Lyle Shelton in 1992.

ARCHERY

World Championships   The most titles won is seven, by Janina Spychajowa-Kurkowska (Poland) in 1931–34, 1936, 1939 and 1947. The most titles won by a man is four, by Hans Deutgen (Sweden), 1947–50. The U.S. has won a record 14 men's and eight women's team titles.

United States   The most individual world titles by a U.S. archer is three, by Rick McKinney: 1977, 1983 and 1985. Darrell Pace won two world titles, (1975, 1979), and two Olympic titles, (1976, 1984). Jean Lee is the only

BULLSEYE!

Hubert van Innis (Belgium) won six gold and three silver medals at the 1900 and 1920 Olympic Games. The most successful U.S. archer at the Olympic Games is Darrell Pace, gold medalist in 1976 and 1984. He was also world champion in 1975 and 1979.

April Moon holds a number of records in the field of flight shooting, the object of which is to fire an arrow as far as possible. On September 13, 1981, in Wendover, UT, using a recurve bow, she fired an arrow an amazing 1,039 yd. 1 ft. 1 in.

ARCHERY RECORDS

Events	Points	Possible	Name and Country	Year

MEN (SINGLE FITA ROUNDS)

FITA ....1,354 ....1,440 ....Han Seung-hoon (South Korea) 1994
90 m...............330 ....360 ....Vladimir Yesheyev (USSR) 1990
70 m...............344 ....360 ....Hiroshi Yamamoto (Japan) 1990
50 m...............345 ....360 ....Rick McKinney (U.S.) 1982
30 m...............360 ....360 ....Han Seung-hoon (South Korea) 1994
Team ....4,035 ....4,320 ....South Korea (Kim Kyeng-ho, Han
Seong-narn, Park Kyeng-moo)...........1993

WOMEN (SINGLE FITA ROUNDS)

FITA ....1,375 ....1,440 ....Cho Youn-jeong (South Korea).........1992
70 m............*341 ....360 ....Kim Soo-nyung (South Korea)...........1990
                338 ....360 ....Cho Youn-jeong (South Korea).........1992
60 m...............347 ....360 ....Kim Soo-nyung (South Korea) 1989
50 m...............340 ....360 ....Lim Jung (South Korea) 1994
30 m...............357 ....360 ....Joanne Edens (Great Britain) 1990
Team ....4,094 ....4,320 ....South Korea (Kim Soo-nyung,
Lee Eun-kyung, Cho
Youn-jeong) 1992

unofficial

INDOOR DOUBLE FITA ROUNDS AT 25 METERS

Men ....577 ....600 ....Tom Henrikson (Denmark) 1994
Women ....556 ....600 ....Annette Frederiksen (Sweden)..........1994

INDOOR FITA ROUNDS AT 18 METERS

Men ....596 ....600 ....Magnus Pattersson (Sweden).............1995
Women ....590 ....600 ....Nalalya Valeyeva (Moldova)..............1995

U.S. woman to have won two individual world titles (1950, 1952). Luann Ryon won the Olympic title in 1976 and the world title in 1977.

U.S. Championships The U.S. National Championships were first held in Chicago, IL, August 12–14, 1879, and are staged annually. The most U.S. archery titles won is 17, by Lida Howell (née Scott), from 20 contested between 1883 and 1907. The most men's titles is nine, by Rick McKinney, 1977, 1979–83, 1985–87.

The greatest span of title winning is 29 years, by William Henry Thompson, who was the first U.S. champion in 1879, and won his fifth and last men's title in 1908.

Highest score in 24 hours The highest recorded score over 24 hours by a pair of archers is 76,158, during 70 Portsmouth Rounds (60 arrows per round at 20 yards at 2-foot FITA targets) by Simon Tarplee and David Hathaway at Evesham, England on April 1, 1991. During this attempt Tarplee set an individual record of 38,500.

Greatest draw on a longbow Gary Sentman of Roseberg, OR drew a longbow weighing a record 176 pounds to the maximum draw on the arrow of $28\frac{1}{4}$ inches at Forksville, PA on September 20, 1975.

Longest arrow flight The furthest an arrow has been shot is 2,047 yd. 2 in. by Harry Drake (U.S.), using a crossbow at the Smith Creek Flight Range near Austin, NV on July 30, 1988.

AUTO RACING

Oldest winner The oldest winner of a professionally sanctioned race is Charles F. Grabiak, M.D. (b. March 9, 1920), who was 72 years old when he finished first in a nationally sanctioned auto race in 1992 at Watkins Glen, NY.

DID YOU KNOW?

The oldest auto race in the world still regularly run is the Royal Automobile Club (RAC) Tourist Trophy, first staged on September 14, 1905 on the Isle of Man, Great Britain.

Fastest circuits The highest average lap speed attained on any closed circuit is 250.958 MPH, in a trial by Dr. Hans Liebold (Germany), who lapped the 7.85-mile high-speed track at Nardo, Italy in 1 min. 52.67 sec. in a Mercedes-Benz C111-IV experimental coupé on May 5, 1979. It was powered by a V8 engine with two KKK turbochargers, with an output of 500 hp at 6,200 rpm.

Fastest race The Busch Clash at Daytona, FL covers 50 miles on a 31-degree banked track $2\frac{1}{2}$ miles long. In 1987, Bill Elliott (U.S.) averaged 197.802 MPH in a Ford Thunderbird.

500 miles Al Unser, Jr. (U.S.) set the world record for a 500-mile race when he won the Michigan 500 on August 9, 1990 at an average speed of 189.727 MPH.

NASCAR

Most titles   Two people have won the NASCAR (National Association for Stock Car Auto Racing, Inc.) championship, now called the Winston Cup Championship, a record seven times. Richard Petty (U.S.) won in 1964, 1967, 1971–72, 1974–75 and 1979, and Dale Earnhardt (U.S.) in 1980, 1986–87, 1990–91, and 1993–94. Petty won 200 NASCAR Winston Cup races in 1,185 starts from 1958 to 1992, and his best season was 1967, with 27 wins.

Most consecutive titles   Cale Yarborough is the only driver with three NASCAR championships, winning in 1976–78.

Highest earnings   The NASCAR career money record is $23,706,114 to June 1995, by Dale Earnhardt, who also won a season record $3,353,789 in 1993.

DAYTONA 500

Most titles   The Daytona 500 has been held at the 2½-mile oval Daytona International Speedway in Daytona, FL since 1959. Richard Petty has a record seven wins—1964, 1966, 1971, 1973–74, 1979 and 1981.

Fastest speed   The record average speed for the race is 177.602 MPH, by Buddy Baker in an Oldsmobile in 1980. The qualifying speed record is 210.364 MPH, by Bill Elliott in a Ford Thunderbird in 1987.

Highest earnings   The career earnings record is $1,124,256, by Dale Earnhardt in 16 races, 1979–94.

INDIANAPOLIS 500

Most titles   The Indianapolis 500-mile race (200 laps) was inaugurated in the United States on May 30, 1911. Three drivers have four wins: A.J. Foyt, Jr. (U.S.) in 1961, 1964, 1967 and 1977; Al Unser (U.S.) in 1970–71, 1978 and 1987; and Rick Mears (U.S.) in 1979, 1984, 1988 and 1991.

Fastest speed   The record time is 2 hr. 41 min. 18.404 sec. (185.981 MPH) by Arie Luyendyk (Netherlands) driving a Lola-Chevrolet on May 27, 1990. The record average speed for four laps qualifying is 232.482 MPH by Roberto Guerrero (Colombia) in a Lola-Buick (including a 1-lap record of 232.618 MPH) on May 9, 1992. The track record is 234.107 MPH by Arie Luyendyk on May 9, 1995.

Most starts A.J. Foyt, Jr. has started a record 35 races, 1958–92, and Rick Mears has started from pole position a record six times, 1979, 1982, 1986, 1988–89, and 1991.

Highest earnings The record prize fund is $8,063,550, awarded in 1995. The individual prize record is $1,373,813 by Al Unser, Jr., in 1994. As of June 1995, Rick Mears held the career earnings record of $4,299,392.

CLOSE!

The closest finish to a World Championship race was when Ayrton Senna (Brazil) in a Lotus beat Nigel Mansell (Great Britain) in a Williams by 0.014 seconds in the Spanish Grand Prix at Jerez de la Frontera on April 13, 1986.

Closest finish The closest margin of victory was 0.043 seconds in 1992 when Al Unser, Jr. edged Scott Goodyear.

INDY CAR

Most wins *National Championships* A.J. Foyt, Jr. is the most successful Indy car driver; he has won 67 races and seven championships (1960–61, 1963–64, 1967, 1975 and 1979). The record for the most victories in a season is 10, shared by two drivers: A.J. Foyt, Jr. (1964) and Al Unser (1970).

Most laps led Mario Andretti holds the record for the most laps led in Indy car championships, with 7,587 as of June 1995. He also holds the record for most pole positions, at 67.

Highest career earnings As of October 1994, Al Unser, Jr. had earned $15,379,906 during his career.

FORMULA ONE GRAND PRIX

Most successful drivers The World Drivers' Championship, inaugurated in 1950, has been won a record five times by Juan-Manuel Fangio (Argentina), in 1951 and 1954–57. He retired in 1958, after having won 24 Grand Prix races (two shared) from 51 starts.

Alain Prost (France) holds the records for both the most Grand Prix points in a career, 798.5, and the most Grand Prix victories, 51 from 199 races, 1980–93. The most Grand Prix victories in a year is nine, by Nigel Mansell (Great Britain) in 1992. The most Grand Prix starts is 256, by Ricardo Patrese (Italy), 1977–93.

The greatest number of pole positions is 65, by Ayrton Senna (Brazil) from 161 races (41 wins), 1984–94.

Two U.S. drivers have won the World Drivers' Championship—Phil Hill in 1961, and Mario Andretti in 1978. Andretti has the most Grand Prix wins by a U.S. driver: 12 in 128 races, 1968–82.

Fastest race   The fastest overall average speed for a Grand Prix race on a circuit in current use is 146.284 MPH, by Nigel Mansell (Great Britain) in a Williams-Honda at Zeltweg in the Austrian Grand Prix on August 16, 1987. The qualifying lap record was set by Keke Rosberg (Finland) at 1 min. 05.59 sec., an average speed of 160.817 MPH, in a Williams-Honda at Silverstone in the British Grand Prix on July 20, 1985.

LE MANS

Most wins   The race has been won by Porsche cars 13 times, in 1970–71, 1976–77, 1979, 1981–87, and 1994. The most wins by one man is six, by Jacky Ickx (Belgium), 1969, 1975–77 and 1981–82.

Greatest distance   The greatest distance ever covered in the 24-hour *Grand Prix d'Endurance* on the old Sarthe circuit at Le Mans, France is 3,315.203 miles, by Dr. Helmut Marko (Austria) and Gijs van Lennep (Netherlands) in a 4,907-cc flat-12 Porsche 917K Group 5 sports car, June 12–13, 1971.

The record for the greatest distance ever covered for the current circuit is 3,313.150 miles (average speed 137.047 MPH) by Jan Lammers (Netherlands), Johnny Dumfries and Andy Wallace (both from Great Britain) in a Jaguar XJR9 on June 11–12, 1988.

Fastest lap   The race lap record (now an 8.411-mile lap) is 3 min. 21.27 sec. (average speed 150.429 mph) by Alain Ferté (France) in a Jaguar XRJ-9 on June 10, 1989. Hans Stück (West Germany) set the practice lap speed record of 156.377 MPH.

RALLYING

Longest rally   The Singapore Airlines London–Sydney Rally was held over 19,329 miles from Covent Garden, London, England on August 14, 1977 to Sydney Opera House, Australia. It was won on September 28, 1977 by Andrew Cowan, Colin Malkin and Michael Broad in a Mercedes 280E.

Monte Carlo   The Monte Carlo Rally (first run in 1911) has been won a record four times by Sandro Munari (Italy), in 1972, 1975, 1976 and 1977; and by Walter Röhrl (West Germany) (with co-driver Christian Geistdorfer) in 1980 and 1982–84, each time in a different car.

World Championship   Juha Kankkunen (Finland) has won the World Drivers' Championships (instituted 1979) on a record four occasions, 1986–87, 1991 and 1993. The most wins in a season is six, by Didier Auriol (France) in 1992. The most wins in World Championship races is 21, by Juha Kankkunen.

DRAG RACING

Piston-engined   The lowest elapsed time recorded by a piston-engined dragster from a standing start for 440 yards is 4.665 seconds, by Larry Dixon (U.S.) in Englishtown, NJ on May 19, 1995. The highest terminal velocity at the end of a 440-yard run is 314.46 MPH, by Kenny Bernstein (U.S.) in Pomona, CA on October 30, 1994.

In the Funny Car category, John Force (U.S.) had the quickest run at

4.939 seconds on October 1, 1994, in Topeka, KS. A top speed of 306.33 MPH was achieved by Al Hofmann (U.S.) in Englishtown, NJ on May 19, 1995.

For a gasoline-driven piston-engined car, the lowest elapsed time is 6.948 seconds, by Warren Johnson (U.S.) on March 10, 1995 in Baytown, TX. On the same day, Johnson set the highest terminal velocity mark of 199.15 MPH.

The lowest elapsed time for a gasoline-driven piston-engined motorcycle is 7.503 seconds, by David Schultz on March 10, 1995 in Baytown, TX. Schultz also set the highest terminal velocity mark at 182.14 MPH on June 4, 1995 in Dinwiddie, VA.

NHRA titles Since 1975, The National Hot Rod Association (NHRA) World Championship Series (inaugurated 1951) has been known as the NHRA Winston Drag Racing Series.

Top Fuel Joe Amato has won a record five national titles: 1984, 1988 and 1990–92.

Funny Car Two drivers have won a record four national titles: Don Prud-homme, 1975–78, and Kenny Bernstein, 1985–88.

Pro Stock Bob Glidden has won a record 10 national titles, 1974–75, 1978–80 and 1985–89.

Pro Stock Motorcycle David Schultz has won a record five national titles, in 1987–88, 1991, and 1993–94.

BADMINTON

World Championships Individual In this competition, instituted in 1977 and staged biennially, a record five titles have been won by Park Joo-bong (South Korea)—men's doubles, 1985 and 1991, and mixed doubles, 1985, 1989 and 1991.

Three Chinese players have won two individual world titles—men's singles: Yang Yang, 1987 and 1989; women's singles: Li Lingwei in 1983 and 1989; Han Aiping in 1985 and 1987.

Team The most wins in the men's World Team Badminton Championship for the Thomas Cup (instituted 1948) is nine, by Indonesia (1958, 1961, 1964, 1970, 1973, 1976, 1979, 1984 and 1994).

The most wins in the women's World Team Badminton Championship for the Uber Cup (instituted 1956) is five, by Japan (1966, 1969, 1972, 1978 and 1981) and China (1984, 1986, 1988, 1990 and 1992).

United States Championships The competition was first held in 1937 and has since been staged annually.

Most titles Judy Devlin Hashman won a record 31 U.S. titles: 12 women's singles, 1954, 1956–63, 1965–67; 12 women's doubles, 1953–55, 1957–63, 1966–67 (7 with her sister Susan Devlin); and seven mixed doubles, 1956–59, 1961–62, 1967. David Freeman won seven singles titles: 1939–42, 1947–48, 1953.

Longest winning streak The longest continuous winning streak achieved by an American badminton team is 338 wins to June 20, 1994, by Miller Place High School, Miller Place, NY.

Longest badminton rally In the men's singles final of the 1987 All-England Championships between Morten Frost (Denmark) and Icuk Sugiarto (Indonesia), there were two successive rallies of over 90 strokes.

Shortest badminton game In the 1992 Olympic Games in Barcelona, Spain, Christine Magnusson (Sweden) beat Martine de Souza (Mauritius) 11–1, 11–0 in 8 min. 30 sec.

BASEBALL

MAJOR LEAGUE

Longest sports strike The longest strike in the history of professional sports was in major league baseball, August 12, 1994–April 4, 1995—a total of 234 days. For the first time in 90 years, the World Series was not held.

Most games played Pete Rose played in a record 3,562 games with a record 14,053 at-bats, for the Cincinnati Reds (NL), 1963–78 and 1984–86, the Philadelphia Phillies (NL), 1979–83, and the Montreal Expos (NL), 1984. Cal Ripken Jr., shortstop for the Baltimore Orioles (AL), played in his 2,131st successive game on September 6, 1995.

Most home runs Career Hank Aaron holds the major league career record with 755 home runs—733 for the Milwaukee (1954–65) and Atlanta (1966–74) Braves (NL) and 22 for the Milwaukee Brewers (AL) 1975–76. On April 8, 1974 he bettered the previous record of 714 by Babe Ruth (1895–1948). Ruth hit his home runs in 8,399 times at bat, achieving the highest home run percentage of 8.5 percent.

Josh Gibson (1911–47) of the Homestead Grays and Pittsburgh Crawfords, Negro League clubs, hit an estimated 900 home runs in his career, including an unofficial season record of 84 in 1931. These totals are believed to include exhibition games.

Season The major league record for home runs in a season is 61, by Roger Maris (1934–85) for the New York Yankees (AL) in 162 games in 1961. The most official home runs in a minor league season is 72, by Joe Bauman of the Roswell Rockets of the Longhorn League in 1954.

Game   The most home runs in a major league game is four, first achieved by Bobby Lowe (1868–1951) for Boston vs. Cincinnati on May 30, 1894. The feat has been achieved a further 11 times since then.

Consecutive games   The most home runs hit in consecutive games is eight, set by Dale Long for the Pittsburgh Pirates (NL), May 19–28, 1956, and tied by Don Mattingly for the New York Yankees (AL), on July 18, 1987, and by Ken Griffey Jr., Seattle Mariners (AL) on July 28, 1993.

Grand slams   Seven players have hit two grand slams in a single game. They are: Tony Lazzeri (1903–46) for the New York Yankees (AL) on May 24, 1936; Jim Tabor (1916–53) for the Boston Red Sox (AL) on July 4, 1939; Rudy York (1913–70) for the Boston Red Sox (AL) on July 27, 1946; Diamond Jim Gentile for the Baltimore Orioles (AL) on May 9, 1961; Tony Cloninger for the Atlanta Braves (NL) on July 3, 1966; Jim Northrup for the Detroit Tigers (AL) on June 24, 1968; and Frank Robinson for the Baltimore Orioles (AL) on June 26, 1970.

Don Mattingly of the New York Yankees (AL) hit six grand slams in 1987, the most in one season. Lou Gehrig hit 23 grand slams during his 16 seasons with the New York Yankees (AL), 1923–39, the most in one lifetime.

Fastest base runner   The fastest time for circling bases is 13.3 seconds, by Ernest Swanson in Columbus, OH in 1931, at an average speed of 18.45 MPH.

Most career hits   The career record for most hits is 4,256, by Pete Rose. Rose's record hits total came from a record 14,053 at-bats, which gave him a career batting average of .303.

On September 6, 1995, Cal Ripken Jr., shortstop for the Baltimore Orioles, broke Lou Gehrig's record for the most successive games. He played in 2,131 consecutive games. He received a 22-minute standing ovation for his accomplishment. (*Allsport [U.S.]/J. Rettaliata*)

Most consecutive hits Pinky Higgins had 12 consecutive hits for the Boston Red Sox (AL) in a 4-game span, June 19–21, 1938. This was equaled by Moose Dropo for the Detroit Tigers (AL), July 14–15, 1952. Joe DiMaggio hit in a record 56 consecutive games for the New York Yankees (AL) in 1941; he went to bat 223 times, with 91 hits, totaling 56 singles, 16 doubles, 4 triples and 15 home runs.

Largest baseball bat The Baseball Hall of Fame in Cooperstown, NY possesses a baseball bat over 11 feet long. It was turned from a telephone pole by Ernst Anderson of Gardner, MA. The citizens of Gardner presented the bat to Ted Williams of the Boston Red Sox (AL) on August 25, 1946.

Home runs and stolen bases The only player to have hit 40 or more home runs and have 40 stolen bases in a season was Jose Canseco for the Oakland Athletics (AL) in 1988. His totals were 42 and 40 respectively.

Longest home run The longest measured home run in a major league game was 643 feet, by Mickey Mantle for the New York Yankees vs. Detroit Tigers on September 10, 1960 at Briggs Stadium in Detroit.

Most stolen bases As of June 30, 1995, Rickey Henderson of the Oakland Athletics (AL) had stolen a record 1,130 bases. Henderson also holds the mark for most stolen bases in a season, which he set in 1982 when he stole 130 bases.

Don Mattingly of the New York Yankees has the highest career fielding percentage. (*Allsport/ S. Dunn*)

MAJOR LEAGUE RECORDS

American League (AL)
National League (NL)

Career Batting Records

Batting average	.367	Ty Cobb (Detroit–AL, Philadelphia–AL) 1905–28
Runs scored	2,245	Ty Cobb 1905–28
Runs batted in (RBI's)	2,297	Hank Aaron (Milwaukee, Atlanta–NL, Milwaukee–AL) 1954–76
Base hits	4,256	Pete Rose (Cincinnati–NL, Philadelphia–NL, Montreal–NL) 1963–86
Total bases²	6,856	Hank Aaron (Milwaukee, Atlanta–NL, Milwaukee–AL) 1954–76

Season Batting Records

Batting average	.438	Hugh Duffy (Boston–NL; 236 hits in 539 at-bats) 1894
1900–present	.424	Rogers Hornsby (St. Louis–NL; 227 hits in 536 at-bats) 1924
Runs scored	196	Billy Hamilton (Philadelphia–NL; in 131 games) 1894
1900–present	177	Babe Ruth (New York–AL; in 152 games) 1921
Runs batted in (RBI's)	190	Hack Wilson (Chicago–NL; in 155 games) 1930
Base hits	257	George Sisler (St. Louis–AL; 631 times at bat, 143 games) 1920
Singles	202	"Willie" Keeler (Baltimore–NL; in 128 games) 1898
1900–present	198	Lloyd Waner (Pittsburgh–NL; in 150 games) 1927
Doubles	67	Earl Webb (Boston–AL; in 151 games) 1931
Triples	36	Owen Wilson (Pittsburgh–NL; in 152 games) 1912
Total bases	457	Babe Ruth (New York–AL); 85 singles, 44 doubles, 16 triples, 59 home runs 1921

Single-Game Batting Records

Runs batted in (RBI's)	12	Jim Bottomley (St. Louis–NL) vs. Brooklyn .... Sep. 16, 1924
	12	Mark Whiten (St. Louis–NL) vs. Cincinnati .... Sep. 7, 1993
Base hits	9	Johnny Burnett (Cleveland–AL; in 18 innings) .... Jul. 10, 1932
Total bases	18	Joe Adcock (Milwaukee–AL); 1 double, 4 home runs ... Jul. 31, 1954

Career Pitching Records

Games won	511	Cy Young (in 906 games; Cleveland, St. Louis, Boston–NL and Cleveland, Boston–AL) 1890–1911
Shutouts	110	Walter Johnson (Washington–AL; in 802 games) 1907–27
Strikeouts	5,714	Nolan Ryan (New York–NL, California–AL, Houston–NL, Texas–AL) 1968–93

Season Pitching Records

Games won	60	"Old Hoss" Radbourn (Providence–NL; and 12 losses) 1884
1900–present	41	Jack Chesbro (New York–AL) 1904
Shutouts	16	George Bradley (St. Louis–NL; in 64 games) 1876
1900–present	16	Grover Alexander (Philadelphia–NL; 48 games) 1916
Strikeouts	513	Matt Kilroy (Baltimore–AL) 1886
1900–present	383	Nolan Ryan (California–AL) 1973

Single-Game Pitching Records

Strikeouts (9 innings)	20	Roger Clemens (Boston–AL) vs. Seattle ....Apr. 29, 1986
Strikeouts in extra innings	21	Tom Cheney (Washington–AL) vs. Baltimore (16 innings) ....Sep. 12, 1962

Greg Maddux of the Atlanta Braves is the first major league pitcher to win the coveted Cy Young Award three years in succession, 1992–94. His first success was with the Chicago Cubs. (*Allsport [U.S.]/S. Dunn*)

Most walks Babe Ruth holds the record for career walks, 2,056, and the single-season record, 170 in 1923.

Three players share a record six walks for a single game: Walt Wilmot, of the Chicago White Stockings (NL, later known as the Chicago Cubs), August 22, 1891; Jimmie Foxx of the Boston Red Sox (AL), June 16, 1938, and Andre Thornton of the Cleveland Indians (AL), May 2, 1984 in a game that went 18 innings.

Most strikeouts The batter with the career strikeout record is Reggie Jackson, who struck out 2,597 times in 21 seasons with four teams. The season record is 189, by Bobby Bonds, right fielder for the San Francisco Giants in 1970. The longest run of games without striking out is 115, by Joe Sewell while playing third base for the Cleveland Indians (AL) in 1929.

Most games won by a pitcher Cy Young had a record 511 wins and a record 749 complete games from a total of 906 games and 815 starts in his career for the Cleveland Spiders (NL) 1890–98, the St. Louis Cardinals (NL) 1899–1900, the Boston Red Sox (AL) 1901–08, the Cleveland Indians (AL) 1909–11 and the Boston Braves (NL) 1911. He pitched a record total of 7,356 innings.

The career record for most pitching appearances is 1,070, by Hoyt Wilhelm for nine teams, 1952–72; he set the career record with 124 wins as a relief pitcher (in addition to 19 wins as a starting pitcher). The season's record is 106 appearances, by Mike Marshall for the Los Angeles Dodgers (NL) in 1974.

Most consecutive games won by a pitcher New York Giants (NL) pitcher Carl Hubbell won 24 consecutive games—16 in 1936 and 8 in 1937.

Longest baseball throw Glen Gorbous (Canada) threw a baseball 445 ft. 10 in. on August 1, 1957.

Most shutouts Walter Johnson pitched 110 shutouts in his 21-season career with the Washington Senators (AL), 1907–27. Don Drysdale pitched six consecutive shutouts for the Los Angeles Dodgers (NL), May 14–June 4, 1968. Orel Hershiser pitched a record 59 consecutive shutout innings for the Los Angeles Dodgers (NL), August 30–September 28, 1988.

Most no-hitters Nolan Ryan, playing for the Texas Rangers (AL) against the Toronto Blue Jays (AL), pitched his record seventh no-hitter on May 1, 1991. Johnny Vander Meer of the Cincinnati Reds (NL) is the only player in baseball history to have pitched consecutive no-hitters, from June 11 to June 15, 1938.

Most walks Nolan Ryan holds the record for the greatest number of walks, giving up 2,795 between 1966 and 1993.

Perfect game A perfect nine-inning game, in which the pitcher allowed the opposition no hits, no runs and did not allow a man to reach first base, was first achieved by John Lee Richmond for Worcester, MA against Cleveland in the NL on June 12, 1880. There have been 14 perfect games over nine innings, but no pitcher has achieved this feat more than once.

On May 26, 1959 Harvey Haddix, Jr. for Pittsburgh pitched a perfect 12 innings against Milwaukee in the National League, but lost in the 13th.

SHORT!

The shortest major league player was eddie Gaedel, who measured 3 ft. 7 in. and weighed 65 pounds. Gaedel pinch-hit for the St. Louis Browns (AL) vs. the Detroit Tigers (AL) on August 19, 1951; wearing number $^1/_8$, the batter with the smallest-ever major league strike zone walked on four pitches.

Most saves Bobby Thigpen saved a record 57 games for the Chicago White Sox (AL) in 1990. The career record for saves is 453 as of June 30, 1995 by Lee Smith in his 16th season, playing for the Chicago Cubs (NL) 1980–87; the Boston Red Sox (NL) 1988–90; the St. Louis Cardinals (NL) 1990–93; the New York Yankees (AL) 1993; the Baltimore Orioles (AL) 1994; and the California Angels (AL) 1995.

Highest career fielding percentage The highest career fielding percentage (.996) is shared by three people: Wes Parker, Los Angeles Dodgers (NL), 1964–72; Steve Garvey, Los Angeles Dodgers (NL), 1969–87; and Don Mattingly, New York Yankees (AL), 1982–95.

Youngest player The Cincinnati Reds (NL) pitcher Joe Nuxhall played one game on June 10, 1944, at age 15 yr. 314 days.

Oldest player Satchel Paige pitched for the Kansas City A's (AL) at 59 yr. 78 days on September 25, 1965.

WORLD SERIES RECORDS

American League (AL), National League (NL)

Most wins	22......New York Yankees–AL	1923–78
Most series played	14......Yogi Berra (New York Yankees–AL)	1947–63
Most series played by pitcher	11......Whitey Ford (New York Yankees–AL)	1950–64

World Series Career Records

Batting average (min. 75 at-bats)	.391......Lou Brock (St. Louis Cardinals–NL; 34 hits in 87 at-bats, 3 series)	1964–68
Runs scored	42......Mickey Mantle (New York Yankees–AL)	1951–64
Runs batted in (RBI's)	40......Mickey Mantle (New York Yankees–AL)	1951–64
Base hits	71......Yogi Berra (New York Yankees–AL)	1947–63
Home runs	18......Mickey Mantle (New York Yankees–AL)	1951–64
Victories pitching	10......Whitey Ford (New York Yankees–AL)	1950–64
Strikeouts	94......Whitey Ford (New York Yankees–AL)	1950–64

World Series Single Series Records

Batting average (4 or more games)	.750	Billy Hatcher (Cincinnati Reds–NL; 9 hits in 12 at-bats in four-game series)	1990
Runs scored	10	Reggie Jackson (New York Yankees–AL)	1977
Runs batted in (RBI's)	12	Bobby Richardson (New York Yankees–AL)	1960
Base hits (7-game series)	13	Bobby Richardson (New York Yankees–AL)	1960
	13	Lou Brock (St. Louis Cardinals–NL)	1968
	13	Marty Barrett (Boston Red Sox–AL)	1986
Home runs	5	Reggie Jackson (New York Yankees–AL; in 20 at-bats)	1977
Victories pitching	3	Christy Matthewson (New York Yankees–AL; in five-game series)	1905
	3	Jack Coombs (Philadelphia A's–AL; in five-game series)	1910
		Ten other pitchers have won three games in more than five games.	
Strikeouts	35	Bob Gibson (St. Louis Cardinals–NL; in 7 games)	1968
	23	Sandy Koufax (Los Angeles Dodgers–NL; in 4 games)	1963

World Series Game Records

Home runs	3	Babe Ruth (New York Yankees–AL) vs. St. Louis Cardinals	Oct. 6, 1926
	3	Babe Ruth (New York Yankees–AL) vs. St. Louis Cardinals	Oct. 9, 1928
	3	Reggie Jackson (New York Yankees–AL) vs. Los Angeles Dodgers	Oct. 18, 1977
Runs batted in (RBI's) in a game	6	Bobby Richardson (New York Yankees–AL) vs. Pittsburgh Pirates	Oct. 8, 1960
Strikeouts by pitcher in a game	17	Bob Gibson (St. Louis Cardinals–NL) vs. Detroit Tigers	Oct. 2, 1968
Perfect game (9 innings)		Don Larsen (New York Yankees–AL) vs. Brooklyn Dodgers	Oct. 8, 1956

Tallest player   The tallest major leaguers of all time are two pitchers measuring 6 ft. 10 in.: Randy Johnson, who played in his first game for the Montreal Expos (NL) on September 15, 1988, and Eric Hillman, who debuted for the New York Mets (NL) on May 18, 1992.

Most Valuable Player Award   The most selections in the annual vote (instituted in 1931) of the Baseball Writers' Association for Most Valuable Player of the Year (MVP) in the major leagues is three, won by: *National League*: Stan Musial (St. Louis), 1943, 1946, 1948; Roy Campanella (Brooklyn), 1951, 1953, 1955; Mike Schmidt (Philadelphia), 1980–81, 1986; Barry Bonds (Pittsburgh, San Francisco), 1990, 1992–93; *American League*: Jimmie Foxx (Philadelphia), 1932–33, 1938; Joe DiMaggio (New York), 1939, 1941, 1947; Yogi Berra (New York), 1951, 1954–55; Mickey Mantle (New York), 1956–57, 1962.

Cy Young Award   In the competition for this prize, awarded annually from 1956 on to the outstanding pitcher in the major leagues, the most wins is four, by Steve Carlton (Philadelphia Phillies), 1972, 1977, 1980 and 1982.

The only pitcher to win three consecutive Cy Young Awards is Greg Maddux (Chicago Cubs/Atlanta Braves), 1992–94.

Dwight Gooden (b. November 16, 1964) of the New York Mets became the youngest pitcher to win the Cy Young Award in 1985 by unanimous vote of the 24 sportswriters who make the selection.

Longest game   The longest game was a minor league game in 1981 that lasted 33 innings. At the end of nine innings the score was tied, 1–1, with the Rochester (NY) Red Wings battling the home team Pawtucket (RI) Red Sox. At the end of 21 innings it was tied 2–2, and at the end of 32 innings, the score was still 2–2, at which point the game was suspended. Two months later, play was resumed, and 18 minutes later, Pawtucket scored one run and won. The winning pitcher was the Red Sox's Bob Ojeda.

The Chicago White Sox (AL) played the longest major league ballgame in elapsed time—8 hr. 6 min.—beating the Milwaukee Brewers, 7–6, in the 25th inning on May 9, 1984 in Chicago. The game started on Tuesday night and was still tied at 3–3 when the 1 A.M. curfew caused suspension until Wednesday night. The most innings in a major league game were 26, when the Brooklyn Dodgers (NL) and the Boston Braves (NL) played to a 1–1 tie on May 1, 1920.

Shortest game   In the shortest major league game on record, the New York Giants (NL) beat the Philadelphia Phillies (NL), 6–1, in nine innings in 51 minutes on September 28, 1919. (A minor league game, Atlanta vs. Mobile in the Southern Association on September 19, 1910, took 33 minutes.)

Around the majors   Wayne Zumwalt of Colorado Springs, CO attended a major league baseball game at all 28 major league stadiums in 28 consecutive days, from June 10 to July 7, 1993.

Most successful managers   Connie Mack managed in the major leagues for a record 53 seasons and achieved a record 3,731 regular-season victories (and a record 3,948 losses)—149 wins and 134 losses for the Pittsburgh Pirates (NL) 1894–96, and 3,582 wins and 3,814 losses for the Philadelphia Athletics (AL), a team he later owned, 1901–50.

The most successful in the World Series was Casey Stengel, who managed the New York Yankees (AL) to seven wins in 10 World Series, winning in 1949–53, 1956 and 1958, and losing in 1955, 1957 and 1960.

Joe McCarthy also led the New York Yankees to seven wins, 1932, 1936–39, 1941, 1943, and his teams lost in 1929 (Chicago) and 1942 (New York). He had the highest win percentage of managers who achieved at least 1,500 regular-season wins, with .615—2,125 wins and 1,333 losses in his 24-year career with the Chicago Cubs (NL) 1926–30, the New York Yankees (AL) 1931–46, and the Boston Red Sox (AL) 1948–50, during which he never had an overall losing season.

Most players in a family   On August 19, 1992, Bret Boone made his major league debut for the Seattle Mariners (AL), making the Boone family the first 3-generation family in major league history. Boone's father, Bob Boone, played 19 seasons in the majors, 1972–90, and his grandfather, Ray Boone, played from 1948 to 1960.

Most valuable baseball card   One of the six known baseball series cards of Honus Wagner was sold at Sotheby's, New York for $451,000 on March 22, 1991. The buyers were Bruce McNall, owner of the Los Angeles Kings hockey club, and team member Wayne Gretzky.

WORLD SERIES

Most wins   The most wins in the World Series is 22, by the New York Yankees, 1923–78, during a record 33 Series appearances. The most wins by a National League team is 9, by the St. Louis Cardinals in 1926, 1931, 1934, 1942, 1944, 1946, 1964, 1967 and 1982.

DID YOU KNOW?

Three players have won the World Series Most Valuable Player award twice: Sandy Koufax (Los Angeles, NL, 1963, 1965), Bob Gibson (St. Louis, NL, 1964, 1967) and Reggie Jackson (Oakland, AL, 1973; New York, AL, 1977).

LEAGUE CHAMPIONSHIP SERIES

Most series played   Reggie Jackson has played in 11 series, with the Oakland Athletics (AL), 1971–75; New York Yankees (AL), 1977–78 and 1980–81; California Angels (AL), 1982, 1986.

Most games played   The record for most games played is 45, by Reggie Jackson. Jackson played for the Oakland Athletics (AL) from 1971–75; the New York Yankees (AL) from 1977–78 and 1980–81; and the California Angels (AL) during the 1982 and 1986 seasons.

Batting average (minimum 50 at-bats)   Playing for the California Angels (AL, 1986) and the Toronto Blue Jays (AL, 1991–93), Devon White had a batting average of .392 during 74 at-bats in 20 games.

Most series pitched   Bob Welch has pitched in eight, with the Los Angeles Dodgers (NL), 1978, 1981, 1983, 1985; and the Oakland Athletics (AL), 1988–90 and 1992.

Most games pitched   The record for most games pitched is 15, held by two pitchers: Tug McGraw, New York Mets (NL), 1969, 1973, Philadelphia Phillies (NL), 1976–78, 1980; and Dennis Eckersley, Chicago Cubs (NL), 1984, Oakland Athletics (AL), 1988–90, 1992.

COLLEGE BASEBALL

NCAA Division I regular season   Hitting records   The most career home runs was 100, by Pete Incaviglia for Oklahoma State in three seasons, 1983–85. The most career hits was 418, by Phil Stephenson for Wichita State in four seasons, 1979–82.

Pitching records   Don Heinkel won 51 games for Wichita State in four seasons, 1979–82. John Powell struck out 602 batters for Auburn University in five seasons, 1990–94.

College World Series   The first College World Series was played in 1947 in Kalamazoo, MI. Since 1950, the College World Series has been played annually at Rosenblatt Stadium in Omaha, NE.

Most championships   The most wins in Division I is 11, by the University of Southern California (USC) in 1948, 1958, 1961, 1963, 1968, 1970–74 and 1978.

Most home runs   The record for most career home runs in the College World Series is four, shared by five players: Bud Hollowell (University of Southern California), 1963; Pete Incaviglia (Oklahoma State), 1983–85; Ed Sprague (Stanford University), 1987–88; Gary Hymel (Louisiana State University), 1990–91; and Lyle Mouton (Louisiana State University), 1990–91.

Most hits   Keith Moreland of the University of Texas holds the record for most career hits in the College World Series, with 23 in three series, 1973–75.

Most wins   The record for most career wins in the College World Series is four, shared by nine pitchers: Bruce Gardner (University of Southern California), 1958, 1960; Steve Arlin (Ohio State), 1965–66; Bert Hooten (University of Texas at Austin), 1969–70; Steve Rogers (University of Tulsa), 1969, 1971; Russ McQueen (University of Southern California), 1972–73; Mark Bull (University of Southern California), 1973–74; Greg Swindell (University of Texas), 1984–85; Kevin Sheary (University of Miami of Florida), 1984–85; Greg Brummett (Wichita State), 1988–89.

BASKETBALL

Highest score   Iraq scored 251 points against Yemen (33) at the 1982 Asian Games.

Most points   Mats Wermelin, 13 years old (Sweden), scored all 272 points in a 272–0 win in a regional boys' basketball tournament in Stockholm, Sweden on February 5, 1974.

The record score by a woman is 156 points by Marie Boyd (later Eichler) of Central High School, Lonaconing, MD in a 163–3 defeat of Ursaline Academy, Cumbria on February 25, 1924.

Dribbling   Ashrita Furman (U.S.) dribbled a basketball without "traveling" a distance of 83 miles in 24 hours at the National Stadium, Suva, Fiji, January 6–7, 1994.

Longest goal   Christopher Eddy scored a field goal measured at 90 ft. 2¼ in. for Fairview High School vs. Iroquois High School in Erie, PA on February 25, 1989.

Nikki Fierstos scored a field goal of about 79 feet, the longest by a woman, on January 2, 1993 at Huntington North High School, Huntington, IN.

Shooting skills   The greatest goal-shooting demonstration was by Thomas Amberry (U.S.), who scored 2,750 consecutive free throws in Seal Beach, CA on November 15, 1993. On June 11, 1992, Jeff Liles scored 231 out of 240 attempts in 10 minutes at Southern Nazarene University, Bethany, OK. He repeated this total of 231 (241 attempts) on June 16. This speed record is achieved using one ball and one rebounder. In one minute, from seven scoring positions, Jeff Liles scored 25 out of 29 attempts in Bethany, OK on September 18, 1994.

In 24 hours, Fred Newman scored 20,371 free throws from a total of 22,049 taken (92.39 percent) at Caltech, Pasadena, CA, September 29–30, 1990.

Steve Bontrager (U.S.) of the British team Polycell Kingston scored 21 points in one minute from seven positions in a demonstration on October 29, 1986.

DUNK!

Joey Johnson of San Pedro, CA successfully dunked a basketball at a rim height of 11 ft. 7 in. at the One-on-One Collegiate Challenge on June 25, 1990 at Trump Plaza Hotel and Casino in Atlantic City, NJ.

Most valuable basket Don Calhoun, a spectator at a Chicago Bulls home game on April 14, 1993, sank a basket from the opposite foul line—a distance of 75 feet—and won $1 million. He was randomly picked from the crowd to try his luck as part of a promotional stunt.

NATIONAL BASKETBALL ASSOCIATION

Most championships The Boston Celtics have won a record 16 NBA titles—1957, 1959–66, 1968–69, 1974, 1976, 1981, 1984 and 1986.

Highest attendance In the 1994–95 season, the NBA had a record regular-season attendance of 18,516,484.

Most games played Kareem Abdul-Jabbar played in a record 1,560 NBA regular-season games over 20 seasons, totaling 57,446 minutes played, for the Milwaukee Bucks, 1969–75, and the Los Angeles Lakers, 1975–89.

The most successive games played is 906, by Randy Smith for the Buffalo Braves, the San Diego Clippers, the Cleveland Cavaliers and the New York Knicks, from February 18, 1972 to March 13, 1983.

The record for most complete games played in one season is 79, by Wilt Chamberlain for Philadelphia in 1962, when he was on court for a record 3,882 minutes. Chamberlain went through his entire career of 1,045 games without fouling out. Moses Malone played his 1,212th consecutive game without fouling out to the end of the 1994/95 season. In his career, Malone has played 1,329 games, fouling out on only five occasions.

Most minutes played The career record for minutes played is 57,446 by Kareem Abdul-Jabbar, Milwaukee Bucks, 1969–75, and Los Angeles Lakers, 1975–89. The season record is 3,882 minutes, by Wilt Chamberlain for the Philadelphia Warriors, 1961–62. The single-game record is 69 minutes, by Dale Ellis for the Seattle SuperSonics vs. Milwaukee Bucks on November 9, 1989 in a 5-overtime game.

Despite retiring at the end of the 1993 season, Michael Jordan, the most prolific scorer of modern times, returned to the NBA during the 1994/95 season after playing minor league baseball. (*Allsport* [*U.S.*]/ *J. Daniel*)

Highest scoring average The highest average during the regular season for players exceeding 10,000 points is 32.2 points per game, by Michael Jordan, who scored 21,998 points in 684 games for the Chicago Bulls, 1984–95. The season record is 50.4 per game, set by Wilt Chamberlain, Philadelphia Warriors, 1961–62.

Playoffs The career scoring average record for the playoffs is held by Michael Jordan, at 34.4 points per game. He scored 4,165 points in 121 games, 1984–95.

Most assists John Stockton (Utah Jazz) made 10,394 assists, 1984–95.

NBA RECORDS

Career Records

Points	38,387	Kareem Abdul-Jabbar: Milwaukee Bucks, Los Angeles Lakers 1970–89
Field-goal percentage	.599	Artis Gilmore: Chicago Bulls, San Antonio Spurs, Boston Celtics; min. 2,000 field goals...1977–88
Free throws made	8,531	Moses Malone: Buffalo Braves, Houston Rockets, Philadelphia 76ers, Washington Bullets, Atlanta Hawks, Milwaukee Bucks, San Antonio Spurs 1976–95
Free-throw percentage	.900	Rick Barry: San Francisco / Golden State Warriors, Houston Rockets; 3,818 from 4,243 attempts (technically .89983) 1965–80
Field goals	15,837	Kareem Abdul-Jabbar 1970–89
3-point field goals	1,119	Dale Ellis: Dallas Mavericks, Seattle SuperSonics, Milwaukee Bucks, San Antonio Spurs
Rebounds	23,924	Wilt Chamberlain: Philadelphia / San Francisco Warriors, Philadelphia 76ers, Los Angeles Lakers ....1983–95 ...1960–73
Steals	2,310	Maurice Cheeks: Philadelphia 76ers, San Antonio Spurs, New York Knicks, Atlanta Hawks, New Jersey Nets...1979–93
Assists	10,394	John Stockton: Utah Jazz..1984–95

Season Records

Points	4,029	Wilt Chamberlain: Philadelphia Warriors 1962
Field-goal percentage	.727	Wilt Chamberlain: Los Angeles Lakers; 426 of 586 attempts 1972
Free throws made	840	Jerry West: Los Angeles Lakers; from 977 attempts 1966
Free-throw percentage	.958	Calvin Murphy: Houston Rockets; 206 of 215 attempts 1981
Field goals	1,597	Wilt Chamberlain: Philadelphia Warriors 1962
3-point field goals	172	Vernon Maxwell: Houston Rockets 1990–91
Rebounds	2,149	Wilt Chamberlain: Philadelphia Warriors 1961
Assists	1,164	John Stockton: Utah Jazz 1991
Steals	301	Alvin Robertson: San Antonio Spurs 1986

Single-Game Records

Points	100	Wilt Chamberlain: Philadelphia Warriors vs. New York Knicks ....Mar. 2, 1962
Field goals	36	Wilt Chamberlain ....Mar. 2, 1962
3-point field goals	10	Brian Shaw: Miami Heat vs. Milwaukee Bucks ....Apr. 8, 1993
	10	Joe Dumars: Detroit Pistons vs. Minnesota Timberwolves ....Nov. 8, 1994

Free throws made	28	Wilt Chamberlain	Mar. 2, 1962
	28	Adrian Dantley: Utah Jazz vs. Houston Rockets	Jan. 5, 1984
Rebounds	55	Wilt Chamberlain: Philadelphia Warriors vs. Boston Celtics	Nov. 24, 1960
Assists	30	Scott Skiles: Orlando Magic vs. Denver Nuggets	Dec. 30, 1990
Steals	11	Larry Kenon: San Antonio Spurs vs. Kansas City Kings	Dec. 26, 1976

NBA PLAYOFF RECORDS

Career Records

Most games played	237	Kareem Abdul-Jabbar: Milwaukee Bucks, Los Angeles Lakers	1970–89
Points	5,762	Kareem Abdul-Jabbar (in 237 playoff games)	1970–89
Field goals	2,356	Kareem Abdul-Jabbar	1970–89
Free throws made	1,213	Jerry West: Los Angeles Lakers; from 1,507 attempts	1961–74
Assists	2,142	Magic Johnson: Los Angeles Lakers	1980–91
Rebounds	4,104	Bill Russell: Boston Celtics	1957–69

Series Records

Points	284	Elgin Baylor: Los Angeles Lakers (vs. Boston Celtics); in 7 games	1962
Field goals	113	Wilt Chamberlain: San Francisco (vs. St. Louis); in 6 games	1964
Free throws made	86	Jerry West: Los Angeles Lakers (vs. Baltimore); in 6 games	1965
Rebounds	220	Wilt Chamberlain: Philadelphia 76ers (vs. Boston Celtics); in 7 games	1965
Assists	115	John Stockton: Utah Jazz (vs. Los Angeles Lakers); in 7 games	1988

Single-Game Records

Points	63	Michael Jordan: Chicago Bulls (vs. Boston Celtics); includes two overtime periods	Apr. 20, 1986
	61	Elgin Baylor: Los Angeles Lakers (vs. Boston Celtics)	Apr. 14, 1962
Field goals	24	Wilt Chamberlain: Philadelphia 76ers vs. Syracuse Nationals; in 42 attempts	Mar. 14, 1960
	24	John Havlicek: Boston Celtics (vs. Atlanta Hawks); in 36 attempts	Apr. 1, 1973
	24	Michael Jordan: Chicago Bulls (vs. Cleveland Cavaliers); in 45 attempts	May 1, 1988
Free throws made	30	Bob Cousy: Boston Celtics (vs. Syracuse Nationals); includes four overtime periods and 32 attempts	Mar. 21, 1953
	23	Michael Jordan: Chicago Bulls (vs. New York Knicks); in 28 attempts	May 14, 1989
Rebounds	41	Wilt Chamberlain: Philadelphia 76ers (vs. Boston Celtics)	Apr. 5, 1967
Assists	24	Magic Johnson: Los Angeles Lakers (vs. Phoenix Suns)	May 15, 1984
	24	John Stockton: Utah Jazz (vs. Los Angeles Lakers)	May 17, 1988

Most blocked shots   The record for most blocked shots in an NBA game is 17, by Elmore Smith for Los Angeles vs. Portland in Los Angeles on October 28, 1973. The season record is 456, by Mark Eaton, Utah Jazz during the 1984–85 season. The career mark is held by Kareem Abdul-Jabbar, at 4,657.

Most ejections   The career record for ejections (for a player) is 127, by Vern Mikkelsen, Minneapolis Lakers, 1950–59. The season mark is 26, by Don Meineke, Fort Wayne Pistons, 1952–53.

Most personal fouls   Kareem Abdul-Jabbar had 4,657 personal fouls called on him in his career. The single-season record is 386, by Darryl Dawkins, New Jersey Nets, 1983–84. The NBA record for most fouls in a game is eight, committed by Don Otten, Tri-Cities vs. Sheboygan on November 24, 1949.

Most Valuable Player   Kareem Abdul-Jabbar was elected the NBA's Most Valuable Player a record six times, 1971–72, 1974, 1976–77 and 1980.

Youngest and oldest players   Bill Willoughby made his debut for the Atlanta Hawks on October 23, 1975 at 18 yr. 156 days. The oldest NBA regular player was Kareem Abdul-Jabbar, who made his last appearance for the Los Angeles Lakers at age 42 yr. 59 days in 1989.

Tallest player   The tallest player in NBA history is Gheorge Muresan (Romania) of the Washington Bullets, at 7 ft. 7 in. He made his pro debut in 1994.

Highest score   The highest aggregate score in an NBA game is 370, when the Detroit Pistons (186) beat the Denver Nuggets (184) in overtime in Denver, CO on December 13, 1983. The record in regulation time is 320, when the Golden State Warriors beat Denver 162–158 in Denver on November 2, 1990. The most points in a half is 107, by the Phoenix Suns in the first half vs. the Denver Nuggets on November 11, 1990. The most points

John Stockton (Utah Jazz) surpassed Magic Johnson's career assists record during the 1994/95 season, ending the year with a total of 10,394 (1984–95). He has led the NBA for eight consecutive seasons, 1988–95, equaling the record of Bob Cousy (Boston, 1953–60). (*Allsport* [*U.S.*]/*S. Dunn*)

DID YOU KNOW?

The Los Angeles Lakers won a record 33 NBA games in succession from November 5, 1971 to January 7, 1972, as during the 1971/72 season they won a record 69 games with 13 losses.

in a quarter is 58, in the fourth quarter, by Buffalo vs. Boston on October 20, 1972.

Greatest winning margin   The greatest winning margin in an NBA game is 68 points, by which the Cleveland Cavaliers, 148, beat the Miami Heat, 80, on December 17, 1991.

Most successful coaches   The most successful coach in NBA history is Lenny Wilkens, with a career coaching record of 968–814 through the 1994/95 season. Wilkens coached for the Seattle SuperSonics (1969–72, 1977–85), the Portland Trail Blazers (1974–76), the Cleveland Cavaliers (1986–93), and the Atlanta Hawks (1994–95).

Pat Riley has the highest winning percentage, with a .717 average (756 wins, 299 losses), coaching the Los Angeles Lakers (1981–90) and the New York Knicks (1991–95).

The most games coached is 1,804, by Bill Fitch: Cleveland Cavaliers, 1970–79; Boston Celtics, 1979–83; Houston Rockets, 1983–88; New Jersey Nets, 1989–92; and Los Angeles Clippers, 1994–95. Fitch's career totals 862 wins and 942 losses.

Playoffs   Pat Riley has won a record 137 playoff games, 102 with the Los Angeles Lakers (1981–90) and 35 with the New York Knicks (1992–95).

NCAA RECORDS

Most wins   In this competition, first held in 1939, the record for most Division I titles is 11, by the University of California at Los Angeles (UCLA), 1964–65, 1967–73, 1975 and 1995.

Most Valuable Player   The only player to have been voted the Most Valuable Player in the NCAA final three times has been Lew Alcindor of UCLA in 1967–69. Alcindor subsequently changed his name to Kareem Abdul-Jabbar.

Highest score   The NCAA aggregate record is 399, when Troy State (258) beat De Vry Institute, Atlanta (141) in Troy, AL on January 12, 1992. Troy's total was also the highest individual team score in a game.

Most points scored   The most points scored in an NCAA game is 113, by Clarence "Bevo" Francis, Rio Grande (Div. II), vs. Hillsdale on February 2, 1954. Pete Maravich, Louisiana State (Div. I) holds the season record. He scored 1,381 points in 1970 (522 field goals and 337 free throws). The

NCAA MEN'S DIVISION I RECORDS

Career Records

Points	3,667	Pete Maravich: Louisiana State 1968–70
Field goals	1,387	Pete Maravich: Louisiana State 1968–70
Best percentage	.690	Ricky Need: Appalachian State 1991–94
3-point field goals	.401	Doug Day: Radford 1990–93
Free throws	905	Dickie Hemric: Wake Forest 1952–55
Rebounds	2,201	Tom Gola: La Salle 1952–55
Assists	1,076	Bobby Hurley: Duke 1990–93
Blocked shots	453	Alonzo Mourning: Georgetown 1989–92
Steals	376	Eric Murdock: Providence 1988–91

Season Records

Points	1,381	Pete Maravich: Louisiana State 1970
Field goals	522	Pete Maravich: Louisiana State (from 1,168 attempts) 1970
Best percentage	.746	Steve Johnson: Oregon State 1981
3-point field goals	158	Darrin Fitzgerald: Butler (in 362 attempts) 1987
Free throws	355	Frank Selvy: Furman (in 444 attempts) 1954
Best percentage	.959	Craig Collins: Penn State 1985
Rebounds	734	Walt Dukes: Seton Hall (in 33 games) 1953
Assists	406	Mark Wade: Nevada–Las Vegas 1987
Blocked shots	207	David Robinson: Navy (in 35 games) 1986
Steals	150	Mookie Blaylock: Oklahoma 1988

Game Records

Points	100	Frank Selvy: Furman (vs. Newberry) ...... Feb. 13, 1954
Field goals	41	Frank Selvy: Furman ...... Feb. 13, 1954
3-point field goals	14	Dave Jamerson: Ohio (vs. Charleston) ...... Dec. 21, 1989
	14	Askia Jones: Kansas State (vs. Fresno State) ...... Mar. 24, 1994
Free throws	30	Pete Maravich: Louisiana State (vs. Oregon State) ...... Dec. 22, 1969
Rebounds	51	Bill Chambers: William and Mary (vs. Virginia) ...... Feb. 14, 1953
Assists	22	Tony Fairly: Baptist (vs. Armstrong State) ...... Feb. 9, 1987
	22	Avery Johnson: Southern-B.R. vs. Texas Southern) ...... Jan. 25, 1988
	22	Sherman Douglas: Syracuse (vs. Providence) ...... Jan. 28, 1989
Blocked shots	14	David Robinson: Navy (vs. North Carolina–Wilmington) ...... Jan. 4, 1986
	14	Shawn Bradley: BYU (vs. Eastern Kentucky) ...... Dec. 7, 1990
Steals	13	Mookie Blaylock: Oklahoma (vs. Centenary) ...... Dec. 12, 1987
	13	Mookie Blaylock: Oklahoma (vs. Loyola Marymount) ...... Dec. 17, 1988

NCAA WOMEN'S DIVISION I CHAMPIONSHIP GAME RECORDS

Team Records

Most championships	3 Tennessee	1987, 1989, 1991
Points	97 Texas (vs. USC)	1986
Field goals	40 Texas (vs. USC)	1986
Best percentage	.588 Texas (vs. USC; 40–68)	1986
3-point field goals	11 Stanford (vs. Auburn)	1990
Rebounds	57 Old Dominion (vs. Georgia)	1985
Assists (since 1985)	22 Texas (vs. USC)	1986
Blocked shots (since 1988)	7 Tennessee (vs. Auburn)	1989
Steals (since 1988)	12 Louisiana Tech (vs. Auburn)	1988
	12 Louisiana Tech (vs. North Carolina)	1994

Individual Records

Points	47 Sheryl Swoopes: Texas Tech (vs. Ohio State)	1993
Field goals	16 Sheryl Swoopes: Texas Tech (vs. Ohio State)	1993
Best percentage	.889 Jennifer White: Louisiana Tech (vs. USC; 8–9)	1983
3-point field goals (since 1988)	6 Katy Steding: Stanford (vs. Auburn)	1990
Rebounds	23 Charlotte Smith: North Carolina (vs. Louisiana Tech)	1994
Assists (since 1985)	10 Kamie Ethridge: Texas (vs. USC)	1986
	10 Melissa McCray: Tennessee (vs. Auburn)	1989
Blocked shots (since 1988)	5 Sheila Frost: Tennessee (vs. Auburn)	1989
Steals (since 1988)	6 Erica Westbrooks: Louisiana Tech (vs. Auburn)	1988

career scoring record is 4,045 points, held by Travis Grant, Kentucky State (Div. II), 1969–72.

Most goals The single-game field goal record is 41, by Frank Selvy, Furman (Div. I) vs. Newberry on February 13, 1954. The season record is 539, by Travis Grant, Kentucky State in 1972. Grant also holds the career mark, at 1,760.

Most assists The most assists in a game is 26, by Robert James, Kean (Div. III) vs. New Jersey Tech on March 11, 1989. The season mark is 406, by Mark Wade, UNLV (Div. I) in 1987. The career record is 1,076, by Bobby Hurley, Duke (Div. I), 1990–93.

Consecutive records (Division I) Individual The record for scoring 10 or more points in consecutive games is 115, by Lionel Simmons for La Salle, 1987–90. The consecutive 50-plus points tally is three games, by Pete Maravich, Louisiana State, February 10–15, 1969. The longest field goal streak is 25, by Ray Voelkel, American, over nine games from November 24 to December 16, 1978. The single-game mark is 16 field goals hit by Doug Grayson, Kent vs. North Carolina on December 6, 1967.

The record for consecutive 3-point shots made is 15, by Todd Leslie, Northwestern, over four games, December 15–28, 1990.

Team UCLA set the NCAA mark for consecutive victories (including the playoffs) at 88 games. The streak started on January 30, 1971 and ended on January 19, 1974, when the Bruins were defeated by Notre Dame, 71–70.

Most successful coaches The coach with the most victories in NCAA Division I competition is Adolph Rupp at Kentucky, with 876 wins (and 190 losses), 1931–72. The highest winning percentage for a Division I coach is .837 (625 wins, 122 losses), by Jerry Tarkanian, Long Beach State, 1969–73; UNLV, 1974–92. John Wooden coached UCLA to 10 NCAA titles.

Henry Iba coached the most games, 1,105, with Northwest Missouri State 1930–33, Colorado 1934, and Oklahoma State 1935–70. Iba's career record was 767 wins and 338 losses.

Lenny Wilkens is the NBA's most successful coach. (*Allsport [U.S.]/ J. Daniel*)

Longest coaching career In his 48-year career Phog Allen coached four teams: Baker, 1906–08; Kansas, 1908–09, 1920–56; Haskell, 1909; and Central Missouri State, 1913–19.

Largest attendance The highest paid attendance for a college game was 68,112, for Louisiana State's 87–64 victory over Notre Dame at the Louisiana Superdome, New Orleans, LA on January 20, 1990.

Women's The record for a women's college game is 23,912, in Knoxville, TN for a game between the University of Tennessee and the University of Texas on December 9, 1987.

WOMEN'S BASKETBALL

Women's championships In this competition, first held in 1982, the record for most Division I titles is three, by Tennessee, 1987, 1989 and 1991. The regular-season game aggregate record is 261, when St. Joseph's (Indiana) beat North Kentucky 131–130 on February 27, 1988.

Most successful coaches Jody Conradt of the University of Texas has won the most games in Women's NCAA Division I competition, with 654 victories through the 1994/95 season.

The coach with the highest winning percentage is Leon Barmore of Louisiana Tech, who compiled a .857 average (366 wins, 61 losses), 1985–95.

Most points Pearl Moore scored 4,061 points in her college career: 177 points in eight games for Anderson Junior College, Anderson, SC, and 3,884 points for Francis Marion College, Florence, SC, 1975–79. Francis Marion was a member of the Association of Intercollegiate Athletics for Women (AIWA) during Moore's career.

NCAA DIVISION I SCORING RECORDS

Vertical dunk On December 21, 1984, at Randolph County Armory, Elkins, WV, Georgeann Wells became the first woman to dunk the ball in an NCAA game. Wells, who measures 6 ft. 7 in., performed the feat when her team, West Virginia, played Charleston.

Most points The career points leader in NCAA Division I competition is Patricia Hoskins of Mississippi Valley State, with 3,122 points (1985–89).

REBOUND!

Wanda Ford of Drake set the women's career and season rebound records, at 1,887 and 534 respectively. Her career spanned 1983–86, and she set the season mark in 1985. The single-game record is 40 rebounds, by Deborah Temple, Delta State vs. Alabama-Birmingham, February 14, 1983.

The season record is 974 points, by Cindy Brown, Long Beach State in 1987. Brown also holds the single-game mark; she scored 60 points vs. San Jose State on February 16, 1987.

Most assists The most helpful player in NCAA history is Suzie McConnell, Penn State. She holds the career mark, at 1,307, 1984–88, and the single-season mark, with 355 assists in 1987. Michelle Burden, Kent, has the most assists in a game, 23, vs. Ball State on February 6, 1991.

Most field goals The all-time leader for field goals is Joyce Walker, Louisiana State, with 1,259, 1981–84. The season mark was set by Clemson's Barbara Kennedy in 1982, when she hit 392 goals. The single-game record is 27, by Lorri Bauman, Drake vs. Southwest Missouri State, January 6, 1984.

Highest scores The highest-scoring game was Virginia's defeat of North Carolina State, 123–120, for an aggregate of 243 points. Played on January 12, 1991, the game went to three overtimes.

The most points scored by a team in one game is 149, by Long Beach State, in their defeat of San Jose State (69 points) on February 16, 1987.

OTHER RECORDS

Olympic Games Six men and two women have won two Olympic gold medals: Bob Kurland in 1948 and 1952; Bill Houghland in 1952 and 1956; Michael Jordan, Patrick Ewing, and Chris Mullin, all in 1984 and 1992; Burdette Eliele Haldorson in 1956 and 1960; Anne Theresa Donovan and Theresa Edwards, both in 1984 and 1988.

Most titles Olympic The United States has won 10 men's Olympic titles. From the time the sport was introduced to the Games in 1936 until 1972, the U.S. won 63 consecutive matches in the Olympic Games, until it lost 51–50 to the USSR in the disputed final match in Munich, Germany. Since then it has won a further 29 matches and has had another loss to the USSR (in 1988). The women's title has been won a record three times by the USSR, in 1976, 1980 and 1992 (by the Unified team from the republics of the former USSR). The U.S. team won the title in 1984 and 1988.

World The USSR has won the most titles in both the men's World Championships (instituted 1950) with three (1967, 1974 and 1982) and women's (instituted 1953), with six (1959, 1964, 1967, 1971, 1975 and 1983). Both Yugoslavia and the U.S. have also won three men's world titles: Yugoslavia in 1970, 1978 and 1990, and the U.S. in 1954, 1986 and 1994.

BIATHLON

Most titles Olympic The most Olympic individual titles is two, won by Magnar Solberg (Norway), in 1968 and 1972; and Franz-Peter Rötsch (East Germany) in both 10 km and 20 km in 1988. The USSR won six 4 ×

7.5-km relay titles, 1968–88. Aleksandr Tikhonov, who was a member of the first four teams, also won a silver in the 1968 20 km.

World Frank Ullrich (East Germany) has won a record six individual world titles—four in 10 km, 1978–81, including the 1980 Olympics, and two in 20 km, 1982–83. Aleksandr Tikhonov was on 10 winning Soviet relay teams, 1968–80, and won four individual titles. The Biathlon World Cup (instituted 1979) was won four times by Frank Ullrich, 1978 and 1980–82; and by Franz-Peter Rötsch (East Germany), 1984–85 and 1987–88.

Women The first World Championships were held in 1984. The most individual titles is three, by Anne-Elinor Elvebakk (Norway), 10 km 1988, 7.5 km 1989–90. Kaya Parve (USSR) has won six titles, two individual and four relay, 1984–86, 1988. A women's biathlon was included in the 1992 Olympics. Myriam Bédard (Canada) is the only double Olympic champion. She won the 7.5 km and 15 km events in 1994.

United States National Championships In this competition, first held in 1965 in Rosendale, NY, men's events have been staged annually. Women's events were first included in 1982.

Most titles Lyle Nelson has won seven National Championships: five in the 10 km, 1976, 1979, 1981, 1985 and 1987; two in the 20 km, 1977 and 1985. Anna Sonnerup holds the women's record with five titles: three in the 7.5 km, 1986–87 and 1989; and two in the 15 km, 1989 and 1991.

BILLIARDS

Most titles The greatest number of World Championships (instituted 1870) won by one player is eight, by John Roberts, Jr. (Great Britain), in 1870 (twice), 1871, 1875 (twice), 1877 and 1885 (twice). The record for world amateur titles is four, by Robert James Percival Marshall (Australia), in 1936, 1938, 1951 and 1962.

Youngest champion The youngest winner of the world professional title is Mike Russell, age 20 yr. 49 days when he won in Leura, Australia on July 23, 1989.

Highest breaks The highest certified break made by the anchor cannon is 42,746, by William Cook (England) from May 29 to June 7, 1907.

The official world record under the then balkline rule is 1,784, by Joe Davis in the United Kingdom Championship on May 29, 1936.

Under the "two pot" rule, restored on January 1, 1983, the highest break is Michael Ferreira's (India) 962 unfinished, in a tournament in Bombay, India on April 29, 1986.

Fastest century In 1941, Walter Lindrum made an official 100 break in 46.0 seconds in Sydney, Australia.

THREE CUSHION

Most titles　Willie Hoppe (U.S.) won 51 billiards championships in all forms, spanning the pre- and post-international era, 1906–52.

Union Mondiale de Billiard (UMB)　Raymond Ceulemans (Belgium) has won 20 UMB world Three Cushion championships (1963–73, 1975–80, 1983, 1985 and 1990).

BOBSLED AND LUGE

BOBSLEDDING

Oldest sled run　The oldest and most famous sled run is the Cresta Run, which was constructed in St. Moritz, Switzerland in 1902.

Oldest sledder　The oldest person to travel the whole length of the Cresta Run is Robin Todhunter (Great Britain), who completed the course at age 83 yr. 239 days on February 2, 1987.

Most titles　The Olympic 4-man bob title (instituted 1924) has been won five times by Switzerland (1924, 1936, 1956, 1972 and 1988). The Olympic 2-man bob title (instituted 1932) has been won four times by Switzerland (1948, 1980, 1992 and 1994). The most gold medals won by an individual is three, by Meinhard Nehmer (East Germany) and by Bernhard Germeshausen (East Germany) in the 1976 2-man, 1976 and 1980 4-man events. The most medals won is seven (one gold, five silver, one bronze) by Bogdan Musiol (East Germany), 1980–92.

World and Olympic　The world 4-man bob title (instituted 1924) has been won 20 times by Switzerland (1924, 1936, 1939, 1947, 1954–57, 1971–73, 1975, 1982–83, 1986–90, 1993), including its five Olympic victories. Switzerland won the 2-man title 17 times (1935, 1947–50, 1953, 1955, 1977–80 and 1982–83, 1987, 1990, 1992 and 1994), including its four Olympic successes.

Eugenio Monti was a member of 11 world championship crews, eight 2-man and three 4-man, in 1957–68.

United States　Two American bobsledders have won two gold medals: driver Billy Fiske and crewman Clifford Grey in 1928 and 1932. At age 16

DID YOU KNOW?

The oldest age at which a gold medal has been won in any Winter Olympic sport is 49 yr. 7 days, for James Jay O'Brien (U.S.) in 4-man bob in 1932.

yr. 260 days in 1928, Fiske was America's youngest-ever Winter Games gold medalist.

LUGEING

Most titles   The most successful rider in the World Championships was Thomas Köhler (East Germany), who won the single-seater title in 1962, 1964 (Olympic) and 1967, and shared the 2-seater title in 1965, 1967 and 1968 (Olympic). Georg Hackl (GDR/Germany) has won four single-seater titles, 1989, 1990, 1992 (Olympic) and 1994 (Olympic). Margit Schumann (East Germany) won five women's titles, 1973–75, 1976 (Olympic) and 1977.

United States   No American luger has won a medal in the Olympic Games. Wendell Suckow won a gold medal in men's singles at the 1993 World Luge Championships in Calgary, Canada.

United States National Championships   Most titles   Frank Masley has won a record six men's championships, 1979, 1981–83 and 1987–88. Bonny Warner, 1983–84, 1987–88 and 1990, and Cammy Miller, 1985, 1989 and 1991–93, have each won a record five women's titles.

Fastest lugeing speed   The fastest recorded speed is 92.3 MPH, by Duncan Kennedy (U.S.) at the World Luge Championships in Winterberg, Germany, on January 27, 1991.

BOWLING

Highest bowling score—24 hours   A team of six scored 242,665 at Dover Bowl, Dover, DE, March 18–19, 1995. During this attempt a member of the team, Richard Ranshaw, set an individual record of 51,064.

United States   The American record is held by a team of six called the Brunswick Thursday Nite Stars, who scored 209,072 at Brunswick Sharptown Lanes, Houston, TX, June 20–21, 1991.

Largest bowling center   The Fukuyama Bowl, Osaka, Japan has 144 lanes. The Tokyo World Lanes Center, Japan, now closed, had 252 lanes.

Consecutive strikes, spares and splits   The record for most consecutive strikes is 40, by Jeanne Maiden. Mabel Henry of Winchester, KY had 30 consecutive spares in the 1986/87 season. Shirley Tophigh of Las Vegas, NV holds the unenviable record of rolling 14 consecutive splits in 1968/69.

World Championships   The World (*Fédération Internationale des Quilleurs*) Championships were instituted for men in 1954 and for women in 1963. The highest pinfall in the individual men's event is 5,963 (in 28 games) by Ed Luther (U.S.) in Milwaukee, WI on August 28, 1971.

For the current schedule of 24 games the men's record is 5,261, by Rick

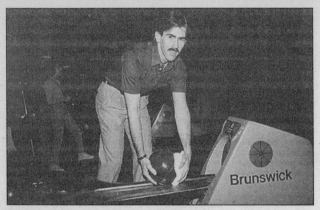

Although there are claims for a perfect 3-game score of 900, the highest sanctioned score is 899, by Tom Jordan in Union, NJ, in 1989.

Steelsmith (U.S.). The women's record is 4,894, by Sandra Jo Shiery (U.S.), both in Helsinki, Finland in June 1987.

The World Cup (instituted 1965) is contested annually by the national champions of each member of FIQ. The most wins is three, by Paeng Nepomuceno (Philippines), 1976, 1980 and 1992.

Highest scores The highest individual score for three sanctioned games (out of a possible 900) is 899, by Thomas Jordan (U.S.) in Union, NJ on March 7, 1989. He followed with a 299, setting a 4-game series record of 1,198 pins.

The record by a woman is 865, by Anne Marie Duggan of Edmond, OK on July 18, 1993.

PERFECT!

Walter Ray Williams Jr. bowled four perfect games in one tournament, in Mechanicsburg, PA in 1993. Kelly Coffman rolled eight perfect games on the 1994 tour.

Youngest 300 bowler Scott Owsley of Fontana, CA scored 300 at age 10 yr. 9 mo. 6 days on March 26, 1994. The youngest girl to roll a 300 game is Nicole Long of Columbia, MO, at age 12 yr. 5 mo. on May 27, 1995.

Oldest 300 bowler Jerry Whelman of Port St. Lucie, FL scored 300 on April 15, 1992, at age 81. The oldest woman to score 300 is Evelyn Culbert of Austin, MN at Echo Lanes, Austin, MN on April 4, 1993, at age 66.

PROFESSIONAL BOWLERS ASSOCIATION (PBA)

Most titles · Earl Anthony (U.S.) has won a lifetime total of 41 PBA titles. The record number of titles won in one PBA season is eight, by Mark Roth of Lake Heights, NJ, in 1978.

Consecutive titles · Three bowlers have won three consecutive professional tournaments—Dick Weber, in 1959, 1960 and 1961; Johnny Petraglia in 1971; and Mark Roth in 1977.

Perfect games · A total of 210 perfect (300-pin) games were bowled in PBA tournaments in 1993, the most ever for one year.

Grand Slam · The first bowler to accumulate the four legs of bowling's Grand Slam was Mike Aulby: National Championship (1979); U.S. Open (1989); ABC Masters (1989); and Firestone Tournament of Champions (1995).

Triple Crown · The first bowler to accumulate the three legs of the triple crown was Billy Hardwick: National Championship (1963); Firestone Tournament of Champions (1965); U.S. Open (1969). Hardwick's feat was matched by Johnny Petraglia: Firestone (1971); U.S. Open (1977); National (1980); by Pete Weber: Firestone (1987); U.S. Open (1988); National (1989); and by Mike Aulby: National (1979); U.S. Open (1989); Firestone (1995).

PBA TOUR SCORING RECORDS

Games	Score	Bowler	Site	Year
6	1,635	Norm Duke	Peoria, IL	1994
8	2,165	Billy Hardwick	Tokyo, Japan	1968
12	3,061	Norm Duke	Peoria, IL	1994
16	4,015	Carmen Salvino	Sterling Heights, MI	1980
18	4,696	Norm Duke	Peoria, IL	1994
24	5,826	Kelly Coffman	Riverside, CA	1993

PBA Tour

U.S. Open · The most wins in this tournament is four, by two bowlers: Don Carter (1953–54, 1957–58), and Dick Weber (1962–63, 1965–66).

PBA National Championship · The most wins in this tournament is six, by Earl Anthony in 1973–75 and 1981–83.

Firestone Tournament of Champions · The most wins in this tournament is three, by Mike Durbin in 1972, 1982 and 1984.

Highest earners · Pete Weber had won a record $1,715,423 in PBA competitions through July 10, 1995.
Mike Aulby of Indianapolis, IN holds the single-season earnings mark of $298,237, reached in 1989.

LADIES PROFESSIONAL BOWLERS TOUR (LPBT)

Most titles Lisa Wagner has won 28 tournaments in her 14-year career, 1980–95. Patty Costello won a season high seven tournaments in 1976.

Highest earnings Aleta Sill has won a career record $688,681 in prize money through June 1, 1995. She also had the season high record in 1994, with $126,325 in earnings.

AMERICAN BOWLING CONGRESS (ABC)

Highest scores The highest individual score for three games is 899, by Thomas Jordan in Union, NJ on March 7, 1989 (see BOWLING: HIGHEST SCORES). The highest 3-game team score is 3,868, by Hurst Bowling Supplies of Luzerne, PA on February 23, 1994.

The highest season average attained in sanctioned competition is 247.9, by Jeff Phipps of Salem, OR in the 1992/93 season.

The all-time ABC-sanctioned 2-man single-game record is 600, held jointly by the teams of John Cotta (300) and Steve Larson (300) on May 1, 1981, at the Manteca, CA Bowling Association Tournament; Jeff Mraz and Dave Roney of Canton, OH on November 8, 1987 in the Ann Doubles Classic in Canton, OH; William Gruner and Dave Conway of Oceanside, CA on February 27, 1990; Scott Williams and Willie Hammar of Utica, MI on January 7, 1990; and Darrell Guertin and George Tignor of Rutland, VT on February 20, 1993.

Perfect scores The highest number of sanctioned 300 games is 51, by Mike Whalin of Cincinnati, OH.

Two perfect games were rolled back-to-back *twice* by three bowlers: Al Spotts of West Reading, PA, on March 14, 1982 and February 1, 1985; Gerry Wright of Idaho Falls, ID, on January 9, 1992 and February 26, 1992; and Steve Gehringer of Reading, PA on October 3, 1991 and February 7, 1992.

WOMEN'S INTERNATIONAL BOWLING CONGRESS (WIBC)

Highest scores Elizabeth Johnson of Niagara Falls, NY had a record 234 single-season average in the 1993/94 season. Patty Ann of Appleton, WI had a record 5-year composite average of 227 through the 1985/86 season.

The highest 5-woman team score for a 3-game series is 3,536, by Contour Power Grips on August 29, 1994.

Perfect games Jeanne Nacarrato (née Maiden) of Tacoma, WA has rolled 21 perfect games to set the WIBC career record. She also set a record of 40 consecutive strikes in 1986 and rolled an 864 on games of 300–300–264.

BOXING

Most knockdowns in title fight   Vic Toweel (South Africa) knocked down Danny O'Sullivan of London, England 14 times in 10 rounds in their world bantamweight fight in Johannesburg, South Africa on December 2, 1950, before the latter retired.

Longest fight   The longest recorded world title fight with gloves was between Andy Bowen of New Orleans and Jack Burke in New Orleans, LA, April 6–7, 1893. It lasted 110 rounds, 7 hr. 19 min. (9:15 P.M.-4:34 A.M.), and was declared a no-contest (later changed to a draw).

Most fights without loss   Between 1989 and 1992, Buck Smith (U.S.) went undefeated for 106 fights (5 draws).

Pedro Carrasco (Spain) won 83 consecutive fights from April 22, 1964 to September 3, 1970, drew once and had a further nine wins, for an undefeated streak of 93 fights (1 draw).

Highest attendance   The greatest paid attendance at a boxing match is 132,274 for four world title fights at Aztec Stadium, Mexico City on February 20, 1993, headed by the WBC light-welterweight defense by Julio César Chávez (Mexico) over Greg Haugen (U.S.).

The indoor record is 63,350, at the Muhammad Ali vs. Leon Spinks fight in the Superdome, New Orleans, LA on September 15, 1978.

The highest nonpaying attendance is 135,132, at the Tony Zale vs. Billy Pryor fight at Juneau Park, Milwaukee, WI on August 16, 1941.

Lowest attendance   The smallest attendance at a world heavyweight title fight was 2,434, at the Cassius Clay vs. Sonny Liston fight in Lewiston, ME on May 25, 1965. Clay changed his name to Muhammad Ali after the bout.

KNOCKOUT!

The greatest number of finishes classed as "knockouts" in a career (1936–63) is 145 (129 in professional bouts), by Archie Moore (born Archibald Lee Wright; U.S.).

WORLD HEAVYWEIGHT

Longest-reigning heavyweight champion   Joe Louis (U.S.) was champion for 11 yr. 252 days, from June 22, 1937, when he knocked out James Joseph Braddock in the eighth round in Chicago, IL, until announcing his retirement on March 1, 1949. During his reign Louis made a record 25 defenses of his title.

Shortest-reigning heavyweight champion Tony Tucker (U.S.) was IBF champion for 64 days, May 30–August 2, 1987, the shortest duration of a title won and lost in the ring.

Most recaptures Muhammad Ali (b. Cassius Clay) is the only man to have regained the heavyweight championship twice. Ali first won the title on February 25, 1964, defeating Sonny Liston. He defeated George Foreman on October 30, 1974, after having been stripped of the title by the world boxing authorities on April 28, 1967. He won the WBA title from Leon Spinks on September 15, 1978, having previously lost to him on February 15, 1978.

Lightest heavyweight champion Robert James "Bob" Fitzsimmons of Great Britain weighed 165 pounds when he won the title by knocking out James J. Corbett in Carson City, NV on March 17, 1897.

Heaviest heavyweight champion Primo Carnera (Italy), the "Ambling Alp," who won the title from Jack Sharkey in New York City on June 29, 1933, scaled 260½ pounds for this fight, but he reached his peak weight, 270 pounds, on March 1, 1934. He had an expanded chest measurement of 54 inches and the longest reach at 85½ inches (fingertip to fingertip).

Oldest heavyweight champion George Foreman (U.S.; b. January 22, 1949) was 45 yr. 287 days old when he knocked out Michael Moorer (U.S.) in Las Vegas, NV on November 5, 1994 for the WBA/IBF heavyweight title.

Youngest heavyweight champion Mike Tyson (U.S.) was 20 yr. 144 days old when he beat Trevor Berbick (U.S.) to win the WBC version in Las Vegas, NV on November 22, 1986. He added the WBA title when he beat James "Bone-crusher" Smith on March 7, 1987 at 20 yr. 249 days. He became undisputed champion on August 2, 1987 when he beat Tony Tucker (U.S.) for the IBF title.

George Foreman lands a heavy right on Michael Moorer on his way to winning the world heavyweight title. (*Allsport [U.S.]/H. Stein*)

Greatest weight difference When Primo Carnera (Italy), 270 pounds, fought Tommy Loughran (U.S.), 184 pounds, for the world heavyweight title in Miami, FL on March 1, 1934, there was a weight difference of 86 pounds between the two fighters. Carnera won the fight on points.

WORLD CHAMPIONS—ANY WEIGHT

Longest reign The Joe Louis heavyweight duration record of 11 yr. 252 days stands for all divisions.

Shortest reign Tony Canzoneri (U.S.) was world light-welterweight champion for 33 days, May 21 to June 23, 1933, the shortest period for a boxer to have won and lost the world title in the ring.

Youngest world champion Wilfred Benitez of Puerto Rico was 17 yr. 176 days old when he won the WBA light-welterweight title in San Juan, Puerto Rico on March 6, 1976.

Oldest world champion Archie Moore, who was recognized as a light-heavyweight champion up to February 10, 1962 when his title was removed, was then believed to be between 45 and 48 years old.

Longest fight The longest world title fight (under Queensberry Rules) was that between the lightweights Joe Gans (U.S.) and Oscar Matthew "Battling" Nelson, the "Durable Dane," in Goldfield, NV on September 3, 1906. It was terminated in the 42nd round when Gans was declared the winner on a foul.

Most recaptures The only boxer to win a world title five times at one weight is "Sugar Ray" Robinson (U.S.; b. Walker Smith, Jr.), who beat Carmen Basilio (U.S.) in Chicago Stadium, IL on March 25, 1958 to regain the world middleweight title for the fourth time.

Most title bouts The record number of title bouts in a career is 37, of which 18 ended in "no decision," by 3-time world welterweight champion Jack Britton (U.S.) in 1915–22. The record for most contests without a "no decision" is 29, including a record 28 wins by Julio César Chávez (Mexico), 1984–94.

Greatest "tonnage" The highest aggregate weight recorded in any fight is 699 pounds, when Claude "Humphrey" McBride (Oklahoma), 339½

CHAMP!

Rocky Marciano (U.S.) is the only world champion at any weight to have won every fight of his professional career, from March 17, 1947 to September 21, 1955 (he announced his retirement on April 27, 1956); 43 of his 49 fights were won by knockouts or stoppages.

pounds, knocked out Jimmy Black (Houston, TX), 359½ pounds, in the third round in Oklahoma City, OK on June 1, 1971.

AMATEUR

Olympic titles Only two boxers have won three Olympic gold medals: southpaw László Papp (Hungary), middleweight winner 1948, light-middleweight winner 1952 and 1956; and Teófilo Stevenson (Cuba), heavyweight winner 1972, 1976 and 1980.

The only man to win two titles in one Olympic celebration was Oliver L. Kirk (U.S.), who won both bantam and featherweight titles in St. Louis, MO in 1904, but he needed only one bout in each class.

Youngest The youngest Olympic boxing champion was Jackie Fields (U.S.), who won the 1924 featherweight title at age 16 yr. 162 days. The minimum age for Olympic boxing competitors is now 17.

Oldest gold medalist Richard Gunn (Great Britain) won the Olympic featherweight gold medal on October 27, 1908 in London, England at age 37 yr. 254 days.

World Championships A record of five world titles (instituted 1974) have been won by Félix Savon (Cuba), heavyweight winner 1986, 1989, 1991, and 91 kg 1993 and 1995.

Most U.S. titles The most titles won is five, by middleweight W. Rodenbach, 1900–04.

BUNGEE JUMPING

Greatest jump Chris Allum holds the record for jumping the greatest distance off a fixed structure—822 feet off the New River Gorge Bridge, WV, in October 1992.

CANOEING

Most titles Olympics Gert Fredriksson (Sweden) won a record six Olympic gold medals, 1948–60. He added a silver and a bronze, for a record eight medals.

The most by a woman is four, by Birgit Schmidt (née Fischer; Germany, formerly GDR), 1980–92.

The most gold medals won at one Games is three, by Vladimir Parfenovich (USSR) in 1980 and by Ian Ferguson (New Zealand) in 1984.

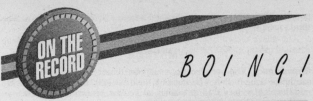
BOING!

"Just imagine jumping off a building," muses Chris Allum. "Your ears peel back against your head. Your hair whips back. All the water comes out of your eyes. You see the ground coming toward you at tremendous speed. And then you bounce."

Not only does Allum hold the record for jumping the greatest distance off a fixed structure (822 feet off the New River Gorge Bridge in West Virginia), he's also been instrumental in the United States in popularizing the safe pursuit of bungee jumping using a thick elastic cable attached to a harness to break the fall. An electrician by trade in his native New Zealand, Allum now runs Triple C Sports Management, and has "jumped" 130,000 people worldwide, ages seven to 84, without incident.

Just don't ask why. Allum replies, "That's like asking someone, 'Why are you a lawyer?' Bungee jumping gives you a lot of confidence. It makes you feel that you're in control of your life. You've made a decision about doing something unusual and you tell yourself, 'If I can get myself

Greatest jump
Chris Allum holds the record for jumping the greatest distance off a fixed structure—822 feet off the New River Gorge Bridge, WV, in October 1992.

through this then I can get through other stuff.' It's a release of tension, and for me, of course, it pays the rent."

Allum's next challenge is bungee jumping from a blimp during ESPN's Extreme Games. And he'll continue his bungee business from cranes, even though, he says, they're "not as nice" as bridges. "It's much nicer to walk through woods and then get to the edge of something and jump off." Amen!

World   Including the Olympic Games, a record 24 titles have been won by Birgit Schmidt, 1979–93.

The men's record is 13, by Gert Fredriksson, 1948–60; Rüdiger Helm (East Germany), 1976–83; and Ivan Patzaichin (Romania), 1968–84.

United States   The only American canoeist to have won two Olympic gold medals is Greg Barton, who won in K1 and K2 1,000 m events in 1988. He also has a U.S. record three medals, as he took bronze in K1 1,000 m in 1984.

Most U.S. titles   Marcia Smoke won 35 U.S. national titles between 1962 and 1981. The men's record is 33 U.S. titles, by Ernest Riedel between 1930 and 1948, mostly in kayak events.

ROLL OVER!

Colin Brian Hill achieved 1,000 hand rolls in 31 min. 55.62 sec. in Consett, England in March 1987. He also achieved 100 rolls in 2 min. 39.2 sec. in London, England in February 1987 and 3,700 continuous rolls in Durham, England in May 1989.

Fastest speed   The German 4-man kayak Olympic champions in 1992 in Barcelona, Spain covered 1,000 m in 2 min. 52.17 sec. in a heat on August 4. This represents an average speed of 12.98 MPH. At the 1988 Olympics in Seoul, South Korea, the Norwegian four achieved a 250 m split of 42.08 seconds between 500 m and 750 m for a speed of 13.29 MPH.

Longest journey   Father and son Dana and Donald Starkell paddled from Winnipeg, Manitoba, Canada by ocean and river to Belem, Brazil, a distance of 12,181 miles, from June 1, 1980 to May 1, 1982. All portages were human-powered. Without portages or aid of any kind, the longest journey is one of 6,102 miles, by Richard H. Grant and Ernest "Moose" Lassy, circumnavigating the eastern United States via Chicago, New Orleans, Miami, New York City and the Great Lakes from September 22, 1930 to August 15, 1931.

24 hours   Zdzislaw Szubski paddled 157.1 miles in a Jaguar K1 canoe on the Vistula River, Wockawek to Gdansk, Poland, September 11–12, 1987.

Flat water   Marinda Hartzenberg (South Africa) paddled, without benefit of current, 137.13 miles on Loch Logan, Bloemfontein, South Africa, December 31, 1990–January 1, 1991.

Open sea   Randy Fine (U.S.) paddled 120.6 miles along the Florida coast, June 26–27, 1986.

Greatest lifetime distance in a canoe   Fritz Lindner of Berlin, Germany totaled 64,278 miles of canoeing from 1928 to 1987.

Eskimo rolls Ray Hudspith achieved 1,000 rolls in 34 min. 43 sec. at the Elswick Pool, Newcastle-upon-Tyne, England on March 20, 1987. He completed 100 rolls in 3 min. 7.25 sec. at Killingworth Leisure Centre, Tyne and Wear, England on March 3, 1991.

Randy Fine (U.S.) completed 1,796 continuous rolls at Biscayne Bay, Miami, FL on June 8, 1991.

Canoe raft A raft of 568 kayaks and canoes, organized by the Nottinghamshire County Scout Council with the help of scouts from other counties, was held together by hands only, while free floating for 30 seconds on the River Trent, Nottingham, England on June 30, 1991.

Longest race The Canadian Government Centennial Voyageur Canoe Pageant and Race from Rocky Mountain House, Alberta to the Expo 67 site in Montreal, Quebec was 3,283 miles. Ten canoes represented Canadian provinces and territories. The winner of the race, which took from May 24 to September 4, 1967, was the Province of Manitoba canoe *Radisson*.

Fastest Rhine crossing The fastest time to paddle the length of the River Rhine is 10 days 12 hr. 9 min. by Frank Palmer (Great Britain), May 15–25, 1988. The supported team record is 7 days 23 hr. 31 sec. by the RAF Laarbruch Canoe Club, led by Andy Goodsell (Great Britain), May 17–24, 1989.

CRICKET

TEST CRICKET

Career records The most runs scored by an individual is 11,174, by Allan Border (Australia) in 156 Tests, 1978–94. The most wickets taken by a bowler is 434, by Kapil Dev (India) in 131 Tests, 1978–94. The most dismissals by a wicket-keeper is 355, by Rodney Marsh (Australia), in 96 Tests, 1970–84. The most catches by a fielder is 156, by Allan Border in 156 Tests, 1978–94.

The best all-around Test career record is that of Kapil Dev, with 5,248 runs, 434 wickets and 64 catches in 131 matches, 1978–94.

ONE-DAY CRICKET

World Cup The West Indies are the only double winners, in 1975 and 1979.

International Team The highest innings scored by a team is 363–7 (55 overs) by England vs. Pakistan in Nottingham, England on August 20, 1992. The lowest completed innings total is 43 by Pakistan vs. the West Indies in Cape Town, South Africa on February 25, 1993. The largest victory margin is 232 runs by Australia vs. Sri Lanka (323–2 to 91), in Adelaide, Australia on January 28, 1985.

Individual The highest individual score is 189 not out by Viv Richards for the West Indies vs. England in Manchester, England on May 31, 1984. The best bowling analysis is 7–37 by Aqib Javed for Pakistan vs. India in Sharjah, UAE on October 25, 1991. The best partnership is 263 by Aamir Sohail (134) and Inzamam-ul-Haq (137 not out) for Pakistan vs. New Zealand in Sharjah on April 20, 1994.

Career The most matches played is 273 by Allan Border (Australia), 1979–94. The most runs scored is 8,648 (av. 41.37) by Desmond Haynes (West Indies) in 238 matches, 1977–94; this total includes a record 17 centuries. The most wickets taken is 273 by Wasim Akram (Pakistan) in 189 matches, 1985–95. The most dismissals is 204 (183 catches, 21 stumpings) by Jeff Dujon (West Indies) in 169 matches, 1981–91. The most catches by a fielder is 127 by Border.

NATIONAL CRICKET CHAMPIONSHIPS

Australia The premier event in Australia is the Sheffield Shield, an interstate competition contested since 1891–92. New South Wales has won the title a record 42 times.

England The major championship in England is the County Championships, an intercounty competition officially recognized since 1890. Yorkshire has won the title a record 30 times.

India The Ranji Trophy is India's premier cricket competition. It is contested on a zonal basis, culminating in a playoff competition. Bombay has won the tournament a record 32 times.

New Zealand Since 1975, the major championship in New Zealand has been the Shell Trophy. Auckland has won the competition a record five times.

Pakistan Pakistan's national championship is the Quaid-e-Azam Trophy, established in 1953. Karachi has won the trophy a record nine times.

South Africa The Currie Cup, donated by Sir Donald Currie, was first contested in 1889. Transvaal has won the competition (called the Castle Cup since 1991/92) a record 28 times.

DID YOU KNOW?

Five women's World Cups have been staged in cricket. Australia has won three times, in 1978, 1982 and 1988. The highest individual score in this competition is 143 not out by Lindsay Reeler for Australia vs. Netherlands in Perth, Australia on November 29, 1988.

West Indies The Red Stripe Cup, established in 1966, is the premier prize played for by the association of Caribbean islands (plus Guyana) that form the West Indies Cricket League. Barbados has won the competition 14 times.

CROQUET

International trophy The MacRobertson Shield (instituted 1925 and held every three years) has been won a record nine times by Great Britain, in 1925, 1937, 1956, 1963, 1969, 1974, 1982, 1990 and 1993.

A record seven appearances have been made by John G. Prince (New Zealand), in 1963, 1969, 1975, 1979, 1982, 1986 and 1990; on his debut he was the youngest-ever international, at 17 yr. 190 days.

World Championships The most wins is three, by Robert Fulford (Great Britain), 1990, 1992 and 1994.

USCA National Championships The first United States Championships were played in 1977. J. Archie Peck has won the singles title four times, 1977, 1979–80 and 1982. Ted Prentis has won the doubles title four times with three different partners, 1978, 1980–81 and 1988. The teams of Ted Prentis and Ned Prentis (1980–81), Dana Dribben and Ray Bell (1985–86), and Reid Fleming and Debbie Cornelius (1990–91) have each won the doubles title twice. The New York Croquet Club has won a record six National Club Championships, 1980–83, 1986 and 1988.

CROSS-COUNTRY RUNNING

World Championships The greatest margin of victory is 56 seconds or 390 yards by Jack Holden (England) at Ayr Racecourse, Strathclyde, Scotland on March 24, 1934.

United States The U.S. has never won either of the men's team races, but Lynn Jennings has won the women's individual title three times, 1990–92, and Craig Virgin won the men's individual race twice, in 1980–81.

Most wins England has the most team victories, with 45 for the men's team. The U.S. and the USSR each have a record eight women's team victories.

The greatest team domination was by Kenya in Auckland, New Zealand on March 26, 1988. Kenya's senior men's team finished eight men in the first nine, with a low score of 23 (six to score), and its junior men's team set a record low score, 11 (four to score) with six in the first seven.

At the 1995 World Cross-Country Championships, Kenya won the men's senior team title for a record 10th time in succession. The winner of the individual title was Paul Tergat (9). (*Allsport/C. Mason*)

Kenya won the men's senior team title for a record 10th time in succession at the 1995 World Cross-Country Championships.

The greatest number of individual victories is five, by John Ngugi (Kenya), 1986–89 and 1992; by Doris Brown-Heritage (U.S.), 1967–71; and by Grete Waitz (née Andersen; Norway), 1978–81 and 1983.

Most appearances Marcel van de Wattyne (Belgium) ran in a record 20 races, 1946–65. The women's record is 16, by Jean Lochhead (Wales), 1967–79, 1981, 1983–84.

U.S. National Championships In this competition, first staged in 1890, the most wins in the men's race is eight, by Pat Porter, 1982–89. The most wins in the women's championships is eight, by Lynn Jennings, 1985 and 1987–93.

Largest cross-country field The largest recorded field in any cross-country race was 11,763 starters (10,810 finished), in the 18.6-mile Lidingöloppet, near Stockholm, Sweden on October 3, 1982.

CURLING

Most titles Canada has won the men's World Championships 23 times, 1959–64, 1966, 1968–72, 1980, 1982–83, 1985–87, 1989–90 and 1993–95.

The most women's World Championships (instituted 1979) is eight, by Canada (1980, 1984–87, 1989, 1993–94).

United States The U.S. has won the men's world title four times, with Bud Somerville skip on the first two winning teams, 1965 and 1974.

United States National Championship *Men* In this competition, first held in 1957, two curlers have been skips on five championship teams: Bud Somerville (Superior, WI Curling Club in 1965, 1968–69, 1974, 1981), and Bruce Roberts (Hibbing Curling Club, MN in 1966–67, 1976–77, 1984). Bill Strum of the Superior, WI Curling Club has been a member of five title teams, in 1965, 1967, 1969, 1974 and 1978.

Women In this competition, first held in 1977, Nancy Langley (Seattle, WA) has been the skip of a record four championship teams, 1979, 1981, 1983 and 1988.

The Labatt Brier (formerly the Macdonald Brier 1927–79) The Brier is the Canadian Men's Curling championship. The competition was first held at the Granite Club, Toronto in 1927. The most wins is 23, by Manitoba (1928–32, 1934, 1936, 1938, 1940, 1942, 1947, 1949, 1952–53, 1956, 1965, 1970–72, 1979, 1981, 1984 and 1992). Ernie Richardson (Saskatchewan) has been winning skip a record four times (1959–60, 1962–63). His brothers Arnold and Sam Richardson were also members of each championship team.

BONSPIEL!

The largest curling tournament in the world is the Manitoba Curling Association Bonspiel, held annually in Winnipeg, Canada. In 1988, there were 1,424 4-man teams, a total of 5,696 curlers, using 187 sheets of curling ice.

Fastest game Eight curlers from the Burlington Golf and Country Club curled an 8-end game in 47 min. 24 sec., with time penalties of 5 min. 30 sec., in Burlington, Ontario, Canada on April 4, 1986, following rules agreed on with the Ontario Curling Association. The time is taken from when the first rock crosses the near hogline until the game's last rock comes to a complete stop.

Longest curling throw The longest throw of a curling stone was a distance of 576 ft. 4 in., by Eddie Kulbacki (Canada) at Park Lake, Neepawa, Manitoba, Canada on January 29, 1989. The attempt took place on a specially prepared sheet of curling ice on frozen Park Lake, a record 1,200 feet long.

Largest rink The Big Four Curling Rink, Calgary, Alberta, Canada, opened in 1959 and closed in 1989. Ninety-six teams and 384 players were accommodated on two floors, each with 24 sheets of ice.

CYCLING

Fastest speed   The fastest speed ever achieved on a bicycle is 152.284 MPH, by John Howard (U.S.) behind a windshield at Bonneville Salt Flats, UT on July 20, 1985. Considerable help was provided by the slipstreaming effect of the lead vehicle.

The 24-hour record behind pace is 1,216.8 miles, by Michael Secrest at Phoenix International Raceway, AZ, April 26–27, 1990.

Fastest rollercycling speed   James Baker (U.S.) achieved a record speed of 153.2 MPH at El Con Mall, Tucson, AZ on January 28, 1989.

Most titles   *Olympic*   The most gold medals won is three, by Paul Masson (France) in 1896; Francisco Verri (Italy) in 1906; Robert Charpentier (France) in 1936; and Daniel Morelon (France) in 1968 and 1972.

Burton Cecil Down (U.S.) won a record six medals at the 1904 Games—two gold, three silver and one bronze. The only American woman to win a cycling gold medal is Connie Carpenter-Phinney, who won the individual road race in 1984. She became the first woman to compete in both the Winter and the Summer Olympics, as she had competed as a speed skater in 1972.

World   World Championships are contested annually. They were first staged for amateurs in 1893 and for professionals in 1895.

The most wins in a particular event is 10, by Koichi Nakano (Japan), professional sprint 1977–86.

The most world titles won by a U.S. cyclist is five, in women's 3 km pursuit, by Rebecca Twigg, 1982, 1984–85, 1987 and 1993. The most successful man is Greg LeMond, winner of the individual road race in 1983 and 1989.

United States   National cycling championships have been held annually since 1899. Women's events were first included in 1937.

Leonard Nitz has won the most titles, 16: five pursuit (1976 and 1980–83); eight team pursuit (1980–84, 1986 and 1988–89); two 1-km timetrial (1982 and 1984); and one criterium (1986). Rebecca Twigg has won 14 titles in women's events: five time trials (1982, 1984, 1986, 1993–94); one points race (1984); one match sprint (1984); five pursuits (1981–82, 1984, 1986, 1992); one criterium (1993); and one road race (1983).

HIGH-WHEELING!

In 1992, Stephen Carter set the record for crossing the United States on a high-wheel cycle. The journey took 33 days 7 hr.

Tour de France   The greatest number of wins in the Tour de France is five, by Jacques Anquetil (France), 1957, 1961–64; Eddy Merckx (Belgium),

1969–72 and 1974; and Bernard Hinault (France), 1978–79, 1981–82 and 1985. Greg LeMond (U.S.) became the first American winner in 1986, and returned from serious injury to win again in 1989 and 1990.

The closest race ever was in 1989, when after 2,030 miles over 23 days (July 1–23) Greg LeMond, who completed the Tour in 87 hr. 38 min. 35 sec., beat Laurent Fignon (France) in Paris, France by only eight seconds.

The fastest average speed was 24.547 MPH, by Miguel Indurain (Spain) in 1992.

Women   The inaugural women's Tour de France was staged in 1984. Jeannie Longo (France) has won the event a record four times, 1987–90.

TOUR DE FRANCE STAGE WINS

Rider	Stages
Eddy Merckx (Belgium)	35
Bernard Hinault (France)	28
André Leducq (France)	25
André Darrigade (France)	22
Nicolas Frantz (Luxemburg)	20

Longest one-day race   The longest single-day "massed start" road race is the Bordeaux–Paris, France event of 342–385 miles. Paced over all or part of the route, the highest average speed was 29.32 MPH, by Herman van Springel (Belgium) for 363.1 miles in 13 hr. 35 min. 18 sec., in 1981.

Cross-America   The trans-America solo record recognized by the Ultra-Marathon Cycling Association is 8 days 3 hr. 11 min., by Rob Kish from Costa, CA to New York, in the 1992 Race Across AMerica. The women's record is 9 days 8 hr. 54 min., by Seana Hogan, also in the Race Across AMerica.

Most wins   Five cyclists have won two titles: Bob Fourney, 1990–91; Lon Haldeman, 1982–83; Rob Kish, 1992, 1994; Susan Notorangelo, 1985, 1989; and Pete Penseyres, 1984, 1986. Seana Hogan has won the Women's Division three times: 1992–93 and 1994.

Cycling the length of the Americas   Daniel Buettner, Bret Anderson, Martin Engel and Anne Knabe cycled the length of the Americas, from Prudhoe Bay, AK to the Beagle Channel, Ushuaia, Argentina from August 8, 1986 to June 13, 1987. They cycled a total distance of 15,266 miles.

Cross-Canada   The trans-Canada record is 13 days 9 hr. 6 min., by Bill Narasnek of Lively, Ontario, cycling 3,751 miles from Vancouver, British Columbia to Halifax, Nova Scotia, July 5–18, 1991.

Greatest distance   Thomas Godwin (Great Britain), cycling every day during the 365 days of 1939, covered 75,065 miles, or an average of 205.65

THE HOUR

The Hour is the most famous of cycling records, and the earliest noted achievement for it was 25.508 km (15.85 miles) by F.L. Dodds at Cambridge University Ground, Cambridge, England on March 25, 1876. The first popularly known holder of the record, however, was Henri Desgrange, who cycled 35.525 km (22.07 miles). He had only learned to ride a bicycle the previous year. Desgrange later organized the Tour de France, and the great names in the history of this race, such as Jacques Anquetil, Eddy Merckx and Miguel Indurain, have all made their mark on the Hour. The current best was set by Tony Rominger, with 55.291 km (34.36 miles).

The current women's record for the Hour is 47.112 km (29.27 miles) by Catherine Marsal (above) in Bordeaux, France on April 29, 1995.

CYCLING RECORDS

These records are those recognized by the Union Cycliste Internationale (UCI).
From January 1, 1993, its severely reduced list no longer distinguished between those set by professionals and amateurs, indoor and outdoor, at altitude and at sea level.

	min : sec	Name and Country	Place	Date
MEN				
Unpaced Standing Start				
1 km	1:02.091	Maic Malchow (East Germany)	Colorado Springs, CO	Aug. 28, 1986
4 km	4:20.894	Graeme Obree (Great Britain)	Hamar, Norway	Aug. 19, 1993
4 km team	4:03.822	Australia	Hamar, Norway	Aug. 20, 1993
Unpaced Flying Start				
200 meters	0:10.099	Vladimir Adamashvili (USSR)	Moscow, USSR	Aug. 6, 1990
500 meters	0:26.649	Aleksandr Kirichenko (USSR)	Moscow, USSR	Oct. 29, 1988
Unpaced—One Hour	55.291 km	Tony Rominger (Switzerland)	Bordeaux, France	Nov. 6, 1994
WOMEN				
Unpaced Standing Start				
500 m	0:33.438	Galina Yenyukhina (Russia)	Moscow, Russia	Apr. 29, 1993
3 km	3:37.347	Rebecca Twigg (U.S.)	Hamar, Norway	Aug. 20, 1993
Unpaced Flying Start				
200 meters	0:10.831	Olga Slyusareva (USSR)	Moscow, USSR	Aug. 6, 1990
500 meters	0:29.655	Erika Salumäe (USSR)	Moscow, USSR	Aug. 6, 1987
Unpaced—One Hour	47.112 km	Catherine Marsal (France)	Bordeaux, France	Apr. 29, 1995

miles per day. Continuing his effort, he went on to complete 100,000 miles in 500 days to May 14, 1940.

Jay Aldous and Matt DeWaal cycled 14,290 miles on an around-the-world trip from Place Monument, Salt Lake City, UT in 106 days, from April 2, to July 16, 1984.

Tal Burt (Israel) circumnavigated the world (13,523 road miles) from Place du Trocadero, Paris, France in 77 days 14 hr., from June 1 to August 17, 1992.

Greatest distance in one hour   The greatest distance covered in one hour is 122.28 km, by Leon Vanderstuyft (Belgium) on the Montlhéry Motor Circuit, France, on September 30, 1928, achieved from a standing start paced by a motorcycle.

Cycle touring   Walter Stolle amassed a record 402,000 miles, January 24, 1959–December 12, 1976. Starting from Romford, England, he visited 159 countries. From 1922 to December 25, 1973, Tommy Chambers of Glasgow, Scotland rode a verified total of 799,405 miles.

Visiting every continent, John W. Hathaway (Great Britain) of Vancouver, British Columbia, Canada covered 50,600 miles from November 10, 1974 to October 6, 1976.

Ronald and Sandra Slaughter hold the U.S. record for tandem bicycling, having traveled 18,077.5 miles around the world from December 30, 1989 to July 28, 1991.

The most participants in a bicycle tour were 31,678, in the 56-mile London-to-Brighton Bike Ride (England) on June 19, 1988. However, it is estimated that 45,000 cyclists took part in the 44-mile Tour de l'Ile de Montréal, Canada on June 7, 1992. The most participants in a tour in excess of 1,000 km is 2,037 (from 2,157 starters) for the Australian Bicentennial Caltex Bike Ride from Melbourne to Sydney, November 26–December 10, 1988.

Highest-altitude cycling   Canadians Bruce Bell, Philip Whelan and Suzanne MacFadyen cycled at an altitude of 22,834 feet on the peak of Mt. Aconcagua, Argentina on January 25, 1991. This feat was matched by Mozart Hastenreiter Catão (Brazil) on March 11, 1993 and by Tim Sumner (Great Britain) and Jonathan Greene (Great Britain) on January 6, 1994.

CYCLO-CROSS

The greatest number of World Championships (instituted 1950) has been won by Eric de Vlaeminck (Belgium), with the Amateur and Open in 1966 and six Professional titles in 1968–73.

DARTS

PROFESSIONAL DARTS

Most titles   Eric Bristow (Great Britain) has the most wins in the World Masters Championship (instituted 1974) with five, 1977, 1979, 1981 and

1983–84; the most in the World Professional Championship (instituted 1978) with five, 1980–81 and 1984–86; and the most in the World Cup Singles (instituted 1977) with four, 1983, 1985, 1987 and 1989.

SCORING RECORDS

Fewest darts The lowest number of darts thrown for a score of 1,001 is 19, by Cliff Inglis (Great Britain) (160, 180, 140, 180, 121, 180, 40) at the Bromfield Men's Club, Devon, England on November 11, 1975; and by Jocky Wilson (Great Britain) (140, 140, 180, 180, 180, 131, Bull) at The London Pride, Bletchley, England on March 23, 1989.

A score of 2,001 in 52 darts was achieved by Alan Evans (Great Britain) in Ferndale, Wales on September 3, 1976.

A score of 3,001 in 73 darts was thrown by Tony Benson at the Plough Inn, Gorton, England on July 12, 1986. Linda Batten set a women's 3,001 record of 117 darts at the Old Wheatsheaf, London, England on April 2, 1986.

A score of 100,001 was achieved in 3,579 darts by Chris Gray at the Dolphin, Cromer, England on April 27, 1993.

Roy Blowes (Canada) was the first person to achieve a 501 in nine darts, "double-on, double-off," at the Widgeons Pub, Calgary, Canada on March 9, 1987. His scores were: bull, treble 20, treble 17, five treble 20s and a double 20 to finish.

Highest score Team The highest score in 24 hours is 1,722,249, by the Broken Hill Darts Club (eight players) in Broken Hill, New South Wales, Australia, September 28–29, 1985.

The women's record is 744,439 by a team of eight players from the Lord Clyde, London, England, October 13–14, 1990.

Doubles The highest score by a 2-man team retrieving their own darts, in 10 hours, is 465,919 by Jon Archer and Neil Rankin on November 17, 1990 at the Royal Oak, Cossington, Leicester, England.

Individual The highest score in 24 hours by an individual is 566,175, by Russell Locke in Hugglescote, England, September 17–18, 1993.

Bulls and 25s An 8-member team scored 526,750 points at the George Inn, Morden, England, July 1–2, 1994.

Million and One Up Men (8 players) 36,583 darts by a team at Buzzy's Pub and Grub, Lynn, MA, October 19–20, 1991.

Women (8 players) 70,019 darts by The Delinquents darts team at the Top George Pub, Combe Martin, England, September 11–13, 1987.

10-hour bulls (individual) 1,320, by John Lowe (U.S.) at The Unicorn Tavern, Chesterfield, England on October 27, 1994.

10-hour trebles 3,056, by Paul Taylor (Great Britain) at the Woodhouse Tavern, Leytonstone, England on October 19, 1985.

10-hour doubles   3,265, by Paul Taylor at the Lord Brooke, Walthamstow, England on September 5, 1987.

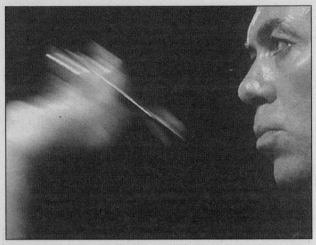

John Lowe set the record for the most bulls in 10 hours; he hit 1,320 bull's-eyes, beating the previous record by 59. (*Allsport/H. Boylan*)

SPEED RECORDS

The fastest time taken to complete three games of 301, finishing on doubles, is 1 min. 38 sec., by Ritchie Gardner on the British TV show *Record Breakers*, on September 12, 1989.

The record time for going around the board clockwise in "doubles" at arm's length is 9.2 seconds, by Dennis Gower at the Millers Arms, Hastings, England on October 12, 1975.

The record for around-the-board in numerical order is 14.5 seconds by Jim Pike at the Craven Club, Newmarket, England in March 1944.

The record for this feat at the 9-foot throwing distance, retrieving own darts, is 2 min. 13 sec. by Bill Duddy at The Plough, London, England on October 29, 1972.

EQUESTRIAN SPORTS

CARRIAGE DRIVING

Most team titles World Championships were first held in 1972. Three team titles have been won by Great Britain, 1972, 1974 and 1980; by Hungary, 1976, 1978 and 1984; and by the Netherlands, 1982, 1986 and 1988.

Most individual titles Two individual titles have been won by György Bárdos (Hungary), 1978 and 1980; by Tjeerd Velstra (Netherlands), 1982 and 1986; and by Ijsbrand Chardon (Netherlands), 1988 and 1992.

Most animals in a hitch Floyd Zopfi of Stratford, WI has driven 52 llamas in a hitch on several occasions since 1990, with the lead llamas (four abreast) on reins 150 feet long.

Coaching The longest horse-drawn procession was a cavalcade of 68 carriages that measured 3,018 feet "nose to tail," organized by the Spies Traveling Company of Denmark on May 7, 1986. It carried 810 people through the woods around Copenhagen to celebrate the coming of spring.

HITCHED!

The only man to drive 48 horses in a single hitch is Dick Sparrow of Zearing, IA, 1972–77. The lead horses were on reins 135 feet long.

DRESSAGE

Olympic Games and World Championships Germany (West Germany 1968–90) has won a record eight team Olympic gold medals, 1928, 1936, 1964, 1968, 1976, 1984, 1988 and 1992, and has the most team wins, seven, at the World Championships (instituted 1966). Dr. Reiner Klimke (West Germany) has won a record six Olympic golds (team 1964–88, individual, 1984). He won individual bronze in 1976, for a record seven medals overall, and is the only rider to have won two world titles, on Mehmed in 1974 and on Ahlerich in 1982. Henri St. Cyr (Sweden) won two individual Olympic gold medals, in 1952 and 1956. This was equaled by Nicole Uphoff (Germany) in 1992; she had previously won in 1988.

World Cup This competition (instituted 1986) has had two double winners: Christine Stückelberger (Switzerland) on Gauguin de Lully, 1987–88, and Monica Theodorescu (Greece) on Ganimedes Tecrent, in 1993–94.

SHOW JUMPING

Olympic Games   The most Olympic gold medals won by a rider is five, by Hans-Günter Winkler (West Germany)—four team wins in 1956, 1960, 1964 and 1972 and the individual Grand Prix in 1956. He also won team silver in 1976 and team bronze in 1968, for a record seven medals overall.

The most team wins in the Prix des Nations is six, by Germany in 1936, 1956, 1960, 1964 and as West Germany in 1972 and 1988.

The lowest score obtained by a winner is no faults, by Frantisek Ventura (Czechoslovakia) on Eliot, 1928; Alwin Schockemöhle (West Germany) on Warwick Rex, 1976; and Ludger Beerbaum (Germany) on Classic Touch, in 1992.

Pierre Jonquères d'Oriola (France) uniquely won the individual gold medal twice, in 1952 and 1964.

United States   Two U.S. riders have won individual gold medals: Bill Steinkraus won in 1968 and also won two silvers and a bronze, 1952–68; and Joe Fargis won both individual and team gold medals in 1984 as well as team silver in 1988.

GUESS WHAT?

Q. WHAT WAS THE HIGHEST JUMP BY A DOG?

A. LOOK IN "DOGS" (LIVING WORLD)

World Championships   The men's World Championships (instituted 1953) have been won twice by Hans-Günter Winkler (1954–55) and Raimondo d'Inzeo (Italy) (1956 and 1960).

The women's title (1965–74) was won twice by Janou Tissot (née Lefebvre; France) on Rocket (1970 and 1974). A team competition was introduced in 1978, and the most wins is two, by France, 1982 and 1990.

President's Cup   Instituted in 1965 for Nations Cup teams, it has been won a record 14 times by Great Britain, in 1965, 1967, 1970, 1972–74, 1977–79, 1983, 1985–86, 1989 and 1991.

World Cup   In this competition, instituted in 1979, double winners have been Conrad Homfeld (U.S.), 1980 and 1985; Ian Millar (Canada), 1988 and 1989; and John Whitaker (Great Britain), 1990–91.

Jumping   The official *Fédération Equestre Internationale* records are: high jump, 8 ft. 1¼ in., by Huasó, ridden by Capt. Alberto Larraguibel Morales (Chile) at Viña del Mar, Santiago, Chile on February 5, 1949; long jump over water, 27 ft. 6¾ in., by Something, ridden by André Ferreira (South Africa) in Johannesburg, South Africa on April, 25 1975.

THREE-DAY EVENT

Olympic Games and World Championships Charles Pahud de Mortanges (Netherlands) won a record four Olympic gold medals: team 1924 and 1928, individual (riding Marcroix) 1928 and 1932.

Bruce Davidson (U.S.) is the only rider to have won two world titles (instituted 1966), on Irish Cap in 1974 and on Might Tango in 1978.

United States J. Michael Plumb has won a record six medals for the United States: team gold 1976 and 1984, and four silver medals, team 1964, 1968 and 1972, and individual 1976. Tad Coffin is the only U.S. rider to have won both team and individual gold medals, in 1976.

Badminton Horse Trials Lucinda Green (née Prior-Palmer; Great Britain) has won the Badminton Three-Day Event (instituted 1949) a record six times, in 1973 (on Be Fair), 1976 (Wide Awake), 1977 (George), 1979 (Killaire), 1983 (Regal Realm) and 1984 (Beagle Bay).

FENCING

Most titles *Olympic* The most individual Olympic gold medals won is three, by Ramón Fonst (Cuba) in 1900 and 1904 (two); and by Nedo Nadi (Italy) in 1912 and 1920 (two). Nadi also won three team gold medals in 1920, making five gold medals at one celebration, the record for fencing. Aladár Gerevich (Hungary) won seven golds—one individual and six team.

Edoardo Mangiarotti (Italy), with six gold, five silver and two bronze, holds the record of 13 Olympic medals in fencing. He won them for foil and épée from 1936 to 1960.

The most gold medals won by a woman is four (one individual, three team) by Yelena Novikova (née Belova; USSR) from 1968 to 1976, and the women's record for all medals is seven (two gold, three silver, two bronze) by Ildikó Sági (formerly Ujlaki, née Retjö; Hungary), 1960–76.

World The greatest number of individual world titles won is five, by Aleksandr Romankov (USSR), in foil 1974, 1977, 1979, 1982 and 1983. Christian d'Oriola (France) won four world foil titles, 1947, 1949, 1953–54, as well as two individual Olympic titles (1952 and 1956).

Four women foilists have won three world titles: Helene Mayer (Germany), 1929, 1931, 1937; Ilona Schacherer-Elek (Hungary), 1934–35, 1951; Ellen Müller-Preis (Austria), 1947, 1949–50; and Cornelia Hanisch (West Germany), 1979, 1981, 1985. Of these only Ilona Schacherer-Elek also won two individual Olympic titles (1936 and 1948).

The longest time span for winning an individual world or Olympic title is 20 years, by Aladár Gerevich (Hungary) in saber, 1935–55.

United States National Championships The most U.S. titles won in one weapon is 13 in saber, by Peter Westbrook, in 1974, 1975, 1979–86, 1988, 1989 and 1995. The women's record is 10 in foil, by Janice Romary in 1950–51, 1956–57, 1960–61, 1964–66 and 1968.

The most men's individual foil championships won is eight, by Michael Marx in 1977, 1979, 1982, 1985–87, 1990 and 1993. L.G. Nunes won the most épée championships, with six—1917, 1922, 1924, 1926, 1928 and 1932. Vincent Bradford won a record number of women's épée championships, with four in 1982–84 and 1986.

NCAA Championship Division I   *Men*   This event was inaugurated in 1941 and was combined with the team title in 1989. It was won a record 12 times by New York University (1947, 1954, 1957, 1960–61, 1966–67, 1970–71, 1973–74, 1976).

Michael Lofton (New York University) has won the most titles in a career, with four victories in saber, 1984–87. Abraham Balk (New York University) is the only man to win two individual titles in one year, 1947 (foil, épée).

Women   Wayne State (MI) has won the most titles in this event (inaugurated 1982), with three (1982, 1988–89).

Caitlin Bilodeaux (Columbia-Barnard) and Molly Sullivan (Notre Dame) have both won the individual title twice—Bilodeaux in 1985 and 1987; Sullivan in 1986 and 1988.

Team   In 1990, the NCAA team competition was combined for the first time. Penn State has won the team title three times (1990–91, 1995).

DID YOU KNOW?

The only U.S. Olympic fencing champion was Albertson Van Zo Post, who won the men's single sticks and team foil (with two Cubans) at the 1904 Games.

FIELD HOCKEY

Most Olympic medals   India was Olympic champion from 1928 until 1960, when Pakistan beat India 1–0 in Rome. India had its eighth win in 1980.

United States   U.S. men won the bronze medal in 1932, but only three teams played that year; U.S. women won the bronze in 1984.

World Cup   The World Cup for men was first held in 1971, and for women in 1974. The most wins are: *(men)* four by Pakistan, 1971, 1978, 1982 and 1994; *(women)* five by Netherlands, 1974, 1978, 1983, 1986 and 1990.

GOAL!

The greatest number of goals scored in international hockey is 267, by Paul Litjens (Netherlands) in 177 games.

MEN

Highest international score   The highest score was achieved when India defeated the U.S. 24–1 in Los Angeles, CA in the 1932 Olympic Games.

Most international appearances   Heiner Dopp represented West Germany 286 times between 1975 and 1990, indoors and out.

Best goalkeeping   Richard Allen (India) did not concede a goal at the 1928 Olympic tournament and gave up only a total of three in 1936.

Fastest goal in an international field hockey game   John French scored seven seconds after the bully-off for England vs. West Germany in Nottingham, England on April 25, 1971.

WOMEN

Most international appearances   Alison Ramsay has made a record 250 international appearances, 143 for Scotland and 107 for Great Britain, 1982–95.

United States   Sheryl Johnson made a record 137 appearances for the U.S., 1978–89.

Highest scores   The highest score in an international game was when England beat France 23–0 in Merton, London, England on February 3, 1923.

NCAA Division I   In this competition, inaugurated in 1981, Old Dominion University, Norfolk, VA has won the most championships with seven titles: 1982–84, 1988 and 1990–92.

FISHING

Largest single catch   The largest officially ratified fish ever caught on a rod was a great white shark (*Carcharodon carcharias*) weighing 2,664 pounds and measuring 16 ft. 10 in. long, caught on a 130-pound test line by Alf Dean in Denial Bay, near Ceduna, South Australia on April 21, 1959. A great white shark weighing 3,388 pounds was caught by Clive Green off Albany, Western Australia on April 26, 1976 but will remain unratified because whale meat was used as bait.

In June 1978, a great white shark measuring 20 ft. 4 in. long and weighing over 5,000 pounds was harpooned and landed by fishermen in the harbor of San Miguel, Azores.

The largest marine animal killed by *hand* harpoon was a blue whale 97 feet long, by Archer Davidson in Twofold Bay, New South Wales, Australia in 1910. Its jawbone measured 23 ft. 4 in. and its tail flukes 20 feet across.

The largest fish ever taken underwater was an 804-pound giant black grouper, by Don Pinder of the Miami Triton Club, FL in 1955.

World Freshwater Championship France won the European title in 1956 and 12 world titles between 1959 and 1990. The individual title has been won a record three times by Robert Tesse (France), 1959–60 and 1965; and by Bob Nudd (England), 1990–91, 1994.

The record weight (team) is 76.52 pounds in three hours by West Germany on the Neckar in Mannheim, Germany on September 21, 1980. The individual record is 37.45 pounds, by Wolf-Rüdiger Kremkus (West Germany) in Mannheim on September 20, 1980. The most fish caught is 652,

---

LONGEST FIGHT

The longest recorded individual fight with a fish is 37 hours, by Bob Ploeger (U.S.) with a King salmon on July 12–13, 1989.

---

by Jacques Isenbaert (Belgium) in Danaújváros, Hungary on August 27, 1967.

IGFA The heaviest freshwater category recognized by the International Game Fish Association is for the sturgeon; the record weight in this category is 468 pounds, caught by Joey Pallotta III on July 9, 1983 off Benicia, CA.

Fly fishing World fly fishing championships were inaugurated by the CIPS (Confédération de la Pêche Sportive) in 1981. The most team titles is five, by Italy, 1982–84, 1986, 1992. The most individual titles is two, by Brian Leadbetter (Great Britain), 1987 and 1991.

Casting The longest freshwater cast ratified under ICF (International Casting Federation) rules is 574 ft. 2 in., by Walter Kummerow (Germany), for the Bait Distance Double-Handed 30 g event held in Lenzerheide, Switzerland in the 1968 Championships.

At the currently contested weight of 17.7 g, known as 18 g Bait Distance, the longest Double-Handed cast is 457 ft. ¹/₂ in., by Kevin Carriero (U.S.) in Toronto, Ontario, Canada on July 24, 1984.

The longest Fly Distance Double-Handed cast is 319 ft. 1 in., by Wolfgang Feige (Germany) in Toronto, Ontario, Canada on July 23, 1984.

FOOT FEAT

Andy Linder (left) and Ted Martin (*Hans T. Martin*)

When Andy Linder met Ted Martin at a footbag tournament in 1988, the doubles record for keeping a footbag in the air was 33,000 kicks. "We had each done higher than that individually," recalls Andy, "so we figured we had a good chance of beating it together." Martin puts it a little differently: "I beat him at singles. Then we teamed up."

The rest, as they say, is history. Linder and Martin, both Illinois residents, set a record of 64,792 kicks in 1989. These days their record stands at 100,001—and nobody else is in sight. Together and separately, they dominate the sport, with six men's records between them.

Linder, 30, is a psychotherapist with a soccer background. "I stopped playing soccer at 18 when I injured my knee. I had been close to the record for soccer kicks—about 32,000—at the time. I converted my soccer style into footbag. I was able to progress pretty fast."

Martin, 35, manufactures contact lenses, and uses his talent for detail to craft his own footbags of leather from old purses and gloves. He was introduced to footbag by his college roommate, and "decided to get very good in it." To train, he rides his bicycle 40–50 miles at a time, lifts weights, and kicks the footbag 10,000 times a day. Certainly part of his talent is for concentration. "You have to be flexible, quick. One miss and it's over."

How do Linder and Martin create their magical teamwork? "We don't spend all that much time together, actually," says Linder. "We train on our own and only get together to practice passing. The key thing is that we feel we can depend on each other. When Ted has the bag and has to do a certain number of kicks, I have full faith that he'll do it."

Men's doubles The record is 100,001 hacks, by Andy Linder and Ted Martin (both U.S.) on April 9, 1994 in Mount Prospect, IL. The pair kept the footbag aloft for 15 hr. 38 min. 40 sec.

FOOTBAG

This sport, also sometimes known by the brand names Hackeysack and Sipa Sipa, originated in Oregon in 1972. Its inventor was John Stalberger (U.S.).

Men's singles   Ted Martin (U.S.) kept a footbag airborne for 51,155 consecutive kicks or hacks in 7 hr. 1 min. 37 sec., at the Green/White Soccer Center, Chicago, IL on May 29, 1993.

Women's singles   Constance Constable (U.S) holds the record, with 17,669 kicks in 2 hr. 58 min. 19 sec. on May 27, 1995, in Menlo Park, CA.

Men's doubles   The record is 100,001 hacks, by Andy Linder and Ted Martin (both U.S.) on April 9, 1994 in Mount Prospect, IL. The pair kept the footbag aloft for 15 hr. 38 min. 40 sec.

Women's doubles   The record is 34,543 kicks (5 hr. 38 min. 22 sec.), by Constance Constable and Tricia George (both U.S.) on February 18, 1995.

Most kicks in five minutes   Andy Linder (U.S.) achieved 956 kicks in five minutes on May 5, 1995 in Malta, IL. The women's record is 749, by Tricia George (U.S.) on May 27, 1995, in Menlo Park, CA.

Largest footbag circle   The largest continuous circle of people playing footbag was 862. This gathering was staged at Colorado State University in Fort Collins on June 24, 1986.

FOOTBALL

NATIONAL FOOTBALL LEAGUE (NFL) RECORDS

Most championships   The Green Bay Packers have won a record 11 NFL titles, 1929–31, 1936, 1939, 1944, 1961–62, 1965–67.

Most consecutive wins (regular season and playoffs)   The Chicago Bears have won 18 consecutive games twice, in 1933–34 and 1941–42. This was matched by the Miami Dolphins in 1972–73 and by the San Francisco 49ers in 1989–90. The most consecutive games without defeat is 25, by the Canton Bulldogs (22 wins and 3 ties) in 1921–23.

Most games played   George Blanda played in a record 340 games in a record 26 seasons in the NFL, for the Chicago Bears (1948–58), the Baltimore Colts (1950), the Houston Oilers (1960–66), and the Oakland Raiders (1967–75).
   The most consecutive games played is 282, by Jim Marshall for the Cleveland Browns (1960) and the Minnesota Vikings (1961–79).

NFL RECORDS

Most Points
Career 2,002, George Blanda (Chicago Bears, Baltimore Colts, Houston Oilers, Oakland Raiders), 1949–75. **Season** 176, Paul Hornung (Green Bay Packers), 1960. **Game** 40, Ernie Nevers (Chicago Cardinals), Nov. 28, 1929.

Most Touchdowns
Career 139, Jerry Rice (San Francisco 49ers), 1985–94. **Season** 24, John Riggins (Washington Redskins), 1983. **Game** 6, Ernie Nevers (Chicago Cardinals), Nov. 28, 1929; William "Dub" Jones (Cleveland Browns) Nov. 25, 1951; Gale Sayers (Chicago Bears), Dec. 12, 1965.

Most Yards Gained Rushing
Career 16,726, Walter Payton (Chicago Bears), 1975–87. **Season** 2,105, Eric Dickerson (Los Angeles Rams), 1984. **Game** 275, Walter Payton (Chicago Bears), Nov. 20, 1977. **Highest career average** 5.22 yd. per game (12,352 yd. from 2,359 attempts), Jim Brown (Cleveland Browns), 1957–65.

Most Yards Gained Receiving
Career 14,004, James Lofton (Green Bay Packers, Los Angeles Raiders, Buffalo Bills, Los Angeles Rams, Philadelphia Eagles), 1978–93. **Season** 1,746, Charley Hennigan (Houston Oilers), 1961. Game 336, Willie "Flipper" Anderson (Los Angeles Rams), Nov. 26, 1989.

Most Yards Gained Passing
Career 47,003, Fran Tarkenton (Minnesota Vikings, New York Giants), 1961–78. **Season** 5,084, Dan Marino (Miami Dolphins), 1984. **Game** 554, Norm Van Brocklin (Los Angeles Rams), Sep. 28, 1951.

Passing Attempts
Career 6,467, Fran Tarkenton (Minnesota Vikings, New York Giants), 1961–78. **Season** 691 Drew Bledsoe (New England Patroits), 1994. **Game** 70 Drew Bledsoe (New England Patriots), Nov. 13, 1994.

Most Passes Completed
Career 3,686, Fran Tarkenton (Minnesota Vikings, New York Giants), 1961–78. **Season** 404, Warren Moon (Houston Oilers), 1991. **Game** 45 (from 70 attempts), Drew Bledsoe (New England Patroits), Nov. 13, 1994. **Consecutive** 22, Joe Montana (San Francisco 49ers), Nov. 29, 1987 vs. Cleveland Browns (5); Dec. 6, 1987 vs. Green Bay Packers (17).

Pass Receptions
Career 934, Art Monk (Washington Redskins), 1980–95. **Season** 122, Cris Carter (Minnesota Vikings), 1994. **Game** 18, Tom Fears (Los Angeles Rams), Dec. 3, 1950.

Field Goals
Career 373, Jan Stenerud (Kansas City Chiefs, Green Bay Packers, Minnesota Vikings), 1967–85. **Season** 35, Ali Haji-Sheikh (New York Giants), 1983. **Game** 7, Jim Bakken (St. Louis Cardinals), Sep. 24, 1967; Rich Karlis (Minnesota Vikings), Nov. 5, 1989.

Punting
Career 1,154, Dave Jennings (New York Giants, New York Jets), 1974–87. **Season** 114, Bob Parsons (Chicago Bears), 1981. **Game** 15, John Teltschik (Philadelphia Eagles vs. New York Giants), Dec. 6, 1987.

Sacks
Career 145, Reggie White (Philadelphia Eagles, Green Bay Packers), 1985–94. **Season** 22, Mark Gastineau (New York Jets), 1984. **Game** 7, Derrick Thomas (Kansas City Chiefs vs. Seattle Seahawks), Nov. 11, 1990.

Most Interceptions
Career 81, Paul Krause (Washington Redskins, Minnesota Vikings), 1964–79. **Season** 14, Dick "Night Train" Lane (Los Angeles Rams), 1952. **Game** 4; 16 players have achieved this feat.

DID YOU KNOW?

On January 3, 1993, the Buffalo Bills, playing at home in the AFC Wild Card game, trailed the Houston Oilers 35–3 with 28 minutes remaining. The Bills eventually won the game in overtime, overcoming a deficit of 32 points—the largest in NFL history.

Longest run from scrimmage   Tony Dorsett completed a touchdown after a run of 99 yards for the Dallas Cowboys vs. the Minnesota Vikings on January 3, 1983.

Longest field goal   The longest field goal was 63 yards, by Tom Dempsey for the New Orleans Saints vs. the Detroit Lions, November 8, 1970.

Longest pass completion   A pass completion of 99 yards has been achieved on seven occasions and has always resulted in a touchdown. The most recent was a pass from Stan Humphries to Kelvin Martin of the San Diego Chargers against the Seattle Seahawks on September 18, 1994.

Longest punt   The record is held by Steve O'Neal, who achieved a punt of 98 yards for the New York Jets vs. the Denver Broncos on September 21, 1969.

Longest interception return   The longest interception return is 103 yards, by two players: Vencie Glenn, San Diego Chargers vs. Denver Broncos, November 29, 1987; and Louis Oliver, Miami Dolphins vs. Buffalo Bills, October 4, 1992, both for touchdowns.

Longest kickoff return   Three players share the record for a kickoff return at 106 yards: Al Carmichael, Green Bay Packers vs. Chicago Bears, October 7, 1956; Noland Smith, Kansas City Chiefs vs. Denver Broncos, December 17, 1967; and Roy Green, St. Louis Cardinals vs. Dallas Cowboys, October 21, 1979. All three players scored touchdowns.

Longest punt return   Robert Bailey, of the Los Angeles Rams, set the record for the longest punt return at 103 yards, while playing against the New Orleans Saints on October 23, 1994.

Most successful coaches   The most successful coach in NFL history is Don Shula, with 338 victories—73 with the Baltimore Colts (1963–69) and 265 with the Miami Dolphins (1970–present). The highest winning percentage was .740, achieved by Vince Lombardi (1913–70): 105 wins, 35 losses and 6 ties with the Green Bay Packers, 1959–67, and the Washington Redskins, 1969.

THE SUPER BOWL

The Super Bowl was first held in 1967 between the winners of the NFL and AFL championships. Since 1970, it has been contested by the winners of

During the 1994 season, Jerry Rice of the San Francisco 49ers (80) broke the career record for most touchdowns. At the Super Bowl, he set a number of game and career records with the assistance of MVP Steve Young (8). Young also threw the fastest touchdown in Super Bowl history—1 min. 24 sec.—to Jerry Rice. (*Allsport[U.S.]/O. Greule and R. Stewart*)

the National and American Conferences of the NFL. The most wins is five, by the San Francisco 49ers in 1982, 1985, 1989–90 and 1995.

Most appearances   The Dallas Cowboys have played in seven Super Bowls: V, VI, X, XII, XIII, XXVII and XXVIII. The Cowboys have won four and lost three.

Don Shula has coached six Super Bowls: Baltimore Colts, 1968; Miami Dolphins, 1971–73, 1982, 1984. He won two games and lost four.

Highest scores   The highest aggregate score was 75 points, set when the San Francisco 49ers beat the San Diego Chargers 49–26 in Superbowl XXIX on January 29, 1995.

Smallest margin of victory   The narrowest margin of victory was one point, when the New York Giants defeated the Buffalo Bills 20–19 on January 27, 1991.

Individual game records   *Points*   The most points scored is 18, by: Roger Craig, San Francisco 49ers (vs. Denver Broncos, 1989); Jerry Rice, San Francisco 49ers (vs. Denver Broncos, 1989 and vs. San Diego Chargers, 1995); and Ricky Watters, San Francisco 49ers (vs. San Diego Chargers, 1995).

Touchdowns   The most touchdowns thrown is 6, by Steve Young, San Francisco 49ers (vs. San Diego Chargers, 1995). The most touchdowns scored is 3, by three players: Roger Craig, San Francisco 49ers (vs. Miami Dolphins, 1984); Jerry Rice, San Francisco 49ers (vs. Denver Broncos, 1989 and vs. San Diego Chargers, 1995); and Ricky Watters, San Francisco 49ers (vs. San Diego Chargers, 1995).

Yards gained   The most yards gained rushing is 204, by Timmy Smith, Washington Redskins (vs. Denver Broncos, 1987). The most yards gained passing is 357, by Joe Montana, San Francisco 49ers (vs. Cincinnati Bengals, 1988). The most yards gained receiving is 215, by Jerry Rice, San Francisco 49ers (vs. Cincinnati Bengals, 1988).

Completions   The most completions thrown is 31, by Jim Kelly, Buffalo Bills (vs. Dallas Cowboys, 1994). The highest pass completion mark is 88 percent (22–25) by Phil Simms, New York Giants (vs. Denver Broncos, 1986).

Receptions   The most receptions is 11, by two players: Dan Ross, Cincinnati Bengals (vs. San Francisco 49ers, 1981) and Jerry Rice, San Francisco 49ers (vs. Cincinnati Bengals, 1988).

COLLEGE FOOTBALL (NCAA)

Team records   *Most wins*   Michigan has won 747 games out of 1,029 played, 1879–1995.

Highest winning percentage   The highest winning percentage is .760, by Notre Dame. The Fighting Irish have won 729, lost 216 and tied 42 out of 987 games played, 1887–1995.

Career records (Divisions I-A, I-AA, II and III) *Points scored* 528, Carey Bender, Coe College (Div. III), 1991–94.

Rushing (yards) 6,320, Johnny Bailey, Texas A&I (Div. II), 1986–89.

Passing (yards) 15,031, Ty Detmer, Brigham Young (Div. I-A), 1988–91.

Receptions (yards) 4,693, Jerry Rice, Mississippi Valley (Div. I-AA), 1981–84.

Receptions (most) 301, Jerry Rice, Mississippi Valley (Div. I-AA), 1981–84.

Field goals (game) 8, Goran Lingmerth, Northern Arizona (Div. I-AA). Booting 8 out of 8 kicks, Lingmerth set the record on October 25, 1986 vs. Idaho.

Longest streak The University of Oklahoma won 47 successive games 1953–57, until they were beaten 7–0 by Notre Dame. The longest unbeaten streak is 63 (59 won, 4 tied) by Washington, 1907–17, ended by a 27–0 loss to California.

Most successful coaches In Division I-A competition, Paul "Bear" Bryant won more games than any other coach, with 323 wins over 38 years: Maryland 1945, Kentucky 1946–53, Texas A&M 1954–57 and Alabama 1958–82. He led Alabama to five national titles and 15 bowl wins, including seven Sugar Bowls. The best win percentage in Division I-A was .881, by Knute Rockne (1888–1931), with 105 wins, 12 losses and 5 ties, 12,847 points for and 667 against, at Notre Dame 1918–30. In overall NCAA competition, Eddie Robinson, Grambling (Division I-AA) holds the mark for most victories, with 388 through 1993.

National College Football Champions The most wins in the national journalists' poll, established in 1936 to determine the college team of the year, is eight, by Notre Dame, in 1943, 1946–47, 1949, 1966, 1973, 1977 and 1988.

Bowl games The oldest college bowl game is the Rose Bowl. It was first played on January 1, 1902 at Tournament Park, Pasadena, CA, when Michigan beat Stanford 49–0. The University of Southern California

---

CROWD!

The highest college football game attendances were estimated crowds of 120,000 at Soldier Field, Chicago, IL on November 26, 1927, when Notre Dame beat Southern California 7–6, and on October 13, 1928, when Notre Dame beat Navy 7–0. The highest average attendance for home games was 106,217, by Michigan in 1994.

NCAA DIVISION I-A INDIVIDUAL RECORDS

Points

Game ....48 ....Howard Griffith (Illinois vs. Southern Illinois; 8 touchdowns) ....Sep. 22, 1990
Season ....234 ....Barry Sanders (Oklahoma State; 39 touchdowns in 11 games) 1988
Career ....423 ....Roman Anderson (Houston; 70 field goals, 213 point-after-touchdowns) 1988–91

Total yardage

Game ....732 ....David Klingler (Houston vs. Arizona State; 716 passing, 16 rushing) ....Dec. 1, 1990
Season ....5,221 ....David Klingler (Houston; 5,140 passing, 81 rushing) 1990
Career ....14,665 ....Ty Detmer (Brigham Young; 15,031 passing, 366 rushing) 1988–91

Yards gained rushing

Game ....396 ....Tony Sands (Kansas vs. Missouri) ....Nov. 23, 1991
Season ....2,628 ....Barry Sanders (Oklahoma State; 344 rushes in 11 games, record av. 238.9) 1988
Career ....6,082 ....Tony Dorsett (Pittsburgh) 1973–76

Yards gained passing

Game ....716 ....David Klingler (Houston vs. Arizona State) ....Dec. 1, 1990
Season ....5,188 ....Ty Detmer (Brigham Young) 1990
Career ....15,031 ....Ty Detmer (Brigham Young; completed 958 of 1,530) 1988–91

Pass completions

Game ....48 ....David Klingler (Houston vs. SMU) ....Oct. 20, 1990
Season ....374 ....David Klingler (Houston) 1990
Career ....958 ....Ty Detmer (Brigham Young; 1,530 attempts) 1988–91

Touchdown passes

Game ....11 ....David Klingler (Houston vs. Eastern Washington) ....Nov. 17, 1990
Season ....54 ....David Klingler (Houston) 1990
Career ....121 ....Ty Detmer (Brigham Young) 1988–91

Pass receptions

Game	23	Randy Gatewood (UNLV vs. Idaho)	Sep. 17, 1994
Season	142	Emmanuel Hazard (Houston)	1989
Career	266	Aaron Turner (Pacific)	1989–92

Yards gained receiving

Game	363	Randy Gatewood (UNLV vs. Idaho)	Sep. 17, 1994
Season	4,357	Ryan Yarborough (Wyoming)	1990–93
Career	4,345	Aaron Turner (Pacific)	1989–92

Pass interceptions

Game	5	Dan Rebsch (Miami [Ohio] vs. Western Michigan; 88 yards; three others with less yards)	Nov. 4, 1972
Season	14	Al Worley (Washington; 130 yards, in 10 games)	1968
Career	29	Al Brosky (Illinois; 356 yards, 27 games)	1950–52

Touchdowns (receiving)

Game	6	Tim Delaney (San Diego State vs. New Mexico State)	Nov. 15, 1969
Season	22	Emmanuel Hazard (Houston)	1989
Career	43	Aaron Turner (Pacific)	1989–92

Field goals

Game	7	Mike Prindle (West Michigan vs. Marshall)	Sep. 29, 1984
	7	Dale Klein (Nebraska vs. Missouri)	Oct. 19, 1985
Season	29	John Lee (UCLA)	1984
Career	80	Jeff Jaeger (Washington)	1983–86
Consecutive	30	Chuck Nelson (Washington)	1981–82

Touchdowns

Game	8	Howard Griffith (Illinois vs. Southern Illinois)	Sep. 22, 1990
Season	39	Barry Sanders (Oklahoma State)	1988
Career	65	Anthony Thompson (Indiana)	1986–89

(USC) has a record 19 wins in the Rose Bowl. The University of Alabama has made a record 47 bowl appearances and has had 27 wins (including 18 wins in 31 "big four" appearances). Most wins in the other "big four" bowl games: Orange Bowl: 11, Oklahoma; Sugar Bowl: 8, Alabama; Cotton Bowl: 9, Texas. Alabama, Georgia, Georgia Tech and Notre Dame are the only four teams to have won each of the "big four" bowl games.

Heisman Memorial Trophy   Archie Griffin of Ohio State won the Heisman Memorial Trophy in 1974 and again in 1975, making him the only double winner. The University of Notre Dame has had more Heisman Trophy winners than any other school, with a total of seven selections.

GAMES

Shortest backgammon game   Alan Malcolm Beckerson devised a game of 16 throws in 1982.

Biggest board game   The world's biggest commercially available board game is "Galaxion," created by Cerebe Design International of Hong Kong. The board measures 33 by 33 inches.

Most expensive board game   The deluxe version of *Outrage!*, produced by Imperial Games of Southport, England, retails for £3,995 ($6,392).
The object of the game is to steal the Crown Jewels from the Tower of London.

Card holding   Ralf Laue held 326 standard playing cards in a fan in one hand, so that the value and color of each one was visible, in Leipzig, Germany, on March 18, 1994.

Card throwing   Jim Karol of Catasauqua, PA threw a standard playing card 201 feet at Mount Ida College, Newton Centre, MA on October 18, 1992.

Shortest solitaire game   The shortest time taken to complete the game of solitaire is 10.0 seconds, by Stephen Twigge in Scissett Baths, England on August 2, 1991.

BINGO

Largest house   The largest "house" in bingo sessions was 15,756, at the Canadian National Exhibition, Toronto on August 19, 1983, staged by the Variety Club of Ontario Tent Number 28. There was total prize money of $Cdn250,000 with a record 1-game payout of $Cdn100,000.

Earliest and latest full house   A "full house" call occurred on the 15th number by Norman A. Wilson at Guide Post Working Men's Club, Bedlington, England on June 22, 1978; by Anne Wintle of Brynrethin, Wales, on a bus trip to Bath, England on August 17, 1982; and by Shirley Lord at Kahibah Bowling Club, New South Wales, Australia on October 24, 1983.

"House" was not called until the 86th number at the Hillsborough Working Men's Club, Sheffield, England on January 11, 1982. There were 32 winners.

CHECKERS

World champion Walter Hellman (U.S.) won a record eight world titles during his tenure as world champion, 1948–75.

Youngest and oldest national champion Asa A. Long became the youngest U.S. national champion, at age 18 yr. 64 days, when he won in Boston, MA on October 23, 1922. He became the oldest, age 79 yr. 334 days, when he won his sixth title in Tupelo, MS on July 21, 1984. He was also world champion 1934–38.

Most opponents Charles Walker played a record 306 games simultaneously, winning 300, drawing 5 and losing 1, at Dollywood, Pigeon Force, TN on October 22, 1994.

The largest number of opponents played without a defeat or draw is 172, by Nate Cohen of Portland, ME in Portland on July 26, 1981. This was not a simultaneous attempt, but consecutive play over a period of four hours.

In 1933, Newell W. Banks played 140 games simultaneously in Chicago, IL; he won 133 and drew seven. His total playing time was 145 minutes, thus averaging about one move per second. In 1947, he played blindfolded for four hours per day for 45 consecutive days, winning 1,331 games, drawing 54 and losing only two, while playing six games at a time.

Longest game In competition, the prescribed rate of play is not less than 30 moves per hour, with the average game lasting about 90 minutes. In 1958, a game between Dr. Marion Tinsley (U.S.) and Derek Oldbury (Great Britain) lasted 7 hr. 30 min. (played under the 5-minutes-a-move rule).

CHESS

World Championships World champions have been officially recognized since 1886. The longest undisputed tenure was 26 yr. 337 days, by Dr. Emanuel Lasker of Germany, 1894–1921.

The women's world championship title was held by Vera Francevna Stevenson-Menchik (USSR, later Great Britain) from 1927 until her death in 1944, and was successfully defended a record seven times.

Judit Polgar was just 15 yr. 150 days old when she qualified as the youngest ever Grand Master on December 20, 1991, a record overtaken by compatriot Peter Leko (14 yr. 145 days) in January 1994. (*Gamma/Gifford-Liaison*)

United States   The first American to be regarded as world champion was Paul Charles Morphy in 1858.

Team   The USSR won the biennial men's team title (Olympiad) a record 18 times between 1952 and 1990, with Russia winning twice, in 1992 and 1994. The women's title has been won 11 times by the USSR from its introduction in 1957 to 1986, with Georgia winning in 1992 and 1995.

The U.S. has won the men's title five times: 1931, 1933, 1935, 1937 and 1976.

Youngest world champion   Maya Chiburdanidze (USSR; b. January 17, 1961) won the women's title in 1978 when she was only 17. Gary Kasparov (USSR) won the title on November 9, 1985 at age 22 yr. 210 days.

Oldest world champion   Wilhelm Steinitz (Austria, later U.S.) was 58 yr. 10 days when he lost his title to Lasker on May 26, 1894.

Most active world champion   Anatoliy Karpov (USSR) in his tenure as champion, 1975–85, averaged 45.2 competitive games per year, played in 32 tournaments and finished first in 26.

Youngest Grand Master   The youngest individual to qualify as an International Grand Master is Peter Leko (Hungary), at age 14 yr. 145 days on January 30, 1994. The youngest female Grand Master is Judit Polgar (Hungary), at age 15 yr. 150 days on December 20, 1991.

United States   The youngest U.S. Grand Master was Bobby Fischer (b. March 9, 1943) in 1958.

Youngest Master   In August 1981, Stuart Rachels of Birmingham, AL became the youngest person in the history of the United States Chess Foundation to achieve a master rating, at age 11 yr. 10 mo.

Highest rating   The highest rating ever attained on the officially adopted Elo System (devised by Arpad E. Elo) is 2,805, by Gary Kasparov (USSR) at the end of 1992.

The women's record is held by Judit Polgar, who achieved a peak rating of 2,630 at the end of 1993.

Fewest games lost by a world champion   José Raúl Capablanca (Cuba) lost only 34 games (out of 571) in his adult career, 1909–39. He was unbeaten from February 10, 1916 to March 21, 1924 (63 games) and was world champion 1921–27.

U.S. Championships   The most wins since the U.S. Championships became determined by match play competition in 1888 is eight, by Bobby Fischer, 1957–66.

Most opponents   The record for most consecutive games played is 663, by Vlastimil Hort (Czechoslovakia, later Germany) over 32½ hours in Porz, Germany, October 5–6, 1984. He played 60–120 opponents at a time, scoring over 80 percent wins and averaging 30 moves per game. He also holds the record for most games played simultaneously, 201 during 550 consecutive games of which he lost only 10, in Seltjarnes, Iceland, April 23–24, 1977.

Eric G.J. Knoppert (Netherlands) played 500 games of 10-minute chess against opponents, averaging 2,002 on the Elo scale, September 13–16, 1985. He scored 413 points (1 for win, ½ for draw), a success rate of 82.6 percent.

Slowest moves   In a 15-hour chess game between Louis Paulsen (Germany) and Paul Charles Morphy (U.S.) at the first American Chess Congress, NY on October 29, 1857 (before time clocks were used), a total of 56 moves were made. The game ended in a draw, Paulsen having used about 11 hours of play.

Grand Master Friedrich Sämisch (Germany) ran out of the allotted time (2 hr. 30 min. for 45 moves) after only 12 moves, in Prague, Czechoslovakia, in 1938.

The slowest move played since time clocks were introduced was in Vigo, Spain in 1980 when Francisco R. Torres Trois took 2 hr. 20 min. for his seventh move vs. Luis M. C. P. Santos.

Oldest chess pieces   The oldest chess pieces were found in Nashipur, and were dated to around A.D. 900.

MOVING!

The Master chess game with the most moves on record was one of 269 moves, when Ivan Nikolić drew with Goran Arsović in a Belgrade, Yugoslavia tournament, on February 17, 1989. The game took a total of 20 hr. 15 min.

CONTRACT BRIDGE

Biggest tournament The Epson World Bridge Championship, held June 20–21, 1992, was contested by more than 102,000 players playing the same hands, at over 2,000 centers worldwide.

Most world titles The World Championship (Bermuda Bowl) has been won 13 times by Italy's Blue Team (*Squadra Azzura*), 1957–59, 1961–63, 1965–67, 1969, 1973–75; and by the U.S., 1950–51, 1953–54, 1970–71, 1976–77, 1979, 1981, 1983, 1985, 1987. Italy also won the team Olympiad in 1964, 1968 and 1972, and the U.S. won in 1988. Giorgio Belladonna was on all the Italian winning teams.

The U.S. has a record six wins in the women's world championship for the Venice Trophy, 1974, 1976, 1978, 1987, 1989 and 1991, and three women's wins in the World Team Olympiad, 1976, 1980 and 1984.

Most world championship hands In the 1989 Bermuda Bowl in Perth, Australia, Marcel Branco and Gabriel Chagas (both Brazil) played a record 752 out of a possible 784 boards.

Perfect deals in bridge The mathematical odds against dealing 13 cards of one suit are 158,753,389,899 to 1; the odds against a named player receiving a "perfect hand" consisting of all 13 spades are 635,013,559,599 to 1. The odds against each of the four players' receiving a complete suit (a "perfect deal") are 2,235,197,406,895,366,368,301,559,999 to 1.

Possible bridge auctions The number of possible auctions with North as dealer is 128,745,650,347,030,683,120,231,926,111,609, 371,363,122,697,557.

CRIBBAGE

Rare hands Five maximum 29-point hands have been achieved by Sean Daniels of Astoria, OR, 1989–92. Paul Nault of Athol, MA had two such hands within eight games in a tournament on March 19, 1977.

Most points in 24 hours The most points scored by a team of four, playing singles in two pairs, is 126,414, by Mark Fitzwater, Eddie Pepper, Mark Perry and Gary Watson at The Green Man, Potton, England, May 8–9, 1993.

DOMINOES

Domino toppling The greatest number set up single-handedly and toppled is 281,581 out of 320,236, by Klaus Friedrich, 22, in Fürth, Germany on January 27, 1984. The dominoes fell within 12 min. 57.3 sec., having taken 31 days (10 hours daily) to set up.

Thirty students at Delft, Eindhoven and Twente Technical Universities in the Netherlands set up 1,500,000 dominoes representing all the European Community countries. Of these, 1,382,101 were toppled by one push on January 2, 1988.

Domino stacking Edwin Sirko successfully stacked 401 dominoes on a single supporting domino on August 4, 1994 in Irvine, CA.

HORSESHOE PITCHING

World Championships   *Most titles (men)*   Ted Allen (U.S.) has won 10 world titles: 1933–35, 1940, 1946, 1953, 1955–57 and 1959.

Most titles (women)   Vicki Winston (née Chapelle) has won a record 10 women's titles: 1956, 1958–59, 1961, 1963, 1966–67, 1969, 1975 and 1981.

Longest perfect game   At the 1968 World Championship, Elmer Hohl (Canada) threw 56 consecutive ringers.

Most perfect games   In World Championship play, only three pitchers have thrown perfect games: Guy Zimmerman (U.S.), 1948; Elmer Hohl (Canada), 1968; and Jim Walters (U.S.), 1993.

JUMP ROPE

10-mile skip–run   Vadivelu Karunakaren (India) jumped rope 10 miles in 58 minutes in Madras, India, February 1, 1990.

Most turns of the rope   *One hour*   14,628, by Park Bong Tae (South Korea) in Pusan, South Korea, July 2, 1989. Robert Commers holds the U.S. record, with 13,783, in Woodbridge, NJ, May 13, 1989.

On a single rope, team of 90   196, by students from the Ino Elementary School, Toyama, Japan, August 21, 1994.

On a tightrope   358 (consecutive), by Julian Albulet (U.S.) in Las Vegas, NV, July 2, 1990.

Most on a rope (minimum 12 turns obligatory)   260, by students of the Yorkton Regional High School, Yorkton, Saskatchewan, Canada, on May 28, 1992.

TWISTER!

The greatest number of participants in a game of Twister is 4,160 people, at the University of Massachusetts of Amherst on May 2, 1987. Allison Culler won the game.

SCRABBLE

Highest scores   The highest competitive game score is 1,049 by Phil Appleby in June 1989. His opponent scored 253, and the margin of victory, 796 points, is also a record. His score included a single turn of 374 for the word "OXIDIZERS."

The highest competitive single-turn score recorded, however, is 392, by Dr. Saladin Karl Khoshnaw (of Kurdish origin) in Manchester, England in April 1982. He laid down "CAZIQUES," which means "native chiefs of West Indian aborigines."

United States   The highest score in a tournament game (American-style competitive) is 770 points by game inventor Mark Lansberg (Los Angeles) at the Scrabble tournament in Eagle Rock, CA on June 13, 1993. His opponent, Alan Stern, scored 338 points; their combined total of 1,108 points is also a record for American-style competitive tournament play.

Most tournaments   Chuck Armstrong, a hospital worker from Saline, MI, won the most tournaments—65 to the end of 1989.

GOLF

Oldest club   The oldest club of which there is written evidence is the Gentlemen Golfers (now the Honourable Company of Edinburgh Golfers) formed in March 1744. The Royal Burgess Golfing Society of Edinburgh, Scotland claims to have been founded in 1735.

United States   Two golf clubs claim to be the first established in the United States: the Foxburg Golf Club, Clarion Co., PA (1887) and St. Andrews Golf Club of Yonkers, NY (1888).

Largest tournament   The Volkswagen Grand Prix Open Amateur Championship in Great Britain attracted a record 321,778 (206,820 men and 114,958 women) competitors in 1984.

Longest course   The world's longest course is the par-77 8,325-yard International Golf Club in Bolton, MA from the "Tiger" tees, remodeled in 1969 by Robert Trent Jones.

Great Britain's Laura Davies is currently the world's number one woman golfer. In 1994, she won eight tournaments on five tours: three in the U.S., two in Europe, one in Japan, one in Thailand and one in Australia. (*Allsport/D. Cannon*)

Largest green   Probably the largest green in the world is that of the par-6 695-yard fifth hole at the International Golf Club, Bolton, MA, with an area greater than 28,000 square feet.

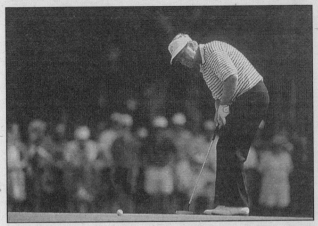

Jack Nicklaus is the only golfer to have won each of golf's four Majors at least three times, and the only golfer to have won the U.S. Amateur twice. (*Allsport [U.S.]/G. Newkirk*)

Biggest bunker   The biggest bunker is Hell's Half Acre on the 585-yard seventh hole of the Pine Valley course, Clementon, NJ. It is generally regarded as the world's most trying course.

Longest hole   The seventh hole (par-7) of the Satsuki Golf Course, Sano, Japan measures 964 yards.

United States   The longest hole in the United States is the 841-yd. 12th hole at Meadows Farm Golf Course in Locust Grove, VA.

Longest drive   The longest recorded drive on a standard course is one of 515 yards, by Michael Hoke Austin of Los Angeles, CA in the U.S. National Seniors Open in Las Vegas, NV on September 25, 1974.

Kelly Robbins struck the longest recorded drive by a woman, 429.7 yards, at the Elmira Corning Regional Airport in Corning, NY on May 22, 1995.

Longest putt   The longest recorded holed putt in a professional tournament is 110 feet: by Jack Nicklaus in the 1964 Tournament of Champions; and by Nick Price in the 1992 United States PGA Championship.

Bob Cook (U.S.) sank a putt measured at 140 ft. 2¾ in. on the 18th at St. Andrews, Scotland in the International Fourball Pro Am Tournament on October 1, 1976.

SCORES

Lowest 18 holes *Men* At least four players have played a long course (over 6,561 yards) in a score of 58—most recently Monte Carlo Money (U.S.), at the par-72, 6,607-yard Las Vegas Municipal Golf Club, NV on March 11, 1981.

The PGA tournament record for 18 holes is 59 (30 + 29), by Al Geiberger in the second round of the Danny Thomas Classic, on the 72-par 7,249-yard Colonial Golf Club course, Memphis, TN on June 10, 1977; and by Chip Beck in the third round of the Las Vegas Invitational, on the 72-par 6,979-yard Sunrise Golf Club course, Las Vegas, NV on October 11, 1991.

Women The lowest score on an 18-hole course over 5,000 yards is 60 (31 + 29) by Wanda Morgan, on the Westgate and Birchington Golf Club course, Kent, England, on July 11, 1929.

The lowest recorded score in an LPGA tour event on an 18-hole course (over 5,600 yards) is 62 (30 + 32) by Mickey Wright (U.S.) on the Hogan Park Course (par-71, 6,286 yards) in Midland, TX, November 1964; Vicki Fergon at the 1984 San Jose Classic, San Jose, CA; Laura Davies (Great Britain) (32 + 30) at the Rail Golf Club, Springfield, IL, August 31, 1991; and Hollis Stacy (U.S.) (30 + 32) at the Meridian Valley CC, Seattle, WA, September 18, 1992.

Lowest 72 holes *Men* Horton Smith scored 245 (63, 58, 61 and 63) for 72 holes on the 4,700-yard course (par-64) at Catalina Country Club, CA to win the Catalina Open, December 21–23, 1928.

The lowest 72 holes in a PGA tour event is 257 (60, 68, 64, 65), by Mike Souchak in the 1955 Texas Open in San Antonio.

Women Trish Johnson (Great Britain) scored 242 (64, 60, 60, 58; 21 under par) in the Bloor Homes Eastleigh Classic at the Fleming Park Course (4,402 yards) in Eastleigh, England, July 22–25, 1987.

The lowest score in an LPGA tour event is 267 (68, 66, 67, 66), by Betsy King in the 1992 Mazda LPGA championship.

Most consecutive birdies The official PGA tour record is eight, recorded by three players: Bob Goalby, during the fourth round of the 1961 St. Petersburg Open; Fuzzy Zoeller, during the opening round of the 1976 Quad Cities Open; and Dewey Arnette, during the opening round of the 1987 Buick Open.

Most shots under par 35, by Tom Kite at the 90-hole 1993 Bob Hope Chrysler Classic, February 11–14, 1993.

Fastest rounds *Individual* With wide variations in the lengths of courses, speed records, even for rounds under par, are of little comparative value. The fastest round played with the golf ball coming to rest before each new stroke is 27 min. 9 sec., by James Carvill at Warrenpoint Golf Course, County Down, Northern Ireland (18 holes, 6,154 yards) on June 18, 1987.

Team The 35 members of the Team Balls Out Diving completed the 18-hole 5,516-meter John E. Clark course in Point Micu, CA in 9 min. 39 sec. on November 16, 1992. They scored 71.

Most holes in 24 hours On foot Ian Colston, 35, played 22 rounds plus five holes (401 holes in all) at Bendigo Golf Club, Victoria, Australia (par-73, 6,061 yards), November 27–28, 1971.

Using golf carts David Cavalier played 846 holes at Arrowhead Country Club, North Canton, OH (9 holes, 3,013 yards), August 6–7, 1990. The women's record is held by Cyndy Lent (U.S.), who played 509 holes at Twin Lakes Country Club, Twin Lakes, WI on August 7–8, 1994.

Most holes in 12 hours Doug Wert played 440 holes in 12 hours on the 6,044-yard course at Tournament Players Club, Coral Springs, FL on June 7, 1993.

Most holes played in a week Steve Hylton played 1,128 holes at the Mason Rudolph Golf Club (6,060 yards), Clarksville, TN, August 25–31, 1980. Using a golf cart for transport, Colin Young completed 1,260 holes at Patshull Park Golf Club (6,412 yards), Pattingham, England, July 2–9, 1988.

World One-Club Championship Thad Daber (U.S.), with a 6-iron, played the 6,037-yard Lochmore Golf Club course, Cary, NC in 70 to win the 1987 World One-Club Championship.

MEN'S CHAMPIONSHIP RECORDS

Grand Slam The four grand slam events are, in order of play, the Masters, the U.S. Open, the British Open and the PGA Championship. No player has won all four events in one calendar year. Ben Hogan came closest to succeeding in 1951, when he won the first three legs, but he could not return to the United States from Britain in time for the PGA Championship. Jack Nicklaus has won the most major championships, with 18 professional titles (6 Masters, 4 U.S. Opens, 3 British Opens and 5 PGA Championships). Nicklaus has also won two U.S. Amateur titles, which are often included in calculating major championship victories.

Masters (played on the 6,925-yard Augusta National Golf Course, GA, first in 1934)

Most wins Jack Nicklaus has won six green jackets (1963, 1965–66, 1972, 1975, 1986). Two players have won consecutive Masters: Jack Nicklaus (1965–66) and Nick Faldo (Great Britain; 1989–90).

Lowest total aggregate 271, by Jack Nicklaus (67, 71, 64, 69) in 1965, and by Raymond Loran Floyd (65, 66, 70, 70) in 1976.

U.S. Open (inaugurated 1895)

Most wins Four players have won the title four times: Willie Anderson (1901, 1903–05), Bobby Jones (1923, 1926, 1929–30), Ben Hogan (1948, 1950–51, 1953) and Jack Nicklaus (1962, 1967, 1972, 1980). The only player to gain three successive titles was Willie Anderson, from 1903 to 1905.

Lowest total aggregate The lowest 72-hole score is 272, achieved by two players: Jack Nicklaus, 272 (63, 71, 70, 68) on the lower course (7,015

PGA TOUR ALL-TIME SCORING RECORDS

Lowest score (9 holes)	27	Mike Souchak, Texas Open (back nine) 1955
	27	Andy North, B.C. Open (back nine) 1975
Lowest score (18 holes)	59	Al Geiberger, Danny Thomas Memphis Classic (2nd round) ...1977
	59	Chip Beck, Las Vegas Invitational (3rd round) 1991
Lowest score (36 holes)	125	Gay Brewer, Pensacola Open (2nd and 3rd rounds) 1967
	125	Ron Streck, Texas Open (3rd and 4th rounds) 1978
	125	Blaine McCallister, Hardee's Golf Classic (2nd and 3rd rounds) ...1988
Lowest score (54 holes)	189	Chandler Harper, Texas Open (2nd, 3rd and 4th rounds) ...1954
Lowest score (72 holes)	257	Mike Souchak, Texas Open 1955
Most shots under par	27	Ben Hogan, Portland Invitational 1945
	27	Mike Souchak, Texas Open 1955
Fewest putts (18 holes)	18	Sam Trahan, IVB-Philadelphia Golf Classic (4th round) ...1979
	18	Mike McGee, Federal Express St. Jude Classic (1st round) ...1987
	18	Kenny Knox, MCI Heritage Classic (1st round) 1989
	18	Andy North, Anheuser Busch Golf Classic (2nd round) ...1990
	18	Jim McGovern, Federal Express St. Jude Classic (2nd round) ...1992
Fewest putts (72 holes)	93	Kenny Knox, MCI Heritage Classic 1989

All records listed are for 72-hole tournaments.

PGA Tour

yards) at Baltusrol Country Club, NJ, June 12–15, 1980; and Lee Janzen (67, 67, 69, 69), also at Baltusrol, June 17–20, 1993.

British Open (inaugurated 1860)

Most wins Harry Vardon won a record six titles, in 1896, 1898–99, 1903, 1911 and 1914. Tom Morris, Jr. is the only player to have won four successive British Opens, from 1868 to 1872 (the event was not held in 1871).

Lowest total aggregate 267 (66, 68, 69, 64) by Greg Norman (Australia) at Royal St. George's, in July 1993.

Professional Golfers Association (PGA) Championship (inaugurated 1916)

Most wins Two players have won the title five times: Walter Hagen (1921, 1924–27) and Jack Nicklaus (1963, 1971, 1973, 1975, 1980). Walter Hagen won a record four consecutive titles from 1924 to 1927.

Lowest total aggregate 269, by Nick Price (67, 65, 70, 67) at Seven Hills Country Club, Tulsa, OK, in 1994.

WOMEN'S CHAMPIONSHIP RECORDS

Grand Slam The Grand Slam of women's golf has consisted of four tournaments since 1955. The format has changed many times. Since 1983, the U.S. Open, LPGA Championship, du Maurier Classic and Nabisco Dinah Shore have been the major events. Patty Berg has won 15 professional Grand Slam events: U.S. Open (1), Titleholders (7), Western Open (7); the latter two are now defunct. She also won one U.S. Amateur title.

U.S. Open (inaugurated 1946)

Most wins The most wins is four, by Betsy Rawls, 1951, 1953, 1957 and 1960, and by Mickey Wright, in 1958–59, 1961 and 1964.

Lowest total aggregate The lowest 72-hole aggregate is 277, by Liselotte Newman (Sweden) in 1988, and by Patty Sheehan (U.S.) in 1994.

Ladies Professional Golfers Association (LPGA) Championship (inaugurated 1955)

Most wins The most wins is four, by Mickey Wright in 1958, 1960–61 and 1963.

Lowest total aggregate The lowest score for 72 holes is 267, by Betsy King at the Bethesda Country Club, MD in 1992.

Du Maurier Classic (inaugurated 1973)

Most wins Pat Bradley holds the record for most wins, with three titles won in 1980, 1985–86.

Lowest total aggregate The lowest score for 72 holes is 272, by Jody Rosenthal in 1987.

Nabisco Dinah Shore (inaugurated 1972)

Most wins The most wins is three, by Amy Alcott (1983, 1988 and 1991).

Lowest total aggregate The lowest score for 72 holes is 273, by Amy Alcott in 1991.

INDIVIDUAL RECORDS

Highest earnings. PGA and LPGA circuits The all-time top professional money-winner is Tom Kite (U.S.) with $9,261,125 from 1982 to June 4, 1995. Nick Price (Zimbabwe) won a season's record $1,499,927 in 1994.

The record career earnings for a woman is $5,027,628 to May 26, 1995, by Betsy King. The season record for a woman is $863,578, by Beth Daniel in 1990.

Most times leading money winner Jack Nicklaus has been the PGA tour leading money winner eight times—1964–65, 1967, 1971–73, 1975–76. Kathy Whitworth headed the LPGA list eight times—1965–68, 1970–73.

Most tournament wins Byron Nelson (U.S.) won 18 tournaments (plus one unofficial) in one year, including a record 11 consecutively from March 8 to August 4, 1945.

The LPGA record for one year is 13, by Mickey Wright (1963). She also holds the record for most wins in scheduled events, with four between August and September 1962 and between May and June 1963, a record matched by Kathy Whitworth between March and April 1969.

Successive wins Between May and June 1978, Nancy Lopez won all five tournaments that she entered; however, these events did not follow each other and are therefore not considered consecutive tournament victories.

Career wins Sam Snead, who turned professional in 1934, won 84 official PGA tour events, 1936–65. The LPGA record is 88, by Kathy Whitworth, 1959–91.

Oldest winner Sam Snead won a PGA tournament at age 52 yr. 312 days at the 1965 Greater Greensboro Open.

Greatest winning margin The greatest margin of victory in a professional tournament is 21 strokes, by Jerry Pate (U.S.), who won the Colombian Open with 262, December 10–13, 1981.

Bobby Locke (South Africa) achieved the greatest winning margin in a PGA tour event by 16 strokes in the Chicago Victory National Championship in 1948.

NCAA Championships Two golfers have won three NCAA titles: Ben Daniel Crenshaw of the University of Texas in 1971–73, tying with Tom Kite in 1972; and Phil Mickelson of Arizona State University in 1989–90, 1992.

Highest shot on Earth   Gerald Williams (U.S.) played a shot from the summit of Mt. Aconcagua (22,834 feet), Argentina on January 22, 1989.

Oldest player to score his age   The oldest player to achieve a score equal to his age is C, Arthur Thompson (1869–1975) of Victoria, British Columbia, Canada, who scored 103, on the Uplands course of 6,215 yards in 1973.

Golf ball balancing   Lang Martin balanced seven golf balls vertically on a flat surface without adhesive in Charlotte, NC on February 9, 1980.

DID YOU KNOW?

The most first-place prize money ever won is $1 million, in the Sun City Challenge, 1987–91, Bophuthatswana, South Africa. The greatest total prize money is $2.7 million (including a $550,000 first prize) for the Johnnie Walker World Championship at Tryall Golf Course, Montego Bay, Jamaica in 1992, 1993 and 1994.

HOLES IN ONE

Longest hole in one   The longest hole ever sunk in one shot was the "dogleg" 480-yard fifth at Hope Country Club, AR by L. Bruce on November 15, 1962.

The women's record is 393 yards, by Marie Robie on the first hole of the Furnace Brook Golf Club, Wollaston, MA on September 4, 1949.

Consecutive holes in one   There are at least 20 cases of "aces" being achieved in two consecutive holes, of which the greatest was Norman L. Manley's unique "double albatross" on the par-4 330-yard seventh and par-4 290-yard eighth holes on the Del Valle Country Club course, Saugus, CA on September 2, 1964.

The first woman to record consecutive "aces" was Sue Prell, on the 13th and 14th holes at Chatswood Golf Club, Sydney, Australia on May 29, 1977.

Youngest and oldest   The youngest golfer recorded to have shot a hole in one is Coby Orr (5 years) of Littleton, CO on the 103-yard fifth at the Riverside Golf Course, San Antonio, TX in 1975. The youngest girl is Nicola Mylonas (10 yr. 64 days) on the 133-yard 1st at South Course, Nudgee, Australia on September 18, 1993.

The youngest American girl to score an ace was Kimberly C. Smith, at the Skaneateles Country Club, Skaneateles, NY on June 14, 1992, at age 12.

The oldest golfers to have performed this feat are: *(men)* 99 yr. 244 days, Otto Bucher (Switzerland) on the 130-yard 12th at La Manga Golf Club, Spain on January 13, 1985; *(women)* 95 yr. 257 days, Erna Ross on the 112-yard 17th at The Everglades Club, Palm Beach, FL on April 23, 1986.

Most rewarding hole in one On November 1, 1992, Jason Bohn (U.S.) won $1 million when he made a hole in one during a charity contest. He aced the 136-yard second hole at the Harry S. Pritchett Gold Course in Tuscaloosa, AL using a 9-iron, having paid $10 to enter the event.

HANDY!

The lowest recorded score for throwing a golf ball around 18 holes (over 6,000 yards) is 82, by Joe Flynn (U.S.), 21, at the 6,288-yard Port Royal course, Bermuda on March 27, 1975.

TEAM COMPETITIONS

World Cup (formerly Canada Cup) The World Cup (formerly Canada Cup) has been won most often by the U.S., with 20 victories between 1955 and 1994.

The only men to have been on six winning teams are Arnold Palmer (1960, 1962–64, 1966–67) and Jack Nicklaus (1963–64, 1966–67, 1971 and 1973). Only Nicklaus has taken the individual title three times (1963–64, 1971).

The lowest aggregate score for 144 holes is 536, by the U.S., Fredrick Stephen Couples and Davis Love III, in Dorado, Puerto Rico, November 10–13, 1994.

The lowest individual score is 269, by Roberto de Vicenzo (Argentina) in 1970.

Ryder Cup The U.S. has won 23 to 5 (with 2 ties) to 1993.

Arnold Palmer has won the most Ryder Cup matches, with 22 out of 32 played, with 2 halved and 8 lost, in six contests from 1963 to 1973. Christy

Fred Couples and Davis Love III celebrate winning golf's World Cup in Dorado, Puerto Rico, November 10–13, 1994. It was the U.S.'s record 20th success and the third in succession for Couples and Love. *(Allsport/S. Munday)*

O'Connor, Sr. (Ireland) played in a record 10 contests, 1955–73. Three players have played in eight U.S. Ryder Cup teams: Billy Casper (1965–75), Raymond Floyd (1969–93) and Lanny Wadkins (1977–93).

Walker Cup   The series was instituted in 1921 (for the Walker Cup since 1922 and now held biennially). The U.S. has won 30 matches, Great Britain and Ireland 3 (in 1938, 1971 and 1989), and the 1965 match was tied.

Jay Sigel (U.S.) has won a record 18 matches, with 5 halved and 10 lost, 1977–93. Joseph Boynton Carr (Great Britain & Ireland) played in 10 contests, 1947–67.

Curtis Cup   The biennial ladies' Curtis Cup match between the U.S. and Great Britain & Ireland was first held in 1932. The U.S. has won 20 to 1994, Great Britain & Ireland six (1952, 1956, 1986, 1988, 1992 and 1994), and three matches have been tied.

GREYHOUND RACING

Oldest club   St. Petersburg Kennel Club, located in St. Petersburg, FL, which opened on January 3, 1925, is the oldest greyhound track in the world still in operation on its original site.

Derby   Two greyhounds have won the American Derby twice, in Taunton, MA: Real Huntsman in 1950–51, and Dutch Bahama in 1984–85.

Fastest greyhound   *United States*   My Bold Girl ran $5/16$ mile in 29.58 seconds at Bluffs Run, Council Bluffs, IA in 1994. P's Rambling ran $3/8$-mile in 36.43 seconds in Hollywood, FL in 1987. Runaround Sue ran a $7/16$-mile track in 42.57 seconds in Hollywood, FL in 1991.

HOTDOG!

The fastest speed at which any greyhound has been timed is 41.83 MPH (400 yards in 19.57 seconds) by Star Title on the straightaway track in Wyong, New South Wales, Australia on March 5, 1994.

Most wins   The most career wins is 143, by JR's Ripper of Multnomah, Fairview, OR and Tucson, AZ, 1982–86.

The most wins in a year is 61, by Indy Ann in Mexico and the United States in 1956.

The most consecutive victories is 37, by J.J. Doc Richard, owned by Jack Boyd, as of May 31, 1995.

Highest earnings   The career earnings record is held by Mo Kick with $314,067, 1990–94.

The most money won in a single greyhound race is $130,000, by Design Time at the 1994 Great Greyhound Futurity, in the Woodlands, Kansas City, KS.

Most stakes victories   Real Huntsman achieved 10 wins from 1949 to 1951, including the American Derby twice.

Longest odds   Apollo Prince won at odds of 250–1 at Sandown Greyhound Race Course, Springvale, Victoria, Australia on November 14, 1968.

GYMNASTICS

Largest gymnastics/aerobics display   The largest number of participants was 26,017 for the Great Singapore Workout 93 at Padang Field, Singapore on October 3, 1993.

World Championships   Women   The greatest number of titles won in the World Championships (including Olympic Games) is 12 individual wins and six team, by Larisa Latynina (née Diriy; USSR), 1954–64.

The USSR won the team title on 21 occasions (11 world and 10 Olympic).

Men   Vitaliy Scherbo (Belarus) won 11 individual titles and one team title between 1992 and 1994. Boris Shakhlin (USSR) won 10 individual titles and three team titles, 1954–64.

The USSR won the team title a record 13 times (eight World Championships, five Olympics) between 1952 and 1992.

United States   Shannon Miller has won five gold medals, in all-around, floor exercise and uneven bars in 1993 and all-around and beam in 1994. The men's record is three gold medals, by Kurt Thomas, in floor exercise in 1978–79 and horizontal bar in 1979.

Youngest champions   Aurelia Dobre (Romania) won the women's overall world title at age 14 yr. 352 days on October 23, 1987. Daniela Silivas (Romania) revealed in 1990 that she was born on May 9, 1971, a year later than previously claimed, so that she was age 14 yr. 185 days when she won the gold medal for balance beam on November 10, 1985.

The youngest male world champion was Dmitriy Bilozerchev (USSR), at 16 yr. 315 days in Budapest, Hungary on October 28, 1983.

Olympics   The USSR won the women's title 10 times (1952–80, 1988 and 1992). The successes in 1992 were by the Unified Team from the republics of the former USSR. The men's title has been won a record five times, by Japan (in 1960, 1964, 1968, 1972 and 1976) and the USSR (1952, 1956, 1980, 1988 and 1992).

Vera Cáslavská-Odlozil (Czechoslovakia) has won the most individual gold medals, with seven, three in 1964 and four (one shared) in 1968.

The most men's individual gold medals is six, by Boris Shakhlin, one in 1956, four (two shared) in 1960 and one in 1964; and by Nikolay Yefimovich (USSR), one in 1972, four in 1976 and one in 1980.

Larisa Latynina won six individual gold medals and was on three winning teams, 1956–64, earning nine gold medals. She also won five silver and four bronze, 18 in all—an Olympic record.

The most medals won by a male gymnast is 15, by Nikolay Andrianov (USSR)—seven gold, five silver and three bronze, 1972–80.

Aleksandr Dityatin (USSR) is the only man to win a medal in all eight categories in the same Games, with three gold, four silver and one bronze in Moscow in 1980.

Vitaliy Scherbo (Belarus) won a record six golds at one Games in 1992, adding four individual titles to the all-around and team gold that he had won with the Unified Team.

United States   The best U.S. performances were in the 1904 Games, when there was only limited international participation. Anton Heida won five gold medals and a silver, and George Eyser, who had a wooden leg, won three gold, two silver and a bronze medal. Mary Lou Retton won a women's record five medals in 1984—gold in all-around, two silver and two bronze.

U.S. Championships   Alfred A. Jochim (1902–81) won a record seven men's all-around U.S. titles, 1925–30 and 1933, and a total of 34 in all events, between 1923 and 1934. The women's record is six all-around, 1945–46 and 1949–52, and 39 in all exercises, including 11 in succession on balance beam, 1941–51, by Clara Marie Schroth Lomady.

Shannon Miller (U.S.), at just 17, has won more World and Olympic titles than any other American gymnast.
(Allsport/Vandystadt/ Y. Guicbaoua)

EXERCISES—SPEED AND STAMINA

Records are for the most repetitions of the following activities within the given time span.

Chins—consecutive 370, Lee Chin-yong (South Korea) at Backyon Gymnasium, Seoul, South Korea on May 14, 1988.

Chins—consecutive, one arm, from a ring 22, Robert Chisnall at Queen's University, Kingston, Ontario, Canada on Dec. 3, 1982. (Also 18 two-finger chins, 12 one-finger chins.)

Parallel bar dips—1 hour 3,726, Kim Yang-ki (South Korea) at the Rivera Hotel, Seoul, South Korea on Nov. 28, 1991.

Sit-ups—24 hours 70,715, Lou Scripa, Jr. at Beale Airforce Base, Marysville, CA on Dec. 1–2, 1992.

Push-ups—24 hours 46,001, Charles Servizio (U.S.) at Fontana City Hall, Fontana, CA on Apr. 24–25, 1993.

Push-ups—one arm, 5 hours 8,151, Alan Rumbell (Great Britain) at the Gym 'N' Slym, St. Albans, Great Britain on Jun. 26, 1993.

Push-ups—fingertip, 5 hours 7,011, Kim Yang-ki (South Korea) at the Swiss Guard Hotel, Seoul, South Korea on Aug. 30, 1990.

Push-ups—consecutive, one finger 124, Paul Lynch (Great Britain) at the Hippodrome, London, England on Apr. 21, 1992.

Push-ups in a year Paddy Doyle (Great Britain) achieved a documented 1,500,230 push-ups from October 1988 to October 1989.

Leg lifts—12 hours 41,788, Lou Scripa, Jr. at Jack La Lanne's American Health & Fitness Spa, Sacramento, CA on Dec. 2, 1988.

Somersaults Ashrita Furman performed 8,341 forward rolls in 10 hr. 30 min. over 12 miles 390 yd., Lexington to Charleston, MA on Apr. 30, 1986.

Somersaults—backwards Shigeru Iwasaki somersaulted backwards 54.68 yd. in 10.8 sec. in Tokyo, Japan on Mar. 30, 1980.

Squats—1 hour 4,289, Paul Wai Man Chung at the Yee Gin Kung Fu of Chung Sze Health (HK) Association, Kowloon, Hong Kong on Apr. 5, 1993.

Squat thrusts—1 hour 3,552, Paul Wai Man Chung at the Yee Gin Kung Fu of Chung Sze Kung Fu (HK) Association, Kowloon, Hong Kong on Apr. 21, 1992.

Burpees—1 hour 1,840, Paddy Doyle at the Bull's Head, Polesworth, England on Feb. 6, 1994.

Pummel horse double circles—consecutive 97, Tyler Farstad (Canada) at Surrey Gymnastic Society, Surrey, British Columbia on Nov. 27, 1993.

Static wall sit (Samson's chair) 11 hr. 5 min., Rajikumar Chakraborty (India) at Panposh Sports Hostel, Rourkel, India on Apr. 22, 1994.

NCAA Championships **Men** The men's competition was first held in 1932. The most team championships won is nine, by two colleges: University of Illinois, 1939–42, 1950, 1955–56, 1958, 1989; and Pennsylvania State University, 1948, 1953–54, 1957, 1959–61, 1965, 1976.

The most individual titles in a career is seven, by Joe Giallombardo,

---

10 OUT OF 10!

Hans Eugster (Switzerland) scored a perfect 10.00 in the compulsory parallel bars at the 1950 World Championships. Nadia Comaneci (Romania) was the first to achieve a perfect score (10.00) in the Olympics, and achieved seven perfect scores in all in Montreal, Canada in July 1976.

University of Illinois, tumbling, 1938–40, all-around title, 1938–40, and floor exercise, 1938; and by Jim Hartung, University of Nebraska, all-around title, 1980–81, rings, 1980–82, and parallel bar, 1981–82.

Women The women's competition was first held in 1982. The most team championships is eight, by the University of Utah, 1982–86, 1990, 1992 and 1994.

The most individual titles in a career is five, by Missy Marlowe, University of Utah—all-around title, 1992, balance beam, 1991–92, uneven bars, 1992, floor exercise, 1992.

Modern rhythmic gymnastics The most overall individual world titles in modern rhythmic gymnastics is three, by Maria Gigova (Bulgaria) in 1969, 1971 and 1973 (shared). Bulgaria has a record eight team titles, in 1969, 1971, 1981, 1983, 1985, 1987, 1989 (shared) and 1993. Bianka Panova of Bulgaria won all four apparatus gold medals, all with maximum scores, and won a team gold in 1987.

Lilia Ignatova (Bulgaria) has won two individual World Cup titles, in 1983 and 1986. Marina Lobach (USSR) won the 1988 Olympic title with perfect scores for all six disciplines.

HOCKEY

NATIONAL HOCKEY LEAGUE (NHL)

Most wins The Montreal Canadiens won a record 60 games and 132 points (with 12 ties) in 80 games played in 1976/77; their eight losses were also a record, the least ever in a season of 70 or more games. The highest percentage of wins in a season was .875, by the Boston Bruins, with 30 wins in 44 games, 1929/30.

The longest undefeated run during a season—35 games (25 wins and 10 ties)—was established by the Philadelphia Flyers, October 14, 1979–January 6, 1980.

The most goals scored in a season is 446, by the Edmonton Oilers in 1983/84, when they also achieved a record 1,182 points.

The most assists recorded in a season was the 737 by the Edmonton Oilers during the 1985–86 season.

The most power-play goals scored in a season is 119, by the Pittsburgh Penguins during the 1988–89 season. The most shorthanded goals scored in a season is 36, by the Edmonton Oilers during the 1983/84 season.

Most goals in a game The NHL record is 21 goals, when the Montreal Canadiens beat Toronto St. Patrick's, 14–7, in Montreal on January 10, 1920, and the Edmonton Oilers beat the Chicago Blackhawks, 12–9, in Chicago on December 11, 1985. The NHL single-team record is 16, by the Montreal Canadiens vs. the Québec Bulldogs (3), in Québec City on November 3, 1920.

Fastest goals Toronto scored eight goals in 4 min. 52 sec. vs. the New York Americans on March 19, 1938.

SHUTOUT!

The most shutouts in a season is 22, in just 44 games, 1928/29, all by George Hainsworth (Montreal Canadiens) who also achieved a record low goals-against average of .98 that season.

INDIVIDUAL RECORDS

Most games played Gordie Howe played in 1,767 NHL regular-season games (and 157 playoff games) over 26 seasons, 1946–71, for the Detroit Red Wings, and in 1979/80 for the Hartford Whalers.

Fastest goals Joseph A.C. Provost (Montreal Canadiens) scored after four seconds vs. Boston Bruins in the second period in Montreal on November 9, 1957. Denis J. Savard (Chicago Blackhawks) equaled this feat on January 12, 1986 vs. Hartford Whalers in the third period in Chicago. From the opening whistle, the fastest is five seconds, by Doug Smail (Winnipeg Jets) vs. St. Louis Blues in Winnipeg on December 20, 1981, and by Bryan John Trottier (New York Islanders) vs. Boston Bruins in Boston on March 22, 1984. Bill Mosienko (Chicago Blackhawks) scored three goals in 21 seconds vs. New York Rangers on March 23, 1952.

Most goals, assists and points Career Wayne Gretzky is the NHL's all-time leader in goals, assists and points. During his career (Edmonton Oilers 1979–88, Los Angeles Kings 1988–94) he has scored 814 goals, 1,692 assists and 2,506 points.

Season   The most goals scored in a season in the NHL is 92, in the 1981/82 season by Wayne Gretzky for the Edmonton Oilers. In 1985/86, he scored a record 215 points, including a record 163 assists.

Game   The most goals in an NHL game is seven, by Michael Joe Malone in Québec's 10–6 win over Toronto St. Patricks in Québec City on January 31, 1920.

The most assists in an NHL game is seven, once by Billy Taylor for Detroit, 10–6 vs. Chicago on March 16, 1947, and three times by Wayne Gretzky for Edmonton, 8–2 vs. Washington on February 15, 1980, 12–9 vs. Chicago on December 11, 1985, and 8–2 vs. Québec on February 14, 1986.

The record number of assists in one period is five, by Dale Hawerchuk, for the Winnipeg Jets vs. the Los Angeles Kings on March 6, 1984.

DID YOU KNOW?

The longest game, and the longest single shutout, was 2 hr. 56 min. 30 sec. (playing time) when the Detroit Red Wings beat the Montreal Maroons 1–0 in the sixth period of overtime at the Forum, Montreal, at 2:25 A.M. on March 25, 1936.

Consecutive games   Harry Broadbent scored in 16 consecutive games for Ottawa in the 1921/22 season.

Most points in one game   The NHL record for most points scored in one game is 10, by Darryl Sittler—six goals, four assists for the Toronto Maple Leafs vs. the Boston Bruins in an NHL game in Toronto on February 7, 1976.

Period   The most points in one period is six, by Bryan Trottier—three goals and three assists in the second period, for the New York Islanders vs. the New York Rangers (9–4) on December 23, 1978. Nine players have a record four goals in one period.

Most consecutive games played   A record of 964 consecutive games played was achieved by Doug Jarvis for the Montreal Canadiens, the Washington Capitals and the Hartford Whalers from October 8, 1975 to October 10, 1987.

Most consecutive 50-or-more-goal seasons   Mike Bossy (New York Islanders) scored at least 50 goals in nine consecutive seasons from 1977/78 through 1985/86. Wayne Gretzky (Edmonton Oilers, Los Angeles Kings) has also scored at least 50 goals in one season nine times, but his longest streak is eight seasons.

Most consecutive points   The most consecutive games scoring points was 51, by Wayne Gretzky from October 5, 1983 to January 27, 1984 for the Edmonton Oilers.

Goaltending   Terry Gordon Sawchuk played a record 971 games as a goal-tender, for the Detroit Red Wings, the Boston Bruins, the Toronto Maple Leafs, the Los Angeles Kings and the New York Rangers, from 1949 to 1970. He achieved a record 435 wins (to 337 losses, and 188 ties). Jacques Plante, with 434 NHL wins, surpassed Sawchuk's figure by adding 15 wins in his one season in the WHA, for a total of 449 in 868 games.

Bernie Parent achieved a record 47 wins in a season, with 13 losses and 12 ties, for Philadelphia in 1973/74.

Most successful goaltending   The most shutouts played by a goaltender in an NHL career is 103, by Terry Sawchuck of Detroit, Boston, Toronto, Los Angeles and New York Rangers, between 1949 and 1970. Gerry Cheevers (Boston Bruins) went a record 32 successive games without a defeat in 1971/72. George Hainsworth completed 22 shutouts for the Montreal Canadiens in 1928/29. Alex Connell played 461 min. 29 sec. without con-ceding a goal for Ottawa in the 1928/29 season. Roy Worters saved 70 shots for the Pittsburgh Pirates vs. the New York Americans on December 24, 1925.

Defensemen   Paul Coffey (Edmonton Oilers 1980–87, Pittsburgh Penguins 1988–92, Los Angeles Kings 1992–93, Detroit Red Wings 1993) holds the record for most goals (358), assists (978) and points (1,336) by a defenseman. He scored a record 48 goals in 1985/86. Bobby Orr (Boston Bruins) holds the single-season marks for assists (102) and points (139), both of which were set in 1970/71.

Player awards   The Hart Trophy, awarded annually starting with the 1923/24 season by the Professional Hockey Writers Association as the Most Valuable Player award of the NHL, has been won a record nine times by Wayne Gret-zky, 1980–87, 1989. Gretzky has also won the Art Ross Trophy a record 10 times, 1981–87, 1990–91 and 1992–94; this trophy has been awarded annually since 1947/48 to the NHL season's leading scorer. Bobby Orr of Boston won the James Norris Memorial Trophy, awarded annually starting with the 1953/54 season to the league's leading defenseman, a record eight times, 1968–75.

Most successful coach   Scotty Bowman holds the records for most victories, highest winning percentage and most games coached by an NHL coach. He won 880 games (110, St. Louis Blues 1967–71; 419, Montreal Canadiens 1971–79; 210, Buffalo Sabres 1979–87; 95, Pittsburgh Penguins, 1991–93; 46, Detroit Red Wings, 1993–94). His career record is 880 wins, 410 losses, 234 ties for a record .654 winning percentage from a record 1,524 games.

HAT TRICK!

The most hat tricks (three or more goals in a game) in a career is 49, by Wayne Gretzky through the 1994/95 season for the Edmonton Oilers and the Los Angeles Kings. Gretzky also holds the record for most hat tricks in a season, 10, in both the 1982 and 1984 seasons for the Oilers.

STANLEY CUP

The Stanley Cup has been won most often by the Montreal Canadiens, with 24 wins in 1916, 1924, 1930–31, 1944, 1946, 1953, 1956–60, 1965–66, 1968–69, 1971, 1973, 1976–79, 1986, 1993 from a record 33 finals. The longest Stanley Cup final game was settled after 115 min. 13 sec., in the third period of overtime, when the Edmonton Oilers beat the Boston Bruins 3–2 on May 15, 1990.

Henri Richard played on 11 winning teams for the Montreal Canadiens, 1956–73.

Most games played   Larry Robinson played in 227 Stanley Cup playoff games, for the Montreal Canadiens (1973–89) and the Los Angeles Kings (1990–92).

Highest scores   Wayne Gretzky (Edmonton Oilers, Los Angeles Kings) has scored a record 346 points in Stanley Cup games, a record 110 goals and a record 236 assists. Gretzky scored a playoff record 47 points (17 goals, record 30 assists) in 1985. The most goals in a season is 19, by Reggie Leach for Philadelphia in 1976 and by Jari Kurri (Finland) for Edmonton in 1985.

Five goals in a Stanley Cup game were scored by Newsy LaLonde in Montreal's 6–3 victory over Ottawa on March 1, 1919; by Maurice Richard in Montreal's 5–1 win over the Toronto Maple Leafs on March 23, 1944; by

---

STREAK!

Bryan Trottier (New York Islanders) scored a point in 27 playoff games over three seasons (1980–82), scoring 16 goals and 26 assists for 42 points.

Darryl Glen Sittler for Toronto's 8–5 victory over Philadelphia on April 22, 1976; by Reggie Leach for Philadelphia's 6–3 victory over the Boston Bruins on May 6, 1976; and by Mario Lemieux for the Pittsburgh Penguins' 10–7 win over Philadelphia on April 25, 1989. Reggie Leach (Philadelphia) scored at least one goal in nine consecutive playoff games in 1976. The streak started on April 17, vs. the Toronto Maple Leafs, and ended on May 9, when he was shut out by the Montreal Canadiens. Overall, Leach scored 14 goals during his record-setting run.

A record six assists in a game were achieved by Mikko Leinonen (Finland) for the New York Rangers in their 7–3 victory over Philadelphia on April 8, 1982, and by Wayne Gretzky for Edmonton's 13–3 victory over Los Angeles on April 9, 1987, when his team set a Stanley Cup game record of 13 goals. The most points in a game is eight, by Patrik Sundström (Sweden), three goals and five assists, for the New Jersey Devils (10) vs. the Washington Capitals (4) on April 22, 1988; and by Mario Lemieux, five goals and three assists, for the Pittsburgh Penguins (10) vs. the Philadelphia Flyers (7) on April 25, 1989.

Goaltending Two players share the record of 15 shutouts in a playoff career: Jacques Plante, of the Montreal Canadiens (1953–63) and the St. Louis Blues (1969–70), and Clint Benedict, of the Montreal Maroons (1917–30). The record for most victories in a playoff career is 88, by Billy Smith for the New York Islanders (1975–88).

Defensemen During his career with the Edmonton Oilers, 1980–87, Paul Coffey set marks for the most points in a playoff game (6) and in a season (37)—both set in 1985. Also in 1985, Coffey set the record for most goals by a defenseman in a playoff season, with 12 in 18 games. The record for most goals in a game by a defenseman is three, shared by eight players: Bobby Orr (Boston Bruins vs. Montreal Canadiens, April 11, 1971); Dick Redmond (Chicago Blackhawks vs. St. Louis Blues, April 4, 1973); Denis Potvin (New York Islanders vs. Edmonton Oilers, April 17, 1981); Paul Reinhart twice (Calgary Flames vs. Edmonton Oilers, April 14, 1983; vs. Vancouver Canucks, April 8, 1984); Doug Halward (Vancouver Canucks vs. Calgary Flames, April 7, 1984); Al Iafrate (Washington Capitals vs. New York Islanders, April 26, 1993); Eric Desjardins (Montreal Canadiens vs. Los Angeles Kings, June 3, 1993); Gary Suter (Chicago Blackhawks vs. Toronto Maple Leafs, April 24, 1994); and Brian Leetch (Ottawa Senators vs. New York Rangers, May 22, 1995).

Most valuable player The Conn Smythe Trophy for the most valuable player in the playoffs has been awarded annually since 1965. It has been won twice by: Bobby Orr (Boston), 1970 and 1972; Bernie Parent (Philadelphia), 1974 and 1975; Wayne Gretzky (Edmonton), 1985 and 1988; Mario Lemieux (Pittsburgh), 1991 and 1992; and Patrick Roy (Montreal), 1986 and 1993.

Most successful coaches Toe Blake coached the Montreal Canadiens to eight championships (1956–60, 1965–66, 1968), the most of any coach. Scotty Bowman holds the record for most playoff wins at 152: 26, St. Louis Blues, 1967–71; 70, Montreal Canadiens, 1971–79; 18, Buffalo Sabres, 1979–87; 23, Pittsburgh Penguins, 1991–93; 15, Detroit Red Wings, 1993–95.

WORLD CHAMPIONSHIPS AND OLYMPIC GAMES

World Championships were first held for amateurs in 1920 in conjunction with the Olympic Games, which were also considered world championships up to 1968. Since 1976, the World Championships have been open to professionals. The USSR won 22 world titles between 1954 and 1990 (with Russia winning a further title in 1993), including the Olympic titles of 1956, 1964 and 1968. It has a record eight Olympic titles with a further five in 1972, 1976, 1984, 1988 and 1992 (as the Unified Team). The longest Olympic career is that of Richard Torriani (Switzerland; 1911–88) from 1928 to 1948. The most gold medals won by any player is three, achieved by Soviet players Vitaliy Davydov, Anatoliy Firsov, Viktor Kuzkin and Aleksandr Ragulin in 1964, 1968 and 1972, and by Vladislav Tretyak in 1972, 1976 and 1984.

Women's World Championships   The first three world championships have been won by Canada, 1990, 1992 and 1994.

Most goals   The greatest number of goals recorded in a world championship match was when Australia beat New Zealand 58–0 in Perth on March 15, 1987.

Fastest goals   In minor leagues, Per Olsen scored two seconds after the start of the match for Rungsted against Odense in the Danish First Division in Hørsholm, Denmark on January 14, 1990. Three goals in 10 seconds was achieved by Jørgen Palmgren Erichsen for Frisk vs. Holmen in a junior league match in Norway on March 17, 1991. The Skara Ishockeyclubb, Sweden scored three goals in 11 seconds against Örebro IK in Skara on October 18, 1981. The Vernon Cougars scored five goals in 56 seconds against the Salmon Arm Aces in Vernon, British Columbia, Canada on August 6, 1982. The Kamloops Knights of Columbus scored seven goals in 2 min. 22 sec. vs. the Prince George Vikings on January 25, 1980.

HORSE RACING

Highest prizes   The highest prize money won for a day's racing is $10 million, for the Breeders' Cup series of seven races staged annually since 1984. Included each year is a record $3 million for the Breeders' Cup Classic.

Breeders' Cup   Pat Day has a record eight wins in Breeders' Cup races: Classic (1984, 1990); Distaff (1986, 1991); Turf (1987); Juvenile Fillies (1987, 1994); and Juvenile (1994).

Highest earnings   Pat Day has won a record $9,551,000 in Breeders' Cup racing, 1984–93.

Biggest payout   Anthony A. Speelman and Nicholas John Cowan (both Great Britain) won $1,627,084.40, after federal income tax of $406,768.00 was withheld, on a $64 9-horse accumulator at Santa Anita Racetrack, Arcadia, CA on April 19, 1987. Their first seven selections won, and the payout was for a jackpot accumulated over 24 days.

Most successful owners   The most lifetime wins by an owner is 4,775, by Marion H. Van Berg (1895–1971), in North America, in 35 years. The most wins in a year is 494, by Dan R. Lasater (U.S.) in 1974. The greatest amount won in a year is $6,881,902, by Sam-Son Farm in North America in 1991.

Most successful trainers   Jack Charles Van Berg (U.S.) has the greatest number of wins in a year, 496 in 1976. The career record is 6,362, by Dale Baird (U.S.) from 1962 to the end of 1993. The greatest amount won in a year is $17,842,358, by D. Wayne Lukas (U.S.) in 1988; he has won a record $140,024,750 in his career.

HORSES

Oldest thoroughbred   The greatest age recorded for a thoroughbred racehorse is 42 years, in the case of the chestnut gelding Tango Duke (foaled 1935), owned by Carmen J. Koper of Barongarook, Victoria, Australia. The horse died on January 25, 1978.

Most successful horse   The horse with the best win–loss record was Kincsem, a Hungarian mare foaled in 1874, who was unbeaten in 54 races (1876–79) throughout Europe, including the Goodwood Cup (Great Britain) of 1878.

Longest winning sequence   Camarero, foaled in 1951, was undefeated in 56 races in Puerto Rico from April 19, 1953 to his first defeat on August 17, 1955 (in his career to 1956, he won 73 of 77 races).

Career   Chorisbar (foaled 1935) won 197 of his 325 races in Puerto Rico, 1937–47. Lenoxbar (foaled 1935) won 46 races in one year, 1940, in Puerto Rico from 56 starts.

GUESS WHAT?

Q. HOW TALL WAS THE TALLEST HORSE?

A. LOOK IN "HORSES" (LIVING WORLD)

United States   The most career wins in the United States is 89, by Kingston in 138 starts, 1886–94. This included 33 in stakes races, but the horse with the most wins in stakes races in the U.S. is Exterminator (foaled 1915), with 34 between 1918 and 1923. John Henry (foaled 1975) won a record 25 graded stakes races, including 16 at Grade 1, 1978–84. On his retirement in 1984, his career prize money was $6,597,947, nearly twice as much as the next best. Of 83 races, he won 39, was second 15 times and third 9 times.

Same race   Doctor Syntax (foaled 1811) won the Preston Gold Cup on seven successive occasions, 1815–21.

Triple Crown winners   The Triple Crown (Kentucky Derby, Preakness Stakes, Belmont Stakes) has been achieved 11 times, most recently by Af-

---

DID YOU KNOW?

The most valuable animals are racehorses. The most ever paid for a yearling was $13.1 million on July 23, 1985 in Keeneland, KY by Robert Sangster and partners for Seattle Dancer.

Sunday Silence holds the record for most money won in a year. He won the Kentucky Derby (center jockey) and the Preakness Stakes, and was second in the Belmont Stakes, winning over $4.5 million in 1989. (*Bob Thomas/Joyner*)

firmed in 1978. Eddie Arcaro is the only jockey to have ridden two Triple Crown winners, Whirlaway in 1941 and Citation in 1948. Two trainers have schooled two Triple Crown winners: James Fitzsimmons, Gallant Fox in 1930 and Omaha in 1935; Ben A. Jones, Whirlaway in 1941 and Citation in 1948.

Greatest winnings The career earnings record is $6,679,242, by the 1987 Kentucky Derby winner Alysheba (foaled 1984), 1986–88. Alysheba's career record was 11 wins, 8 seconds and 2 thirds from 26 races. The most prize money earned in a year is $4,578,454, by Sunday Silence (foaled 1986) in 1989. The record was set in nine races, Sunday Silence winning seven times and finishing second twice.

The leading money-winning mare is Dance Smartly (foaled 1988), with $3,263,346 in North America, 1990–92.

The one-race record is $2.6 million, by Spend a Buck (foaled 1982), for the Jersey Derby, Garden State Park, NJ on May 27, 1985, of which $2 mil-

---

DID YOU KNOW?

Willie Shoemaker (U.S.), whose racing weight was 97 pounds at 4 ft. 11 in., rode a record 8,833 winners out of 40,350 mounts from his first ride on March 19, 1949 to his retirement on February 3, 1990. Laffit Pincay, Jr. (U.S.) earned a career record $186,267,029 from 1964 to May 1, 1995.

lion was a bonus for having previously won the Kentucky Derby and two preparatory races at Garden State Park.

Fastest horses   The fastest race speed recorded is 43.26 MPH, by Big Racket, 20.8 seconds for ³/₄ mile, in Mexico City, Mexico on February 5, 1945. The 4-year-old carried 114 pounds. The record for 1¹/₂ miles is 37.82 MPH, by 3-year-old Hawkster (carrying 121 pounds) at Santa Anita Park, Arcadia, CA on October 14, 1989, with a time of 2 min. 22.8 sec.

JOCKEYS

Most successful jockeys   The most races won by a jockey in a year is 598, in 2,312 rides, by Kent Jason Desormeaux (U.S.) in 1989. The greatest amount won in a year is 3,133,742,000 yen ($28.4 million) by Yutaka Take (Japan) in Japan in 1993. The greatest amount won in the United States in a year is $14,877,298, by José Adeon Santos (U.S.) in 1988. Mike Smith (U.S.) rode a season record 62 stakes race winners in 1993.

Most wins   One day   The most winners ridden in one day is nine, by Chris Antley (U.S.) on October 31, 1987. They consisted of four in the afternoon at Aqueduct, NY and five in the evening at The Meadowlands, East Rutherford, NJ.

One card   The most winners ridden on one card is eight, by six riders, most recently (and in fewest rides) by Pat Day, in only nine rides in Arlington, IL on September 13, 1989.

Consecutive   The longest winning streak is 12, by Sir Gordon Richards (Great Britain)—one race in Nottingham, England on October 3, six out of six at Chepstow on October 4, and the first five races next day at Chepstow, in 1933; and by Pieter Stroebel in Bulawayo, Southern Rhodesia (now Zimbabwe), June 7 to July 7, 1958.

United States   The longest consecutive winning streak for an American jockey is nine races, by Albert Adams (U.S.) at Marlboro Racetrack, MD over three days, September 10–12, 1930. He won the last two races on September 10, all six races on September 11 and the first race on September 12.

HARNESS RACING

Most successful horses   The trotter Goldsmith Maid won an all-time record 350 races (including dashes and heats), 1864–77. The career record tally for a pacer is 262 wins (including dashes and heats) by Single G, 1918–26. The season record is 65 races, by the pacer Victory Hy in 1950. The record for a trotter is 53 victories, by Make Believe in 1949.

Most successful driver   The most successful sulky driver in North American harness racing history is Herve Filion of Québec, Canada, who had achieved 14,712 wins and prize earnings of $84,697,340 through June 25, 1995. The most wins in a year is 843, by Walter Case (U.S.) in 1992. The most wins in a day is 12, by Mike Lechance at Yonkers Raceway, NY on June 23, 1987.

HARNESS RACING MILE RECORDS

Trotting		Horse (driver)	Place	Date
World	1:51	*Pine Chip*	Lexington,	
		(John Campbell)	KY	Oct. 1, 1994
Race	1:51 4/5	*Beat the Wheel*	East Rutherford,	
		(Cat Manzi)	NJ	Jul. 7, 1994

Pacing				
World	1:46 1/5	*Cambest*	Springfield,	
		(Bill O'Donnell)	IL	Aug. 16, 1993
Race	1:48 2/5	*Staying Together*	East Rutherford,	
		(Bill O'Donnell)	NJ	Jun. 19, 1993

John D. Campbell (U.S.) has the highest career earnings, $132,240,609 through June 24, 1995. This includes a season record of $11,620,878 in 1990, when he won 543 races.

Triple Crown *Trotters* The Triple Crown consists of three races: Hambletonian, Kentucky Futurity, and Yonkers Trot. Six trotters have won the Triple Crown. Stanley Dancer is the only driver to win two Triple Crowns, 1968 and 1972.

Hambletonian: The record time is 1 min. 53 1/5 sec., by American Winner, driven by Ron Pierce in 1993.

Kentucky Futurity: The race record time is 1 min. 52 3/5 sec., by Pine Chip, driven by John Campbell in 1993.

Yonkers Trot: The race record time is 1 min. 56 2/5 sec., by American Winner, driven by Ron Pierce, in 1993.

Pacers The Triple Crown consists of three races: Cane Pace, Little Brown Jug, and Messenger Stakes. Seven horses have won the Triple Crown, each with different drivers.

Cane Pace: The race record time is 1 min. 51 2/5 sec., by Riyadh, driven by Jim Morrill Jr., in 1993.

Little Brown Jug: The race record time is 1 min. 52 sec., by Life Sign, driven by John Campbell, in 1993.

Messenger Stakes: The race record time is 1 min. 51 sec., by Cam's Card Shark driven by John Campbell, in 1994.

Highest price The highest price paid was $19.2 million for Nihilator (a pacer), who was syndicated by Wall Street Stable and Almahurst Stud Farm in 1984.

Greatest winnings For any harness horse the record amount is $4,907,307, by the trotter Peace Corps, 1988–93.

The single-season record is $2,264,714 by the pacer Cam's Card Shark in 1994.

The largest-ever purse was $2,161,000, for the Woodrow Wilson 2-year-old race over one mile at The Meadowlands, East Rutherford, NJ on August 16, 1984. Of this sum a record $1,080,500 went to the winner, Nihilator, driven by William O'Donnell.

MAJOR RACING RECORDS

Triple Crown

Race (instituted)	Record Time	Most Wins by a Jockey	Most Wins by a Trainer	Most Wins by an Owner	Largest Field
Kentucky Derby (1875) 1¼ miles Churchill Downs, Louisville, KY	1 min. 59.4 sec. Secretariat, 1973	5—Eddie Arcaro 1938, '41, '45, '48, '52 5—Bill Hartack 1957, '60, '62, '64, '69	6—Ben Jones 1938, '41, '44, '48, '49, '52	8—Calumet Farm 1941, '44, '48, '49, '52, '57, '58, '68	23 (1974)
Preakness Stakes (1873) 1 mile 1½ furlongs Pimlico, Baltimore, MD	1 min. 53.2 sec. Tank's Prospect, 1985	6—Eddie Arcaro '48, '50, '51, '55, '57	7—Robert Wyndham Walden 1875, '78, '79, '80, '81, '82, '88	5—George Lorillard 1878, '79, '80, '81, '82	18 (1928)
Belmont Stakes (1867) 1½ miles Belmont Park, NY	2 min. 24.0 sec. Secretariat, 1973 (By a record 31 lengths)	6—Jimmy McLaughlin 1882, '83, '84, '86, '87, '88 6—Eddie Arcaro 1941, '42, '45, '48, '52, '55	8—James Rowe Sr. 1883, '84, 1901, '04, '07, '08, '10, '13	5—Dwyer Bros. 1883, '84, '86, '87, '88 5—James R. Keene 1901, '04, '07, '08, '10 5—William Woodward Sr. (Belair Stud) 1930, '32, '35, '36, '39	15 (1983)

Famous International Races

Race	Fastest time	Most wins, jockey	Most wins, trainer	Most wins, owner	Races (first year)
Derby (1780) 1½ miles Epsom Downs, Great Britain	2 min. 33.8 sec. Mahmoud, 1936 2 min. 33.84 sec. Kahyasi, 1988 (Electronically timed)	9—Lester Piggott 1954, '57, '60, '68, '70, '72, '76, '77, '83	7—Robert Robson 1793, 1802, '09, '10, '15, '17, '23 7—John Porter 1868, 82, '83, '86, '90, '91, '99 7—Fred Darling 1922, '25, '26, '31, '38, '40, '41	5—3rd Earl of Egremont 1782, 1804, '05, '07, '26 5—HH Aga Khan III 1930, '35, '36, '48, '52	34 (1862)
Prix de l'Arc de Triomphe (1920) 1 mile 864 yd. Longchamp, France	2 min. 26.3 sec. Trempolino, 1987	4—Jacques Doyasbère 1942, '44, '50, '51 4—Frédéric Freddy Head 1966, '72, '76, '79 4—Yves Saint-Martin 1970, '74, '82, '84 4—Pat Eddery 1980, '85, '86, '87	4—Charles Semblat 1942, '44, '46, '49 4—Alec Head 1952, '59, '76, '81 4—François Mathet 1950, '51, '70, '82	6—Marcel Boussac 1936, '37, '42, '44, '46, '49	30 (1967)
VRC Melbourne Cup (1861) 1 mile 1,739 yd. Flemington, Victoria, Australia	3 min. 16.3 sec. Kingston Rule, 1990	4—Bobby Lewis 1902, '15, '19, '27 4—Harry White 1974, '75, '78, '79	9—Bart Cummings 1965, '66, '67, '74, '75, '77, '79, '90, '91	4—Etienne de Mestre 1861, '62, '67, '78	39 (1890)
Grand National (1839) 4½ miles Aintree, Liverpool, Great Britain	8 min. 47.8 sec. Mr. Frisk, 1990	5-George Stevens 1856, '63, '64, '69, '70	4—Fred Rimell 1956, '61, '70, '76	3—James Machell 1873, '74, '76 3—Sir Charles Assheton-Smith 1893, 1912, '13 3—Noel Le Mare 1973, '74, '77	66 (1929)

HURLING

Most titles *All-Ireland* The greatest number of All-Ireland Championships won by one team is 27, by Cork, between 1890 and 1990. The greatest number of successive wins is four, by Cork (1941–44).

Most appearances The most appearances in All-Ireland finals is 10, shared by Christy Ring (Cork and Munster) and John Doyle (Tipperary). They also share the record of All-Ireland medals, won with eight each. Ring's appearances on the winning side were in 1941–44, 1946 and 1952–54, while Doyle's were in 1949–51, 1958, 1961–62 and 1964–65. Ring also played in a record 22 interprovincial finals (1942–63), and was on the winning side 18 times.

Highest and lowest scores The highest score in an All-Ireland final (60 minutes) was in 1989, when Tipperary, 41 (4 goals, 29 points) beat Antrim, 18 (3 goals, 9 points). The record aggregate score was when Cork, 39 (6 goals, 21 points) defeated Wexford, 25 (5 goals, 10 points), in the 80-minute final of 1970. A goal equals three points. The highest individual score was by Nick Rackard (Wexford), who scored 7 goals and 7 points against Antrim in the 1954 All-Ireland semifinal. The lowest score in an All-Ireland final was when Tipperary (1 goal, 1 point) beat Galway (zero) in the first championship at Birr in 1887.

Largest crowd The largest crowd was 84,865 for the All-Ireland Final between Cork and Wexford at Croke Park, Dublin in 1954.

ICE AND SAND YACHTING

Fastest speeds *Ice* The fastest speed officially recorded is 143 MPH, by John D. Buckstaff in a Class A stern-steerer on Lake Winnebago, WI in 1938. Such a speed is possible in a wind of 72 MPH.

Sand The official world record for a sand yacht is 66.48 MPH, set by Christian-Yves Nau (France) in *Mobil* in Le Touquet, France on March 22, 1981, when the wind speed reached 75 MPH. A speed of 88.4 MPH was attained by Nord Embroden (U.S.) in *Midnight at the Oasis* on Superior Dry Lake, CA on April 15, 1976.

Largest ice yacht The largest ice yacht was *Icicle*, built for Commodore John E. Roosevelt for racing on the Hudson River, NY in 1869. It was 68 ft. 11 in. long and carried 1,070 square feet of canvas.

Speeds in excess of 50 MPH are often reached in the sport of sand yachting. The highest speed ever attained is 88.4 MPH. (*Allsport/ B. Martin*)

ICE SKATING

Largest rink The world's largest indoor ice rink is in the Moscow Olympic Arena, which has an ice area of 86,800 square feet. The five rinks at Fujikyu Highland Skating Center in Japan total 285,243 square feet.

Barrel jumping on ice skates The official distance record is 29 ft. 5 in. over 18 barrels, by Yvon Jolin in Terrebonne, Québec, Canada on January 25, 1981. The women's record is 22 ft. 5¼ in. over 11 barrels, by Marie Josée Houle in Lasalle, Quebec, Canada on March 1, 1987.

FIGURE SKATING

Most titles *Olympic* The most Olympic gold medals won by a figure skater is three: by Gillis Grafström (Sweden) in 1920, 1924 and 1928 (also silver medal in 1932); by Sonja Henie (Norway) in 1928, 1932 and 1936;

and by Irina Rodnina (USSR) with two different partners in the pairs in 1972, 1976 and 1980.

Triple Crown   Karl Schäfer (Austria) and Sonja Henie achieved double "Triple Crowns" (world, Olympic and European or U.S. titles won in the

---

LONG JUMP!

Robin Cousins (Great Britain) jumped 19 ft. 1 in. in an axel jump, and 18 feet with a back flip on Richmond Ice Rink, Richmond, England on November 16, 1983.

---

same year), both in the years 1932 and 1936. This feat was repeated by Katarina Witt (East Germany) in 1984 and 1988.

World   The greatest number of men's individual world figure skating titles (instituted 1896) is 10, by Ulrich Salchow (Sweden) in 1901–05 and 1907–11. The women's record (instituted 1906) is also 10 individual titles, by Sonja Henie between 1927 and 1936. Irina Rodnina won 10 pairs titles (instituted 1908), four with Aleksey Ulanov, 1969–72, and six with her former husband Aleksandr Zaitsev, 1973–78. The most ice dance titles (instituted 1952) won is six, by Lyudmila Pakhomova and her husband Aleksandr Gorshkov (USSR), 1970–74 and 1976. They also won the first-ever Olympic ice dance title in 1976.

Dick Button set U.S. records with two Olympic gold medals, 1948 and 1952, and five world titles, 1948–52. Five women's world titles were won by Carol Heise, 1956–60, as well as the 1960 Olympic gold.

United States   The U.S. Championships were first held in 1914. The most titles won by an individual is nine, by Maribel Y. Vinson, 1928–33 and 1935–37. She also won six pairs titles, and her aggregate of 15 titles is equaled by Therese Blanchard (née Weld), who won six individual and nine pairs titles between 1914 and 1927. The men's individual record is seven, by Roger Turner, 1928–34, and by Dick Button, 1946–52.

Highest marks   The highest tally of maximum six marks awarded in an international championship was 29, to Jayne Torvill and Christopher Dean (both Great Britain) in the World Ice Dance Championships in Ottawa, Canada, March 22–24, 1984. This comprised seven in the compulsory dances, a perfect set of nine for presentation in the set pattern dance, and 13 in the free dance, including another perfect set from all nine judges for artistic presentation. In their career Torvill and Dean received a record total of 136 sixes.

The most by a soloist is seven: by Donald Jackson (Canada) in the World Men's Championship in Prague, Czechoslovakia in 1962; and by Midori Ito (Japan) in the World Women's Championships in Paris, France in 1989.

SPEED SKATING

Most medals　*Olympic*　The most Olympic gold medals ever won in speed skating is six, by Lidiya Skoblikova (USSR) in 1960 (two) and 1964 (four).

The men's record is five, by Clas Thunberg (Finland), in 1924 and 1928 (including one tied); and by Eric Heiden (U.S.), uniquely at one Games on Lake Placid, NY in 1980.

The most medals won is seven, by Clas Thunberg, who won a silver and a bronze in addition to his five gold medals, and by Ivar Ballangrud (Norway), four gold, two silver and a bronze, 1928–36.

World　The greatest number of world overall titles (instituted 1893) won by any skater is five—by Oscar Mathisen (Norway) in 1908–09 and 1912–14; by Clas Thunberg in 1923, 1925, 1928–29 and 1931; and by Karin Kania (née Enke; East Germany) in 1982, 1984, 1986–88. Kania also won a record six overall titles at the World Sprint Championships, 1980–81, 1983–84, 1986–87. A record six men's sprint overall titles have been won by Igor Zhelezovskiy (USSR/Belarus), 1985–86, 1989 and 1991–93.

United States　Eric Heiden won a U.S. record three overall world titles, 1977–79. He also won four overall titles at the World Sprint Championships, 1977–80. His sister Beth Heiden became the only U.S. women's all-around champion in 1979. Bonnie Blair has won a U.S. women's record three overall World Sprint Championships, 1989, 1994–95. Sheila Young has also won three, 1973, 1975–76. Bonnie Blair has won more Olympic medals—five gold and one bronze—than any other U.S. citizen.

World Short-Track Championships　The most successful skater in these championships (instituted 1978) has been Sylvie Daigle (Canada), women's overall champion in 1979, 1983 and 1989–90.

Longest race　The "Elfstedentocht" ("Tour of the Eleven Towns"), which originated in the 17th century, was held in the Netherlands, 1909–63, and again in 1985 and 1986, covering 200 km (124 miles 483 yards). The weather does not permit an annual race in the Netherlands, so alternative "Elfstedentocht" have taken place on Lake Vesijärvi, near Lahti, Finland; Ottawa River, Canada; and Lake Weissensee, Austria. The record time for 200 km is: *(men)* 5 hr. 40 min. 37 sec., by Dries van Wijhe (Netherlands); and *(women)* 5 hr. 48 min. 8 sec., by Alida Pasveer (Netherlands), both on Lake Weissensee (altitude 3,609 feet), Austria on February 11, 1989. Jan-Roelof Kruithof (Netherlands) won the race nine times—1974, 1976–77, 1979–84. An estimated 16,000 skaters took part in 1986.

Greatest 24-hour distance　Martinus Kuiper (Netherlands) skated a record 339.67 miles in 24 hours in Alkmaar, Netherlands in December 1988.

SPEED SKATING RECORDS

Meters	min. : sec.	Name and Country	Place	Date
MEN				
500	35.76	Dan Jansen (U.S.)	Calgary, Canada	Jan. 30, 1994
1,000	1:12.37	Yasunori Miyabe (Japan)	Calgary, Canada	Mar. 26, 1994
1,500	1:51.29	Johann-Olav Koss (Norway)	Hamar, Norway	Feb. 16, 1994
3,000	3:56.16	Thomas Bos (Netherlands)	Calgary, Canada	Mar. 3, 1992
5,000	6:34.96	Johann-Olav Koss	Hamar, Norway	Feb. 13, 1994
10,000	13:30.55	Johann-Olav Koss	Hamar, Norway	Feb. 20, 1994
WOMEN				
500	38.69	Bonnie Blair (U.S.)	Calgary, Canada	Feb. 12, 1995
1,000	1:17.65	Christa Rothenburger (now Luding) (East Germany)	Calgary, Canada	Feb. 26, 1988
1,500	1:59.30†	Karin Kania (East Germany)	Medeo, USSR	Mar. 22, 1986
3,000	4:09.32	Gunda Niemann (née Kleeman) (Germany)	Calgary, Canada	Mar. 25, 1994
5,000	7:03.26	Gunda Niemann	Calgary, Canada	Mar. 26, 1994

† Set at high altitude.

SHORT TRACK

MEN

500	42.99	Mirko Vuillermin (Italy)	Graz, Austria	Jan. 21, 1995
1,000	1:28.47	Mike McMillen (New Zealand)	Denver, CO	Apr. 4, 1992
1,500	2:22.36	Eric Flaim (U.S.)	Beijing, China	Mar. 21, 1993
3,000	5:00.83	Chae Ji-hoon (South Korea)	Lake Placid, NY	Jan. 16, 1993
5,000 relay	7:10.95	New Zealand	Beijing, China	Mar. 28, 1993

WOMEN

500	45.60	Zhang Yanmei (China)	Beijing, China	Mar. 27, 1993
1,000	1:34.07	Nathalie Lambert (Canada)	Hamar, Norway	Nov. 7, 1993
1,500	2:27.38	Chun Lee-Kyung (South Korea)	Jaca, Spain	Feb. 23, 1995
3,000	5:17.59	Won Hye-kyung (South Korea)	Asahikawa, Japan	Dec. 6, 1993
3,000 relay	4:26.56	Canada	Beijing, China	Mar. 28, 1993

JAI ALAI (PELOTA VASCA)

World Championships The *Federacion Internacional de Pelota Vasca* stages World Championships every four years (the first in 1952). The most successful pair have been Roberto Elias and Juan Labat (Argentina), who won the *Trinquete Share* four times, 1952, 1958, 1962 and 1966. Labat won a record seven world titles in all between 1952 and 1966. Riccardo Bizzozero (Argentina) also won seven world titles in various *Trinquete* and *Frontón corto* events, 1970–82. The most wins in the long court game Cesta

---

FRONTÓN!

The world's largest frontón (enclosed stadium) is the Palm Beach Jai Alai, West Palm Beach, which has a seating capacity of 6,000 and covers three acres.

Punta is three, by José Hamuy (Mexico; 1934–83), with two different partners, 1958, 1962 and 1966.

Fastest speed An electronically measured ball velocity of 188 MPH was recorded by José Ramon Areitio (Spain) at the Newport Jai Alai, RI on August 3, 1979.

Longest domination The longest domination as the world's No. 1 player was enjoyed by Chiquito de Cambo (France; born Joseph Apesteguy) from the beginning of the century until he was succeeded in 1938 by Jean Urruty (France).

Largest crowd The record attendance for a jai alai contest was 15,052 people at the World Jai Alai in Miami, FL on December 27, 1975. The frontón, which is the oldest in the United States (1926), has a seating capacity of 3,884.

JUDO

Most titles *World and Olympic* World Championships were inaugurated in Tokyo, Japan in 1956. Women's championships were first held in 1980 in New York. Yashiro Yamashita won nine consecutive Japanese titles from 1977 to 1985; four world titles (Over 95 kg in 1979, 1981 and 1983; Open in

1981); and the Olympic Open category in 1984. He retired undefeated after 203 successive wins between 1977 and 1985. Two other men have won four world titles—Shozo Fujii (Japan), Under 80 kg 1971, 1973 and 1975, Under 78 kg 1979; and Naoya Ogawa (Japan), Open 1987, 1989, 1991 and Over 95 kg 1989.

The only men to have won two Olympic gold medals are Wilhelm Ruska (Netherlands), Over 93 kg and Open in 1972; Peter Seisenbacher (Austria), 86 kg 1984 and 1988; Hitoshi Saito (Japan), Over 95 kg 1984 and 1988; and Waldemar Legien (Poland), 78 kg 1988 and 86 kg 1992. Ingrid Berghmans (Belgium) has won a record six women's world titles (first held 1980): Open 1980, 1982, 1984 and 1986 and Under 72 kg in 1984 and 1989. She has also won four silver medals and a bronze. She won the Olympic 72 kg title in 1988, when women's judo was introduced as a demonstration sport.

The only U.S. judo players to win world titles were Michael Swain, in the men's 71 kg class in 1987, and Ann-Maria Bernadette Burns in the women's 56 kg in 1984.

Most throws Brian Woodward and David Norman completed 33,681 judo throws in 10 hours in Rainham, England on April 10, 1994.

Jiu-Jitsu The World Council of Jiu-Jitsu Organization has staged World Championships biennially since 1984. The Canadian team has been the winner on each occasion.

KARATE

World Championships Great Britain has won a record six world titles (instituted 1970) in the kumite team event, in 1975, 1982, 1984, 1986, 1988 and 1990. Two men's individual kumite titles have been won by Pat McKay (Great Britain) in Under 80 kg, 1982 and 1984; Emmanuel Pinda (France) in Open, 1984, and Over 80 kg, 1988; Thierry Masci (France) in Under 70 kg, in 1986 and 1988; and José Manuel Egea (Spain) in Under 80 kg, 1990 and 1992. Four women's kumite titles have been won by Guus van Mourik (Netherlands) in Over 60 kg, in 1982, 1984, 1986 and 1988. Three individual kata titles have been won by: *(men)* Tsuguo Sakumoto (Japan) in 1984, 1986 and 1988; *(women)* Mie Nakayama (Japan) in 1982, 1984 and 1986, and Yuki Mimura (Japan) in 1988, 1990 and 1992.

"Tokey" Hill is the only American ever to win a gold medal at the Karate World Championships in Madrid, Spain. He won the 80 kg division on November 27, 1980.

LACROSSE

MEN

Most titles *World* The U.S. has won six of the seven World Championships, in 1967, 1974, 1982, 1986, 1990 and 1994. Canada won the other world title in 1978, beating the U.S. 17–16 in overtime; this was the first tied international match.

NCAA National champions were determined by committee from 1936; since 1971 they have been decided by NCAA playoffs. Johns Hopkins University has the most wins overall: seven NCAA titles between 1974 and 1987, and six wins and five ties between 1941 and 1970.

Most points The record for most points in the NCAA lacrosse tournament is 25, by Eamon McEneaney (Cornell) in 1977 and Tim Goldstein (Cornell) in 1987. Both players played in three games. Two players are tied with 12 points in one championship game: Ed Mullen scored 12 for Maryland vs. Navy in the 1976 championship game; and Gary Gait scored 12 on May 22, 1988, for Syracuse vs. Navy.

Highest score The highest score in an international lacrosse match is Scotland's 34–3 win over Germany in Greater Manchester, England on July 25, 1994.

In 1994, the U.S. beat Australia 21–7 to secure the World Cup lacrosse title for the sixth time. (*Allsport/A. Want*)

The first reported playing of lacrosse by women was in 1886. The women's game has evolved separately from the men's game, so the rules now differ considerably.

World Championships/World Cup The first World Cup was held in 1982, replacing the world championships that had been held three times since 1969. The U.S. has won four times, in 1974, 1982, 1989 and 1993.

NCAA The NCAA first staged a women's national championship in 1982.

Most titles Maryland has won the most titles, with three: 1986, 1992 and 1995.

MODERN PENTATHLON

Most titles World András Balczó (Hungary) won the record number of world titles (instituted 1949), six individual and seven team. He won the world individual title in 1963, 1965–67 and 1969 and the Olympic title in 1972. His seven team titles (1960–70) comprised five world and two Olympic.

The USSR has won a record 15 world and four Olympic team titles. Hungary has also won a record four Olympic team titles and 10 world titles.

Women's World Championships were first held in 1981, replacing the World Cup, which began in 1978. Poland has won a record five women's world team titles: 1985, 1988–91; Great Britain won three world titles, 1981–83, and three World Cups, 1978–80. Eva Fjellerup (Denmark) has won the individual title four times, 1990–91, 1993–94.

The only U.S. modern pentathletes to win world titles have been Robert Nieman, 1979, when the men's team also won, and Lori Norwood (women's) in 1989.

Olympic The greatest number of Olympic gold medals won in pentathlon is three, by András Balczó, a member of the winning team in 1960 and 1968 and the 1972 individual champion.

DID YOU KNOW?

The women's U.S. National pentathlon championship was first held in 1977; Kim Dunlop (née Arata) has won a record nine titles (1979–80, 1984–89 and 1991). The men's championship was inaugurated in 1955. Mike Burley has won a record four titles (1977, 1979, 1981, 1985).

Lars Hall (Sweden) has uniquely won two individual championships (1952 and 1956). Pavel Serafimovich Lednyev (USSR) won a record seven medals (two team gold, one team silver, one individual silver, three individual bronze), 1968–80.

MOTORCYCLE RACING

Oldest race   The oldest continuous motorcycle races in the world are the Auto-Cycle Union Tourist Trophy (TT) series, first held on the 15.81 mile "Peel" (St. John's) course in the Isle of Man, Great Britain on May 28, 1907, and still run in the island on the "Mountain" circuit.

Earliest race   The first reported race in the United States was won by George Holden of Brooklyn, NY in 1903, recording 14 min. 57.2 sec. for 10 miles.

Fastest circuits   The highest average lap speed attained on any closed circuit is 160.288 MPH, by Yvon du Hamel (Canada) on a modified 903-cc 4-cylinder Kawasaki Z1 at the 31-degree banked 2.5-mile Daytona International Speedway, FL in March 1973. His lap time was 56.149 seconds.

The fastest road circuit used to be Francorchamps circuit near Spa, Belgium, then 8.77 miles long. It was lapped in 3 min. 50.3 sec. (average speed 137.150 MPH) by Barry Sheene (Great Britain) on a 495-cc 4-cylinder Suzuki during the Belgian Grand Prix on July 3, 1977. On that occasion he set a record time for this 10-lap (87.74-mile) race of 38 min. 58.5 sec. (average speed 135.068 MPH).

Longest circuit   The 37.73-mile "Mountain" circuit on the Isle of Man, over which the Tourist Trophy (TT) races have been run since 1911, has 264 curves and corners and is the longest used for any motorcycle race.

Most successful riders   Giacomo Agostini (Italy) won 122 races (68 in 500 cc, 54 in 350 cc) in the World Championship series between April 24, 1965 and September 25, 1977, including a record 19 in 1970, a season's total also achieved by Mike Hailwood (Great Britain) in 1966.

The record number of career wins for any one class is 75, by Rolf Biland in sidecar.

Angel Roldan Nieto (Spain) won a record seven 125-cc titles, 1971–72, 1979, 1981–84, and he also won a record six titles in 50 cc, 1969–70, 1972,

---

MEAN MACHINES!

Japanese Yamaha machines won 45 World Championships between 1964 and 1992.

1975–77. Phil Read (Great Britain) won a record four 250-cc titles, 1964–65, 1968, 1971.

Sidecar Rolf Biland (Switzerland), won seven world sidecar titles, 1978–79, 1981, 1983 and 1992–94.

World Championships The most World Championship titles (instituted by the *Fédération Internationale Motocycliste* in 1949) won is 15, by Giacomo Agostini—seven in 350 cc, 1968–74, and eight in 500 cc in 1966–72, 1975. He is the only man to have won two World Championships in five consecutive years (350-cc and 500-cc titles, 1968–72).

The most world titles won by an American motorcyclist is four, by Eddie Lawson, in 500 cc in 1984, 1986, 1988–89.

In 1994, Michael Doohan won a record six successive races in the 500-cc class.

Trials A record six World Trials Championships have been won by Jordi Tarrès (Spain), 1987, 1989–91, 1993–94.

Youngest and oldest world champions Loris Capirossi (Italy) is the youngest to win a World Championship. He was 17 yr. 165 days old when he won the 125-cc title on September 16, 1990. The oldest was Hermann-Peter Müller of West Germany, who won the 250-cc title in 1955 at the age of 46.

In 1994, Michael Doohan won nine 500-cc races, including a record six in succession, breaking the record set by Giacomo Agostini in 1972. (*Allsport/M. Cooper*)

MOTO-CROSS

World Championships Joël Robert (Belgium) won six 250-cc Moto-cross World Championships (1964, 1968–72). Between April 25, 1964 and June 18, 1972 he won a record 50 250-cc Grand Prix.

Eric Geboers (Belgium) has uniquely won all three categories of the Moto-cross World Championships, in 125 cc in 1982 and 1983, 250 cc in 1987 and 500 cc in 1988 and 1990.

BORN TO REV

She was a fearless 3-year-old on a Suzuki with training wheels. She competed for the first time at age 6, and admits she was "a little freaked out by all those little boys going so fast." Now, after becoming a world champion moto-cross racer at 14, she definitely doesn't get freaked out anymore.

Kristy Shealy beat women from countries as diverse as Switzerland, New Zealand and Ukraine to win the Women's World Cup when it was held in 1994 in her home state of Texas. This year she defends her crown in Milan. On the way, Shealy will take on the nationals, test her mettle in her first competition against men, do exhibitions, and—in between—practice two or three times a day, with several races a week.

"My trainer works on my riding skills with me, and teaches me a whole lot of attitude," Shealy says. "Moto-cross is half body, half mind. You're outside, going up and down hills, doing doubles—jumping from one jump to the other—and triples—jumping over one jump to another."

How fast does she travel? She turns to her father and asks, "Dad? How fast are we going?" The answer comes back: "Fifty, fifty-five, sixty-five . . ."

Aside from a dislocated hip, Shealy hasn't been injured while racing. "My mind's in top shape," she says. "I tell myself, 'These guys are not better than me. I can run with them.'"

Besides future trophies, bigger and better sponsorships, and interviews with Ted Turner, surely there's a big, powerful motorcycle in Shealy's future. Then again, maybe not. "What I'd like is a long limousine car."

Youngest champion The youngest female moto-cross champion in the United States is Kristy Shealy (born December 12, 1978), who, at 14 years of age in 1993, won the women's division in the AMA Amateur/Youth National Motocross at Loretta Lynn's. In the same year, as the only female in the GNC Motocross 21st Annual Texas Series, she became the youngest racer to win in the 125 Novice Class.

(*Action Photos*)

Kristy Shealy

Youngest champion   The youngest-ever moto-cross world champion was Dave Strijbos (Netherlands), who won the 125-cc title at the age of 18 yr. 296 days on August 31, 1986.

United States   The youngest female moto-cross champion in the United States is Kristy Shealy (born December 12, 1978), who, at 14 years of age in 1993, won the women's division in the AMA Amateur/Youth National Motocross at Loretta Lynn's. In the same year, as the only female in the GNC Motocross 21st Annual Texas Series, she became the youngest racer to win in the 125 Novice Class. In March 1994, at age 15, Shealy became the youngest to win in the Ladies class at the GNC International Motocross Final.

OLYMPICS

Most participants   The greatest number of competitors at a Summer Games celebration was 9,369 (6,659 men, 2,710 women), who represented a record 169 nations, in Barcelona, Spain in 1992. The greatest number at a Winter Games was 1,737 (1,216 men, 521 women) representing 64 countries, in Lillehammer, Norway in 1994.

Largest crowd   The largest crowd at any Olympic site was 104,102 in the 1952 ski-jumping competition at the Holmenkøllen, outside Oslo, Norway. Estimates of the number of spectators of the marathon race through

---

DID YOU KNOW?

Christa Luding (née Rothenburger; East Germany) became the first woman to win a medal at both the Summer and Winter Games when she won a silver in the cycling sprint event in 1988. She had previously won medals for speed skating—500 meter gold in 1984, and 1,000 meter gold and 500 meter silver in 1988.

Tokyo, Japan on October 21, 1964 ranged from 500,000 to 1.5 million. The total spectator attendance in Los Angeles in 1984 was given as 5,797,923.

Olympic torch relay   The longest journey of the torch within one country was for the XV Olympic Winter Games in Canada in 1988. The torch arrived from Greece in St. John's, Newfoundland on November 17, 1987 and was transported 11,222 miles (5,088 miles on foot, 4,419 miles by

Baron de Coubertin, initiator of the modern Olympic Games, which celebrates its centennial in 1996 in Atlanta, GA. *(Allsport)*

aircraft/ferry, 1,712 miles by snowmobile and 3 miles by dogsled) until its arrival in Calgary on February 13, 1988.

Most medals   In the ancient Olympic Games, Leonidas of Rhodos won 12 running titles, 164–152 B.C. The most individual gold medals won by a male competitor in the modern Games is 10, by Raymond Clarence Ewry (U.S.) (see TRACK AND FIELD). The women's record is seven, by Vera Cáslavská-Odlozil (Czechoslovakia) (see GYMNASTICS).

The most gold medals won by an American woman is four, by three athletes: Patricia Joan McCormick (née Keller), diving, 1952–56; Evelyn Ashford, track and field, 1984–92; and Janet Evans, swimming, 1988–92. The most medals won by an American woman is eight, by swimmer Shirley Babashoff—gold in 4 ×100 meters freestyle relay 1972 and 1976, and six silver medals 1972–76, a record for any competitor in Olympic history.

Gymnast Larisa Latynina (USSR) won a record 18 medals, and the men's record is 15, by Nikolay Andrianov (see GYMNASTICS). The record at one celebration is eight, by gymnast Aleksandr Dityatin (USSR) in 1980.

The most medals won by an American Olympian is 11, in shooting, by Carl Townsend Osburn from 1912 to 1924—five gold, four silver, two bronze; by Mark Spitz, in swimming, 1968–72—nine gold, one silver, one

MOST MEDALS

WINTER GAMES *(1924–94)*

	Gold	Silver	Bronze	Total
USSR[1]	99	71	71	241
Norway	73	77	64	214
U.S.	53	55	39	147
Austria	36	48	44	128
Germany[2]	45	43	37	125
Finland	36	45	42	123
GDR[3]	39	36	35	110
Sweden	39	26	34	99
Switzerland	27	29	29	85
Italy	25	21	21	67

[1] *Includes Czarist Russia to 1912, CIS 1992, Russia 1994.*
[2] *Includes West Germany 1968–88.*
[3] *GDR (East Germany) 1968–88.*

bronze; and by Matt Biondi, in swimming, 1984–92—eight gold, two silver, one bronze.

The only Olympian to win four consecutive individual titles in the same event was Alfred Adolph Oerter (U.S.), who won the discus in 1956–68. However, Raymond Clarence Ewry (U.S.) won both the standing long jump and the standing high jump at four games in succession, 1900, 1904, 1906 (the Intercalated Games) and 1908. Also, Paul B. Elvstrøm won four successive gold medals in monotype yachting events, 1948–60, but there was a class change (1948 Firefly class, 1952–60 Finn class).

Swimmer Mark Spitz (U.S.) won a record seven golds at one celebration, in Munich in 1972, including three in relays. The most gold medals won in individual events at one celebration is five, by speed skater Eric Heiden (U.S.) at Lake Placid, NY in 1980.

The only man to win a gold medal in both the Summer and Winter Games is Edward Patrick Francis Eagan (U.S.), who won the 1920 light-heavyweight boxing title and was a member of the winning 4-man bob in 1932.

Youngest medal winners The youngest-ever winner was a French boy (whose name is not recorded) who coxed the Netherlands pair in rowing in 1900. He was 7–10 years old and he substituted for Dr. Hermanus Brockmann, who coxed in the heats but proved too heavy. The youngest-ever fe-

MOST MEDALS

SUMMER GAMES *(1896–94)* *

	Gold	Silver	Bronze	Total
USA	789	603	518	1,910
USSR[1]	442	361	333	1,136
Germany[2]	186	227	236	649
Great Britain	177	224	218	619
France	161	175	191	527
Sweden	133	149	171	453
GDR[3]	154	131	126	411
Italy	153	126	131	410
Hungary	136	124	144	404
Finland	98	77	112	287

* *Excludes medals won in Official Art competitions in 1912-1948.*
[1] *Includes Czarist Russia to 1912, CIS 1992, Russia 1994.*
[2] *Germany 1896-9164 and 1992, West Germany 1968–88.*
[3] *GDR (East Germany) 1968–88.*

male champion was Kim Yoon-mi (South Korea), age 13 yr. 83 days, in the 1994 women's 3,000 m short-track speed skating relay event.

United States The youngest American medalist and participant was Dorothy Poynton, who won the springboard diving bronze medal at 13 yr. 23 days in 1928. The youngest American male medalist was Donald Wills Douglas, Jr. with silver in 6-meter yachting in 1932, at 15 yr. 40 days. The youngest American gold medalist was Jackie Fields, who won the 1924 featherweight boxing title at 16 yr. 161 days.

Oldest medal winners Oscar Swahn (Sweden) won a silver medal in running deer shooting at 72 yr. 280 days in 1920.

United States The oldest American Olympic champion was retired minister Galen Spencer, who won a gold medal in the Team Round archery event two days after his 64th birthday in 1904.

The oldest American medalist and Olympic participant was Samuel Harding Duvall, who was 68 yr. 194 days when he was a member of the 1904 silver medal team.

Longest span The longest span of an Olympic competitor is 40 years, by Dr. Ivan Osiier (Denmark) in fencing, 1908–32 and 1948; Magnus Konow

(Norway; 1887–1972) in yachting, 1908–20, 1928 and 1936–48; Paul Elvstrøm (Denmark) in yachting, 1948–60, 1968–72 and 1984–88; and Durward Randolph Knowles (Great Britain 1948, then Bahamas) in yachting, 1948–72 and 1988. Raimondo d'Inzeo competed for Italy in equestrian events at a record eight celebrations from 1948 to 1976, gaining one gold, two silver and three bronze medals. Paul Elvstrøm and Durward Knowles equaled d'Inzeo's achievement in 1988. The longest span by a woman is 28 years, by Anne Jessica Ransehousen (née Newberry; U.S.) in dressage, 1960, 1964 and 1988. Fencer Kerstin Palm (Sweden) competed in a women's record seven competitions, 1964–88.

United States The U.S. record for longest span of Olympic competition by a man is 32 years, by equestrian Michael J. Plumb, who competed in seven Olympics. Janice Lee York Romary competed in fencing in six Games.

ORIENTEERING

Most titles Sweden has won the women's relay nine times—1966, 1970, 1974, 1976, 1981, 1983, 1985, 1989 and 1991. The men's relay has been won a record seven times by Norway—1970, 1978, 1981, 1983, 1985, 1987 and 1989. Three women's individual titles have been won by Annichen Kringstad (Sweden), in 1981, 1983 and 1985. The men's title has been won twice by Åge Hadler (Norway), in 1966 and 1972; Egil Johansen (Norway), in 1976 and 1978; and Øyvin Thon (Norway), in 1979 and 1981.

Most competitors The most competitors in a 1-day orienteering event was 38,000, in the Ruf des Herbstes held in Sibiu, Romania in 1982. The largest event is the 5-day Swedish O-Ringen in Småland, which attracted 120,000 competitors in July 1983.

U.S. National Championships This competition was first held in 1970. Sharon Crawford, of the New England Orienteering Club, has won a record 11 overall women's titles, 1977–82, 1984–87, 1989. Mikell Platt, of the Rocky Mountain Orienteering Club, has won a record seven overall men's titles, 1985 and 1988–93.

Ski orienteering The World Championships in ski orienteering were instituted in 1975. Sweden has won the men's relay five times (1977, 1980, 1982, 1984 and 1990) and Finland has won the women's relay five times (1975, 1977, 1980, 1988 and 1990). The most individual titles is four, by Ragnhild Bratberg (Norway), Classic 1986, 1990, Sprint 1988, 1990. The men's record is three, by Anssi Juutilainen (Finland), Classic 1984, 1988, Sprint 1992.

PARACHUTING

World championships *Team* The USSR won the men's team title a record seven times, in 1954, 1958, 1960, 1966, 1972, 1976 and 1980, and the women's team title six times, in 1956, 1958, 1966, 1968, 1972 and 1976.

Individual Nikolay Ushamyev (USSR) has won the individual title twice, in 1974 and 1980.

Greatest accuracy Dwight Reynolds scored a record 105 daytime dead centers, and Bill Wenger and Phil Munden tied with 43 night-time dead centers, competing as members of the U.S. Army Golden Knights in Yuma, AZ, in March 1978.

With electronic measuring, the official *Fédération Aeronautique Internationale* (FAI) record is 50 dead centers, by Linger Abdurakhmanov (USSR) in Fergana in 1988, when the women's record was set at 41, by Natalya Filinkova (USSR).

Paragliding The greatest distance flown is 176.4 miles, by Alex François Louw (South Africa) from Kuruman, South Africa on December 31, 1992. The women's distance record is 79.8 miles, by Judy Leden (Great Britain) from Vryburg, South Africa on December 9, 1992. The height gain record is 14,849 feet, by Robby Whittal (Great Britain), in Brandvlei, South Africa on January 6, 1993. All these records were tow launched.

Nigel Horder scored four successive dead centers at the Dutch Open, Flevhof, Netherlands on May 22, 1983.

POLO

Oldest polo club The oldest existing polo club in the United States is Meadow Brook Polo Club, Jericho, NY, founded in 1879.

World Championships The first World Championships were held in Berlin, Germany in 1989. The U.S. won the title, defeating Great Britain 7–6 in the final.

The United States Open Championship has been won 28 times by the Meadow Brook Polo Club, in 1916, 1920, 1923–41, 1946–51 and 1953.

Highest score The highest aggregate number of goals scored in an international polo match is 30, when Argentina beat the U.S. 21–9 in Meadowbrook, Long Island, NY in 1936.

Highest handicap The highest handicap based on six 7½-minute "chukkas" is 10 goals, introduced in the United States in 1891. A total of 56 players have received 10-goal handicaps.

MAN DROPS, RECORD RISES

Don Kellner started jumping out of planes in 1961, three years after sport parachuting was introduced in the United States. As of October 1994, he had 21,000 jumps to his credit. That's an average of 636 jumps a year, 53 jumps a month, 13 jumps a week, almost 2 a day.

At that rate (and at age 59), no one knows where Kellner will end up. But how did he get started? "I was in an airborne outfit in the service, but I never needed to jump. After carrying the stupid parachute around for so long, I wanted to try it." When he heard of someone 50 miles from his home who was going parachuting, he decided to go along. "He had one jump," Kellner grins, "so he knew all about it. We packed our own parachutes and took off. I jumped. The parachute worked. I have no idea why, but it did."

Before long, Kellner was jumping all the time and began teaching others. These days he has a full-time business out of a small airport in eastern Pennsylvania. Kellner feels compelled to keep parachuting; the second-place record holder is hot on his trail. "It's tough to stay number one," he says. Darlene, his wife (they were married in mid-air) and partner, flies the planes.

Kellner says it can sometimes be hard to convince novices to jump. "I don't blame them," he admits. "I'm scared to death each time I leave the airplane. By the time I land with new jumpers, I have to hold them on the ground. They're floating. No words can describe the feeling."

Most sport parachuting descents

Don Kellner (U.S.) had made 21,000 descents in various locations as of October 2, 1994.

(Photos courtesy of Don Kellner)

Parachute Records

First *Tower* [1] • Louis-Sébastien Lenormand (1757–1839), quasi parachute, Montpellier, France, 1783.

Balloon • André-Jacques Garnerin (1769–1823), 2,230 ft., Monceau Park, Paris, France, Oct. 22, 1797.

Aircraft • *Man:* "Captain" Albert Berry, an aerial exhibitionist, St. Louis, MO, Mar. 1, 1912. *Woman:* Mrs. Georgina "Tiny" Broadwick (b. 1893), Griffith Park, Los Angeles, CA, Jun. 21, 1913.

Longest-Duration Fall • Lt. Col. Wm H. Rankin (USMC) 40 min. due to thermals, North Carolina, Jul. 26, 1956.

Longest-Delayed Drop *Man* • Capt. Joseph W. Kittinger,[2] 84,700 ft. (16.04 miles), from balloon at 102,800 ft., Tularosa, NM, Aug. 16, 1960.

Woman • Elvira Fomitcheva (USSR), 48,556 ft. over Odessa, USSR, Oct. 26, 1977.

Base Jump *Highest* • Nicholas Feteris and Dr. Glenn Singleman from the "Great Trango Tower" at 19,300 ft. in Karakoram, Pakistan, Aug. 26, 1992. *Jumps from buildings and claims for lowest base jumps will not be accepted.*

Mid-Air Rescue *Earliest* • Miss Dolly Shepherd (1886-1983) brought down Miss Louie May on her single 'chute from balloon at 11,000 ft., Longton, England, Jun. 9, 1908.

Lowest • Eddie Turner saved Frank Farnan (unconscious), who had been injured in a collision after jumping out of an aircraft at 13,000 ft. He pulled his ripcord at 1,800 ft.—less than 10 seconds from impact—over Clewiston, FL on Oct. 16, 1988.

Escape *Highest* • Flt. Lt. J. de Salis (RAF) and Fg. Off. P. Lowe (RAF), 56,000 ft., Monyash, Derby, England, Apr. 9, 1958.

Lowest • S/Ldr. Terence Spencer (DFC, RAF), 30–40 ft., Wismar Bay, Baltic, Apr. 19, 1945.

Landing *Highest* • Ten USSR parachutists,[3] 23,405 ft., Lenina Peak, USSR, May 1969.

Cross-Channel (Lateral Fall) • Sgt. Bob Walters with three soldiers and two British Royal Marines, 22 miles from 25,000 ft., Dover, Great Britain to Sangatte, France, Aug. 31, 1980.

Total Sport Parachuting Descents *Man* • Don Kellner (U.S.), 21,000, various locations up to Oct. 2, 1994.

Woman • Valentina Zakoretskaya (USSR), 8,000, over USSR, 1964–80.

24-Hour Total *Man* • Dale Nelson (U.S.), 301 (in accordance with United States Parachute Association rules), PA, May 26–27, 1988.

Woman • Cheryl Stearns (U.S.), 255 at Lodi, CA, Nov. 26–27, 1987.

Most Traveled • Kevin Seaman from a Cessna Skylane (pilot Charles E. Merritt), 12,186 miles, jumps in all 50 states, Jul. 26–Oct. 15, 1972.

Heaviest Load • Space shuttle *Columbia*, booster rocket retrieval, 80 ton capacity, triple array, each 120 ft. in diameter, Atlantic, off Cape Canaveral, FL, Apr. 12, 1981.

Highest Canopy Formation • 37, a team of French parachutists at Brienne le Chateau, Troyes, France, held for 13 sec. on Aug. 16, 1992.

Largest Free-fall Formation • 216, from 23 countries, held for 8.21 seconds from 21,000 ft. over Bratislava, Slovakia, Aug. 19, 1994 (unofficial).

200, from 10 countries, held for 6.47 sec. from 16,500 ft., Myrtle Beach, SC, Oct. 23, 1992 (record recognized by FAI).

Women • 100, from 20 countries, held for 5.97 sec., from 17,000 ft., Aéreodrome du Cannet des Maures, France, Aug. 14, 1992.

Oldest *Man* • Edwin C. Townsend (d. Nov. 7, 1987), 89 years, Vermillion Bay, LA, Feb. 5, 1986.

Woman • Mrs. Sylvia Brett (Great Britain), 80 yr. 166 days, Cranfield, England, Aug. 23, 1986.

Oldest Tandem *Man* • Edward Royds-Jones, 95 yr. 170 days, Dunkeswell, England, Jul. 2, 1994.

Woman • Corena Leslie (U.S.), 89 years 326 days, Buckeye Airport, Sun Valley, AZ, Jun. 11, 1992.

Survival from Longest Fall without Parachute • Vesna Vulovic (Yugoslavia), air hostess in DC–9 that blew up at 33,330 ft. over Srbská Kamenice, Czechoslovakia (now Czech Republic), Jan. 26, 1972.

[1] *The king of Ayutthaya, Siam in 1687 was reported to have been amused by an ingenious athlete parachuting with two large umbrellas. Faustus Verancsis is reputed to have descended in Hungary with a framed canopy in 1617.*
[2] *Maximum speed in rarefied air was 625.2 mph at 90,000 ft.—marginally supersonic.*
[3] *Four were killed.*

DEAD CENTER!

The Men's Night Accuracy Landing record on an electronic score pad is 31 consecutive dead centers, by Vladimir Buchenev (USSR) on October 30, 1986. The women's record is 21, by Inessa Stepanova (USSR) in Fergana on October 18, 1988.

A match of two 40-goal teams has been staged on three occasions—in Argentina in 1975, in the United States in 1990, and in Australia in 1991.

Most chukkas   The greatest number of chukkas played on one ground in a day is 43. This was achieved by the Pony Club on the Number 3 Ground in Kirtlington Park, England on July 31, 1991.

POOL

14.1 CONTINUOUS POOL
(AMERICAN STRAIGHT POOL)

World Championship   The two most dominant 14.1 players were Ralph Greenleaf (U.S.), who won the "world" professional title six times and defended it 13 times (1919–37), and Willie Mosconi (U.S.), who dominated the game from 1941 to 1956, and also won the title six times and defended it 13 times.

Longest consecutive run   The longest consecutive run in 14.1 recognized by the Billiard Congress of America (BCA) is 526 balls, by Willie Mosconi in March 1954 during an exhibition in Springfield, OH. Michael Eufemia is reported to have pocketed 625 balls at Logan's Billiard Academy, Brooklyn, NY on February 2, 1960, but this run has never been ratified by the BCA.

Most balls pocketed   The greatest number of balls pocketed in 24 hours is 16,497, by Paul Sullivan in Selby, England, April 16–17, 1993.

Pool pocketing speed   The record times for pocketing all 15 balls in a speed competition are: *(men)* 35.4 seconds, by Dave Pearson at the 701 club, Failsworth, England on December 9, 1993; *(women)* 42.28 seconds, by Susan Thompson at the Ferry Inn, Holmsgarth, Shetland Isles on January 28, 1995.

POWERBOAT RACING

APBA Gold Cup   The American Power Boat Association (APBA) Gold Cup race has been won a record ten times by Chip Hanauer (U.S.), 1982–88, 1992–93 and 1995.

The highest average speed for the race is 149.160 MPH, also set by Hanauer, piloting *Miss Budweiser* in Detroit, MI on June 4, 1995.

Longest races   The longest offshore race was the Port Richborough, London, England to Monte Carlo Marathon Offshore international event. The race extended over 2,947 miles in 14 stages, June 10–25, 1972. It was won by *H.T.S.* (Great Britain), driven by Mike Bellamy, Eddie Chater and Jim Brooker, in 71 hr. 35 min. 56 sec., for an average of 41.15 MPH. The longest circuit race is the 24-hour race held annually on the River Seine in Rouen, France.

FASTEST WATER SPEED

Kenneth Peter Warby achieved 300 knots (345.48 MPH) on Blowering Dam Lake, New South Wales, Australia on November 20, 1977 in his unlimited hydroplane *Spirit of Australia*.

Fastest water speed The official world water speed record is 275.8 knots (511.11 kilometers per hour) set on October 8, 1978 by Kenneth Peter Warby on Blowering Dam Lake, New South Wales, Australia.

Mary Rife of Flint, TX set a women's unofficial record of 206.72 MPH in her blown fuel hydro *Proud Mary* in Tulsa, OK on July 23, 1977. Her official record is 197 MPH.

PROJECTILE THROWING

Longest throw The longest independently authenticated throw of any inert object heavier than air is 1,265 ft. 9 in., for a lead weight with a long string tail attached, which was thrown by David Engvall in El Mirage, CA on October 17, 1993. The record for an object without any velocity-aiding feature is 1,257 feet by Scott Zimmerman, with a flying ring on July 8, 1986 in Fort Funston, CA.

Records achieved with other objects:

Boomerang juggling Consecutive catches with two boomerangs, keeping at least one boomerang aloft at all times, 502, by Chet Snouffer (U.S.) in Geneva, Switzerland in 1992.

Boomerang throwing The greatest number of consecutive 2-handed catches is 817, by Michael Girvin (U.S.) on July 17, 1994 in Oakland, CA.

Longest out-and-return distance, 489 ft. 3 in., by Michel Dufayard (France) on July 5, 1992 in Shrewsbury, England.

Longest flight duration (with self-catch), 2 min. 59.94 sec. by Dennis Joyce (U.S.) in Bethlehem, PA, June 25, 1987.

Brick ...146 ft. 1 in. (standard 5-pound building brick), Geoff Capes (Great Britain) in Orton Goldhay, England on July 19, 1978.

Cow chip tossing The greatest distance achieved under the "non-sphericalization and 100 percent organic" rule (established in 1970) is 266 feet, by Steve Urner at the Mountain Festival, Tehachapi, CA in 1981.

Egg (fresh hen's) ... 323 ft. 2½ in. (without breaking it), Johnny Dell Foley to Keith Thomas in Jewett, TX on November 12, 1978.

Flying disc throwing (formerly Frisbee) The World Flying Disc Federation distance records are: *(men)* 647 ft. 7 in., by Niclas Bergehamn (Sweden) on August 11, 1993 in Linköping, Sweden; *(women)* 426 ft. 10 in., by Amy Bekken (U.S.) on July 25, 1990 in La Habra, CA.

The throw, run and catch records are: *(men)* 303 ft. 11 in., by Hiroshi Oshima (Japan) on July 20, 1988 in San Francisco, CA; *(women)* 196 ft. 11 in., by Judy Horowitz (U.S.) on June 29, 1985 in La Mirada, CA.

The 24-hour distance records for a pair are: *(men)* 367.94 miles, by Conrad Damon and Pete Fust (U.S.) on April 24–25, 1993 in San Marino, CA; *(women)* 115.65 miles, by Jo Cahow and Amy Berard (U.S.), December 30–31, 1979 in Pasadena, CA.

The records for maximum time aloft are: *(men)* 16.72 seconds, by Don Cain (U.S.) on May 26, 1984 in Philadelphia, PA; *(women)* 11.81 seconds, by Amy Bekken (U.S.) on August 1, 1991.

Haggis The record distance for throwing a haggis weighing 1 lb. 8 oz. is 180 ft. 10 in., by Alan Pettigrew (Great Britain) in Loch Lomond, Scotland on May 24, 1984.

Rolling pin ... 175 ft. 5 in. (two pounds), Lori La Deane Adams at Iowa State Fair, IA on August 21, 1979.

Slingshot ... 1,565 ft. 4 in. (50-inch-long sling and a 2¼-ounce dart), David P. Engvall in Baldwin Lake, CA on September 13, 1992.

Spear throwing ... 660 ft. 3 in. (using an atlatl or hand-held device that fits onto a short spear), Wayne Brian in Rexburg, ID on September 16, 1993.

RACQUETBALL

World Championships First held in 1982, the International Amateur Racquetball Federation (IARF) World Championships have been held biennially since 1984. The United States has won all seven team titles, in 1981, 1984, 1986 (tie with Canada), 1988, 1990, 1992 and 1994. Egan Inoue (U.S.) has won the most men's singles titles with two, in 1986 and 1990. Three women have won the world singles championships twice: Cindy Baxter (U.S.) in 1981 and 1986; Heather Stupp (Canada) in 1988 and 1990; and Michelle Gould (née Gilman; U.S.), in 1992 and 1994.

RAPPELING

Rappeling   A team of four Royal Marines set an overall distance record of 3,627 feet, by each rappeling down the Boulby Potash Mine, Cleveland, England from 25 feet below ground level to the shaft bottom on November 2, 1993.

The longest descent down the side of a building is one of 1,465 feet by two teams of twelve people representing the Royal Marines from Great Britain and the Canadian School of Rescue Training. All 24 people rappeled to the ground from the Space Deck of the CN Tower in Toronto, Ontario, Canada on July 1, 1992. Two ropes were used, the first member of each team reaching the ground at exactly the same time.

The greatest distance rappeled by a team of 10 in an 8-hour period is 45 miles, by Royal Marines from the Commando Training Centre in Lympstone, England. They achieved the record by rappeling 1,382 times down the side of the Civic Centre in Plymouth, England on May 22, 1993.

RODEO

Largest rodeo   The National Finals Rodeo is organized by the Professional Rodeo Cowboys Association (PRCA) and the Women's Professional Rodeo Association (WPRA). The 1991 Finals had a paid attendance of 171,414 for 10 performances. In 1992, a record $2.6 million in prize money was offered for the event.

Most world titles   The record number of all-around titles (awarded to the leading money winner in a single season in two or more events) in the PRCA World Championships is six, by Larry Mahan (U.S.) in 1966–70 and 1973; Tom Ferguson, 1974–79; and Ty Murray, 1989–94. Jim Shoulders of Henrietta, TX won a record 16 World Championships in four events between 1949 and 1959.

Earnings records   Roy Cooper holds the career rodeo earnings mark at $1,489,698 through June 1995. The record figure for prize money in a single season is $297,896 by Ty Murray in 1993.

Fastest times   The fastest time recorded for calf-roping under the current PRCA rules is 6.7 seconds, by Joe Beaver in West Jordan, UT in 1986, and the fastest time for steer wrestling is 2.4 seconds, by James Bynum in Marietta, OK in 1955; Carl Deaton in Tulsa, OK in 1976; and Gene Melton in Pecatonica, IL in 1976. The fastest team roping time is 3.7 seconds, by Bob Harris and Tee Woolman in Spanish Fork, UT in 1986.

BULL!

The top bucking bull Red Rock dislodged 312 riders, 1980–88, and was finally ridden to the 8-second bell by Lane Frost (1963–89; world champion bull rider, 1987) on May 20, 1989.

Women's barrel racing   The greatest number of titles won in women's barrel racing is 10, by Charmayne Rodman, 1984–93.

Youngest rodeo champions   The youngest winner of a world title in rodeo is Anne Lewis (b. September 1, 1958), who won the WPRA barrel racing title in 1968, at 10 years of age. Ty Murray (b. October 11, 1969) is the youngest cowboy to win the PRCA All-Around Champion title, at age 20, in 1989.

Bull riding   The highest-ever score in bull riding was 100 points out of a possible 100, by Wade Leslie on Wolfman Skoal in Central Point, OR in 1991.

Saddle bronc riding   The highest scored saddle bronc ride is 95 out of a possible 100, by Doug Vold on Transport in Meadow Lake, Saskatchewan, Canada in 1979. Descent, a saddle bronc owned by Beutler Brothers and Cervi Rodeo Company, received a record six PRCA Saddle Bronc of the Year awards, 1966–69, 1971–72.

LOOPY!

Using a 100-foot rope, Kalvin Cook spun a loop of 95 feet at the Hacienda Hotel, Las Vegas, NV on March 27, 1994.

Bareback riding   Joe Alexander of Cora, WY scored 93 out of a possible 100 on Marlboro in Cheyenne, WY in 1974. Sippin' Velvet, owned by Bernis Johnson, has been awarded a record five PRCA Bareback Horse of the Year titles: 1978, 1983–84 and 1986–87.

Texas skips   Vince Bruce (U.S.) performed 4,001 Texas skips (jumps back and forth through a large, vertical spun loop) on July 22, 1991 at the Empire State Building, New York City.

ROLLER SPORTS

INLINE SKATING

World championships   The first world championships took place in 1992. Derek Parra of Dover, DE was the overall world track champion in 1993 and the overall road champion for 1994. Heather Laufer, Kansas City, MO, was the 1994 women's world champion.

Speed records   In the 1994 championships in Gujan Mestras, France, Derek Parra (U.S.) broke two records: the 1,500 meter, 2 min. 6.42 sec.; and the 42 km marathon, 1 hr. 4 min. 27.986 sec. The Atlanta-based International Inline Skating Association regulates the following world records:

One hour   Haico Bauma (Netherlands) skated 22.11 miles in one hour on August 16, 1994 in Gronigen, Netherlands. The women's record is held by Karin Verhoef (Netherlands), who accomplished 18.98 miles on August 14, 1990 in Vriezenveen, Netherlands.

Six hours   Jonathan Seutter (U.S.) holds the men's 6-hour road record, having skated 91.35 miles on February 2, 1991 in Long Beach, CA. The women's record is 90.54 miles, by Kimberly Pavek (U.S.) on October 30, 1993 in Minneapolis, MN.

12 hours   Jonathan Seutter bladed 177.63 miles in 12 hours on February 2, 1991 in Long Beach, CA. Kimberley Ames (U.S.) is the women's record holder, with 162.26 miles on October 2, 1994 in Portland, OR.

24 hours   The 24-hour world record is held by Kimberly Ames, who skated 283.07 miles on October 2, 1994 in Portland, OR. The men's 24-hour record is held by Jonathan Seutter, who bladed 271.25 miles on October 31, 1993 in Minneapolis, MN.

ROLLER SKATING

Most titles   *Speed*   The most world speed titles won is 18, by two women: Alberta Vianello (Italy), eight track and 10 road, 1953–65; and Annie Lambrechts (Belgium), one track and 17 road, 1964–81, at distances from 500 meters to 10,000 meters.

Blades of Glory

She's a chemist for Nike who created a polymer used to give sandals increased traction. He's a chimney sweep equipped with a top hat, tails and the traditional lucky handshake. Together, they're out to dominate the inline skating distance record.

Kimberly Ames holds the record for skating 283 miles in 24 hours. She broke the record held by her coach, Jonathan Seutter. It was Ames who coached Seutter when he set his record, and it is most likely Ames who will hold the record until Seutter decides to go for it again. "There's nobody in the world I'd rather have break my record than her," Seutter graciously concedes.

Ames feels she succeeded at the record attempt because of her mental strength and agility. "I've been running hard since I was 13. I've only been skating inline since January 1993, but I caught on fast. I've always been a fairly strong person, and the training program we devised made it so there were no surprises physically or mentally."

That training involved skating up Mount Hood in Oregon at breakneck speed, to the Timberline Lodge where the movie *The Shining* was shot. Did coach Seutter look like Jack Nicholson to her by the time she got there? Ames just smiles. "I kind of enjoyed the climb. It was so intense. I knew if I could do that I'd be able to do the record."

The record attempt itself took place on a circular route in a smoothly paved industrial park, and involved a crew of six, a massage therapist, three separate computers for timing, four printers, canopies for crew members, clothing, equipment, a liquid diet for Ames, and, of course, backup Walkmans.

"It was a relief to start," Ames recalls. "Once I got to the starting line I knew all I had to do was just skate." Alas, victory may be short-lived. "I figure I could do 310 miles in 24 hours," Seutter states. "I'll have no mercy next time. If she's really nice to me, I won't try."

Inline skating speed records

The 24-hour world inline skating record is held by Kimberly Ames (U.S.), who skated 283.07 miles on October 2, 1994 in Portland, OR.

(Tara Gurry Peterson)

Figure   The records for combined figure and free skating titles are five, by two men, Karl Heinz Losch (West Germany) in 1958–59, 1961–62 and 1966, and Sandro Guerra (Italy), 1987–89 and 1991–92, and one woman, Rafaella del Vinaccio (Italy), 1988–92. The most world pair titles is six, by Tammy Jeru (U.S.) in 1983–86 (with John Arishita), and in 1990–91 (with Larry McGrew).

Speed skating   The fastest speed posted in an official world record is 27.46 MPH, when Luca Antoniel (Italy) recorded 24.678 seconds for 300 meters on a road in Bello, Colombia on November 15, 1990. The women's record is 25.04 MPH, by Marisa Canofoglia (Italy) for 300 meters on the road in Grenoble, France on August 27, 1987. The world records for 10,000 meters on a road or track are: *(men)* 14 min. 55.64 sec., Giuseppe de Persio (Italy) in Gujan-Mestras, France on August 1, 1988; *(women)* 15 min. 58.022 sec., Marisa Canofoglia (Italy) in Grenoble, France on August 30, 1987.

Roller limbo   On May 10, 1993, Syamala Gowri roller-skated under a limbo bar set at 4.7 inches in Hyderabad, India.

ROLLER HOCKEY

Most titles   Portugal has won most titles, with 14: 1947–50, 1952, 1956, 1958, 1960, 1962, 1968, 1974, 1982, 1991 and 1993.

ROWING

Most Olympic medals   Seven oarsmen have won three gold medals: John Brenden Kelly (U.S.), who won in single sculls (1920) and double sculls (1920 and 1924); his cousin, Paul Vincent Costello (U.S.), double sculls (1920, 1924 and 1928); Jack Beresford, Jr. (Great Britain), single sculls (1924), coxless fours (1932) and double sculls (1936); Vyacheslav Nikolayevich Ivanov (USSR), single sculls (1956, 1960 and 1964); Siegfried Brietzke (East Germany), coxless pairs (1972) and coxless fours (1976, 1980); Pertti Karppinen (Finland), single sculls (1976, 1980 and 1984); and Steven Redgrave (Great Britain), coxed fours (1984) and coxless pairs (1988 and 1992).

World Championships   Rowing championships distinct from the Olympic Games were first held in 1962, and were held every four years at first, but from 1974 were held annually, except in Olympic years.

The most gold medals won at World Championships and Olympic Games is nine, in coxed pairs, by Guiseppe and Carmine Abbagnale (Italy); World in 1981–82, 1985, 1987, 1989–91, and Olympics, in 1984 and 1988. Francesco Esposito (Italy) has won nine titles in lightweight events; coxless pairs, 1980–84, 1988 and 1994, and coxless fours in 1990 and 1992. In women's events, Yelena Tereshina (USSR) has won a record seven golds, all in eights, in 1978–79, 1981–83 and 1985–86.

The most wins in single sculls is five, by Peter-Michael Kolbe (West Germany), 1975, 1978, 1981, 1983 and 1986; Pertti Karppinen, 1979 and 1985, and with his three Olympic wins (above); Thomas Lange (Germany), 1987, 1989 and 1991 and two Olympics 1988 and 1992; and in the women's events by Christine Hahn (née Scheiblich; East Germany), 1974–75, 1977–78 (and the 1976 Olympic title).

Collegiate Championships   The first intercollegiate boat race in the United States was between Harvard and Yale in 1852. The Intercollegiate Rowing Association (IRA) was formed in 1895, and in 1898 inaugurated the Varsity Challenge Cup, which was recognized as the national championship. In 1982, the United States Rowing Assocation introduced the National Collegiate Championships, and this race now decides the national champion. Overall, Cornell University has won the most national championships, with 25 titles (all Varsity Cup wins). Since 1982, Harvard University has won six titles (1983, 1985, 1987–89, 1992).

The women's national championship was inaugurated in 1979. The University of Washington has won a record seven times (1981–85, 1987–88).

DID YOU KNOW?

The longest annual rowing race is the annual Tour du Lac Leman, Geneva, Switzerland for coxed fours (the 5-man crew taking turns as cox) over 99 miles. The record winning time is 12 hr. 52 min., by LAGA Delft, Netherlands on October 3, 1982.

Fastest speed   The record time for 2,187 yards on non-tidal water is 5 min. 24.28 sec. (13.79 MPH) by an eight from Hansa Dortmund (Germany), in Essen, Germany on May 17, 1992.

The women's record is 5 min. 59.26 sec., by Romania in Lake Barrington, Tasmania, Australia, in November 1990. The single sculls record is 6 min. 38.97 sec. (11.21 MPH), by Xeno Müller (Switzerland) in Lucerne, Switzerland, on July 17, 1994. On the same occasion, Silken Laumann (Canada) set a women's record of 7 min. 17.09 sec.

Greatest 24-hour distance   The greatest distance rowed in 24 hours (upstream and downstream) is 141.26 miles, by six members of Dittons Skiff & Punting Club on the River Thames between Hampton Court and Teddington, England on June 3–4, 1994.

International Dragon Boat Race   In this race, instituted in 1975 and held annually in Hong Kong, the fastest time achieved for the 700-yard course is 2 min. 27.45 sec., by the Chinese Shun De team on January 30, 1985. Teams have 28 members—26 rowers, one steersman and one drummer.

RUGBY

Records are based on the scoring system that was in use at the time.

Rugby all-arounder Canadian international Barrie Burnham scored all possible ways—try, conversion, penalty goal, drop goal, goal from mark—for Meralomas vs. Georgians (20–11) in Vancouver, British Columbia, Canada on February 26, 1966.

Highest rugby posts The world's highest rugby union goal posts are 110 ft. $1/2$ in. high, at the Roan Antelope Rugby Union Club, Luanshya, Zambia.

OLYMPIC GAMES

In competitions held 1900–24, the only double gold medalist was the United States, which won in 1920 and 1924, defeating France in the final on both occasions.

WORLD CUP

The World Cup has been held on three occasions, 1987, 1991 and 1995, with the winners being New Zealand, Australia and South Africa respectively. The highest team score was New Zealand's 145–17 victory over Japan in Bloemfontein, South Africa on June 4, 1995. The individual match record was 45 (20 conversions, 1 try), by Simon Culhane (New Zealand) vs. Japan in Bloemfontein, South Africa on June 4, 1995. The leading scorer in the tournament was Gavin Hastings (Scotland), with 227 points. The most at a single tournament was 126, by Grant Fox (New Zealand), in 1987.

HIGHEST SCORES

Teams The highest score in any full international was when Hong Kong beat Singapore 164–13 in a World Cup qualifying match in Kuala Lumpur, Malaysia, on October 27, 1994.

Individuals *Most points scored* Ashley Billington (Hong Kong) scored 50 points (10 tries) in the World Cup qualifying match in Kuala Lumpur, Malaysia, on October 27, 1994, when Hong Kong won 164–13.

Most penalty goals The most penalty goals kicked in a match is eight, by Mark Andrew Wyatt (Canada) vs. Scotland in St. John, New Brunswick, Canada on May 25, 1991; Neil Roger Jenkins (Wales) vs. Canada in Cardiff, Wales on November 10, 1993; Santiago Meson (Argentina) vs. Canada in Buenos Aires, Argentina on March 12, 1995; Gavin Hastings (Scotland) vs. Tonga in Pretoria, South Africa on May 30, 1995; and Thierry Lacroix (France) vs. Ireland at Durban, South Africa on June 10, 1995.

Career In all internationals, Michael Patrick Lynagh scored a record 911 points in 72 matches for Australia, 1984–95. The most tries is 63, by David Campese in 91 internationals for Australia, 1982–95.

SEVEN-A-SIDES

Hong Kong Sevens The record of seven wins is held by Fiji, 1977–78, 1980, 1984, 1990–92.

SHOOTING

Most Olympic medals Carl Townsend Osburn (U.S.) won 11 medals, in 1912, 1920 and 1924—five gold, four silver and two bronze. The only marksman to have won three individual gold medals is Gudbrand Gudbrandsönn Skatteboe (Norway), in 1906. Separate events for women were first held in 1984.

Bench rest shooting The smallest group on record at 1,000 yards is 3.960 inches, by Frank Weber (U.S.) with a .308 Baer Magnum in Williamsport, PA on November 14, 1993.

The smallest at 500 meters (546 yards) is 1.5 inches, by Ross Hicks (Australia) using a .30–06 rifle of his own design in Canberra, Australia on March 12, 1994.

Clay pigeon The most world titles have been won by Susan Nattrass (Canada) with six, 1974–75, 1977–79, 1981. The record number of clay birds shot in an hour is 4,557, by John Cloherty (U.S.) in Seattle, WA on August 31, 1992.

The maximum 200/200 was achieved by Ricardo Ruiz Rumoroso at the Spanish Clay Pigeon Championships in Zaragossa on June 12, 1983.

Noel D. Townend achieved the maximum 200 consecutive down-the-line targets in Nottingham, England on August 21, 1983.

BANG!

The Easingwold Rifle and Pistol Club (Yorkshire, England) team of John Smith, Edward Kendall, Phillip Kendall and Paul Duffield scored 120,242 points (averaging 95.66 per card), August 6–7, 1983.

SHOOTING—INDIVIDUAL RECORDS

In 1986, the International Shooting Union (UIT) introduced new regulations for determining major championships and world records. Now the leading competitors undertake an additional round with a target subdivided to tenths of a point for rifle and pistol shooting, and an extra 25 shots for trap and skeet. Harder targets have since been introduced, and the table below shows the world records, as recognized by the UIT, for the 13 Olympic shooting disciplines, giving in parentheses the score for the number of shots specified plus the score in the additional round.

	Score	Name and Country	Place	Date
MEN				
Free Rifle 50 m 3 × 40 shots	1,287.9	(1,186 + 101.9) ...Rajmond Debevec (Slovenia)	Munich, Germany	Aug. 29, 1992
Free Rifle 50 m 60 shots prone	703.5	(599 + 104.5) ...Jens Harskov (Denmark)	Zürich, Switzerland	Jun. 6, 1991
Air Rifle 10 m 60 shots	699.4	(596 + 103.4) ...Rajmond Debevec (Yugoslavia)	Zürich, Switzerland	Jun. 8, 1990
Free Pistol 50 m 60 shots	672.5	(575 + 97.5) ...Sergey Pyzhyanov (Russia)	Milan, Italy	Jun. 15, 1993
Rapid-Free Pistol 25 m 60 shots	699.7	(596 + 107.5) ...Ralf Schumann (Germany)	Barcelona, Spain	Jun. 8, 1994
Air Pistol 10 m 60 shots	695.1	(593 + 102.1) ...Sergey Pyzhyanov (USSR)	Munich, Germany	Oct. 13, 1989
Running Target 50 m 30 + 30 shots	679	(582 + 97) ...Lubos Racansky (Czechoslovakia)	Munich, Germany	May 30, 1991
WOMEN				
Standard Rifle 50 m 3 × 20 shots	689.3	(590 + 99.3) ...Vessela Letcheva (Bulgaria)	Munich, Germany	Aug. 28, 1992
Air Rifle 10 m 40 shots	500.8	(399 + 101.8) ...Valentina Cherkasova (USSR)	Los Angeles, CA	Mar. 23, 1991
Sport Pistol 25 m 60 shots	696.2	(594 + 102.2) ...Diana Jorgova (Bulgaria)	Milan, Italy	May 31, 1994
Air Pistol 10 m 40 shots	492.4	(392 + 100.4) ...Lieslotte Breker (West Germany)	Zagreb, Yugoslavia	May 18, 1989
OPEN				
Trap 200 targets	148	(124 + 24) ...Giovanni Pellielo (Italy)	Fagnano, Italy	Jun. 5, 1993
	148	(124 + 24) ...Marco Venturini (Netherlands)	Barcelona, Spain	Jun. 15, 1993
Skeet 200 targets	149	(124 + 25) ...Dean Clark (U.S.)	Barcelona, Spain	Jun. 20, 1993

SKATEBOARDING

Distance   Eleftherios Argiropoulos covered 271.3 miles in 36 hr. 33 min. 17 sec. in Ekali, Greece, November 4–5, 1993.

Fastest speed   The stand-up record is 55.43 MPH, by Roger Hickey, in San Demas, CA in 1990.

Highest jump   The high-jump record is 5 ft. 5¾ in., by Trevor Baxter of Burgess Hill, England in Grenoble, France on September 14, 1982.

Longest jump   At the World Professional Championships in Long Beach, CA, on September 25, 1977, Tony Alva, 19, jumped 17 barrels (17 feet).

SKIING

Most titles   *World/Olympic Championships—Alpine*   The greatest number of titles were won by Christl Cranz of Germany, with seven individual—four slalom (1934, 1937–39) and three downhill (1935, 1937, 1939), and five combined (1934–35, 1937–39). Cranz also won the gold medal for the combined in the 1936 Olympics. The most won by a man is seven, by Anton "Toni" Sailer (Austria), who won all four in 1956 (giant slalom, slalom, downhill and the non-Olympic Alpine combination) and the downhill, giant slalom and combined in 1958.

The only U.S. skier to win two Olympic gold medals has been Andrea Mead-Lawrence, in slalom and giant slalom in 1952.

INFERNO!

The longest downhill race is the Inferno in Switzerland, 9.8 miles from the top of the Schilthorn to Lauterbrunnen. The record number of entries was 1,401 in 1981, and the record time was 13 min. 53.40 sec. by Urs von Allmen (Switzerland) in 1991.

World/Olympic Championships—Nordic   The first World Nordic Championships were those of the 1924 Winter Olympics in Chamonix, France.

The greatest number of titles won is 11, by Gunde Svan (Sweden), seven individual—15 km 1989, 30 km 1985 and 1991, 50 km 1985 and 1989, and Olympics, 15 km 1984, 50 km 1988; and four relays—4 ×10 km, 1987 and 1989, and Olympics, 1984 and 1988. The most titles won by a woman is 11, by Yelena Välbe (née Trubizinina; Russia), with six individual and five relay, 1989–95. The most medals is 23, by Raisa Petrovna Smetanina (USSR), including seven gold, 1974–92. Ulrich Wehling (East Germany) has also won four Nordic combined, winning the World Championship in 1974 and the Olympic title, 1972, 1976 and 1980—the only skier to win the

---

MOST OLYMPIC SKIING TITLES

MEN

Alpine	3	Toni Sailer (Austria)	Downhill, slalom, giant slalom 1956
	3	Jean-Claude Killy (France)	Downhill, slalom, giant slalom 1968
	3	Alberto Tomba (Italy)	Slalom, giant slalom 1988; giant slalom 1992
Nordic	5	Bjorn Daehlie (Norway)	15 km, 50 km, 4 × 10 km 1992; 10 km, 15 km 1994
Jumping	4	Matti Nykänen (Finland)	70 m hill 1988; 90 m hill 1984, 1988; team 1988

WOMEN

Alpine	3	Vreni Schneider (Switzerland)	Giant slalom, slalom 1988; slalom 1994
Nordic	6	Lyubov Yegorova (Russia)	10 km, 15 km, 4 × 5 km 1992; 5 km, 10 km, 4 × 5 km 1994

---

same event at three successive Olympics. The record for a jumper is five, by Birger Ruud (Norway), in 1931–32 and 1935–37. Ruud is the only person to win Olympic events in each of the dissimilar Alpine and Nordic disciplines. In 1936, he won the ski-jumping and the Alpine downhill (which was not then a separate event, but only a segment of the combined event).

World Cup The World Cup was introduced for Alpine events in 1967 and for Nordic events in 1981. The most individual event wins is 86 (46 giant slalom, 40 slalom from a total of 287 races) by Ingemar Stenmark (Sweden) in 1974–89, including a men's record 13 in one season in 1978/79, of which 10 were part of a record 14 successive giant slalom wins from March 18, 1978 to January 21, 1980. Franz Klammer (Austria) won a record 25 downhill races, 1974–84. Annemarie Moser (née Pröll; Austria) won a women's record 62 individual event wins, 1970–79. She had a record 11 consecutive downhill wins from December 1972 to January 1974. Vreni Schneider (Switzerland) won a record 13 events and a combined including all seven slalom events in 1988/89.

The Nation's Cup, awarded on the combined results of the men's and women's competition in the World Cup, has been won a record 16 times by Austria—1969, 1973–80, 1982, 1990–95.

United States   The most successful U.S. skier was Phillip Mahre, winner of the overall title three times, 1981–83, with two wins in giant slalom and one in slalom. The most successful U.S. woman was Tamara McKinney, overall winner 1983, giant slalom 1981 and 1983, and slalom 1984.

The only American to win a Nordic skiing World Cup title was William Koch, in cross-country in 1982.

The Russian relay team, winners of the 1994 Olympic 4 × 5 km race, includes two of the most successful Nordic skiers ever—Lyubov Yegorova (far left), winner of a record six Olympic golds, and Yelena Välbe (second left), winner of a record four World Cup titles.
(Allsport/S. Botterill)

Longest ski-jump   The longest ski-jump ever recorded is 636 feet, by Piotr Fijas (Poland) in Planica, Yugoslavia on March 14, 1987. The women's record is 367 feet, by Eva Ganster (Austria), in Bischofshofen, Austria on January 7, 1994. The longest dry ski-jump is 302 feet, by Hubert Schwarz (West Germany) in Berchtesgarten, Germany on June 30, 1981.

Fastest speed   The official world record, as recognized by the International Ski Federation, is 241.448 MPH, by Jeffrey Hamilton (U.S.) on April 21, 1993, and the fastest by a woman is 139.808 MPH, by Karine Dubouchet (France) on April 14, 1995, both in Vars, France. On April 16, 1988 Patrick Knaff (France) set a 1-legged record of 115.306 MPH.

The fastest average speed in the Olympic downhill race is 64.95 MPH, by

Jeffrey Hamilton (U.S.), the world's fastest skier, sports some of the aerodynamic equipment needed to reach speeds in excess of 150 MPH. (Allsport/Vandystadt/Zoom)

During 1994, Lucy Dicker and Arnie Wilson skied a total of 3,678 miles and 472,050 vertical feet at 237 resorts in 13 countries on 5 continents.

William D. Johnson (U.S.), in Sarajevo, Yugoslavia on February 16, 1984. The fastest in a World Cup downhill is 69.8 MPH, by Armin Assinger (Austria) in Sierra Nevada, Spain on March 15, 1993.

Fastest speed—cross-country The record time for a 50-km race in a major championship is 1 hr. 54 min. 46 sec., at an average speed of 16.24 MPH, by Aleksey Prokurorov (Russia), at Thunder Bay, Canada on March 19, 1994.

Longest run The longest all-downhill ski run in the world is the Weissfluhjoch-Küblis Parsenn course, near Davos, Switzerland, which measures 7.6 miles. The run from the Aiguille du Midi top of the Chamonix lift (vertical lift 9,052 feet) across the Vallée Blanche is 13 miles.

Long-distance Nordic In 24 hours, Seppo-Juhani Savolainen covered 258.2 miles in Saariselkä, Finland, April 8–9, 1988. The women's 24-hour record is 205.05 miles, by Sisko Kainulaisen in Jyväskylä, Finland, March 23–24, 1985.

In 48 hours Bjørn Løkken (Norway) covered 319 mi. 205 yd., March 11–13, 1982.

Alpine During 1994, Lucy Dicker and Arnie Wilson (both Great Britain) skied every day in an around-the-world expedition. They skied a total 3,678 miles and 472,050 vertical feet at 237 resorts in 13 countries on 5 continents.

Longest races The world's longest Nordic ski race is the Vasaloppet, at 55.3 miles. There were a record 10,934 starters on March 6, 1977 and a record 10,650 finishers on March 4, 1979. The fastest time is 3 hr. 48 min. 55 sec., by Bengt Hassis (Sweden) on March 2, 1986.

The Finlandia Ski Race, 46.6 miles from Hämeenlinna to Lahti, on February 26, 1984, had a record 13,226 starters and 12,909 finishers.

Freestyle skiing The first World Championships were held in Tignes, France in 1986. Titles are awarded in ballet, moguls, aerials and combined. Edgar Grospiron (France) has won a record three titles: moguls, 1989, 1991 and 1995. Grospiron has also won an Olympic title, in 1992. The most Overall titles in the World Cup (instituted 1980) is 10, by Connie Kissling (Switzerland), 1983–92. The men's record is four, by Eric Laboureix (France), 1986–87, 1990–91.

Longest ski lift The longest gondola ski lift is 3.88 miles long, in Grindelwald-Männlichen, Switzerland (in two sections, but one gondola).

Ski-bob Fastest speed The fastest speed attained is 103.1 MPH, by Erich Brenter (Austria), in Cervinia, Italy in 1964.

World Championships The only ski-bobbers to retain a world championship are: *(men)* Alois Fischbauer (Austria), 1973 and 1975; Robert Mühlberger (West Germany), 1979 and 1981; *(women)* Gerhilde Schiffkorn (Austria), 1967 and 1969; Gertrude Geberth (Austria), 1971 and 1973.

GRASS SKIING

Most titles   The biennial World Championships (now awarded for Super G, giant slalom, slalom and combined) were first held in 1979. The most titles won is 14, by Ingrid Hirschhofer (Austria), 1979–93. The most by a man is seven, by Erwin Gansner (Switzerland), 1981–87, and Rainer Grossman, 1985–93. The feat of winning all four titles in one year has been achieved by *(men)* Erwin Gansner, 1987, and Rainer Grossman, 1991, and by *(women)* Katja Krey (West Germany), 1989, and Ingrid Hirschhofer, 1993.

Fastest speed   Klaus Spinka (Austria) set a record of 57.21 MPH in Waldassen, Germany on September 24, 1989.

SLED DOG RACING

Iditarod trail   Now recognized as the world's most prestigious sled dog race, the Iditarod trail is also the oldest established trail. It has existed since 1910 and has been raced annually since 1967 by dog teams, 1,049 miles from Anchorage to Nome, AK. The inaugural winner, Dick Wilmarth, took 20 days 49 min. 41 sec. to complete the course, beating 33 other racers.

The fastest time was set by Doug Swingley (U.S.) in 1995 with 9 days 2 hr. 42 min. 19 sec. Rick Swenson (U.S.) has won the race a record five times (1977, 1979, 1981–82 and 1991).

Longest trail   The longest race is the 1,243-mile Benergia Trail from Esso to Markovo, Russia, now established as an annual event. The 1991 race was won by Pavel Lazarev in 10 days 18 hr. 17 min. 56 sec.

Largest team   On February 8, 1988, Rev. Donald Ewen McEwen, owner-musher of Nekanesu Kennels, Eldorado, Ontario, Canada, drove a 76-dog sled for two miles single-handedly on the ice and around the shore of Lingham Lake. The team, consisting of 25 Siberian huskies and 51 Alaskan huskies, was assembled for the filming of a British TV commercial.

SNOOKER

Most world titles   The world professional title was won a record 15 times by Joe Davis, on the first 15 occasions it was contested, 1927–40 and 1946. The most wins in the Amateur Championships have been two—by Gary Owen (England) in 1963 and 1966; Ray Edmonds (England) in 1972 and 1974; and Paul Mifsud (Malta) in 1985–86.

Stephen Hendry, winner of the 1995 World Championship, made a 147 break during his semifinal win over Jimmy White. He is only the third person to achieve this during the championship's history. (*Allsport/ M. Cooper*)

Maureen Baynton (née Barrett) won a record eight Women's Amateur Championships between 1954 and 1968, as well as seven in billiards.

Youngest World Champion The youngest man to win a world title is Stephen O'Connor (Ireland), who was 18 yr. 40 days when he won the World Amateur Snooker Championship in Colombo, Sri Lanka on November 25, 1990. Stephen Hendry (Scotland) became the youngest World Professional champion, at 21 yr. 106 days on April 29, 1990.

Stacey Hillyard (Great Britain; b. September 15, 1969) won the Women's World Amateur Championship in October 1984 at age 15.

Highest breaks Over 200 players have achieved the maximum break of 147. The first to do so was E.J. "Murt" O'Donoghue (New Zealand) in Griffiths, New South Wales, Australia on September 26, 1934. The first officially ratified 147 was by Joe Davis against Willie Smith in London, England on January 22, 1955. Cliff Thorburn (Canada) has scored two tournament 147 breaks (in the World Professional Championship), on April 23, 1983 and March 8, 1989. Peter Ebdon (Great Britain), James

---

CLEAN BREAK!

The highest break in snooker by a woman in competition is 137, by Stacey Hillyard (Great Britain) in the General Portfolio's Women's Classic in Aylesbury, England on February 23, 1992.

Wattana (Thailand) and Stephen Hendry (Great Britain) have also achieved this feat.

Longest unbroken run   From March 17, 1990 to his defeat by Jimmy White on January 13, 1991, Stephen Hendry won five successive titles and 36 consecutive matches in ranking tournaments. During the summer of 1992, Ronnie O'Sullivan won 38 consecutive matches, but these were in qualifying competitions.

SNOWSHOEING

Fastest speed   The IASSRF (International Amateur SnowShoe Racing Federation) record for covering one mile is 5 min. 56.7 sec., by Nick Akers of Edmonton, Alberta, Canada on February 3, 1991. The 100 meter record is 14.07 seconds, by Jeremy Badeau in Canaseraga, NY on May 31, 1991.

SOARING

Most titles   The most World Individual Championships (instituted 1937) won is four, by Ingo Renner (Australia) in 1976 (Standard class), 1983, 1985 and 1987 (Open).

The most titles won by a U.S. pilot is two, by George Moffat, in the Open category, 1970 and 1974.

Women's altitude records   The women's single-seater world record for absolute altitude is 41,460 feet, by Sabrina Jackintell (U.S.) in an Astir GS on February 14, 1979.

HANG GLIDING

World Championships   The World Team Championships (officially instituted in 1976) have been won most often by Great Britain (1981, 1985, 1989 and 1991).

World records   The *Fédération Aéronautique Internationale* recognizes world records for rigid-wing, flex-wing and multiplace flex-wing. The following records are for the greatest distance in each category—all by flex-wing gliders.

Men   Greatest distance in straight line and declared goal distance: 303.3 miles, Larry Tudor (U.S.), Hobbs Airpark, NM to Elkhart, KS, July 3, 1990.

Height gain: 14,250 feet, Larry Tudor, Owens Valley, CA, August 4, 1985.

Out and return distance: 192.8 miles, Larry Tudor and Geoffrey Loyns (Great Britain), Owens Valley, June 26, 1988.

Triangular course distance: 121.79 miles, James Lee (U.S.), Wild Horse Mesa, CO, July 4, 1991.

Women   Greatest distance: 208.6 miles, Kari Castle (U.S.), Owens Valley, July 22, 1991.

Height gain: 13,025 feet, Judy Leden (Great Britain), Kuruman, South Africa, December 1, 1992.

Out and return distance in a single turn: 181.5 miles, Kari Castle, Hobbs Airpark, July 1, 1990.

Declared goal distance: 132.04 miles, Liavan Mallin (Ireland), Owens Valley, July 13, 1989.

Triangular course distance: Judy Leden, 70.9 miles, Kössen, Austria, June 22, 1991.

SOCCER

Ball control   Ricardinho Neves (Brazil) juggled a regulation soccer ball for 19 hr. 5 min. 31 sec. nonstop with feet, legs and head, without the ball ever touching the ground, at the Los Angeles Convention Center, CA, on July 15–16, 1994. The heading record is 7 hr. 16 min. by Tomas Lundman (Sweden) at Valstrum Centrum, Märsta, Sweden on November 26, 1994.

THE FIFA WORLD CUP

Three wins have been achieved by Brazil, in 1958, 1962 and 1970; Italy, in 1934, 1938 and 1982; and West Germany, in 1954, 1974 and 1990.

Team records   *Most appearances*   Brazil is the only country to qualify for all 15 World Cup tournaments.

Most goals   The most goals scored in one game occurred when New Zealand beat Fiji 13–0 in a qualifying game in Auckland on August 15, 1981. The highest score during the final stages is 10, scored by Hungary in a 10–1 defeat of El Salvador in Elche, Spain on June 15, 1982. The highest

---

HAT TRICK!

Pelé (Brazil) is the only player to have played on three winning teams, 1958, 1962 and 1970. He played during the 1962 Finals, but was injured before the final match and was unable to play in it.

game aggregate in the finals tournament is 12, when Austria defeated Switzerland 7–5 in Lausanne, Switzerland on June 26, 1954.

Tournament The greatest number of goals in a single finals tournament is 27 (five games) by Hungary in 1954. Brazil has scored the most overall, with 159 in 73 games.

Individual records *Most goals* The most goals scored in a final is three, by Geoff Hurst for England vs. West Germany on July 30, 1966.

Most games played Four players have appeared in 21 games in the finals tournament: Uwe Seeler (West Germany) 1958–70; Wladyslaw Zmuda (Poland) 1974–86; Diego Maradona (Argentina), 1982–94; and Lothar Matthaüs (Germany), 1982–94.

DID YOU KNOW?

It was reported on June 1, 1993 that in a league soccer match between Sportivo Ameliano and General Caballero in Paraguay, referee William Weiler ejected 20 players. Trouble flared after two Sportivo players were thrown out, a 10-minute fight ensued, and Weiler then dismissed a further 18 players, including the rest of the Sportivo team. Not suprisingly, the game was abandoned.

Most goals scored The most goals scored in one tournament is 13, by Just Fontaine (France) in 1958, in six games. The most goals scored in a career is 14, by Gerd Muller (West Germany), 10 goals in 1970 and four in 1974.

WOMEN'S WORLD CUP

The U.S. won the inaugural World Cup in 1991, beating Norway 2–1 in the final. The second competition, in 1995, was won by Norway, which beat Germany 2–0 in the final.

OLYMPIC GAMES

The leading gold medal winner is Hungary, with three wins (1952, 1964, 1968). The highest Olympic score is 17, by Denmark vs. France in 1908. A record 126 nations took part in qualifying for the 1992 tournament.

NCAA DIVISION I CHAMPIONSHIPS

Men In this competition, first held in 1959, the University of St. Louis has won the most Division I titles with 10 victories, including one tie: 1959–60, 1962–63, 1965, 1967, 1969–70, 1972–73.

Women   In this competition, first held in 1982, the University of North Carolina has won a record 10 Division I titles. Its victories came in 1982–84, 1986–92.

Largest soccer crowds   The top attendance for a soccer match in the United States was 101,799, for France's 2–0 Olympic final win over Brazil at the Rose Bowl, Pasadena, CA on August 11, 1984.

SOFTBALL

Most titles   The U.S. has won the men's World Championship (instituted 1966) five times, 1966, 1968, 1976 (shared), 1980 and 1988, and the women's title (instituted 1965) five times, in 1974, 1978, 1986, 1990 and 1994.

U.S. National Championships   The most wins in the fast pitch championships (first held in 1933) for men is 10, by the Clearwater (Florida) Bombers, 1950–73, and for women is 23, by the Raybestos Brakettes of Stratford, CT, 1958–92.

Slow pitch championships have been staged annually since 1953 for men and since 1962 for women. Three wins for men have been achieved by Skip Hogan A.C. of Pittsburgh, 1962, 1964–65, and by Joe Gatliff Auto Sales of Newport, KY, 1956–57, 1963. At super slow pitch, four wins have been achieved by Steele's Silver Bullets, Grafton, OH, 1985–87 and 1990. The Dots of Miami, FL have a record five women's titles, playing as the Converse Dots, 1969; Marks Brothers, 1974–75; North Miami Dots, 1974–75; and Bob Hoffman Dots, 1978–79.

SQUASH

World Championships   Jahangir Khan (Pakistan) won six World Open (instituted 1976) titles, 1981–85 and 1988, and the International Squash Rackets Federation (ISRF) world individual title (formerly World Amateur,

UNBEATEN!

Heather McKay was unbeaten at squash from 1962 to 1980. Jahangir Khan was unbeaten from his loss to Geoff Hunt at the British Open on April 10, 1981 until Ross Norman (New Zealand) ended his sequence in the World Open final on November 11, 1986.

instituted 1967) in 1979, 1983 and 1985. Jansher Khan (Pakistan) has also won six World Open titles, in 1987, 1989–90, 1992–93 and 1994. Geoffrey B. Hunt (Australia) won four World Open titles, 1976–77 and 1979–80 and three World Amateur, 1967, 1969 and 1971. The most women's World Open titles is five, by Susan Devoy (New Zealand), 1985, 1987 and 1990–92.

Australia (1967, 1969, 1971, 1973, 1989 and 1991) and Pakistan (1977, 1981, 1983, 1985, 1987 and 1993) have each won six men's world titles. England won the women's title in 1985, 1987, 1989 and 1990, following Great Britain's win in 1979.

Most titles Open Championship The most wins in the Open Championship held annually in Britain is 10, by Jahangir Khan, in successive years, 1982–91. Hashim Khan (Pakistan) won seven times, 1950–55 and 1957, and also won the Vintage title six times, 1978–83.

The most British Open women's titles is 16, by Heather Pamela McKay (née Blundell [Australia]) from 1961 to 1977. She also won the World Open title in 1976 and 1979.

United States The U.S. amateur squash championships were first held for men in 1907 and for women in 1928; the most singles wins is six, by Stanley W. Pearson, 1915–17 and 1921–23. G. Diehl Mateer won a record 11 men's doubles titles between 1949 and 1966 with five different partners. Sharif Khan (Pakistan) won a record 13 North American Open Championships (instituted 1953), 1969–74 and 1976–82. Alicia McConnell has won a record seven women's national championships (1982–88).

Longest and shortest championship matches The longest recorded competitive match was one of 2 hr. 45 min. when Jahangir Khan beat Gamal Awad (Egypt) 9–10, 9–5, 9–7, 9–2, the first game lasting a record 1 hr. 11 min., in the final of the Patrick International Festival in Chichester, England on March 30, 1983. Philip Kenyon (England) beat Salah Nadi (Egypt) in just 6 min. 37 sec. (9–0, 9–0, 9–0) in the British Open at Lamb's Squash Club, London, England on April 9, 1992.

Most international appearances The men's record is 122 by David Gotto for Ireland. The women's record is 108 by Marjorie Croke (née Burke) for Ireland, 1981–93.

SURFING

Most titles World Amateur Championships were inaugurated in May 1964 in Sydney, Australia. The most titles is three, by Michael Novakov (Australia), who won the Kneeboard event in 1982, 1984 and 1986. A World Professional series was started in 1975. The men's title has been won five times, by Mark Richards (Australia), 1975 and from 1979 to 1982, and the women's title (instituted 1979) four times, by Frieda Zamba (U.S.), 1984–86, 1988; and by Wendy Botha (Australia, formerly South Africa), 1987, 1989, 1991–92.

HIGHEST WAVE RIDDEN

Waimea Bay, HI reputedly provides the most consistently high waves, often reaching the ridable limit of 30–35 feet. The highest wave ever ridden was the tsunami of "perhaps 50 feet" that struck Minole, HI on April 3, 1868, and was ridden to save his life by a Hawaiian named Holua.

Youngest surfing champion Frieda Zamba was 19 years old when she won the 1984 title. The youngest men's champion was Kelly Slater (U.S.), who won the 1992 crown at age 20.

Highest career earnings The career earnings leader through 1993 is Tom Carroll (Australia) with $488,434. The women's leader is Pam Burridge (Australia), with $220,540.

Longest ride About four to six times each year, ridable surfing waves break in Matanchen Bay near San Blas, Nayarit, Mexico, making rides of *c.* 5,700 feet possible.

SWIMMING

Fastest swimmer In a 25-yard pool, Tom Jager (U.S.) achieved an average speed of 5.37 MPH for 50 yards in 19.05 seconds in Nashville, TN on March 23, 1990.

Most world records *Men:* 32, Arne Borg (Sweden), 1921–29. *Women:* 42, Ragnhild Hveger (Denmark), 1936–42. For currently recognized events (only metric distances in 50-meter pools) the most is (*men*) 26, by Mark Andrew Spitz (U.S.), 1967–72, and (*women*) 23, by Kornelia Ender (East Germany), 1973–76. The most by a U.S. woman is 15, by Debbie Meyer, 1967–70.

The most world records set in a single pool is 86, in the North Sydney, Australia pool between 1955 and 1978. This total includes 48 imperial distance records, which ceased to be recognized in 1969.

Most world titles In the World Championships (instituted 1973) the most medals won is 13, by Michael Gross (West Germany)—5 gold, 5 silver and 3 bronze, 1982–90. The most medals won by a woman is 10, by Kornelia Ender, with eight gold and two silver in 1973 and 1975. The most gold medals won is six (two individual and four relay) by Jim Montgomery (U.S.) in 1973 and 1975. The most medals won in a single championship is seven, by Matt Biondi (U.S.)—3 gold, 1 silver, 3 bronze, in 1986.

The most gold medals won by an American woman is five, by Tracy

Caulkins, all in 1978; she also won a silver. The most medals overall is nine, by Mary T. Meagher—2 gold, 5 silver, 2 bronze, 1978–82.

U.S. Championships   Tracy Caulkins won a record 48 U.S. swimming titles and set 60 U.S. records in her career, 1977–84. The men's record is 36 titles, by Johnny Weissmuller (born Janos Weiszmuller), 1921–28.

Largest pool   The largest swimming pool in the world is the seawater Orthlieb Pool in Casablanca, Morocco. It is 1,574 feet long and 246 feet wide, and has an area of 8.9 acres.

The largest land-locked pool in use is Willow Lake in Warren, OH. It measures 600 by 150 feet.

The greatest spectator accommodation is 13,614 in Osaka, Japan.

Sponsored swim   The greatest amount of money collected in a charity swim was £122,983.19 (*c.* $350,000) in "Splash '92," organized by the Royal Bank of Scotland Swimming Club and held at the Royal Commonwealth Pool, Edinburgh, Scotland on January 25–26, 1992 with 3,218 participants.

The record for an event staged at several pools was £548,006.14 (*c.* $986,400) by Penguin Swimathon '88; 5,482 swimmers participated at 43 pools throughout London, England, February 26–28, 1988.

Most Golden Gate crossings   Joseph Bruno has crossed the Golden Gate strait 61 times. He first performed the feat on September 17, 1933. His latest crossing was on September 11, 1993, two months short of his 81st birthday.

Youngest to cross the Golden Gate   Andrew Pinetti swam the strait on August 11, 1993, when he was 10 years old.

OLYMPIC RECORDS

Most medals   *Men*   The greatest number of Olympic gold medals won is nine, by Mark Spitz (U.S.): 100 m and 200 m freestyle, 1972; 100 m and 200 m butterfly, 1972; 4 × 100 m freestyle, 1968 and 1972; 4 × 200 m freestyle, 1968 and 1972; 4 × 100 m medley, 1972. All but one of these performances (the 4 × 200 m freestyle of 1968) were also new world records. He also won a silver (100 m butterfly) and a bronze (100 m freestyle) in 1968, for a record 11 medals. His record seven medals at one Games in 1972 was equaled by Matt Biondi (U.S.), who took five gold, a silver and a bronze in 1988. Biondi has also won a record 11 medals in total, winning a gold in 1984, and two golds and a silver in 1992.

Women   The record number of gold medals won by a woman is six, by Kristin Otto (East Germany) in Seoul in 1988: 100 m freestyle, backstroke and butterfly, 50 m freestyle, 4 × 100 m freestyle and 4 × 100 m medley. Dawn Fraser (Australia) is the only swimmer to have won the same event, the 100 m freestyle, on three successive occasions (1956, 1960 and 1964). The most gold medals won by a U.S. woman is three, by 14 swimmers.

The most medals won by a woman is eight, by three swimmers: Dawn Fraser—four golds (100 m freestyle, 1956, 1960 and 1964, 4 × 100 m freestyle, 1956) and four silvers (400 m freestyle, 1956, 4 × 100 m freestyle, 1960 and 1964, 4 × 100 m medley, 1960); Kornelia Ender—four golds (100

SWIMMING RECORDS (set in 50-meter pools)

Event	min. : sec.	Name and Country	Place	Date
MEN				
Freestyle				
50 meters	21.81	Tom Jager (U.S.)	Nashville, TN	Mar. 24, 1990
100 meters	48.21	Aleksandr Popov (Russia)	Monte Carlo, Monaco	Jun. 18, 1994
200 meters	1:46.69	Giorgis Lamberti (Italy)	Bonn, Germany	Aug. 15, 1989
400 meters	3:43.80	Kieren Perkins (Australia)	Rome, Italy	Sep. 9, 1994
800 meters	7:46.00	Kieren Perkins (Australia)	Victoria, Canada	Aug. 24, 1994
1,500 meters	14:41.66	Kieren Perkins (Australia)	Victoria, Canada	Aug. 24, 1994
4 × 100 meter relay	3:16.53	United States (Christopher Jacobs, Troy Dalbey, Tom Jager, Matt Biondi)	Seoul, South Korea	Sep. 25, 1988
4 × 200 meter relay	7:11.95	EUN (Dmitriy Lepikov, Vladimir Pychenko, Venyamin Tayanovich, Yevgeniy Sadoviy)	Barcelona, Spain	Jul. 27, 1992
Breaststroke				
100 meters	1:00.95	Karoly Gutler (Hungary)	Sheffield, England	Aug. 3, 1993
200 meters	2:10.16	Michael Barrowman (U.S.)	Barcelona, Spain	Jul. 29, 1992
Butterfly				
100 meters	52.84	Pablo Morales (U.S.)	Orlando, FL	Jun. 23, 1986
200 meters	1:55.22	Dennis Pankratov (Russia)	Canet-en-Roussillon, France	Jun. 14, 1995
Backstroke				
100 meters	53.86	Jeff Rouse (U.S.—relay leg)	Barcelona, Spain	Jul. 31, 1992
200 meters	1:56.57	Martin Lopez-Zubero (Spain)	Tuscaloosa, AL	Nov. 23, 1991
Medley				
200 meters	1:58.16	Jani Nikanor Sievenen (Finland)	Rome, Italy	Sep. 11, 1994
400 meters	4:12.30	Tom Dolan (U.S.)	Rome, Italy	Sep. 6, 1994
4 × 100 meter relay	3:36.93	United States (David Berkoff, Richard Schroeder, Matt Biondi, Christopher Jacobs)	Seoul, South Korea	Sep. 25, 1988
	3:36.93	United States (Jeff Rouse, Nelson Diebel, Pablo Morales, Jon Olsen)	Barcelona, Spain	Jul. 31, 1992

WOMEN

Freestyle

50 meters	24.51	Le Jingyi (China)	Rome, Italy	Sep. 11, 1994
100 meters	54.01	Le Jingyi (China)	Rome, Italy	Sep. 5, 1994
200 meters	1:56.78	Franziska van Almsick (Germany)	Rome, Italy	Sep. 6, 1994
400 meters	4:03.85	Janet B. Evans (U.S.)	Seoul, South Korea	Sep. 22, 1988
800 meters	8:16.22	Janet B. Evans (U.S.)	Tokyo, Japan	Aug. 20, 1989
1,500 meters	15:52.10	Janet B. Evans (U.S.)	Orlando, FL	Mar. 26, 1988
4 × 100 meter relay	3:37.91	China (Le Jingyi, Shan Ying, Le Ying, Lu Bin)	Rome, Italy	Sep. 7, 1994
4 × 200 meter relay	7:55.47	East Germany (Manuela Stellmach, Astrid Strauss, Anke Möhring, Heike Friedrich)	Strasbourg, France	Aug. 18, 1987

Breaststroke

100 meters	1:07.69	Samantha Riley (Australia)	Rome, Italy	Sep. 9, 1994
200 meters	2:24.76	Rebecca Brown (Australia)	Brisbane, Australia	Mar. 16, 1994

Butterfly

100 meters	57.93	Mary Terstegge Meagher (U.S.)	Milwaukee, WI	Aug. 16, 1981
200 meters	2:05.96	Mary Terstegge Meagher (U.S.)	Milwaukee, WI	Aug. 13, 1981

Backstroke

100 meters	1:00.16	He Cihong (China)	Rome, Italy	Sep. 11, 1994
200 meters	2:06.62	Krizstina Egerszegi (Hungary)	Athens, Greece	Aug. 25, 1991

Medley

200 meters	2:11.65	Li Lin (China)	Barcelona, Spain	Jul. 30, 1992
400 meters	4:36.10	Petra Schneider (East Germany)	Guayaquil, Ecuador	Aug. 1, 1982
4 × 100 meter relay	4:01.67	China (He Cihong, Dai Guohong, Liu Limin, Le Jingyi)	Rome, Italy	Sep. 11, 1994

EUN=Unified Team

U.S. NATIONAL SWIMMING RECORDS (set in 50-meter pools)

Event	Time	Name	Place	Date
MEN				
Freestyle				
50 meters	21.81	Tom Jager	Nashville, TN	Mar. 24, 1990
100 meters	48.42	Matt Biondi	Austin, TX	Aug. 10, 1988
200 meters	1:47.72	Matt Biondi	Austin, TX	Aug. 8, 1988
400 meters	3:48.06	Matt Cetlinski	Austin, TX	Aug. 11, 1988
800 meters	7:52.45	Sean Killion	Clovis, CA	Jul. 27, 1987
1,500 meters	15:01.51	George DiCarlo	Indianapolis, IN	Jun. 30, 1984
4 × 100 meter relay	3:16.53	United States (Christopher Jacobs, Troy Dalbey, Tom Jager, Matt Biondi)	Seoul, South Korea	Sep. 23, 1988
4 × 200 meter relay	7:12.51	United States (Troy Dalbey, Matthew Cetlinski, Douglas Gjertsen, Matt Biondi)	Seoul, South Korea	Sep. 21, 1988
Breaststroke				
100 meters	1:01.40	Nelson Diehl	Indianapolis, IN	Mar. 1, 1992
	2:10.16	Seth Van Neerdan	Indianapolis, IN	Aug. 14, 1994
200 meters		Michael Barrowman	Barcelona, Spain	Jul. 29, 1992
Butterfly				
100 meters	52.84	Pablo Morales	Orlando, FL	Jun. 23, 1986
200 meters	1:55.69	Melvin Stewart	Perth, Australia	Jan. 12, 1991
Backstroke				
100 meters	53.86	Jeff Rouse	Barcelona, Spain	Jul. 31, 1992
200 meters	1:58.66	Royce Sharp	Indianapolis, IN	Mar. 3, 1992
Medley				
200 meters	2:00.11	David Wharton	Tokyo, Japan	Aug. 20, 1989
400 meters	4:12.30	Tom Dolan	Rome, Italy	Sep. 6, 1994
4 × 100 meter relay	3:36.93	United States (David Berkoff, Richard Schroeder, Matt Biondi, Christopher Jacobs)	Seoul, South Korea	Sep. 25, 1988

WOMEN

Freestyle

50 meters	25.18	Amy Van Dyken	Rome, Italy	Sep. 11, 1994
100 meters	54.48	Jenny Thompson	Indianapolis, IN	Mar. 1, 1992
200 meters	1:57.90	Nicole Haislett	Barcelona, Spain	Jul. 27, 1992
400 meters	4:03.85	Janet B. Evans	Seoul, South Korea	Sep. 22, 1988
800 meters	8:16.22	Janet B. Evans	Tokyo, Japan	Aug. 20, 1989
1,500 meters	15:52.10	Janet B. Evans	Orlando, FL	Mar. 26, 1988
4 × 100 meter relay	3:39.46	United States Team (Nicole Haislett, Dara Torres, Angel Martino, Jenny Thompson)	Barcelona, Spain	Jul. 28, 1992
4 × 200 meter relay	8:02.12	United States (Betsy Mitchell, Mary Terstegge Meagher, Kim Brown, Mary Alice Wayte)	Madrid, Spain	Aug. 22, 1986

Breaststroke

100 meters	1:08.17	Anita Nall	Barcelona, Spain	Jul. 29, 1992
200 meters	2:25.35	Anita Nall	Indianapolis, IN	Mar. 2, 1992

Butterfly

100 meters	57.93	Mary T. Meagher	Brown Deer, WI	Aug. 16, 1981
200 meters	2:05.96	Mary T. Meagher	Brown Deer, WI	Aug. 13, 1981

Backstroke

100 meters	1:00.82	Lea Loveless	Barcelona, Spain	Jul. 30, 1992
200 meters	2:08.60	Betsy Mitchell	Orlando, FL	Jun. 27, 1986

Medley

200 meters	2:11.91	Summer Sanders	Barcelona, Spain	Jul. 28, 1992
400 meters	4:37.58	Summer Sanders	Barcelona, Spain	Jul. 26, 1992
4 × 100 meter relay	4:02.54	United States (Lea Loveless, Anita Nall, Crissy Ahmann-Leighton, Jenny Thompson)	Barcelona, Spain	Jul. 30, 1992

SHORT-COURSE SWIMMING RECORDS

(set in 25-meter pools)

Event	min. : sec.	Name & Country	Place	Date
MEN				
Freestyle				
50 meters	21.50	Aleksandr Popov (Russia)	Desenzano, Italy	Mar. 13, 1994
100 meters*	46.74	Aleksandr Popov (Russia)	Gelsenkirchen, Germany	Mar. 19, 1994
200 meters	1:43.64	Giorgio Lamberti (Italy)	Bonn, Germany	Feb. 11, 1990
400 meters	3:40.46	Danyon Loader (New Zealand)	Sheffield, England	Feb. 11, 1995
800 meters	7:34.90	Kieren Perkins (Australia)	Sydney, Australia	Jul. 25, 1993
1,500 meters	14:26.52	Kieren Perkins (Australia)	Auckland, New Zealand	Jul. 15, 1993
4 × 50 meters	1:27.62	Sweden	Stavanger, Norway	Dec. 2, 1994
4 × 100 meters	3:12.11	Brazil	Palma de Mallorca, Spain	Dec. 5, 1993
4 × 200 meters	7:05.17	West Germany	Bonn, Germany	Feb. 9, 1986
Backstroke				
50 meters	24.37	Jeff Rouse (U.S.)	Sheffield, England	Feb. 12, 1995
100 meters	51.43	Jeff Rouse (U.S.)	Sheffield, England	Apr. 11, 1993
200 meters	1:52.51	Martin Zubero (Spain)	Gainesville, FL	Apr. 10, 1991
Breaststroke				
50 meters	27.00	Mark Warnecke (Germany)	Gelsenkirchen, Germany	Feb. 18, 1995
100 meters	59.07	Philip John Rogers (Australia)	Melbourne, Australia	Aug. 29, 1993
200 meters	2:07.80	Philip John Rogers (Australia)	Melbourne, Australia	Aug. 28, 1993
Butterfly				
50 meters	23.55	Mark Foster (Great Britain)	Sheffield, England	Feb. 11, 1995
100 meters	52.07	Marcel Gery (Canada)	Leicester, England	Feb. 23, 1990
200 meters	1:53.05	Franck Esposito (France)	Paris, France	Mar. 26, 1994
Medley				
100 meters	53.78	Jani Sievinen (Finland)	Espoo, Finland	Nov. 21, 1992
200 meters	1:54.65	Jani Sievinen (Finland)	Kuopio, Finland	Jan. 21, 1994
400 meters	4:07.10	Jani Sievinen (Finland)	Malmo, Sweden	Feb. 9, 1992
4 × 50 meters	1:38.01	Germany	Stavanger, Norway	Dec. 3, 1994
4 × 100 meters	3:32.57	U.S.	Palma de Mallorca, Spain	Dec. 2, 1993

WOMEN

Freestyle

50 meters	24.23	Le Jingyi (China)	Palma de Mallorca, Spain	Dec. 3, 1993
100 meters	53.01	Le Jingyi (China)	Palma de Mallorca, Spain	Dec. 2, 1993
200 meters	1:55.84	Franziska van Almsick (Germany)	Beijing, China	Jan. 9, 1983
400 meters	4:02.05	Astrid Strauss (East Germany)	Bonn, Germany	Feb. 8, 1987
800 meters	8:15.34	Astrid Strauss (East Germany)	Bonn, Germany	Feb. 6, 1987
1,500 meters	15:43.31	Petra Schneider (East Germany)	Gainesville, FL	Jan. 10, 1982
4 × 50 meters	1:40.63	Germany	Espoo, Finland	Nov. 22, 1992
4 × 100 meters	3:35.97	China	Palma de Mallorca, Spain	Dec. 4, 1993
4 × 200 meters	7:52.45	China	Palma de Mallorca, Spain	Dec. 2, 1993

Backstroke

50 meters	27.64	Bai Xiuyu (China)	Desenzano, Italy	Mar. 12, 1994
100 meters	58.50	Angel Martino (U.S.)	Palma de Mallorca, Spain	Dec. 3, 1993
200 meters	2:06.09	He Cihong (China)	Palma de Mallorca, Spain	Dec. 5, 1993

Breaststroke

50 meters	31.19	Louise Karlsson (Sweden)	Espoo, Finland	Nov. 21, 1992
100 meters	1:06.58	Dai Guohong (China)	Palma de Mallorca, Spain	Dec. 4, 1993
200 meters	2:21.99	Dai Guohong (China)	Palma de Mallorca, Spain	Dec. 3, 1993

Butterfly

50 meters	26.56	Angela Kennedy (Australia)	Sheffield, England	Feb. 12, 1995
100 meters**	58.77	Angela Kennedy (Australia)	Gelsenkirchen, Germany	Feb. 18, 1995
200 meters	2:05.65	Mary Meagher (U.S.)	Gainesville, FL	Jan. 2, 1981

Medley

100 meters	1:01.03	Louise Karlsson (Sweden)	Espoo, Finland	Nov. 22, 1992
200 meters	2:07.79	Allison Wagner (U.S.)	Palma de Mallorca, Spain	Dec. 5, 1993
400 meters	4:29.00	Dai Guohong (China)	Palma de Mallorca, Spain	Dec. 2, 1993
4 × 50 meters	1:52.44	Germany	Espoo, Finland	Nov. 21, 1992
4 × 100 meters	3:57.73	China	Palma de Mallorca, Spain	Dec. 5, 1993

*Hand timed for first leg.
**Slower than long-course bests.

m and 200 m freestyle, 100 m butterfly, and 4 × 100 m medley in 1976) and four silvers (200 m individual medley, 1972, 4 × 100 m medley, 1972, 4 × 100 m freestyle, 1972 and 1976); and Shirley Babashoff (U.S.), who won two golds (4 × 100 m freestyle, 1972 and 1976) and six silvers (100 m freestyle, 1972, 200 m freestyle, 1972 and 1976, 400 m and 800 m freestyle, 1976, 4 × 100 m medley, 1976).

Most individual gold medals   The record number of individual gold medals won is four, by Charles Meldrum Daniels (U.S.): 100 m freestyle, 1906 and 1908, 220 yd freestyle, 1904, 440 yd freestyle, 1904; by Roland Matthes (East Germany) with 100 m and 200 m backstroke in 1968 and 1972; by Mark Spitz and Kristin Otto (see MOST MEDALS); and by the divers Pat McCormick and Greg Louganis (see DIVING).

DIVING

Most Olympic medals   The most medals won by a diver is five, by Klaus Dibiasi (Austria), three gold, two silver, 1964–76; and by Greg Louganis (U.S.), four golds, one silver, 1976, 1984–88. Dibiasi is the only diver to win the same event (highboard) at three successive Games (1968, 1972 and 1976). Two divers have won the highboard and springboard doubles at two Games: Pat McCormick (née Keller), 1952 and 1956, and Greg Louganis, 1984 and 1988.

Most world titles   Greg Louganis (U.S.) won a record five world titles—highboard in 1978, and both highboard and springboard in 1982 and 1986, as well as four Olympic gold medals, in 1984 and 1988. Three gold medals in one event have also been won by Philip Boggs (U.S.)—springboard, 1973, 1975 and 1978.

United States Championships   Most titles   Greg Louganis has won a record 47 national titles: 17 in 1 m springboard; 17 in 3 m springboard; 13 in platform. In women's competition Cynthia Potter has won a record 28 titles.

Highest scores   Men   Greg Louganis achieved record scores at the 1984 Olympic Games in Los Angeles, CA, with 754.41 points for the 11-dive springboard event and 710.91 for the highboard. In non-Olympic competitions, Louganis also set the record for the springboard, with 755.49 points at the 1983 U.S. International in Fort Lauderdale, FL. The record for the highboard is 718 points, awarded to Sun Shewei at the 1994 China Open in Wuhan, China.

Women   In 1988, Gao Min (China) won 614.07 points in a 10-dive springboard event at Dive Canada, in Québec, Canada. Chi Bin (China) holds

---

GUESS WHAT?

Q. HOW DEEP CAN A BIRD DIVE?

A. LOOK IN "BIRDS" (LIVING WORLD)

---

the highboard record for her eight dives at the 1994 China Open in Wuhan, China, which earned a score of 516.31 points.

High diving The highest regularly performed head-first dives are those of professional divers from La Quebrada ("The Break in the Rocks") in Acapulco, Mexico, a height of 87½ feet. The base rocks, 21 feet out from the takeoff, necessitate a leap of 27 feet out. The water is 12 feet deep.

The world record high dive from a diving board is 176 ft. 10 in., by Olivier Favre (Switzerland) in Villers-le-Lac, France on August 30, 1987.

The women's record is 120 ft. 9 in., by Lucy Wardle (U.S.) in Ocean Park, Hong Kong on April 6, 1985.

LONG-DISTANCE SWIMMING

Longest swims The greatest recorded distance ever swum is 1,826 miles down the Mississippi River between Ford Dam near Minneapolis, MN and Carrollton Ave., New Orleans, LA, by Fred P. Newton of Clinton, OK from July 6 to December 29, 1930. He was in the water for 742 hours.

Greatest 24-hour distance Anders Forvass (Sweden) swam 63.3 miles at the 25-meter Linköping public swimming pool, Sweden, October 28–29, 1989. In a 50-meter pool, Evan Barry (Australia) swam 60.08 miles, at Carss Park, Sydney, Australia, April 21–22, 1995.

The women's record is 58.17 miles, by Susie Maroney (Australia) at Chandler Aquatic Centre, Brisbane, Australia, July 2–3, 1993.

Long-distance relays The New Zealand national relay team of 20 swimmers swam a record 113.59 miles in Lower Hutt, New Zealand in 24 hours, passing 100 miles in 20 hr. 47 min. 13 sec., December 9–10, 1983. The 24-hour club record by a team of five is 100.99 miles, by the Portsmouth Northsea SC at the Victoria Swimming Centre, Portsmouth, England, March 4–5, 1993. The women's record is 88.93 miles by the City of Newcastle ASC, December 16–17, 1986. The most participants in a 1-day swim relay is 2,375, each swimming a length, at Liverpool High School, Liverpool, New York, NY, May 20–21, 1994.

Underwater swimming Paul Cryne (Great Britain) and Samir Sawan al Awami (Qatar) swam 49.04 miles in 24 hours from Doha, Qatar to Umm Said and back, February 21–22, 1985, using sub-aqua equipment. They were swimming under water for 95.5 percent of the time. A relay team of six swam 94.44 miles in a swimming pool in Olomouc, Czechoslovakia, October 17–18, 1987.

DID YOU KNOW?

The fastest swim around Manhattan Island in New York City was in 5 hr. 53 min. 57 sec., by Kris Rutford (U.S.) on August 29, 1992. Shelley Taylor set the women's record, 6 hr. 12 min. 29 sec., on October 15, 1985

CHANNEL SWIMMING

As of May 1995, there had been 6,333 attempts to swim the English Channel by 4,363 people. Of these, 467 individuals (310 men and 157 women) from 47 countries have made 732 successful crossings: 683 solo, 20 double and 3 triple.

Alison Streeter has crossed the English Channel a record 27 times.
(*Mike Griggs*)

OLDEST CHANNEL SWIMMERS

Bertram Clifford Batt (Australia) was 67 yr. 241 days old when he swam from Cap Gris-Nez, France to Dover, England in 18 hr. 37 min. on August 19–20, 1987. Susan Fraenkel (South Africa; b. April 22, 1948), was 46 yr. 93 days old when she swam the Channel in 12 hr. 5 min. on July 24, 1994.

Fastest crossing The official Channel Swimming Association (founded 1927) record is 7 hr. 17 min., by Chad Hundeby (California), from Shakespeare Beach, Dover, to Cap Gris-Nez, France, on September 27, 1994.

The women's record is 7 hr. 40 min., by Penny Dean (California) from Shakespeare Beach, Dover to Cap Gris-Nez, France, on July 29, 1978.

The fastest France–England time is 8 hr. 5 min., by Richard Davey (Great Britain) in 1988.

The fastest crossing by a relay team is 6 hr. 52 min. (England to France), by the U.S. National Swim Team on August 1, 1990. They went on to complete the fastest two-way relay in 14 hr. 18 min.

Fastest double crossing Philip Rush (New Zealand) completed the fastest double crossing in 16 hr. 10 min. on August 17, 1987. He also completed the fastest triple crossing in 28 hr. 21 min., August 17–18, 1987.

The women's record is 17 hr. 14 min., by Susie Maroney (Australia) on July 23, 1991.

Most Channel conquests   Michael Read (Great Britain) made 31 crossings between August 24, 1969 and August 19, 1984. The most by a woman is 27, by Alison Streeter from 1982 to the end of 1994 (including a record seven crossings in one year in 1992).

Merv Sharp of Weymouth, England has completed a crossing over (by plane), on (by ferry), in (swam seven times) and under (by train) the English Channel.

TABLE TENNIS

Most titles   *World*   *(instituted 1926)* G. Viktor Barna (b. Győző Braun; Hungary) won a record five singles, 1930, 1932–35, and eight men's doubles, 1929–35, 1939, in the World Championships (first held in 1926).

Angelica Rozeanu (Romania) won a record six women's singles, 1950–55, and Maria Mednyanszky (Hungary) won seven women's doubles, 1928, 1930–35. With two more at mixed doubles and seven team, Viktor Barna won 22 world titles in all, while 18 were won by Maria Mednyanszky.

The most men's team titles (Swaythling Cup) is 12, by Hungary, 1927–31, 1933–35, 1938, 1949, 1952 and 1979.

The women's record (Marcel Corbillon Cup) is 11, by China, 1965, and eight successive, 1975–89 (biennially), 1993 and 1995.

United States   The U.S. won the Swaythling Cup in 1937 and the Corbillon Cup in 1937 and 1949. Ruth Aarons was the women's world champion in 1936 and 1937, sharing the title in the latter year.

No American has won the men's world singles title, but James McClure won three men's doubles titles, with Robert Blattner in 1936–37 and with Sol Schiff in 1938.

U.S. Championships   U.S. national championships were first held in 1931. Leah Neuberger (née Thall) won a record 21 titles between 1941 and 1961: nine women's singles and 12 women's doubles. Richard Miles won a record 10 men's singles titles between 1945 and 1962.

The longest span for winning a national championship is 61 years, by Keith Gledhill. He won the U.S. National Boys' Doubles Championship (with Sidney Wood) in 1926. In 1987, he won the U.S. National 75 and Over Doubles Championship (with Elbert Lewis).

Counter hitting   The record number of hits in 60 seconds is 173, by Jackie Bellinger and Lisa Lomas (née Bellinger), at the Northgate Sports Centre, Ipswich, England, on February 7, 1993.

With a paddle in each hand, Gary D. Fisher of Olympia, WA completed 5,000 consecutive volleys over the net in 44 min. 28 sec. on June 25, 1975.

TAEKWONDO

Most titles   Chung Kook-hyun (South Korea) won a record four world titles: as a light-middleweight in 1982 and 1983 and as a welterweight in 1985 and 1987. Lynette Love (U.S.) also took four world titles, all in the heavyweight category, in 1985, 1987, 1988 and 1991.

Most consecutive U.S. titles   Lynette Love (heavyweight) and Dae Sung Lee (finweight) held national titles from 1979 to 1987.

TEAM HANDBALL

Most championships   *Olympic*   The USSR won five titles—(men) 1976, 1988 and 1992 (by the Unified Team from the republics of the former USSR), (women) 1976 and 1980. South Korea has also won two women's titles, in 1988 and 1992.

World Championships (instituted 1938)   For indoor handball (now the predominant version of the game), the most men's titles won is four, by Romania, 1961, 1964, 1970 and 1974. However, Germany/West Germany won the outdoor title five times, 1938–66, and has won the indoor title twice, 1938 and 1978. Three women's titles have been won by three teams: Romania, 1956, 1960 (both outdoor) and 1962 (indoor); the GDR, 1971, 1975 and 1978 (all indoor); and the USSR, 1982, 1986 and 1990 (all indoor).

Highest score   The highest score in an international match was when the USSR beat Afghanistan 86–2 in the "Friendly Army Tournament" in Miskolc, Hungary in 1981.

TENNIS

Longest match   The longest match in a grand slam tournament is 5 hr. 26 min. between Stefan Edberg (Sweden) and Michael Chang (U.S.) for the semifinal of the U.S. Championships, September 12–13, 1992. Edberg won 6–7, 7–5, 7–6, 5–7, 6–4.

Fastest service   The fastest service timed with modern equipment is 138 MPH, by Steve Denton (U.S.) in Beaver Creek, CO on July 29, 1984. The women's best is 115 MPH by Brenda Shultz (Netherlands) and Jana

Novotna (Czechoslovakia), both at the 1993 Wimbledon Championships, on June 25 and July 1, respectively.

DID YOU KNOW?

The only known example of a "golden set" (winning a set 6–0 without dropping a single point, i.e., winning 24 consecutive points) in professional tennis was achieved by Bill Scanlon (U.S.) against Marcos Hocevar (Brazil) in the first round of the WCT Gold Coast Classic in Del Ray, FL on February 22, 1983. Scanlon won the match 6–2, 6–0.

Grand Slam The grand slam for a tennis player is winning all four of the major singles titles—the Australian Open, French Open, Wimbledon and U.S. Open—in the same calendar year. The first man to win the grand slam was Don Budge (U.S.) in 1938. The first man to achieve the grand slam twice was Rodney George "Rod" Laver (Australia), as an amateur in 1962 and again in 1969, when the titles were open to professionals.

Four women have achieved the grand slam: Maureen Catherine Connolly (U.S.), in 1953; Margaret Jean Court (née Smith; Australia) in 1970; Martina Navratilova in 1983–84; and Steffi Graf (Germany) in 1988, when she also won the women's singles Olympic gold medal.

The most singles championships won in grand slam tournaments is 24, by Margaret Court (11 Australian, 5 U.S., 5 French, 3 Wimbledon), 1960–73. She also won the U.S. Amateur in 1969 and 1970 when this was held, as well as the U.S. Open. The men's record is 12, by Roy Stanley Emerson (Australia), 6 Australian, 2 each French, U.S., Wimbledon, 1961–67.

The first doubles pair to win the grand slam were the Australians Frank Allan Sedgeman and Kenneth Bruce McGregor in 1951.

Pam Shriver (U.S.) with Martina Navratilova won a record eight successive grand slam tournament women's doubles titles, and 109 successive matches in all events, from April 1983 to July 1985.

The most grand slam tournament wins by a doubles partnership is 20, by Althea Louise Brough (U.S.) and Margaret Evelyn du Pont (née Osborne; U.S.)—12 U.S., 5 Wimbledon, 3 French, 1942–57; and by Martina Navratilova and Pam Shriver—7 Australian, 5 Wimbledon, 4 French, 4 U.S., 1981–89.

GUESS WHAT?

Q. WHO IS THE WORLD'S MOST TITLED PERSON?

A. LOOK IN "HONORS, DECORATIONS AND AWARDS" (HUMAN WORLD)

United States   The most singles wins in grand slam tournaments by a U.S. player is 19, by Helen Wills Moody—8 Wimbledon, 7 U.S. and 4 French.

Martina Navratilova (formerly of Czechoslovakia) has won a total of 55 grand slam titles—18 singles, a world record 31 women's doubles and 6 mixed doubles. Billie Jean King (née Moffit) has the most of U.S.-born players, with 39 titles—12 singles, 16 women's doubles and 11 mixed doubles.

During the 1994 season, Arantxa Sánchez Vicario (Spain) won a women's record $2,943,665, winning two of the major tournaments, the French and U.S. Opens. (*Allsport/C. Brunskill*)

WIMBLEDON CHAMPIONSHIPS

Most wins *Women* Billie Jean King won a record 20 titles between 1961 and 1979—6 singles, 10 women's doubles and 4 mixed doubles. Elizabeth Montague Ryan (U.S.) won a record 19 doubles (12 women's, seven mixed) titles from 1914 to 1934.

Men The greatest number of titles by a man was 13, by Hugh Laurence Doherty (Great Britain) with 5 singles titles (1902–06) and a record 8 men's doubles (1897–1901, 1903–05) partnered by his brother Reginald Frank (Great Britain).

United States The most titles won by a U.S. man is eight, by John McEnroe—singles 1981, 1983 and 1984; men's doubles 1979, 1981, 1983–84 (all with Peter Fleming), and 1992 (with Michael Stich).

Singles Martina Navratilova won a record nine titles, 1978–79, 1982–87 and 1990. The most men's singles wins since the Challenge Round was abolished in 1922 is five consecutively, by Björn Borg (Sweden) in 1976–80. William Charles Renshaw (Great Britain) won seven singles, in 1881–86 and 1889.

Youngest champions The youngest champion was Lottie Dod (Great Britain), who was 15 yr. 285 days when she won in 1887. The youngest male champion was Boris Becker (West Germany), who won the men's singles title in 1985 at 17 yr. 227 days.

DID YOU KNOW?

The longest tiebreak was 26–24 for the fourth and decisive set of a first round men's doubles at the Wimbledon Championships on July 1, 1985. Jan Gunnarsson (Sweden) and Michael Mortensen (Denmark) defeated John Frawley (Australia) and Victor Pecci (Paraguay) 6–3, 6–4, 3–6, 7–6.

U.S. OPEN

Most wins Margaret Evelyn du Pont won a record 25 titles between 1941 and 1960. She won a record 13 women's doubles, 9 mixed doubles and 3 singles. The men's record is 16, by Bill Tilden, including seven men's singles, 1920–25, 1929—a record for singles shared with: Richard Dudley Sears, 1881–87; William A. Larned, 1901–02, 1907–11; and in women's singles by Molla Mallory (née Bjurstedt), 1915–16, 1918, 1920–22, 1926; and Helen Wills Moody, 1923–25, 1927–29, 1931.

Youngest champions The youngest champion was Vincent Richards, who was 15 yr. 139 days when he won the men's doubles with Bill Tilden in 1918. The youngest singles champion was Tracy Ann Austin, who was 16 yr. 271 days when she won the women's singles in 1979.

FRENCH OPEN

Most wins (from international status 1925)   Margaret Court won a record 13 titles—5 singles, 4 women's doubles and 4 mixed doubles, 1962–73. The men's record is 9, by Henri Cochet (France)—4 singles, 3 men's doubles and 2 mixed doubles, 1926–30. The singles record is seven, by Chris Evert (U.S.), 1974–75, 1979–80, 1983, 1985–86. Björn Borg won a record six men's singles, 1974–75, 1978–81.

Youngest champions   The youngest doubles champions were the 1981 mixed doubles winners Andrea Jaeger, at 15 yr. 339 days, and Jimmy Arias, at 16 yr. 296 days. The youngest singles winners were Monica Seles (Yugoslavia), who won the 1990 women's title at 16 yr. 169 days in 1990, and Michael Chang (U.S.), who won the men's title at 17 yr. 109 days in 1989.

AUSTRALIAN OPEN

Most wins   Margaret Jean Court won the women's singles 11 times (1960–66, 1969–71 and 1973) as well as eight women's doubles and two mixed doubles, for a record total of 21 titles. A record six men's singles were won by Roy Stanley Emerson, 1961 and 1963–67. Thelma Dorothy Long (née Coyne) won a record 12 women's doubles and four mixed doubles for a record total of 16 doubles titles. Adrian Karl Quist won 10 consecutive men's doubles from 1936 to 1950 (the last eight with John Bromwich) and three men's singles.

Youngest champions   The youngest champions were Rodney W. Heath, age 17 when he won the men's singles in 1905, and Monica Seles (Yugoslavia), who won the women's singles at 17 yr. 55 days in 1991.

OLYMPIC GAMES

A record four gold medals, as well as a silver and a bronze, were won by Max Decugis (France), 1900–20. A women's record five medals (one gold, two silver, two bronze) were won by Kitty McKane (later Mrs. Godfree; Great Britain) in 1920 and 1924.

INTERNATIONAL TEAM

Davis Cup (instituted 1900)   The most wins in the Davis Cup, the men's international team championship, was 30, by the U.S. between 1900 and 1992. The most appearances for Cup winners is eight, by Roy Emerson (Australia), 1959–62, 1964–67. Bill Tilden (U.S.) played in a record 28 matches in the final, winning a record 21—17 out of 22 singles and four out of six doubles. He was on seven winning sides, 1920–26, and then on four losing sides, 1927–30.

Nicola Pietrangeli (Italy) played a record 163 rubbers (66 ties), 1954 to 1972, winning 120. He played 109 singles (winning 78) and 54 doubles (winning 42).

John McEnroe has played for the U.S. team on 31 occasions, 1978 through 1992. He also has the most wins—60 matches in Davis Cup competition (41 singles and 19 doubles).

Federation Cup (instituted 1963 and known as the Fed Cup from 1995)   The most wins in the Federation Cup, the women's international team championship, is 14, by the U.S. between 1963 and 1990. Virginia Wade (Great Britain) played each year, 1967–83, in a record 57 ties, playing 100 rubbers, including 56 singles (winning 36) and 44 doubles (winning 30). Chris Evert won her first 29 singles matches, 1977–86. Her overall record, 1977–89, is 40 wins in 42 singles and 16 wins in 18 doubles matches.

Martina Navratilova retired from singles competition at the end of the 1994 season. In a career that spanned three decades, Navratilova won a world record 167 singles tournaments and 165 doubles titles. *(Allsport/G. Prior)*

Highest earnings Pete Sampras (U.S.) won a men's season's record of $4,857,812 and Arantxa Sánchez Vicario (Spain) a women's record of $2,943,665, both in 1994.

The career earnings records are (men) $20,512,417 by Ivan Lendl (Czechoslovakia, now U.S.) to retirement, and (women) $20,283,727 by Martina Navratilova to her retirement on November 15, 1994. Navrativlova won a world record 167 singles tournaments and 165 doubles titles. Earnings from special restricted events and team tennis are not included.

Pete Sampras achieved the record for the greatest first-place prize money ever won, with $2 million, when he won the Grand Slam Cup on December 16, 1990 in Munich, Germany. In the final he beat Brad Gilbert (U.S.) 6–3, 6–4, 6–2. Gilbert received $1 million, also well in excess of the previous record figure.

The highest total prize money was $9,022,000 for the 1993 U.S. Open Championships.

Largest crowd A record 30,472 people were at the Astrodome, Houston, TX on September 20, 1973, when Billie Jean King beat Bobby Riggs (U.S.). The record for a standard tennis match is 25,578 in Sydney, Australia on December 27, 1954, in the Davis Cup Challenge Round (first day), Australia vs. U.S.

Longest game The longest singles game was one of 37 deuces (80 points) between Anthony Fawcett (Rhodesia) and Keith Glass (Great Britain) in the first round of the Surrey Championships in Surbiton, England on May 26, 1975. It lasted 31 minutes.

Noëlle van Lottum and Sandra Begijn played a game lasting a total 52 minutes during the semifinals of the Dutch Indoor Championships in Ede, Gelderland on February 12, 1984.

TRACK AND FIELD

Fastest speed An analysis of split times in each 10 meters in the 1988 Olympic Games 100 m final in Seoul, South Korea on September 24, 1988, won by Ben Johnson (Canada) in 9.79 seconds (average speed 22.85 MPH), with Carl Lewis (U.S.) finishing in 9.92 seconds, showed that both Johnson and Lewis reached a peak speed (40 m–50 m and 80 m–90 m respectively) of 0.83 seconds for 10 m, i.e., 26.95 MPH. Johnson's record was later disallowed as a result of his positive drug test for steroids. In the women's final, Florence Griffith Joyner was timed at 0.91 seconds for each 10 m from 60 m–90 m, i.e., 24.58 MPH.

Most track records in a day Jesse Owens (U.S.) set six world records in 45 minutes in Ann Arbor, MI on May 25, 1935, with a 9.4-second 100 yards at 3:15 P.M., a 26 ft. 8¼ in. long jump at 3:25 P.M., a 20.3-second 220 yards (and 200 m) at 3:45 P.M., and a 22.6-second 220 yards (and 200 m) low hurdles at 4 P.M.

Highest jump above own head　The greatest height cleared above an athlete's own head is 23¼ inches, by Franklin Jacobs (U.S.), 5 ft. 8 in. tall, who jumped 7 ft. 7¼ in. in New York City, on January 27, 1978. The greatest height cleared by a woman above her own head is 12¾ inches, by Yolanda Henry (U.S.), 5 ft. 6 in. tall, who jumped 6 ft. 6¾ in. in Seville, Spain on May 30, 1990.

Most Olympic titles　The most Olympic gold medals won is 10 (an absolute Olympic record), by Raymond Clarence Ewry (U.S.) in the standing high, long and triple jumps in 1900, 1904, 1906 and 1908.

Women　The most gold medals won by a woman is four, shared by Fanny E. Blankers-Koen (Netherlands), with 100 m, 200 m, 80 m hurdles and 4 × 100 m relay, 1948; Betty Cuthbert (Australia), with 100 m, 200 m, 4 × 100 m relay, 1956 and 400 m, 1964; Bärbel Wöckel (née Eckert; East Germany), with 200 m and 4 × 100 m relay in 1976 and 1980; and Evelyn Ashford (U.S.), 100 m and 4 × 100 m relay in 1984, 4 × 100 m relay in 1988 and 1992.

Most wins at one Games　The most gold medals at one Games is five, by Paavo Johannes Nurmi (Finland) in 1924: 1,500 m, 5,000 m, 10,000 m cross-country, 3,000 m team and cross-country team. The most in individual events is four, by Alvin Christian Kraenzlein (U.S.) in 1900: 60 m, 110 m hurdles, 200 m hurdles and long jump.

Most Olympic medals　The most medals won is 12 (nine gold and three silver), by Paavo Nurmi (Finland) in the Games of 1920, 1924 and 1928.

Women　The most medals won by a woman athlete is seven, by Shirley Barbara de la Hunty (née Strickland; Australia) with 3 gold, 1 silver and 3 bronze in the 1948, 1952 and 1956 Games. A reappraisal of the photo-finish indicates that she finished third, not fourth, in the 1948 200 m event, thus unofficially increasing her medal haul to eight. Irena Szewinska (née Kirszenstein; Poland) won 3 gold, 2 silver and 2 bronze in 1964, 1968, 1972 and 1976, and is the only woman athlete to win a medal in four successive Games.

United States　The most Olympic medals won is 10, by Ray Ewry (see MOST OLYMPIC TITLES). The most by a woman is five, by Delorez Florence Griffith Joyner: silver in 200 m in 1984, gold in 100 m, 200 m and 4 × 100 m relay, silver in 4 × 400 m relay in 1988, and Evelyn Ashford: gold in 100 m and 4 × 100 m relay in 1984, gold in 4 × 100 m relay and silver in 100 m in 1988, and gold in 4 × 100 m relay in 1992.

　　Four gold medals at one Games were won by Alvin Kraenzlein (see above). Jesse Owens in 1936 and Carl Lewis in 1984 both won four gold medals at one Games, both in 100 m, 200 m, long jump and the 4 × 100 m relay.

Olympic champions　*Oldest and youngest*　The oldest athlete to win an Olympic title was Irish-born Babe McDonald (b. McDonnell; U.S.), who was age 42 yr. 26 days when he won the 56-lb. weight throw in Antwerp, Belgium on August 21, 1920. The oldest female champion was Lia Manoliu (Romania), age 36 yr. 176 days when she won the discus in Mexico City on October 18, 1968. The youngest gold medalist was Barbara Pearl Jones

TRACK AND FIELD RECORDS—*Women*

World records for the women's events scheduled by the International Amateur Athletic Federation.

Running	min. : sec.	Name & Country	Place	Date
100 meters	10.49	Delorez Florence Griffith Joyner (U.S.)	Indianapolis, IN	Jul. 16, 1988
200 meters	21.34	Delorez Florence Griffith Joyner (U.S.)	Seoul, South Korea	Sep. 29, 1988
400 meters	47.60	Marita Koch (East Germany)	Canberra, Australia	Oct. 6, 1985
800 meters	1:53.28	Jarmila Kratochvílová (Czechoslovakia)	Münich, Germany	Jul. 26, 1983
1,000 meters	2:30.6	Tatyana Providokhina (USSR)	Podolsk, USSR	Aug. 20, 1978
	2:30.67	Christine Wachtel (East Germany)	Berlin, Germany	Aug. 17, 1990
1,500 meters	3:50.46	Qu Yunxia (China)	Beijing, China	Sep. 11, 1993
1 mile	4:15.61	Paula Ivan (Romania)	Nice, France	Jul. 10, 1989
2,000 meters	5:25.36	Sonia O'Sullivan (Ireland)	Edinburgh, Scotland	Jul. 8, 1994
3,000 meters	8:06.11	Wang Junxia (China)	Beijing, China	Sep. 13, 1993
5,000 meters	14:37.33	Ingrid Kristiansen (née Christensen; Norway)	Stockholm, Sweden	Aug. 5, 1986
10,000 meters	29:31.78	Wang Junxia (China)	Beijing, China	Sep. 8, 1993

Hurdling				
100 meters (2' 9")	12.21	Yordanka Donkova (Bulgaria)	Stara Zagora, Bulgaria	Aug. 20, 1988
400 meters (2' 6")	52.74	Sally Jane Janet Gunnell (Great Britain)	Stuttgart, Germany	Aug. 19, 1993

Relays

	m			
4 × 100 meters	41.37	East Germany	Canberra, Australia	Oct. 6, 1985
		(Silke Gladisch [now Möller], Sabine Rieger [now Günther], Ingrid Auerswald [née Brestrich], Marlies Göhr [née Oelsner])		
4 × 200 meters	1:28.15	East Germany	Jena, Germany	Aug. 9, 1980
		(Marlies Göhr [née Oelsner], Romy Müller [née Schneider], Bärbel Wöckel [née Eckert], Marita Koch)		
4 × 400 meters	3:15.17	USSR	Seoul, South Korea	Oct. 1, 1988
		(Tatyana Ledovskaya, Olga Nazarova [née Grigoryeva], Maria Pinigina [née Kulchunova], Olga Bryzgina [née Vladykina])		
4 × 800 meters	7:50.17	USSR	Moscow, USSR	Aug. 5, 1984
		(Nadezhda Olizarenko [née Mushta], Lyubov Gurina, Lyudmila Borisova, Irina Podyalovskaya)		

Field Events

	m	ft.	in.			
High jump	2.09	6	10¹/₄	Stefka Kostadinova (Bulgaria)	Rome, Italy	Aug. 30, 1987
Pole vault	4.13	13	6¹/₂	Daniela Brtov (Czech Republic)	Wesel, Germany	Jun. 24, 1995
Long jump	7.52	24	8¹/₂	Galina Chistyakova (USSR)	Leningrad, USSR	Jun. 11, 1988
Triple jump	15.09	49	6	Anna Biryukova (née Dereyankina; Russia)	Stuttgart, Germany	Aug. 21, 1993
Shot 8 lb. 13 oz.	22.63	74	3	Natalya Lisovskaya (USSR)	Moscow, USSR	Jun. 7, 1987
Discus 2 lb. 3 oz.	76.80	25	20	Gabriele Reinsch (East Germany)	Neubrandenburg, Germany	Jul. 9, 1988
Javelin 24 lb. 7 oz.	80.00	26	25	Petra Felke (East Germany)	Potsdam, Germany	Sep. 9, 1988

Heptathlon

7,291 points	Jacqueline Joyner-Kersee (U.S.)	Seoul, South Korea	Sep. 23–24 1988

(100 m hurdles 12.69 sec.; High jump 6 ft. 1¹/₄ in.: Shot 51 ft. 10 in.; 200 m 22.56 sec.; Long jump 23 ft. 10 in.; Javelin 149 ft. 9 in.; 800 m 2 min. 08.51 sec.)

Yolanda Chen was the first woman to triple jump 15 meters indoors when she won the 1995 World Championships in Barcelona, Spain.
(Allsport/G. Mortimore)

(U.S.), who at 15 yr. 123 days was a member of the winning 4 × 100 m relay team, in Helsinki, Finland on July 27, 1952. The youngest male champion was Bob Mathias (U.S.), age 17 yr. 263 days when he won the decathlon at the London Games, August 5–6, 1948.

The oldest Olympic medalist was Tebbs Lloyd Johnson (Great Britain), age 48 yr. 115 days when he was third in the 1948 50,000 m walk. The oldest woman medalist was Dana Zátopková (Czechoslovakia), age 37 yr. 348 days when she was second in the javelin in 1960.

World Championships   Quadrennial World Championships, distinct from the Olympic Games, were inaugurated in 1983, when they were held in Helsinki, Finland. In 1991, the event became a biennial championship. The most medals won is 10, by Carl Lewis (U.S.)—eight gold, in 100 m, long jump and 4 × 100 m relay in 1983; 100 m, long jump and 4 × 100 m relay in 1987; 100 m and 4 × 100 m relay, 1991; silver in long jump in 1991; and bronze in 200 m in 1993; and by Merlene Ottey (Jamaica)—two gold, in 200 m in 1993 and 4 × 100 m relay in 1991; two silver, in 100 m in 1993 and 200 m in 1983; and six bronze, in 100 m and 200 m in 1987 and 1991 and in 4 × 100 m relay in 1983 and 1993.

The most gold medals won by a woman at the World Championships is four, by Jackie Joyner-Kersee (U.S.)—long jump 1987, 1991; heptathlon 1987, 1993.

Indoor   First held as the World Indoor Games in 1985, they are now staged biennially. The most individual titles is four, shared by Stefka Kostadinova (Bulgaria), high jump 1985, 1987, 1989, 1993; by Mikhail

Shchennikov (Russia), 5,000 m walk 1987, 1989, 1991, 1993; and by Sergey Bubka (Ukraine), pole vault 1985, 1987, 1991, 1995.

Youngest record breaker   The youngest individual record breaker is Wang Yan (China), who set a women's 5,000 m walk record at age 14 yr. 334 days with 21 min. 33.8 sec. in Jian, China on March 9, 1986. The youngest male is Thomas Ray (Great Britain) at 17 yr. 198 days when he pole-vaulted 11 ft. 2³/₄ in. on September 19, 1879 (prior to IAAF ratification).

U.S. Championships   The most American national titles won in all events, indoors and out, is 65, by Ronald Owen Laird in various walks events between 1958 and 1976. Excluding the walks, the record is 41, by Stella Walsh (née Walasiewicz), who won women's events between 1930 and 1954—33 outdoors and 8 indoors.

The most wins outdoors in one event in AAU/TAC history is 11, by James Sarsfield Mitchel in 56 lb weight in 1888, 1891–97, 1900, 1903, 1905; Stella Walsh, in 220 yd/200 m 1930–31, 1939–40, 1942–48, and in long jump 1930, 1939–46, 1948 and 1951; Maren Seidler in shot 1967–68, 1972–80; and Dorothy Dodson in javelin 1939–49.

Noureddine Morceli, one of the top middle-distance runners of the decade, holds the record for the mile, 1,500 m and 3,000 m. (*Allsport/Vandystadt/ R. Martin*)

TRACK AND FIELD RECORDS—Men

World records for the men's events scheduled by the International Amateur Athletic Federation.
Fully automatic electric timing is mandatory for events up to 400 meters.

Running	min. : sec.	Name & Country	Place	Date
100 meters	9.85*	Leroy Burrell (U.S.)	Lausanne, Switzerland	Jul. 6, 1994
200 meters	19.72†	Pietro Mennea (Italy)	Mexico City, Mexico	Sep. 12, 1979
400 meters	43.29	Butch Reynolds, Jr. (U.S.)	Zürich, Switzerland	Aug. 17, 1988
800 meters	1:41.73	Sebastian Coe (Great Britain)	Florence, Italy	Jun. 10, 1981
1,000 meters	2:12.18	Sebastian Coe (Great Britain)	Oslo, Norway	Jul. 11, 1981
1,500 meters	3:28.86	Noureddine Morceli (Algeria)	Rieti, Italy	Sep. 6, 1992
1 mile	3:44.39	Noureddine Morceli (Algeria)	Rieti, Italy	Sep. 5, 1993
2,000 meters	4:50.81	Said Aouita (Morocco)	Paris, France	Jul. 16, 1987
3,000 meters	7:25.11	Noureddine Morceli (Algeria)	Monte Carlo, Monaco	Aug. 2, 1994
5,000 meters	12:55.30	Moses Kiptanui (Kenya)	Rome, Italy	Jun. 8, 1995
10,000 meters	26:43.53	Haile Gebrselassie (Ethiopia)	Hengelo, Netherlands	Jun. 5, 1995
20,000 meters	56:55.6	Arturo Barrios (Mexico)	La Flèche, France	Mar. 30, 1991
25,000 meters	1 hr. 13:55.8	Toshihiko Seko (Japan)	Christchurch, New Zealand	Mar. 22, 1981
30,000 meters	1 hr. 29:18.8	Toshihiko Seko (Japan)	Christchurch, New Zealand	Mar. 22, 1981
1 hour	13.111 miles	Arturo Barrios (Mexico)	La Flèche, France	May 30, 1991

* Ben Johnson (Canada) ran 100 m in 9.79 seconds at Seoul, South Korea on Sep. 24, 1988, but was subsequently disqualified when he tested positive for steroids: He later admitted to having taken drugs over many years, and this also invalidated his 9.83 sec at Rome, Italy on Aug. 30, 1987.
† This record was set at high altitude—Mexico City 7,349 ft. Best mark at low altitude: 200 m: 19.73 sec., Michael Marsh (U.S.) Barcelona, Spain, August 5, 1992.

Hurdling				
110 meters (3' 6")	12.91	Colin Jackson (Great Britain)	Stuttgart, Germany	Aug. 20, 1993
400 meters (3' 0")	46.78	Kevin Young (U.S.)	Barcelona, Spain	Aug. 6, 1992
3,000 meter steeplechase	8:02.08	Moses Kiptanui (Kenya)	Zürich, Sweden	Aug. 20, 1992

Relays

	m/time			Team	Location	Date
4 × 100 meters	37.40			United States	Barcelona, Spain	Aug. 8, 1992
				(Mike Marsh, Leroy Burrell, Dennis Mitchell, Carl Lewis)		
	37.40			United States	Stuttgart, Germany	Aug. 21, 1993
				(John A. Drummond Jr, Andre Cason, Dennis A. Mitchell, Leroy Burrell)		
4 × 200 meters	1:18.68			Santa Monica Track Club	Walnut, CA	Apr. 17, 1994
				(Mike Marsh, Leroy Burrell, Floyd Heard, Carl Lewis)		
4 × 400 meters	2:54.29			United States	Stuttgart, Germany	Aug. 21, 1993
				(Andrew Valmon, Quincy Watts, Butch Reynolds, Michael Johnson)		
4 × 800 meters	7:03.89			Great Britain	London, England	Aug. 30, 1982
				(Peter Elliott, Garry Peter Cook, Steven Cram, Sebastian Coe)		
4 × 1,500 meters	14:38.8			West Germany	Cologne, Germany	Aug. 17, 1977
				(Thomas Wessinghage, Harald Hudak, Michael Lederer, Karl Fleschen)		

Field Events

	m	ft.	in.	Athlete	Location	Date
High jump	2.45	8	0½	Javier Sotomayor (Cuba)	Salamanca, Spain	Jul. 27, 1993
Pole vault	6.14*	20	1¾	Sergey Bubka (Ukraine)	Sestriere, Italy	Jul. 31, 1994
Long jump	8.95	29	4½	Mike Powell (U.S.)	Tokyo, Japan	Aug. 30, 1991
Triple jump	17.97	58	11½	Willie Banks (U.S.)	Indianapolis, IN	Jun. 16, 1985
Shot 16 lb.	23.12	75	10¼	Randy Barnes (U.S.)	Los Angeles, CA	May 20, 1990
Discus 4 lb. 8 oz.	74.08	243	0	Jürgen Schult (East Germany)	Neubrandenburg, Germany	Jun. 6, 1986
Hammer 16 lb.	86.74	284	7	Yuriy Sedykh (USSR)	Stuttgart, Germany	Aug. 30, 1986
Javelin	95.66	313	10	Jan Zelezny (TCH)	Sheffield, England	Aug. 29, 1993

Decathlon

8,891 points				Dan O'Brien (U.S.)	Talence, France	Sep. 4–5, 1992

(1st day: 100 m 10.43 sec., Long jump 26 ft. ¼ in., Shot put 54 ft. 9¼ in., High jump 6 ft. 9½ in., 400 m 48.51 sec.) (2nd day: 110 m hurdles 13.98 sec., Discus 159 ft. 4 in., Pole vault 16 ft. 4¾ in., Javelin 205 ft. 4 in., 1,500 m 4:42.10 sec.)

*This record was set at high altitude. Best mark at low altitude: 20 ft. 1¼ in. by Sergey Bubka in Tokyo, Japan, Sep. 19, 1992.

Longest winning sequence Iolanda Balas (Romania) won a record 150 consecutive competitions in high jump, 1956–67. The record in a track event is 122, in 400 m hurdles, by Edwin Corley Moses (U.S.) between his loss to Harald Schmid (West Germany) in Berlin, Germany on August 26, 1977 and his loss to Danny Lee Harris (U.S.) in Madrid, Spain on June 4, 1987.

Javier Sotomayor holds both the indoor and outdoor high jump world records and was the first man to clear eight feet. (*Allsport/ G. Mortimore*)

Longest running races The longest race ever staged was the 1929 transcontinental race from New York City to Los Angeles, CA (3,665 miles). Johnny Salo (b. Finland) was the winner in 1929 in 79 days, from March 31, to June 18. His elapsed time was 525 hr. 57 min. 20 sec. (averaging 6.97 MPH).

The longest race staged annually is the New York 1,300 Mile race, held since 1987, in Flushing Meadows–Corona Park, Queens, NY. The fastest time to complete the race is 16 days 19 hr. 31 min. 47 sec. by Al Howie (Great Britain), from September 16 to October 3, 1991.

Longest runs The longest run by an individual is one of 11,134 miles around the United States, by Sarah Covington-Fulcher (U.S.), starting and finishing in Los Angeles, CA, from July 21, 1987 to October 2, 1988. Al Howie (Great Britain) ran across Canada, from St. Johns, Newfoundland to Victoria, British Columbia, a distance of 4,533.2 miles, in 72 days 10 hr. 23 min., from June 21 to September 1, 1991. Robert J. Sweetgall (U.S.) ran 10,608 miles around the perimeter of the United States, starting and finishing in Washington, D.C., from October 9, 1982 to July 15, 1983. Ron Grant (Australia) ran around Australia, 8,316 miles in 217 days 3 hr. 45 min., from March 28 to October 31, 1983. Max Telford (New Zealand; b. Hawick, Scotland) ran 5,110 miles from Anchorage, AK to Halifax, Nova Scotia, in 106 days 18 hr. 45 min. from July 25, to November 9, 1977.

The fastest time for the cross-America run is 46 days 8 hr. 36 min., by Frank Giannino, Jr. (U.S.) for the 3,100 miles from San Francisco to New York from September 1 to October 17, 1980. The women's trans-America record is 69 days 2 hr. 40 min., by Mavis Hutchinson (South Africa) from March 12 to May 21, 1978.

JACKIE JO!

"The record is the dessert," Jackie Joyner-Kersee says. "I gotta do the main course first." As a multi-

ple record holder, Joyner-Kersee is eating cheesecake these days. "I'm not conscious all the time of my record; your mark (e.g., points in the heptathlon) is your target—the standard to shoot for."

World Championships

Jackie Joyner-Kersee holds the women's record for World Championship gold medals, with four—long jump, 1987, 1991, and heptathlon, 1987, 1993.

Joyner-Kersee holds the world record in the heptathlon and the national record in the long jump. Although all her accomplishments are important to her, "being the first woman to score 7,000 points in the heptathlon is definitely my favorite."

Also close to her heart is making people realize that multi-events are not just men's domain any more. "I hope that in the future, I can help educate people so that young girls can do this event without being looked upon strangely by their peers."

Joyner-Kersee's education never ends. She continues to strive for greater challenges and accomplishments. "Track teaches me a lot—I have to go up against myself, there's no one else to look to."

What does Jackie Joyner-Kersee foresee in the future? The 1996 Olympics in Atlanta, of course. "Discipline and hard work . . . and always believing in the total being. It's the philosophy I live by."

TRACK AND FIELD RECORDS

U.S. National Records— *Women*

Running

	min. : sec.	Name	Place	Date
100 meters	10.49	Florence Griffith Joyner	Indianapolis, IN	Jul. 16, 1988
200 meters	21.34	Florence Griffith Joyner	Seoul, South Korea	Sep. 29, 1988
400 meters	48.83	Valerie Ann Brisco	Los Angeles, CA	Aug. 6, 1984
800 meters	1:56.90	Mary Slaney (née Decker)	Berne, Switzerland	Aug. 16, 1985
1,000 meters	2:34.04	Julie Jenkins	Berlin, Germany	Aug. 17, 1990
1,500 meters	3:57.12	Mary Slaney	Stockholm, Sweden	Jul. 26, 1983
1 mile	4:16.71	Mary Slaney	Zürich, Switzerland	Aug. 21, 1985
2,000 meters	5:32.7	Mary Slaney	Eugene, OR	Aug. 3, 1984
3,000 meters	8:25.83	Mary Slaney	Rome, Italy	Sep. 7, 1985
5,000 meters	14:56.07	Annette Peters	Berlin, Germany	Aug. 27, 1993
10,000 meters	31:19.89	Lynn Jennings	Barcelona, Spain	Aug. 7, 1992
Marathon	2 hr. 21:21	Joan Samuelson (née Benoit)	Chicago, IL	Oct. 20, 1985

Hurdling

	min. : sec.	Name	Place	Date
100 meters	12.46	Gail Devers	Stuttgart, Germany	Aug. 20, 1993
400 meters	52.79	Sandra Farmer-Patrick	Stuttgart, Germany	Aug. 19, 1993

Relays

	min. : sec.	Name	Place	Date
4 × 100 meters	41.49	National Team (Michelle Finn, Gwen Torrance, Wendy Vereen, Gail Devers)	Stuttgart, Germany	Aug. 22, 1993
4 × 200 meters	1:32.55	Louisiana State University (D'Andre Hill, Karen Boone, Eureka Hall, Cheryl Taplin)	Philadelphia, PA	Apr. 30, 1994
4 × 400 meters	3:15.51	National Team (Denean Howard, Diane Lynn Dixon, Valerie Brisco, Florence Griffith Joyner)	Seoul, South Korea	Oct. 1, 1988
4 × 800 meters	8:17.09	Athletics West (Susan Addison, Lee Arbogast, Mary Decker, Chris Mullen)	Walnut, CA	Apr. 24, 1983

Field Events

	ft.	in.			
High jump	6	8	Louise Ritter	Austin, TX	Jul. 8, 1988
	6	8	Louise Ritter	Seoul, South Korea	Sep. 30, 1988
Pole vault	13	1¼	Melissa Price	Walnut, CA	Jun. 24, 1995
Long jump	24	7	Jacqueline Joyner-Kersee	New York, NY	May 22, 1994
Triple jump	46	8¼	Sheila Hudson Standwick	New Orleans, LA	Jun. 21, 1992
	46	8¼	Sheila Hudson Standwick	Knoxville, TN	Jun. 16, 1994
Shot	66	2½	Ramona Pagel (née Ebert)	San Diego, CA	Jun. 25, 1988
Discus	216	10	Carol Cady	San Jose, CA	May 31, 1986
Javelin	227	5	Kate Schmidt	Fürth, Germany	Sep. 11, 1977

Heptathlon

7,291 points		Jacqueline Joyner-Kersee	Seoul, South Korea ...... Sep. 23-24, 1988

(100 m hurdles 12.69 sec.; High jump 6 ft. 1¼ in.; Shot 51 ft. 10 in.;
200 m 22.56 sec.; Long jump 23 ft. 10 in.; Javelin 149 ft. 9 in.;
800 m 2 min. 08.51 sec.

TRACK AND FIELD RECORDS

U.S. National Records—*Men*

Running	min. : sec.	Name	Place	Date
100 meters	9.85	Leroy Burrell	Lausanne, Switzerland	Jul. 6, 1994
200 meters	19.73	Mike Marsh	Barcelona, Spain	Aug. 6, 1992
400 meters	43.29	"Harry "Butch" Reynolds, Jr.	Zürich, Switzerland	Aug. 17, 1988
800 meters	1:42.60	Johnny Gray	Koblenz, Germany	Aug. 28, 1985
1,000 meters	2:13.9	Rick Wohlhuter	Oslo, Norway	Jul. 30, 1974
1,500 meters	3:29.77	Sydney Maree	Cologne, Germany	Aug. 25, 1985
1 mile	3:47.69	Steve Scott	Oslo, Norway	Jul. 7, 1982
2,000 meters	4:52.44	Jim Spivey	Lausanne, Switzerland	Sep. 15, 1987
3,000 meters	7:33.37	Sydney Maree*	London, England	Jul. 17, 1982
	7:35.33	Bob Kennedy	Nice, France	Jul. 18, 1994
5,000 meters	13:01.15	Sydney Maree	Oslo, Norway	Jul. 27, 1985
10,000 meters	27:20.56	Marcus Nenow	Brussels, Belgium	Sep. 5, 1986
15,000 meters	43:39.8	Bill Rodgers	Boston, MA	Aug. 9, 1977
20,000 meters	58:25.0	Bill Rodgers	Boston, MA	Aug. 9, 1977
25,000 meters	1 hr. 14:11.8	Bill Rodgers	Saratoga, NY	Feb. 21, 1979
30,000 meters	1 hr. 31:49	Bill Rodgers	Saratoga, NY	Feb. 21, 1979
1 hour	12 mil 1,350 yd.	Bill Rodgers	Boston, MA	Aug. 9, 1977
Marathon	2 hr. 08:47.	Robert Kempainen**	Boston, MA	Apr. 18, 1994

*Prior to obtaining US citizenship. ** Course overall downhill, and with following wind. Official U.S. record: 2 hr. 10:04, by Pat Peterson, London, Apr. 23, 1989.*

Hurdling				
110 meters	12.92	Roger Kingdom	Zürich, Switzerland	Aug. 16, 1989
400 meters	46.78	Kevin Young	Barcelona, Spain	Aug. 6, 1992
3,000 meter steeplechase	8:09.17	Henry Marsh	Koblenz, Germany	Aug. 28, 1985

Relays

	ft.	in.			
4 × 100 meters		37.40	National Team	Barcelona, Spain	Aug. 8, 1992
			(Michael Marsh, Leroy Burrell, Dennis Mitchell, Carl Lewis)		
		37.40	National Team	Stuttgart, Germany	Aug. 21, 1993
			(Jon Drummond, Andre Cason, Dennis Mitchell, Leroy Burrell)		
4 × 200 meters		1:18.68	Santa Monica Track Club	Walnut, CA	Apr. 17, 1994
			(Michael Marsh, Leroy Burrell, Floyd Heard, Carl Lewis)		
4 × 400 meters		2:54.29	National Team	Stuttgart, Germany	Aug. 21, 1993
			(Andrew Valmon, Quincy Watts, Butch Reynolds, Michael Johnson)		
4 × 800 meters		7:06.5	Santa Monica Track Club	Walnut, CA	Apr. 26, 1986
			(James Robinson, David Mack, Earl Jones, Johnny Gray)		
4 × 1,000 meters		14:46.3	National Team	Bourges, France	Jun. 24, 1969

Field Events

	ft.	in.			
High jump	7	10½	Charles Austin	Zürich, Switzerland	Aug. 7, 1991
Pole vault	19	7	Scott Huffman	Knoxville, TN	Jun. 18, 1994
Long jump	29	4½	Mike Powell	Tokyo, Japan	Aug. 30, 1991
Triple jump	58	11½	Willie Banks	Indianapolis, IN	Jun. 16, 1985
Shot	75	10¼	Randy Barnes	Westwood, LA	May 20, 1990
Discus*	237	4	Ben Plunknett	Stockholm, Sweden	Jul. 7, 1981
Hammer	270	8	Lance Deal	Knoxville, TN	Jun. 17, 1994
Javelin	281	2	Tom Pukstys	Kuortane, Finland	Jun. 26, 1993

Ratified despite the fact that it was achieved after a positive drug test.

Decathlon

8,891 points	Dan O'Brien	Talence, France .... Sep. 4–5, 1992

(1st day: 100 m 10.43 sec..; Long jump 26 ft. ¼ in.; Shot put 54 ft. 9¼ in.; High jump 6 ft. 9½ in.; 400 m 48.51 sec..)
(2nd day: 110 m hurdles 13.98 sec..; Discus 159 ft. 4 in.; Pole vault 16 ft. 4¾ in.; Javelin 205 ft. 4 in.; 1,500 m 4:42.10 sec.)

Jan Zelezny sends
the javelin on its
way to the world
record distance of
95.66 meters in
Sheffield, England.
(*Allsport/
G. Mortimore*)

Mass relays The record for 100 miles by 100 runners from one club is 7 hr. 53 min. 52.1 sec., by the Baltimore Road Runners Club, Towson, MD on May 17, 1981. The women's record is 10 hr. 33 min. 38.81 sec. on August 10, 1994, by the Syracuse Chargers Running Club, NY. The record for 100×100 m is 19 min. 14.19 sec., by a team from Antwerp in Merksem, Belgium on September 23, 1989.

The longest relay ever run was 10,806 miles by 23 runners of the Melbourne Fire Brigade, around Australia on Highway No. 1, in 50 days 43 min., from August 6 to September 25, 1991. The most participants is 6,500—260 teams of 25—for the Batavierenrace from Nijmegen to Enschede, Netherlands on April 25, 1992. The greatest distance covered in 24 hours by a team of 10 is 302.281 miles, by Puma Tyneside RC at Monkton Stadium, Jarrow, England, September 10–11, 1994.

United States The greatest distance covered by an American team of 10 runners in 24 hours is 271.974 miles, by students of Marcus High School in Flower Mound, TX, May 17–18, 1991.

Greatest mileage Douglas Alistair Gordon Pirie (Great Britain), who set five world records in the 1950s, estimated that he had run a total distance of 216,000 miles in 40 years up to 1981.

The greatest competitive distance run in a year is 5,502 miles, by Malcolm Campbell (Great Britain) in 1985.

Joggling *3 objects* Owen Morse (U.S.), 100 m in 11.68 seconds, 1989, and 400 m in 57.32 seconds, 1990. Kirk Swenson (U.S.), one mile in 4 min.

43 sec., 1986, and 5,000 m (3.1 miles) in 16 min. 55 sec., 1986. Ashrita Furman (U.S.), marathon—26 mi. 385 yd.—in 3 hr. 22 min. 32.5 sec., 1988, and 50 miles in 8 hr. 52 min. 7 sec., 1989. Michael Hout (U.S.), 110 m hurdles in 18.9 seconds, 1993. Albert Lucas (U.S.), 400 m hurdles in 1 min. 7 sec., 1993. Owen Morse, Albert Lucas, Tuey Wilson and John Wee (all U.S.), one mile relay in 3 min. 57.38 sec., 1990.

5 objects Owen Morse (U.S.), 100 m in 13.8 seconds, 1988. Bill Gillen (U.S.), 1 mile in 7 min. 41.01 sec., 1989, and 3.1 miles in 28 min. 11 sec., 1989.

MARATHON

Fastest marathon There are no official records for the marathon, and it should be noted that courses may vary in severity. The following are the best times recorded on courses whose distances have been verified.

Men 2 hr. 6 min. 50 sec., by Belayneh Dinsamo (Ethiopia) in Rotterdam, Netherlands on April 17, 1988.

Women 2 hr. 21 min. 6 sec., by Ingrid Kristiansen (née Christensen; Norway) in London, England on April 21, 1985.

Boston Marathon First run by 15 men on April 19, 1897 over a distance of 24 mi. 1,232 yd., the Boston Marathon is the world's oldest annual marathon. The full marathon distance was first run in 1927.

The most wins is seven, by Clarence DeMar, in 1911, 1922–24, 1927–28 and 1930.

Rosa Mota (Portugal) has a record three wins, 1987–88 and 1990, in the women's competition.

The course record for men is 2 hr. 7 min. 15 sec. by Cosmas Ndeti (Kenya) in 1994. The women's record is 2 hr. 21 min. 45 sec., by Uta Pippig (Germany) in 1994.

John A. Kelley (U.S.) finished the Boston Marathon 62 times through 1993, winning twice, in 1933 and 1945.

New York City Marathon In the 1994 New York City Marathon, there were a record 29,735 finishers.

Grete Waitz (née Andersen; Norway) was the women's winner nine times, in 1978–80, 1982–86 and 1988. Bill Rodgers (U.S.) had a record four wins, 1976–79.

The course record for men is 2 hr. 8 min. 1 sec., by Juma Ikangaa (Tan-

TRACK AND FIELD RECORDS—Indoor

Track performances around a turn must be made on a track of circumference no longer than 200 meters.

MEN

Running	min. : sec.	Name & Country	Place	Date
50 meters	5.61*	Manfred Kokot (East Germany)	East Berlin, Germany	Feb. 4, 1973
	5.61*	James Sanford (U.S.)	San Diego, CA	Feb. 20, 1981
60 meters	6.41*	Andre Cason (U.S.)	Madrid, Spain	Feb. 14, 1992
200 meters	20.25	Linford Christie (Great Britain)	Liévin, France	Feb. 19, 1995
400 meters	44.63	Michael Johnson (U.S.)	Atlanta, GA	Mar. 4, 1995
800 meters	1:44.84	Paul Ereng (Kenya)	Budapest, Hungary	Mar. 4, 1989
1,000 meters	2:15.26	Noureddine Morceli (Algeria)	Birmingham, England	Feb. 22, 1992
1,500 meters	3:34.16	Noureddine Morceli (Algeria)	Seville, Spain	Feb. 28, 1991
1 mile	3:49.78	Eamonn Coghlan (Ireland)	East Rutherford, NJ	Feb. 27, 1983
3,000 meters	7:35.15	Moses Kiptanui (Kenya)	Ghent, Belgium	Feb. 12, 1995
5,000 meters	13:20.4	Suleiman Nyambui (Tanzania)	New York, NY	Feb. 6, 1983
50 meter hurdles	6.25	Mark McKoy (Canada)	Kobe, Japan	Mar. 5, 1986
60 meter hurdles	7.30	Colin Jackson (Great Britain)	Sindelfingen, Germany	Mar. 6, 1994

Ben Johnson (Canada) ran 50 m in 5.55 sec. at Ottawa, Canada on Jan. 31, 1987 and 60 m in 6.41 sec. at Indianapolis, IN on Mar. 7, 1987, but these were invalidated due to his admission, following his disqualification at the 1988 Olympics, of having taken drugs over many years.

Relays

4 × 200 meters	1:22.11	United Kingdom	Glasgow, Scotland	Mar. 3, 1991
		(Linford Christie, Darren Braithwaite, Ade Mafe, John Regis)		
4 x 400 meter	3:03.05	Germany	Seville, Spain	Mar. 10, 1991
		(Rico Lieder, Jens Carlowitz, Karsten Just, Thomas Schönlebe)		

Walking

5,000 meters....18:07.08*....Mikhail Schennikov (Russia)....Moscow, Russia....Feb. 14, 1995

Field Events

	m	ft.	in.			
High jump	2.43	7	11½	Javier Sotomayor (Cuba)	Budapest, Hungary	Mar. 4, 1989
Pole vault	6.15	20	2¼	Sergey Nazarovich Bubka (Ukraine)	Donetsk, Ukraine	Feb. 21, 1993
Long jump	8.79	28	10¼	Carl Lewis (U.S.)	New York, NY	Jan. 27, 1984
Triple jump	17.77	58	3½	Leonid Voloshin (Russia)	Grenoble, France	Feb. 6, 1994
Shot	22.66	74	4¼	Randy Barnes (U.S.)	Los Angeles, CA	Jan. 20, 1989

Heptathlon

6,476 points ....Dan O'Brien (U.S.)....Toronto, Canada....Mar. 13–14, 1993
(60 m 6.67 sec.; Long jump 7.84 m; Shot 16.02 m; High jump 2.13 m; 60 m hurdles 7.85 sec.; Pole vault 5.20 m; 1,000 m 2:57.96)

WOMEN

Running

50 meters	5.96....Irina Privalova (Russia)	Madrid, Spain	Feb. 9, 1995
60 meters	6.92....Irina Privalova (Russia)	Madrid, Spain	Feb. 11, 1993
60 meters	6.92....Irina Privalova (Russia)	Madrid, Spain	Feb. 9, 1995
200 meters	21.87....Merlene Ottey (Jamaica)	Liévin, France	Feb. 13, 1994
400 meters	49.59....Jarmila Kratochvílová (Czechoslovakia)	Milan, Italy	Mar. 7, 1982
800 meters	1:56.40....Christine Wachtel (East Germany)	Vienna, Austria	Feb. 13, 1988
1,000 meters	2:33.93*....Inna Yevseyeva (Ukraine)	Moscow, Russia	Feb. 7, 1992
1,500 meters	4:00.27....Doina Melinte (Romania)	East Rutherford, NJ	Feb. 9, 1990
1 mile	4:17.14....Doina Melinte (Romania)	East Rutherford, NJ	Feb. 19, 1990
3,000 meters	8:33.82....Elly van Hulst (Netherlands)	Budapest, Hungary	Mar. 14, 1989
5,000 meters	15:03.17....Elizabeth McColgan (Great Britain)	Birmingham, England	Feb. 22, 1992
50 meter hurdles	6.58....Cornelia Oschkenat (East Germany)	Berlin, Germany	Feb. 20, 1988
60 meter hurdles	7.69**....Lyudmila Narozhilenko (USSR)	Chelyabinsk, Russia	Feb. 4, 1993

* unratified

** Narozhilenko recorded a time of 7.63 in. Seville, Spain on November 4, 1993, but was disqualified on a positive drugs test.

Relays

4 × 200 meters	1:32.55	S.C. Eintracht Hamm (West Germany)	Dortmund, Germany	Feb. 19, 1988

(Helga Arendt, Silke-Beate Knoll, Mechthild Kluth, Gisela Kinzel)

4 × 400 meters	3:27.22	Germany	Seville, Spain	Mar. 10, 1992

(Sandra Seuser, Katrin Schreiter, Annet Hesselbarth, Grit Breuer)

Walking

3,000 meters	11:44.00	Alina Ivanova (Ukraine)	Moscow, Russia	Feb. 7, 1992

Field Events

	m	ft.	in.			
High jump	2.07	6	9½	Heike Henkel (Germany)	Karlsruhe, Germany	Feb. 9, 1992
Pole Vault	4.15	13	5¼	Sun Caiyun (China)	Erfurt, Germany	Feb. 15, 1995
Long jump	7.37	24	2¼	Heike Drechsler (East Germany)	Vienna, Austria	Feb. 13, 1988
Triple jump	15.03	49	3½	Yolanda Chen (Russia)	Barcelona, Spain	Mar. 11, 1995
Shot	22.50	73	10	Helena Fibingerová (Czechoslovakia)	Jablonec, Czechoslovakia	Feb. 19, 1977

Pentathlon

4,991 points		Irina Belova (Russia)	Berlin, Germany	Feb. 14–15, 1992

(60 m hurdles 8.22 sec.; High jump 1.93 m; Shot 13.25 m; Long jump 6.67 m; 800 m 2:10.26)

HURDLING TO HEAVEN?

(Don Bennett)

JOGGLING
Michael Hout of Kettering, OH completed the 110 m hurdles while juggling three balls in 18.9 seconds on June 24, 1993.

What does Michael Hout do when he isn't leaping over hurdles at top speed while juggling balloons full of sand? He might be juggling bowling balls, dressing up as a clown on stilts, or riding his unicycle in a parade while strumming a guitar. Just as likely: He might be writing a sermon, working with a youth group, or carrying out some of the many responsibilities of a Lutheran pastor, husband, and father of three.

Like other record holders, Hout overcame a lot to reach his *Guinness* goal. "At first I just wanted exercise. The joggling was something to motivate me. I wanted just to be able to do the hurdles without dropping the balls." The trouble was that this record had to be set in competition—and few people wanted him in their races. "One person told me to join the circus. Another suggested I work to make joggling an Olympic event and compete there. Then, when I finally got into a race, I found out about joggling among other people, with legs flying, elbows jostling."

One hurdle Hout didn't face was convincing his congregation, Good Shepherd Church in Kettering, OH, to support him. Nowadays, he'd be preaching to the converted: "There are 60 or 70 people in our congregation who juggle. We have a great time at church picnics."

What does his superior think? "I can't quote what the bishop said," Hout says. "He kind of looks at me and says, 'Staying out of trouble?' "

ULTRA LONG DISTANCE RECORDS

Track	hr.: min.: sec.	Name and Country	Place	Date
MEN				
50 km	2:48:06	Jeff Norman (Great Britain)	Manchester, England	Jun. 7, 1980
50 miles	4:51:49	Don Ritchie (Great Britain)	London, England	Mar. 12, 1983
100 km	6:10:20	Don Ritchie (Great Britain)	London, England	Oct. 28, 1978
100 miles	11:30:51	Don Ritchie (Great Britain)	London, England	Oct. 15, 1977
200 km	15:11:10*	Yiannis Kouros (Greece)	Montauban, France	Mar. 15–16, 1985
200 miles	27:48:35	Yiannis Kouros (Greece)	Montauban, France	Mar. 15–16, 1985
500 km	60:23:00	Yiannis Kouros (Greece)	Colac, Australia	Nov. 26–29, 1984
500 miles	105:42:09	Yiannis Kouros (Greece)	Colac, Australia	Nov. 26–30, 1984
1,000 km	136:17:00	Yiannis Kouros (Greece)	Colac, Australia	Nov. 26–Dec. 1, 1984
	kilometers			
24 hours	285.362	Yiannis Kouros (Greece)	Surgères, France	Mar. 6–7, 1995
48 hours	470.781	Yiannis Kouros (Greece)	Surgères, France	Mar. 6–8, 1995
6 days	1,023.200	Yiannis Kouros (Greece)	Colac, Australia	Nov. 26–Dec. 1, 1984
Road	**hr.:min.:sec.**			
50 km	2:43:38	Thompson Magawana (South Africa)	Claremont–Kirstenbosch, South Africa	Apr. 12, 1988
50 miles	4:50:21	Bruce Fordyce (South Africa)	London–Brighton, England	Sep. 25, 1983
1,000 miles	10 days 10:30:35	Yiannis Kouros (Greece)	New York City	May 21–30, 1988
	kilometers			
24 hours	286.463	Yiannis Kouros (Greece)	New York City	Sep. 28–29, 1985
6 days	1,028.370	Yiannis Kouros (Greece)	New York City	May 21–26, 1988

WOMEN

Track	hr: min.: sec.			
50 km	3:30:23	Ann Trason (U.S.)	Santa Rosa, CA	Mar. 18, 1995
50 miles	6:07:58	Linda Meadows (Australia)	Burwood, Australia	Jun. 18, 1994
100 km	7:50:09	Ann Trason (U.S.)	Hayward, CA	Aug. 3–4, 1991
100 miles	14:29:44	Ann Trason (U.S.)	Santa Rosa, CA	Mar. 18–19, 1989
200 km	19:28:48**	Eleanor Adams (Great Britain)	Melbourne, Australia	Aug. 19–20, 1989
200 miles	39:09:03	Hilary Walker (Great Britain)	Blackpool, England	Nov. 5–6, 1988
500 km	77:53:46	Eleanor Adams (Great Britain)	Colac, Australia	Nov. 13–15, 1989
500 miles	130:59:58	Sandra Barwick (New Zealand)	Campbelltown, Australia	Nov. 18–23, 1990

kilometers				
1 hour	18.084	Silvana Cruciata (Italy)	Rome, Italy	May 4, 1981
24 hours	240.169	Eleanor Adams (Great Britain)	Melbourne, Australia	Aug. 19–20, 1989
48 hours	366.512	Hilary Walker (Great Britain)	Blackpool, England	Nov. 5–7, 1988
6 days	883.631	Sandra Barwick (New Zealand)	Campbelltown, Australia	Nov. 18–24, 1990

Road	hr.:min.:sec.			
30 km	1:38:27	Ingrid Kristiansen (Norway)	London, England	May 10, 1987
50 km	3:08:13	Frith van der Merwe (South Africa)	Claremont–Kirstenbosch, South Africa	Mar. 25, 1989
50 miles	5:40:18	Ann Trason (U.S.)	Houston, TX	Feb. 23, 1991
100 km	7:09:44	Ann Trason (U.S.)	Amiens, France	Sep. 27, 1993
100 miles	13:47:41	Ann Trason (U.S.)	Queens, NY	May 4, 1991
200 km	19:08:21	Sigrid Lomsky (Germany)	Basel, Switzerland	May 1–2, 1993
1,000 km	(indoors) 19:00:31	Eleanor Adams (Great Britain)	Milton Keynes, England	Feb. 3–4, 1990
1,000 km	7 days 1:11:00	Sandra Barwick (New Zealand)	Queens, NY	Sep. 16–23, 1991
1,000 miles	12 days 14:38:40	Sandra Barwick (New Zealand)	Queens, NY	Sep. 16–29, 1991

*Where superior to track bests and run on properly measured road courses. It should be noted that road times must be assessed with care as course conditions can vary considerably. ** No stopped time known.

zania), in 1989. Lisa Ondieki (Australia) set the course record for women, 2 hr. 24 min. 40 sec., in 1992.

Highest altitude The highest start for a marathon is the biennially held Everest Marathon, first run on November 27, 1987. It begins at Gorak Shep at 17,100 feet and ends at Namche Bazar, 11,300 feet. The fastest times to complete this race are *(men)* 3 hr. 59 min. 4 sec., by Jack Maitland in 1989; *(women)* 5 hr. 32 min. 43 sec., by Cath Proctor, in 1993.

Most competitors A record 29,735 people finished the New York City Marathon on November 6, 1994. A record 11 men ran under 2 hr. 10 min. in Boston, MA on April 18, 1994 although the course is downhill overall and there was a strong following wind on the point-to-point course. A record nine women finished in under 2 hr. 30 min. in the first Olympic marathon for women in Los Angeles on August 5, 1984.

Most marathons run by an individual Norm Frank has run 565 marathons of 26 mi. 385 yd. or longer from 1965 to July 1, 1995.

Three marathons in three days The fastest combined time for three marathons in three days is 8 hr. 22 min. 31 sec., by Raymond Hubbard (Belfast, Northern Ireland: 2 hr. 45 min. 55 sec.; London, England: 2 hr. 48 min. 45 sec.; and Boston: 2 hr. 47 min. 51 sec.), April 16–18, 1988.

Oldest marathon finishers Dimitrion Yordanidis (Greece) was aged 98 when he completed a marathon in Athens, Greece on October 10, 1976 in 7 hr. 33 min. The women's record was set by Thelma Pitt-Turner (New Zealand) in August 1985 when she completed the Hastings, New Zealand Marathon in 7 hr. 58 min. at age 82.

Half marathon   The distance of half the full marathon has become established in recent years as one of the most popular for road races. In 1992, the IAAF held the first official world championships at this distance.

The world best time on a properly measured course is 59 min. 47 sec. by Moses Tanui (Kenya) in Milan, Italy on April 3, 1993.

Ingrid Kristiansen (Norway) ran 66 min. 40 sec. in Sandes, Norway on April 5, 1987, but the measurement of the course has not been confirmed. Liz McColgan ran 67 min. 11 sec. in Tokyo, Japan on January 26, 1992, but the course was 33 m downhill, a little more than the allowable 1 in 1,000 drop.

Baby carriage-pushing   Tabby Puzey pushed a baby carriage while running the Abingdon half marathon in Abingdon, England, on April 13, 1986 in 2 hr. 4 min. 9 sec.

Backwards running   Bud Badyna (U.S.) ran the fastest backwards marathon in 3 hr. 53 min. 17 sec. in Toledo, OH on April 24, 1994. He also ran 10 km in 45 min. 37 sec. in Toledo on July 13, 1991. Donald Davis (U.S.) ran one mile in 6 min. 7.1 sec. at the University of Hawaii on Febru-

---

IN REVERSE!

Arvind Pandya of India ran backwards across the United States, from Los Angeles to New York, in 107 days, August 18–December 3, 1984. He also ran backwards from John O'Groat's to Land's End (Great Britain) in 26 days 7 hr., April 6–May 2, 1990.

---

ary 21, 1983. Ferdie Ato Adoboe (Ghana) ran 100 yards in 12.7 seconds at Smith College, Northampton, MA on July 25, 1991.

Greatest 1,000-hour distance   Ron Grant (Australia) ran 1.86 miles within an hour, every hour, for 1,000 consecutive hours in New Farm Park, Brisbane, Queensland, Australia from February 6 to March 20, 1991.

Roof of the world run   Ultra runner Hilary Walker ran the length of the Friendship Highway from Lhasa, Tibet to Kathmandu, Nepal, a distance of 590 miles, in 14 days 9 hr. 36 min. from September 18 to October 2, 1991. The run was made at an average altitude of 13,780 feet.

WALKING

Most titles   Four-time Olympian Ronald Owen Laird of the New York Athletic Club won a total of 65 U.S. national titles from 1958 to 1976, plus four Canadian championships.

Most Olympic medals   Walking races have been included in the Olympics since 1906. The only walker to win three gold medals has been Ugo Frige-

TRACK WALKING RECORDS

The International Amateur Athletic Federation recognizes men's records at 20 km, 30 km, 50 km and 2 hours, and women's at 5 km and 10 km.

Event	hr.:min.:sec..	Name and Country	Place	Date
MEN				
10 km	38:02.60	Jozef Pribilinec (Czechoslovakia)	Banská Bystrica, Czechoslovakia	Aug. 30, 1985
20 km	1:17:25.6	Bernardo Segura (Mexico)	Fana, Norway	May 7, 1994
30 km	2:01:44.1	Maurizio Damilano (Italy)	Cuneo, Italy	Oct. 4, 1992
50 km	3:41:28.2	René Piller (France)	Fana, Norway	May 7, 1994
1 hour	15,577 m	Bernardo Segura (Mexico)	Fana, Norway	May 7, 1994
2 hours	29,572 m	Maurizio Damilano (Italy)	Cuneo, Italy	Oct. 4, 1992
WOMEN				
3 km	11:48.24	Ileana Salvador (Italy)	Padua, Italy	Aug. 19, 1993
5 km	20:07.52	Beate Anders (East Germany)	Rostock, Germany	Jun. 23, 1990
10 km	41:56.23	Nadezhda Ryashkina (USSR)	Seattle, WA	Jul. 24, 1990

rio (Italy) with the 3,000 m in 1920, and 10,000 m in 1920 and 1924. He also holds the record for most medals, with four (he won the bronze medal in 50,000 m in 1932), a total shared with Vladimir Stepanovich Golubnichiy (USSR), who won gold medals for the 20,000 m in 1960 and 1968, the silver in 1972 and the bronze in 1964.

Longest race   The race from Paris to Colmar (until 1980 from Strasbourg to Paris) in France (instituted 1926 in the reverse direction), now about 325 miles, is the world's longest annual race walk.

The fastest performance is by Robert Pietquin (Belgium), who walked 315 miles in the 1980 race in 60 hr. 1 min. 10 sec. (after deducting 4-hour compulsory stops). This represents an average speed of 5.25 MPH. Roger Quémener (France) has won a record seven times, 1979, 1983, 1985–89. The first woman to complete the race was Annie van der Meer (Netherlands), who was tenth in 1983 in 82 hr. 10 min.

Greatest 24-hour distance   Jesse Castenada (U.S.) walked 142 mi. 440 yd. in Albuquerque, NM, September 18–19, 1976. The best 24-hour distance by a woman is 131.27 miles, by Annie van der Meer-Timmerman (Netherlands) in Rouen, France, May 10–11, 1986.

Backwards walking   Plennie L. Wingo walked a total distance of 8,000 miles backwards from Santa Monica, CA to Istanbul, Turkey from April 15, 1931 to October 24, 1932. The longest distance recorded for walking backwards in 24 hours is 95.40 miles, by Anthony Thornton (U.S.) in Minneapolis, MN, December 31, 1988 to January 1, 1989.

ROAD WALKING

It should be noted that the severity of the road race courses and the accuracy of their measurement may vary, sometimes making comparisons of times unreliable.

WORLD BESTS

MEN
30 km: 2 hr. 2 min. 41 sec., Andrey Perlov (USSR) at Sochi, USSR on Feb. 19, 1989.

50 km: 3 hr. 37 min. 41 sec., Andrey Perlov (USSR) at Leningrad, USSR on Aug. 5, 1989.

WOMEN
10 km: 41 min. 29 sec., Larisa Ramazonova (Russia) in Izhevsk on Jun. 8, 1995.

20 km: 1 hr. 29 min. 40 sec., Kerry Saxby at Varnamo, Sweden on May 13, 1988.

50 km: 4 hr. 50 min. 28 sec., Kora Sommerfield (Australia) at Neuilly-sur-Marne, France on Sep. 13, 1993.

Walking on hands   The distance record for walking on hands is 870 miles, by Johann Hurlinger of Austria, who in 55 daily 10-hour stints averaged 1.58 MPH from Vienna, Austria to Paris, France in 1900. The 4-man relay team of David Lutterman, Brendan Price, Philip Savage and Danny Scannell covered one mile in 24 min. 48 sec. on March 15, 1987 in Knoxville, TN.

HAND STAND!

Shin Don-mok of South Korea completed a 50-meter inverted sprint in 17.44 seconds at the Toda Sports Center, Saitama, Japan on November 14, 1986.

TRAMPOLINING

World Championships   World Championships were instituted in 1964 and have been held biennially since 1968. The most titles won is nine, by Judy Wills (U.S.)—a record 5 individual 1964–68, 2 pairs 1966–67 and 2 tumbling 1965–66. The men's record is 5, by Aleksandr Moskalenko (Russia), 3 individual 1990–94, and 2 pairs 1992–94. Brett Austine (Australia) won three individual titles in double mini, 1982–86.

United States Championships   Most titles   Stuart Ransom has won 12 national titles: 6, individual (from 1975 to 1976, 1978–80 and 1982); 3, synchronized (1975, 1979–80); and 3 in double mini-tramp, in 1979–80 and 1982. Karl Heger has also won 12 titles: 4, individual (1991–94); 2, synchronized (1982, 1986); and 6, double mini-tramp (1986, 1991–94). Leigh Hennessy has won a record 10 women's titles: 1, individual (1978); 8, synchronized (1972–73, 1976–78, 1980–82); and 1, double mini-tramp (1978).

Most somersaults   Christopher Gibson performed 3,025 consecutive somersaults in Shipley Park, Derbyshire, England on November 17, 1989.

The most complete somersaults performed in one minute is 75, by Richard Cobbing of Lightwater, England, in London, England on November 8, 1989. The most baranis in a minute is 78, by Zoe Finn of Chatham, England in London, England on January 25, 1988.

TRIATHLON

The triathlon combines long-distance swimming, cycling and running. Distances for each of the phases can vary, but for the best-established event—the Hawaii Ironman—competitors first swim 2.4 miles, then cycle 112 miles, and finally run a full marathon of 26 mi. 385 yd.

Fastest triathlon The fastest times recorded over the Ironman distances are: (*men*) 8 hr. 1 min. 32 sec., by Dave Scott (U.S.) at Lake Biwa, Japan on July 30, 1989, and (*women*) 8 hr. 55 min., by Paula Newby-Fraser (Zimbabwe), in Roth, Germany on July 12, 1992.

IRONMAN!

The oldest triathlete to finish the Ironman Triathlon was 73-year-old Walt Stack in 1981. Swimming 2.4 miles, cycling 112 miles and running 26 mi. 385 yd., Stack completed the course in a time of 26 hr. 20 min., the longest elapsed time ever.

World Championships After earlier abortive efforts, a world governing body, *L'Union Internationale de Triathlon* (UIT), was founded in Avignon, France on April 1, 1989, staging the first official World Championships in August 1989.

A World Championship race has been held annually in Nice, France from 1982; the distances are 3,200 m, 120 km and 32 km respectively, with the swim increased to 4,000 m from 1988 on. Mark Allen (U.S.) has won 10 times, 1982–86, 1989–93. Paula Newby-Fraser has a record four women's wins, 1989–92. The fastest times are: (*men*) 5 hr. 46 min. 10 sec. in 1988, by Mark Allen; (*women*) 6 hr. 27 min. 6 sec. in 1988, by Erin Baker (New Zealand).

Hawaii Ironman Dave Scott has won the Ironman six times—1980, 1982–84, 1986–87. Mark Allen holds the record for fastest time, at 8 hr. 7 min. 45 sec. in 1993. The women's event has been won a record seven times by Paula Newby-Fraser, in 1986, 1988–89, 1991–94. Newby-Fraser holds the course record for women at 8 hr. 55 min. 28 sec. on October 10, 1992.

TUG OF WAR

Most titles   The most successful team at the World Championships has been England, which has won 16 titles in all categories, 1975–93. Sweden has won the 520 kg and the 560 kg three times at the Womens' World Championships (held biennially since 1986), 1986–94.

Longest pulls   *Duration*   The longest recorded pull (prior to the introduction of AAA rules) is one of 2 hr. 41 min. when "H" Company beat "E" Company of the 2nd Battalion of the Sherwood Foresters (Derbyshire Regiment) in Jubbulpore, India on August 12, 1889. The longest recorded pull under AAA rules (in which lying on the ground or entrenching the feet is not permitted) is one of 24 min. 45 sec. for the first pull between the Republic of Ireland and England during the world championships (640 kg

One of the 20-person teams competes in the record-breaking 3,962-yard contest between Freedom Square and Independence Square in Lodz, Poland on May 28, 1994.

class) in Malmö, Sweden on September 18, 1988. The record time for "The Pull" (instituted 1898), across the Black River, between freshman and sophomore teams at Hope College, Holland, MI, is 3 hr. 51 min. on September 23, 1977, but the method of bracing the feet precludes this replacing the preceding records.

Greatest distance   The record distance for a tug of war contest is 3,962 yards, between Freedom Square and Independence Square, in Lodz, Poland on May 28, 1994.

VOLLEYBALL

Most Olympic titles   The sport was introduced to the Olympic Games for both men and women in 1964. The USSR won a record three men's (1964, 1968 and 1980) and four women's (1968, 1972, 1980 and 1988) titles. The only player to win four medals is Inna Valeryevna Ryskal (USSR), who won women's silver medals in 1964 and 1976 and golds in 1968 and 1972. The record for men is held by Yuriy Mikhailovich Poyarkov (USSR), who won gold medals in 1964 and 1968 and a bronze in 1972; and by Katsutoshi Nekoda (Japan), who won gold in 1972, silver in 1968 and bronze in 1964.

United States   The U.S. won the men's championship in 1984 and 1988. Three men played on each of the winning teams and on the only U.S. teams to win the World Cup (1985) and World Championships (1986): Craig Buck, Karch Kiraly and Stephen Timmons. Karch Kiraly is the only player to win an Olympic gold medal and the beach volleyball World Championship.

Most world titles in volleyball   World Championships were instituted in 1949 for men and in 1952 for women. The USSR won six men's titles (1949, 1952, 1960, 1962, 1978 and 1982) and five women's (1952, 1956, 1960, 1970 and 1990).

BEACH VOLLEYBALL

U.S. Championships   Most wins   Four players have won five titles: Sinjin Smith (U.S.), 1979 and 1981 (with K. Kiraly), 1982, 1988 and 1990 (with Randy Stoklos); Karch Kiraly (U.S.), 1979 and 1981 (with S. Smith), and

---

GUESS WHAT?

Q.   WHERE IS THE LARGEST RECREATIONAL BEACH?

A.   LOOK IN "BUILDINGS FOR ENTERTAINMENT" (BUILDINGS & STRUCTURES)

1992, 1993 and 1994 (with Kent Steffes); and Mike Dodd (U.S.) and Tim Hovland (U.S.), who teamed up to win the 1983, 1985–87 and 1989 titles.

AVP Tour   Most wins   Sinjin Smith (U.S.) has won a record 139 AVP tour events, 1977–95.

Highest earnings   Karch Kiraly has the highest career earnings, reaching $1,784,974 as of June 5, 1995.

WATER POLO

Most Olympic titles   Hungary has won the Olympic tournament most often, with six wins, in 1932, 1936, 1952, 1956, 1964 and 1976.

Five players share the record of three gold medals: Britons George Wilkinson, in 1900, 1908, 1912; Paul Radmilovic, and Charles Sidney Smith, in 1908, 1912, 1920; and Hungarians Deszö Gyarmati and György Kárpáti, in 1952, 1956 and 1964. Paul Radmilovic also won a gold medal for 4×200 m freestyle swimming in 1908.

United States   U.S. teams took all the medals in 1904, but there were no foreign contestants. Since then, their best result has been silver in 1984 and 1988.

World Championships   This competition was first held at the World Swimming Championships in 1973. The most wins is two, by the USSR, 1975 and 1982; Yugoslavia, 1986 and 1991; and Italy, 1978 and 1994. A women's competition was introduced in 1986, when it was won by Australia. The Netherlands won the title in 1991, and Hungary won in 1994.

Most goals   The greatest number of goals scored by an individual in an international match is 13, by Debbie Handley for Australia (16) vs. Canada (10) at the World Championship in Guayaquil, Ecuador in 1982.

Most international appearances   The greatest number of international appearances is 412, by Aleksey Stepanovich Barkalov (USSR), 1965–80.

U.S. National Championships   In this competition, inaugurated in 1891, the New York Athletic Club has won a record 25 men's championships: 1892–96, 1903–04, 1906–08, 1922, 1929–31, 1933–35, 1937–39, 1954, 1956, 1960–61, 1971. The women's championship was first held in 1926; the Industry Hills Athletic Club (California) has won a record five titles: 1980–81, 1983–85.

WATERSKIING

Most titles World Overall Championships (instituted 1949) have been won four times by Sammy Duvall (U.S.), in 1981, 1983, 1985 and 1987, and three times by two women, Willa Worthington McGuire (U.S.), in 1949–50 and 1955, and Liz Allan-Shetter (U.S.), in 1965, 1969 and 1975. Liz Allan-Shetter has won a record eight individual championship events and is the only person to win all four titles—slalom, jumping, tricks and overall—in one year, in Copenhagen, Denmark in 1969. Patrice Martin (France) has won a men's record seven titles. The U.S. has won the team championship on 17 successive occasions, 1957–89.

United States U.S. national championships were first held at Marine Stadium, Jones Beach State Park, Long Island, NY on July 22, 1939. The most overall titles is nine, by Carl Roberge, 1980–83, 1985–88, and 1990. The women's record is eight titles, by Willa Worthington McGuire, 1946–51 and 1954–55, and by Liz Allan-Shetter, 1968–75.

Fastest speed The fastest waterskiing speed recorded is 143.08 MPH, by Christopher Michael Massey (Australia) on the Hawkesbury River, Windsor, New South Wales, Australia on March 6, 1983. Donna Patterson Brice set a women's record of 111.11 MPH in Long Beach, CA on August 21, 1977.

Most skiers towed by one boat A record 100 waterskiers were towed on double skis over a nautical mile by the cruiser *Reef Cat* in Cairns, Queensland, Australia on October 18, 1986. This feat, organized by the Cairns and District Powerboat and Ski Club, was then replicated by 100 skiers on single skis.

BAREFOOT WATERSKIING

The barefoot duration record is 2 hr. 42 min. 39 sec., by Billy Nichols (U.S.) on Lake Weir, FL in 1978. The backwards barefoot record is 1 hr. 27 min. 3.96 sec., by Steve Fontaine in Jupiter, FL, in 1989.

Barefoot World Championships (instituted 1978) The most overall titles is four, by Kim Lampard (Australia), 1980, 1982, 1985, 1986; and the men's record is three, by Brett Wing (Australia), 1978, 1980, 1982. The team title has been won five times by Australia, 1978, 1980, 1982, 1985 and 1986.

The official barefoot speed record is 135.74 MPH, by Scott Michael Pellaton over a ¼-mile course in Chandler, CA, in November 1989. The wom-

Richard Mainwaring (Great Britain), holder of the world barefoot jumping record, launches himself off the end of the ramp.

en's record is 73.67 MPH, by Karen Toms (Australia) on the Hawkesbury River, Windsor, New South Wales, March 31, 1984.

The fastest official speed backwards barefoot is 62 MPH, by Robert Wing (Australia) on April 3, 1982.

The barefoot jump record is: *(men)* 90 ft. 3 in., by Richard Mainwaring in Thurrock, England on August 20, 1994; and *(women)* 54 ft. 5 in., by Sharon Stekelenberg (Australia) in 1991.

Walking on water Rémy Bricka (France) "walked" across the Atlantic Ocean on waterskis 13 ft. 9 in. long in 1988. Leaving Tenerife, Canary Islands on April 2, 1988, he covered 3,502 miles, arriving in Trinidad on May 31, 1988.

He also set a speed record of 7 min. 7.41 sec. for 1,094 yards in the Olympic pool in Montreal, Canada on August 2, 1989.

LONGEST JET-SKI JOURNEY

Richard Chenoweth, Brian Peterson and Dan Walker rode their Yamaha Wave Runners from Pascagoula, MS to Key West, FL, a distance of 922.2 miles, between March 31 and April 6, 1994.

Wearing 11-foot waterski shoes, called Skijaks, and using a twin-bladed paddle, David Kiner walked 155 miles on the Hudson River from Albany, NY to Battery Park, New York City. His walk took him 57 hours, June 22–27, 1987.

WEIGHTLIFTING

Most titles *Olympic* Norbert Schemansky (U.S.) won a record four Olympic medals: gold, middle heavyweight 1952; silver, heavyweight 1948; bronze, heavyweight 1960 and 1964.

World The most world title wins (overall), including Olympic Games, is eight, by John Henry Davis (U.S.) in 1938, 1946–52; Tommy Kono (U.S.) in 1952–59; Vasiliy Alekseiev (USSR), 1970–77; and Naim Suleymanoğlü (Turkey; previously Neum Shalamanov [Bulgaria]), 1985–86, 1988–89, 1991–94.

Two American women have won world titles. In the 82 kg category, Karyn Marshall won a title in 1987 by lifting a total of 220 kg (a 95 kg

snatch and a 125 kg clean and jerk). In 1994, Robin Byrd-Goad won a 50 kg title with a total weight of 175 kg.

United States The most U.S. national titles won is 13, by Anthony Terlazzo, in 137 lb, 1932 and 1936, and in 148 pounds, 1933, 1935, 1937–45.

Youngest world record holder Naim Suleimanov (later Neum Shalamanov [Bulgaria]; now Naim Suleymanoğlü of Turkey) set 56 kg world records for clean and jerk (160 kg) and total (285 kg), at 16 yr. 62 days, in Allentown, NJ on March 26, 1983.

Oldest world record holder The oldest is Norbert Schemansky (U.S.), who snatched 164.2 kg in the then unlimited Heavyweight class, aged 37 yr. 333 days, in Detroit, MI on April 28, 1962.

Women's World Championships These are held annually; the first was held in Daytona Beach, FL in October 1987. Women's world records have been ratified for the best marks at these championships. The most gold medals is 12, by Peng Liping (China) with snatch, jerk and total in the 52 kg class each year, 1988–89 and 1991–92; and Milena Trendafilova (Bulgaria), 67.5 kg/70 kg classes, 1989–93.

POWERLIFTING

Most world titles The winner of the most world titles is Hideaki Inaba (Japan) with 17, in 52 kg, 1974–83, 1985–91. Lamar Gant (U.S.) holds the

---

OOMPH!

The first man to clean and jerk more than three times his body weight was Stefan Topurov (Bulgaria), who lifted 396¾ pounds in Moscow, USSR on October 24, 1983.

---

record for an American with 15 titles, in 56 kg, 1975–77, 1979, 1982–84; and in 60 kg, 1978, 1980–81 and 1986–90. The most by a woman is six, by Beverley Francis (Australia), in 75 kg 1980, 1982; 82.5 kg 1981, 1983–85. Sisi Dolman (Netherlands) has also won six world titles, in the 52 kg class, in 1985–86 and in 1988–91.

Timed lifts 24 hours A deadlifting record of 5,960,631 pounds was set by a team of 10 from Her Majesty's Prison, Wayland, England, May 10–11, 1993. The 24-hour deadlift record by an individual is 818,121 pounds, by

Turkish lifter Halil Mutlu is holder of all three weightlifting world records in the 54 kg weight category. (*Allsport/D. Leab*)

POWERLIFTING RECORDS (All weights in kilograms)

Class	Squat	Bench Press	Deadlift	Total
MEN				
52 kg	270...Andrzej Stanashek (Pol.) 1994	177.5...Andrzej Stanashek 1994	256...E.S. Bhaskaran (Ind.) 1993	587.5...Hideaki Inaba (Jap.) 1987
56 kg	260...Magnus Karlsson (Swe.) 1994	175...Magnus Karlsson 1993	289.5...Lamar Gant (U.S.) 1982	625...Lamar Gant 1982
60 kg	295.5...Magnus Karlsson (Swe.) 1994	180.5...Magnus Karlsson 1993	310...Lamar Gant 1988	707.5...Joe Bradley (U.S.) 1982
67.5 kg	300...Jessie Jackson (U.S.) 1987	200...Kristoffer Hulecki (Swe.) 1985	316...Daniel Austin (U.S.) 1991	762.5...Daniel Austin 1989
75 kg	328...Ausby Alexander (U.S.) 1989	217.5...James Rouse (U.S.) 1980	337.5...Daniel Austin (U.S.) 1994	850...Rick Gaugler (U.S.) 1982
82.5 kg	379.5...Mike Bridges (U.S.) 1982	240...Mike Bridges 1981	357.5...Veli Kumpuniemi (Fin.) 1980	952.5...Mike Bridges 1982
90 kg	375...Fred Hatfield (U.S.) 1980	255...Mike MacDonald (U.S.) 1980	372.5...Walter Thomas (U.S.) 1982	937.5...Mike Bridges 1980
100 kg	423...Ed Coan (U.S.) 1994	261.5...Mike MacDonald 1977	390...Ed Coan 1982	1035...Ed Coan 1994
110 kg	415...Kirk Karwoski (U.S.) 1994	270...Jeffrey Magruder (U.S.) 1982	395...John Kuc (U.S.) 1980	1000...John Kuc 1980
125 kg	440...Kirk Karwoski (U.S.) 1993	278.5...Tom Hardman (U.S.) 1982	387.5...Lars Norén (Swe.) 1987	1005...Ernie Hackett (U.S.) 1982
125+ kg	447.5...Shane Hamman (U.S.) 1994	310...Antony Clark (U.S.) 1994	406...Lars Norén 1988	1100...Bill Kazmaier 1981
WOMEN				
44 kg	156...Raija Koskinen (Fin.) 1995	82.5...Irina Krylova (Rus.) 1993	165...Nancy Belliveau (U.S.) 1985	365...Jacquline Janot (Fra.) 1993
48 kg	160.5...Raija Koskinen 1994	93...Isuko Watanabe (Jap.) 1994	182.5...Majik Jones (U.S.) 1984	400...Elena Yamkich (Rus.) 1994
52 kg	175.5...Mary Jeffrey (née Ryan; U.S.) 1991	105...Mary Jeffrey 1991	197.5...Diana Rowell (U.S.) 1984	452.5...Mary Jeffrey 1991
56 kg	191...Mary Jeffrey 1989	115...Mary Jeffrey 1988	220.5...Carrie Boudreau (U.S.) 1995	517.5...Carrie Boudreau 1995
60 kg	210...Beate Amdahl (Nor.) 1993	115...Eriko Himeno (Jap.) 1995	213...Ruthi Shafer 1983	502.5...Vicki Steenrod 1985
67.5 kg	230...Ruthi Shafer (U.S.) 1984	120...Vicki Steenrod (U.S.) 1990	244...Ruthi Shafer 1984	565...Ruthi Shafer 1984
75 kg	240.5...Yelena Sukhoruk (Ukr.) 1995	142.5...Liz Odendaal (Neth.) 1989	252.5...Yelena Sukhoruk 1995	605...Yelena Sukhoruk 1995
82.5 kg	240...Cathy Millen (N.Z.) 1991	150.5...Cathy Millen 1993	257.5...Cathy Millen 1993	637.5...Cathy Millen 1993
90 kg	260...Cathy Millen 1994	160...Cathy Millen 1994	260...Cathy Millen 1994	682.5...Cathy Millen 1994
90+ kg	277.5...Juanita Trujillo (U.S.) 1993	157.5...Ulrike Herchenhein (Ger.) 1993	240...Ulrike Herchenhein (Ger.) 1994	640...Juanita Trujillo 1994

WEIGHTLIFTING RECORDS—MEN

From January 1, 1993, the International Weightlifting Federation (IWF) introduced modified weight categories, thereby making the then world records redundant. This is the current list for the new weight categories with, for some events, world standards that have yet to be met.

Bodyweight	Lift.	kg	lb	Name and Country	Place	Date
54 kg *119 lb.*	Snatch	130.5	*287½*	Halil Mutlu (Turkey)	Warsaw, Poland	May 3, 1995
	Jerk	160	*352¾*	Halil Mutlu (Turkey)	Istanbul, Turkey	Nov. 18, 1994
	Total	290	*639¼*	Halil Mutlu (Turkey)	Istanbul, Turkey	Nov. 18, 1994
59 kg *130 lb.*	Snatch	140	*308½*	Hafiz Suleymanoğlü	Warsaw, Poland	May 3, 1995
	Jerk	170	*370¼*	Nikolai Pershalov (Bulgaria)	Warsaw, Poland	May 3, 1995
	Total	305	*672¼*	Nikolai Pershalov (Bulgaria)	Melbourne, Australia	Nov. 13, 1993
64 kg *141 lb.*	Snatch	147.5	*325*	Naim Suleymanoğlü (Turkey)*	Istanbul, Turkey	Nov. 20, 1994
	Jerk	182.5	*402¼*	Naim Suleymanoğlü (Turkey)*	Istanbul, Turkey	Nov. 20, 1994
	Total	330	*727½*	Naim Suleymanoğlü (Turkey)*	Istanbul, Turkey	Nov. 20, 1994
70 kg *154¼ lb.*	Snatch	160	*352¾*	Fedail Guler (Turkey)	Istanbul, Turkey	Nov. 21, 1994
	Jerk	192.5	*424¼*	Yotov Yoto (Bulgaria)	Sokolov, Czech Republic	May 5, 1994
	Total	350	*760½*	Fedail Guler (Turkey)	Istanbul, Turkey	Nov. 21, 1994
76 kg *167½ lb.*	Snatch	170	*374¾*	Ruslan Savchenko (Ukraine)	Melbourne, Australia	Nov. 16, 1993
	Jerk	207.5	*457½*	Pablo Lara (Cuba)	Mar del Plata, Argentina	Mar. 14, 1995
	Total	370	*815¾*	Ruslan Savchenko (Ukraine)	Melbourne, Australia	Nov. 16, 1993
83 kg *183 lb.*	Snatch	175.5	*387*	Sergo Chakhoyan	Istanbul, Turkey	Nov. 23, 1994
	Jerk	210.5	*464*	Sunay Bolut (Turkey)	Istanbul, Turkey	Nov. 23, 1994
	Total	382.5	*843¼*	Marc Huster (Germany)	Istanbul, Turkey	Nov. 23, 1994
91 kg *200½ lb.*	Snatch	186	*410*	Aleksey Petrov (Russia)	Istanbul, Turkey	Nov. 24, 1994
	Jerk	228	*502½*	Aleksey Petrov (Russia)	Istanbul, Turkey	Nov. 24, 1994
	Total	412.5	*909¼*	Aleksey Petrov (Russia)	Sokolov, Czech Republic	May 7, 1994
99 kg *218½ lb.*	Snatch	192.5	*424¼*	Sergey Syrtsov (Russia)	Istanbul, Turkey	Nov. 25, 1994
	Jerk	225.5	*501½*	Sergey Syrtsov (Russia)	Istanbul, Turkey	Nov. 25, 1994
	Total	417.5	*920¼*	Sergey Syrtsov (Russia)	Istanbul, Turkey	Nov. 25, 1994
108 kg *238 lb.*	Snatch	200	*441*	Timour Taimazov (Ukraine)	Istanbul, Turkey	Nov. 26, 1994
	Jerk	235.5	*519*	Timour Taimazov (Ukraine)	Istanbul, Turkey	Nov. 26, 1994
	Total	435	*959*	Timour Taimazov (Ukraine)	Istanbul, Turkey	Nov. 26, 1994
Over 108 kg	Snatch	205	*452*	Aleksandr Kurlovich (Belarus)	Istanbul, Turkey	Nov. 27, 1994

	Jerk	253	*557¾*	Aleksandr Kurlovich (Belarus)	Istanbul, Turkey	Nov. 27, 1994
	Total	457.5	*992*	Aleksandr Kurlovich (Belarus)	Istanbul, Turkey	Nov. 27, 1994

* *Formerly Naim Suleimanov or Neum Shalamanov of Bulgaria.*

WEIGHTLIFTING RECORDS—WOMEN

46 kg *101¼ lb.*	Snatch	80.5	*177¼*	Yun Yanhong (China)	Istanbul, Turkey	Nov. 18, 1994
	Jerk	102.5	*226*	Guang Hong (China)	Hiroshima, Japan	Oct. 3, 1994
	Total	182.5	*402¼*	Guang Hong (China)	Hiroshima, Japan	Oct. 3, 1994
50 kg *110¼ lb.*	Snatch	87.5	*193*	Liu Xiuhia (China)	Hiroshima, Japan	Oct. 3, 1994
	Jerk	110.5	*243½*	Liu Xiuhia (China)	Hiroshima, Japan	Oct. 3, 1994
	Total	197.5	*435¼*	Liu Xiuhia (China)	Hiroshima, Japan	Oct. 3, 1994
54 kg *119 lb.*	Snatch	92.5	*204*	Zhang Juhua (China)	Hiroshima, Japan	Oct. 3, 1994
	Jerk	112.5	*248*	Long Yuiling (China)	Shilong, China	Dec. 16, 1993
	Total	202.5	*446¼*	Zhang Juhua (China)	Hiroshima, Japan	Oct. 3, 1994
59 kg *130 lb.*	Snatch	98.5	*217*	Zou Feie (China)	Istanbul, Turkey	Nov. 21, 1994
	Jerk	123.5	*272¼*	Zou Feie (China)	Istanbul, Turkey	Nov. 21, 1994
	Total	220	*485*	Chen Xiaomin (China)	Hiroshima, Japan	Oct. 4, 1994
64 kg *141 lb.*	Snatch	105	*231½*	Li Hongyun (China)	Istanbul, Turkey	Nov. 22, 1994
	Jerk	130	*286½*	Li Hongyun (China)	Istanbul, Turkey	Nov. 22, 1994
	Total	235	*518*	Li Hongyun (China)	Istanbul, Turkey	Nov. 22, 1994
70 kg *154¼ lb.*	Snatch	102.5	*226*	Tang Weifang (China)	Hiroshima, Japan	Oct. 4, 1994
	Jerk	128.5	*281*	Zhou Meihong (China)	Istanbul, Turkey	Nov. 23, 1994
	Total	230	*507*	Tang Weifang (China)	Hiroshima, Japan	Oct. 4, 1994
76 kg *167¼ lb.*	Snatch	105.5	*232½*	Hua Ju (China)	Hiroshima, Japan	Oct. 5, 1994
	Jerk	140	*308½*	Zhang Guimei (China)	Shilong, China	Dec. 18, 1993
	Total	235	*518*	Zhang Guimei (China)	Shilong, China	Dec. 18, 1993
83 kg *183 lb.*	Snatch	108	*238*	Zhang Xiaoli (China)	Hiroshima, Japan	Oct. 5, 1994
	Jerk	132.5	*292*	Maria Urrutia (Colombia)	Istanbul, Turkey	Nov. 25, 1994
	Total	237.5	*523½*	Zhang Xiaoli (China)	Hiroshima, Japan	Oct. 5, 1994
+83 kg	Snatch	105.5	*232½*	Li Yajuan (China)	Hiroshima, Japan	Oct. 5, 1994
	Jerk	155	*341½*	Li Yajuan (China)	Melbourne, Australia	Nov. 20, 1993
	Total	260	*573*	Li Yajuan (China)	Melbourne, Australia	Nov. 20, 1993

Anthony Wright at Her Majesty's Prison, Featherstone, England, August 31–September 1, 1990.

12 hours   An individual bench press record of 1,181,312 pounds was set by Chris Lawton at the Waterside Wine Bar, Solihull, England on June 3, 1994.

A bench press record of 8,873,860 pounds was set by a 9-man team from the Forum Health Club, Chelmsleywood, England, July 18–19, 1987. An individual bench press record of 1,231,150 pounds was set by Paul Goodall at the Copthorne Hotel, Plymouth, England, March 12–13, 1991. A squat record of 4,780,994 pounds was set by a 10-man team from St. Albans Weightlifting Club and Ware Boys Club, Hertfordshire, England, July 20–21, 1986. A record 133,380 arm-curling repetitions using three 48¼-pound weightlifting bars and dumbbells was achieved by a team of nine from Intrim Health and Fitness Club in Gosport, England, August 4–5, 1989.

WRESTLING

Most Olympic titles   Three Olympic titles have been won by Carl Westergren (Sweden), in 1920, 1924 and 1932; Ivar Johansson (Sweden), in 1932 (two) and 1936; and Aleksandr Vasilyevich Medved (USSR), in 1964, 1968 and 1972. Four Olympic medals were won by Eino Leino (Finland) in freestyle 1920–32; and by Imre Polyák (Hungary) in Greco-Roman in 1952–64.

United States   Three U.S. wrestlers have won two Olympic freestyle titles: George Nicholas Mehnert, flyweight in 1904 and bantamweight in 1908; John Smith, featherweight in 1988 and 1992; and Bruce Baumgartner, super-heavyweight in 1984 and 1992. The only U.S. men to win a Greco-Roman title are Steven Fraser in light-heavyweight and Jeffrey Blatnick in super-heavyweight in 1984.

Most World titles   The freestyler Aleksandr Medved (USSR) won a record 10 World Championships, 1962–64, 1966–72 in three weight categories.

United States   The most world titles won by a U.S. wrestler is six (four world, two Olympic), by John Smith, featherweight 1987–92.

STRUGGLE!

The longest recorded wrestling bout was 11 hr. 40 min., when Martin Klein (Russia) beat Alfred Asikáinen (Finland) for the Greco-Roman 75-kg "A" event silver medal in the 1912 Olympic Games in Stockholm, Sweden.

Most wins   In international competition, Osamu Watanabe (Japan), the 1964 Olympic freestyle 63 kg champion, was unbeaten and did not concede a score in 189 consecutive matches. Outside of FILA sanctioned competition, Wade Schalles (U.S.) won 821 bouts from 1964 to 1984, with 530 of these victories by pin.

NCAA Division I Championship   Including five unofficial titles, Oklahoma State has won a record 30 NCAA titles, in 1928–31, 1933–35, 1937–42, 1946, 1948–49, 1954–56, 1958–59, 1961–62, 1964, 1966, 1968, 1971, 1989–90 and 1994. The University of Iowa has won the most consecutive titles, with nine championships, 1978–86.

Heaviest heavyweight   The heaviest wrestler in Olympic history was Chris Taylor (U.S.), bronze medalist in the super-heavyweight class in 1972, who stood 6 ft. 5 in. tall and weighed over 420 pounds.

FILA introduced an upper weight limit of 286 pounds for international competition in 1985.

DID YOU KNOW?

Sumo's origins in Japan date from *c.* 23 B.C. The heaviest-ever *rikishi,* or wrestler, is Samoan-American Salevaa Fuali Atisnoe of Hawaii, alias Konishiki, who weighed in at 580 pounds at Tokyo's Ryogaku Kokugikau on January 4, 1993. He is also the first foreign *rikishi* to attain the second highest rank of *ozeki,* or champion. Weight is gained by eating large quantities of a high-protein stew called *chankonabe.*

SUMO

Most successful sumo wrestlers   The most successful wrestlers have been *yokozuna* (grand champion) Sadaji Akiyoshi, alias Futabayama, winner of 69 consecutive bouts in the 1930s; *yokozuna* Koki Naya, alias Taiho, who won the Emperor's Cup 32 times up to his retirement in 1971; and the *ozeki* Tameemon Torokichi, alias Raiden, who in 21 years (1789–1810) won 254 bouts and lost only 10, for the highest-ever winning percentage of 96.2. Taiho and Futabayama share the record of eight perfect tournaments without a single loss.

Yokozuna   Mitsugu Akimoto, alias Chiyonofuji, set a record for domination of one of the six annual tournaments by winning the Kyushu Basho for eight successive years, 1981–88. He also holds the record for most career wins, 1,045, and *Makunoiuchi* (top division) wins, 807. He retired in May 1991 but remains in sumo as a training coach.

Hawaiian-born Jesse Kuhaulua, now a Japanese citizen named Daigoro

Watanabe, alias Takamiyama, was the first non-Japanese to win an official top-division tournament, in July 1972, and in September 1981 he set a record of 1,231 consecutive top-division bouts.

Kenji Hatano, alias Oshio, contested a record 1,891 bouts in his 26-year career, 1962–88, the longest in modern sumo history. Yukio Shoji, alias Aobajo, contested a record 1,631 consecutive bouts in his 22-year career, 1964–86.

Katsumi Yamanaka, alias Akinoshima, set a new *kinboshi* (gold star) record of 13 upsets over *yokozuna* by a *maegashira*.

Chad Rowan (b. Hawaii), alias Akebono, scored a majority of wins for a record 18 consecutive tournaments, March 1988–March 1991. He became the first foreign *rikishi* to be promoted to the top rank of *yokozuna*, in 1993. He is the tallest (6 ft. 8 in.) and heaviest (467½ pounds) *yokozuna* in sumo history.

Youngest The youngest of the 64 men to attain the rank of *yokozuna* was Toshimitsu Ogata, alias Kitanoumi, in July 1974 at age 21 yr. 2 mo. He set a record in 1978, winning 82 of the 90 bouts that top *rikishi* fight annually.

YACHTING

Oldest race The oldest race for any type of craft on either fresh or salt water is the Chicago-to-Mackinac race on Lakes Michigan and Huron, first sailed in 1898. It was held again in 1904, and has been held almost every year since then. The record for the course (333 nautical miles) is 1 day 1 hr. 50 min. (average speed 12.89 knots), set in 1987 by the sloop *Pied Piper*, owned by Dick Jennings (U.S.).

GUESS WHAT?

Q. WHAT IS THE LARGEST SAILING VESSEL?

A. LOOK IN "SHIPS" (TRANSPORT)

Olympic titles The first sportsman ever to win individual gold medals in four successive Olympic Games was Paul B. Elvstrøm (Denmark), in the Firefly class in 1948 and the Finn class in 1952, 1956 and 1960. He also won eight other world titles in a total of six classes. The lowest number of penalty points by the winner of any class in an Olympic regatta is three points (five wins, one disqualified and one second in seven starts) by *Superdocious* of the Flying Dutchman class (Lt. Rodney Stuart Pattisson and Iain Somerled Macdonald-Smith), in Acapulco Bay, Mexico in October 1968.

The America's Cup was contested for the 29th time in 1995, and for only the second time the U.S. was defeated. The New Zealand boat *Black Magic I*, a syndicate by record-breaking yachtsman Peter Blake, beat *Young America* 5–0. Here, Blake lifts the cup in celebration. *(Allsport [U.S.]/S. Dunn)*

United States   The only U.S. yachtsman to have won two gold medals is Herman Frasch Whiton, in 6-meter class, in 1948 and 1952.

America's Cup   The America's Cup was originally won as an outright prize (with no special name) by the schooner *America* on August 22, 1851 in Cowes, Great Britain and was later offered by the New York Yacht Club as a challenge trophy.

There have been 29 challenges since August 8, 1870, with the United States winning on every occasion until 1983, when *Australia II*, skippered by John Bertrand and owned by a Perth syndicate headed by Alan Bond, beat *Liberty* 4–3 in Newport, RI, the narrowest series victory ever. In San Diego in 1995, the United States lost again, 5–0, to New Zealand's *Black Magic I*, skippered by Russell Coutts and owned by an Auckland syndicate headed by Peter Blake.

Dennis Walter Conner (U.S.) has been helmsman of American boats

---

GUESS WHAT?

Q. WHAT IS THE 36-MILE BATH TUB RACE RECORD?

A. LOOK IN "FANTASTIC FEATS" (HUMAN ACHIEVEMENTS)

---

five times in succession: in 1980, when he successfully defended; in 1983, when he steered the defender, but lost; in 1987, when the American challenger regained the trophy; in 1988, when he again successfully defended; and in 1995, when he lost. He was also starting helmsman in 1974, with Ted Hood as skipper.

The largest yacht to have competed in the America's Cup was the 1903 defender, the gaff rigged cutter *Reliance*, with an overall length of 144 feet, a record sail area of 16,160 square feet and a rig 175 feet high.

Longest sailing race   The Vendée Globe Challenge, first held in Les Sables d'Olonne, France on November 26, 1989, has a nonstop circumnavigated distance of 22,500 nautical miles and is for boats between 50–60 feet, sailed single-handedly. The record time on the course is 109 days 8 hr. 48 min. 50 sec., by Titouan Lamazou (France) in the sloop *Ecureuil d'Aquitaine*, which finished in Les Sables on March 19, 1990.

The oldest regular transglobal sailing race is the quadrennial Whitbread Round the World race (instituted August 1973) organized by the British Royal Naval Sailing Association. It starts in England, but the course and the number of legs with stops at specified ports are varied from race to race. The distance for the 1993–94 race was 32,000 nautical miles from Southampton, England and return, with stops and restarts in Punta del Este, Uruguay; Fremantle, Australia; Auckland, New Zealand; Punta del Este, Uruguay; and Fort Lauderdale, FL.

Fastest speeds   The fastest speed reached under sail on water by any craft over a 500-meter timed run is 46.25 knots, by Simon McKeon and Tim Daddo (Australia) in the trifoiler *Yellow Pages Endeavour c.* October 26,

1993 in Shallow Inlet near Melbourne. The women's record is held by boardsailer Babethe Coquelle (France), who achieved 40.05 knots in Tarifa, Spain in July 1993.

The fastest speed by a true yacht is 36.22 knots (41.68 MPH), by Jean Saucet (France) in *Charante Maritime* on the Bassin de Thau, near Sete, on October 5, 1992.

The record for a boat is 43.55 knots (80.65 kilometers per hour) by *Longshot*, steered by Russell Long (U.S.) in Tarifa, Spain in July 1992.

United States The American with the best time under sail over a 500-meter run is Jimmy Lewis, with 38.68 knots in Saintes Maries-de-la-Mer, Camargue, France in February 1988.

Most competitors The most boats ever to start in a single race was 2,072 in the Round Zeeland (Denmark) race on June 21, 1984, over a course of 235 nautical miles.

The largest transoceanic race was the ARC (Atlantic Rally for Cruisers), when 204 boats of the 209 starters from 24 nations completed the race from Las Palmas de Gran Canaria (Canary Islands) to Barbados in 1989.

Boardsailing (windsurfing) World Championships were first held in 1973 and the sport was added to the Olympic Games in 1984, when the winner was Stephan van den Berg (Netherlands), who also won five world titles 1979–83.

Longest sailboard A sailboard of 165 feet was constructed in Fredrikstad, Norway. It was first sailed on June 28, 1986.

The longest snake of sailboards was made by 70 windsurfers in a row at the Sailboard Show '89 event in Narrabeen Lakes, Manly, Australia on October 21, 1989.

The Trifoiler *Yellow Pages Endeavour*, piloted by Simon McKeon and Tim Daddo (both Australian) achieved the highest speed on water by any craft.

LETTERS TO THE EDITOR

VÄXJÖ
11/11-1994

HELLO GUINNESS BOOK OF RECORDS

IF YOU DON'T PUBLISH THIS LETTER IN THE BOOK OF RECORDS FOR THE
SILLIEST BLACKMAIL LETTER I'AM GOING TELL MUM.

BYE BYE IN THE MUSHROOM WOOD FROM

JOHAN RAGNARSSON

DEAR GUINNESS BOOK

OF RECORDS

We received around 10,000 record claims and suggestions
from all over the world in 1994. Of those, only about 30 made
their way into the book as totally new categories. Our reasons
for turning down claims vary. Sometimes the achievement is
just too specialized; sometimes we are simply strapped for
space. In any case, many more of the letters we receive de-
serve recognition, and so, for the second time, we are giving
you a sample of the record-breakers and would-be record-
breakers who didn't quite make it into the book.

Schoolchildren from Gettysburg Elementary School in Clovis, CA really stretched themselves to make the world's longest rubber band; after tying thousands of bands together, they painstakingly measured it with the help of their teacher, Jeff Ogas. The result was a rubber band more than 19 miles long.

This bandy stick, 34 ft. 9 in. long and weighing 793 pounds, was made by teacher Kent Eriksson and students of the Wood Technology Program at Ovanaker Sweden College in Trov, Sweden, 1993–94.

A giant tape-measure 131 feet long was made by IMAX and displayed at the V & A Waterfront in Cape Town, South Africa on December 11, 1994.

VÄXJÖ
11/11-1994

HELLO GUINNESS BOOK OF RECORDS

IF YOU DON'T PUBLISH THIS LETTER IN THE BOOK OF RECORDS FOR THE SILLIEST BLACKMAIL LETTER I'AM GOING TELL MUM.

BYE BYE IN THE MUSHROOM WOOD FROM

JOHAN RAGNARSSON

We don't normally include new "firsts"—we prefer records that are beatable—but this one we couldn't resist. Mel Lastman, mayor of North York, Ontario, Canada, was so determined to meet any sales challenge put to him that he set out to become the first person to sell a refrigerator to an Inuit. He did it in March 1965 as part of a publicity stunt for his appliance business, Bad Boy Appliances and Furniture Limited.

Mary Jane Sorgel of Mequon, WI can twirl a baton, cheerleader-style, while her dog Muffy sits on her head. In 1994, Sorgel performed the balancing act on a live television broadcast from a 747 at an altitude of 25,000 feet.

Eleanor and Daniel Campanaro of Bangor, PA wrote to us at the suggestion of friends who thought their unusual tradition deserved recognition. Eleanor and Daniel have their picture taken in their wedding clothes every year on their anniversary. This picture was taken on their latest—their 44th.

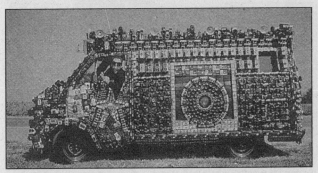

Harrod Blank, a filmmaker and car artist from El Cerrito, CA, made a "Camera Van" by covering a van with 1,705 cameras. Ten of these can actually take pictures and 40 can flash simultaneously; the look of amazement on people's faces as they set eyes on the creation for the first time makes for some excellent snaps. The Camera Van took Blank one year and $10,000 to make.

Although we receive inquiries about fruit displays from time to time, we've never received an apple-chain claim before. This one was assembled in Litomerice, Czech Republic, and included 2,986 apples, all from different trees and grown by different individuals. The chain was created as part of a local trade fair and each apple was an entrant in the "Apple of the Year" contest.

EXTRA! EXTRA!

HUMAN BEING

***Memorizing* pi** (p. 28–29)   Hiroyuki Goto, 21, of Tokyo, Japan recited *pi* to 42,195 places at the NHK Broadcasting Centre, Tokyo on February 18, 1995.

Hemodialysis United States (p. 36)   Carl Toscano of Haverhill, MA has been on hemodialysis since May 31, 1967.

LIVING WORLD

Top show dog (p. 60)   The greatest number of Best-in-Show awards won by any dog in all-breed shows is 275, by the German shepherd bitch Altana's Mystique (b. May 1987). The dog was formerly owned by Mrs. Jane Firestone and is now owned and trained by James A. Moses of Alpharetta, GA.

Largest undivided leaf (p. 104)   A leaf of the water lily *Victoria amazonica* (Longwood hybrid) growing in the Princess of Wales Conservatory of the Royal Botanic Gardens, Kew, England measured 8 ft. 6½ in. in July 1995.

Tree planting (p. 107)   The most trees planted by no more than 300 volunteers is 2,589, by 218 students of Peel Hall Primary School and Joseph Eastham High, New Madamswood, England on March 14, 1995.

One of the water lilies at the Royal Botanic Gardens, Kew, England produced an 8-ft.-6½-in. leaf. (*Royal Botanic Gardens, Kew*)

EARTH AND SPACE

Highest-priced diamond (p. 154)   A 100.10-carat pear-shaped "D" flawless diamond was sold for $16,548,750 at Sotheby's, Geneva, Switzerland in May 1995. It was purchased by Sheikh Ahmed Fitaihi for his chain of jewelry shops in Saudi Arabia.

SCIENCE AND TECHNOLOGY

Largest objects orbited (p. 195)   The heaviest object was the combined Russian *Mir 1* space station and U.S. space shuttle *Atlantis*, which docked on June 29, 1995 and together weighed 245.8 tons.

Most time in space United States (p. 198)   Norm Thagard has spent more time in space than any other American astronaut. He left Earth with the Russian team Mir 18 on a *Soyuz* spacecraft on March 14, 1995 and returned July 7, 1995 on the U.S. shuttle *Atlantis*, after 115 days 9 hr. 44 min. in space.

BUILDINGS AND STRUCTURES

Largest reataurant chain (p. 224)   The world's largest restaurant company is PepsiCo of Purchase, NY—operator of Pizza Hut, Taco Bell and Kentucky Fried Chicken—with 27,000 outlets around the world. Assets in 1994 were $24.79 billion, with profits for that year of $1.75 billion and with employees numbering 471,000 worldwide.

Tallest LEGO tower (p. 234)   A Lego tower measuring 73.5 feet high was built in Madrid, Spain, October 7–10, 1994.

TRANSPORT

Oldest active sailing ship (p. 252)   Following the sinking of the *Maria Asumpta* in June 1995, the *Star of India* (formerly the *Euterpe*) is the oldest active sailing vessel. Built on the Isle of Man in 1863, it is 205 feet long, with a gross tonnage of 1,318, and is operated by the Maritime Museum Association of San Diego, CA.

Oldest car to cross the United States Electric (p. 269) Raymond H. Carr drove from Astoria, OR to Atlantic City, NJ in a 1912 Baker Electric Runabout, May 28–July 3, 1995.

Highest mileage (p. 269) As of July 10, 1995, Albert Klein's VW Beetle had traveled 1,579,040 miles.

Oldest driver (p. 270) Edward Newsom of Brighton, England was still driving on July 22, 1995, his 104th birthday. Since he bought his first car in 1914, a Ford Model T, he has never made an insurance claim.

Most miles traveled on railroads *United States* (p. 283) H. Frank Martin of Muscatine, IA traveled 22,857 unduplicated miles on Amtrak, May 13–June 13, 1994.

Fastest circumnavigation (flying) *Antipodal points* (p. 293) David Sole traveled around the world on scheduled flights, taking in exact antipodal points, in 64 hr. 2 min., May 2–5, 1995. Leaving from London Heathrow, he flew to Madrid, Spain, back to Heathrow, and then to Napier, New Zealand via Singapore and Auckland. From Napier he went by helicopter to Ti Tree Point, the point exactly opposite Madrid Airport on the other side of the world. Returning to London via Los Angeles, Sole traveled a total distance of 25,917 miles.

Plane pulling (p. 296–97) A team of 60 people pulled a British Airways Boeing 747 weighing 226 tons a distance of 328 feet in 61.0 seconds at Heathrow Airport, London, England on May 25, 1995.

Largest paper aircraft (p. 305) The largest flying paper airplane, with a wingspan of 45 ft. 10 in., was constructed by a team of students from the

Ray Carr crosses the finish line in his 1912 Baker Electric Runabout. (*Baker Command Center/Jeffrey Anderson*)

Juanita Carmichael is the world's longest-serving flight attendant.
(*American Airlines*)

Faculty of Aerospace Engineering at Delft University of Technology, Netherlands and flown on May 16, 1995. It was launched indoors and flew a distance of 114 ft. 2 in.

Longest-serving flight attendant   Juanita Carmichael has been a flight attendant on American Airlines since July 10, 1944.

ARTS AND ENTERTAINMENT

Largest painting (p. 307)   A painting of Elvis Presley measuring 76,726 square feet was completed by students of Savannah College of Art and Design and members of the local community in Tybee Island, GA on April 8, 1995.

Largest mural (p. 309)   The Pueblo Levee Project in Colorado has produced the largest mural in the world, at 178,200 square feet.

Oldest author (p. 329)   Sarah Louise Delany's second book, *The Delany Sisters' Book of Everyday Wisdom*, was published by Kodansha America in October 1994, when she was 105 years old. Her sister and co-author, A. Elizabeth Delany, was 103.

Highest printings (p. 329)   The highest order for an initial print-run of a work of fiction is 2.8 million, ordered by Doubleday for John Grisham's sixth novel, *The Rainmaker*. Grisham's novels are reported to have sold 55 million copies to date, and worldwide box-office takings for three films made from his books (*The Firm*, *The Pelican Brief* and *The Client*) have reached $572 million.

Most widely syndicated comic strip (p. 333) Jim Davis's comic strip *Garfield*, which first appeared on June 19, 1978, currently appears in 2,547 newspapers in 83 countries and 26 languages.

Most drums played (p. 339) Rory Blackwell of Starcross, England played 400 separate drums in 16.2 seconds at Finlake Leisure Park, near Chudleigh, England on 29 May 1995.

Oldest opera singer (p. 345) Ukrainian bass Mark Reizen (b. July 3, 1895) sang the substantial role of Prince Gremin in Tchaikovsky's *Eugene Onegin* at the Bolshoi Theatre in Moscow on his 90th birthday.

Largest country line dance (p. 352) A total of 3,197 people danced to 10 minutes of music, including "Boot Scootin' Boogie," in Rowlett, TX on July 1, 1995.

Longest dancing dragon (p. 352) The longest dancing dragon measured 5,550 feet from the end of its nose to the tip of its tail. A total of 610 people brought the dragon to life on May 19, 1995, making it dance for more than five minutes at Tiantan (Temple of Heaven), Beijing, China.

Highest box office gross (p. 359) *Batman Forever* (Warner Brothers) broke records for both highest opening-day box office gross and highest single-day gross by bringing in $20 million on June 16, 1995.

BUSINESS AND LAW

Richest man (p. 386) The richest private individual is Microsoft founder Bill Gates. *Forbes* magazine reported in July 1995 that Gates was worth an estimated $12.9 billion.

Cynthia-Jean (Baba), the longest-lactating goat, at her 16th birthday party.

Longest-lactating goat Cynthia-Jean (Baba), owned by Carolyn Freund-Nelson of Northport, NY, has lactated continuously since June 1980. Baba celebrated her 16th birthday on April 14, 1995.

Greatest damages Sexual harassment (p. 409) The record award in a sexual harassment case was $50 million to Peggy Kimzey, a former employee of the Warsaw, MO Wal-Mart. The award of punitive damages was made by a jury in Jefferson City, MO on June 28, 1995. The jury also awarded Kimzey $35,000 for humiliation and mental anguish and $1 in lost wages. Wal-Mart said it would appeal.

HUMAN ACHIEVEMENTS

Brick carrying (p. 455) The greatest distance achieved for carrying a 9-pound brick in one ungloved hand using an uncradled downward pincer grip is 71.03 miles, by Ashrita Furman of Jamaica, NY on June 3–4, 1995.

Snowman (p. 463) The tallest was 96 ft. 7 in. high and was made by a team of local residents at Ohkura Village, Yamagata, Japan. It took 10 days and nights to build the snowman, which was completed on March 10, 1995.

Step-ups (p. 463) Fred Burton of Cheadle, England completed 2,469 step-ups in an hour on July 8, 1995, using a 15-inch-high exercise bench.

Deepest dive (p. 473) The record depth for the *ill-advised and dangerous* activity of breath-held diving is 417 feet, by Francisco "Pipin" Ferreras off Key Largo, FL in December 1994. He was under water for 2 min. 22 sec.

Burrito (p. 478) A burrito weighing 4,217 pounds and measuring 3,112.99 feet in length was created by El Pollo Loco in Anaheim, CA on July 31, 1995.

Cookie (p. 480) An oatmeal chocolate chip cookie with an area of 2,000 square feet, measuring 40 by 50 ft, was made in Peterborough, Ontario, Canada on May 20, 1995. It was decorated with Italian buttercream icing and covered with chocolate chips and toasted coconut.

Largest party Teddy bear picnic (p. 487) The largest teddy bear picnic ever staged was attended by 33,573 bears and their owners at Dublin Zoo, Dublin, Ireland on June 24, 1995.

Bottle collections (p. 488) Peter Broeker of Geesthacht, Germany has a collection of 8,131 unduplicated full beer bottles from 110 countries.

Buttons Teacher Ellen Dambach and students of Rolling Hills Primary School, Vernon, NJ collected 1,000,000 clothing buttons between January and June 1995.

Credit cards (p. 490) Walter Cavanagh's collection has now reached 1,394, worth a total of more than $1.65 million in credit. His wallet weighs 38 lb. 8 oz.

Can pyramid (p. 489) Ten science students at University College Dublin, Belfield, Ireland built a pyramid of 5,525 empty cans in 30 minutes on February 14, 1995.

Lei (p. 494) A 7-mile-long ti-leaf lei was made by students and staff of Samuel Wilder King Intermediate School and residents of Kaneohe, HI in October 1990.

SPORTS AND GAMES

Archery records (table, p. 501) *Men's FITA round, 50 m* 348, Han Seuong-hoon (South Korea), 1994.

Women's FITA rounds, 60 m 349, He Ying (China), 1995.

Tour de France (p. 548) Miguel Induráin won the Tour de France for a record-equaling fifth time in 1995, having previously won 1991–94.

Cycling records (table, p. 551) *Unpaced—one hour* Yvonne McGregor (Great Britain) set a women's record when she cycled 47.411 km (29.459 miles) in one hour in Manchester, England on June 17, 1995.

Domino stacking (p. 574) Aleksandr Bendikov of Mogilev, Belarus stacked 522 dominoes on a single supporting domino in September 1994.

Most turns of a jump rope *On a tightrope* (p. 575) 521 (consecutive), by Walfer Guerrero (Colombia) in Haarlem, Netherlands on June 1, 1995.

Total sport parachuting descents *Woman* (table, p. 624) Cheryl Stearns (U.S.), 10,100, various locations, mainly in the United States, up to August 2, 1995.

24-hour total parachute descents *Man* (table, p. 624) Jay Stokes (U.S.), 331 (in accordance with United States Parachute Association rules), Raeford, NC, May 30–31, 1995.

Flying disc throwing (p. 628) The World Flying Disc Federation distance records are: (men) 656 ft. 2 in., by Scott Stokely (U.S.) on May 14, 1995 in Fort Collins, CO; (women) 447 ft. 3 in., by Anni Kreml (U.S.) on August 21, 1994, also in Fort Collins, CO.

Spear throwing (p. 628) The record distance for throwing a spear (using an atlatl or hand-held device which fits onto it) is 848 ft. 6½ in. by David Engvall in Aurora, CO on July 15, 1995.

Rappeling (p. 629)   The greatest distance rappeled by 10 people in an 8-hour period is 67.68 miles, by a team from the British 10th (Volunteer) Battalion, Parachute Regiment. They rappeled 1,427 times down the side of Barclays Bank on Fenchurch Street, London, England on May 6, 1995.

Track and field records—Women 5000 m (table, p. 672)   14:36.45, Fernanda Ribeiro (Portugal) in Hechtel, Belgium on July 22, 1995.

Miguel Induráin won the Tour de France for the fifth time in 1995. (*Allsport*)

Pole vault   4.17 m *13 ft. 8 in.*, Daniela Bártová (Czech Republic) in Gisingen, Austria on July 15, 1995.

Track and field records—Men 1500 m (table, p. 676)   3:27.37, Noureddine Morceli (Algeria) in Nice, France on July 12, 1995.

2000 m   4:47.88 Noureddine Morceli (Algeria) in Paris, France on July 3, 1995.

Long jump   8.96 m *29 ft. 4³/₄ in.*, Iván Pedroso (Cuba) in Sestriere, Italy on July 29, 1995.

Triple jump   17.98 m *58 ft. 11³/₄ in.*, Jonathan Edwards (Great Britain) in Salamanca, Spain on July 18, 1995.

Longest jet-ski journey (p. 702)   Gary Frick of Ocean City, MD traveled 5,040 miles along the United States coastline on a stand-up Kawasaki 650sx Jet Ski. He left Lubec, ME on June 5, 1993 and arrived in Seattle, WA on September 16, 1993.

Timed lifts (p. 704)   A team of 10 deadlifted 6,057,237 pounds in 24 hours at Her Majesty's Prison, Belmarsh, Thamesmead, England on June 25–26, 1995.

INDEX

A

abbreviations 319
absorbency 162
Academy Awards *see* Oscars
accelerator, particle *see* particle
  accelerator
accidents *see* disasters
acidity 161
acoustic guitar 339
acquired immune deficiency
  syndrome *see* AIDS
acronym 319
actors and actresses
  all genres (number of roles
    portrayed) 355
  screen: age/durability 363; earnings
    359; generations in family 363;
    Oscar winners 365
  stage: durability 355; number of
    roles 355; one-man shows
    354–355; Tony winners 354
  television: commercials 372
acuity, auditory 45, *46*
acuity, visual 27
advanced age *see also* centenarians
  airline passenger 296
  airline pilots 290, 296
  astronauts 199
  ballroom dancers 352
  baseball player 513
  basketball player (NBA) 524
  bobsledders 532
  bowlers to score 300 534
  boxers (pro/amateur) 538, 539,
    540
  bride/bridegroom 475
  checkers champion 571
  chess champion 572
  English Channel swimmers 662
  golfers 583
  governor 437
  heads of state/prime ministers 435,
    441–442
  judge 411
  marathon finishers 692
  members of Congress: House
    speaker 438; representatives/
    senators 438, 439
  mother 6
  motorcycle racing champion 613
  mountain climbers 469
  movie director 362
  movie performer 363; Oscar winner
    365
  musicians 343
  Olympic medalists 619; boxing 540;
    track and field 671, 674; winter
    games 532
  opera singers 345, 724
  parachutists 625
  president (U.S.) 436
  soldier 449
  triathlete 697
  twins *16,* 9, 16
  vice-president (U.S.) 437
  weightlifting world record holder
    703
  world record breakers/champions
    (all sports) 498, 685
advance sales (Broadway show) 355
adventure 468–474
advertising
  magazines 334
  newspapers 333
  signs 374
  television 372
aerial acts 375
aerobatics 499
aerobics 586
Aeroflot (Russian state airline) 292
age *see* advanced age; longevity; youth
agriculture 396–408
aid, foreign *see* foreign aid
AIDS (acquired immune deficiency
  syndrome) 33, 41
aircraft 286–305 *see also* air racing;
  parachuting; space flight
  disasters 67, *67,* 424, 425
  flights 286–297; historic 286–287,
    290; nonstop 292, 293; passenger
    load 291; scheduled 292–293, 722
  personal records: flight attendant
    723, *723;* pilots/passengers
    296–297, *297*
  size/weight 290–291
  speed 291, 293–295, 301, 302
  types: airships 302–303, 375;
    balloons 303–304; bombers *see*
    bombers; gyrocopters 302;
    helicopters 301–302; jet airliners
    291–292, 294; model planes

Z